AF580934

CASSATT

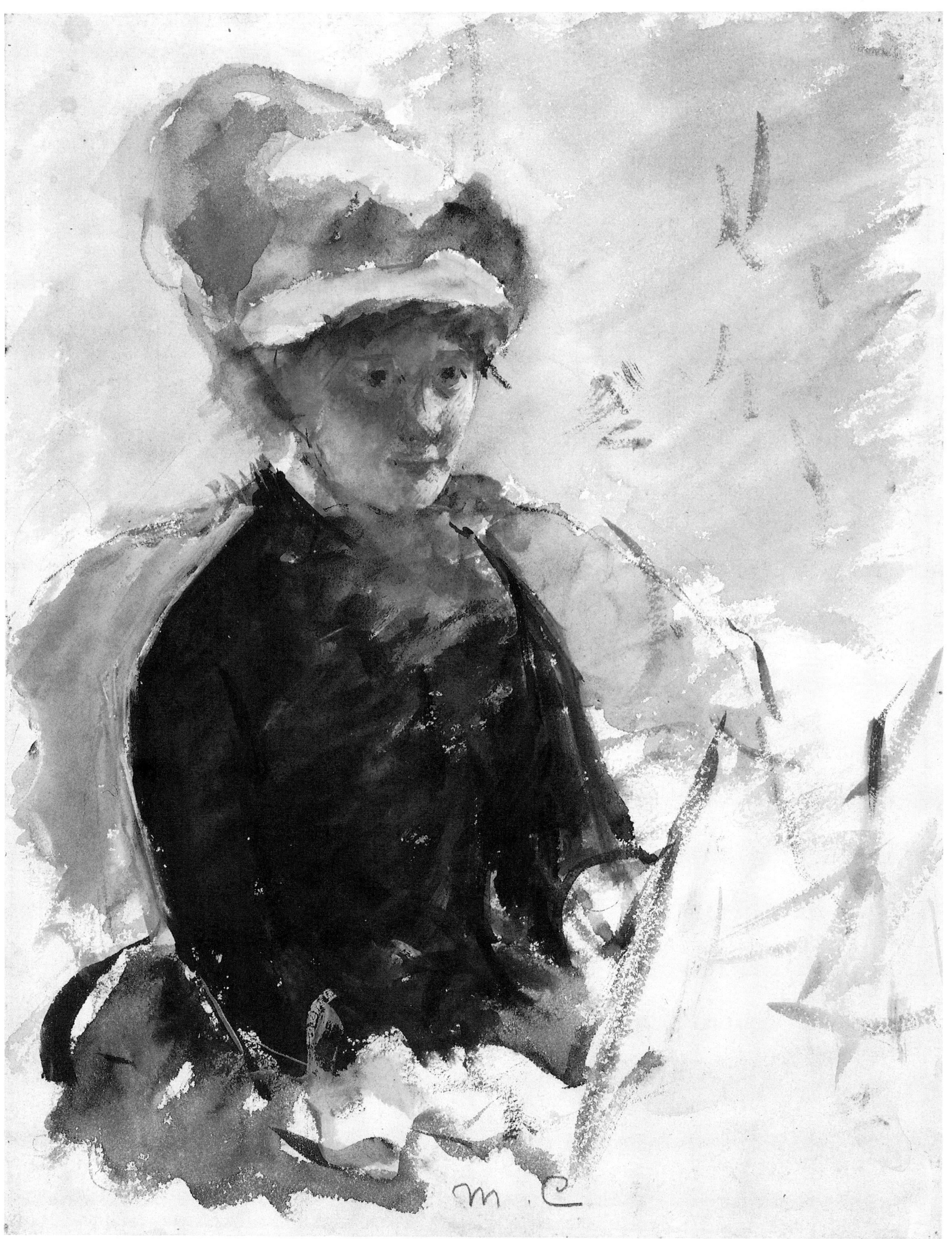
M. C

CASSATT

A RETROSPECTIVE

Edited by Nancy Mowll Mathews

Hugh Lauter Levin Associates, Inc.

Designed by Ken Scaglia
Copyedited by Deborah Teipel Zindell
Printed in China
ISBN: 0-88363-256-x

FRONTISPIECE: *Self-Portrait.* c. 1880. Watercolor on paper. 13 x 9 5⁄8 in. (33 x 24.4 cm). National Portrait Gallery, Smithsonian Institution. Photograph: Art Resource, New York.

CONTENTS

ACKNOWLEDGMENTS

It has been almost twenty-five years since I compiled my first Mary Cassatt bibliography in preparation for my dissertation, "Mary Cassatt and the Modern Madonna of the Nineteenth-Century" (Institute of Fine Arts, New York University, 1980). During the intervening years, I have compiled many other bibliographies on Cassatt for courses, books, and exhibitions. But none has been so satisfying as the one for this volume, *Cassatt: A Retrospective*, because it allows, for the first time, the major writings on Cassatt to be brought together, in English, for an American audience. I hope it will serve as a convenient reference as well as an illuminating tour through the avenues of thought about Cassatt, her life, and her work over the years. For the opportunity to assemble these writings and the related works of art, I am most grateful to the publisher, Hugh Lauter Levin, and the editor, Jeanne-Marie Perry Hudson, whose decisions and expertise brought this book into existence.

Since I have drawn so heavily on the knowledge gained in previous Cassatt projects, I would like to acknowledge once again those who have guided me in my Cassatt research from dissertation to the present undertaking: Linda Nochlin and the late Gert Schiff who were my dissertation advisors; the late Adelyn Breeskin who so generously opened her research and photo files to me for almost fifteen years until her death in 1986; my colleagues Suzanne Lindsay, Barbara Shapiro, and Lee Edwards for expanding the body of Cassatt knowledge; Henry and Audrey Haldeman who have organized the Haldeman family archives; and Pamela Ivinski, formerly of the Cassatt Catalogue Raisonné project, whose meticulous research has added much to the field. Above all, I would like to thank once again the descendants of Mary Cassatt for their generous cooperation in allowing reproductions of Cassatt's art and writings as well as the other owners of Cassatt materials, both public and private, who have shared their collections with us.

This book could not have been accomplished without the invaluable contributions of my research assistant, Lydia Hemphill. I am indebted to her for tracking down obscure authors and other historical figures to enrich the annotations and for providing both form and substance to the annotations and chronology. I would also like to acknowledge my colleagues at the Williams College Museum of Art for their support in this and the many other projects that shape our work together. Finally, my thanks go to my mother, Slava Matejka Mowll, and to Ingrid Montecino, who have given me the desire and the ability to write books such as these.

—Nancy Mowll Mathews

BIBLIOGRAPHICAL INDEX

All texts included in this volume have been reproduced from the original documents. Inconsistencies in grammar, punctuation, and spelling have been maintained to preserve the documents' authenticity.

Personal letters have been reproduced by permission of the authors' heirs. A source list of the letters' locations can be found on page 349.

Achille Segard, *Un peintre des enfants et des mères.* Librairie Paul Ollendorf, Paris, 1913.

"Woman's Position in Art," *The Crayon;* VIII, February 1861.

Earl Shinn [Edward Strahan], "The First American Art Academy," *Lippincott's Magazine,* February-March 1872.

Achille Segard, *Un peintre des enfants et des mères.* Librairie Paul Ollendorf, Paris, 1913.

May Alcott Nieriker, *Studying Art Abroad, and How To Do It Cheaply.* Roberts Brothers, Boston, 1879.

Lois Marie Fink, *American Art at the Nineteenth-Century Paris Salons.* Cambridge University Press, Cambridge, Massachusetts, and National Museum of American Art, Smithsonian Institution, Washington, D.C., 1990.

Emile Zola. *His Masterpiece* [*L'Oeuvre*]. Allan Sutton Publishing Limited, 1986. Translated by E.A. Vizetelly, 1902.

Henry Bacon. *A Parisian Year.* Roberts Brothers, Boston, 1882.

Elisabeth Luther Cary, "The Scrip: Recent Acquisitions of Modern Art in the Wilstach Collection," *International Studio;* vol. 35, no. 137, July 1908.

"The Philadelphia Academy Exhibition," *The Art Journal*; vol 2, 1876.

May Alcott Nieriker, *Studying Art Abroad, and How To Do It Cheaply.* Roberts Brothers, Boston, 1879.

George Moore, "Sex in Art," *Modern Painting.* W. Scott, London, 1893.

Clive Holland, "Lady Art Students' Life in Paris," *The Studio;* vol. XXX, no. 127, October 1903.

Caroline Ticknor, *May Alcott: A Memoir.* Little, Brown and Company, 1928.

Louisa May Alcott, "Diana and Persis" [c. 1879, unpublished manuscript]. Reprinted by permission of the Houghton Library, Harvard University and the literary heirs of Louisa May Alcott.

Gustave Geffroy, "Mary Cassatt," *La Vie artistique;* 3e série, Paris 1893.

Achille Segard, *Un peintre des enfants et des mères.* Librairie Paul Ollendorf, Paris, 1913.

"Exhibition of the Society of American Artists," *The Art Journal,* 1879.

William C. Brownell, "The Younger Painters of America," *Scribner's Monthly;* vol. 22, no. 3, July 1881.

Samuel Isham, *The History of American Painting.* Macmillan, New York, 1910.

George Moore, *Reminiscences of the Impressionist Painters.* The Tower Press Booklets, no. 3. Maunsel & Co., Ltd., Dublin, 1906.

Margaret Breuning, "Cassatt and Morisot," *Magazine of Art;* vol. 23, no. 12, December 1939.

Karl Madsen, from the Danish newspaper *Politiken,* November 9, 1889.

Marcel Guerin, ed., *Degas Letters.* Bruno Cassirer, Oxford, 1949.

Achille Segard, *Un peintre des enfants et des mères.* Librairie Paul Ollendorf, Paris, 1913.

Ambroise Vollard, *Recollections of a Picture Dealer.* Little, Brown, and Co., Boston, 1936.

Louisine Havemeyer, *Sixteen to Sixty: Memoirs of a Collector.* © 1930, 1993 by The Metropolitan Museum of Art. Reprinted with permission.

"The Exhibition of Independent Artists," *The American Register,* May 17, 1879.

Louis Duranty, "La quatrième exposition faite par un groupe d'artistes indépendants," *La Chronique des arts et de la curiosité;* no. 16, April 19, 1879.

Georges Lafenestre, "Les Expositions d'art: les indépendants et les aquarellistes," *Revue des deux mondes,* May 15, 1879.

Armand Silvestre, "Le Monde des Arts—Exposition de la rue des Pyramides," *La Vie Moderne,* April 24, 1880.

Charles Ephrussi, "Expositions des artistes indépendents," *Gazette des Beaux Arts;* vol. 21, May 1880.

Albert Wolff, "Courriers de Paris," April 10, 1881.

Achille Segard, *Un peintre des enfants et des mères.* Librairie Paul Ollendorf, Paris, 1913.

Joris-Karl Huysmans, "L'Exposition des Indépendants en 1881," *L'Art Moderne.* G. Charpentier, Paris, 1883.

Achille Segard, *Un peintre des enfants et des mères.* Librairie Paul Ollendorf, Paris, 1913.

Christian Brinton, "Concerning Miss Cassatt and Certain Etchings," *The International Studio;* vol. 27, no. 105, November 1905.

Gustave Geffroy, "Mary Cassatt," *La Vie Artistique,* 1893.

Achille Segard, *Un peintre des enfants et des mères.* Librairie Paul Ollendorf, Paris, 1913.

Nancy Mowll Mathews, "Beauty, Truth, and the Artist's Mirror: A Drypoint by Mary Cassatt," *Source: Notes in the History of Art;* vol. 4, nos. 2–3, Winter/Spring 1985. Reprinted by permission of Source: Notes in the History of Art, © 1985.

Yveling Rambaud, "Miss Cassatt," *L'Art dans les Deux Mondes,* vol. 22, no. 1, November 1890.

Georges Lecomte, *L"Art Impressioniste d'après la collection privée de M. Durand-Ruel.* Typographie Chamerot et Renouard, Paris, 1892.

Gardner Teall, "Mother and Child: The Theme Developed in the Art of Mary Cassatt," *Good Housekeeping Magazine;* vol. 50, no. 2, February 1910.

Frank Weitenkampf, "Some Women Etchers," *Scribner's Magazine;* vol. 45, no. 6, December 1909.

Frank Weitenkampf, "The Dry-Points of Mary Cassatt," *Print Collector's Quarterly;* vol. 6, 1916.

Grace Gassette, "Mary Cassatt: Painter and Etcher," *The Art Review;* vol. 17, no. 3, December 1908.

"Expositions à Paris: Pastellistes Français, Peintres-Graveurs—Camille Pissarro, Mary Cassatt," *L'Art Moderne;* vol. 11, no. 17, April 26, 1891.

Cecilia Waern, "Some Notes on French Impressionism," as first published in *Atlantic Monthly;* vol. 69, no. 414, April 1892.

Félix Fénéon, "Cassatt, Pissarro," from *Le Chat Noir* in *Oeuvres plus que complètes,* edited by Joan U. Halperin. © Librairie Droz, Geneva, 1970.

Achille Segard, *Un peintre des enfants et des mères.* Librairie Paul Ollendorf, Paris, 1913.

Camille, Pissarro, *Letters to His Son Lucien,* edited by John Rewald. Peregrine Smith, Inc., Salt Lake City, 1981.

Louisine Havemeyer, *Sixteen to Sixty: Memoirs of a Collector.* © 1930, 1993 by The Metropolitan Museum of Art. Reprinted with permission.

Maud Howe Elliott, *Art and Handicraft in the Woman's Building.* Rand, McNally and Co., Chicago, 1894.

Lucy Monroe, "Chicago Letter," *The Critic;* vol. 22, no. 582, April 15, 1893.

"Woman's Work in the Fine Arts," *The Art Amateur;* vol. 29, no. 1, June 1893.

André Mellério, "Miss Cassatt," *Exposition Mary Cassatt.* Galeries Durand-Ruel, November-December 1893.

A. de Lostalot, "Exposition des oeuvres de Miss Mary Cassatt," *La Chronique des arts et de la curiosité;* vol. 19, no. 38, December 9, 1893.

Florence Finch Kelly, "Painters of Sea and Shore," *The Hampton Magazine,* August 1907.

Achille Segard, *Un peintre des enfants et des mères.* Librairie Paul Ollendorf, Paris, 1913.

Frederick Sweet, *Miss Mary Cassatt: Impressionist from Pennsylvania.* Copyright © 1966 by the University of Oklahoma Press.

Anna Robeson Burr, *The Portrait of a Banker: James Stillman.* Duffield & Co., New York, 1928.

"Pictures by Mary Cassatt," *The New York Times,* April 18, 1895. Reprinted courtesy of *The New York Times.*

The Collector; vol. 6, no. 13, May 1, 1895.

The Art Amateur; vol. 32, no. 6, May 1895.

William Walton, "Miss Mary Cassatt," *Scribner's Magazine;* vol. 19, no. 3, March 1896.

Louisine Havemeyer, *Sixteen to Sixty: Memoirs of a Collector.* © 1930, 1993 by The Metropolitan Museum of Art. Reprinted with permission.

Arthur Hoeber, "Mary Cassatt," *The Century Magazine;* vol. 57, no. 5, March 1899.

"Miss Mary Cassatt," *The Art Amateur;* vol. 38, no. 6, May 1898.

Edgar P. Richardson, "Sophisticates and Innocents Abroad," *Art News;* vol. 53, no. 2, April 1954. © Art News, New York.

Louisine Havemeyer, *Sixteen to Sixty: Memoirs of a Collector.* © 1930, 1993 by The Metropolitan Museum of Art. Reprinted with permission.

Anna Lea Merritt, "A Letter to Artists: Especially Women Artists," *Lippincott's Magazine;* vol. LXV, no. 387, March 1900.

Frederick Sweet, *Miss Mary Cassatt: Impressionist from Pennsylvania.* Copyright © 1966 by the University of Oklahoma Press.

Louisine Havemeyer, *Sixteen to Sixty: Memoirs of a Collector.* © 1930, 1993 by The Metropolitan Museum of Art. Reprinted with permission.

Camille Mauclair, "Un Peintre de l'enfance," *L'Art et Decoratif,* August 1902.

Muriel Cidlokowska, "Painters' Ideals of Childhood," *International Studio;* vol. 78, no. 322, March 1924.

"Artists Every Child Should Know," *American Childhood;* vol. 12, no. 8, April 1927.

"Un Peintre de l'enfance," *Les Modes;* vol 4, no. 38, February 1904.

Helen W. Henderson, "Centenary Exhibition of the Pennsylvania Academy of the Fine Arts," *Brush and Pencil;* vol. XV, no. 3, March 1905.

Sidney Allen, "The Value of the Apparently Meaningless and Inaccurate," *Camera Work;* no. 3, July 1903.

Elisabeth Luther Cary, "The Art of Mary Cassatt," *Artists Past and Present: Random Studies.* Moffat, Yard & Co., New York, 1909.

Lula Merrick, "The Art of Mary Cassatt: Talent, Intelligence, Industry and Poetic Feeling Have Placed an American Girl in the Front Rank of Contemporary Painters," *Delineator;* vol 74, no. 2, August 1909.

André Mellério, "Mary Cassatt," *L'Art et les artistes;* vol. 12, November 1910.

"Mary Cassatt's Achievement: Its Value to the World of Art," *The Craftsman;* vol. 19, no. 6, March 1911.

"The Most Eminent of Living American Women Painters," *Current Literature;* vol. 46, no. 2, February 1909.

Achille Segard, *Un peintre des enfants et des mères.* Librairie Paul Ollendorf, Paris, 1913.

"At the Loan Exhibition for Woman Suffrage," *The Evening Post Saturday Magazine,* New York, April 3, 1915. © 1915 *The Saturday Evening Post.*

"Address Delivered by Mrs. H.O. Havemeyer at the Loan Exhibition." Knoedler Galleries, April 6, 1915.

Anna Louise Thorne, "My Afternoon with Mary Cassatt," *School Arts Magazine;* vol. 59, no. 9, May 1960. Courtesy of *School Arts Magazine.*

Forbes Watson, "Philadelphia Pays Tribute to Mary Cassatt," *The Arts;* vol.11, no. 6, June 1927.

Adelyn Dhome Breeskin, *Mary Cassatt: A Catalogue Raisonné of the Graphic Work.* Smithsonian Institution Press, Washington, D.C., 1979.

George Biddle, "Some Memories of Mary Cassatt," *The Arts;* vol. 10, no. 2, August 1926. Reprinted by permission of Michael Biddle.

"Mary Cassatt," *Journal des Debats;* vol. 33, no. 1689, July 9, 1926.

"The Painter of Children," *Literary Digest;* vol. 90, no. 2, July 10, 1926.

Robert Hallowell, "Mary Cassatt," *The Survey;* vol. 57, no. 5, December 1926.

"Une Retrospective de Mary Cassatt," *Art et Decoration,* July 1930.

Ambroise Vollard, *Recollections of a Picture Dealer.* Little, Brown, and Co., Boston, 1936.

CHRONOLOGY

1844

MAY 22. Mary Stevenson Cassatt is born in Allegheny City, Pennsylvania (now part of Pittsburgh), the fourth of five surviving children of Robert Simpson Cassatt (1806–1891) and Katherine Kelso Cassatt (1816–1895). Her siblings are Lydia Simpson Cassatt (1837–1882), Alexander Johnston Cassatt (1839–1906), Robert Kelso Cassatt (1842–1855), and Joseph Gardner Cassatt (1849–1911).

1848

After a brief move to Pittsburgh, the family moves to Hardwick, their first country house, in Lancaster, Pennsylvania.

1849

The family moves again, this time to Philadelphia.

1850–55

The Cassatts travel in Europe, spending long periods in Paris, Heidelberg, and Darmstadt, where the children attend local schools, and Mary attains fluency in both French and German.

1855

SUMMER. The family returns to the United States, to West Chester, Pennsylvania, after Robbie dies of bone cancer.

1858–60

The Cassatts live at 1436 South Penn Square, Philadelphia, then the second largest city in the United States and the fourth largest in the world.

1860–65

The Cassatts move back and forth between their Philadelphia residence and their country house in Westtown, Chester County, Pennsylvania.

Mary studies at the Pennsylvania Academy of the Fine Arts.

1865

DECEMBER. Mary goes to Paris to further her art education; she takes private lessons from Jean-Léon Gérôme, and spends her time copying works in the Louvre with other young American artists.

1866–67

Cassatt studies with her friend from the Pennsylvania Academy, Eliza Haldeman, under Charles Chaplin, and travels with her to Courances and Ecouen (small art colonies near Paris) to study with various French masters, including Edouard Frère and Paul Soyer.

Cassatt's submission to the Salon is refused.

1868

SPRING. Cassatt's *The Mandolin* is accepted by the Salon; she returns to Paris for the duration of the exhibition. After the Salon she settles in Villiers-le-Bel, near Ecouen, where she studies with Thomas Couture.

1869

SPRING. Cassatt returns to Paris, where her submission to the Salon is refused.

SUMMER. She takes a sketching trip with a friend, Miss Gordon, throughout the Piedmont region of France and Italy and then returns to Ecouen and Paris.

1870

WINTER. Cassatt goes to Rome with her mother and studies with Charles Bellay.

SPRING. Her *Une Contadina di Fabello; val Sesia (Piémont)* is accepted by the Salon.

AUGUST. She returns to her family in Altoona, Pennsylvania, to escape the Franco-Prussian War; the family then moves back to Philadelphia.

1871

Cassatt sets up a studio in Philadelphia, where she befriends Emily Sartain.

SUMMER. She moves with her family to Hollidaysburg, Pennsylvania (near Altoona).

FALL. She visits Pittsburgh and Chicago, where some of her paintings are destroyed in the Great Chicago Fire.

DECEMBER. She returns to Europe with her friend Emily Sartain.

1872

WINTER–SPRING. Cassatt and Sartain work in Parma, Italy, renting rooms at 21 Borgo Riolo.

FALL. Cassatt goes to Madrid and then Seville, where she has a studio at the Casa de Pilatos.

1873

APRIL. Cassatt returns to Paris from Seville for the Salon, where her *Torero and Young Girl* is on view.

SUMMER. She and her mother visit Holland and Belgium, spending the summer in Antwerp.

OCTOBER. After returning to Paris briefly for her mother's departure, Cassatt travels south, stopping over in Parma on her way to Rome.

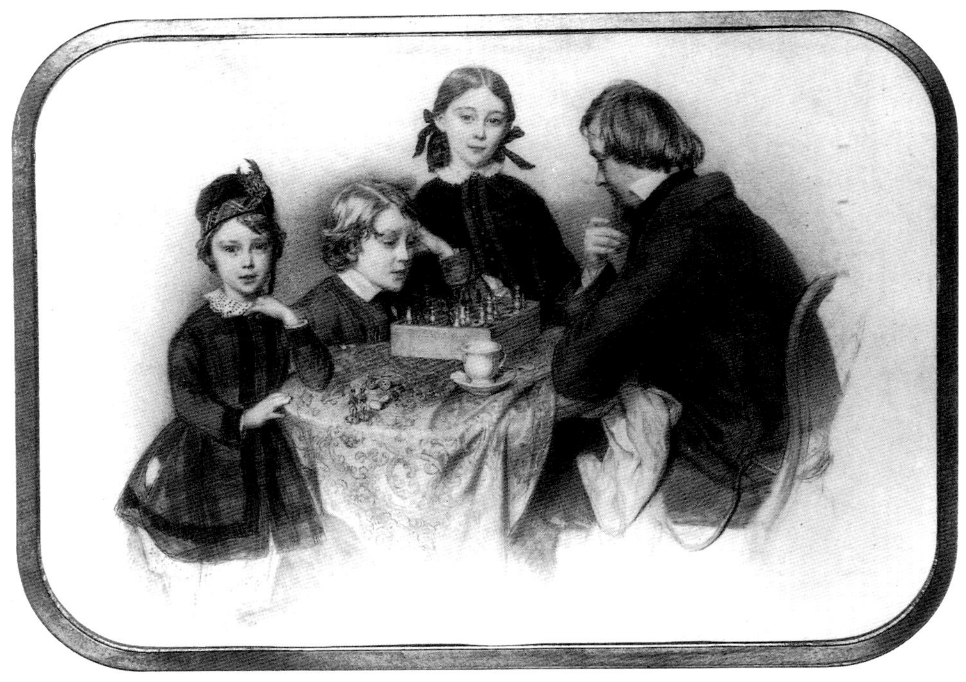

Robert Cassatt and His Children. Drawing of the Cassatt family by Peter Baumgaertner, Heidelberg. 1854. Private collection.

1874

SPRING. Cassatt consults with Charles Bellay in Rome, then returns to Paris in June.

SUMMER. She works with her old teacher, Thomas Couture, in Villiers-le-Bel. Cassatt meets Louisine Elder (later Havemeyer) and the Elder sisters, who are staying at the same boarding house as Emily Sartain in Paris.

FALL. Cassatt settles in at 19, rue de Laval, Paris, and her sister Lydia comes to stay with her. Cassatt works on several portraits—including one of her sister—hoping to attract Americans seeking to have their portraits painted abroad.

1875

SPRING. One of Cassatt's paintings is rejected by the Salon, which causes her severe embarrassment, though another is accepted. Cassatt's friendship with Emily Sartain suffers as a result of gossip surrounding this rejection.

SUMMER. Cassatt takes a trip home to Philadelphia, returning to Paris in August.

1876

SPRING. Cassatt meets May Alcott, painter and sister of Louisa May Alcott. She becomes the subject of many letters between the sisters and ultimately is the model for a character in Louisa May Alcott's unpublished novel about women artists, *Diana and Persis* (1879).

1877

APRIL. Cassatt accepts Edgar Degas's invitation to exhibit with the Impressionist group after her final humiliation over a Salon refusal. She lives and works in the artists' quarter, at 19 rue de Laval.

OCTOBER. Her parents and sister Lydia come to live with her in Paris, at 13, avenue Trudaine. Cassatt sets up a studio outside her home for the first time.

1878

SPRING. The planned Impressionist exhibition falls through, and Cassatt's debut with the group is postponed to 1879.

MAY 1. The International Exposition opens in Paris; Cassatt has a painting in the exhibition of American art in the American Pavilion.

1879

APRIL 10. Cassatt exhibits with the Impressionists for the first time (she participates in their exhibitions again in 1880, 1881, and 1886).

She works with Degas on a proposed (and never realized) print journal, *Le Jour et la nuit,* that would be illustrated with original etchings by Cassatt, Degas, Pissarro, and others.

SUMMER. She travels to England, then retraces her 1869 sketching trip through the Piedmont region, spending the end of the summer in Divonne-les-Bains on Lake Geneva.

FALL. Inspired by other artists around her, Cassatt begins to experiment with printing processes. She executes a large number of theater scenes.

1880

APRIL 1. Cassatt enters eight major paintings and pastels, as well as eight etchings, in the Fifth Impressionist Exhibition.

SUMMER. Cassatt and her family, including Alexander's children, stay at Marly-le-Roi, near Paris. Cassatt spends a great deal of time painting her nieces and nephews.

1881

APRIL 2. The Sixth Impressionist Exhibition opens, to which Cassatt contributes eleven paintings and pastels. She receives favorable reviews.

SUMMER. Cassatt and her family rent "Coeur Volant," a house in Louveciennes, near Paris.

The dealer Paul Durand-Ruel begins representing Cassatt.

1882

SPRING. Conflicts among the members of the Impressionist group cause Cassatt to withdraw from the annual exhibition. Her mother's and sister's health decline.

NOVEMBER 7. Lydia dies from Bright's disease. Aleck and Lois and their children arrive in Paris.

Louisine Elder (Havemeyer) returns to Paris to visit Cassatt.

1884

JANUARY. Cassatt and her mother go to Spain, where her mother suffers severe ill health.

SPRING. Cassatt and her parents move to 14, rue Pierre Charron, Paris.

SUMMER. The family stays at Viarmes, about 20 miles north of Paris.

DECEMBER. Aleck Cassatt and his son Robert come to visit.

1885

SUMMER. Cassatt and her parents stay at Presles, north of Paris.

1886

APRIL 10. Her work is shown in the first major exhibition of Impressionist art in the United States, orchestrated by Paul Durand-Ruel.

MAY. Cassatt helps organize the Eighth Impressionist Exhibition.

SUMMER. Cassatt and her parents spend the summer at Arques-la-Bataille (near Dieppe).

1887

WINTER. Cassatt and her parents move to an apartment at 10, rue de Marignan, which Cassatt would keep for the rest of her life.

SUMMER. They return to Arques-la-Bataille, this time joined by Aleck, Lois, and their children, who were enjoying a year-long residence in Paris.

1888

FALL. Cassatt spends time nursing her ailing parents. She reconciles with her sister-in-law Lois and completes a pastel portrait of her. She also executes a print (drypoint) of another sister-in-law, Jennie (Gardner's wife), and their baby, Gardner. This is the earliest dated example in a series of mother and child images that Cassatt would execute over the remainder of her career.

SUMMER. Cassatt and her parents spend the late summer at Fontainebleau, where she continues to work on her mother and child compositions in prints and in paintings.

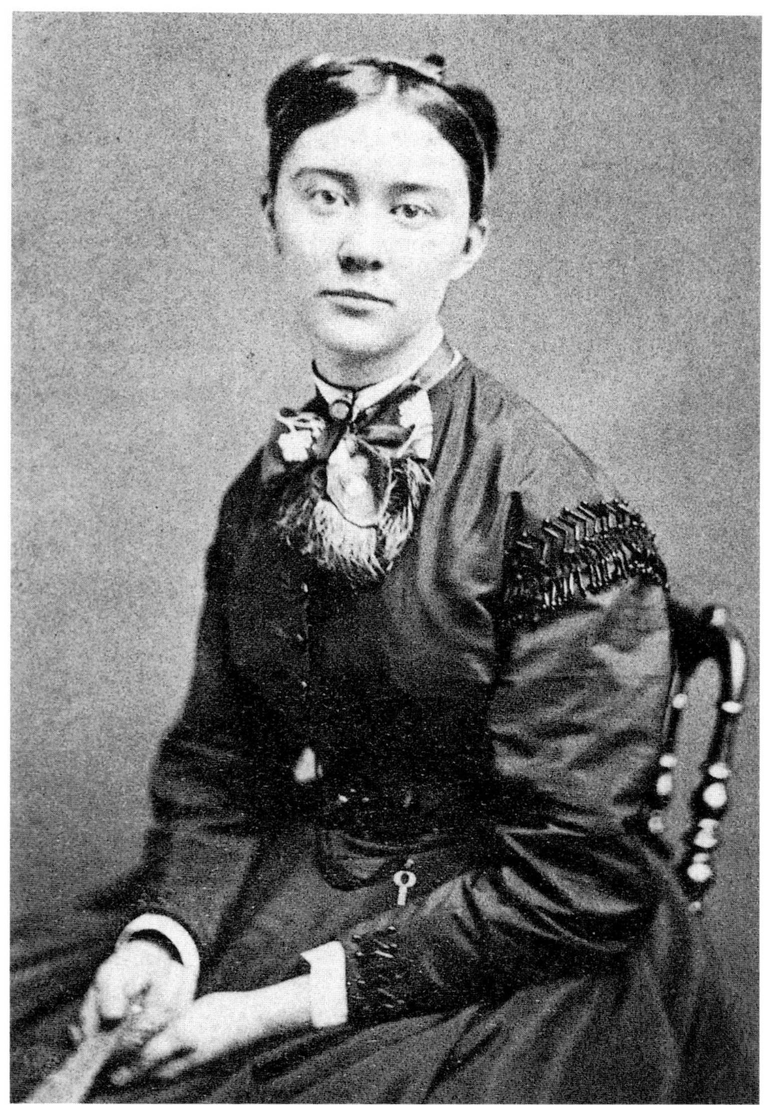

Photograph of Mary Cassatt taken in Paris. c. 1867.
Private collection of Henry B. and Audrey S. Haldeman.

1889

JANUARY. Cassatt's interest in printmaking is revived, and she joins many of her Impressionist friends in a group called Société des Peintres-Graveurs [Society of Painter-Printmakers], which exhibits at the Durand-Ruel gallery.

SUMMER. Cassatt and her parents stay at Septeuil, west of Paris. Cassatt breaks a leg in a horseback riding accident.

FALL. Cassatt renews her friendship with Louisine Havemeyer when the latter visits Paris for the first time since her marriage to H.O. Havemeyer.

1890

MARCH. The Second Exhibition of Painter-Printmakers, for which Cassatt finishes two series of prints, one a set of drypoints, rekindles her enthusiasm for printmaking.

APRIL. A major exhibition of Japanese prints at the École des Beaux-Arts arouses in Cassatt and fellow artist Berthe Morisot a passion for color prints.

SUMMER. Another accident forces Cassatt to convalesce for a time. She and her parents rent "Tournelles," a house in Septeuil, west of Paris.

Cassatt begins work on a series of ten color prints, a project which consumes her for the next nine months.

1891

APRIL. Cassatt's first individual exhibition, consisting of color prints, pastels, and paintings, is held at Galerie Durand-Ruel, Paris

SUMMER. Cassatt and her parents stay at the Château Bachivillers, the country house outside of Paris she rents from 1891 to 1893.

DECEMBER 9. Cassatt's father dies.

1892

WINTER. Cassatt, her mother, Jennie, and Gardner stay in Cap d'Antibes on the Cote d'Azur, then travel to Italy, returning to Paris in April.

APRIL. Cassatt is invited by Bertha Honore Palmer to paint a mural depicting "Modern Woman" for the Woman's Building at the World's Columbian Exposition in Chicago.

SUMMER–WINTER. Cassatt accepts the commission and paints the mural at Bachivillers, where she has a special studio built to accommodate the large size of the work.

1893

FEBRUARY. Cassatt ships the *Modern Woman* mural to Chicago. She executes a number of paintings and color prints inspired by the mural project.

SUMMER. Mother and daughter spend a third summer at Bachivillers, where Paul Durand-Ruel's daughter, Mme. Aude, is their neighbor. Cassatt begins to execute portraits again, usually in pastel, prompting a demand for child portraits.

NOVEMBER. A major retrospective of Cassatt's work is held at the Durand-Ruel gallery, an exhibit of nearly one hundred works, beginning with those executed since 1878, when she first joined the Impressionists. According to one review, half sold within a few weeks.

1894

JANUARY–FEBRUARY. Cassatt and her mother stay at Villa "La Cigaronne," Cap d'Antibes, where she executes *The Boating Party*. Cassatt's niece and namesake, Ellen Mary Cassatt, is born.

SPRING. Cassatt buys and renovates the Château Mesnil-Beaufresne, fifty miles northwest of Paris, a project which extends into the summer; it remains her country house for the rest of her life.

DECEMBER. Cassatt's mother's health worsens.

Berthe Morisot dies in an influenza epidemic, which saddens Cassatt and the art community.

1895

APRIL. The Durand-Ruel Gallery in New York holds Cassatt's first individual exhibition in the United States, showing her mother and child paintings and pastels and the works relating to her mural project, as well as drypoints and color prints.

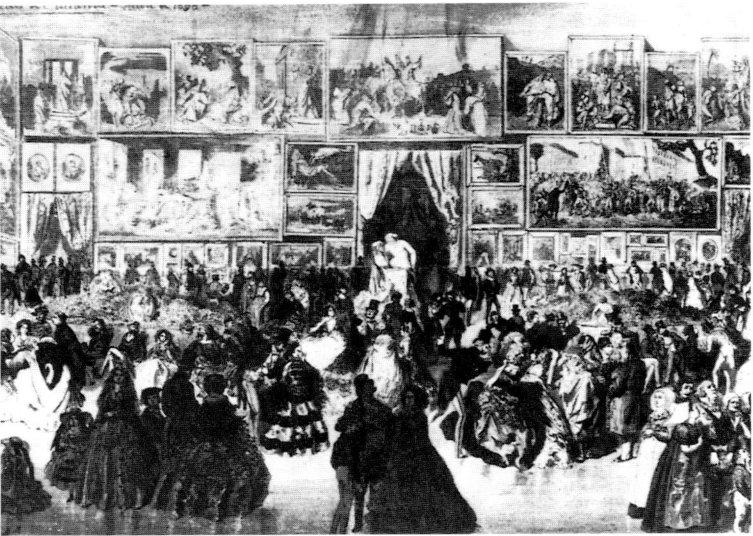

Gustave Doré. *Palais de l'Industrie, Salon de 1868*. Photograph © Bibliothèque Nationale de France, Cabinet des Estampes, Paris.

SUMMER. She works at Mesnil-Beaufresne, setting up her own printing press for a new series of color prints. Louisine Havemeyer comes to visit.

OCTOBER 21. Cassatt's mother dies. After a period of mourning, Cassatt turns to portraiture and the mother and child theme to ease her loss.

1897

This proves to be a productive year for Cassatt; she moves on from her grief over the loss of her mother and into a comfortable rhythm of work.

1898

JANUARY. Cassatt visits the United States for the first time since 1875, arriving in New York and going immediately to Philadelphia, and then to New York, Boston, and Naugatuck, Connecticut, in the company of various artists and collectors; the trip lasts into 1899.

FEBRUARY 28. Cassatt has another show (color prints) at Durand-Ruel in New York. This time she is a witness to the event.

SPRING. In Boston and Connecticut, Cassatt is commissioned to paint a number of portraits. In Connecticut Cassatt meets Theodate Pope, who will be an important friend and correspondent for many years.

SUMMER. Cassatt returns to France and summers at Mesnil-Beaufresne.

1899

Alexander J. Cassatt becomes president of the Pennsylvania Railroad after seventeen years in retirement.

1900

The World's Fair takes place in Paris. Though Cassatt does not appear to exhibit any of her work at the fair, she is discussed as a member of the Impressionist group. Cassatt begins to spend more time at Mesnil-Beaufresne, coming into Paris only when necessary.

1901

SPRING. Cassatt travels to Italy and Spain on a collecting trip with Henry O. and Louisine Havemeyer.

1904

SPRING. Cassatt's *The Caress* is shown at the Seventy-third Annual Exhibition of the Pennsylvania Academy of the Fine Arts, her first work to be shown in her former hometown. She is awarded the Lippincott Prize for *The Caress*. (The painting went on to Chicago, where it won the Norman Wait Harris Prize at the Art Institute's Seventeenth Exhibition.) Cassatt declines all awards and prizes.

DECEMBER 31. Cassatt is named Chevalier of the Legion D'Honneur in France.

1905

Cassatt breaks her long-standing contract with Durand-Ruel in a fury over the fact that he had omitted her from an Impressionist exhibition in London. She turns to another dealer, Ambroise Vollard.

1906

SUMMER. Cassatt rashly burns her stock of early works after giving Vollard a chance to choose from it. Eventually, Cassatt and Durand-Ruel reconcile.

DECEMBER 28. Alexander J. Cassatt dies.

1908

NOVEMBER. Cassatt visits the United States for the last time, to see her friend Louisine Havemeyer on the anniversary of her husband's death.

She goes to a Matisse exhibition with Sarah Sears, where she becomes acquainted with Gertrude, Leo, Michael, and Sarah Stein, American patrons of Matisse.

A Durand-Ruel exhibition of Cassatt's work is seen first in Paris and then sent on tour to New York, Pittsburgh, and Washington, D.C.

1910

DECEMBER. Cassatt travels through Europe to Constantinople, then on to Egypt with her brother Gardner and his family.

1911

JANUARY. The Cassatt party arrives in Cairo for their trip down the Nile; Gardner becomes ill.

MARCH. Cassatt returns to Paris, followed soon after by Gard and his family.

APRIL 5. Gardner dies. Cassatt herself is afflicted by physical maladies and exhaustion stemming from the Egypt trip; she is unable to work for the next two years.

1912

WINTER. Cassatt accompanies friend James Stillman to Cannes.

JUNE. The writer Achille Segard visits Cassatt to interview her for his book, *Mary Cassatt: Un Peintre des enfants et des mères*.

NOVEMBER. Cassatt rents the Villa Angeletto, Grasse, where from 1912 to 1924 Cassatt spends at least six months a year. She renews her friendship with Renoir.

1913

SUMMER. At Beaufresne, Cassatt begins to work in earnest again, resuming the mother and child theme. She begins to have trouble with her eyes.

1914

MARCH. Louisine Havemeyer comes to Grasse for a productive two-month visit with her best friend.

The outbreak of fighting in northern France during World War I forces Cassatt to leave Mesnil-Beaufresne; she spends a major portion of the war years at the Villa Angeletto.

Cataracts are discovered on Cassatt's eyes and for the next five years she will have a series of unsuccessful operations. Her impaired eyesight brings a premature end to her painting.

1915

APRIL 7–27. Cassatt participates in the "Suffrage Loan Exhibition of Old Masters and Works by Edgar Degas and Mary Cassatt," organized by her friend Louisine Havemeyer and held at M. Knoedler & Co., New York.

1917

SEPTEMBER 28. Degas dies.

1918

At the end of the war, Cassatt is able to return to Paris and Beaufresne.

1920

JANUARY. Lois Cassatt dies; her collection of Impressionist paintings, formed by Cassatt mainly in the 1880s, is dispersed to her children and to the art market. Many early Cassatts are seen again.

1923–24

Cassatt finds a group of copper printmaking plates at Mesnil-Beaufresne that she had worked in drypoint, which she believes have never been printed. She has them printed in Paris and puts several editions up for sale. When museums and collectors discover that the plates had indeed been printed twenty years before and they try to tell her so, Cassatt takes offense. The bitter argument that ensues endangers her lifelong friendship with Louisine Havemeyer.

1926

JUNE 14. Mary Cassatt dies at Mesnil-Beaufresne. Memorial exhibitions of her work are held in the United States and France for the next five years.

GENEALOGY

Dennis Cassat — m. — Lydia Simpson
(1776–1807) (1775–1849)
Alexander Johnston — m. — Mary Stevenson
(1784–1832) (1792–1820)
Robert Simpson Cassatt — m. — Katherine Kelso Johnston
(1806–1891) (1816–1895)
Lydia Simpson Cassatt
(1837–1882)
Maria Lois Buchanan — m. — Alexander Johnston Cassatt
(1847–1920) (1839–1906)
Edward Buchanan Cassatt
(1869–1922)
Katharine Kelso Johnston Cassatt
(1871–1905)
Robert Kelso Cassatt
(1873–1944)
Elizabeth (Elsie) Foster Cassatt
(1875–1931)
Robert Kelso Cassatt
(1842–1855)
Mary Stevenson Cassatt
(1844–1926)
Joseph Gardner Cassatt — m. — Eugenia Carter
(1849–1911) (1855–1929)
Joseph Gardner Cassatt
(1886–1955)
Ellen Mary Cassatt
(1894–1966)
Eugenia Cassatt
(1897–1979)

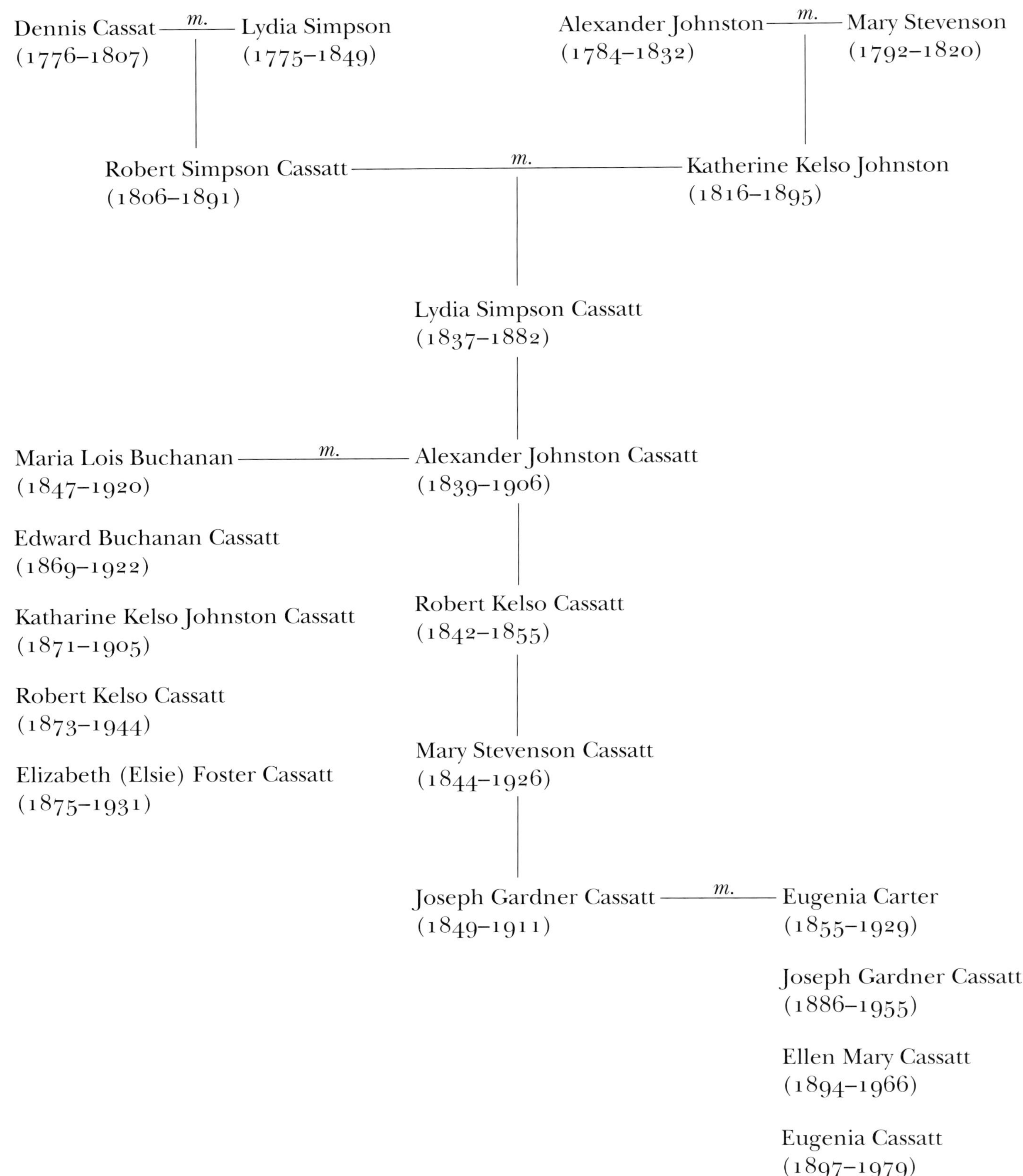

INTRODUCTION

Mary Cassatt achieved fame as an artist and enjoyed the respect and admiration of her colleagues during her long and prolific lifetime. Writings about her art and artistic personality dating from her years as a working artist are, however, somewhat scarce compared to the materials available on many other artists who have achieved comparable fame. This may be partly explained by the fact that although Cassatt was known to express her thoughts and ideas eloquently in conversation, she was not inclined to write them down. While she was known by her friends as a sophisticated analyst of contemporary art and society, both American and French, she left relatively few discursive letters and no diaries, memoirs, or theoretical tracts. Further, society's tendency to minimize women's contributions, even those of successful women like Mary Cassatt, accounts for much of the silence. Many critics discussed the women of the Impressionist group, Cassatt and Berthe Morisot among them, but they were viewed separately and in less depth, resulting in few critical writings that substantively address their art and ideas.

This having been said, the writings that have been assembled here—letters, contemporary literature, critical essays, memoirs, and art historical assessments—nevertheless give us a vivid picture of the art and life of this remarkable woman. These writings document her successes and failures in a world that was difficult for an artist, much less a female artist, to navigate.

Because of her keen intelligence and humanity, Mary Cassatt was able to develop her natural talent in directions that caught the spirit of her times and have proved lasting in their appeal. Her adoption of Impressionism in Paris in the 1870s, when it was the breathtaking new style called "the painting of modern life," and later her interpretation of the mother and child theme, which has never been surpassed, have both contributed to her stature as one of the most important artists of her time. These and the many more ventures that characterize her fifty-plus years as a practicing artist unfold in the writings that follow.

Mary Cassatt was born to a prominent Pittsburgh family with strong ties to Philadelphia. Even though she lived most of her life in Europe, her family back home in Pennsylvania played a major supportive role in her personal and professional affairs. She never relinquished her American citizenship and was engaged in American political debate, including the suffrage movement, until she died. Although the Cassatts were not of the wealthiest class of Americans, they were well off financially because of Mr. Cassatt's astute business and investment career. They could afford to educate their children abroad and, further, they encouraged ambition in both sons and daughters. The strong familial ties and values found in the Cassatt home emboldened both Mary and her older brother Alexander to achieve extraordinary success, Mary as an internationally renowned artist and Alexander as an executive with the Pennsylvania Railroad, and later its president.

Mary Cassatt's decision to begin studying art at the age of sixteen shows that her passion for this occupation took root early. She attended the prestigious Pennsylvania Academy of the Fine Arts where, even though the Civil War was being fought around them, a group of talented men and women assembled who would, like her, make their mark on the art of their times. The painter Thomas Eakins, the sculptor Howard Roberts, and the engraver Emily Sartain were just a few of Cassatt's fellow students who dominated the Philadelphia art scene and also went on to achieve national standing.

When the Civil War ended in 1865 many students from the Pennsylvania Academy sailed for Europe where they took advantage of all available opportunities for art study. They congregated in Paris, where they met frequently at the Louvre for copying exercises but otherwise scattered to the studios of various French masters for the required systematic training. While many American men like Thomas Eakins were accepted into the official École des Beaux-Arts, the women, who were barred from these courses, were forced to receive training on a private basis from the same professors, as Cassatt did with Jean-Léon Gérôme. Women also attended classes specifically for them taught by such artists as Charles Chaplin, Anton Mauve, and Evariste Luminais. In addition to studying with Gérôme, Cassatt went with her friend Eliza Haldeman to Chaplin's classes, which offered the premier training for women in Paris and attracted such prominent French artists as Eva Gonzales.

Artists' colonies that formed in picturesque villages outside of Paris lured many American students interested in landscape and peasant genre painting. Cassatt and Haldeman first stayed in Courances, not far from the Fontainebleau Forest, and then settled in Ecouen and nearby Villiers-le-Bel (north of Paris), where they studied with genre painters Edouard Frère and Paul Soyer and the renegade Salon painter Thomas Couture.

The outbreak of the Franco-Prussian War in 1870 sent foreigners crossing the borders out of harm's way. Cassatt first went south to Rome and then returned to the United States, joining her family in Pennsylvania. However, a year and a half later, as soon as the war was over and she could amass enough money for a return trip, she resumed her studies in Europe. This time she traveled to Italy with Emily Sartain, a professional engraver and daughter of the powerful Philadelphia art figure, John Sartain. Sartain's correspondence with her family during the three years she and Cassatt were in Europe together document Cassatt's charismatic presence in Parma in 1872 and in Paris after 1874, when Cassatt established a studio there.

Other Americans also fell under the spell of the dynamic Miss Cassatt during her early days in Paris and wrote eloquently about her talent and intelligence. The painter May Alcott (later Nieriker), sister of Louisa May Alcott, spoke so admiringly of Cassatt in her letters home to her sister that Louisa included a "Miss Cassal" in *Diana and Persis*, a novel she wrote in 1879 (but did not publish) about American women artists abroad (see page 98). Louisine Elder (later Havemeyer) met Cassatt in 1874 during a short trip to Paris with her family and, in subsequent trips, developed a lifelong friendship with her that produced a rich correspondence between the two. Under Cassatt's tutelage, Havemeyer became one of the great American art collectors of her day. Late in life, she was often asked to speak and write on her friend Mary Cassatt and took these opportunities to convey the monumental stature of Cassatt as an artist and persuasive interpreter of modern art.

As advanced art students and young professionals, Cassatt and her friends concentrated each year on finishing a major work to submit to the Paris Salon—acceptance to which, they felt, would launch their professional careers. None of the Americans wanted to return to the United States without this badge of professional achievement which would help them get commissions and teaching positions back home. Cassatt had paintings accepted to the Salon in 1868, 1870, 1872, 1873, 1874, 1875, and 1876, which established her as one of the leaders of her generation of Americans. Yet, the longer she continued submitting works to the Salon, the more cynical she became about the objectivity of the juries and the more she began to reject the rigid principles of modern art promoted by the Salon system. She had noted that the more radical artists, such as the

Impressionists, were forming their own exhibiting groups in Paris in the late 1860s and 1870s, and in turn, because of her outspoken criticism of official art, the Impressionists took note of her. When the Salon jury refused Cassatt's painting in 1877, she accepted Edgar Degas's suggestion that she cease submitting to the Salon and join the Impressionist group instead.

Not only did joining the Impressionists force her to rethink her method and philosophy of painting, but it irrevocably changed the way Cassatt would conduct her life as a painter. Up to this point she had followed the course typically taken by American artists in Paris—seeking Salon exposure, sending pictures to major exhibitions in the United States, and gearing portraits and genre paintings primarily to American patrons. But exhibiting with the Impressionists meant that her audience was now the French intelligentsia, including not only a small group of progressive collectors, but novelists, critics, politicians, and members of the theatrical and musical worlds as well. She was one of the few Americans accepted into these rarified circles. Furthermore, Cassatt finally abandoned any ideas she might still have had of returning to practice as an artist in her own country. Neither the Impressionist style nor Impressionist exhibition credentials would carry enough weight in American art circles to allow her to establish herself as she had in Paris. A sign that she finally considered herself a permanent expatriate was when she convinced her parents and older sister to move to Paris; this close knit family unit endured for the rest of their lives. Although the Cassatts in Paris maintained ties with their American relatives, they kept their distance from the American colony and lived in a remarkably French style.

The members of the Impressionist group were not just professional colleagues who exhibited together once a year; they were also good friends bound together by their common passion for artistic debate. The men could meet in smoky neighborhood cafés like La Nouvelles Athènes on the Place Pigalle. The women were not to be left out; they rekindled the fiery arguments with and among the men during their frequent social gatherings in one another's homes and studios. The speech was so uncensored that feelings were often wounded, and because of this Cassatt often vowed she would never again speak to Degas, who was apparently the major offender. But Cassatt thrived on the sharpness and level of intellectual exchange which she found had no equal in the American artistic community. Opinionated and argumentative herself, she felt she had found her true home in this group.

Cassatt's debut as an Impressionist in the exhibition of 1879 was marked appropriately by several paintings of young women at the theater—a subject often called "le début," referring both to the introduction of these young women to society and to the opening night of the performance. Both references bespoke Cassatt's position as newcomer to the group and to her unveiling of a style completely new to her. Cassatt's Impressionist paintings were so different from the works she had been painting previously that today, if it were not for the signatures, many of her early pieces would likely be attributed to another artist.

Critics heralded her emergence as an Impressionist and immediately connected her style with that of Degas, who was known for taking new converts under his wing. Cassatt was not sorry to be placed alongside Degas, whom she always believed to be the greatest artist of the nineteenth century, but the connection was too narrow. She had also studied and adopted the painterly effects of Berthe Morisot and Auguste Renoir, neither of whom had exhibited with the group in 1879, and she felt that her own version of Impressionism was by no means a simple imitation of Degas or anyone else, a point she returned to again and again toward the end of her life.

One outgrowth of the 1879 exhibition was Cassatt's new interest in printmaking. Up to this point she had spurned the graphic arts, including drawing, as less interesting and expressive than painting. But in the same spirit of change that had made her reject her previous painting style to become an Impressionist, she was suddenly willing to consider printmaking an expressive art, if approached creatively. Although her first efforts in etching went unappreciated (the new journal in which she and Degas expected to publish their prints did not materialize, and the prints she exhibited in the Impressionist exhibition of 1880 were not mentioned by the critics) nevertheless the exercise awakened in her an enduring interest in innovative printmaking. As time went on, her drypoints and later her color prints were widely exhibited and were largely responsible for her international reputation.

In the summer of 1880, the Paris Cassatts hosted a branch of the Philadelphia Cassatts: Mary's brother Alexander, his wife Lois, and their four children. It was a treat for the elder Cassatts, who had not seen their grandchildren for over two years; and it was a revelation for Mary, whose years abroad had previously prevented her from making the acquaintance of her nieces and nephews. It had long been her practice to use family members as models whenever possible, but until now these models had always been adults. When she pulled out her paints to capture the four children, ranging in age from six to eleven, she found a subject that fit both her own taste for unpretentious subjects and the liveliness of style she had learned from Impressionism. When she showed the paintings of the children in the next Impressionist exhibition, in 1881, she received warm praise from critics like Joris-Karl Huysmans, which in turn encouraged her to take up the subject with increasing frequency. In spite of Cassatt's tendency to dismiss the critics, she was inevitably affected by them. Without wanting to compromise her own firm aesthetic values, she desired the favorable opinion of the press and understood that the fame she was working to achieve would come with their help. Critical assessments had a direct relationship to sales, which she also sought actively. She had placed pictures with dealers as early as 1871 and was later to work primarily with the two major modern art galleries, Durand-Ruel and Vollard. To a certain extent her attention to critics and dealers, who tended to promote those women artists who used subjects "appropriate" to their sex, reinforced her own choices, but ultimately may have led her to emphasize subjects such as children and motherhood to the exclusion of others. Looking back on the last years of her artistic production, she told Anna Thorne, a young American admirer, "I sold my soul to the dealers, that's all" (see page 317).

But in the 1880s Cassatt was still exploring new ideas, particularly those having to do with concepts of beauty and ugliness. In 1883 she painted a portrait of Mary Dickinson Riddle, her mother's cousin from Pittsburgh. She had always painted portraits, since, as her mother said, she "had a talent for likenesses" (see page 59). She had even tried to establish herself as a professional portraitist in the mid-1870s when she was searching for direction in the labyrinthine art world of Paris. But her approach was always more truthful than flattering to her sitters, and, since she was never able to attract commissions as easily as did such fashionable portraitists as John Singer Sargent, she gave it up when she became an Impressionist. In her portrait of Mrs. Riddle, Cassatt attempted to balance her incisive treatment of the elderly woman's features with the elegance of the abstract design and the creamy paint surface. Degas was very complimentary of the portrait, but Mrs. Riddle and her family saw only the unflatteringly straightforward depiction of an aging beauty and rejected the portrait. Thirty years later it was being fought over by the Petit Palais and the Metropolitan Museum, where it resides today.

For the next decade, Cassatt experimented with the balance of beauty and ugliness in her paintings of women. On occasion she would deliberately choose unattractive models from whom she would paint beautiful pictures. Other times she would use the power of a strong, muscular model contrasted with a fashionable dress; she often commissioned dresses for her paintings from the most prominent fashion houses of her day. Her portraits continued to be more accurate than pleasing. By the 1890s this aspect of her style was widely discussed, and critics both praised and bemoaned her tendency to eschew conventional beauty in favor of the overall aesthetic effect of the work.

When the last Impressionist exhibition closed in 1886, Cassatt was, for the first time, without a regular forum for showing new work. Since 1868, when she had her first painting accepted to the Salon, she had been able to exhibit in Paris virtually every year. Now she was faced with having to choose whether to turn again to the Salon, which she still felt was too traditional, or to submit works to the new Salon des Indépendents, which was juryless, but was also without any other means of controlling quality. Finally, in 1889 she found a new exhibiting group, the Société des Peintres-Graveurs (Society of Painter-Printmakers). When she entered her new works into the Society's first exhibition, it was clear that her style had changed. The pastel and two prints she showed were all of mothers and children.

Cassatt had begun exploring the mother and child subject in 1888 with a drypoint sketch of her sister-in-law, Jennie Cassatt, holding her baby son, Gardner. From this haunting image, which combined Cassatt's previous theme of the contemplative woman with her more recent interest in painting children, Cassatt went on to develop a series of mother and child images in paintings and prints. Cassatt's handling of this timeless subject contrasted sharply with other versions popular at the time that were either too sentimental or too melodramatic. Her mothers and children were emphatically modern but had the monumentality of the traditional Madonna and Child. They immediately struck a chord with critics, dealers, collectors, and the public at large. Even though Cassatt had been a prominent artist in every phase of her career so far, it was the mother and child theme that brought her lasting fame.

The most telling sign of her new status was the exclusive contract offered to her in 1890 by the well-established dealer in Impressionism, Paul Durand-Ruel. Cassatt had worked with Durand-Ruel over the years, helping him to hold exhibitions and establish a branch of his gallery in New York. He had also sold a number of her works in Paris, but until this point she had not been important enough for him to enter into the kind of agreement he had held over the years with Monet, Pissarro, and Degas, wherein he paid the artist a certain amount per year and received an established number of works in return. The popularity of the mother and child paintings and prints made Cassatt a valuable asset to Durand-Ruel, and, because she was American, Durand-Ruel could promote her successfully in both Paris and New York. He gave her a prominent place in his publications. Also in 1890, the first complete article ever published on her work appeared in the art journal Durand-Ruel sponsored, *L'Art dans les Deux Mondes.* Soon after, her mother and child works were the focus of the chapter on Cassatt in Georges Lecomte's book on the Durand-Ruel collection, *L'Art Impressioniste d'après la collection privée de M. Durand-Ruel* (1892).

In addition to selling paintings, Durand-Ruel also handled the prints made by Impressionist painters such as Degas and Pissarro. In fact, his gallery hosted the exhibitions of the Society of Painter-Printmakers in which Cassatt exhibited the first in her series of mother and child images. In 1891 Durand-Ruel offered Cassatt her first one-person show where she unveiled her set of ten color prints which are now considered among the most important prints made in the nineteenth century. She had intended to send them to the annual exhibition of the Painter-Printmakers, but a xenophobic sentiment that swept the group that year banned non-French artists. Cassatt and Pissarro (a Danish national from the island of St. Thomas) complained to Durand-Ruel, who gave them each their own exhibition space alongside the "patriots."

Of the many complimentary reviews of Cassatt's exhibition, the most evocative was by Félix Fénéon, a critic and proponent of Neo-Impressionism and other avant-garde movements. Fénéon's review in the radical journal *Le Chat Noir* gave Cassatt a presence in the more progressive art circles that had taken the avant-garde mantle from Impressionism. Although Cassatt herself shied away from the increasingly abstract styles that were developing in Paris, her color prints had an unexpected influence on the revolution in graphic arts among the Nabis and other experimental artists.

The critical success of Cassatt's mother and child works and the color prints in the early 1890s also brought attention from a different quarter. In the spring of 1892 she was visited by the committee planning the pavilion that would be dedicated to the accomplishments of women in the World's Columbian Exposition in Chicago in 1893. Simply called the "Woman's Building," it was to have a barrel-vaulted hall of honor which would be decorated on each end by a mural—one showing "Primitive Woman" in servitude, the other showing "Modern Woman" plucking fruit from the tree of knowledge. Cassatt agreed to tackle "Modern Woman," which she painted in brilliant colors in a light-filled outdoor setting. She dressed her models in the latest fashions, but portrayed them plucking fruit as if in a solemn ceremony. The mural was declared a success by Cassatt's associates in Paris and by the more sophisticated critics in Chicago, but to many others it was considered incomprehensible, even "cynical." The negative reactions so far outweighed the positive that a reproduction of the mural in the guide to the fair was eliminated in the second edition. Cassatt seems to have been insulated from the negative reactions; she declined an invitation to Chicago and spent the summer of the fair painting peacefully in the French countryside.

No matter how large a painting it was, the importance of the mural in Chicago paled in Cassatt's estimation beside the fact that Durand-Ruel was launching her first major retrospective exhibition in the fall of 1893, not long after the fair was to close. To triumph in Paris had been her lifelong dream, and now that dream was coming true. She spent the summer working on new paintings, pastels, and color prints, most based on the sketches she had made in preparation for the mural. The new works would hang beside carefully chosen examples from the last fifteen years, or, in other words, since she had become an Impressionist. The first ten years (1868–1878) of her professional career, during which time she had exhibited regularly at the Salon, were of no interest to her. In later years she would choose a few favorites and destroy the rest, forever preventing posterity from fully understanding her early ideas and images.

The exhibition, with a catalogue essay written by the symbolist critic André Mellério, was everything she hoped it would be. In addition to a wide range of critical reactions, including a translation of the catalogue essay for American audiences, the exhibition attracted a number of buyers. Soon afterwards Cassatt was able to buy a country estate, le Mésnil-Beaufresne, where she would spend summers for the rest of her life. A final honor was the request by the Musée Luxembourg, the French national museum of modern art, to buy one of her works for the official state collection. This exhibition marked a high point in Cassatt's life. Although she would continue to paint for another twenty years and was bestowed with many more honors, the wide acceptance that she had gained in the Paris art world in 1893 meant the most to her.

After this success she was anxious to have a major exhibition in New York where, thanks to the efforts of Durand-Ruel, she was becoming well known. She had a number of longtime friends among New York artists, including J. Alden Weir, William Merritt Chase, and William Sartain (Emily's brother). Through their efforts, she had exhibited at the Society of American Artists every year since 1879. Louisine Elder Havemeyer also served as a conduit to art events in New York in her role as collector and patron. But aside from those who had seen her exhibitions in Paris, Cassatt's career was largely unknown to the American public. However, once the first exhibition was arranged in 1895, the response was so great that another was quickly scheduled for 1898. Thereafter Cassatt's works were often on view at Durand-Ruel's New York gallery and were frequently seen in major exhibitions across the country.

When Americans became familiar with her work, they embraced Cassatt as if she had never left her native country. Much to her surprise, the works that had impressed the Parisian avant-garde were also to the taste of the average American. Not only did Cassatt gain the support of the forward-looking artists and connoisseurs in New York, but her mother and child paintings began to be reproduced along with glowing articles in such popular publications as *Good Housekeeping Magazine* (see page 156) and *The Hampton Magazine* (see page 208).

Once Cassatt's works were subjected to mass distribution and were thus separated from the aesthetic theories that had informed them, Cassatt achieved a kind of fame she had never courted and was powerless to control. She shielded herself from frivolous interviews and refused to take a public role in the art world, including serving on juries or boards of arts organizations. She did, however, make time for American art students seeking her advice, and adopted the Art League, an organization for American art students in Paris, as her main community interest. Many of the reminiscences of Mary Cassatt in later years came from students, such as Grace Gassette, Anna Thorne, and George Biddle, who made the pilgrimage to her studio.

By 1910 she had been elevated to near legendary status and dubbed by one critic "the most eminent of American women painters" (see page 292). While this was surely an exaggeration (Cecilia Beaux had by far more success in American art circles at that time), it nevertheless indicates the importance to Americans of Cassatt's stature in France and her association with the increasingly popular Impressionists. In 1913 the first complete book on Cassatt was published in France, placing her among the select few of her generation (Degas, Renoir) to enjoy this honor during their lifetimes. The symbolist writer and poet, Achille Segard, researched and interpreted her paintings and prints, favorably comparing her work to that of Degas, Renoir, and the other Impressionists. He also interviewed her at her country home and, although she was as reticent with him as with others who came to her door, he managed to come closer than anyone to capturing her personality and aesthetic principles at the end of her career. Unfortunately plans to translate and publish the book in the United States fell through, and although the French edition remains a major source for the study of Mary Cassatt, much of Segard's contribution has not been recognized.

Another important voice in the shaping of the Cassatt legend during her lifetime was her old friend Louisine Havemeyer. In 1915 Havemeyer convinced Cassatt to lend her paintings to an exhibition in New York to benefit the campaign for women's suffrage. Cassatt was a lifelong feminist who spoke out frequently against the obstacles facing women artists, but had never before participated in organized feminist activities. Havemeyer, on the other hand, was a leader in the Women's Political Union, a group famous for its annual marches for suffrage down Fifth Avenue in New York. When Havemeyer wrote and spoke on Cassatt as an artist, she portrayed her as a strong, hardworking, original woman consistent with the feminist principles of her day and ours. This vision would stand as a corrective to the many later attempts to portray Cassatt as a lady of leisure who spent her days reading, sewing, and having tea in imitation of her paintings.

Cassatt was forced to stop painting in 1914 when cataracts clouded her vision. Despite numerous operations over the next six years, always bringing the hope that she would be able to work again, her eyesight was never restored. When she lay down her brushes she was only seventy and physically quite fit, so she felt keenly the loss of her greatest passion in life. This personal tragedy was unfairly compounded by the onset of World War I, which displaced her from her beloved Beaufresne and scattered the loyal household staff who had become a family to her. The twelve years until her death in 1926 saw her grow increasingly restless and outspoken in the manner of a profoundly frustrated person. Those who came to know her during this time—George Biddle and Forbes Watson—recorded the ferocious temper of her old age.

When she died, however, she was hardly alone and forgotten. Her fundamental intelligence and engagement in new ideas kept the younger generations coming even to her final bedside, and her generous heart preserved the affection of her oldest friends. Mathilde Valet, her housekeeper and companion for over forty years, was with her to the end, and Louisine Havemeyer came to her gravesite near Beaufresne to plant tea roses in her memory. The obituaries in France and America were lengthy and respectful, indicating that her stature had not waned even during the last decade of inactivity. Memorial exhibitions abounded in Paris, New York, and her hometown of Philadelphia, allowing a new generation to place her in the history of modern art.

In the seventy years since her death, the interpretation of Cassatt's art and artistic personality have undergone many metamorphoses effected by changing cultural values, particularly those having to do with women's place in society. But there has not been a time when her work has fallen out of favor or ceased to be recognized for the contributions it made to the history of Impressionism and the interpretation of the mother and child. In light of the difficulty women have in fixing a firm position in the history of their age, this is an extraordinary achievement worthy of an extraordinary woman.

—Nancy Mowll Mathews
Williamstown, Massachusetts
1996

CASSATT

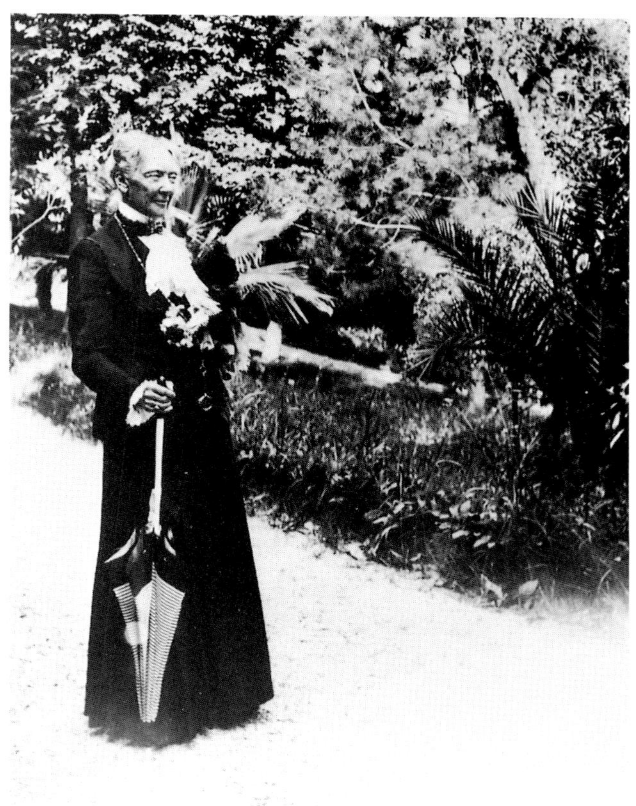

Mary Cassatt in the gardens at the Villa Angeletto in Grasse (near Nice), where she resided during most of World War I. 1911. Photograph courtesy of the Hill-Stead Museum, Farmington, Connecticut.

ACHILLE SEGARD

From *Mary Cassatt: Un Peintre des enfants et des mères*

An Interview with the Artist

1913

Achille Segard (1872–1936), French poet, novelist, and art critic who wrote the first major study of Mary Cassatt's work, drawing on many interviews with the artist, as well as published sources and his own observations of Cassatt's paintings and prints.

A tall, slender, very aristocratic figure dressed in black, leaning on a cane and advancing carefully down the gravelled paths of her park, with its magnificent trees—thus did Miss Mary Cassatt appear to me, the day of my first visit to her, at her beautiful hermitage in Mesnil-Théribus, in the Oise region. I helped her up the front steps. A smile of great goodness illuminated her sober countenance; below curls threaded with silver, her gray-blue eyes, the color of still waters, animated her strong features. She held out to me an energetic and delicate hand, long, thin, hard-working, and lively, a vibrating extension of her sensitivity. We chatted. Along the glassed-in gallery walls, Japanese prints, their lines precise and sure, created an artistic atmosphere. Through a half-open door, one glimpsed a preliminary sketch of a portrait of a child wearing a spring hat accented with tiny red roses, beside a young mother in a rose-red and violet blouse. The extremely elegant arabesque of this group, and the felicitous intensity of the color quickened the conversation with a sort of silent and vivid "presence." The trees in the park were motionless. The silences that interspersed our chat were solemn.

Mesnil-Théribus, a small town fifty miles north of Paris, was the site of Cassatt's country home, Mesnil-Beaufresne.

"I am American," she said, "definitely and frankly American. My family, however, was originally from France. Well before the revocation of the Edict of Nantes—in 1662, to be exact—a Frenchman named Cossart emigrated from France to Holland, then went on to settle in New Amsterdam. His grandson moved to Pennsylvania. That was my father's great-grandfather. My mother is also from a long line of Americans. Her family was originally from Scotland; they immigrated to America around 1700. So our family has been in Pennsylvania a long time, more precisely in Pittsburgh, where I was born. My mother, however, was educated in the French manner. She was raised in part by an American lady who had attended Mme. Campan's school, where there were a fair number of young ladies of the imperial aristocracy. By a twist of fate, this lady had returned to Pittsburgh, where she accepted a few students. From her, my mother learned to speak the purest French, and for the rest of her life she corresponded in French with those of her friends who spoke the language. Her general culture as well as her literary culture were extremely extensive. Our father—a banker in Pittsburgh, though his soul was not at all that of a businessman—was himself imbued with many French ideas, and he devoted himself to our education.

"In my earliest memories I see myself, a little girl of five or six, learning to read in Paris, where my parents had come to consult a physician about one of their children. They remained in Paris for five years. We then returned to Philadelphia, where I received part of my education. Toward 1868, my mother and I returned to Paris for a little over a year. Shortly before the war, that is, around 1868, I decided to become a painter. This also meant that I was deciding to leave for Europe. At the Academy School in Philadelphia one drew, after a fashion, from ancient copies and old plaster casts. There was no teaching. In any case, I believe that painting cannot be taught, and that it is not necessary to study with a master. Museums are all the teachers one needs."

Cassatt's older brother, Robert Kelso Cassatt, suffered from bone cancer. The family moved to Heidelberg in 1853 and then to Darmstadt, where Robbie died in 1855 at age thirteen.

Letter from Alexander J. Cassatt to His Fiancée, Lois Buchanan

On Mary Cassatt's Temperament

November 27, 1867

Alexander J. Cassatt (1839–1906), Cassatt's oldest brother Aleck who graduated from Rensselaer Polytechnic Institute. Entering a career in the railroad, he worked his way up from rodman in 1860 to superintendent of the Pennsylvania Railroad in 1866. He was promoted and transferred to Altoona in 1867 and to Philadelphia in 1871. He served as president of the Pennsylvania Railroad from 1899 to 1906, during which time he oversaw the construction of Pennsylvania Station in New York City.

Maria Lois Buchanan (1847–1920), Alexander's future wife, was the daughter of a Pennsylvania clergyman and niece of James Buchanan, fifteenth president of the United States (1857–61). Aleck and Lois were married on November 25, 1868.

Altoona,
[Pennsylvania]

Dear Miss Lody,

I have been hoping every mail to have an opportunity of inspecting that new purchase of yours. The writing paper, I mean—That was all that I cared for, of course—but I have been disappointed—no, but seriously, if you won't let me come to see you, you ought not to deny me the next biggest pleasure I have. And I am sure if you knew what a very great pleasure it is to me to receive a letter from you, dear heart, you are too good and too kind not to indulge me . . .

I received a letter from my sister Mary the other day—She does not often write to me, knowing that all the family see them anyhow—but on this occasion she did write to me and there is something in the letter about you. I intend to bring it down to show it to you—Mary was always a great favorite of mine. I suppose because our taste was a good deal alike—Whenever it was a question of a walk or a ride or a gallop on horseback, it didn't matter when or in what weather, Mary was already ready, so when I was at home we were together a great deal—We use to have plenty of fights, for she has a pretty quick temper and I was not altogether exempt from that failing myself, but we very soon made friends again—I was in Pittsburgh yesterday and the day before, saw Mrs. Stone and the General there—also Miss Mahon—not your friend but her sister. What a place that Pittsburgh is. I don't think anything could induce me to live there—I did not see the sun while I was there, and yet 10 or 15 miles out of town the day was quite bright—They say it is getting worse every year, and in winter, when fires are kept going in all the private houses it is much worse than in summer. . . .

As I have not heard from you about your going to Wheatland I am beginning to hope that your Uncle has good taste enough not to want you and with that compliment I will say good-bye.

Wheatland in Lancaster, Pennsylvania, was the home of Lois's uncle, President James Buchanan.

Your very much loved.
Yours very sincerely,
A. J. Cassatt

From *The Crayon*
"Woman's Position in Art"
February 1861

In the following article we propose to circulate some ideas bearing upon Art in relation to the gentle sex, to show what a vast field for employment there is open to women, consistent with their organic powers and social relationships. A French writer, M. Lagrange, is our authority. Dancing, Music, and the Drama, he says, are in France the official channels for female artistic capacity, the government providing conservatories for instruction in these branches of art. Why should it not offer the same facilities for instruction in the arts of Design? In advocating the establishment of a *conservatoire* for instruction in Design, M. Lagrange pictures the risks and rewards that fall to the *cantatrice,* the *danseuse* and the actress, and compares these with those that the females are subject to who pursue Drawing, Painting, and Sculpture. The latter pursuits, M. Lagrange contends, are more consonant with the feminine instincts of modesty and privacy, and more worthy of public encouragement. His ideas are of general application, and equally suggestive here as they are in France. . . .

This article is an edited translation of an article by Léon Lagrange, "Du Rang des Femmes dans les Arts" (The Position of Women in the Arts) from the "Gazette des Beaux-Arts" (1860). It is the kind of essay on women artists that Mary Cassatt would have read while she was in art school.

What remains of the fame of dancers and musicians with whose names the dictionaries are full? Of Guimard, a famous *danseuse,* there is no souvenir but that of a sullied reputation and a richly decorated mansion in a depraved taste. Malibran and Pasta charmed the ears of our forefathers—where are the brilliant notes that were warbled from their throats? Borne away by the wind kindred to the breath that uttered them. But the wind could not sweep away the canvas on which Claudine Stella wrote her name to hang by the side of Poussin's in the museums of their common country. Go to the Louvre, go to Florence, and contemplate Madame Le Brun still alive in her graceful portraits.

. . . Rachel Ruisch, the accredited painter to the elector-palatine, and the mother of ten children, held the brush with a firm hand at the ripe old age of eighty. Angelica Kauffman, a skillful musician, viewed music only as a relaxation from labor, devoting herself to painting as the master art of her life.

Claudine Bouzonnet Stella (1636–97); Nicolas Poussin (1594–1665); Marie Louise Elisabeth Vigée-Le Brun (1755–1842), French portraitist, painted the royalty of Europe; Rachel Ruysch (1664–1750), Dutch painter, specialized in floral still life painting; Angelica Kauffmann (1741–1807), Swiss painter working in England, specialized in neoclassical subjects.

In France the old Academy of Painting and Sculpture, more liberal than the present *Institut,* comprehended that it could not justly exclude women; and such was the eagerness of women to avail themselves of its honors, and the readiness of the men to welcome them, that the king was obliged to restrict the number of female academicians to four. . . . Outside of the Academy, from that time to this in France, the name of women artists is legion. They have written themselves on the pages of French art-history as painters of enamels, decorators of royal palaces, accomplished draughtsmen in crayon, and skillful etchers and engravers. In our own day is it necessary to mention the names of Madame O'Connell, Rosa Bonheur, and the sculptress, Mademoiselle Fauveau?

The United States are not left behind in respect to its encouragement of female talent. Like the old Academy in France, our New York Academy of Design has opened its doors to female membership, as can be seen in the name of Miss Anne Hall on its list of academicians. And then has not Miss Hosmer achieved the honor of a State commission to transmit to posterity the marble form of one of its noblest sons.

That Music and Dancing are not the only arts that conduct women to fame and fortune the above instances abundantly demonstrate. Painting, Engraving, and Sculpture, similarly encouraged, promised equal success; they provide a more assured support, in its being better acquired, and a more substantial renown, and especially a calmer and chaster existence. In the crowd of those above referred to, we must admit that some there are who could not be cited as models of domestic life. None, at all events, found in the art to which they were devoted a daily temptation and a lasting snare—a permanent and always craving abyss for victims; none have been placed in that horrible alternative of either abandoning a vocation that supports them, or of dissolving the ties that minister to a pure social intercourse.

Frederique Emile Auguste Miethe O'Connell (1823/28–1885), German painter and etcher working in France, specialized in historical subjects; Rosa Bonheur (1822–99), French painter famous for her monumental paintings of animals; Félicie de Fauveau (1802–1886), French sculptor working in Florence, specialized in historical genre subjects; Anne Hall (1792–1863), American painter of miniatures, and the first woman to be elected a member of the National Academy of Design in New York; Harriet Goodhue Hosmer (1830–1908), American sculptor and poet, center of a group of American women sculptors in Rome.

Exchange between Mary Cassatt and Eliza Haldeman and the Committee on Instruction at the Pennsylvania Academy of the Fine Arts

March 7, 1862

Philadelphia
March 7, 1862

Comm: on Instruction of the Penna: Academy of the Fine Arts

Gentlemen.

We wish to copy one of the Heads in the picture entitled "The Deliverance of Leyden" by Wittkamp. The size of our Canvass to be 20 x 25 inches.

Mary S. Cassatt.
E. J. Haldeman

The Comee are unaware of any reason why the President should not issue the Permit applied for

Comee John Sartain
Joseph Sommerville

Phila March 7th 62

Eliza Haldeman (1843–1910), Mary Cassatt's fellow student, travelling companion, and friend. She attended the Pennsylvania Academy of the Fine Arts from 1860 to 1863, went to France in 1866, and returned to the United States in 1868. She married Philip Figyelmesy in the mid-1870s and had two children. Although she did not pursue a career as an artist, she did publish two books about her family's life abroad.

Johann B. Wittkamp (1820–1885), Dutch painter widely known in Europe and America for such historical subjects as "The Deliverance of Leyden from the Siege by the Spaniards under Valdez in 1574," which was acquired by the Pennsylvania Academy of the Fine Arts in 1851.

John Sartain (1808–1897), father of Emily and William Sartain, was born in London and emigrated upon his marriage in 1830. He was a prominent Philadelphia engraver and publisher of "Sartain's Magazine." His other undertakings included the vice presidency of the Philadelphia School of Design for Women (for which his daughter Emily served as principal) and the directorship of the Pennsylvania Academy of the Fine Arts.

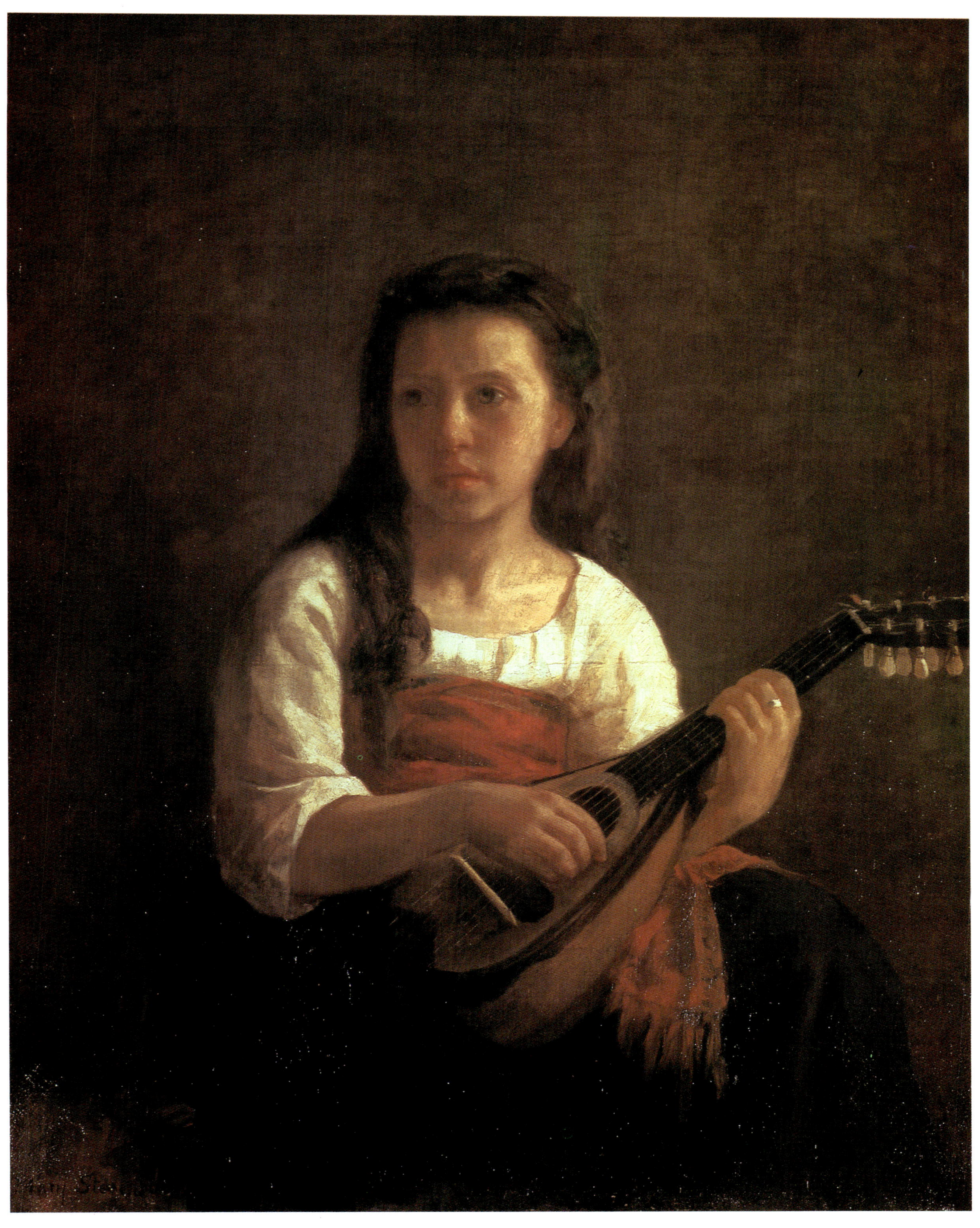

COLORPLATE 1. *The Mandolin Player.* 1868. Oil on canvas. 36 ¼ × 29 in. (92 × 73.6 cm). Private collection.

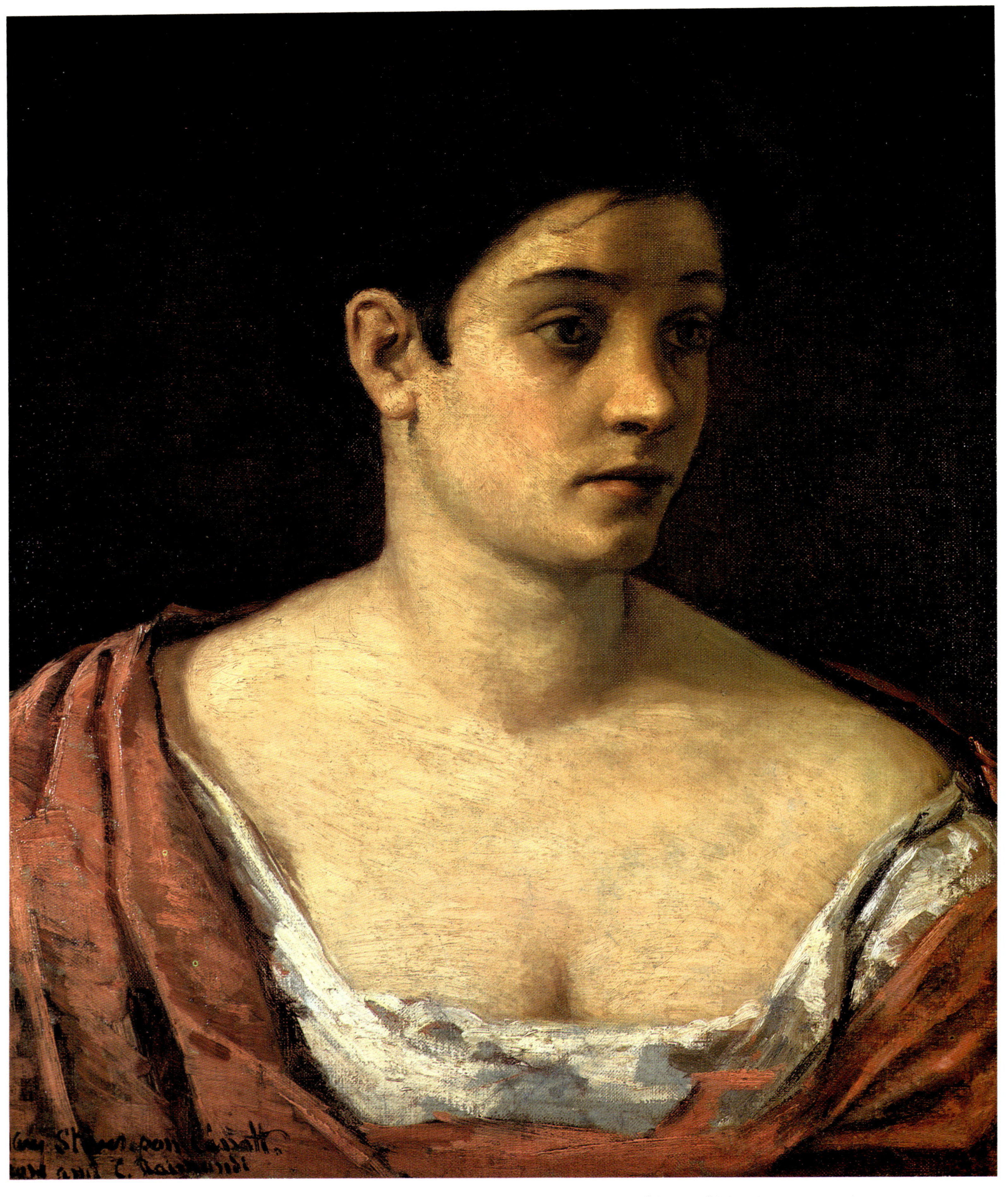

COLORPLATE 2. *Portrait of a Woman.* 1872. Oil on canvas. 23 ¼ × 19 ¾ in. (59 × 50 cm). The Dayton Art Institute. Gift of Mr. Robert Badenhop (1955.67).

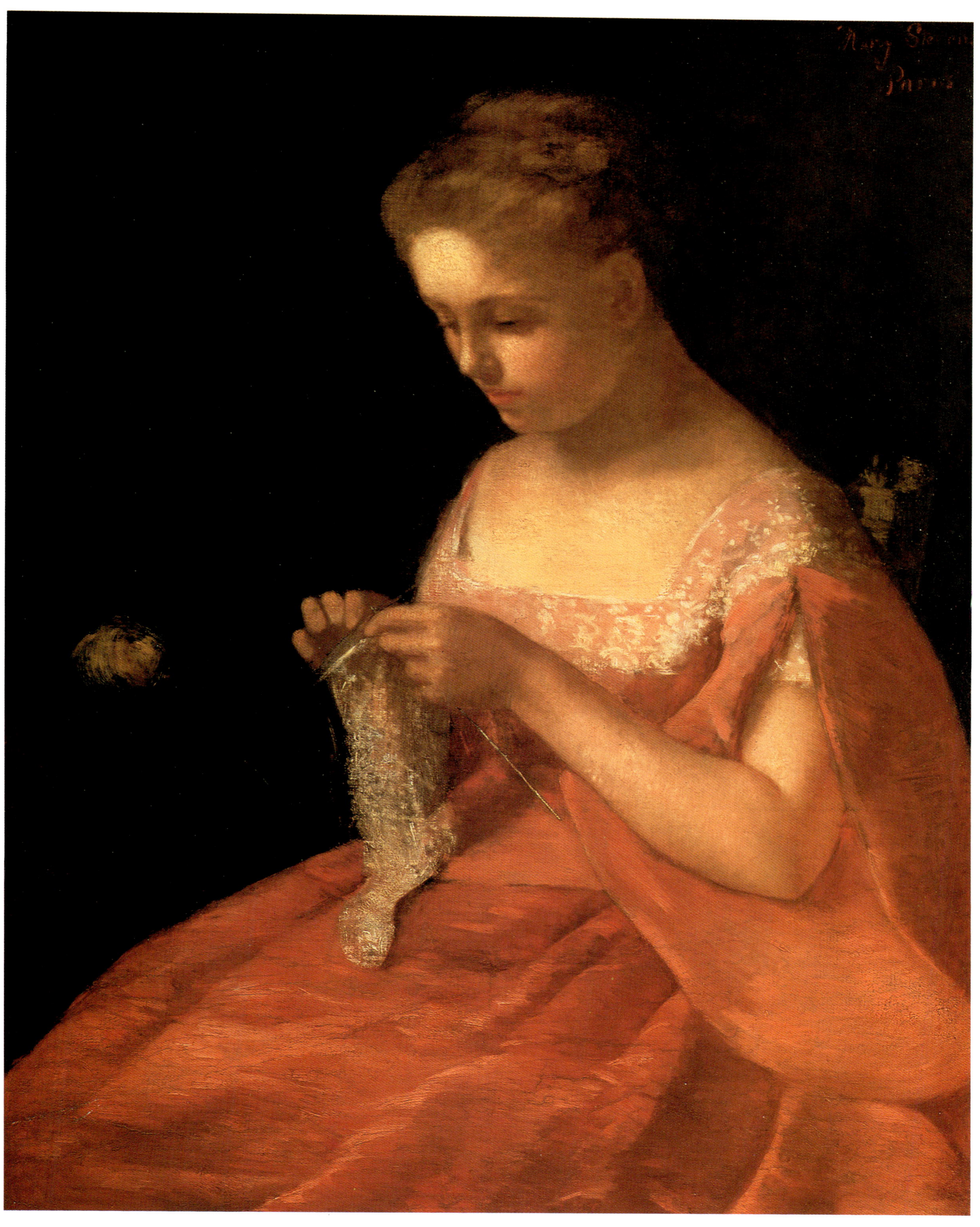

COLORPLATE 3. *The Young Bride.* c. 1869. Oil on canvas. 34 ¾ × 27 ½ in. (88.2 × 69.8 cm). The Montclair Art Museum, Montclair, New Jersey. Gift of the Max Kade Foundation.

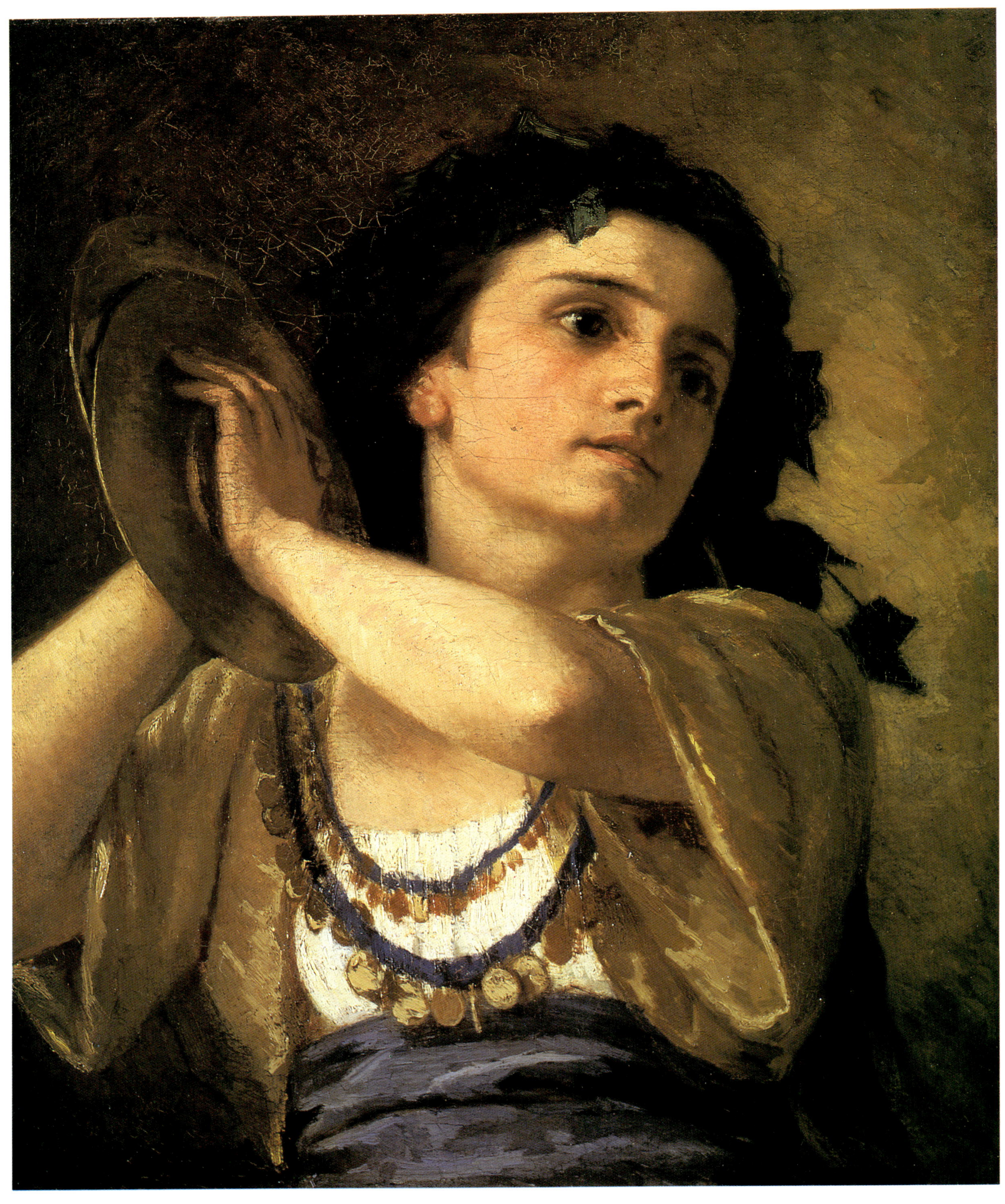

COLORPLATE 4. *Bacchante.* 1872. Oil on canvas. 24 × 19 15/16 in. (61 × 50.6 cm).
The Pennsylvania Academy of the Fine Arts. Gift of John Frederick Lewis.

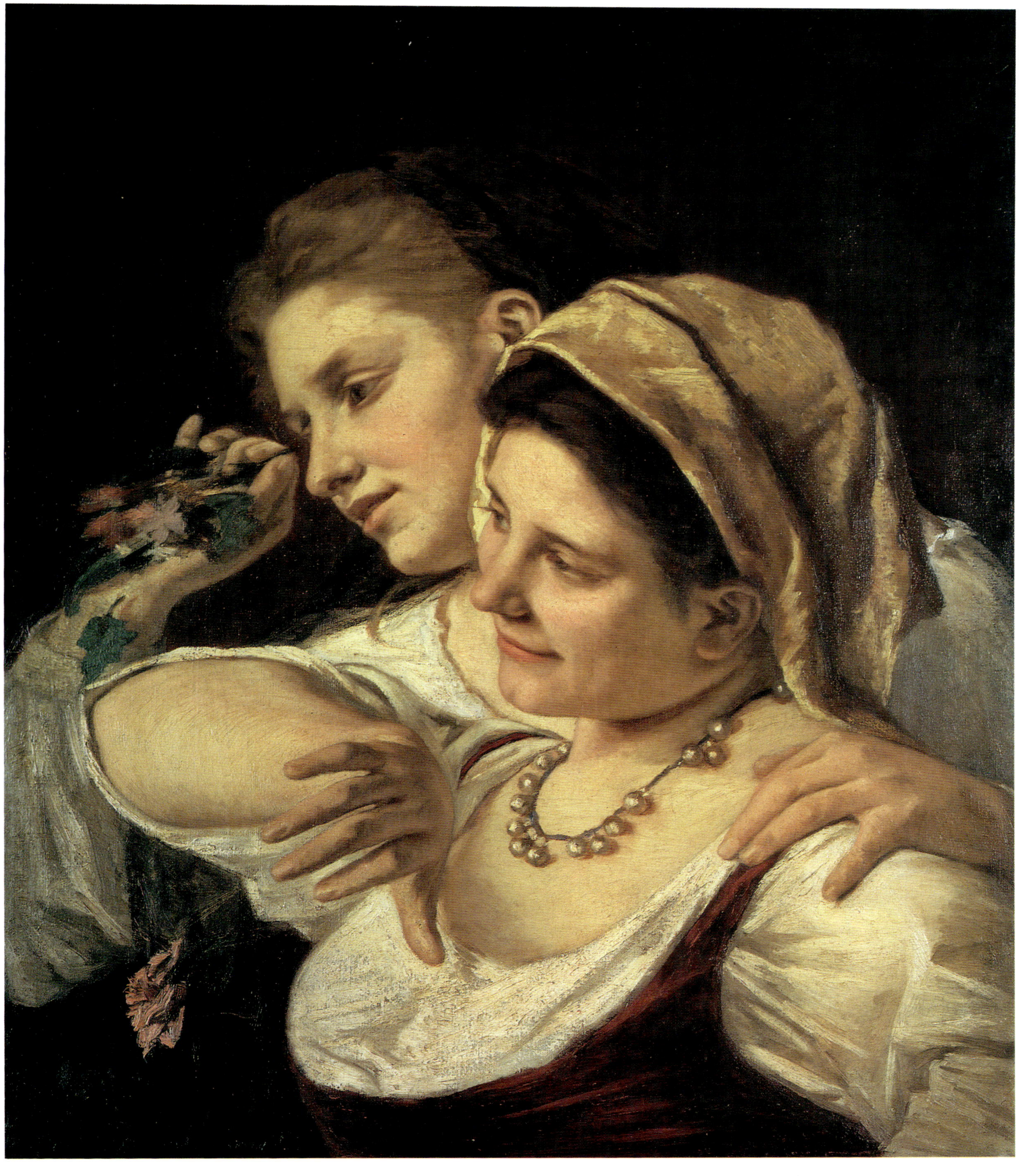

COLORPLATE 5. *Two Women Throwing Flowers During Carnival.* 1872. Oil on canvas. 25 × 21 ½ in. (63.5 × 54.6 cm). Collection of Mr. James J.O. Anderson, Baltimore, Maryland.

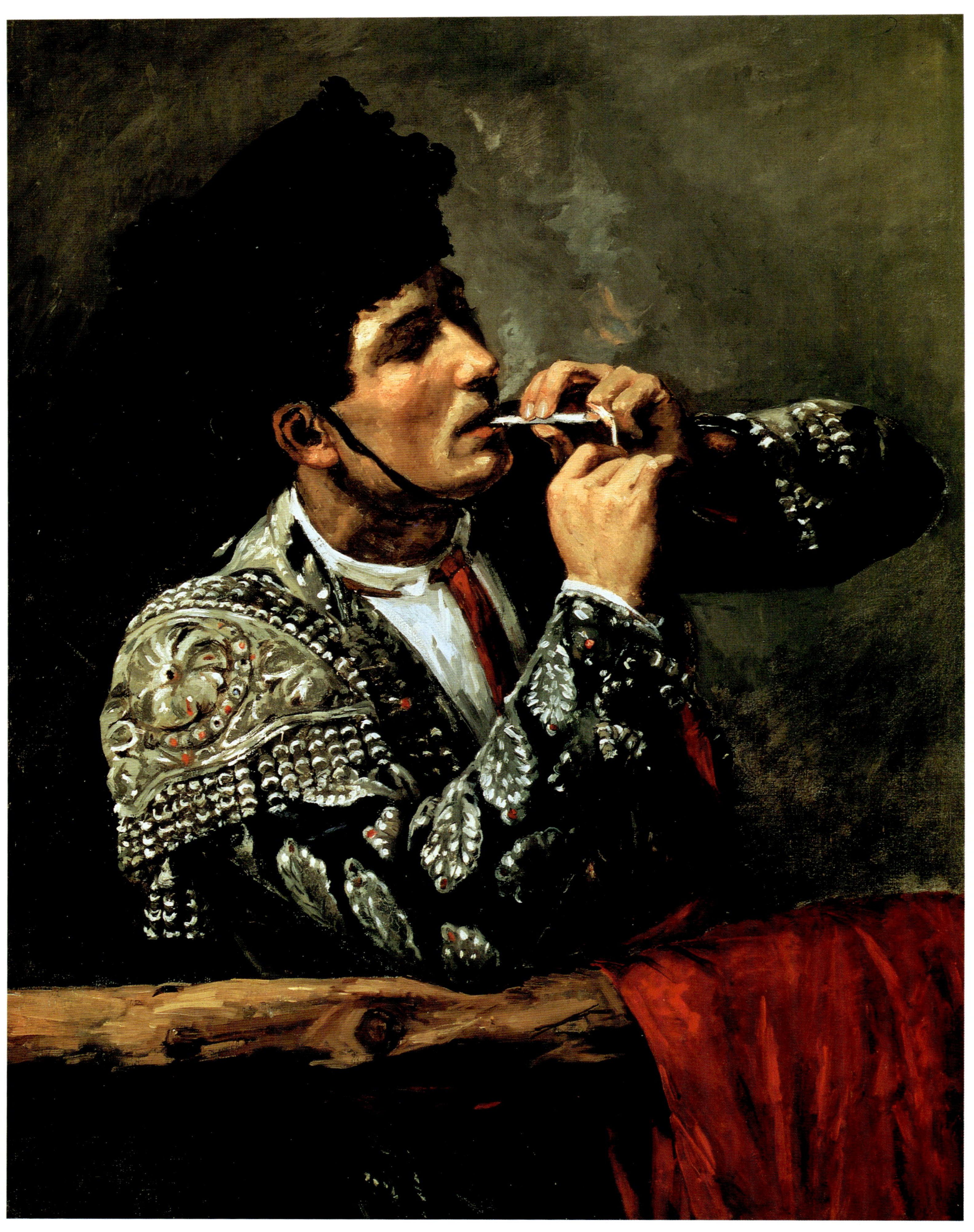

COLORPLATE 6. *Toreador.* 1873. Oil on canvas. 32 1/8 × 25 3/16 in. (81.6 × 64 cm). The Art Institute of Chicago. Gift of Mrs. Sterling Morton. Photograph © The Art Institute of Chicago. All Rights Reserved.

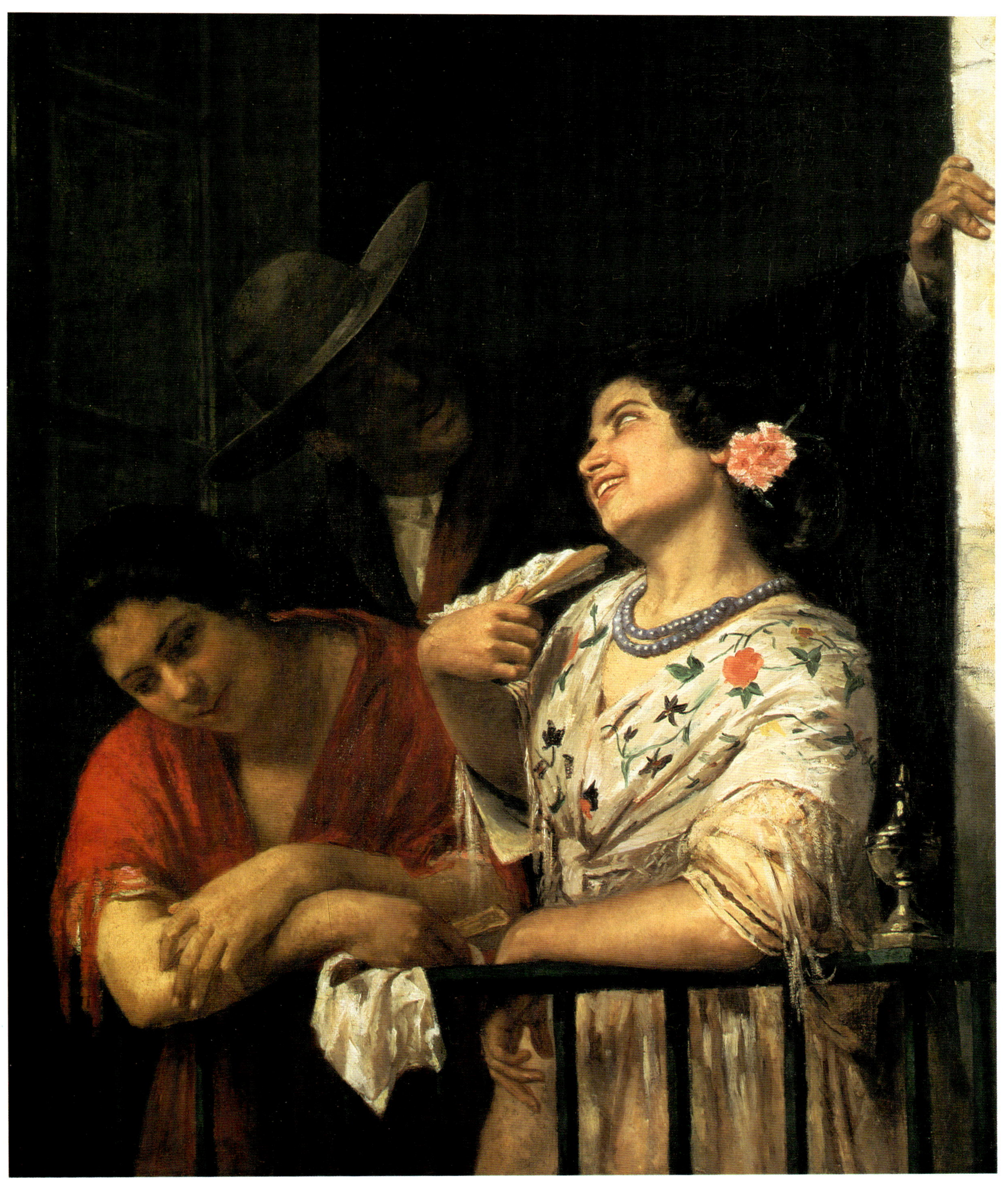

COLORPLATE 7. *On the Balcony.* 1873. Oil on canvas. 39 ¾ × 32 ½ in. (101 × 82.5 cm). Philadelphia Museum of Art. The W.P. Wilstach Collection.

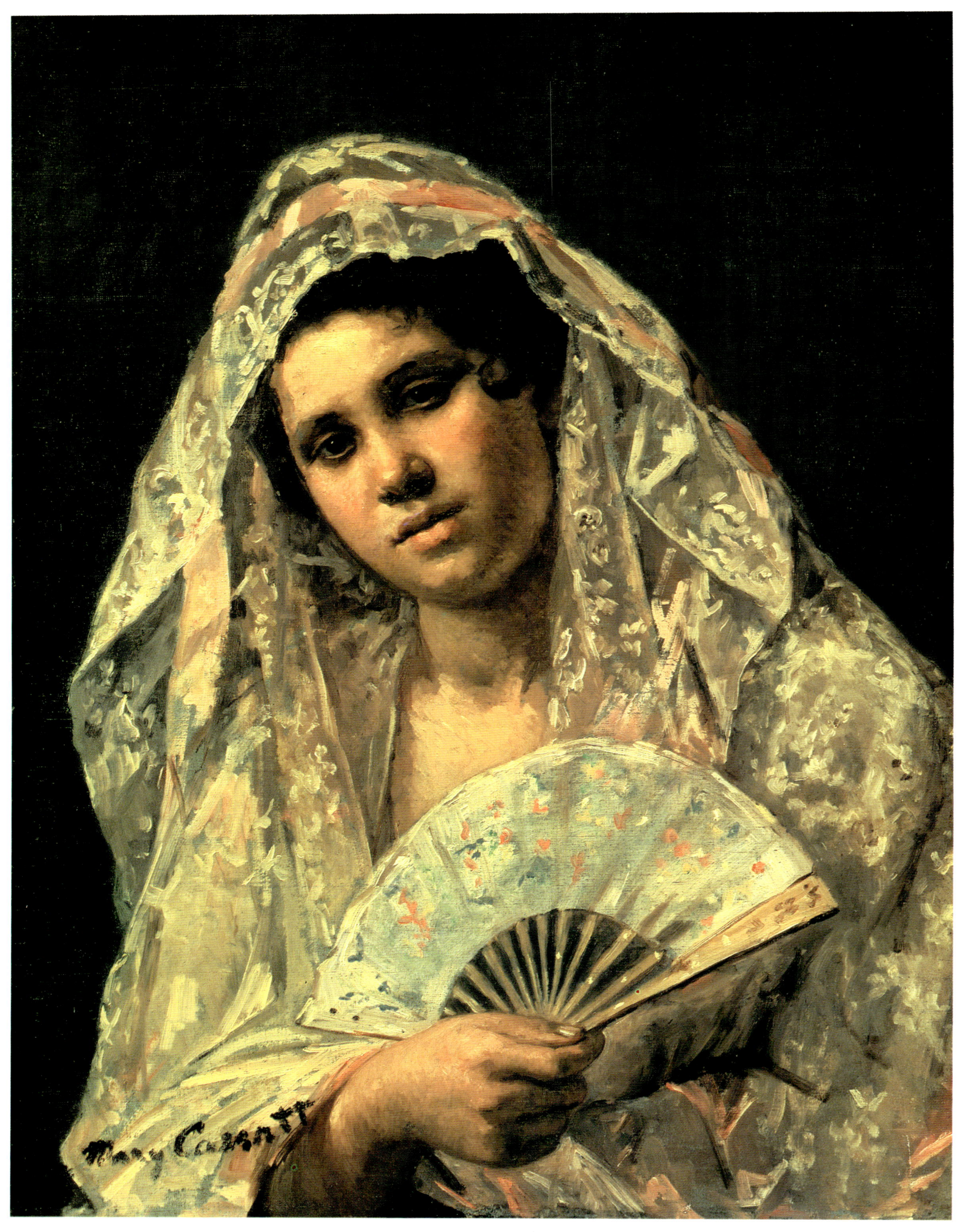

COLORPLATE 8. *Spanish Dancer Wearing a Lace Mantilla.* 1873. Oil on canvas. 25 ½ × 19 ½ in. (65 × 49.5 cm). National Museum of American Art, Washington, D.C. Photograph: Art Resource, New York.

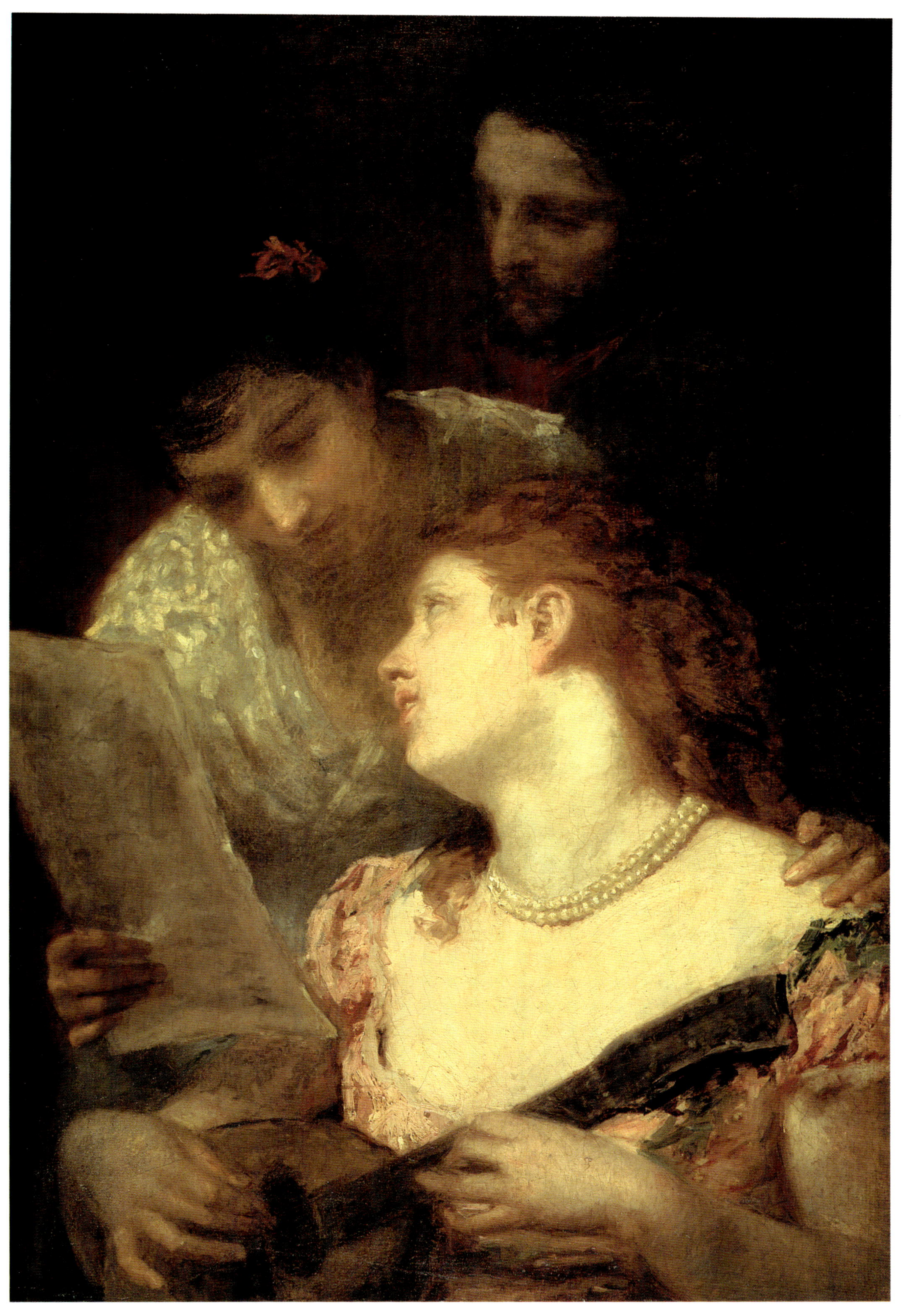

COLORPLATE 9. *A Musical Party.* c. 1874. Oil on canvas. 38 × 26 in. (96.5 × 66 cm). Musée du Petit Palais. Photograph: © Photothèque Musées de la Ville de Paris, SPADEM.

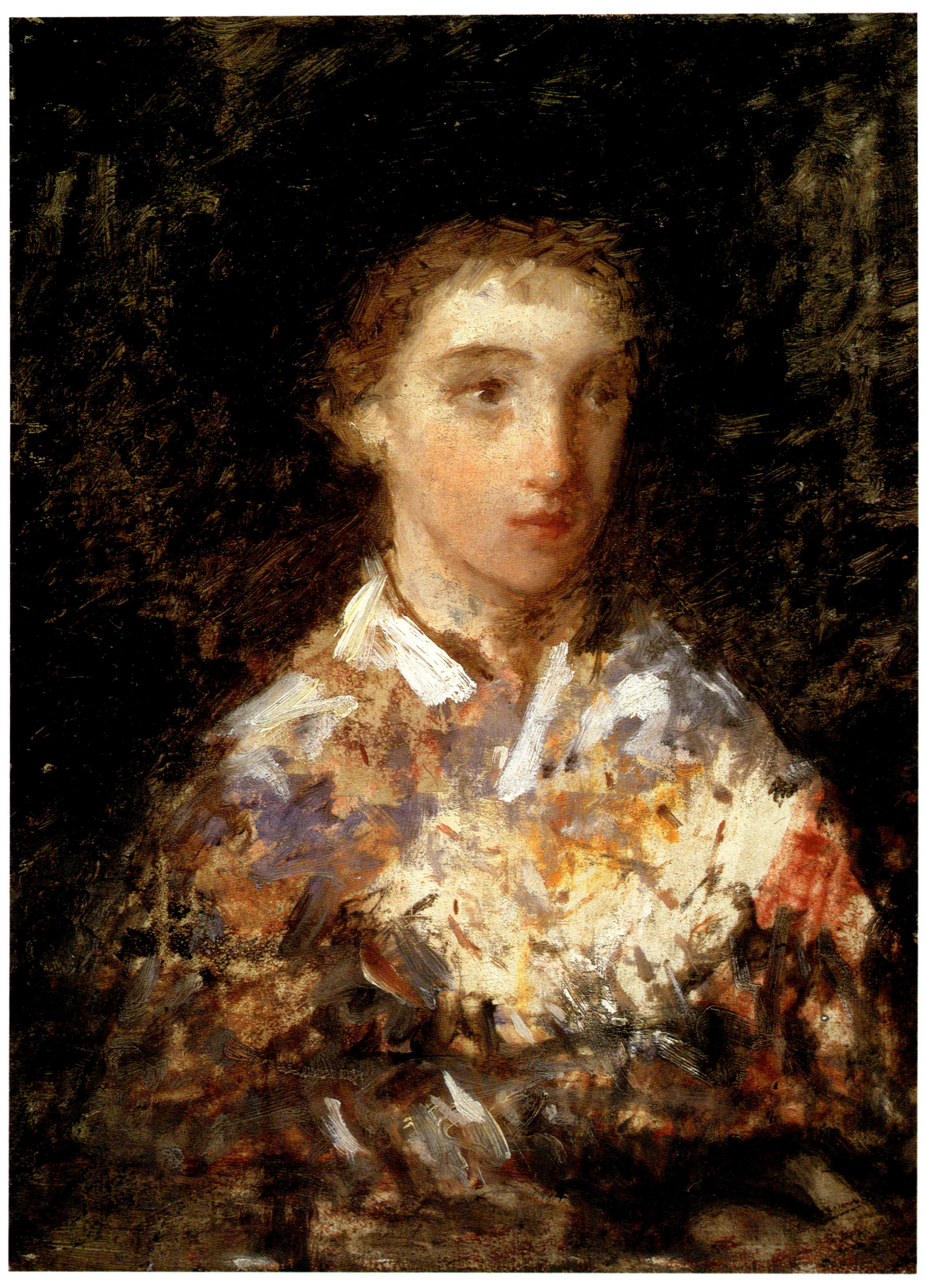

COLORPLATE 10. *Head of a Young Girl.* c. 1874. Oil on panel. 12 ¾ × 9 in. (32.3 × 22.9 cm). Courtesy of Museum of Fine Arts, Boston. Gift of Walter Gay.

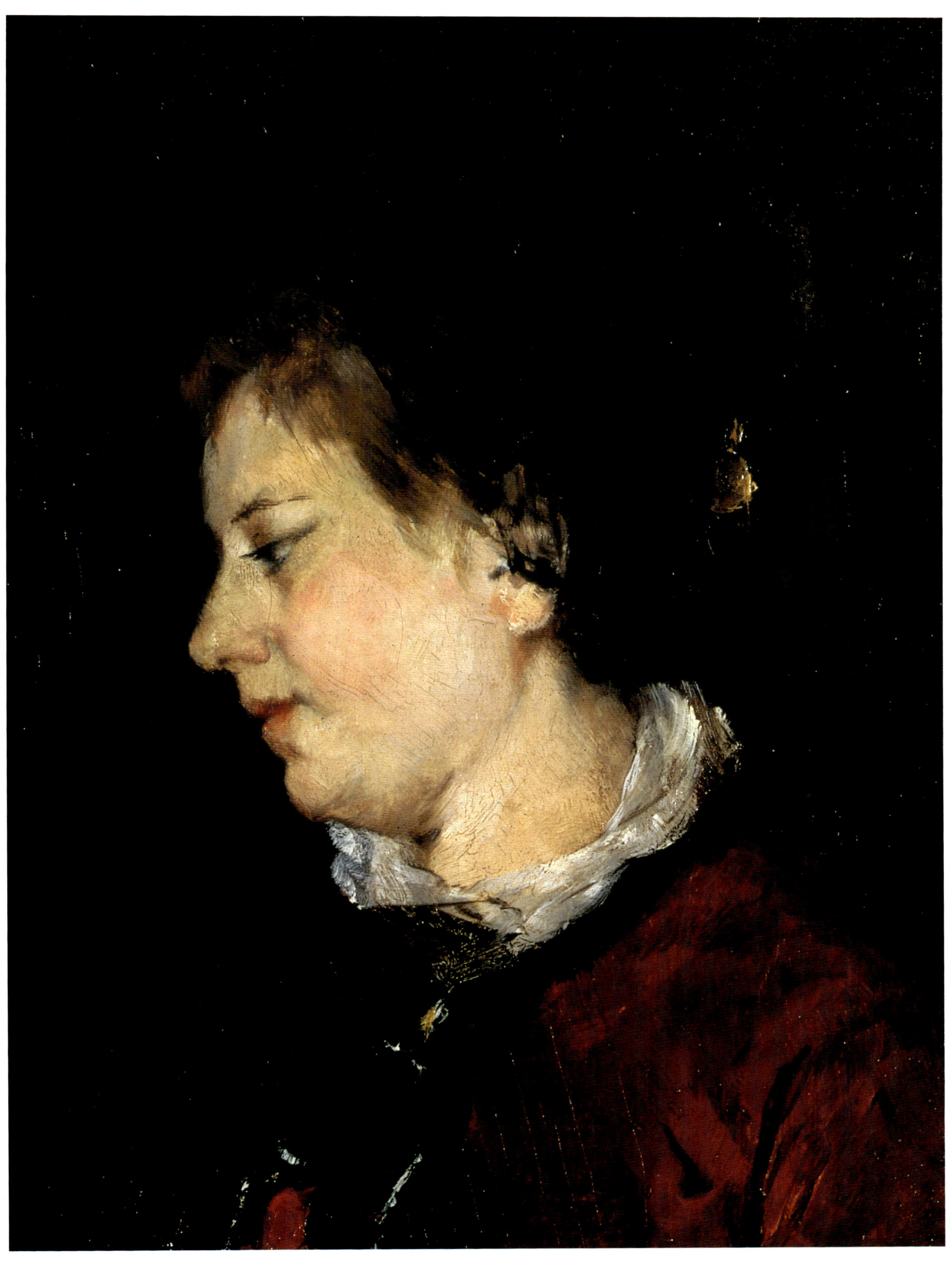

COLORPLATE 11. *Portrait of Madame Sisley*. 1873. Oil on panel. 7 1/8 × 5 3/8 in. (18 × 13.6 cm). Private collection, Toronto.

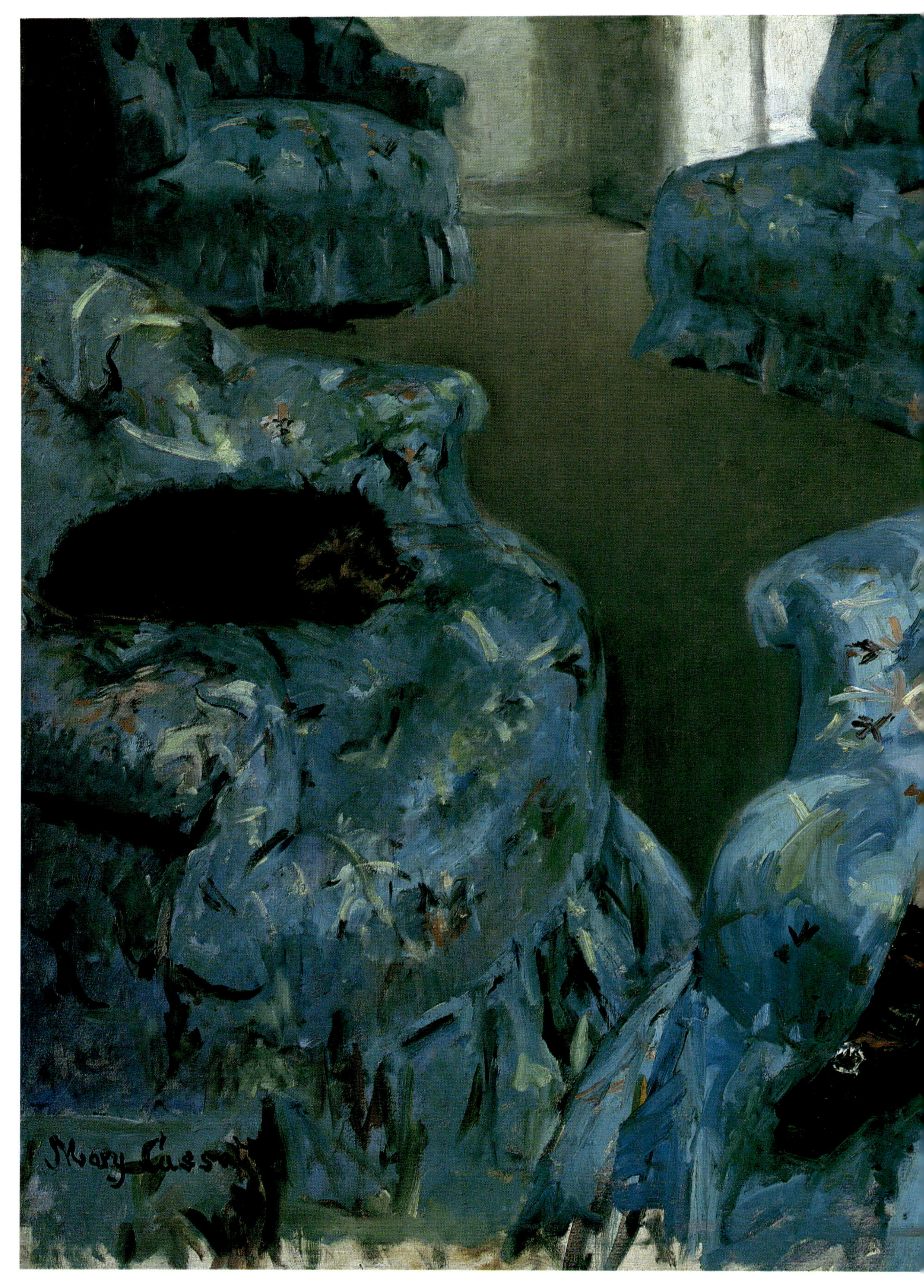

COLORPLATE 12. *Little Girl in a Blue Armchair.* 1878. Oil on canvas. 35 ¼ × 51 ⅛ in. (89.5 × 129.8 cm). National Gallery of Art. Collection of Mr. and Mrs. Paul Mellon. Photograph © Board of Trustees, National Gallery of Art, Washington, D.C.

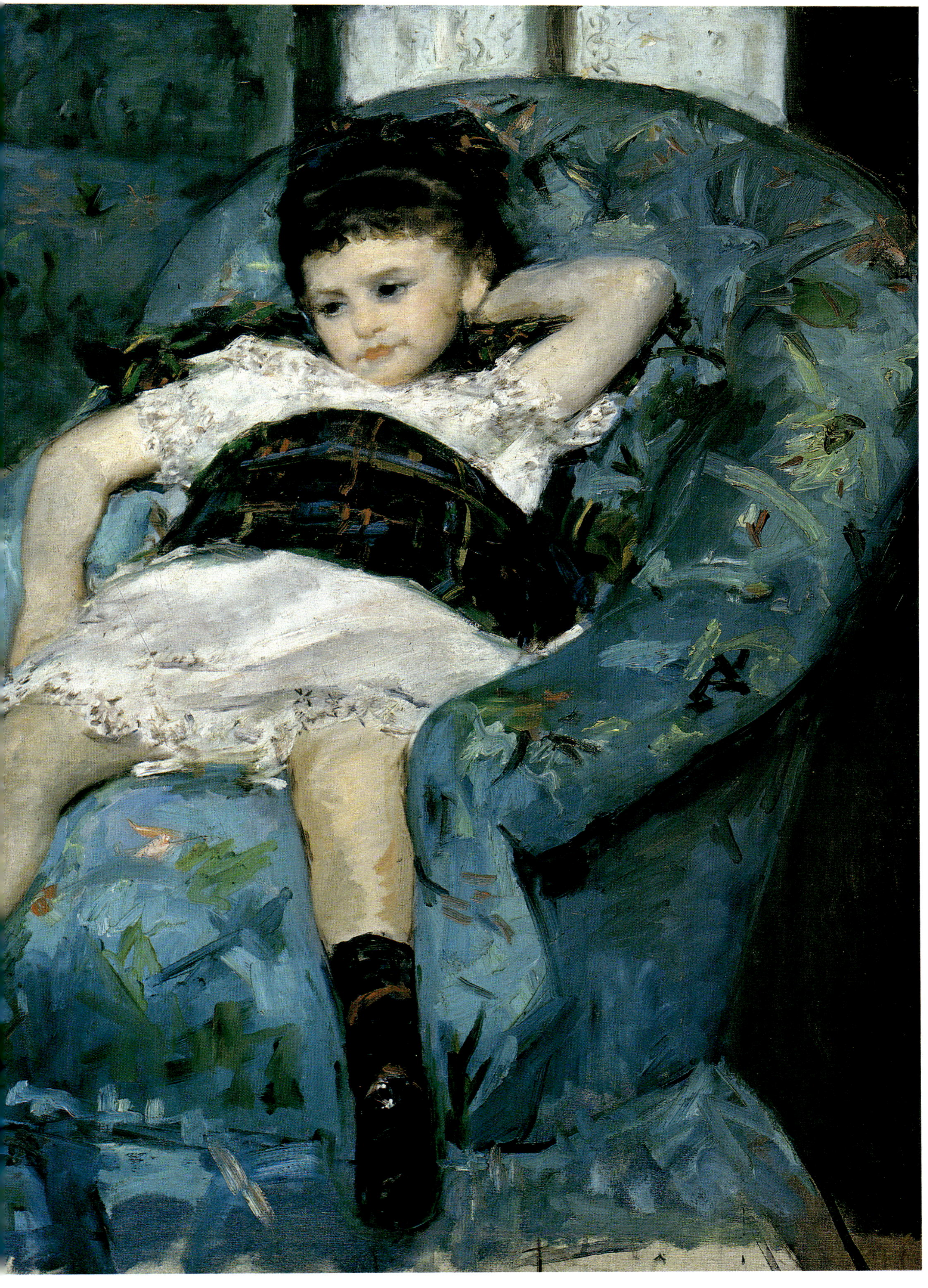

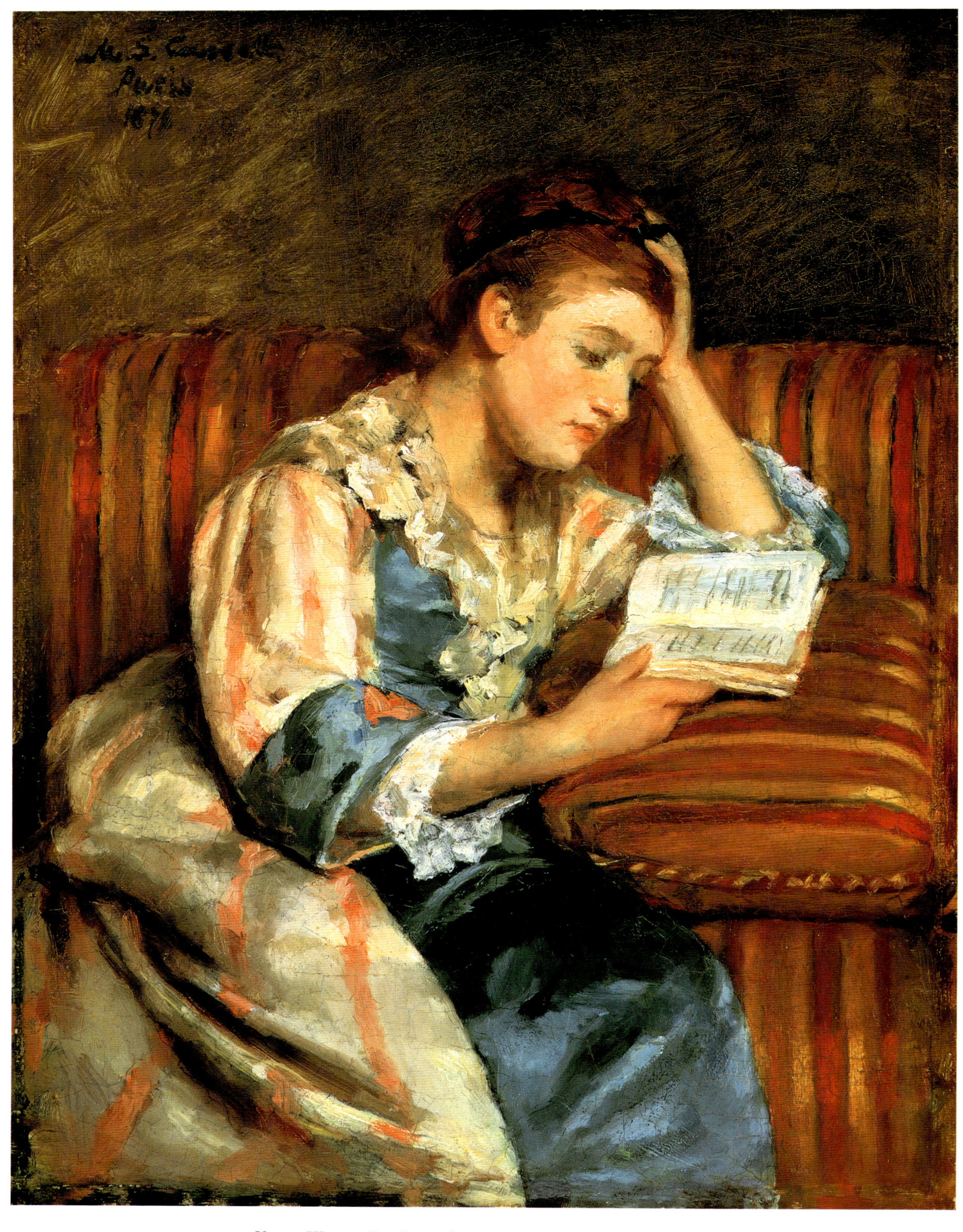

COLORPLATE 13. *Young Woman Reading*. 1875. Oil on panel. 13 ¾ × 10 ½ in. (34.9 × 26.6 cm). Courtesy of Museum of Fine Arts, Boston. Bequest of John T. Spaulding.

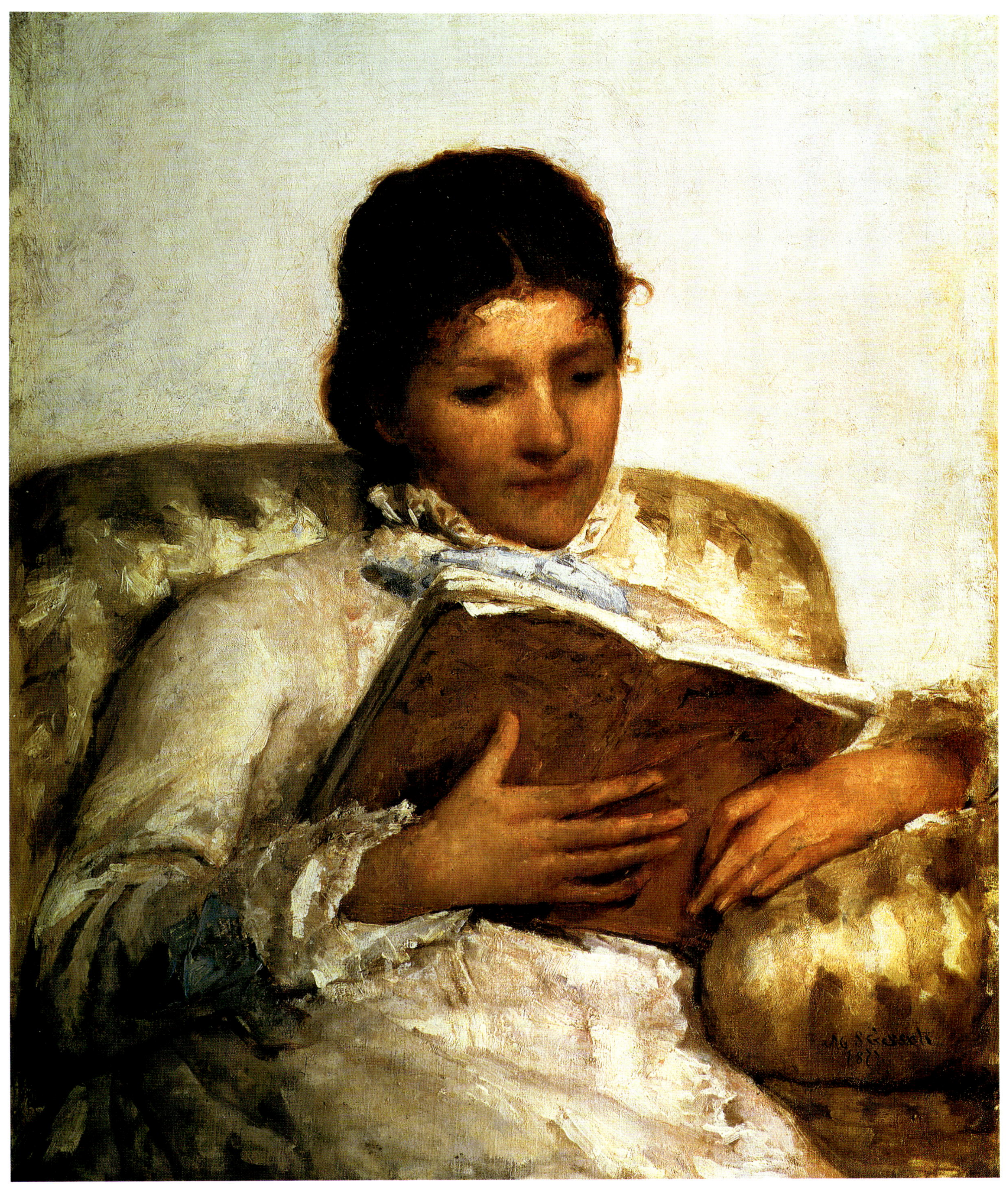

COLORPLATE 14. *The Reader.* 1877. Oil on canvas. 32 × 25 ½ in. (81.2 × 64.7 cm). Private collection. Photograph courtesy of Gerald Peters Gallery, New York.

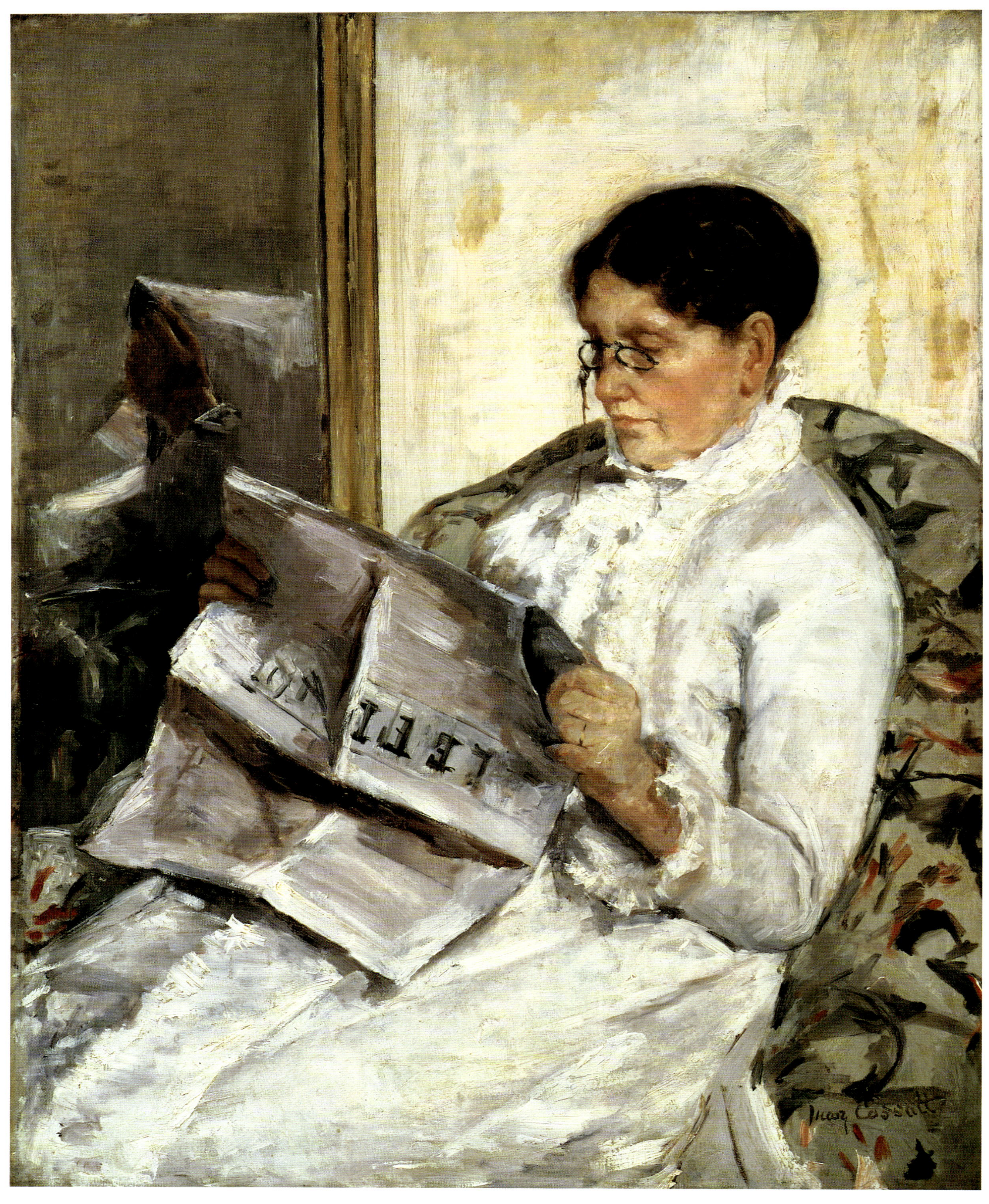

COLORPLATE 15. *Reading Le Figaro.* c. 1877–78. Oil on canvas. 39 ¾ × 32 in. (101 × 81.2 cm). Private collection, Washington, D.C.

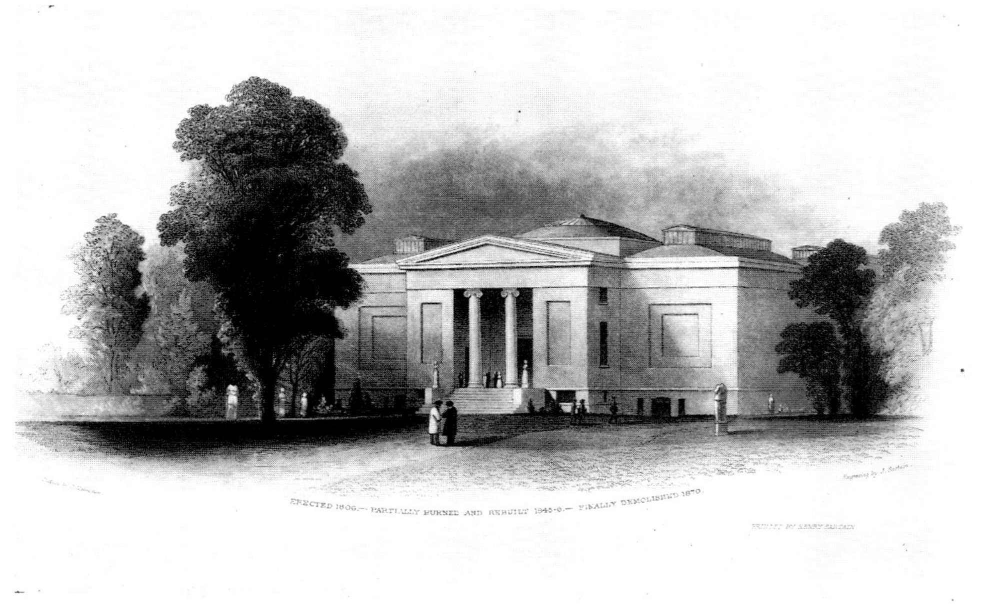

John Sartain. *The Pennsylvania Academy of the Fine Arts, Erected 1806.* Etching, engraving, and aquatint. 4 × 8 7/8 in. (10.2 × 22.5 cm). Courtesy of the Pennsylvania Museum of the Fine Arts, Philadelphia. Dr. Paul J. Sartain Bequest.

Letter from Eliza Haldeman to Her Father, Samuel Haldeman

On Student Life at the Pennsylvania Academy of the Fine Arts

March 7, 1862

Samuel Haldeman (1812–1880), father of Cassatt's friend Eliza, was a prominent and widely published naturalist and philologist. He was professor of natural history and comparative philology at the University of Pennsylvania, the latter from 1868 until his death in 1880.

Philadelphia
March 7, 1862

Dear Father,

I am afraid from my last letter you will think I have given up telling you the news, but as the time grows shorter I find I have so much to do that I have to be even more industrious than usual. In the evening I am tired and this is the first spare moment I have had in the morning for an age.

I made a slight mistake as to the monogram both as to the wood and also Mr. John Stevens, when the artists do not themselves draw all thier designs on wood, receives the credit of them. He (John) has had several in since then but I cannot discribe them. When I come I will show you. Mr Wylie also had one in that he drew on wood, very good. The artists are trying to get up a commic paper in this city, it is to be called "Rack." It is a secret yet, as they don't know whether it will succeed. I have seen some of the drawings, and they are real good.

We had some fun about a week ago. Miss Welch, one of our amature students, that is to say she dont intend to become an artist, wanted to cast the hand of a friend of hers, a gentleman. So they came down one morning and commenced. As she did not know the first thing about casting you may know how she proceeded. Miss Cassatt and I went in to look at her and asked, Why dont you do this! how will that come out? You have too much undercasting here. So she finally found it would be well to have some assistance, introduced us to the gentleman, and asked us to help her which we did, making an excellent cast and flattering the specimen of Genus "Homo" exceedingly. His experience of Artist life was so pleasant that he beged if we were willing to send for a photographer and have the whole scene taken just as we were. We consented and the man came. It was in Mr. Wylies room and the first impression was too dark, so we got Mr Copes permission to go in the galleries and had it taken there with the Gates of Pisa or Paradise for the background and the little bust of Palmer's

Spring and another, on each side. Miss Welch had a hammer and chisel knocking off the plaster. Miss C——— had the plaster dish and spoon which we had used in her hand. Inez Lewis was knocking also, I had a spoon helping Miss C——— and Dr. Smith the owner of the hand in question was behind. It was an excellent picture and he is going to present us each with one when they are finished. . . .

I would like you to send me a little money this week if you can. I need some for art purposes. The last dollar went to Gottschalk's concert. I enjoyed it so much. He played the "Last Hope" and the "Banjo" so you can see I have some new ideas. You must excuse the writing as I am in a great hurry to go to the Academy and the ink is bad. Dont forget the money. Give ever so much love to everybody. . . .

Good bye little Darling and write soon

Eliza

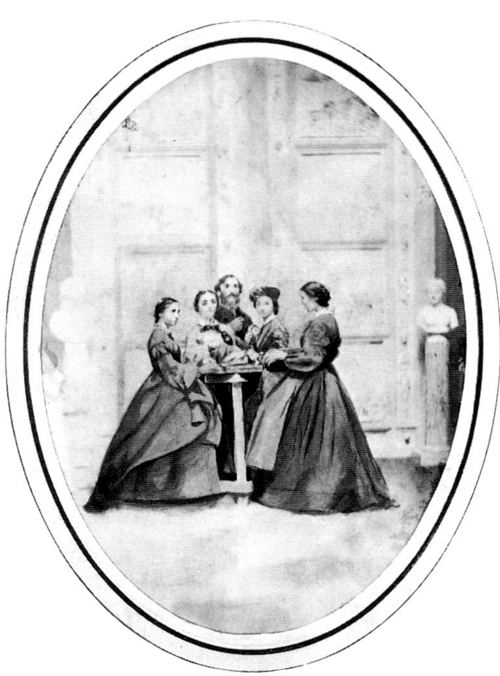

Photograph of (from left to right) Eliza Haldeman, Inez Lewis, Edmund Smith, Rebecca M. Welsh, and Mary Cassatt taken in the Pennsylvania Academy of the Fine Arts. 1862. Courtesy of the Pennsylvania Academy of the Fine Arts Archives, Philadelphia.

EARL SHINN

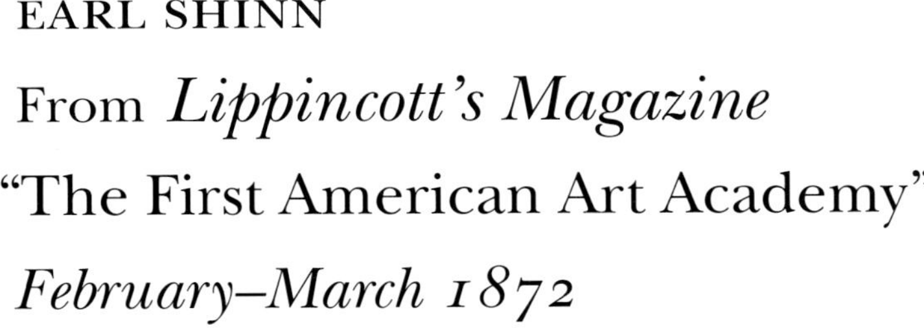

From *Lippincott's Magazine*

"The First American Art Academy"

February–March 1872

Earl Shinn (Edward Strahan) (1838–1886), American artist and critic. He studied at the Pennsylvania Academy of the Fine Arts and knew Cassatt and Thomas Eakins.

The Pennsylvania Academy of the Fine Arts was torn down in 1872. The new building, still standing, was dedicated in 1876.

Certain months ago there tumbled away from the sight of men a silent pale building in the Greek style. . . . A pair of Ionic columns, of very just model and impressively tall, supported the pediment: through the softening stucco, threaded with long zigzag cracks like black lightning, you could see the checkered brick and mortar of which the shafts were built. . . .

Connoisseurs paced the grave old halls immersed in the history of art from the Etruscans downward. Sightseers from the interior took up the Academy as a matter of conscience, entering the first gallery, and telling the whole rosary of the catalogue with the unskeptical regularity of their kind. Lovers made rendezvous, their backs turned to the masterpieces with Love's inimitable contempt. On warm nights of June the externals alone—the cool leafy courts, the shadowy statues, the hawthorn built of scented snow, the open doors through which Lough's *Centaurs* tossed in a flood of light—were an advertisement, and invited to the detailed study within.

Letter from Mary Cassatt to Eliza Haldeman

Youthful Ambition

March 18, 1864

[Cheyney]
Friday, March 18

"Dearest Love do you remember" when we were reading "Timothy Titcombs Letters" that I pointed out to you one passage about husbands & wives when they were seperated for a short time burdening the post with tender epistles. Very well I dont intend to do so but if perfectly convenient to you I will burden the Pennsylvania R.C. with myself & two canvasses (two in case I should spoil one of them) likewise a carpet bag on Wednesday next. You see I am coming earlier than I expected because I want if possible to have my picture dry enough to be varnished before I send it to the 'Cad.' Now please dont let your ambition sleep but finish your portrait of Alice so that I may bring it to town with me & have it framed with mine sent to the Exhibition with mine hung side by side with mine be praised, criticised with mine & finally that some enthusiastic admirer of art and beauty may offer us a thousand dollars a piece for them. "Picture it—think of it!"

Remember all this is only on condition that is perfectly convenient. If you can write so that I may get the letter before Wednesday I shall be much obliged if not I will wait until Thursday. I have been painting all day at your portrait & must finish it—so adieu & believe me your affec. friend

M. S. Cassatt

P.S. Mother thinks that it is likely your mother dont take as much interest in our pictures as we do and wishes you would come here instead of my going to you but we have no one here to compare to Alice & some one else. Much love to your mother and Fanny Ly.

Yours truly
M. S. Cassatt

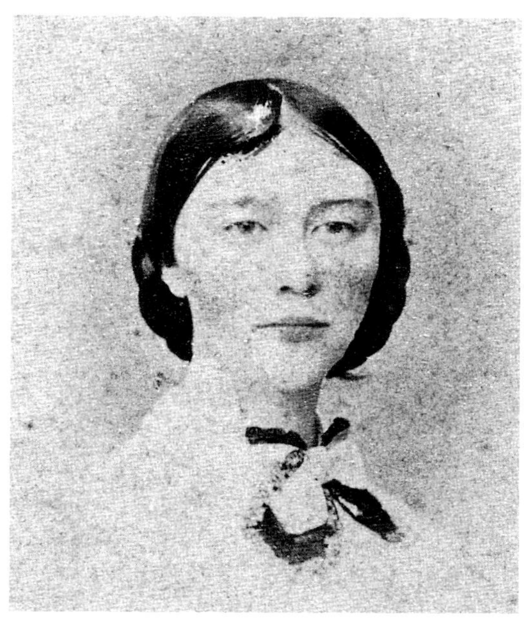

Photograph of Mary Cassatt. c. 1863. Private collection of Henry B. and Audrey S. Haldeman.

Timothy Titcomb (pseudonym of Josiah Gilbert Holland), wrote "Titcomb's Letters to Young People, Single and Married," first published in 1858, which was a book of advice on morals and manners.

The Pennsylvania Academy of the Fine Arts' annual exhibitions included nationally known artists and seldom included students.

Letter from Mary Cassatt to Eliza Haldeman

On Painting in the Country

June 13, 1864

My Dear Ite,

It is not because I have not been industrious that I have not written, although I have not been injuring my health by *too* close application to my drawing. I painted a small portrait of Whiskey for Aleck which he said was very good, and it also had the approval of Theodore who was here the other day. I suspected from something he said that he had either seen you in town or at Chiques, am I right? I have also been drawing the Fighting Gladiators. Have you mended yours yet? You wont find it very easily done, at least I have had a great deal of trouble with my écorchée.

Lyd went down to the fair last week and pronounced it a complete humbug. The Art gallery was not opened but she saw the wonderful baby house, one of the pictures in it was by Mr. Knight. "To what base uses may we not descend?"

I am getting quite dissipated going to West Chester nearly every day, we are going there to a tea party tomorrow night, and a picnic is talked of provided certain contingencies do or do not occur, but I am afraid that will be too much gayity.

If I were talking to you instead of writing I would tell you of a notable flirtation I am carrying on, but I will leave that now until we meet. I find it quite an agreeable employment "Pour passez le temps."

Chiques was Eliza Haldeman's home near Lancaster, Pennsylvania.

The 1864 Sanitary Fair in Philadelphia was one of the exhibitions of arts and industry organized during the Civil War to raise money for Union troops.

Write soon and let me know what you are doing and believe me Yours truly,

Mary S. Cassatt

P.S. You will no doubt be pleased to hear that I expect a visit from the "Graeme" (Graham of Eleventh St. Memory). I heard it from one of his relations.

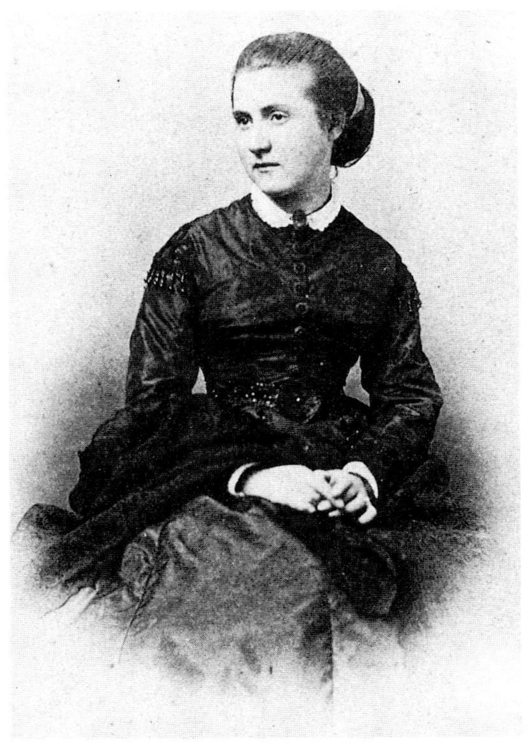

Photograph of Eliza Haldeman taken in Paris. c. 1867. Private collection of Henry B. and Audrey S. Haldeman.

ACHILLE SEGARD

From *Mary Cassatt: Un Peintre des enfants et des mères*

On Cassatt's American Cultural Heritage

1913

America and even England are countries of middling culture. Artistic taste and sense are not commonly found there. Yet it seems as if the great popular masses—which are inorganic, if one judged only from an artistic point of view—obscurely nourish an extremely refined élite and cause it to develop more brilliantly there than elsewhere. I imagine that a Whistler or a Mary Cassatt, rare in any country, is even more rare in England or America than in France. Strictly speaking, theirs are élite natures, exceptional personalities. It is as if the intelligence and sensitivity that are so unstimulated in the massed majority of these great nations gravitate to a small number of individuals, their characteristics typical of all the qualities of the European race, and all the subtleties of European culture. It even happens quite frequently that a slight imbalance adds to these exceptional temperaments a particular kind of charm, to which one is all the more sensitive the more artistic and refined one is oneself. An Edgar Poe or an Oscar Wilde are instances of whatever truth may lie in this observation. The Parisian intellectual milieu is often necessary to these exceptional natures, just as the temperature of a hothouse is indispensable to certain rare plants. Whether in the scientific order or in the purely artistic order, French culture provides the finishing touch to the education of these superior minds, frees them from burdensome ties to surroundings that no longer develop with them, transposes them into the domain of pure intellect, and, finally, permits them to become European examples of a superior humanity.

I have reason to believe that Miss Mary Cassatt's heredity is made up on one side of fairly recent forebears, attached to the land, living on and working the soil that feeds them, silently amassing collective reserves of common sense, uprightness, and physical and moral equilibrium for the distant good of future heirs. Another part of her heredity is made up of bold businessmen, worthy representatives of the new way of understanding life, very hard-working, very active, gifted with that particular kind of imagination that allows the operations of the mind to take place rapidly and to be translated almost immediately into concrete actions. This kind of imagination launches bankers, founders of firms, and builders of railroads. Capital forms and disperses. One complies with the conditions of success. The mind becomes supple. One considers business from a vast point of view. These are men of action, dominated by a few ideas that are elementary but utterly without pettiness. One thinks fast and realizes promptly.

Now let us imagine a young woman who is a stranger to the least concern about money, and gradually developing in a calm atmosphere that contrasts with the businessman's fever. Nowadays, in American life, women, much less young women, do not get involved in the sometimes disorderly movement of commercial contests. We may divine a particularly thorough education: French lessons, precise ideas about the art and literature of all living peoples, visits to museums that encompass all schools, courses taken in an academy in which every professor is of a different nationality from the next. For the average student, this gives rise to all kinds of confusion and can only result in a culture that is superficial and ephemeral. For an élite, these very complexities and contradictions awaken the critical sense, the need to judge and to compare, and the habit of reaching conclusions only through a personal effort of mind and will.

Letter from Eliza Haldeman to Her Father, Samuel Haldeman

On Training with Cassatt

December 4, 1866

Paris
December 4, 1866

Dear Father,

I was strongly reminded of you, of home, and of pleasant May weather today when in passing a florists window I saw three beautiful Cyprideum in bloom. . . . I stood looking at them a long while and did not find them a bit more beautiful than ours the first time we found one. But I was so delighted when I recognized an old friend, and have been thinking of them ever since. . . .

As for art. I made quite a step in my last head a young girl with black hair. Mr. Chaplin said it was good, the first praise he has given me, except his usual "pas mal." Of course it is nothing wonderful, but I am very glad I have done as well. He said I had improved a great deal since I came to him and asked me if I did not feel it myself, to which I answered yes! in fact now, Miss Cassatt and myself are about as "forte" as any there taken all in all, and we have really more prospect of improving rapidly than they have, as it is all ground we have once been over and though in the years that have passed I did not study much still it has made it all familiar to me and though I have the blues often yet it will please you to hear that I am really making progress. Our evening school goes on finely three evenings every week. It is in the quartier Latin and I feel quite like a student when I go there. If I can only study well till spring I know I can do a great deal. The days are never long enough for me and I only know the week has passed by Sunday coming and not painting. My health still keeps very good and if I feel badly I will slacken work so tell the Mother not to be anxious. . . . I am so happy that Mary and I are friends, she is the only bit of home I have here and she never would have stopped writing if there had not been a misunderstanding, she is as kind as she can be. Love to all and a kiss to dear Mother.

Charles Chaplin (1825–1891), French academic painter working in Paris, was at the height of his career in the mid-1860s when Haldeman and then Cassatt first arrived in France. He conducted the most prominent art classes for women in Paris during the 1860s; Haldeman and Cassatt were among his students.

Yours as ever
E. J. Haldeman

MAY ALCOTT NIERIKER

From *Studying Art Abroad, and How To Do It Cheaply*

Advice to Young Women Artists

1879

May Alcott Nieriker (1840–1879), American painter and the fiercely independent youngest sister of writer Louisa May Alcott (and on whom the character Amy from "Little Women" was based). May met and befriended Mary Cassatt in 1876 in Paris and married Ernst Nieriker in 1878. Louisa May Alcott's unpublished "Diana and Persis" was written in honor of her artist sister.

Now that Boston, New York, and Philadelphia have their Fine Art Museums and life classes, there is no longer the same necessity for crossing the Atlantic for an education that existed some years ago. But while the feeling prevails that there is no art world like Paris, no painters like the French, and no incentive to good work equal to that found in a Parisian *atelier,* many will continue to seek in France what, in their estimation, cannot be found in America. To such, especially if women, a few notes, suggestions, and addresses will prove useful in simplifying the *modus operandi* of settling in a foreign city.

Let me impress upon them at the outset the importance of considering well what is one's particular taste or talent, aim or ambition, and to have a definite notion before starting of what one wants to learn, so as to insure the greatest amount of profit and enjoyment in a given time. For I am supposing our particular artist to be no gay tourist, doing Europe according to guide-books, with perhaps a few lessons, here and there, taken only for the name of having been the pupil of some distinguished master, but a thoroughly earnest worker, a lady, and poor, like so many of the profession, wishing to make the most of all opportunities, and the little bag of gold last as long as possible.

Naturally to a painter of the figure or landscape in oils, Paris is the desired goal, where the work of Couture and Millet, Breton, Bonnat, Cabanel, Lefebvre, Duran, and lately Bastien Lepage, offer such splendid examples in drawing and color of the first-named subject, while Rousseau, Corot, Diaz, Dupré, Daubigny, Courbet, and Pelouse display the same truth and *habileté* in their treatment of the landscape, not to mention the gems of the Louvre and Luxembourg always open to a student for reference and copying,—a practice much recommended by French masters to help in the acquirement of certain methods.

Thomas Couture (1815–1879), French historical and portrait painter, taught Puvis de Chavannes, Manet, and Fantin-Latour, as well as many Americans including Mary Cassatt; Jean-François Millet (1814–1875), French painter and a member of the Barbizon School; Jules-Adolphe-Aimé-Louis Breton (1827–1905), French landscape painter; Léon Bonnat (1833–1922), French academic painter, was not particularly admired by Cassatt; Alexandre Cabanel (1823–1889), French painter who taught at the École des Beaux-Arts beginning in 1863; Jules-Joseph Lefebvre (1836–1911), French academic painter who studied at the École des Beaux-Arts and debuted at the Salon in 1855; Charles Émile Auguste Carolus-Duran (1838–1917), fashionable French portraitist and a teacher of John Singer Sargent; Jules Bastien-Lepage (1848–1884), influential French Realist painter; Pierre-Étienne-Théodore Rousseau (1812–67), French landscape painter and member of the Barbizon School; Jean-Baptiste-Camille Corot (1796–1875), French painter and member of the Barbizon School, known for his luminous landscapes and as a forerunner to Impressionism; Barcusse-Virgile Diaz de la Peña (1807–1876), French painter of the Barbizon School; Jules Dupré (1811–1889), French painter of the Barbizon School; Charles-François Daubigny (1817–1879), French landscapist of the Barbizon School; Gustave Courbet (1819–1877), French painter and leader of the Realist movement, which led to such modernist styles as Impressionism; Léon Germain Pelouse (1838–1891), French landscape and portrait painter; Frank Duveneck (1848–1919), American painter influential in spreading the painterly style he learned in Munich.

Much is said just now in favor of the Munich school, and since Duverneck's sudden rise into notice, many have taken their way thither, and thoroughly good work has been the result of months of study. Further than this, I can say nothing but that on my one visit there the gallery was a disappointment, the general refreshing and varnishing, lately given the collection, entirely ruining the effect of many of its best pictures.

Just as naturally will one who seeks instruction in water-color figures and landscapes turn toward London, though the Roman painters possess a fine, strong style in the former subject which cannot be overlooked. However, as every one knows, England's art specialty is water-colors, of which the summer exhibitions give sufficient proof.

Also china painting and decorative art in general flourish in the big city which is acknowledged the great picture-market of the world, and this last fact may be of some importance to an artist if reduced to making pot-boilers, as the saying, "*Live* in Paris, but *sell* in London," was long ago adopted by painters of all nations.

Let us conclude, then, that each of the foregoing considerations has been well thought of, and after due deliberation and all possible study accomplished before starting, that our lady artist decides on a year abroad, and begins preparations in good earnest.

She proceeds to select a large, light trunk, one of French manufacture if possible; for those of American make are very heavy and not proportionately strong, and as every pound in weight is an added item of expense in travelling, this becomes a subject worthy of some consideration. Then packing closely, rolling and pinning every article that can be rolled and pinned, puts in plenty of old underclothes and but few dresses, a strong travelling suit and a black silk being the only important costumes. I say old underclothes, because the grime of London and the acid used by all Parisian *blanchisseuses* soon rot and spoil anything delicate or nicely trimmed, and as the old things become too thin for use, but invaluable as paint-rags (which artists so often have to buy), they are easily replaced by ready-made strong ones at small expense.

If the trunk is too high for sliding under the berth of the state-room, and our artist is sufficiently sensible to prefer going in light marching order on all occasions, she can take only a commodious hand-bag and shawl-strap, letting the trunk go below in the hold. The first-named should contain the necessary changes of linen, paper collars and cuffs (if she is not too proud to wear such), which, like Japanese handkerchiefs, do not require washing, a dressing-case of toilet articles to hang up and sway with the motion of the vessel, gloves, veils, and little things, while into the shawl-strap should be rolled a thick wrap, water-proof, flannel gown, books to read on the passage, and overflowings from the bag.

This comprises all that is strictly needed for a voyage of twelve days across the Atlantic, though the addition of fruit or a supply of preserved ginger to be eaten in the watches of the night will be found a refreshing luxury, not always to be obtained on board.

If not the possessor of a steamer chair, I should advise not buying one on the American side, where the cost is from ten dollars upwards, and being by no means indispensable, any one economically inclined will defer purchasing until the return trip, when very pretty folding chairs of dark wood, suitable even for parlor use afterward, can be procured from Tottenham Court Road furnishing shops, London, or in Liverpool, on going to the steamer, at the low price of ten to fifteen shillings.

Everything, then, being ready, our artist takes passage on a "Cunarder," if she prefers safety, or requires the protecting care of a gallant English captain; but if economy is an object she will try the "Anchor," "National," or "Guion Line," where a deck state-room, for $60, will be found most airy and comfortable, and, accepting what letters and addresses are offered her, push bravely off, to begin her art studies in the Old World. . . .

The American art student, who gives but a week to London and watercolors before passing on to the gayer city Paris for an education in oils, will find it economical, if not provided with a through ticket by the steamer company, to cross the channel by almost any route rather than fashionable Calais and Dover. Say Dieppe and New Haven, for instance, where the fare is but thirty francs, second class, the baggage rates very low, and the boats of the company larger and more comfortable.

Arrived in the metropolis and turning toward what is often called the painters' quarter of the *rive droite* or north side of the Seine (that circuit lying between the *gare du Nord* and *gare St. Lazare,* the Opera House and Montmartre), finds almost every block on Boulevard Clichy, Rochechonart, and the intervening streets entirely given up to studios; for not only do some of the leading masters, like Bonnat, Gérôme, and Müller, meet their classes in that locality, but also have their private residences there.

Jean Léon Gérôme (1824–1904), French academic painter with whom Cassatt studied privately upon her arrival in Paris. A specialist in ancient and Near-Eastern subjects, he studied at the École des Beaux-Arts, where he became a professor in 1863.

All Paris, however, is apt to strike a new-comer as being but one vast studio, particularly if seeing it for the first time of a morning, either in summer or winter, between seven and eight o'clock, when students, bearing paint-box and *toile,* swarm in all directions, hurrying to their *cours;* or still more when artistic excitement reaches its height, during the days appointed for sending work to be examined by the jury of the Salon. Then

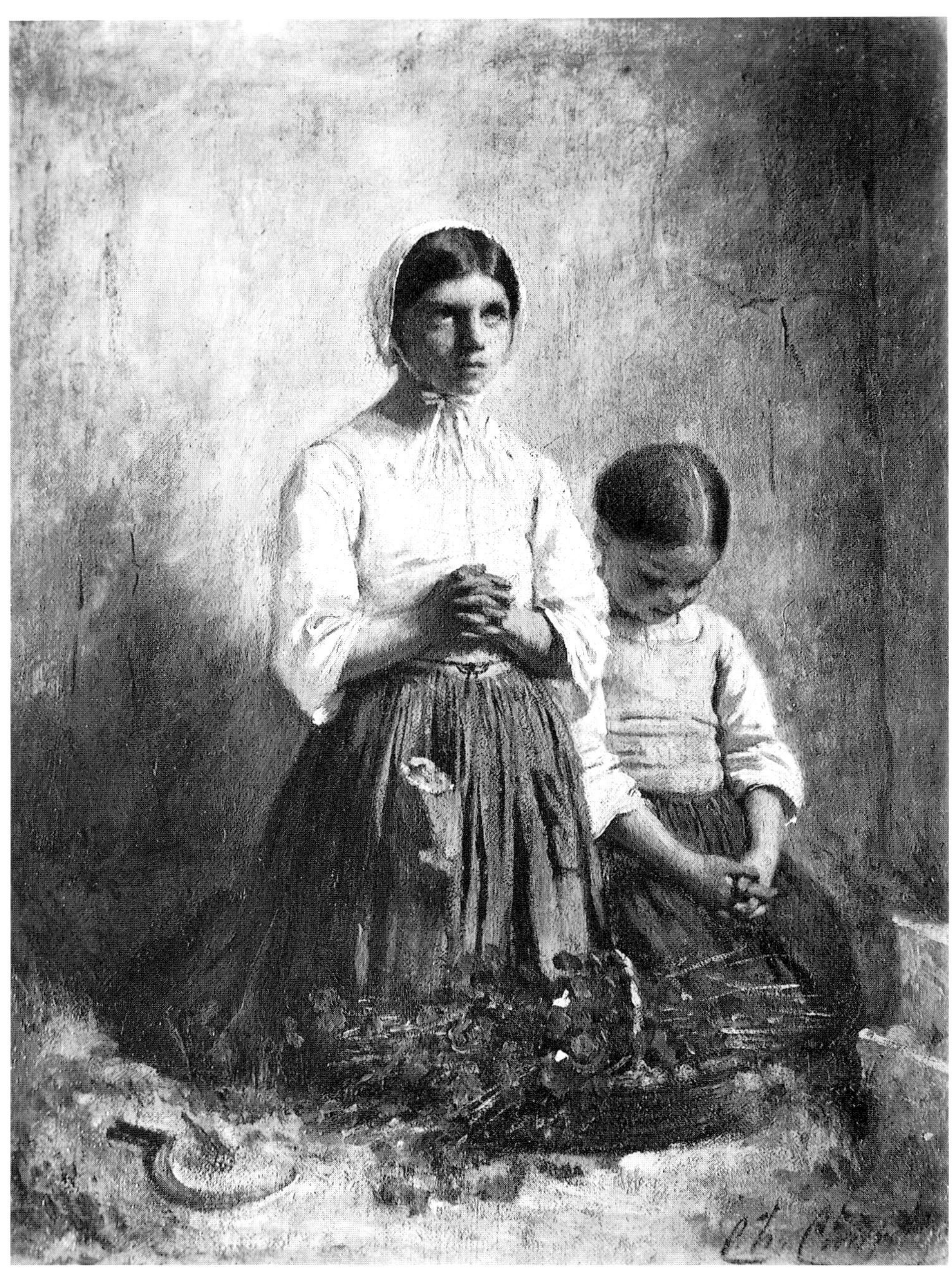

Charles Chaplin. *Devotion.* 1857. Oil on canvas. 10 3/4 × 8 1/2 in. (27.3 × 21.6 cm). Walters Art Gallery, Baltimore.

pictures literally darken the air, borne on men's shoulders and backs, packed in immense vans, or under an arm of the painter himself, all going to the same destination,—the Palais de l'Industrie on the Champs Elysées.

L'École des Beaux Arts, beside Monsieur Jackson and other masters, attracts many to the Latin Quartier for forming another little art world, so a stranger decides each *arrondissement* offers some advantages, and it is not a question of so much importance as in limitless London, where one selects an abode.

But to a party or painter, counting expense and crossing the Atlantic for several years of study in Paris, to hire and furnish an apartment is undoubtedly much cheaper than any hotel or pension can be. For living, until one learns the real French manner of doing it, is quite as high as in America, and a visitor is sadly disappointed if cheapness is expected to be found in anything beyond gloves and Turkey carpets.

To furnish even a small apartment prettily takes time and trouble, as every woman knows, but if one chooses to spend a few hundred francs at Hotel Druot (the great auction-rooms of Paris), a fine collection of useful and ornamental *meubles* may be bought for surprisingly little money, not perhaps quite new, but if carefully selected, suitable to adorn an American studio when no longer needed in France. And as household articles after a year's use, together with bric-à-brac which belongs in the category of "artist's tools of trade," can pass the customs free, the question of heavy duties in transporting such has not to be considered.

It is found very convenient, and even necessary, to number in a party about to settle in Paris one member of a domestic turn of mind, as a *bonne, femme de menagre* and *blanchisseuse* each need careful looking after. For, like the merchants, they seem to consider all foreigners as fair prey, and proceed to fleece such unfortunates to the best of their ability.

It has never been my happy experience to find one of this class who could be called strictly honest, and it becomes almost laughable to see how, like so many among the Irish help of America, they make a decided distinction between the purse and the provisions of a mistress. For though a pile of gold may be safely left for any length of time within reach, everything, from butter to charcoal, is unhesitatingly appropriated in the *cuisine*, and family or relations in the neighborhood luxuriously supported thereon.

Some ladies do not mind such trifles, and quietly submit, paying the thirty francs demanded for service by a *bonne*, beside board, clothes, and lodging, per month without a murmur. Others try to settle this vexed question of help by preparing breakfast and lunch for themselves, only engaging a f*emme de menage*, at five sous per hour, for all other work and cooking the dinner.

I have known ladies coming to Paris for only a short time, wishing to accomplish much shopping or sight-seeing with economy, be very comfortable by taking a room at the "Grande Hotel du Louvre," where by aid of a spirit-lamp a delicious cup of coffee is provided in the morning, lunch taken at a restaurant, in any part of the city where their wanderings may have led them, returning only at night for the substantial *table d'hôte* of the hotel.

Still another way, which has been followed by many students with success, is to hire a furnished room in some small hotel, such as one finds in Rue de Douai, for instance, at a franc per day, make one's breakfast of a roll and cup of coffee, taken at a *crêmerie*, buying lunch *en route* for the studio, and at six o'clock going to the nearest Duval establishment for a dinner, costing from one franc, fifty centimes, upward.

This, amounting in all to about four francs per day, a lady affirmed, judging from her own experience, was by far the cheapest and simplest arrangement possible for one intent on studying art in Paris.

Letter from Eliza Haldeman to Her Cousin, Alice Haldeman

On Painting in a French Village

February 1867

Courances
February

Courances is near Barbizon, on the edge of the Fontainebleau Forest.

My dear Sister,

I suppose Mother has told you that I have left Paris for a little while and am staying with Mary Cassatt for a companion in this little out of the way French village. It is the first time I have been in the country since I left home and you can easily imagine I enjoy it extreamly. The country is very flat and the few hills that one sees are very far off, but the fields are green and the old trees covered with ivy and mistletoe so that you scarcely miss the foliage. Everything is in the most primitive style. The bedroom we have is floored with red tiles, we have a fire place and a wood fire with the accompaniment of tongs shovel and bellows. We have also a bed warmer with a long handle which I need not tell you I make use of every evening much to Marys amusement. I believe she has written a description of my performance in that line to all her friends, and intends painting a picture of the same at some future date. Another amusement is to make candy in the evenings and after several failures we have finally succeeded in becoming quite expert, though Mary says I have no genius for that art. The Chateau and Park which is near are very beautiful. I suppose I appreciate them more as they are the first I have ever seen. We have permission to enter the Park whenever we like and last Sunday I spent two hours walking about in it though without seeing half as it is so large. . . . The cottages of the peasants are also very romantic, we were painting in one today. It is several hundred years old, the rafters are all bare black and wormeaten. The old chimney was beautiful and we were entertained with the music of a spinning wheel and the ticking of a clock, the latter exposing its weights and pendulum some two yds from its unblushing face and weaving like an old woman whenever it struck. The folks were very kind and brought out some pancakes to regale us on. They were laid across the tongs to warm and then the old woman (75 years old) handed them to us in her hands. I eat one mouthful for decencys sake and then put the rest in my pocket when they were not looking and said it was good! The mail is passing so you will excuse my hurry. Love to all, hope you are enjoying yourselves.

EJH

Letter from Eliza Haldeman to Her Mother, Mary Haldeman

On American Painters vs. French Painters

May 15, 1867

Ecouen
May 15, 1867

Ecouen is a small town north of Paris and was the center of the school of genre painting headed by Frère and Soyer.

My darling Mother,

Your letter telling of the arrival of the kid gloves received safely and also the one of the week before that father had forgotten to mark Poste restante, in fact it is useless now to continue that, as we are so well known now and the town is so small that there is no danger of my letters being lost. . . . I think I forgot to tell you we were invited to dinner at Mr. Bacons Sunday before last and went with them in the evening to see the ball the Peasants had at the fête. They are another poor set of artists though now Mr. B. is out of the mire, gets good prices for his pictures and has a pretty house and garden to keep his wife in. He is very communicative and tells funny stories of when he lived in Paris on nothing. One time they did not have a cent in the house and had nothing to eat and finally after a great deal of thought the wife produced some coins she had put away for curiosities and they were able to buy bread. In return for thier hospitality we gave them a Picnic last Sunday. Oysters Champaigne and ham sandwitches, our first entertainment since we are proprietors. . . . You asked me if Mary C.

Henry Bacon (1839–1912), American painter and author who worked in Paris and studied with Gérôme and Cabanel as well as with Frère. He later became known as a specialist in Egyptian subjects. He wrote and illustrated "A Parisian Year" (1882), a book about artists' lives.

was accepted at the exposition, I thought I had told you we had both been refused though we have strong hopes for next year. I dont want to go to Rome till I have painted something for it as I can leave it with a friend here to be sent. Mary wishes to be remembered to you, she laughed when I told her your message and said she wanted to paint *better* than the old masters. Her Mother wants her to become a portrait painter as she has a talent for likenesses and thinks she is very ambitious to want to paint pictures. Her family are now living at Renovo on the railroad with her Brother Aleck C. but I believe they are going to move to Irvington very soon as he is going on another Rail R. Mrs. Cassatt writes that she is tired moving, that being the twentieth time during her life. Mary expects to stay two years more abroad, she is getting on very well and studies hard. I think she has a great deal of talent and industry. One requires the latter living in France, the poeple study so hard and the results are wonderful. Though there is a great deal of talent in the Exposition, nothing equals the French painters. You would not wonder I am what you call ambitious if you could see what I see. The difference between Americans and French is that the former work for money and the latter for fame and then the public appreciate things so much here. You are not allowed to paint badly. But I must stop, excuse my badly written letter but I wrote so closely in order to enclose another to Father. Love to all. Tell our boy I am glad he is improving, that I will be glad to talk French to him when I return. Love to all.

EJH

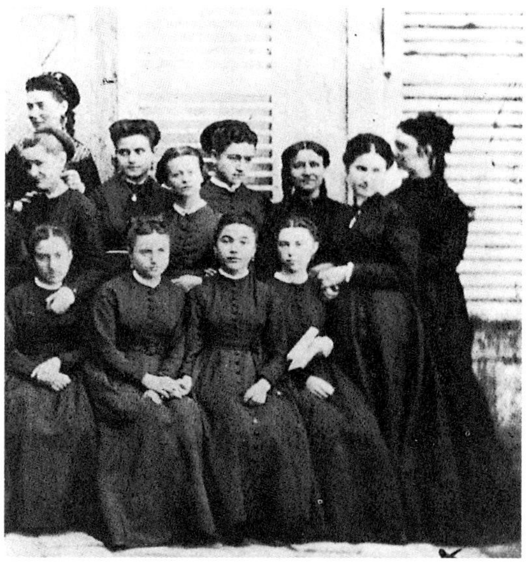

Detail of a photograph of a painting class of Charles Chaplin, Paris. 1866. (Mary Cassatt is at top left; Eliza Haldeman is second from right). Location of original unknown.

The International Exposition held in Paris in 1867 had art exhibits in each nation's pavilion.

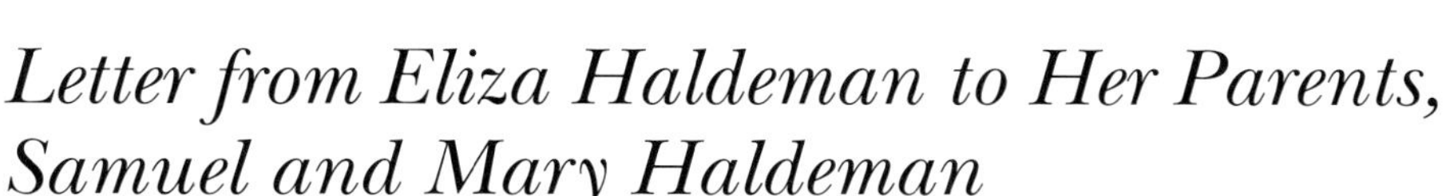

Letter from Eliza Haldeman to Her Parents, Samuel and Mary Haldeman

On Haldeman and Cassatt Being Accepted to the Salon

May 8, 1868

Paris
May 8, 1868

My dear Father & Mother,

I am now in Paris stopping at the Prince Albert Hotel which is opposite the Prince Regent where Father & I staid when we first came to Europe. Miss Cassatt is with me as she has not yet decided where she will go for the summer. & we intend to draw from the pictures in the Louvre and from life until Carsten arrives. . . . I suppose you received the Catalogue of the Exposition and saw my name. I did not know until the day of the opening that my picture had been sent and when I heard it was in I took a good crying spell which lasted three hours. . . . I feel sure I should have been accepted even if Soyer had not touched it and I think it likely I would have been better hung had it not been painted on for this year the Jury are very particular about things being painted on and have rewarded the honest ones with the best places. . . . Mary has also been successful even more so than I as her picture is well hung and was not painted on. Still I think we are pretty equal considering she has been here six months longer than I. Her name in the Catalogue is Stevenson as she dont exhibit under her own name. It is much pleasanter when one is a girl as it avoides publicity. I think

Annual Paris Salon.

Paul Constant Soyer (1823–1903), French genre painter who worked in Ecouen and taught Cassatt during her stay there from 1867 to 1868.

COLORPLATE 1

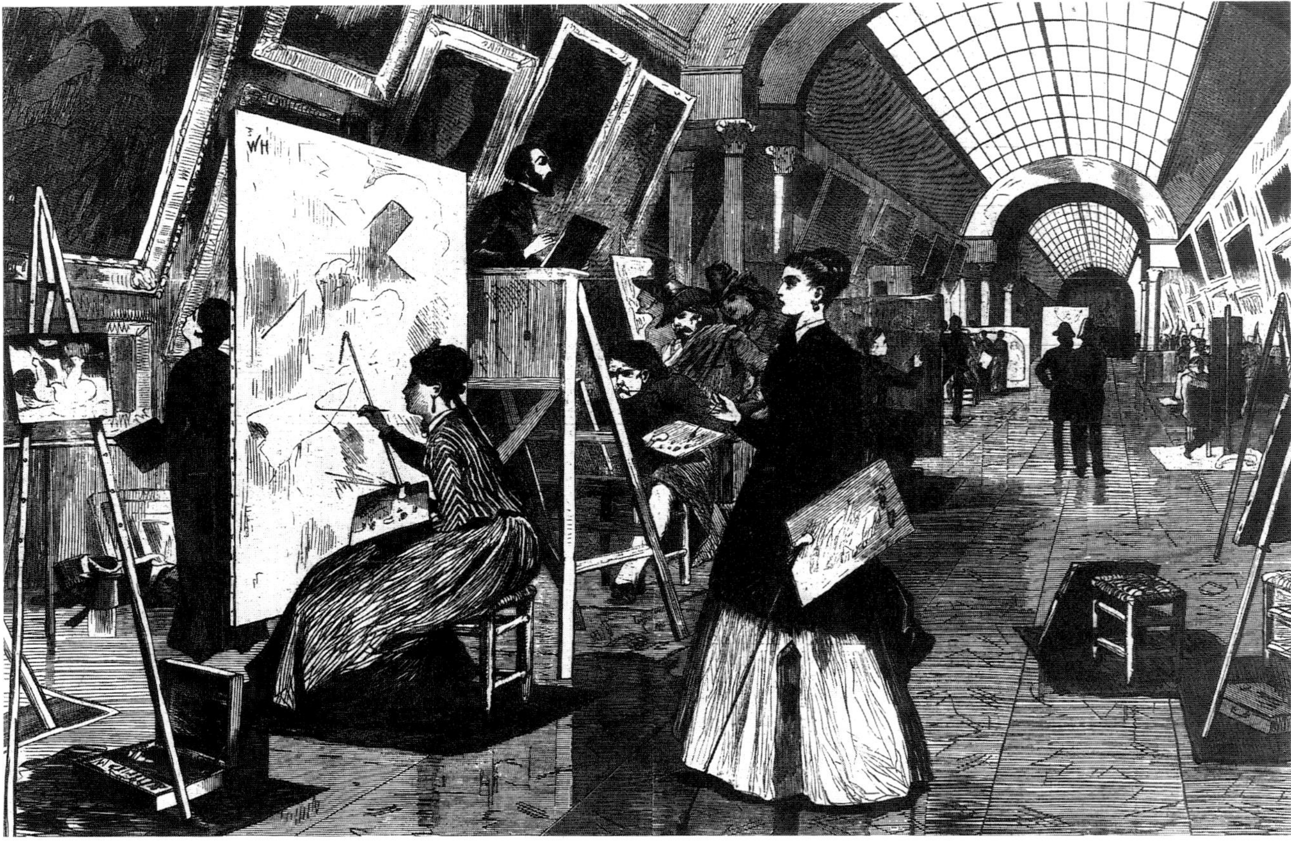

Winslow Homer. *Art Students and Copyists in the Louvre Gallery, Paris.* Wood engraving in *Harper's Weekly,* January 11, 1868. Photograph courtesy of the Library of Congress.

it likely I should have taken another also had I sent my picture myself.

The Exposition is very poor this year as there has been 1200 more pictures accepted than usual in fact almost anything would have passed. There is to be forty medals given though I cannot imagine who there is to deserve them all. Jerome has two very fine pictures. Dorée one large one, a new man Lefebre is the sensation of the year. There has been especial favor shown this time to new beginners, and the old Exampts are all up at the cealing. In fact the pictures of the latter are so bad that I really would not care to be Exampt. Cabanel who used to be so fine who made things equal to Correggio has two horrible portraits. I suppose they are making place for us. In fact the French school is going through a phase. They are leaving the Academy style and each one seaking a new way consequently just now everything is Chaos. But I suppose in the end they will be better for the change. I think by thirty I can get a medal.

Gustave Doré (1832–1883), French painter and illustrator known for his illustrations of Milton, Hugo, and Tennyson. Doré owned a gallery in London.

"Exampts" (Exempts or "hors concours") were artists who had previously won a medal at the Paris Salon and no longer had to submit their work to the jury.

Quite a number of Americans exhibit this year and show a great deal of talent. And the number of women artists is legion. Henrietta Brown has an atrocious picture and in fact the waste of good colors frames and canvas this year is astonishing. . . . Excuse the pen it is a hotel furniture. Much love to all & Believe me very affectionately dear Father & Mother

Your Daughter

Excuse my letter but I have been the last two days at the Exposition and my head is in a whirl. . . .

LOIS MARIE FINK

Lois Marie Fink (b. 1927), American art historian and, from 1970 to 1992, curator of research at the National Museum of American Art, Smithsonian Institution, Washington D.C.

From *American Art at the Nineteenth-Century Paris Salons*

American Women Exhibit at the Paris Salons

1990

American women entered these exhibitions for the first time in the 1860s, enjoying with their male compatriots the opportunity to compete among established professionals. Works at the Salons by female artists were unmistakable because, unlike exhibition catalogues in the United States, where gender was often obscured by the substitution of initials for first names, Salon catalogues clearly identified women by the titles of "Mlle." or "Mme." Since the days of the Royal Academy in the seventeenth and eighteenth centuries, works by women artists appeared in Salon exhibitions, most commonly in the categories of portraiture and miniature painting. At the Second Empire Salons, six women from the United States exhibited, all in the late 1860s and all as painters: Elisabeth Adams and E. Ada Philbrook of Boston; Mary Cassatt and Eliza J. Haldeman of Philadelphia; Elizabeth Jane Gardner of Exeter, New Hampshire; and Jeanette Shepherd Harrison Loop of New York City. Little is known about the careers of Adams, Haldeman, or Philbrook, but the other three continued in long, successful careers. Cassatt and Gardner remained in Paris for the rest of their lives as prominent members of the art community, while Loop returned to New York City.

Elizabeth Jane Gardner (later Bouguereau) came to Paris in 1864 to study art and went on to have a very successful Salon career. Although never close friends, Gardner and Cassatt were the two most important American women artists in Paris for the next three or four decades.

Rejected in 1867, Mary Cassatt yearned for acceptance at the Salons. Her first entry to be approved by the jurors was *La Mandoline* (*The Mandolin*), accepted for the Salon of 1868. Though conventional in theme, Cassatt's portrayal contrasts with the usual depiction of picturesque folk subjects in its focus upon a lone young girl, who appears to be occupied with inner thoughts and feelings, presented to the viewer without supporting details of a setting. The broad manner of handling light and dark is common in French art at this time, while specific qualities of the model's face suggest Cassatt's future strength as a painter. When rejected again in 1869, she was quite discouraged, although she acknowledged that she was not surprised, as she believed that her painting was "not sufficiently finished," a conclusion suggested perhaps by the perfected canvases of her current teacher, Léon Gérôme. Nevertheless, in her disappointment she appealed to Gérôme, hoping his influence might change the decision—but it was too late for him to press the jurors. At the exhibition of 1870 she showed *Une Contadina di Fobello* (*An Italian Peasant Woman*, now unlocated), a subject that, like *The Mandolin*, related to the popular theme of the common folk of Spain and Italy.

COLORPLATE 1

Cassatt's Salon successes brought the artist a new measure of confidence and also promoted her as a marketable painter. Through the showings in 1868 and 1870, she was able to place paintings with Goupil's in New York City. Even so, she seemed not yet able to identify herself as a professional artist, for at these Second Empire Salons she exhibited under her middle name, Mary Stevenson. "It is much pleasanter when one is a girl as it avoides publicity," asserted her friend Eliza Haldeman. In the next decade the Salons would bring Mary Cassatt to the most significant encounter of her career, for that is where Edgar Degas first noticed her paintings.

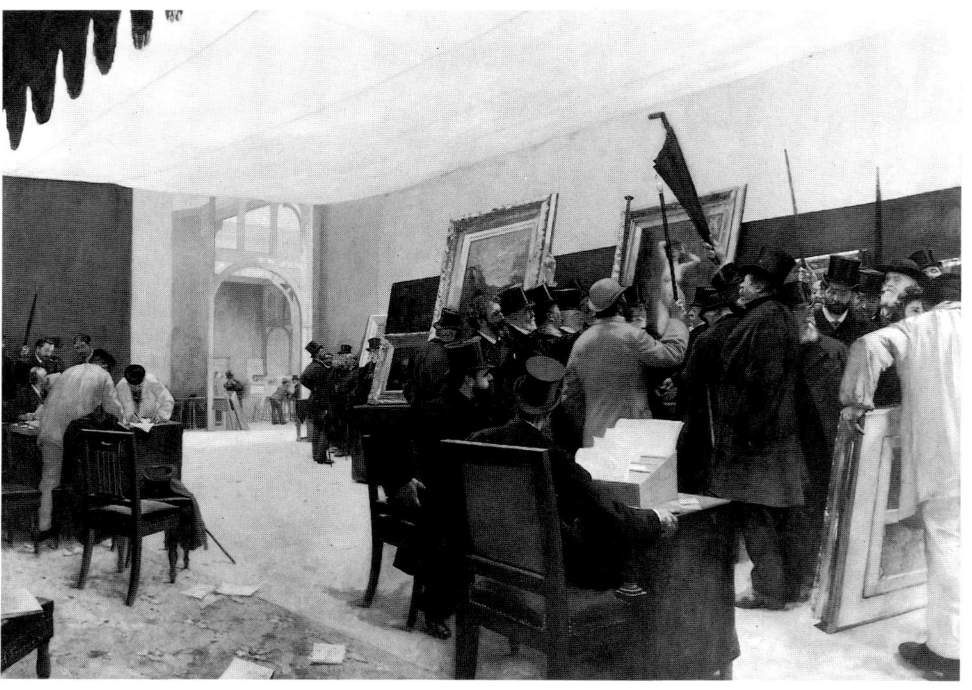

Henri Gervex. *A Meeting of the Painting Jury.* c. 1884–85. Oil on canvas. 117 3/4 × 165 1/4 in. (299 × 419.7 cm). Musée D'Orsay, Paris. Photograph © Réunion des Musées Nationaux.

EMILE ZOLA

From *His Masterpiece*

On the Jury Process at the Paris Salon

1886

Émile Zola (1840–1902), French novelist and art critic. He was the renowned leader of the nineteenth-century school of writing called naturalism, later renamed Realism, which emerged in France in the 1860s in opposition to romanticism and idealism in art and literature. A childhood friend of Cézanne, he was one of the earliest supporters of the Impressionists, but the publication of his novel "L'Oeuvre" in 1886 caused a sensation. The fictional artists and events were only thinly veiled references to actual people and events. Zola's description of the Salon jury gives a good picture of the subjectivity and fallibility of the process. Cassatt was accepted in 1868, 1870, 1872, 1873, 1874, 1875, and 1876. She had paintings rejected in 1869, 1875, and 1877.

The committee work was really a hard task, and even Bongrand's strong legs grew tired of it. It was cut out every day by the assistants. An endless row of large pictures rested on the ground against the handrails, all along the first-floor galleries, right round the Palace; and every afternoon, at one o'clock precisely, the forty committee-men, headed by their president, who was equipped with a bell, started off on a promenade, until all the letters in the alphabet, serving as exhibitors' initials, had been exhausted. They gave their decisions standing, and the work was got through as fast as possible, the worst canvases being rejected without going to the vote. At times, however, discussions delayed the party, there came a ten minutes' quarrel, and some picture which caused a dispute was reserved for the evening revision. Two men, holding a cord some thirty feet long, kept it stretched at a distance of four paces from the line of pictures, so as to restrain the committee-men, who kept on pushing each other in the heat of their dispute, and whose stomachs, despite everything, were ever pressing against the cord. Behind the committee marched seventy museum-keepers in white blouses, executing evolutions under the orders of a brigadier. At each decision communicated to them by the secretaries, they sorted the pictures, the accepted paintings being separated from the rejected ones, which were carried off like corpses after a battle. And the round lasted during two long hours, without a moment's respite, and without there being a single chair to sit upon. The committee-men had to remain on their legs, tramping on in a tired way amid icy draughts, which compelled even the least chilly among them to bury their noses in the depths of their fur-lined overcoats.

Then the three o'clock snack proved very welcome: there was half an hour's rest at a buffet, where claret, chocolate, and sandwiches could be obtained. It was there that the market of mutual concessions was held, that the bartering of influence and votes was carried on. In order that nobody might be forgotten amid the hailstorm of applications which fell upon the committee-men, most of them carried little note-books, which they consulted; and they promised to vote for certain exhibitors whom a colleague protected on condition that this colleague voted for the ones in whom they were interested. Others, however, taking no part in these intrigues, either from austerity or indifference, finished the interval in smoking a cigarette and gazing vacantly about them.

Then the work began again, but more agreeably, in a gallery where there were chairs, and even tables with pens and paper and ink. All the pictures whose height did not reach four feet ten inches were judged there—'passed on the easel,' as the expression goes—being ranged, ten or twelve together, on a kind of trestle covered with green baize. A good many committee-men then grew absent-minded, several wrote their letters, and the president had to get angry to obtain presentable majorities. Sometimes a gust of passion swept by; they all jostled each other; the votes, usually given by raising the hand, took place amid such feverish excitement that hats and walking-sticks were waved in the air above the tumultuous surging of heads. . . .

As it happened, Mazel was in a frightfully bad humour that day. At the outset of the sitting the brigadier had come to him, saying: "There was a mistake yesterday, Monsieur Mazel. A *hors-concours* picture was rejected. You know, No. 2520, a nude woman under a tree."

In fact, on the day before, this painting had been consigned to the grave amid unanimous contempt, nobody having noticed that it was the work of an old classical painter highly respected by the Institute; and the brigadier's fright, and the amusing circumstance of a picture having thus been condemned by mistake, enlivened the younger members of the committee and made them sneer in a provoking manner.

Mazel, who detested such mishaps, which he rightly felt were disastrous for the authority of the School of Arts, made an angry gesture, and drily said:

"Well, fish it out again, and put it among the admitted pictures. It isn't so surprising, there was an intolerable noise yesterday. How can one judge anything like that at a gallop, when one can't even obtain silence?"

He rang his bell furiously, and added:

"Come, gentlemen, everything is ready—a little good will, if you please."

Unluckily, a fresh misfortune occurred as soon as the first paintings were set on the trestle. One canvas among others attracted Mazel's attention, so bad did he consider it, so sharp in tone as to make one's very teeth grate. As his sight was failing him, he leant forward to look at the signature, muttering the while: "Who's the pig———"

But he quickly drew himself up, quite shocked at having read the name of one of his friends, an artist who, like himself, was a rampart of healthy principles. Hoping that he had not been overheard, he thereupon called out:

"Superb! No. 1, eh, gentlemen?"

No. 1 was granted—the formula of admission which entitled the picture to be hung on the line. Only, some of the committee-men laughed and nudged each other, at which Mazel felt very hurt, and became very fierce.

Moreover, they all made such blunders at times. A great many of them eased their feelings at the first glance, and then recalled their words as soon as they had deciphered the signature. This ended by making them cautious, and so with furtive glances they made sure of the artist's name before expressing any opinion. Besides, whenever a colleague's work, some fellow committee-man's suspicious-looking canvas, was brought forward, they took the precaution to warn each other by making signs behind the painter's back, as if to say, "Take care, no mistake, mind; it's his picture." . . .

This general revision was the terrible part of the task. Although, after twenty days' continuous toil, the committee allowed itself forty-eight hours' rest, so as to enable the keepers to prepare the final work, it could not help shuddering on the afternoon when it came upon the assemblage of three thousand rejected paintings, from among which it had to rescue as many canvases as were necessary for the then regulation total of two thousand five hundred admitted works to be complete. Ah! those three thousand pictures, placed one after the other alongside the walls of all the galleries, including the outer one, deposited also even on the floors, and lying there like stagnant pools, between which the attendants devised little paths—they were like an inundation, a deluge, which rose up, streamed over the whole Palais de l'Industrie, and submerged it beneath the murky flow of all the mediocrity and madness to be found in the river of Art. And but a single afternoon sitting was held, from one till seven o'clock—six hours of wild galloping through a maze! At first they held out against fatigue and strove to keep their vision clear; but the forced march soon made their legs give way, their eyesight was irritated by all the dancing colours, and yet it was still necessary to march on, to look and judge, even until they broke down with fatigue. By four o'clock the march was like a rout—the scattering of a defeated army. Some committee-men, out of breath, dragged themselves along very far in the rear; others, isolated, lost amid the frames, followed the narrow paths, renouncing all prospect of emerging from them, turning round and round without any hope of ever getting to the end! How could they be just and impartial, good heavens? What could they select from amid that heap of horrors? Without clearly distinguishing a landscape from a portrait, they made up the number they required in potluck fashion. Two hundred, two hundred and forty—another eight, they still wanted eight more. That one? No, that other. As you like! Seven, eight, it was over! At last they had got to the end, and they hobbled away, saved—free!

HENRY BACON

From *A Parisian Year*

Opening Day at the Salon

1882

The first of May is usually the date on which the painters can for the first time see their works upon the walls of the Salon. They enter the Palais by a small door on the Champs Élysées, and climb the stairs with a mingled feeling of pleasure and apprehension,—pleasure at the thought of seeing so much, and apprehension at the thought that their own work may not show to advantage. Entering the first room produces much the same sensation as entering a well-lighted, crowded ball-room, with this difference,—that one is bewildered and does not know which way to turn, while in the ball room the first thing is to greet the hostess, or, if late, hunt her up in the crowd. The artists, however, do follow something like this custom, for they proceed to hunt up their own pictures, and to greet them as gladly-met friends or disagreeable acquaintances. If one is to be disappointed, it is best to have it over at once. And almost every artist is disappointed at first by the appearance of his picture. It was painted in a special light and placed in the studio to the best advantage, while here it has to take its chance, and the rooms are so large that paintings which in the studio appeared large and ambitious are here dwarfed and subdued. Imagine

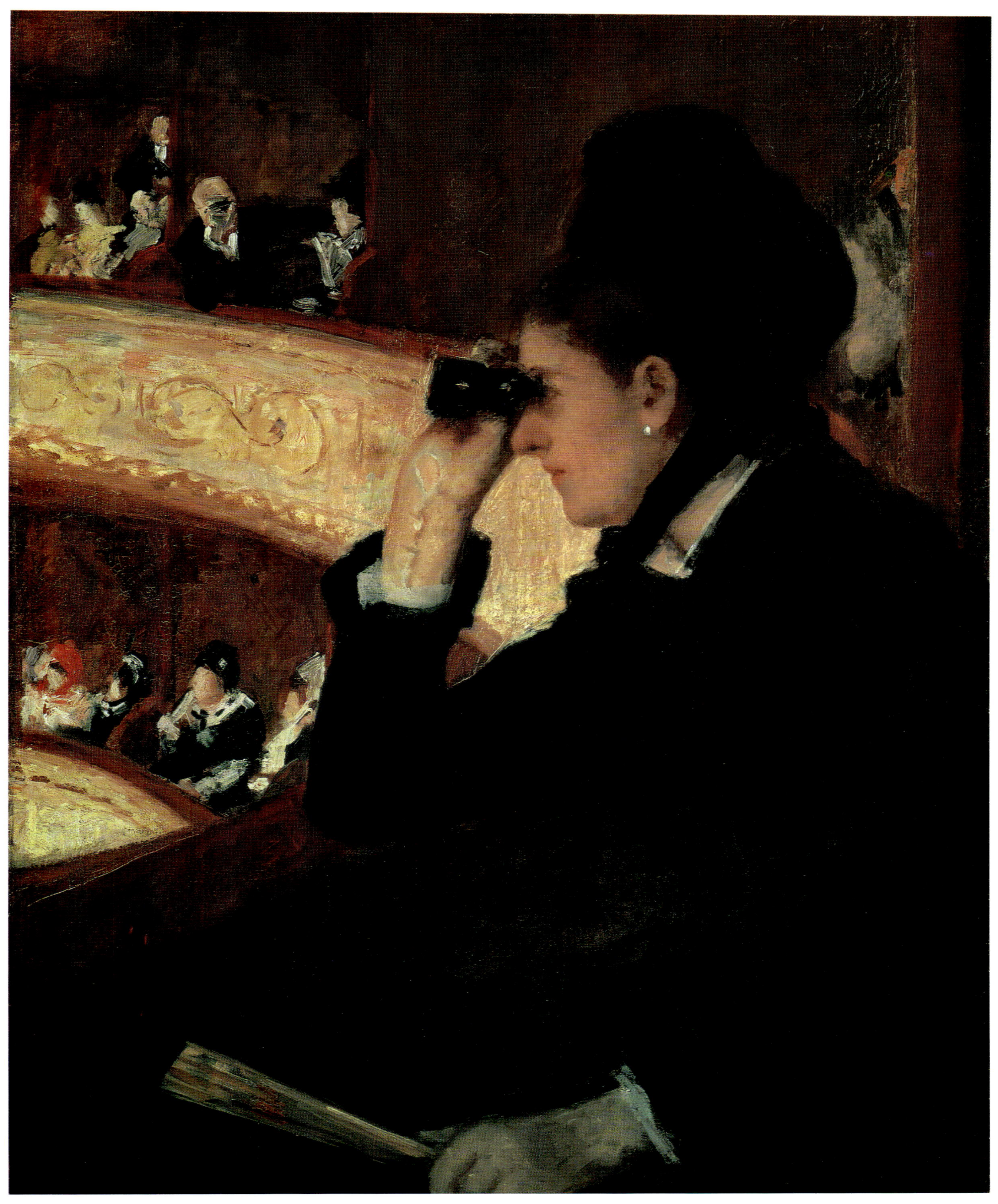

COLORPLATE 16. *At the Opera.* 1879. Oil on canvas. 31 ½ × 25 ½ in. (80 × 64.7 cm). Courtesy of Museum of Fine Arts, Boston. The Hayden Collection.

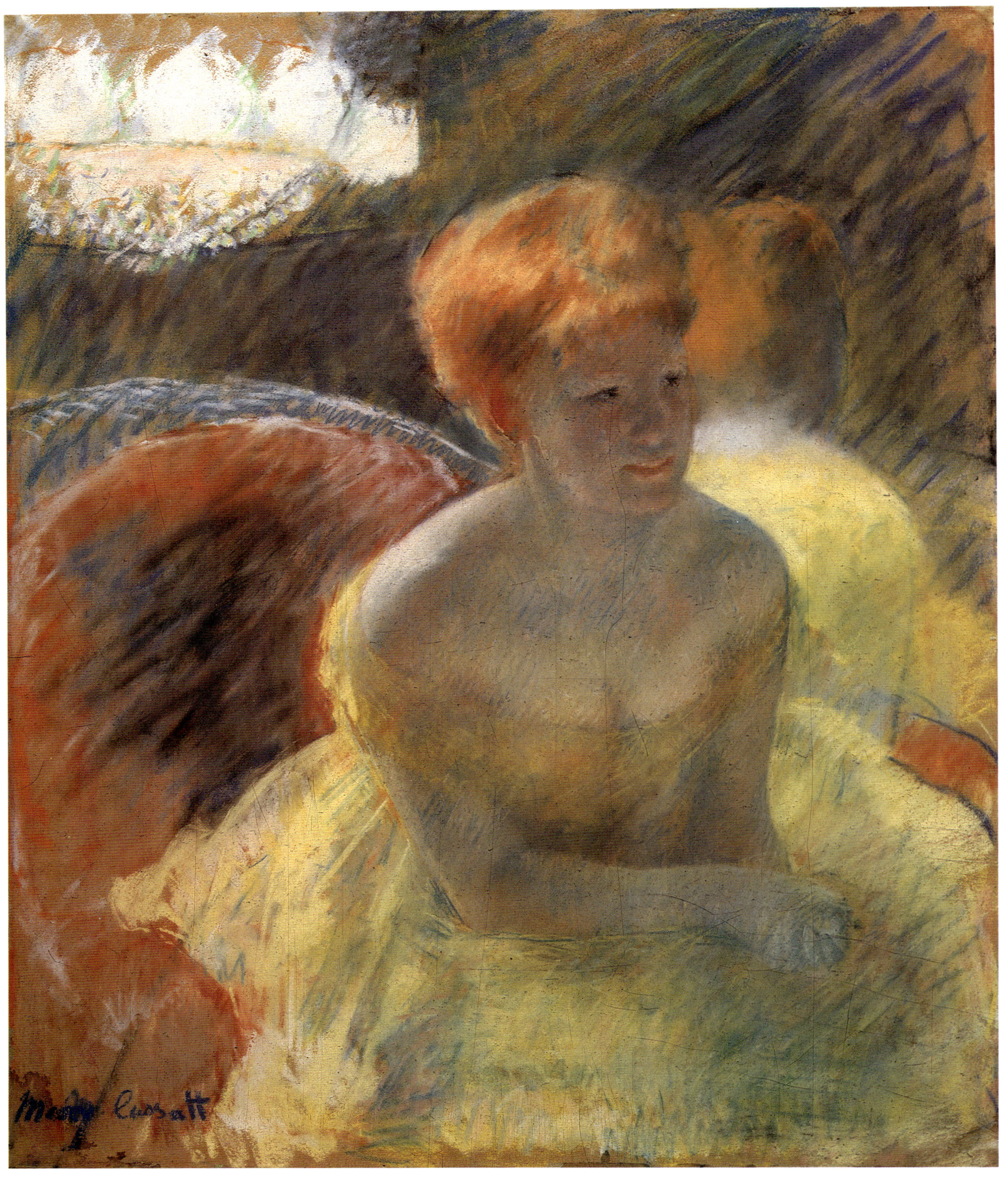

COLORPLATE 17. *At the Theater (Woman in a Loge)*. c. 1879. Pastel on paper. 21 13/16 × 18 1/8 in. (55.4 × 46.1 cm). The Nelson-Atkins Museum of Art, Kansas City, Missouri. Acquired through the generosity of an anonymous donor.

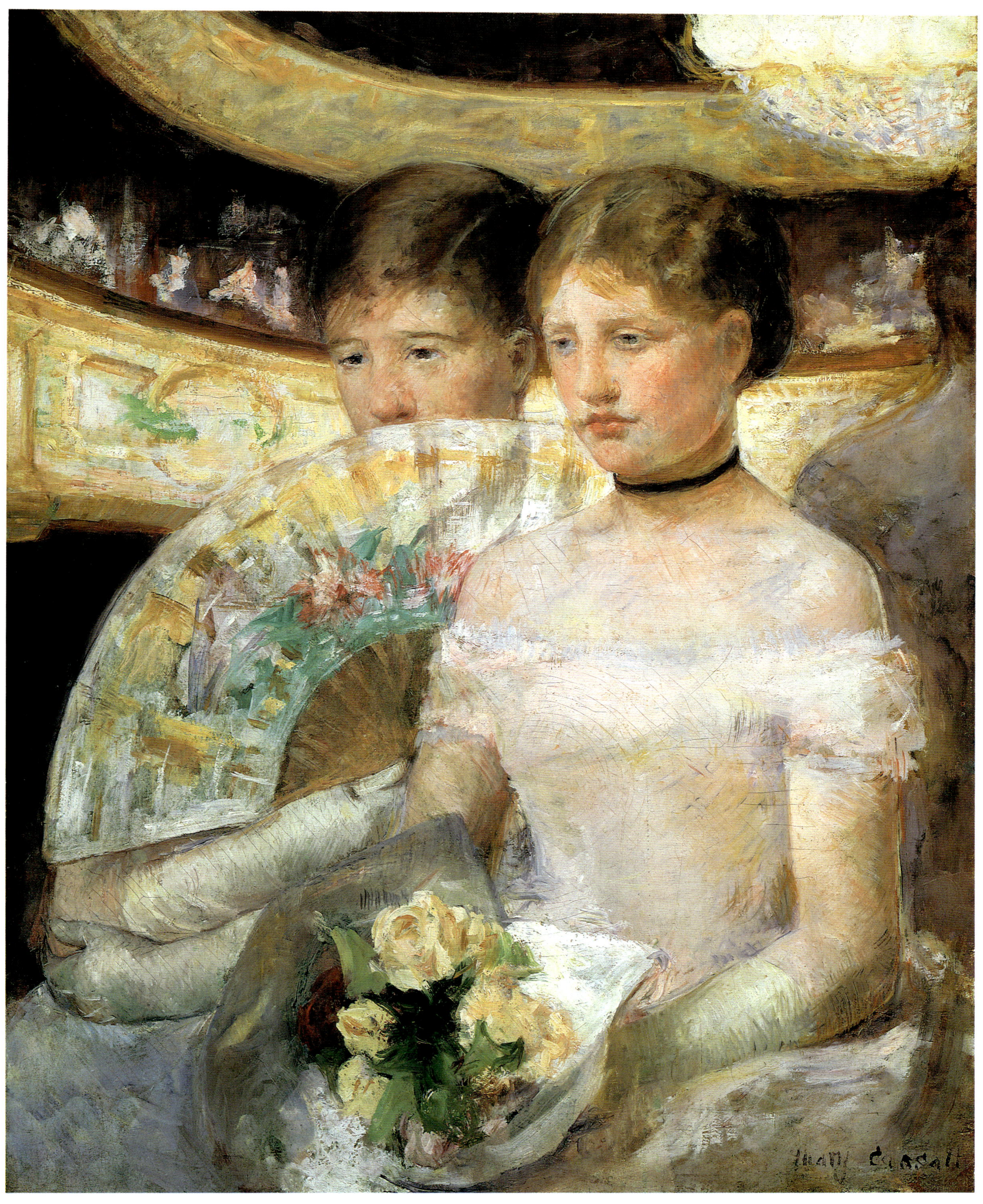

COLORPLATE 18. *The Loge.* 1882. Oil on canvas. 31 ½ × 25 ⅛ in. (80 × 63.8 cm). National Gallery of Art. The Chester Dale Collection. Photograph © Board of Trustees, National Gallery of Art, Washington, D.C.

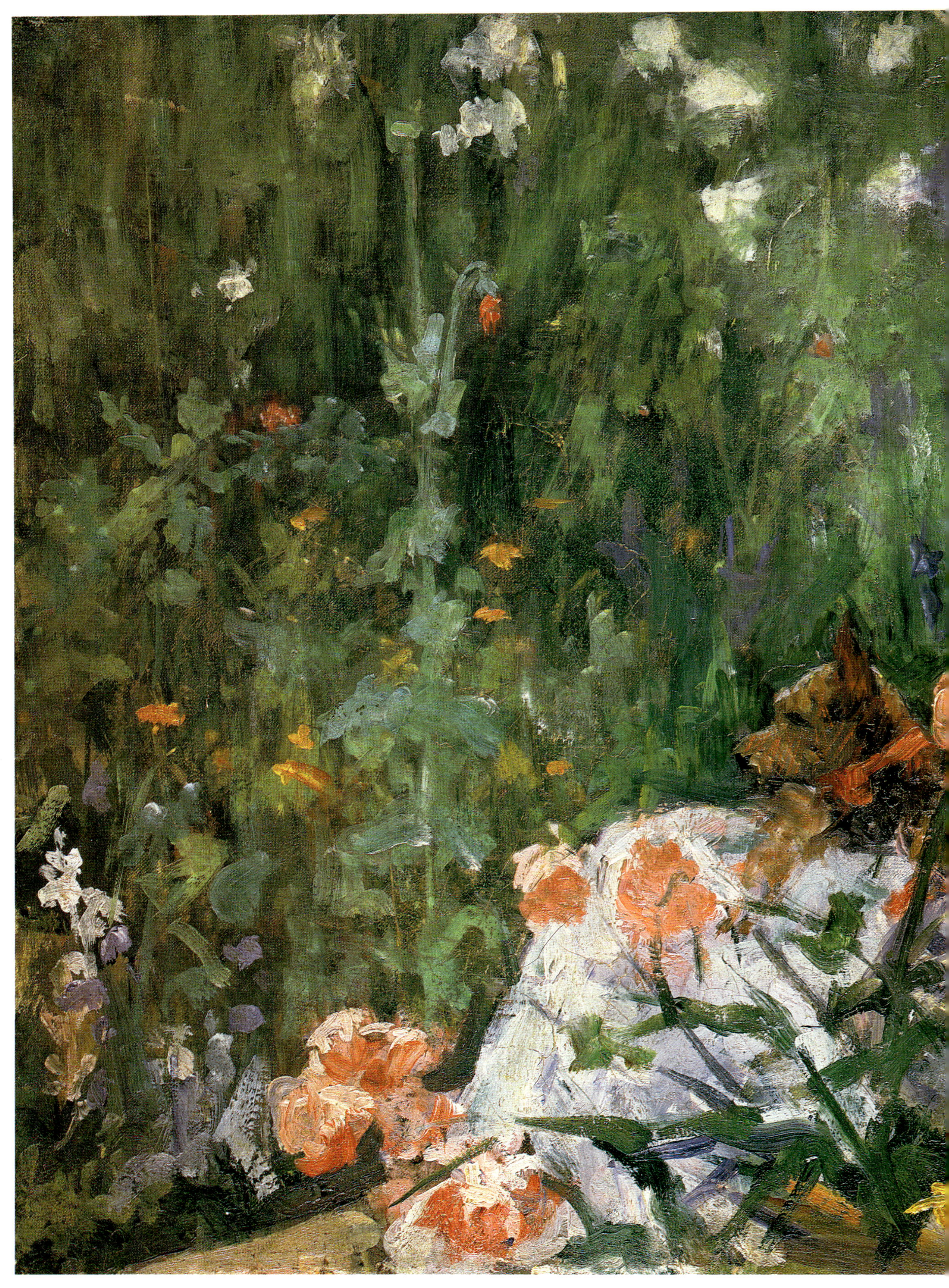

COLORPLATE 19. *Lydia Seated in the Garden with a Dog on Her Lap.* c. 1880. 10 ¾ × 16 in. (27.3 × 40.6 cm). Private collection. Photograph courtesy of Adelson Galleries, Inc., New York.

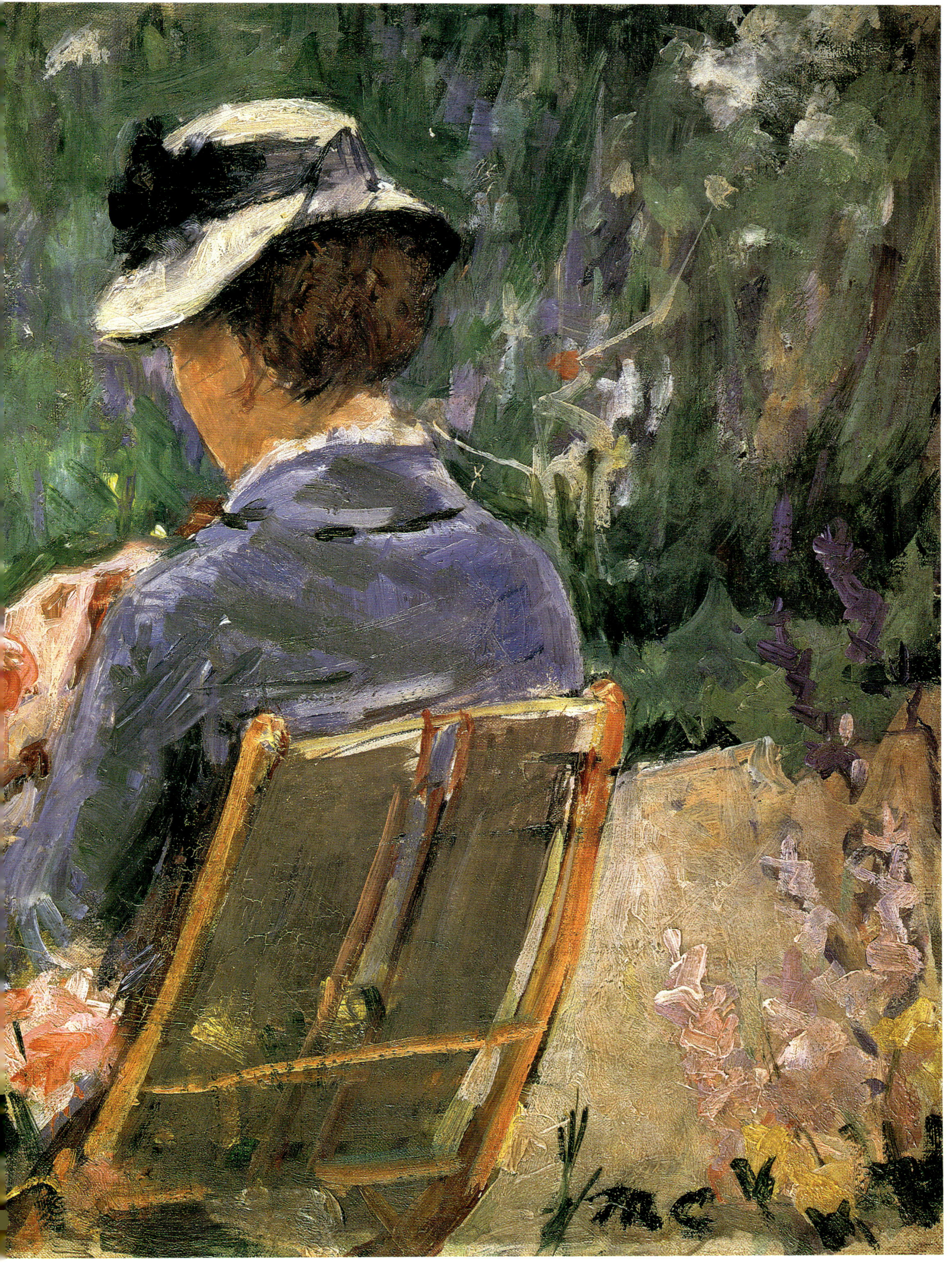

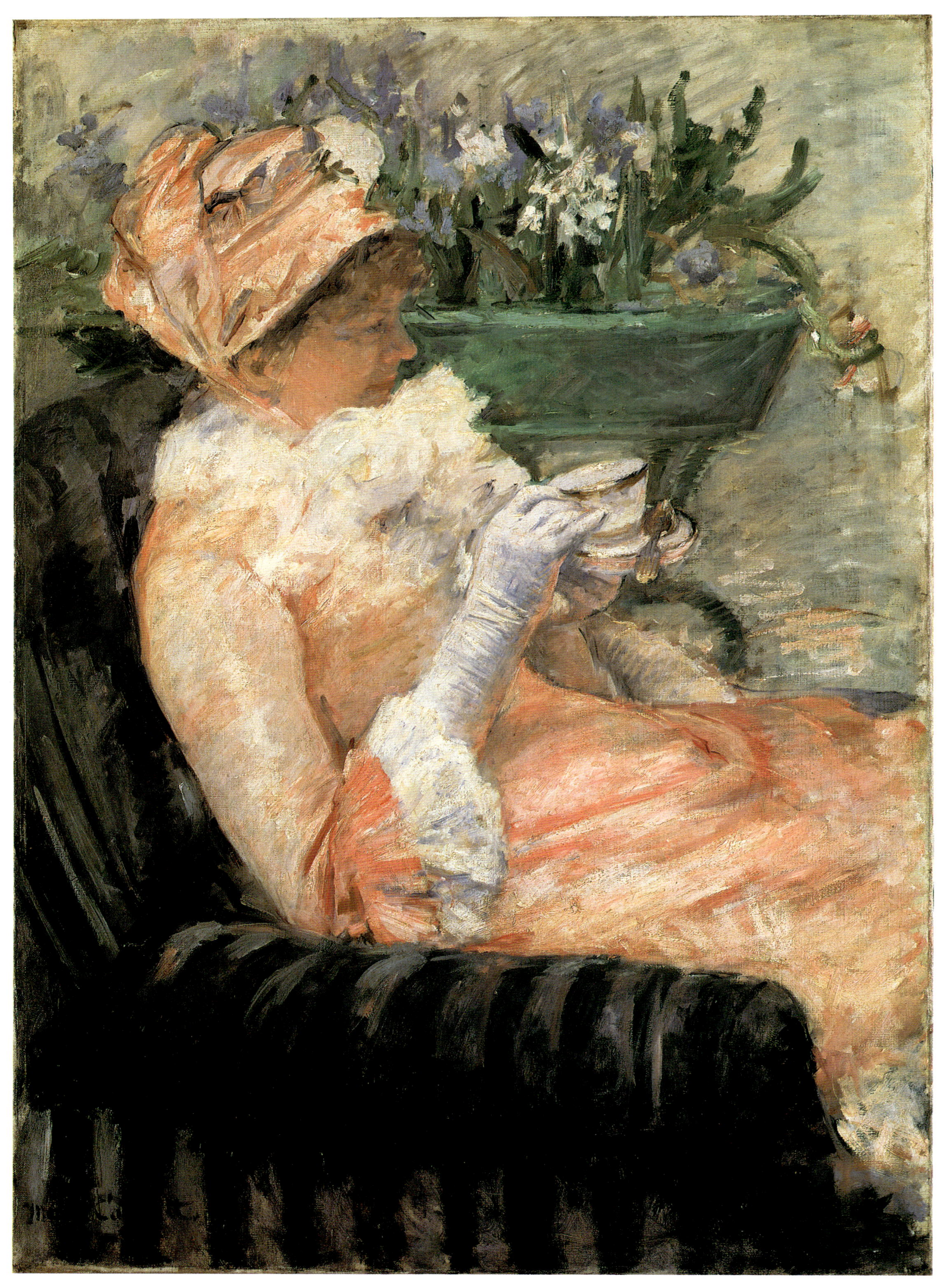

COLORPLATE 20. *The Cup of Tea.* 1879. Oil on canvas. 36 3/8 × 25 3/4 in. (92.4 × 65.4 cm). The Metropolitan Museum of Art, New York. From the collection of James Stillman, gift of Dr. Ernest G. Stillman, 1922 (22.16.17). © 1983 The Metropolitan Museum of Art.

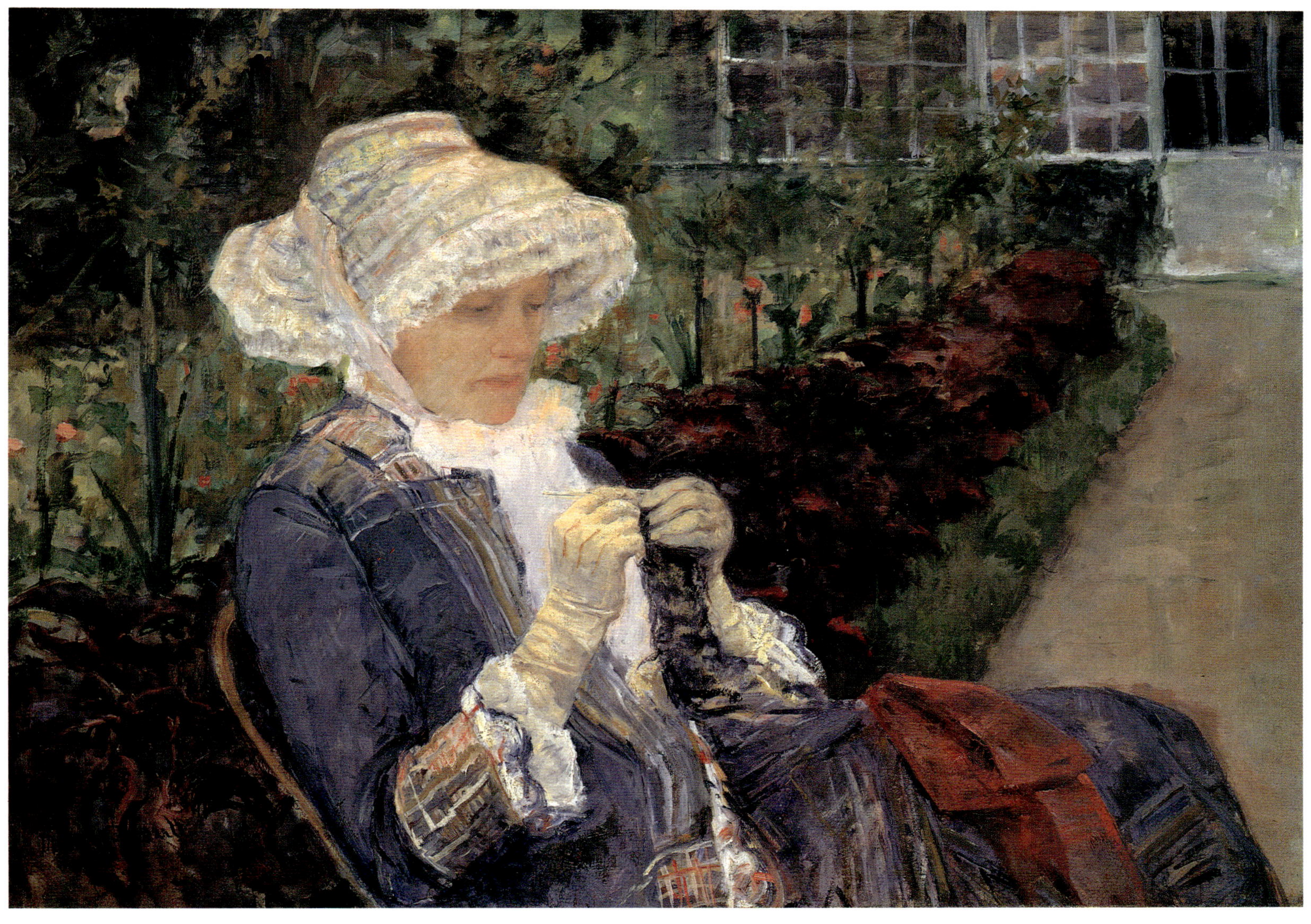

COLORPLATE 21. *Lydia Crocheting in the Garden at Marly.* 1880. Oil on canvas. 26 × 37 in. (66 × 94 cm). The Metropolitan Museum of Art, New York. Gift of Mrs. Gardner Cassatt, 1965 (65.184). © 1993 The Metropolitan Museum of Art.

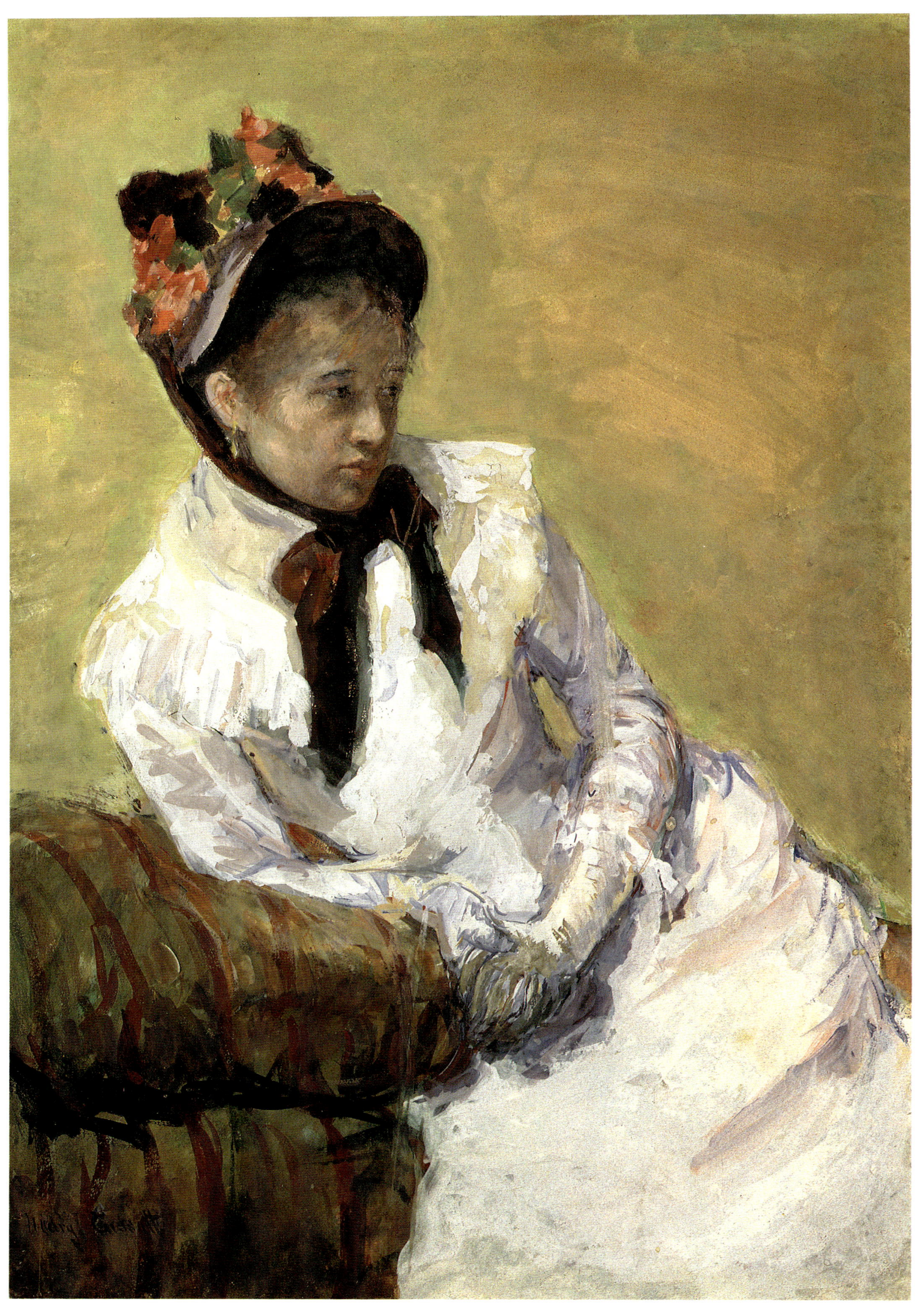

COLORPLATE 22. *Portrait of the Artist.* 1878. Gouache on paper. 23 ½ × 17 ½ in. (59.7 × 44.5 cm). The Metropolitan Museum of Art, New York. Bequest of Edith H. Proskauer, 1975 (1975.319.1). © 1983 The Metropolitan Museum of Art.

twenty-four rooms with nearly three thousand paintings, and you get a faint idea only of the Salon and its magnitude. Some of the rooms are eighty feet square. Many of the large pictures appear as if they had been accepted by the jury as furniture to cover the large walls near the ceiling, which would otherwise have been left vacant. The position coveted by the painter for his production, as has been said, is a place upon the line; for there he is sure of being noticed, and his picture examined. Many visitors follow the iron railing which protects the lower-placed paintings, and only notice those which come opposite their eyes, ignoring those which have necessarily been placed above. As the line is considered a place of honor, it is much coveted. Some of our compatriots who only go to the Salon because "it is the thing," more to be seen than to see, wander around, looking vaguely at the upper rows, never deigning to join the crowd which is examining some choice painting on the line, for fear they should be hidden or their good clothes crushed. But they fulfil their mission. They themselves form an interesting collection of modern works of art,—and are often well painted.

Letter from Mary Cassatt to Her Sister-in-Law, Lois Cassatt

On Painting in the French Alps

August 1, 1869

Beaufort sur Doron, Savoie
August 1, 1869

Beaufort sur Doron, Savoie, is a small town in the French Alps.

My dear Lois,

I have had such a variety of mishaps lately & have changed places so often that most of my correspondents have had a respite, but I begin to think that it is quite time I was hearing from you again. I wrote to Aleck before I left Paris & the day we started I sent him the Consuls certificate; I

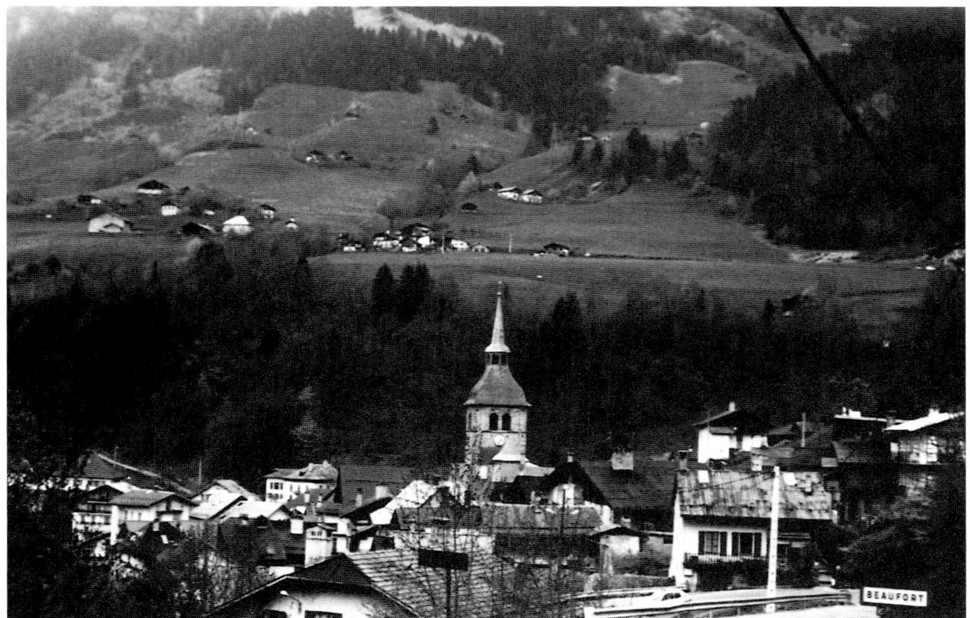

View of Beaufort sur Doron, La Savoie, France.

had been driving about for an hour hunting up our Consul who had moved since I last applied to him & only got the certificate in time to send it from the station just before the cars started. I am here with my friend Miss Gordon from Philadlphia, & we are roughing it most artistically. We made quite a trip before getting here. The first place we stopped at was Maçon where we were perfectly disgusted & from there we went to Aix les bains a very fashionable watering place entirely too gay for two poor painters, at least for one, for although my friend calls herself a painter she is only an amateur and you must know we professionals despise amateurs. So as Aix was too gay we went on into the mountains of Bauges to a place called Les Chesseures [?] our original destination. Unfortunately our hosts had but two beds & as we occupied them both they were obliged to sleep in the barn so we took pity on them & left & after further journeyings we came here. The place is all that we could desire as regards scenery but could be vastly improved as regards accomodations, however as the costumes & surroundings are good for painters we have concluded to put up with all discomforts for a time. These Savoyards are a most civil people & talk a sort of mixture of French & Italien very hard to understand. We are just on the borders of Italy, we took a mountain excursion the other day & waded up to our ankles in snow, but were rewarded by a magnificent view of Mont Blanc & the St. Bernard, however we think we will rest satisfied with that & not try it again as we had to walk some twelve hours. Now my dear Lois I expect to have a long letter from you soon, indeed I dont know whether it is indiscrete but I expect a *very very* interesting piece of news from Altoona before long, it will give me sincere pleasure to hear that it is all satisfactorily over & I may venture to congratulate you beforehand, for my part I want a nephew. Give my love to Aleck & believe me,

The impending arrival of Aleck and Lois's first child, Edward Buchanan Cassatt, born on August 23, 1869.

very affectionately your sister
Mary S. Cassatt

Letter from Mary Cassatt to Emily Sartain

Yearning to Return to Europe

June 7, 1871

Emily Sartain (1841–1927), American painter, mezzotint engraver, and art educator who travelled to Europe with Cassatt in 1871. She studied at the Pennsylvania Academy of the Fine Arts from 1864 to 1870 and exhibited at the Paris Salon in 1875 and in 1883. Sartain was taught mezzotint engraving by her father, also an artist. She served as art editor of the magazine "Our Continent," an illustrated journal published in Philadelphia from 1881 to 1883, and was the principal of the Philadelphia School of Design for Women from 1886 to 1920.

Hollidaysburg
June 7

Hollidaysburg is a riverside town outside of Altoona, Pennsylvania, where the Cassatts rented a house for the summer.

My dear Friend,

I was very glad to hear of your brothers return as I know it must be delightful to be able to talk over your plans with some one who can sympathize with you. Father maintains that one always has more pleasure in anticipation than reality. I am afraid that my pleasure will have to be confined to the first as I have heard several times from New York but nothing in any degree favorable to the sale of my pictures I am beginning to search for a field of operations for next winter nearer home. However as you may be more fortunate than I am, I must tell you what I have forgotten hitherto, that I had an acquaintance a lady artist [Fräulein Beller?] who spent a year or at least a winter near Madrid two years ago, she is a german & her means are very limited so I know the expenses were not great. She lived within a short distance of the city & was able to go in when she pleased, her account of everything was enthusiastic. The climate I have always heard was severe, but I doubt if there is a climate in the world so trying as this of America

William Sartain (1843–1924), Emily Sartain's younger brother, was a painter who also studied at the the Pennsylvania Academy of the Fine Arts and in Paris. He later taught art in Philadelphia and New York.

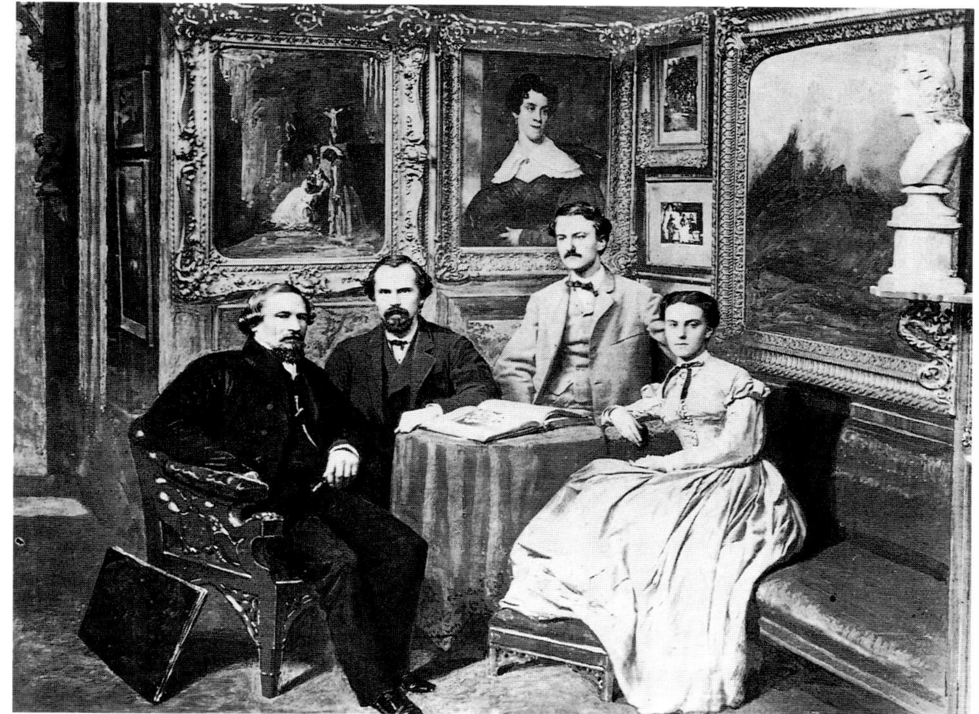

Photograph of Emily Sartain and her family, Philadelphia. c. 1865. Courtesy of the Pennsylvania Academy of the Fine Arts Archives, Philadelphia.

especially Philadelphia, I fancy you would find anything preferable to that. In Rome the hotels & restaurants are dear & yet one can live cheaply. I am in such low spirits over my prospects that although I would prefer Spain I should jump at anything in preference to America, & would look upon any of the places you mention as paradise. I wonder at your being prejudiced against Munich the Gallery is fine & some good artists live there & it is cheap. I suppose though things will be changed since this affair in France. Poor Paris! I am anxious to hear from there but there is no one writing at present. I think you need have no fear as to climate—one can always make oneself comfortable & indeed if one can't one forgets the need of comfort when working hard. Capri is better than Naples & there is quite a colony of artists & it is extremely cheap. Enfin! all this is I am afraid not for me, but in the midst of my misfortunes I can heartily congratulate you on your two new orders & hope you will find some one else, if I am not able who will be able to accompany you. Father is in town today to see about some sort of a vehicle to carry us about the neighbourhood, it has been so oppressively warm that we have not had the energy to settle anything as yet. I suppose I am getting acclimated but I find the process anything but palatable & wish myself in a more congenial climate, Rome last summer even with the fleas was as nothing compared to this place. I am very much obliged for your fathers kind offer about my pictures but for the present I will let them remain where they are. I am working by fits & starts at fathers portrait but it advances slowly he drops asleep while sitting. I commenced a study of our mulatto servant girl but just as I had the mask painted in she gave warning. My luck in this country! I was amused at her finding that I had not made her look like a white person. I have run out of colors & have sent to town for more but they have not arrived yet. Do you know where I could get some good rough canvass? I don't think Janetsky has any. I wonder if Kurz has, if you pass his shop would you kindly ask & let me know. When I have struck a vein of models I will let you know & you must come up. I long to see you & have a talk about art. I cannot tell you what I suffer for the want of seeing a good picture, no amount of bodily suffering occasioned by the want of comforts would seem to be too great a price for the pleasure of living in a country where one could have some art advantages. With kind regards to all

Cassatt had placed two paintings at the Goupil Gallery in New York.

Two new orders for mezzotints.

I remain yours in the Heart
M. S. Cassatt

Quoted in a Letter from William Sartain to His Father

Cassatt's Earliest Known Review from an American Newspaper

March 25, 1872

Miss Mary Stevenson Cassatt has just finished an original painting which all Parma is flocking to see at her studio at the Accademia of that city. Prof. Raimondi and other Italian painters of reputation are quite enthusiastic in regard to our fair young countrywoman's talent which they pronounce to be nearly akin to genius and they offer her every inducement to make Parma her home and to date her works from that city.

Cassatt and Emily Sartain arrived in Parma in late winter 1872. Cassatt had a commission from the bishop of Pittsburgh to paint two copies of Correggio's paintings for the Cathedral of Pittsburgh.

Carlo Raimondi (1809–1883), Italian artist who taught engraving at the Parma Accademia. Raimondi served as Cassatt's mentor while she was in Parma.

Letter from Emily Sartain to Her Father, John Sartain

On Cassatt's Success in Parma, Italy

March 7, 1872

Borgo Riolo No. 21
March 7, 1872

Dear Father,

I finished my last letter to you by saying I had just received a message from Mr. Cornish that he needed his studio—I went round to see him the next day,—so tired and weak I could scarcely walk. . . . In a week, Miss Cassatt will be finished with her studio at the Academy, and I can either take that, or accept Young Raimondi's offer of half of his—He has just taken a room that will come into his possession in a few days—He (as well as Cornish) is going to paint a picture for the Turin exhibition in April—He took a number of his sketches around to Miss Cassatt for her to select which he should finish—

All Parma is talking of Miss Cassatt and her picture, and everyone is anxious to know her—The compliments she receives are overwhelming—At Prof. Caggiati's reception men of talent and distinction to say nothing of titled people, are brought up to be presented, having requested the honor of an introduction—I shine a little, by her reflection—One of the custode yesterday, looking around carefully first to be sure he was not overheard, assured her she was much more "brava" than any of the professors—One of the professors has begged her to come to his studio and give him criticism and advice—This exceeding popularity has its counterbalance—we are not enough to ourselves for my taste. However I suppose it is my only opportunity to see genuine Italian society,—and when I reflect I have been here little more than two months I feel less discouraged.

Edouardo Raimondi took us to Madame Toschi's day before yesterday, at her request. She is an admirable talker, full of vivacity and interest, and can turn a compliment with the most perfect grace—She talks French with the same ease and fluency as Italian, so Miss Cassatt was at home with her—We then went down to the primo piano to call on the Countess Salimberti, who had sent word she would like us to come and see her pictures, her own productions—Notwithstanding she was made honorary member of the Milan Academy for her copy of San Gerolamo, her pictures are about as bad as her reputation, which is saying very little for them—We have had the luck of having a dead set made at us by the three most notorious women of the upper class of Parmagian society,—but fortunately Miss Cassatt tells everything to Prof. Raimondi, so we never have got intimate. There was one woman introduced to Miss Cassatt at Caggiati's, the wife of a colonel, who was so ugly she thought she must be perfectly proper, she was surely safe with her, and so talked with her a great deal—When she mentioned her name to Edouardo R last evening he almost threw himself off his chair with astonishment—He said she was the worst of them all—As they are growing old they are now devout Catholics, and la Caggiati who is a bigotte, receives them and is attempting to rehabilitate them—. . . .

This morning Prof. Raimondi was going to take us out for a drive to Ponte di Tara, a splendid bridge about six miles off built by Maria Louisa, from which there is a splendid view. It was so foggy, it was not worth while to go, so the expedition is postponed till tomorrow—The family always have a horse in summer, and Edouardo is going to try one tomorrow to see if he will do, and he says if he takes him, we can go out driving whenever we want to—I must say they are wonderfully kind—The son seems exactly like an American, just as free and easy, and I am happy to say, without one bit of flirting or nonsense about him—In fact, I was surprised at Caggiati's to see how perfectly free and unconstrained the young girls and young men were with each other,—so entirely different from our preconceived notions of Italians—I might have thought myself with a party of Americans, except that the young girls were so exceedingly polite to each other and to me, whereas at home they generally save up their sweetness for the gentlemen—. . . .

The doctor has ordered Miss Cassatt to ride on horseback,—and of course Prof. Raimondi immediately trots off to inquire about horses etc. He tells her she can go off for a ride of an hour or hour and a half, with a groom behind her (it would not do for her to ride alone here) the expense for it all, the two horses and the man included, would be four francs—eighty cents—Cheap enough, isn't it?—I hope all at home are quite well—Give my love to all the family, to the Schusseles and to all my friends—Hope to hear from you soon—

With much love

Yours
Emily—

Don't you think it would be a good idea for the Academy to order a copy of the San Gerolamo from Miss C—? She expects only $300 for it from the bishop,—and I think it would be nicer for the Academy to have it instead—It is very little money—This suggestion is private,—not pro-bono-pubblico—She knows nothing of it—

E—

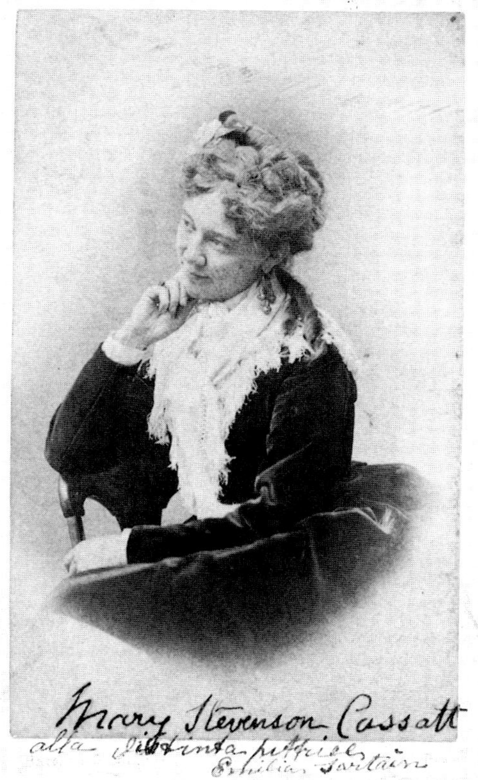

Photograph of Mary Cassatt, age 28, taken in Parma, Italy. 1872. Courtesy of the Pennsylvania Academy of the Fine Arts Archives, Philadelphia.

Letter from Mary Cassatt to Emily Sartain

On Studying in Parma, Italy

June 2, 1872

Parma
Sunday, June 2

My Dear Emily,

If the enclosed don't give you a half hours laugh, I shall think that you have lost all sense of humor. A package was brought in just now containing about twenty copies, and you are honored with the first. Two lines in the paper would have suited me better but I am menaced with a retranslation, & republishing in the *Gazetta di Parma.* Your nice long letter which reached me at last gave me much pleasure. The watch number [?] I had put on at once, and a half hour ago dropped my watch and smashed another number; such is life! My copy is packed and gone, but won't reach Genoa in time for the 5th when a vessel sails for New York so it won't leave for home before the 25th. I wish Mrs. Muzio would get Mr. Ryan to write a line or two for me in the *Register.* I find it has done me good and I am getting anxious to see myself in print; one gets used to anything in this world. Vieille sent me a roll of canvas and some brushes, out of two dozen of the latter I can use 6. Isn't he a sensible individual! He did not send me a bill but I am going to send you some money and write to him to call and you will pay him. I will send twenty five frcs, and I hope after you have paid yourself that there will be enough left to buy a French translation of Jane Eyre for which if you will be kind enough to send it I shall be very much obliged.

"The American Register" was an American newspaper published in Paris.

You don't tell me if you have the life model all day or if you have the nude or in fact any particulars of the Lumenais school, remember I am interested. I am much obliged for what you tell me about my picture I know that it is heavy, but how to get a thing solid & yet keep it easy. Voila! And then I know that the great fault of the modern school is flimsiness, enfin! I shall do better next time. Was'nt I right when I said that the tone of the Antonio Mor here was the tone most in vogue in the French school? Along side of that even the Correggio would seem yellow.

Evariste Vital Luminais (1822–1896), French painter who specialized in animal and hunting scenes and in historical genre. He won medals in the Salon in the 1850s and received the Légion d'Honneur in 1869. Emily Sartain studied with Luminais in Paris from 1872 to 1875. Cassatt did not particularly admire Luminais, and the two had a rather contentious relationship.

Anthonis Moor van Dashorst (c. 1519–1576), Dutch portraitist and court painter.

I have been to here "Piggy" make a speech to the students at the distribution of the prizes, and I was called upon by the Lyndie [?] and Prefect to give some of them, a high honor which I would as leave be spared. Your Edouardo is in Turin, he wrote to me this morning to tell me to go on & see the exhibition for it was excellent, I certainly shall do nothing of the kind, I am sick of Edouard. "Piggy" is a great deal nicer. On the whole I thought it better to send thirty frcs, if there is anything left over it can go toward buying the "Cahier Blue" of Gustave Droz.

I have begun again on my cymbals, changed the background &c it will do for a study and then I am going to have the lame girl, she has a splendid head like a Roman. Everybody sends love especially Angiolina, she is going off to visit her sister, and I don't suppose I shall ever see her again, I like her much; she was delighted with Alfred de Musset, by the way I recommended you particularly. "On ne badine pas avec l'amour," and "Il faut qu'une porte soit ouverte ou fermé." You surely thought those exquisite. Write soon and tell me something to keep me alive. I am tied down here until August and then I hope I shall be able to leave and go either south to Naples or else to Madrid. Kind regards to your Mother and brother, and my inquiring friends and believe me affectionately yours

COLORPLATE 4

Alfred de Musset (1810–1857), French poet, playwright, and novelist.

Mary S. Cassatt

On the whole I think it best to send the printed matter in a separate envelope—

M.S.C.

Letter from Mary Cassatt to Emily Sartain
On Italian Art vs. Spanish Art
January 1, 1873

Seville
New Year's Evening, 1873

My Dear Friend,

This is the first time I have written the above date. Here we are in 73. Happy New Year to you and Mrs. Tolles, and may you make as much improvement as you both desire. It is half past ten, but for some unaccountable reason, I do not feel in the least sleepy, so, I reply at once to your letter which the "Cartero" has just brought me. D'abord! About the tickets for the Theatre Français, it was Miss Biller or rather Fraülein Biller who told me about them; you know that there are always plenty of "sups" about a theater who are given "free tickets" well they are often glad to sell the same, and Miss B spoke to us of a very nice person that she knew who disposed of free entrances, and she gave me the reason that it was because we were art students. We accepted the same without question and frequently went in parties of 10 or 12 from the school in the rue d'Aguessian. The address is Mme. Fourchette no 9 quai Voltaire, as well as I can remember, the tickets cost one franc & entitles you to a seat in the third circle of boxes price 3 frcs, go early, and give 50 centimes to the old woman who takes the cloaks she will give you both good seats; keep your mouth covered, you know I always tell everything but you are wiser and it is no use to let every one know your affaires; however I never can remember that all persons don't take my views of things. Tell Madame Fourchette that I or Miss Biller sent you perhaps she remembers Miss B. best; what I recommend you to do is all right and proper and as I tell you was perfectly approved of at the school.

Everything here goes on as usual. I am all day at Pilats house, and am known as the "Señora of the Casa Pilatos," Sundays and week days, Christmas and New Years day—I get up there sometimes at ten, or half past seldom as late as eleven, and work steadily to five. My present effort is on a canvass of thirty and is three figures life size half way to the knee—All the three heads are forshortened and difficult to pose, so much so that my model asked me if the people who pose for me live long. I have one man's figure the first time I have introduced a mans head into any of my pictures. I had hoped to send something if only a head to the Vienna Exhibition, but I have not the most remote idea of when the pictures must be sent. You say that I have said nothing about the pictures here, but the fine ones are miserably lighted, and many of them inferior to their reputation, there is however a magnificent Zurbaran at the Museo. The great thing here is the odd types and peculiar rich dark coloring of the models, if it were not for that I should not stay, the artists here are perhaps more flattering than they were in Parma, but I think the Spaniards infinitely inferior in education and breeding to the Italians. There is I believe a fine collection of modern paintings owned by an amateur here. Fortuny's Madrazos &c, the gen-

The Casa de Pilatos is the palace of the dukes of Medinaceli in Seville, built in 1520. Cassatt kept a studio in this building during her stay.

COLORPLATE 7

Mariano José Fortuny y Marasal (1838–1874), Spanish artist who became one of the most prominent artists in Europe in the 1870s.

Raimundo de Madrazo y Garret (1841–1920), popular Spanish painter of the 1870s.

tleman called on me, but his gallery is undergoing repairs and I am not to see it yet. Spanish artists see nothing out of their own school, in Madrid everything was inferior to Velasquez in their eyes. I don't know if it was the spirit of contradiction in me but towards the past I got disgusted and found that there were a few other masters who could paint a *little*. It "riled" me to be told as I was constantly that Giorgione and Titian &c was conventional. Now that I have begun to paint from life again, constantly the thought of Correggio's pictures returns to my mind and I am thankful for my six months study in Parma. In all of Velasquez pictures I can think of no beautiful hand, *no!* not *one*. Murillo's hands of the St Elizabeth are exquisite but even in that picture there is a boy scratching his head in the most grotesque manner; indeed throughout I think the Spanish school lack taste. Nowadays everything is fashion however, and at present it is grey color, here is Madrazo paints these gypsies with cheeks like some deep red peaches, and he paints them with Malachite green and white. His modelling and his manner as far as I have seen is fine. I confess that if I did not live to paint life would be dull here, dreadfully dull, nothing absolutely nothing going on, as for the comic opera, it is comic indeed, my only surprise is how people live through it and some of them go every night. I will perhaps add a few lines in the morning, but it is very late, so for the present, good night—

Thursday Evening. I am waiting to begin my first lesson in Spanish—my little man is rather late, I don't intend to take grammer &c I am too tired in the evening to study, but I want to read Lope de Vegas plays, and my little teacher will serve as a walking dictionary, more convenient than looking up all the words I don't know. I confess the "Andalusian salt" doesn't seem to me so "salty," I don't see their great wit.

Lope Félix de Vega Carpio (1562–1635), Spanish poet and playwright.

I have not told you about my second edition of Raimondi, but ah! with a difference. The "intendente" of the Duke of Medina Coeli is a Don Manuel Barrera, he paints very badly himself, but it is he who gave me my studio in the House of Pilate; for he lives there, strange to say although he paints so badly he knows all about art, and has seen so many good artists at work that he can give very good advice, so I profit by it. I suppose you know that the House of Pilate belongs to the Medina Coeli. You were talking of the Exhibition of copies at the Palais d'Industrie, if the one by Reignault is the "lancers" that is the (surrendering of the keys) I have forgotten the name of the town by Velasquez, why Reignault only *commenced* the copy it was finished by some one else. I should think that an Exhibition of copies would be a novelty, I should like to see it. One young Frenchman was copying in Madrid on order from the government, paid 6000 frcs! The copy was *awful*! I wrote to ask you about Harry Moore, for I heard about him here, one of the artists said that when he was here Eakens painted much better than he did. Mother also writes from home that she saw two of his pictures at Haseltines both extremely free in style looked as if they had been painted with a pallet knife, the draperies not well done she says, one was withdrawn, for the artist required $3000 for it! Did I write to you that I heard he did not get on well with his wife? I believe that I have scribbled enough by this time, but if you know anything and can find a minute to write I wish that you would tell me when the pictures must be in Vienna—not that I have much hope of finishing anything in time. Are you going to stay in Paris? Wasnt there some idea of you and Mrs Tolles going to Naples. I was to have gone back to Parma, but I believe I shall not be able to, for I *hope* that mother may be over; besides I think I ought to spend the spring in Madrid. I have little or no desire to go to Granada, the thought of the journey deters me. Father sent me a paper with the account of the laying of the cornerstone of the New Academy, if I were not sure you had seen it I would send it to you, Mr Cope made a brilliant speech! Good bye—my love to you both

very sincerely
Mary S. Cassatt

Alexandre Georges Henri Regnault (1843–1871), French painter, studied at the École des Beaux-Arts and won the Prix de Rome in 1866. He painted in Spain in 1868.

Harry Humphrey Moore (1844–1926), American painter, studied with Gérôme at the École des Beaux-Arts. Moore was a friend and travelling companion of Thomas Eakins.

Thomas Eakins (1844–1916), American painter. Eakins studied at the Pennsylvania Academy in the early 1860s, went to Europe to study in 1866, and returned to Philadelphia in 1870. Cassatt and Eakins had a mutual friend in Emily Sartain.

Charles Field Haseltine (1840–1915), American artist and art dealer in Philadelphia.

ELISABETH LUTHER CARY

From *International Studio* Review of *On the Balcony* July 1908

Elisabeth Luther Cary (1867–1936), American author and art critic. Cary studied art herself but turned to writing and literature and wrote books on several prominent authors and artists. Her career as a journalist began in 1905 when she began her own art journal. In 1908 she became critic to "The New York Times."

COLORPLATE 7

Toward the end of last year a considerable number of pictures, both ancient and modern, were added to the already notable Wilstach Collection in Memorial Hall, Fairmount Park, Philadelphia. The modern pictures of the new group, while hardly, perhaps, of the first importance in the sense of adequately representing the best of the modern masters, give a crisp impression of artists whose talent is of a high order, and have been selected with such eclecticism of taste as to cover a wide range of inspiration and of nationality.

In the early example of Miss Mary Cassatt's work we have a particularly interesting canvas in which the most casual observer may see how firmly the artist's achievement with its high degree of technical development is rooted in her personal endowment. The subject consists of a couple of girls leaning on the railing of a balcony and a man standing in the shadow behind them, talking to one of them, who listens with head upraised. The attitude and gestures are free and animated and give the impression of the class to which the people belong, a class unrestrained by conventions of self-repression and conformity to rigid standards of personal reticence. The handsome young forms are ample and strongly built, the modeling is fuller and closer than in most of Miss Cassatt's later pictures, the foreshortened features of the girl looking up into the man's face are drawn with a thorough mastery of the problems presented by the difficult position, and the hands and arms of both girls are admirably analyzed. The types conform to an ideal which has been consistently adhered to by the artist. The firmness of the flesh, the curve of the strong shoulders, the deep chests and beautifully shaped heads are eloquent of that large and wholesome beauty which Miss Cassatt seems almost to evoke in her models, which certainly is not a general characteristic of modern womanhood, yet which appears in her work with the air of belonging to the essential nature of the persons she portrays.

In the present instance the charm of expression also is great, particularly in the case of the girl leaning with both arms on the balcony. Her half-smiling mouth and musing eyes indicate with much subtlety the idle movement of her thought. The color is brilliant without being bright, and follows a more or less clearly defined path from the pink flower in the hair of the girl at the right to the scarlet shawl of her companion, and the passage of the light, swinging in a free curve from the strip of wall against which the man's hand is pressed across the mass of pale color in the dress of the girl at the right and touching the arms and hand of the girl at the left, to sink almost into shadow where it rests on the man's broad-brimmed hat, shows a careful planning for orderly statement of the pictorial features of the scene. Yet neither the pattern of the light and shade nor the rather intricate linear design is imposed upon the composition, but grow naturally out of it, so that its marked decorative quality appears inevitable. This, of course, is the most expressive and satisfactory kind of decoration and Miss Cassatt's command of it has always insured her place in the front ranks of Impressionism, since it is the masters in that school who recognize the value of the decorative principle which their incompetent followers throw to the winds.

Although Miss Cassatt is an American, and we can no better afford to neglect that fact than we can afford to forget the nationality of Whistler, she owes much to those sources of sound teaching which she intelligently sought abroad, and her talent no less gratefully admits its French bringing up than its American inheritance.

Letter from Emily Sartain to Her Father, John Sartain

On Cassatt's Opinions of Modern Art in 1873

May 8, 1873

88, boulevard Courcelles, Paris
May 8, 1873

Dear Father,

I have been so very much occupied since the Howells have been here, that my letter has been pushed off till the very last minute, although I have lots of things I wanted to talk to you about. . . .

I think I wrote you of the arrival of Miss Cassatt and her mother. Oh how good it is to be with some one who talks understandingly and enthusiastically about Art. I find I soon get tired of even friends who are not interested cordially in painting—I by no means agree with all of Miss C's judgments,—she is entirely too slashing,—snubs all modern Art,—disdains the salon pictures of Cabanel Bonnat and all the names we are used to revere,—but her intolerance comes from the earnestness with which she loves nature and her profession,—so I can sympathize with her—Her own style of painting and the Spanish school which she has been studying all winter is so realistic, so solid,—that the French school in comparison seems washy, unfleshlike and grey—Coming from Italy last winter, the salon made the same effect upon me. I agree with her in a measure in many of her criticisms, but am not so severe and sweeping in my deductions.

By the way, Luminais has seen her Salon picture and a couple of her sketches that I took him—He spoke of them as having a great deal of talent but mostly *talent of the brush*, as [he] called it—You must not repeat this to any one. He also thought it wanting in distinction,—in fact he called it *common*. He said too that he saw the influence of too many masters,—there was no personality in her painting,—he felt in her work, Goya, Couture, etc., etc., not Miss Cassatt—He thought she had wandered about too much,—she ought to settle down in one place, and work out her own style—Somebody else here had told her the same thing. I don't see how he could have derived this conclusion. Her work looks to me so original—But I believe he is right. I told her some of these things in a modified form. I don't think she thinks much of his pictures,—they are not in her school. She talks of leaving Paris next week—for Granada if it is possible to reach there by land,—she is afraid to tempt the Mediterranean. . . .

Francisco José de Goya (1746–1828), Spanish painter and etcher.

I went yesterday with Mary & Mrs. Cassatt, to see the pictures of a Mr. Stewart, a Philadelphian, who is reputed to have the best gallery in Paris. Do you know of him? He has a superb house near the palace of Industry, facing the Seine. It was a great treat—He has four or five Fortuny's in oil, and as many water-colors—I had seen only one water color by him before, never any oil pictures. I was delighted by their color, their force spirit and freedom—One negro or Moor's head, life size, a present to Stewart from

Fortuny,—was superb,—even Miss C. admired it unqualifiedly. . . . Stewart must be immensely rich to live in such style—He entertains his pet artists every Thursday. He invited us to come to see his pictures when we liked, and I hope to go again—Miss Cassatt had been there before. . . .

If Cassatt's go to Granada,—and if they were to give the slightest hint of liking me to join them, I should feel strongly tempted to go down there for the three months Luminais will be away—It would be expensive, I suppose—It is a pity that both Miss C. and I both are so defective in drawing. . . . It is growing dark and it hurts my eyes so much to write at night, that I must say good bye—I must not forget to say both the Howells and Cassatts say that I am looking very very well—I'm afraid I must groan in my letters home, most unwarrantably,—since you seem to have an idea I am overworking myself—I dined with the Cassatt's last night—Had a delicious dinner. . . .

Yours affectionately
Emily—

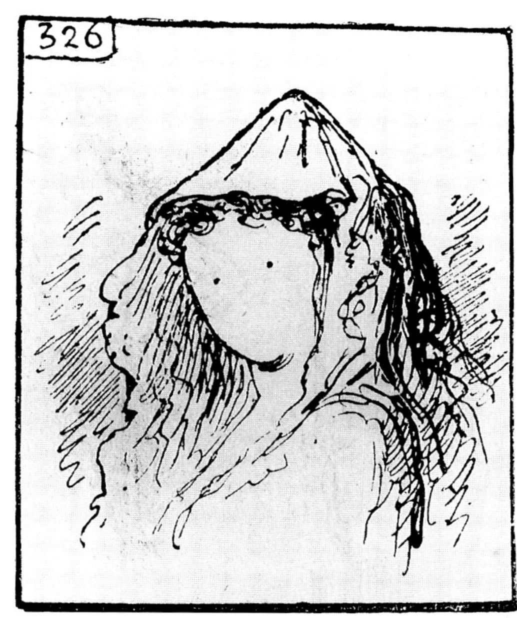

This caricature by the artist-humorist known as STOP (pseudonym of L.P.G.B. Morel-Retz) of Cassatt's painting *Ida* was published in *Le journal amusant,* June 27, 1874. *Ida* was shown in the Salon of 1874, and this caricature is the only survivng record of this important work. Photograph courtesy of the New York Public Library.

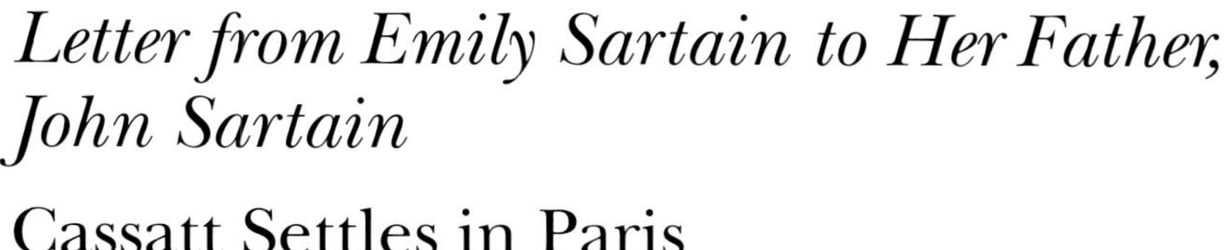

Letter from Emily Sartain to Her Father, John Sartain

Cassatt Settles in Paris

June 17, 1874

Paris
June 17, 1874

My dear Father,

. . . I think I told you that Miss Cassatt is in Paris. She astonished me by telling me she is looking for an atelier here, for next winter. She has always detested Paris so much, that I could scarcely believe it possible, that she would consent to stay here,—but she says she sees it is necessary to be here, to look after her own interests. She thinks it is the fault of her picture dealer that her pictures do not sell. I told you what a washed-out affair she has in the Salon,—but she has a picture now at her dealer's in the Boul. Haussmann, that is superb and delicate in color,—three figures singing. The light on the chest and face of the foreground figure, a blonde, is perfectly dazzling. It is as slovenly in manner and in drawing as her Spanish pochades, however. She says that her Salon head had a great deal of success among artists. I asked Mr. Luminais to look at it, and give me his opinion, but he forgot it. I suppose you know as much as I do, about the probability of her coming home for the summer. It does not seem likely that her mother would have her make the two voyages in so short a time,—suffering as she does on the ocean. . . .

COLORPLATE 9

Trusting all are well,

Yours truly
Emily

From *The Art Journal:* "The Philadelphia Academy Exhibition"

Review of *A Musical Party*

COLORPLATE 9

1876

The present exhibition of paintings and statuary at the Pennsylvania Academy of Fine Arts, which was opened early in May, is a very large one. It includes about five hundred and fifty paintings and a hundred pieces of sculpture. . . . A number of American students, at Paris or Munich, have their pictures here. . . .

Two or three paintings by Miss Mary Cassatt are powerful, and replete with thoughtful individuality. This lady's works are unknown to the New York public, and are so peculiar that it is difficult to define them. *A Musical Party* is her principal production, and shows the heads of three young women, the size of life. One of them has a queer profile face, with the light falling full upon her head and throat and neck, upon which scarcely a degree of shadow defines the forms even about her small, half-averted eyes. A pink ear lies like a shell against her pale cheek, that has a surface soft as velvet, while coarse yellow hair is coiled in masses back from her head into the shadow. Looking at this strange and beautiful piece of colour, and examining the subtile arrangement and the curious hues everywhere full of meaning, the remembrance of Vedder and his mysterious people comes powerfully to mind. We should like to see more of this lady's pictures, but we imagine that, as they have so distinct a character, she cannot paint many of them. A picture that grows into a live thing in the mind of the artist before it is interpreted into paint is usually only of occasional conception. Miss Cassatt has, besides this one, a very charming picture of a child, but it is by her *Musical Party* that we must interpret this interesting artist.

LOUISINE HAVEMEYER

From *Sixteen to Sixty: Memoirs of a Collector*

Reminiscences of Cassatt by Her Best Friend

1930

Louisine Elder Havemeyer (1855–1929), American art collector, suffragist, and philanthropist. In 1874, while visiting Paris with her family, she met Mary Cassatt, who introduced her to the emerging Impressionist circle and advised her in the assembling of a considerable collection of Impressionist paintings. She married Henry O. Havemeyer in 1883. Cassatt and the Havemeyers remained close friends for years, and in 1903 they travelled through Italy together to collect paintings by the Old Masters.

I was only about fifteen years of age when I first met Miss Cassatt. In order to learn French I was living with the family of François Del Sarte, and Miss Cassatt was working in Paris after a year of art study in Seville and several more in Parma. I wondered how she had the courage to go to Spain in the days of the Carlista wars, or to Italy before the bandits were controlled, but she was resourceful, self-reliant, true, and brave, and no one had a better or more truly generous heart.

When we first met in Paris she was very kind to me, showing me the splendid things in the great city, making them still more splendid by opening my eyes to their beauty through her own knowledge and appreciation. I felt then that Miss Cassatt was the most intelligent woman I had ever met, and I cherished every word she uttered and remembered almost every remark she made. It seemed to me no one could see art more understandingly, feel it more deeply or express themselves more clearly than she did.

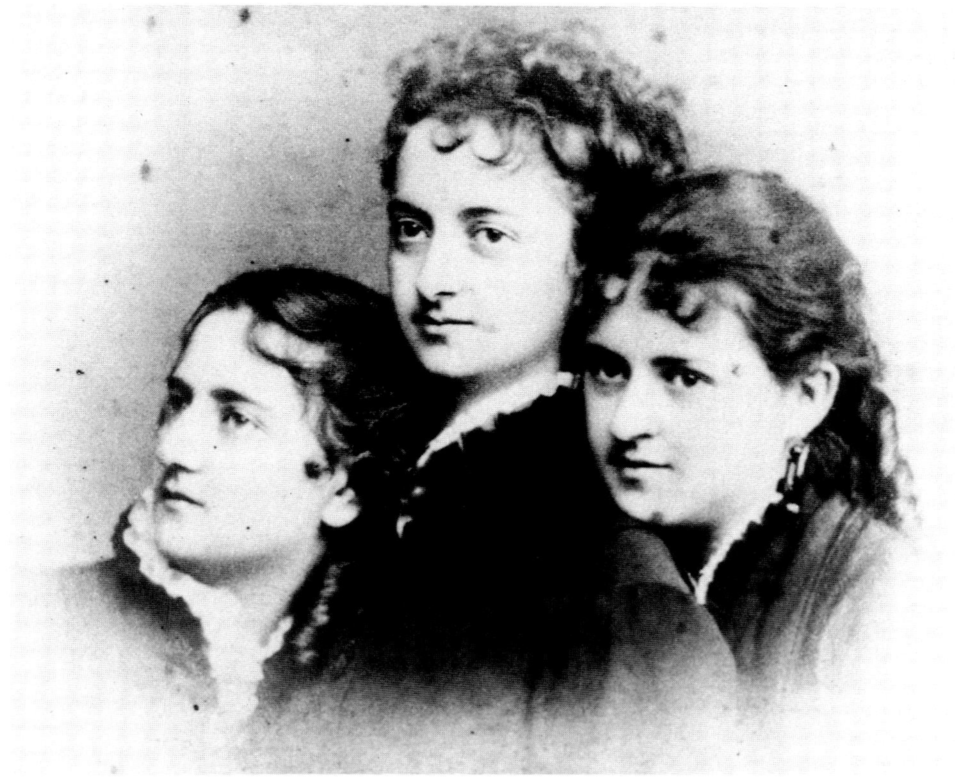

Photograph of the Elder sisters. c. 1872. From left to right, Louisine (Havemeyer), age seventeen; Anne, age nineteen; Adeline, age fifteen. Private collection. Photograph courtesy of J. Watson Webb, Jr.

She opened her heart to me about art while she showed me about the great city of Paris. She took me to the Opera, where, without depleting our pockets, she found a place where we could hear well and could enjoy the fine ballets that were attracting Degas's attention at that very time.

At the Théâtre Français also, she had a resourceful way of avoiding the queue and the interminable wait at the *guichet*. She merely said to the imposing gentleman who sat at the foot of the imposing marble stairway: "Madame D———c has our tickets," and lo! he would bow low and motion us to enter with a *passez Mesdames*, and we would mount to the second balcony, where the good-natured Madame D———c invariably had seats for us in the front of a box. When we were seated, the kind soul would go down to the *guichet* and settle for those mythical tickets at two francs each and accept a modest *pourboire*. . . .

It was really a liberal education to be with Miss Cassatt. Only the dullest mind could fail to retain her original and suggestive remarks, for they stuck like burrs in one's memory and pricked the imagination for many years to come. . . .

Shortly after I met her, her family—her father, mother, and sister came abroad to be with her and ever made their home in France. Her life ever after was an example of devotion to duty. She held duty high before [her] as a pilgrim would his cross. No sacrifice was too great for her to make for her family or for her friends. . . .

I often visited the family during our early friendship, and I remember Mr. Cassatt as a very courteous, tall, white-haired man with a military bearing. Her sister, Lydia, was exactly as represented in Miss Cassatt's portraits of her where she is sitting in an easy chair in the garden beautifully dressed, elegant, and indolent, [one] who graciously allows her sister, the "Martha" of the family, to do a double share in making them all comfortable and happy.

Anyone who had the privilege of knowing Mary Cassatt's mother would know at once that it could be from her and from her only that she and her brother, A.J. Cassatt, inherited their ability. Even in my day, when she was no longer young, she was still powerfully intelligent, executive and masterful and yet with that same sense of duty, that tender sympathy that she had transmitted to her daughter Mary.

I think Mrs. Cassatt had the most alert mind I ever met. She was a fine linguist, an admirable housekeeper, remarkably well read, was interested in everything, and spoke with more conviction and possibly more charm than Miss Cassatt. Even in her last illness, I recall sitting beside her holding her thin hand in mine, filled with pity for the poor sufferer and with regret that this world must lose such a remarkable woman. To poor Miss Cassatt the loss was irreparable. She struggled bravely. At times, like many another lonely soul, she sought to see through the mysterious veil that hides our dear ones and ever after was deeply interested in the science and development of psychic phenomena.

She must have found some hidden strength, for through a friendship of over half a century I could never see that Miss Cassatt grew old. Even in looks she changed but little. It was her personality that impressed and that ripened early. It merely deepened more and more as years passed on. After all, what matters the day of our birth? It is the day of our death that counts, and the memory of Mary Cassatt will last many years after she is gone.

She devoted her life to her art as devotedly as Degas did. She drew a charmed circle about her, and it took credentials of the highest order to be permitted to enter it. She had no time [and] no taste for visiting and could resist meeting princes and princesses with a nonchalance that was amusing.

"I have a right to refuse anyone, for I work from eight to ten hours a day," she would say when she refused a card. Yet when she did entertain, the occasion was not to be forgotten. She would then offer her splendid gifts as royally as a Queen of Sheba and her conversation and quick catching at thoughts was simply entrancing.

"It is no matter what she says," said an enthusiastic admirer, "it is the way she says it."

Although Miss Cassatt's taste was for a quiet life, she often entertained in her apartment in Paris. Her evenings "at home" were attended by many interesting people: diplomats, painters, critics, and writers. Her brilliant mind was like a crystal with many facets. She discussed the Boer War with her friend "the special envoy"; the destiny of museums and art influence with the directors and the leading critics of the day; or realism in literature with some young god of Parnassus. Her luncheons were delightful. I remember one where church and state met at the time of the *séparation*, and it took a Clemenceau to calm the resulting agitation. He wrote an able article and referred to her art as "one of the glories of France."

After one of her dinners, you would find her spellbinding an admiring group of guests, herself a striking personality, beautifully gowned (usually in gray, always high at the neck) her hair parted and waving on each side of a broad forehead, large eyes whose glance came frankly forward to meet yours, a wonderfully flexible mouth, and a nose like Garrick's—remarkable in its modeling, and with those sensitive flaring nostrils which I always said made her an artist in spite of herself. Miss Cassatt's tall figure, which she inherited from her father, had distinction and elegance, and there was no trace of artistic *negligé* or carelessness which some painters affect. Once having seen her, you could never forget her—from her remarkable small foot to the plumed hat with its inevitable tip upon her head and the Brussels lace veil without which she was never seen. She spoke with energy, and you would as soon forget her remarks when she conversed as to forget the motion of her hands. Not even to a Spaniard need she yield anything in the matter of gesture or expressiveness.

"I give myself out too much," she said to me one evening as we drove home from a dinner and she became conscious of her fatigue. Yet her endurance was marvelous. I have seen her entertain a large house party until two in the morning and be ready for another busy day after only a few hours' rest.

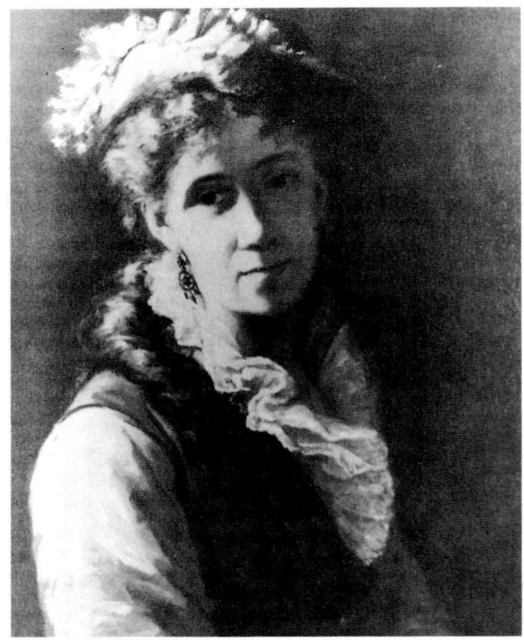

Rose Peckham. *Portrait of May Alcott.* 1877. Oil on canvas. 25 × 21 in. (63.5 × 53.3 cm). Photograph courtesy of the Louisa May Alcott Memorial Association.

MAY ALCOTT NIERIKER

From *Studying Art Abroad, and How To Do It Cheaply*

On the Superiority of Women

1879

An unprejudiced judge of pictures, in Paris, making the tour through the studios of Americans of both sexes, and carefully examining the work found there and at the Salon consecutive seasons, cannot but admit that in many instances that of the women is far superior and, what is somewhat surprising, far stronger in style than most of that done by the men.

If Mr. John Sargent be excepted, whose portrait of Carolus Duran alone undoubtedly places him in the first rank of painters, there is no other male student from the United States in Paris to-day, exhibiting in his pictures the splendid coloring always found in the work of Miss Casatte, from Philadelphia, or the strength and vigor of Miss Dodson's *Deborah*, particularly remarked in this year's Salon.

Sarah Paxton Ball Dodson (1847–1906), American painter, specialized in classical and biblical subjects; Nelie Barbe Hyacinthe Jacquemart (1841–1912), French painter, sculptor, and art collector; Louise Abbéma (1858–1927), French painter and friend of Sarah Bernhardt who executed wall and ceiling paintings for the Sarah Bernhardt Theatre; Sarah Bernhardt (1844–1923), internationally famous French actress and aspiring sculptor.

It is something of a boast for America to possess even these women candidates for artistic honors whose work bears favorable comparison with so much that is excellent done by the men of the same nationality, and that of the French in the great exhibitions; for even among the latter, a nation of painters as it is, the names only of Rosa Bonheur, Nelie Jacquemart, Louise Abbema, and Sara Bernhardt occur as having so far distinguished themselves in art.

GEORGE MOORE

From *Modern Painting*

On the Superiority of Men

1893

George Moore (1852–1933), Irish author, critic, poet, and playwright. He came to Paris to study art in 1873 and began to write criticism in the late 1880s based upon his familiarity with French Impressionism and Symbolist literature. Moore became a friend of Cassatt and the subject of one of her aquatints.

Woman's nature is more facile and fluent than man's. Women do things more easily than men, but they do not penetrate below the surface, and if they attempt to do so the attempt is but a clumsy masquerade in unbecoming costume. In their own costume they have succeeded as queens, courtesans, and actresses, but in the higher arts, in painting, in music, and literature, their achievements are slight indeed—best when confined to the arrangements of themes invented by men—amiable transpositions suitable to boudoirs and fans.

I have heard that some women hold that the mission of their sex extends beyond the boudoir and the nursery. It is certainly not within my province to discuss so important a question, but I think it is clear that all that is best in woman's art is done within the limits I have mentioned. This conclusion is well-nigh forced upon us when we consider what would mean the withdrawal of all that women have done in art. The world would certainly be the poorer by some half-dozen charming novels, by a few charming poems and sketches in oil and water-colour; but it cannot be maintained, at least not seriously, that if these charming triflings were withdrawn there would remain any gap in the world's art to be filled up. Women have created nothing, they have carried the art of men across their fans charmingly, with exquisite taste, delicacy, and subtlety of feelings, and they have hideously and most mournfully parodied the art of men. George Eliot is one in whom sex seems to have hesitated, and this unfortunate hesitation was afterwards intensified by unhappy circumstances. She was one of those women who so entirely mistook her vocation as to attempt to think, and really if she had assumed the dress and the duties of a policeman, her failure could hardly have been more complete. Jane Austen, on the contrary, adventured in no such dismal masquerade; she was a nice maiden lady, gifted with a bright clear intelligence, diversified with the charms of light wit and fancy, and as she was content to be in art what she was in nature, her books live, while those of her ponderous rival are being very rapidly forgotten. *Romola* and *Daniel Deronda* are dead beyond hope of resurrection; *The Mill on the Floss,* being more feminine, still lives, even though its destiny is to be forgotten when *Pride and Prejudice* is remembered.

Sex is as important an element in a work of art as it is in life; all art that lives is full of sex. There is sex in *Pride and Prejudice; Jane Eyre* and *Aurora Leigh* are full of sex; *Romola, Daniel Deronda,* and *Adam Bede* are sexless, and therefore lifeless. There is very little sex in George Sand's works, and they, too, have gone the way of sexless things. When I say that all art that lives is full of sex, I do not mean that the artist must have led a profligate life; I mean, indeed, the very opposite. George Sand's life was notoriously profligate, and her books tell the tale. I mean by sex that concentrated essence of life which the great artist jealously reserves for his art, and through which it pulsates. Shelley deserted his wife, but his thoughts never wandered far from Mary. Dante, according to recent discoveries, led a profligate life, while adoring Beatrice through interminable cantos. So profligacy is clearly not the word I want. I think that gallantry expresses my meaning better.

The great artist and Don Juan are irreparably antagonistic; one cannot contain the other. Notwithstanding all the novels that have been written to prove the contrary, it is certain that woman occupies but a small place in the life of an artist. She is never more than a charm, a relaxation, in his life; and even when he strains her to his bosom, oceans are between them. Profligate, I am afraid, history proves the artist sometimes to have been, but his profligacy is only ephemeral and circumstantial; what is abiding in him is chastity of mind, though not always of body; his whole mind is given to his art, and all vague philanderings and sentimental musings are unknown to him; the women he knows and perceives are only food for it, and have no share in his mental life. And it is just because man can raise himself above the sentimental cravings of natural affection that his art is so infinitely higher than woman's art. "Man's love is from man's life a thing apart"—you know the quotation from Byron, "'Tis woman's whole existence." The natural affections fill a woman's whole life, and her art is only so much sighing and gossiping about them. Very delightful and charming gossiping it often is—full of a sweetness and tenderness which we could not well spare, but always without force or dignity.

In her art woman is always in evening dress: there are flowers in her hair, and her fan waves to and fro, and she wishes to sigh in the ear of him who sits beside her. Her mental nudeness is parallel with her low bodice, it is that and nothing more. She will make no sacrifice for her art; she will not tell the truth about herself as frankly as Jean Jacques, nor will she observe life from the outside with the grave impersonal vision of Flaubert. In music women have done nothing, and in painting their achievement has been almost as slight. It is only in the inferior art—the art of acting—that women approach men. In that art it is not certain that they do not stand even higher.

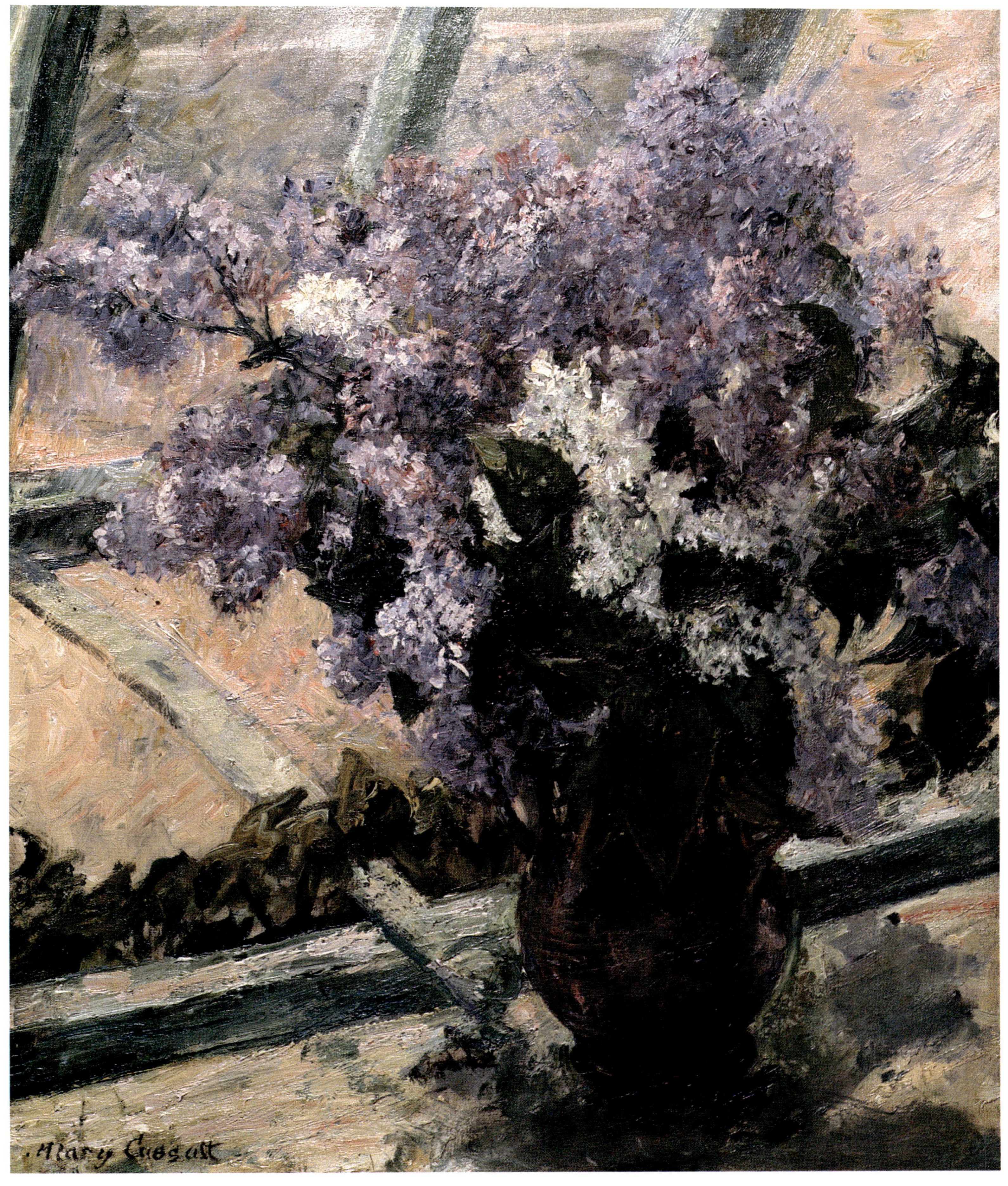

COLORPLATE 23. *Lilacs in a Window.* c. 1880. Oil on canvas. 23 ½ × 19 in. (59.7 × 48.2 cm). Private collection.

COLORPLATE 24. *Alexander J. Cassatt.* 1880. Oil on canvas. 25 ¾ × 36 ⅜ in. (65.4 × 92.4 cm). The Detroit Institute of Arts. Founders Society Purchase, Robert H. Tannahill Foundation Fund. Photograph © The Detroit Institute of Arts.

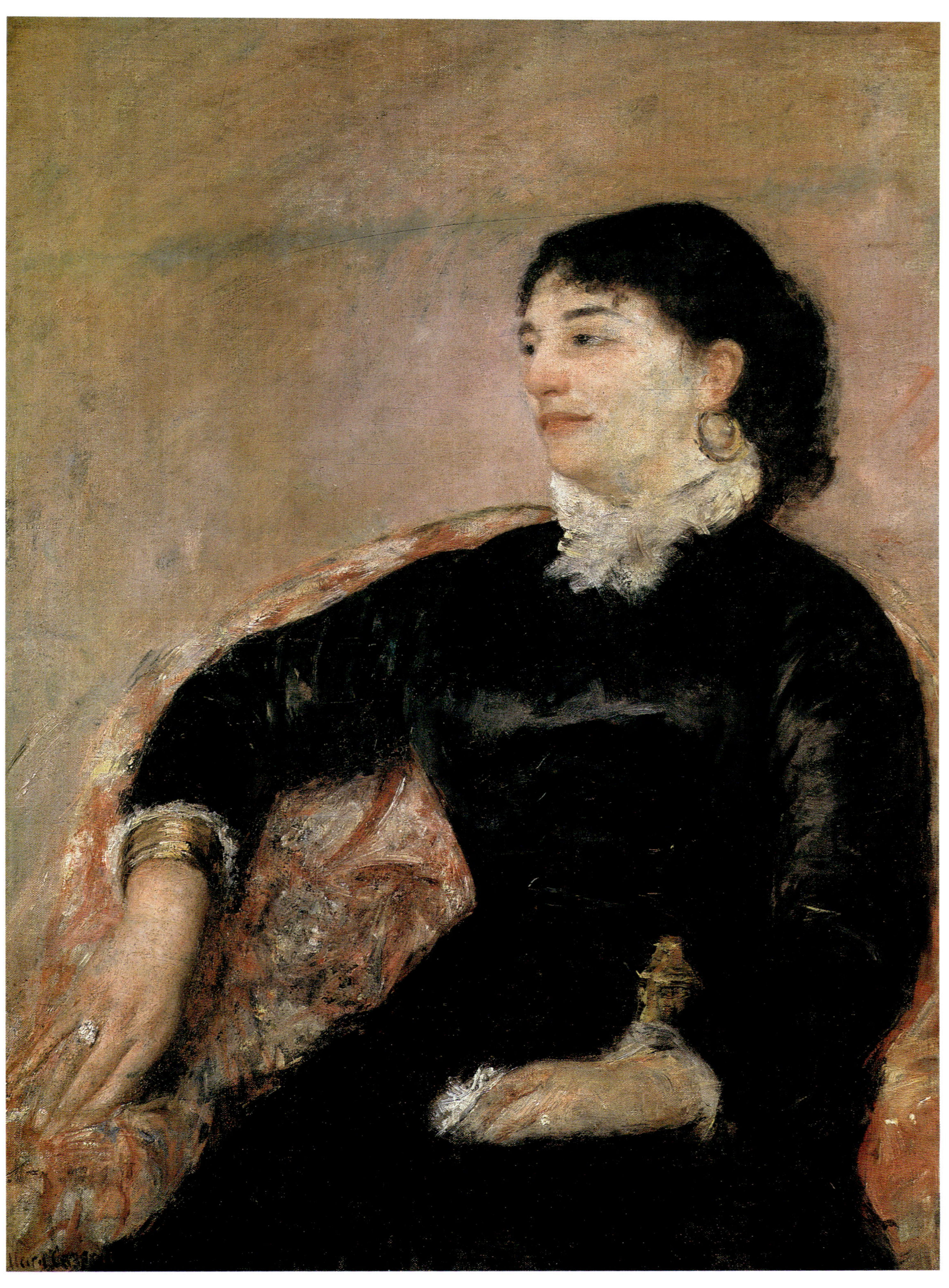

COLORPLATE 25. *Portrait of an Italian Lady.* c. 1879. Oil on canvas. 32 × 23 ⅝ in. (81.2 × 60 cm). Hirshhorn Museum and Sculpture Garden, Smithsonian Institution. Gift of Joseph H. Hirshhorn. Photograph: Lee Stalsworth.

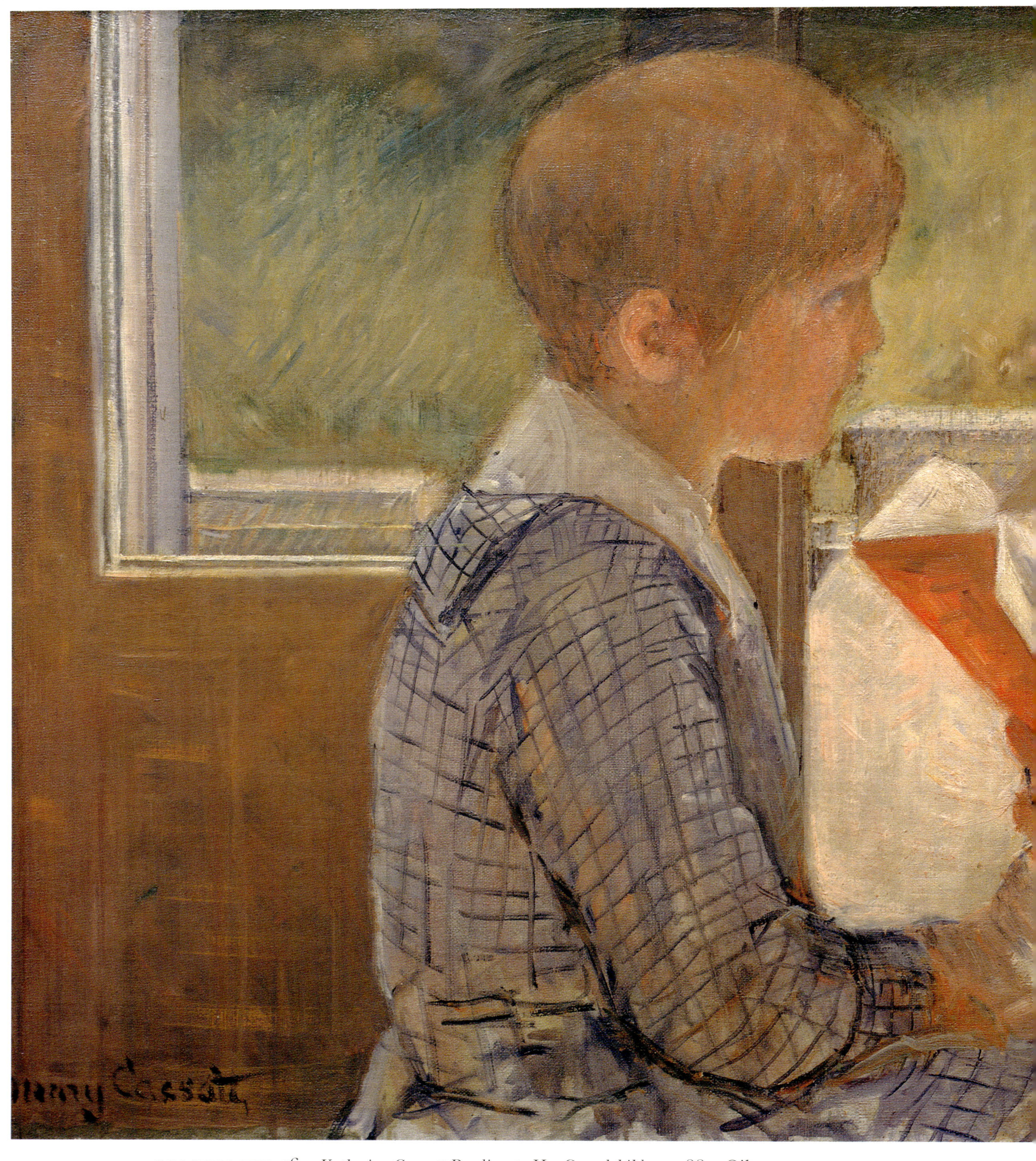

COLORPLATE 26. *Katherine Cassatt Reading to Her Grandchildren.* 1880. Oil on canvas. 22 × 39 ½ in. (55.9 × 100.3 cm). Private collection.

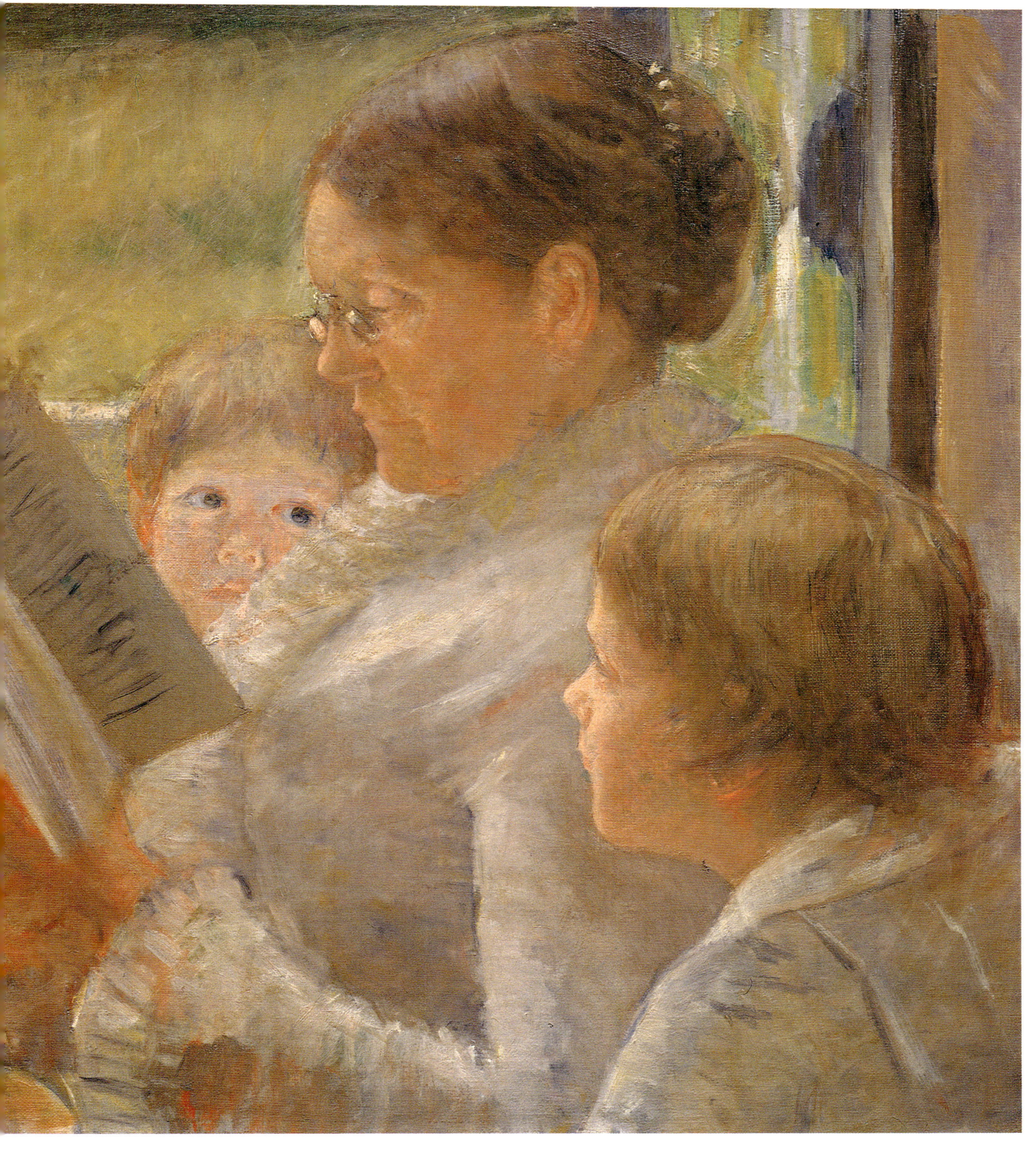

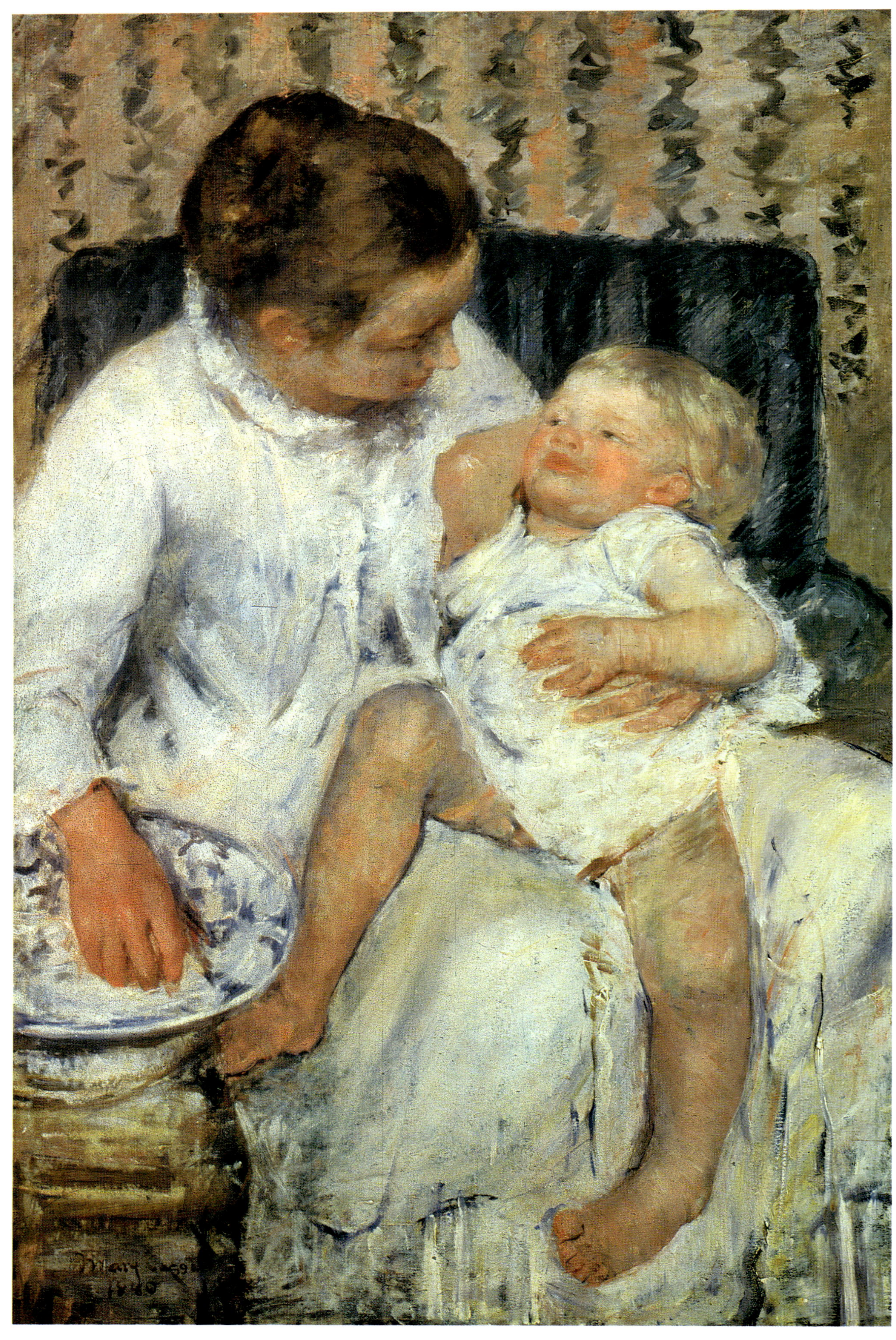

COLORPLATE 27. *Mother About to Wash Her Sleepy Child.* c. 1880. Oil on canvas. 39 7/16 × 25 7/8 in. (100.3 × 65.8 cm). Los Angeles County Museum of Art. Mrs. Fred Hathaway Bixby Bequest.

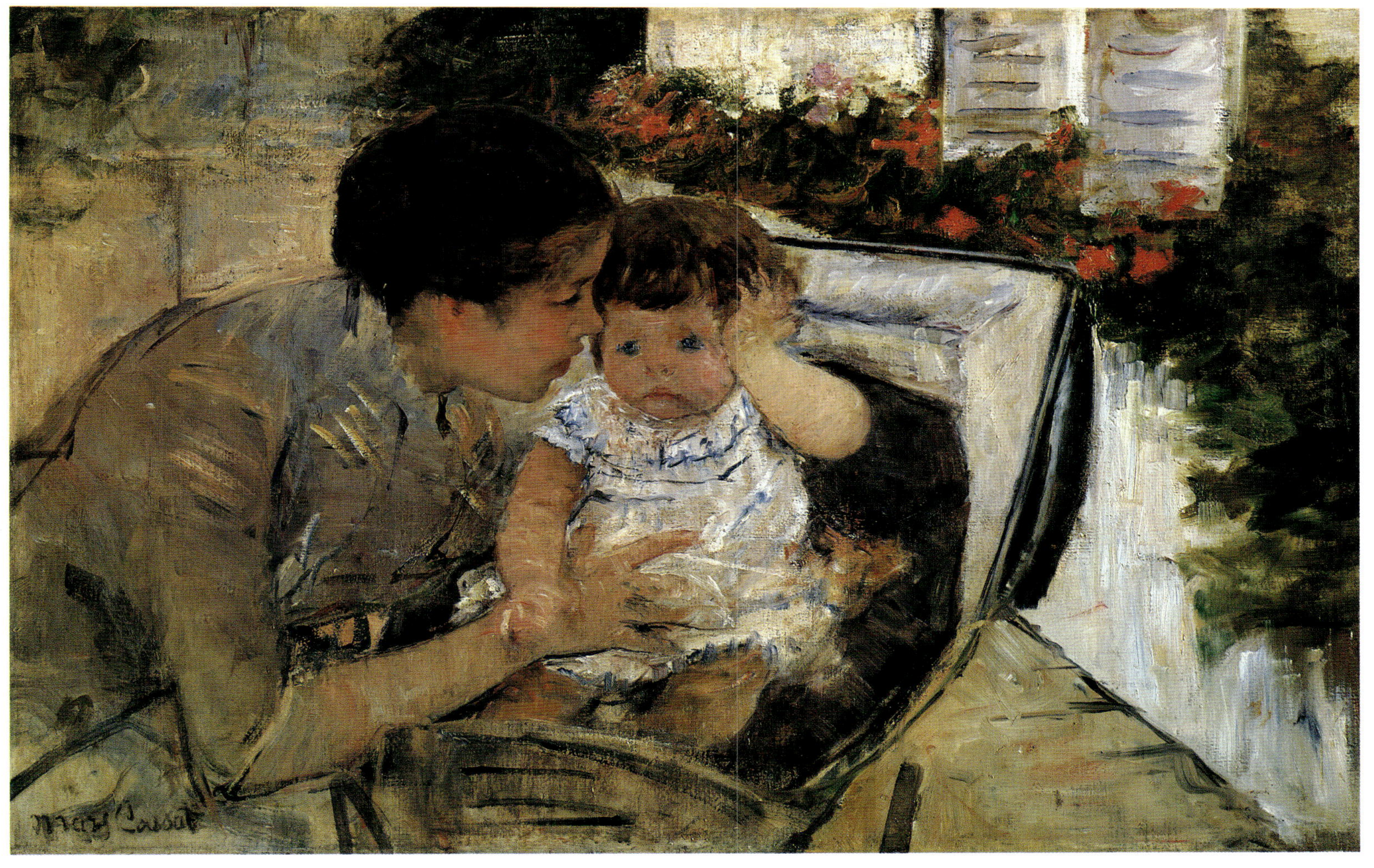

COLORPLATE 28. *Susan Comforting the Baby.* c. 1881. Oil on canvas. 25 ⅝ × 39 ⅜ (65 × 100 cm). The Museum of Fine Arts, Houston. The John A. and Audrey Jones Beck Collection.

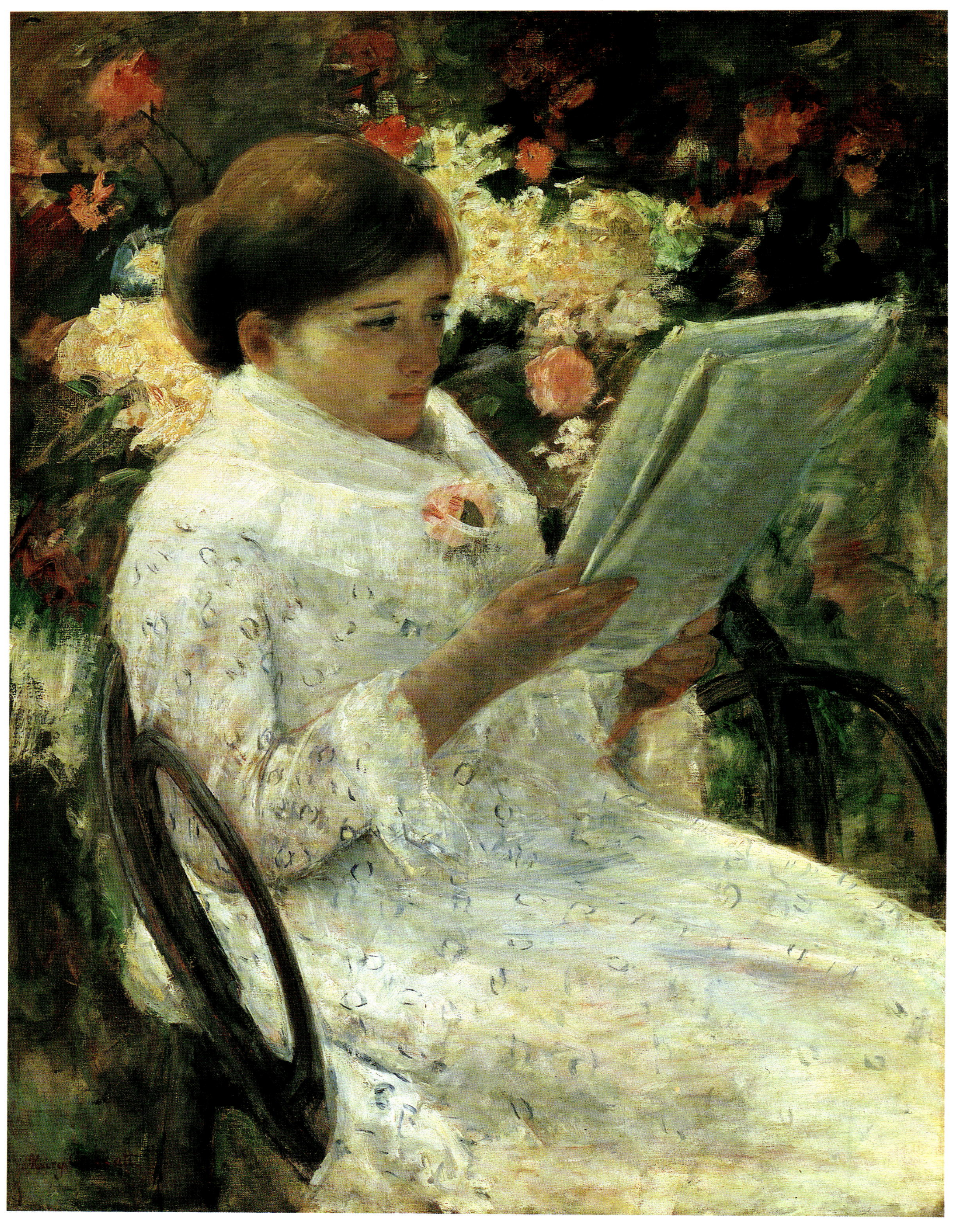

COLORPLATE 29. *Woman Reading in a Garden.* 1880. Oil on canvas. 35 ½ × 25 ⅝ in. (90.1 × 65 cm). The Art Institute of Chicago. Gift of Mrs. Albert J. Beveridge in memory of her aunt, Delia Spencer Field.

CLIVE HOLLAND

From *The Studio*
"Lady Art Students' Life in Paris"
October 1903

Paris has for many years been the Mecca of art students of both sexes. The reason for this is not far too seek. English schools of painting (with few exceptions) do not appear to encourage individuality, and more particularly the individuality of women, in art, however good the technical instruction given may be. Whether it be the glamour which has always enveloped Paris as an art centre, or the attractiveness of life "in the Quarter," it is difficult to say; but true it is, that the lady art students of the present day are going to Paris in increasing numbers. That the life they lead there differs from that led by their male companions, both as regards its freedom and its strenuousness, goes without saying; but it is sufficiently Bohemian for the most enterprising feminine searcher after novelty.

If she be very independent she will eschew the *pension,* run on more or less dull or English lines, in favour of an *appartement au deuxième,* or *au troisième,* working upwards towards the sky above to the *seizième,* according to her worldly wealth, or lack of it. The lady art student who lives *au première* is a *rara avis,* or even perhaps has yet to be discovered. In this little *appartement,* which will in most cases be a bedroom, sitting-room and studio all in one, with a slip of a bathroom and kitchen, if she can afford it, she lives a solitary existence, varied only by the daily visit to the school or *atelier* to which she has attached herself, the incursions of artist friends (if she be emancipated these will be of both sexes); the occasional visit to a place of amusement, when an escort is available; or the equally occasional dinner at a restaurant. When her relatives come over they will be astonished at her emancipation, and they will often wonder how she manages to do most of her own housework, cook, and at the same time take art so seriously. How pretty some of these little *appartements* are, and how interesting! Few women are really untidy by natural inclination, and a girl's studio in Paris is usually a perfection of tidiness, compared with those of most men. In hers, little nicknacks grace the narrow shelf which in his is consecrated to tobacco jar, charred pipes, tubes of paint, a galley-pot of brushes soaking in turpentine, and possibly a razor and shaving brush.

When she has been in the Quarter some little time she will probably have emancipated herself so far that she will even institute little functions in the form of studio teas or musical evenings, at which her girl and even men student friends will gather to drink *thé anglais,* made from a treasured store which she brought with her, or some friend from England has smuggled for her, and discuss other people's work and Art matters in general. How gay some of these little parties are! There is true Bohemian *camaraderie* about them and the visitors who attend them. Some of the art criticism would possibly make academic critics writhe; but it has the merits of outspokenness and point, which, alas! are not always distinguishing features of written art criticism. In the evening, when the shadows begin to fall across the bare floors of these studio-homes, some one will sing, or perhaps—if the owner of the studio possesses a piano, some one will play on it or provide an accompaniment for a violin solo; for the violin has always been a favoured instrument in the Quarter, competing not unsuccessfully in popularity with the *cornet à-piston* of the male students. And although the performers may not be Marie Halls or Kubeliks, there is something about the playing which fits its surroundings and awakes sentiment in the listeners. Memories, perhaps, of some face seen for a moment in passing, or some day in summer twilight spent on the silver Seine, in the woods at Fontainebleau or in the wide fields surrounding some Norman or Breton hamlet frequented by painter-folk.

CAROLINE TICKNOR

From *May Alcott: A Memoir*

Cassatt Entertains in Paris

1928

Caroline Ticknor (1866–1937), American author and editor.

Early in November, 1876, May describes a tea party at Miss Cassatt's beautiful studio, where they met various New York friends, and ate "fluffy cream and chocolate, with French cakes, while sitting in carved chairs, on Turkish rugs, with superb tapestries as a background, and fine pictures on the walls looking down from their splendid frames."

"Statues and articles of *vertu* filled the corners, the whole being lighted by a great antique hanging lamp. We sipped our *chocalat* from superior china, served on an India waiter, upon an embroidered cloth of heavy material. Miss Cassatt was charming as usual in two shades of brown satin and rep, being very lively and a woman of real genius, she will be a first-class light as soon as her pictures get a little circulated and known for they are handled in a masterly way, with a touch of strength one seldom finds coming from a woman's fingers. They would n't suffer if hung with the Thomas Lawrences."

Sir Thomas Lawrence (1769–1830), British portraitist of the grand manner.

LOUISA MAY ALCOTT

From *Diana and Persis*

Cassatt As a Character in a Novel

c. 1879

Louisa May Alcott (1832–1888), American writer who grew up in Boston and Concord, Massachusetts, and author of the famous autobiographical novel, "Little Women." Her sister, May, became acquainted with Mary Cassatt in Paris, and through her sister's descriptions of the artist, used Cassatt as a character in her novel "Diana and Persis," begun in 1879 but never published, which was an exploration of the possibilities of combining motherhood and a career.

We have been a little gay this last week, and as I have made a new friend I will tell you of her, for she is one after your own heart. Miss Cassal comes to the studio to draw when we have a fine model and I liked her strong face the first time I saw it. She liked my work and came very kindly to tell me so one day when I was struggling with a hard lesson, for K would have me draw to the waist when I preferred only the head of our model. She asked me to come and see her and I went. She is a grand woman, full of real genius, I think, and but for her sex would have made a name before now, since all who know her acknowledge her power. She has the modesty of true talent and so is content to do fine things and let others get praised for mediocre work, she biding her time. Her pictures are handled in a mas-

Edouard Krug (1829–1901), French artist and teacher of the women's classes at the Académie Julian, where May Alcott studied.

terly way and with a strength one seldom finds in a woman's fingers. I am told that men are jealous of her, and her "Joel" was refused at the last Salon merely because of its boldness and power. She smiles and paints on tranquilly, content to be felt if not seen. She has money and uses it nobly, not only in helping herself but others, and we have a plan in our heads to get up a school for women, a studio where we can club together and have the best models and masters and a chance to show what we can do with a clear track and fair judges. Her enthusiasm delights me and we shook hands like old friends after my long visit full of the most interesting talk.

This week we went to tea in her studio which is a charming place and the resort of many of the young artists, men as well as women; there last evening, we met fifteen or twenty of them and had a most enjoyable time sitting in antique chairs on Persian rugs with tapestry backgrounds, fine pictures on the walls, pretty things all about us, and the whole lighted by hanging lamps in the most artistic and effective manner. Some of the men sang and we sipped tea and ate ices, but the talk was the best, for it was art, still art. I was much interested in several of these people and in answering my questions Miss C told me some pretty little stories about them, which you will like as they show how kind these artists are to one another. . . .

These and many more like them did Miss C tell me, for she is a sort of refuge to the younger set, being forty and full of maternal sympathy and generosity which is so winning I don't wonder the poor fellows are glad to come to her with their hopes and plans, trials and defeats, and it is both comical and pathetic to hear about them.

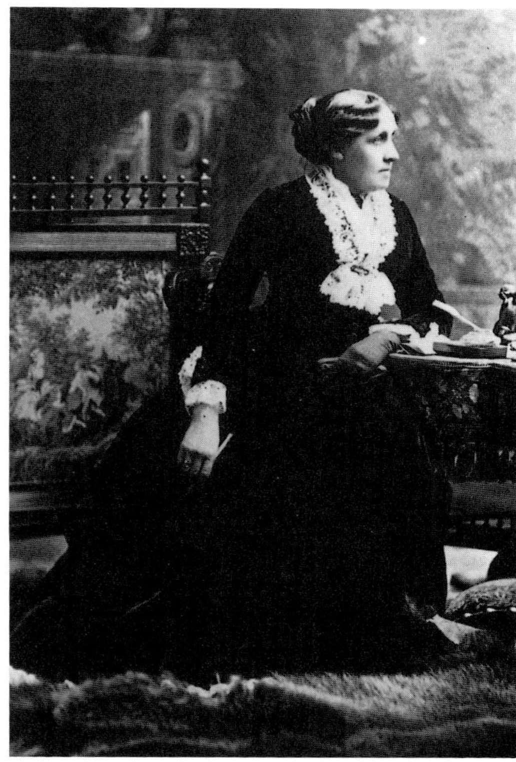

Photograph of Louisa May Alcott. Photograph courtesy of the Concord Free Public Library, Concord, Massachusetts.

"Joel" was a fictitious work.

GUSTAVE GEFFROY

From *La Vie artistique*

Cassatt Encounters Impressionism

1893

Gustave Geffroy (1855–1926), French critic, novelist, and journalist who followed Cassatt's work for decades and contributed regularly to the review "La Justice."

Amid the paintings, pastels, and engravings of Mary Cassatt, one will discover this sensation: a very elegant taste for things, a sustained effort, a stubbornness in capturing a shape, a woman's art influenced by the masters of the group of the Impressionists, as well as a unique grace and will....

She has come from America, from the country almost without history and great with future, from the land of activity where the social experiments are accelerated. When these tradesmen, these industrialists from the other side of the Atlantic, decided to decorate the walls of their houses, to install in their homes the painted poetry of face and landscape, they were obliged to come ask for what they lacked from the European nations, which are equipped with a past and are at peak artistic production. And the young people from over there who felt the desire to create art did as the tradesmen did: they came to Europe. This phenomenon came about entirely naturally: they did not have to go through the stages through which our own young people must pass; they did not have to spend fifteen or twenty years to learn formulas, so that they could then unlearn them, in order to find themselves back before a nature at last revealed.

Imagine, if you will, what efforts are required of a strong and original human being, who is capable of creating his art, and who has had to go through the École des beaux-arts—just to shed the education that masked his individuality. The mediocre succumb. The strong resist, become themselves again, go beyond. But what a waste of time! What years of doubts!

However, these vicissitudes and battles of the will are unknown to the stranger who lands here, his time his own, confident about the morrow. He goes immediately to the latest fashion and assimilates the methods, he astonishes by the facility with which, with a virtuoso air, he executes a painting that is pretty, brilliant, deft—and hollow. Many Americans are like that, as, too, are many of those who come from the north of our Europe.

Miss Mary Cassatt, though, has not gone the way of fashion, of the popular styles, of success, for she has gone to the disparaged Impressionists. A similarity of vision determined this choice, and this vision has expanded, has become increasingly searching; this strong-willed woman has truly learned to paint.

ACHILLE SEGARD

From *Mary Cassatt: Un Peintre des enfants et des mères*

Cassatt Joins the Impressionists

1913

Yet she would bend to them only insofar as these teachings would not stifle what was original in her. She was resistant, and remained so, to any friendship that was too close, to any association that required the sacrifice of a part of oneself, to any group whose fundamental rule was other than the perfect independence of each with regard to all.

She met Degas by chance. The great artist was the friend of a painter named Tourny, who copied famous paintings for M. Thiers. They were strolling together through the 1874 Salon. Tourny brought Degas to the portrait of a young woman that Miss Cassatt had sent to the Salon and that she had painted in Rome. Degas stopped and said: "It's true. This is someone who feels as I do."

* * *

[Cassatt said,] "In 1875, [the Salon] rejected a full-length portrait of my sister, a painting with a light-colored background. I had guessed the reason for their rejection, and I made the background darker. And, indeed, the same portrait was accepted the following year.

"In 1877, I submitted again. They rejected it. That was when Degas made me promise never to submit anything to the Salon again, and to exhibit with his friends in the group of the Impressionists. I agreed gladly. At last I could work absolutely independently, without worrying about the possible opinion of a jury! I had already acknowledged who my true masters were. I admired Manet, Courbet, and Degas. I hated conventional art. I was beginning to live . . ."

The words came rapidly and precisely to her lips. An imperceptible American accent gave certain phrases a characteristic inflection.

Letter from Mary Cassatt to Ambroise Vollard

On *Little Girl in a Blue Armchair*

1903

Ambroise Vollard (1867–1939), French art dealer who, after opening his gallery in 1893, became the sole representative of Cézanne and Gauguin, upon whose work his fame now rests. Cassatt took Vollard as her dealer in 1906 after she became angered with Durand-Ruel and broke her contract with him.

Mesnil-Beaufresne
Tuesday

Dear Sir,

I wanted to come back to your place yesterday to talk to you about the portrait of the little girl in the blue armchair. I did it in 78 or 79—it was the portrait of a child of friends of M. Degas—I had done the child in the armchair, and he found that to be good and advised me on the background, *he even worked on the background*—I sent it to the American section of the Gd. exposition 79 but it was refused. Since M. Degas had thought it good I was furious especially because he had worked on it—at that time it seemed new, and the jury consisted of three people, of which one was a pharmacist! In thinking of the vases that I saw at your place, I see that I have been wrong, I was about to scrape the one that was fired, because I'm sure it won't come out, as with anything a trial run is needed. I'm going to see if I can do something with the other because I'm not very well pleased with the band of lowers.

COLORPLATE 12

World's International Exhibition, actually held in Paris in 1878.

I expect to return to Paris in a week and if you want I will look over the things here that you chose, and also I will sign the two that you took yesterday.

To return to the vases I will do them better in Paris, but on the other hand, I have an abundance of flowers here for models, when it rains I can't work outside—

Please accept my best wishes

Mary Cassatt

ACHILLE SEGARD

From *Mary Cassatt: Un Peintre des enfants et des mères*

On *Little Girl in a Blue Armchair*

1913

COLORPLATE 12

The glow of love! One feels it even in those subjects where the artist probably believed she was putting in nothing of herself.

Here, for example, is a large oil painting that belongs to M. Vollard.

This picture shows a little girl about five years old, her hair hanging down in front, in a white linen dress with a wide plaid belt with a touch of red, but in which the color blue predominates, her legs bare, in dark blue socks with two red stripes, and wearing shoes that look black, but are a very dark Prussian blue. She is seated, almost reclining on an enormous blue pouf and three more large blue poufs (the effect is rather strange) furnish the room with their great big-bellied masses. They look almost like animals, and a small curly-haired griffon terrier with a russet muzzle sleeps on the curve of one of them. Everything rests on a brown floor that, by a trick of perspective, rises very high up in the painting. Two whitish French doors are sketched.

The child's face is quite detailed. It has an expression of gentleness and almost of precocious gravity, but the figure is not here the subject of the painting. What is original and even quite strange, is that the actual characters are the large blue poufs. They seem to live a remote and hidden, yet individual, life, after the fashion of certain animals not endowed with movement, whose primitive organism is barely differentiated from the primitive life of most plants.

What attracted the artist—one feels it quite clearly—was to elevate everyday stuffed seats to the role of figures, and to compose her painting in an unexpected way, her concern being to harmonize great blue areas against a neutral background, a white area, and the amusing details of the plaid belt and the griffon terrier.

The blacks appear to have a part in this picture. However—if one looks closely—one notices that there are none. The darkest areas are deep blues, and they form a colored base, so to speak, on which lean all the variations of blue in order to support each other and set each other off. The real theme of the picture is the pleasure of harmonizing various adjoining blues, arranging them by scales, and deliberately pushing their gradation and variety to the extreme.

It is an entirely visual and pictorial pleasure. There are blue glints even in the whitish panes of the windows. And the construction of these overstuffed poufs—as solid as it is—is rendered with rapid strokes and sketched areas, which, furthermore, by giving them greater importance, emphasize the two points on which, after all, the viewer's attention is to be centered: the child's face and—in second place—the sweet little griffon terrier.

I would like to note that the pictorial instinct in a picture like this is more important than the quality of the execution and the refined taste in the arrangements. Even the painting's subject rejects any idea other than the art of painting, it is painting for painting's sake. Thus, it is a document that manifests a state of mind, and yet one can discern in this picture an order, a style, and a soul, because in the end it expresses an impulse of the artist's soul. Even when she limits herself to thinking only through color and to reveling in this pleasure alone, Miss Mary Cassatt is thinking, and feeling, and succeeding in conveying her intellectual emotion. The blues are astonishingly intensely colored and happily free. It is entirely painterly, in the sense that the subject hardly counts at all and the child itself is seen and executed like the objects around it, but it would be more correct to say that the poufs are seen and executed with the same visual pleasure that the artist felt in looking at this child. The whole is devoid of any vulgarity, very distinguished, very impulsive, very deliberate, and very artistic.

Letter from Mary Cassatt to J. Alden Weir

On the New York Exhibition of the Society of American Artists

March 10, 1878

J. Alden Weir (1852–1919), American painter who had been active in the American art circles in Paris in the 1870s, and was a friend of Cassatt; he too had been a student of Gérôme. He later became a central figure in New York art circles as a proponent of Impressionism.

13, avenue Trudaine
March 10, 1878

My dear Mr. Weir,

Your letter only reached me yesterday evening. Mr. Sargent forwarded it to me from Venice where it had followed him, that accounts for the delay. I thank you very much for all the kind things you say about my work. I only wish I deserved them.

Your exhibition interests me very much. I wish I could have sent something, I am afraid it is too late now. We expect to have our annual exhibition here, and there are so few of us that we are each required to contribute all we have. You know how hard it is to inaugurate anything like independent action among French artists, and we are carrying on a despairing fight & need all our forces, as every year there are new deserters.

I always have a hope that at some future time I shall see New York the artists ground, I think you will create an American school.

You have been so kind to me that I feel thoroughly ashamed of myself for not having done something good enough to send you; next year I will do better; and I hope my artist friends here will send with me.

With many thanks

Very sincerely yours
Mary Cassatt

The Society of American Artists was founded in New York in 1877 as an alternative to the conservative National Academy of Design. Cassatt was invited to join, along with Sargent and Whistler, in 1878.

John Singer Sargent (1856–1925), American painter who was working in Paris with Carolus-Duran in the 1870s when Cassatt first met him.

From *The Art Journal:* "Exhibition of the Society of American Artists"

Review of *Reading Le Figaro*

1879

COLORPLATE 15

The second exhibition of the Society of American Artists opened March 10th, at Kurtz's Gallery, in Twenty-third Street, New York, and closed March 29th, and, like its predecessor of a year ago, attracted a good deal of attention among cultivated people. The collection numbered a hundred and sixty-eight pictures and pieces of statuary, and many of these works were interesting, either for their artistic merit or because they showed freshness of purpose. . . .

Among the technically best pictures in the entire collection was Miss Cassatt's portrait, a capitally drawn figure of an agreeable-looking, middle-aged lady, with a clear skin over her well-formed features, and with soft, brown, wavy hair. It is pleasant to see how well an ordinary person dressed in an ordinary way can be made to look; and we think nobody seeing this lady reading a newspaper through her shell "nippers," and seated so composedly in her white morning-dress, could have failed to like this well-drawn, well-lighted, well-anatomised, and well-composed painting. There was no pretence to a subtle combination of colour in it, of which in her other pictures Miss Cassatt often makes very interesting studies, and one of them is shown in *The Mandolin Player*, but we think there are few people, whether artists or tyros in Art, but would be glad to be so agreeably immortalised.

COLORPLATE 1

WILLIAM C. BROWNELL

From *Scribner's Monthly*
On *At the Opera*
July 1881

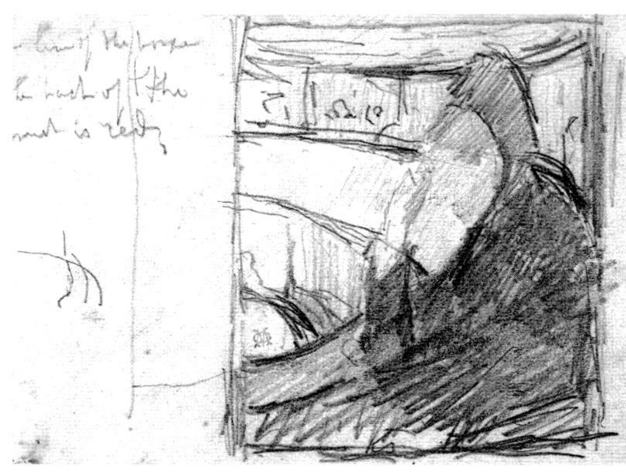

Study for *At the Opera*. c. 1878. Pencil sketch. 4 × 6 in. (10.2 × 15.2 cm). Courtesy of Museum of Fine Arts, Boston. Gift of Dr. Hans Schaeffer.

William C. Brownell (1851–1925), American art and literary critic whose love of modern French art was long-standing. He worked on the staff of "The Nation" from 1879 until 1881 and was the literary adviser to "Scribner's Magazine" for nearly forty years.

COLORPLATE 16

The portrait which Miss Mary S. Cassatt sent from Paris to the Second Exhibition of the Society of American Artists stimulates a lively regret that she should keep her countrymen in comparative ignorance of the work she is doing. If it be said that, judging from that canvas, and from the accompanying *At the Opera*, this seems to lack charm, it is easy to see, on the other hand, that in force few, if any, among American women-artists are her rivals. There is an intelligent directness in her touch, and her entire attitude, beside which a good deal of the painting now abundantly admired seems amateur experimentation. Her work is a good example of the better sort of "impressionism," and the sureness with which, contrary to the frequent notion of it, this proceeds; and perhaps it is especially successful in this respect because Miss Cassatt served an Academic apprenticeship, and "went over" to Dégas and the rest of the school only after she had acquired her powers of expression. One cannot be all things at once, and especially if one determines to be definitely some particular thing; and so many people will temper their acknowledgment and appreciation of Miss Cassatt's success with the recognition of her neglect of, or incapacity for, the poetic and sentimental, not to say spiritual, side of painting. One even feels that to her adoption of a theory may be conveniently ascribed certain prosaic details of her *At the Opera*, for example, which only avoid seeming like *gaucheries* because it is so evident that they are deliberate, intelligent, and well executed.

SAMUEL ISHAM

From *The History of American Painting*
Cassatt as an Impressionist
1910

Samuel Isham (1855–1914), American artist and author whose important book, "The History of American Painting," was published in 1905.

The only school of thirty years ago that has not been generally comprehended by the average art lover is that of Manet, which still finds many insensible to its merits. The whole training at the big studios was in another direction so that, though some admired, yet it found only a single follower among the Americans, but that a notable one, Mary Cassatt.

Édouard Manet (1832–1883), French Impressionist painter and graphic artist who had a reputation as a leader of the avant-garde.

The school of Manet is not a large one, nor do the works of the different members closely resemble each other, for one of the fundamental requirements was a distinct personality. There might even seem to be some doubt about placing Miss Cassatt in it, for her taste was formed by the study of Velasquez in Spain before she settled in Paris; but the classification is sufficiently close to give an idea of her affiliations. Like Manet she sees the world with no desire to alter it to ideal preconceptions, she sees it also in

Diego Rodriguez Velásquez (1599–1660), Spanish painter whose influence on naturalist painting of the later nineteenth century was immense.

large spots of local color, not as contrasting masses of light and shade; these spots she does not weaken by elaborate modelling as Bastien-Le Page did, and unlike him and his followers, she insists that the paint shall be spread in a solid, fine impasto, not broken up in a multitude of small, thin touches.

To do work of this kind requires insight of a peculiar kind, a synthetic mind for form, grasping it instinctively in its simplest, most characteristic mass; and at the same time a most delicate perception of all the refinements of color and tone, for there is no elaborate drawing to hold the picture together, and if the great masses are not perfect in value it falls to pieces. Over these difficulties Miss Cassatt has triumphed, her drawing is sure and characteristic, her coloring subtly harmonized, and she has, moreover, a fine feeling for arrangement, placing the masses of her figures so that they form agreeable patterns; but her painting is painters' painting, and makes its strongest appeal to members of her own craft. By them and by the more enlightened amateurs she is appreciated and honored; but the great public stands aloof, indifferent or hostile. She has never catered to it or given it that obvious prettiness that it loves. Even her color, which is her greatest charm, is made up of subdued whites and grays and pale, sad tones, rarely a touch that is bright and strong, and the drawing is uncompromising in its search for character rather than grace. The average mother and child of real life resembles but remotely the creations of Bouguereau; but the versions by Bouguereau come much nearer to the popular ideals of what babies should be. Miss Cassatt is not to be diverted by such ideals from reality, which has its own beauty,—a beauty which so appeals to her that she seems rather to avoid nature when it runs to a more popular comeliness and so continues to paint stubby toes and pudgy noses, to the delight of the few and the bewilderment of the many.

Adolphe-William Bouguereau (1825–1905), French academic painter known for his allegorical and mythological compositions. He entered the École des Beaux-Arts in 1846 and won the Prix de Rome in 1850. In 1898 he married the American artist Elizabeth Gardner.

This appeal to a restricted few is not a position forced upon Miss Cassatt by repeated rebuffs. From the first she has refused to exhibit in the great annual salons, but in her indifference to their applause and honors she stands alone. All the other Paris-American painters have regularly shown in the big exhibits.

GEORGE MOORE

From *Reminiscences of the Impressionist Painters*

Cassatt on Renoir

1906

Among the Impressionist painters there was an English, I should say an American, Mary Casat. She did not come to the Nouvelle Athenes it is true, but she lived on the Boulevard Extérieur; her studio was within a minute's walk of The Place Pigale, and we used to see her every day. Her art was derived from Degas as Madame Morizot's art was derived from Manet. Madame Morizot, or I should say Berthe Morizot, was Manet's sister-in-law and I remember him saying to me once, "My sister-in-law would not have

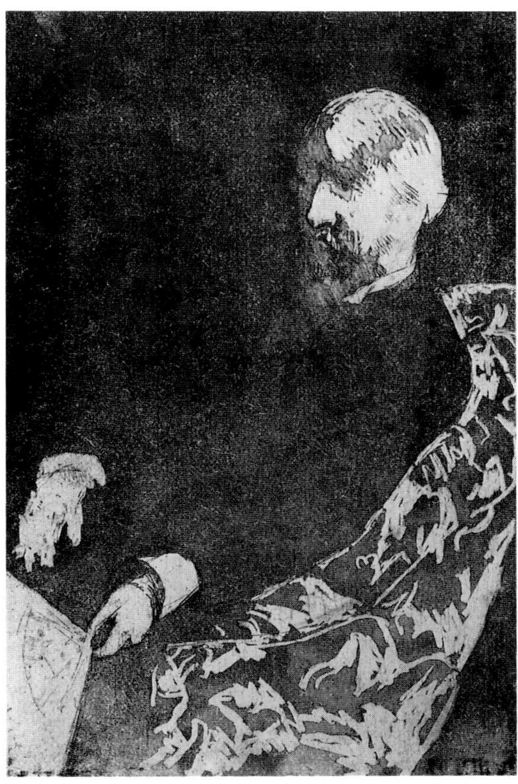

George Moore (second state). c. 1880. Soft-ground etching. 8 3/4 × 5 1/2 in. (22.2 × 14 cm). The Metropolitan Museum of Art, New York. The Rogers Fund. Photograph © The Metropolitan Museum of Art.

existed without me; she did nothing but carry my art across her fan." Berthe Morizot is dead, and her pictures are very expensive—picture dealers do not make presents; but Mary Casat is alive, and she is a rich woman, and I take this opportunity of suggesting that she should be asked to give a picture. But to the anecdote. After an absence of many years I met her in Durand-Ruel's, and at breakfast next day we talked of all the people we had known, and at the end of breakfast she said, "There is one we haven't spoken about, perhaps the greatest of all." I said, "You mean Renoir?" And she accused me of having been always a little indifferent to Renoir's art. I don't think that this is true, or if it is true it is only true in a way.

Pierre-Auguste Renoir (1841–1919), Impressionist painter admired by Cassatt; they became close friends after 1912 when they both spent winters in the south of France.

Berthe Morisot (1841–1895), French Impressionist painter with whom Cassatt had a warm friendship and rivalry. As the two most prominent women in the Impressionist group, critics often compared them—a practice which continues to this day. Morisot married Édouard Manet's brother Eugène in 1874.

Letter from Mary Cassatt to Berthe Morisot

In Praise of Her Work

Fall 1879

13, avenue Trudaine
Friday

Dear Madame,

Your letter found me at Divonne and I waited until my return here to respond. I think I can buy something of Monet's, I wanted to do so before I left. I say "I" but I mean my father. I gave Piette's pictures to Portier to sell and my father told me that he would buy a Monet when the others were sold. I haven't been able to see Portier since my return and I am afraid that he hasn't done what he promised, I will do what I can but you know that it isn't easy to persuade the world.

Trip to the French and Italian Alps in the summer of 1879.

I am so happy that you have done so much work, you will reclaim your place at the exposition with *éclat*, I am very envious of your talent I assure you. This summer I didn't get anything done, we traveled for nearly four weeks, in Piedmont and then to Milan and returned through Switzerland by Lake Maggiore and the Simplon. I saw many things to admire, beautiful frescoes, really I don't see that the moderns have discovered anything about color. It seems to me that we haven't learned anything more about color or drawing.

I would have gone to see you before my departure but my father is never very decisive and I thought that we might return in eight hours.

Bring back many pretty things, and much health and courage, I am eager to see what you have done. The Swedish woman it seems is not happy, her Jule has disappeared, I will try to find another model.

Many kisses to Miss Julie and a thousand best wishes to her mother from their

Berthe Morisot's newborn daughter.

Affectionate friend
Mary Cassatt

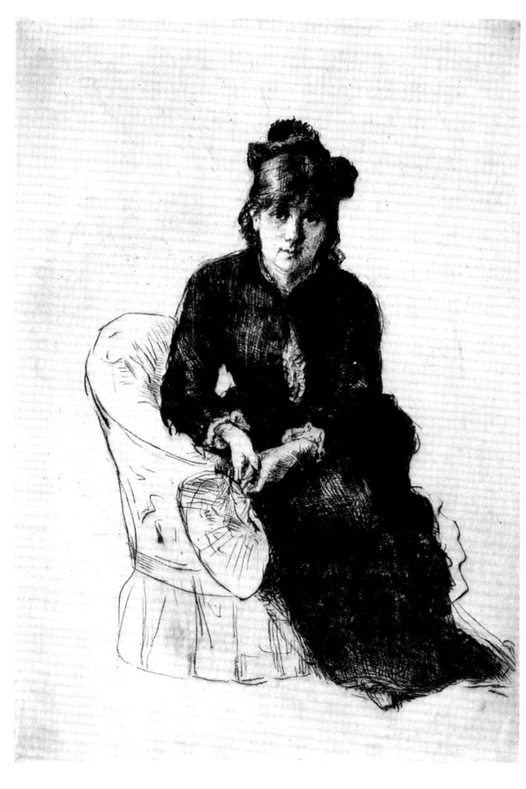

Marcellin Desboutin. *Portrait of Berthe Morisot* (second state). 1876. Drypoint. 10 3/8 × 6 7/8 in. (26.3 × 17.5 cm). Photograph courtesy of William Weston Gallery, London.

MARGARET BREUNING

From *Magazine of Art* "Cassatt and Morisot" *December 1939*

At the Durand-Ruel Gallery there is a showing of the work of two friends, Berthe Morisot and Mary Cassatt, both members in the 70's of that little group of Impressionists then so ignored, now so famous. There is a contrast between these associates and co-workers in temperament and endowment; in achievement it cannot justly be measured because of Morisot's early death. Miss Cassatt's authority and distinction make themselves felt immediately. The accuracy of structure and careful anatomical definition underlying her work, her dispassionate viewpoint even in her themes of motherhood or boudoir *causeries,* her delightful patterns of color and fluent execution were never shown more impressively than in this splendid collection of her work. There are only two notable canvases by Morisot shown here, *Le Lever* and *Le Repos,* but from these fragile, intimate paintings one gets the inescapable impression that here was a real passion for art, an impeccable taste, sensibility and intuitive logic—gifts of the gods of which the artist availed herself continually. But one does not get the impression of a relentless pursuit of craftsmanship, a powerful, unyielding will that never swerved from its pursuit of a definite goal, as one does from Mary Cassatt. Morisot was not a great artist, but a genuine one. She neither capitalized her femininity nor sought to hide it. Because so much of her work is intimate study of adolescence and feminine charm, it is easy to forget how sound it is at its best. Her debt to Corot is evidenced often more plainly than her debt to her other teacher, Manet, although she became more and more preoccupied with light and luminist effects. Her exquisite textures of silvery white, given vitality by unexpected color notes, her final purity of color and individual accents of design foreshadow an accomplishment of greater significance than she lived to realize.

KARL MADSEN

From *Politiken*

Review of *Young Lady in a Loge Gazing to the Right*

November 9, 1889

Karl Madsen (1855–1938), Danish art and theater critic for the liberal newspaper "Politiken" in Copenhagen. This work was included in an exhibition of Impressionist art which included many works from the collection of Paul and Mette Gauguin.

COLORPLATE 17

Curiously enough—and heaven knows how—Degas has got a pupil in the person of the American Miss Mary Cassatt, who is represented by a beautiful pastel, an excellent example of her specific genre. It is a half-length portrait of a young lady, seated in a box at an opera, the background being a large mirror, which reflects the blurred outlines of the chandelier, the curved lines of the balconies, and the young lady's neck and reddish hair. Below, the big half-circle of a Japanese fan forms a fine decorative pattern. The lady is seen almost in profile, and this profile is rendered with a delicacy that one would look for in vain from any Danish artist, past or present. Her nose, her mouth, and her chin, presented in delicate half-tones of light and shade, are superbly drawn. But the best thing in the picture is perhaps her glance—the marvellous rendering of her expressive dark eyes, which are, perhaps, slightly too close to each other. The treatment of the whole subject is at the same time light and firm, and the colours have a singular perfection. This is a picture to make our Danish painters blush for their clumsy hands. One wishes that we could have a teacher like Degas in this country.

Letter from Edgar Degas to Ludovic-Napoléon Lepic

On Cassatt

1879

Ludovic-Napoléon Lepic (1839–89), French artist (and dog breeder). This letter was likely written in the fall of 1879 when Cassatt and Degas were working together on the journal "Le Jour et la nuit," which was never published. During this time Cassatt was investigating the effects of light and shadow in her painting.

Dear Monsieur,

I have been twice too satisfied with your deliveries not to turn to you once again. Could you not either from your kennels and apartments, or from your friends and acquaintances, find me a small griffon, thoroughbred or not (dog or bitch), and send it to me to Paris if an opportunity arises or by carrier. As regards the price I shall not consider that further than you did. However if you should wish to draw on me for a sum exceeding 50 centimes, I should be grateful if you would warn me some months in advance as is always the custom in these parts.

Please accept, Monsieur le Comte, my sincere regards.

E. DEGAS

I think it in good taste to warn you that the person who desires this dog is Mlle. Cassatt, that she approached me, who am known for the quality of my dogs and for my affection for them as for my old friends etc. etc. I also think that it is useless to give you any information about the asker, whom you know for a good painter, at this moment engrossed in the study of the reflection and shadow of flesh or dresses, for which she has the greatest affection and understanding, not that she resigns herself to the use of only *green and red* for this effect which I consider the only salvation, etc. etc. etc.

This distinguished person whose friendship I honour, as you would in my place, asked me to recommend to you the youth of the subject. It is a young dog that she needs, so that he may love her.

By sending with the dog, if you do send the dog, you would give an appreciable pleasure to your requester, by sending with this dog some news of your health and of your noble pursuits.

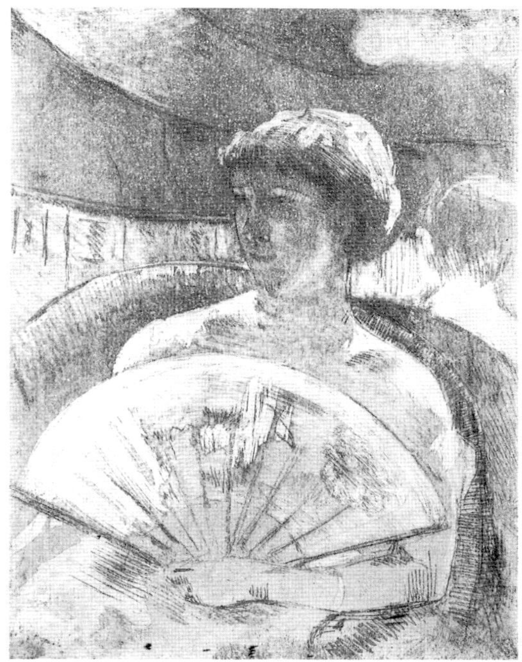

In the Opera Box (No. 2). c. 1880. Soft-ground etching and aquatint, printed in gray-black. 8 5/16 × 6 1/4 in. (21.2 × 15.8 cm). The Museum of Modern Art, New York. Gift of Abby Aldrich Rockefeller. Photograph © The Museum of Modern Art, New York.

ACHILLE SEGARD

From *Mary Cassatt: Un Peintre des enfants et des mères*

On Cassatt's Admiration for Degas

1913

In Degas [Cassatt] had recognized and admired one of the great classical masters of French painting. She had told this to everyone around her, with wonder and delight. Her admiration was all the livelier for being shared by almost no one. She also knew very well that a patient, persistent study of these unappreciated masterpieces was an opportunity for enrichment. She was a disciple only in that her admiration and her patient, solitary study contributed to her training. None of the Impressionists gave her personal lessons. Though it is correct to say that she was Degas's disciple, it is necessary to specify that she earned this appellation more by her admiration for the works that she so persistently studied than by any spoken lessons. The ease and supreme sureness of his rigorous draftsmanship sent her into transports of admiration. She was aware of the novelty of the sentiment, the precision of movement captured in the least characteristic, the refinement of his visual sensitivity. Certain harmonies of almost acid tones gave her the sensation produced by an unripe fruit in the mouth, other harmonies seemed soft and well-blended, as if a kind of very noble, very intellectual tenderness had been crushed beneath the thumb along with the colored pencil. Everything persuaded her that, unbeknownst to itself, France possessed one of the greatest masters of the art of drawing and painting ever to honor a country. Emerging from the museums where she had studied the ancient masters, Miss Mary Cassatt unhesitatingly recognized—in front of the first works of Degas she had the good fortune to see—the continuator of the classical greats. No one helped her make this selection, and she abided by this personal manner of appreciating the works [in] the efforts that she pursued in her solitary studio in order to perfect her art. Since she could permit herself a few luxuries, she happened, some time later, to buy some Degas for two or three hundred francs, in public exhibitions. She only showed them to a few people. She was offended that others disliked them. Now, it should be noted that at the time she had begun to single out Degas's works and to like them, she knew nothing of the painter's personality, not even if he were young or old, or lived in Paris.

AMBROISE VOLLARD

From *Recollections of a Picture Dealer*

Cassatt's Modesty

1936

It was with a sort of frenzy that generous Mary Cassatt labored for the success of her comrades: Monet, Pissarro, Cézanne, Sisley and the rest. But what indifference where her own painting was concerned! What an aversion from "pushing" her work in public. One day at an exhibition, they were fighting for and against the Impressionists. "But," said someone, speaking to Mary Cassatt without knowing who she was, "you are forgetting a foreign painter that Degas ranks very high."

"Who is that?" she asked in astonishment.

"Mary Cassatt."

Without false modesty, quite naturally, she exclaimed, "Oh, nonsense!"

"She is jealous," murmured the other, turning away.

LOUISINE HAVEMEYER

From *Sixteen to Sixty: Memoirs of a Collector*

On Cassatt and Degas

1930

I have been amused, during the long years I have known [Cassatt and Degas], at the little luncheons or dinners that have been planned by friends to effect a reconciliation. I recall one which took place in Paris. Degas and Mary Cassatt had quarreled over the Dreyfus affair. Degas was such an anti-Dreyfusard that he wrote to his lifelong friend Halévy, who was a Jew, not to put his place at the table as he could no longer dine with him on Sundays.

Miss Cassatt was perplexed whether or not to accept her friend's invitation to meet Degas at luncheon.

"By all means accept," said I.

"But this Dreyfus affair!" she objected. "I know he will anger me."

"Don't hesitate," I insisted, "go and silence him for once and for all time."

"But, Louie dear," she said pathetically, "you don't know what a dreadful man he is, he can say anything."

"So can you," I answered and she reluctantly decided to go. Just at that moment Matilde, her good maid, entered with a beautiful new gown over her arm.

"Wear that new gown," I suggested, "and enjoy the repose and assurance the conscious elegance gives you."

Needless to say, Miss Cassatt attended the luncheon while I impatiently awaited her return to learn what had happened.

"Mercy, Louie," she exclaimed, as soon as she saw me, "who do you think sat next to me at table?"

"Degas?" I queried, knowing from her tone I was wrong.

The Dreyfus Affair began in 1894 when Captain Alfred Dreyfus (1859–1935), an Alsatian Jewish officer, was falsely accused of giving information to the Germans. Efforts to exonerate Dreyfus led to political crisis during the Third Republic and caused a renewal of hostility between the Roman Catholic Church and the Republic. Although the evidence against Dreyfus at his court-martial in 1894 was insufficient, he was nevertheless imprisoned. Émile Zola published "J'accuse" in January 1898, an open letter which attacked the army and brought the issue to the public's attention. Dreyfus was finally pardoned and vindicated in 1906, but the affair effected a lingering discredit to the army and eventually led to the rise of radicals in France.

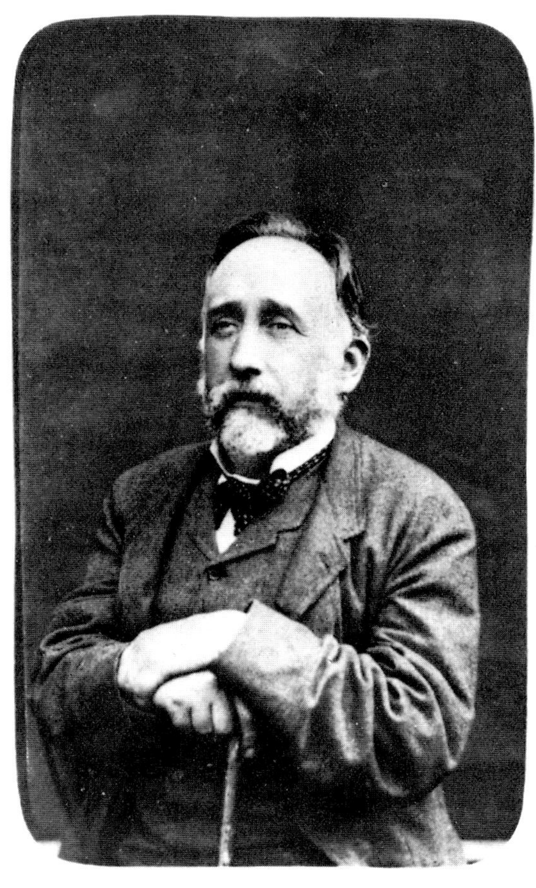

Photograph of Edgar Degas. c. 1855. Photograph

"No! Worse!" she answered, "General Mercier! Would you believe it? And they know how I feel toward him! I wanted to run away!"

"I hope you did nothing of the sort!" I said.

"Oh, no, I couldn't, on account of Degas! He has aged, dear, aged so very much it made me sad, but I was glad to see him, and he was very nice and did not say a disagreeable word."

"Of course, he didn't," I rejoined. How could he? Were they not old, old friends, good comrades, with the deep respect each paid to the other's talent lying firm beneath any momentary differences of opinion?

LOUISINE HAVEMEYER

From *Sixteen to Sixty: Memoirs of a Collector*

Cassatt on Degas's Character

1930

"That was just like Degas," I remarked.

"Exactly," said Miss Cassatt. "Bon diseur de mots, my dear, mauvais caractère. Degas had one sister who married M. Le Febvre, and four brothers, one of whom was a mauvais sujet and the family to save him from ruin gave up everything, the silverware and even the sister's dot were sacrificed. Now Degas's fortune in pictures which should realize several million francs will, of course, go to eight nieces and nephews." Here Miss Cassatt, probably feeling she had brought the biography down to the present time, stopped

"mauvais caractère"; ill-tempered, devilish.

"mauvais sujet"; libertine.

but I saw a look of reminiscence in her eye and a peculiar expression about her mouth, and I pleaded:

"Tell me some more about him."

"Oh, my dear, he is dreadful! He dissolves your will power," she said. "Even the painter Moreau said to Degas after years of friendship, that he could no longer stand his attacks: 'Voyons, Degas, il faut que je mène ma vie! que nous ne nous voyions plus!' (See here, Degas, I must lead my life! Let us no longer meet!)

Gustave Moreau (1826–1898), French painter and teacher influential in the development of Symbolist painting.

"Degas said to me apropos of Sargent (John S. Sargent, portrait painter): 'Un facile peintre, mais pas un artiste' (A skillful painter but not an artist), and of another painter who would like to have been associated with us he said: 'Il n'est pas assez méchant pour nous' (He is not wicked enough for us)." And then after a moment's reflection she continued: "Think of this; one day a young painter seeing Degas in a color shop begged the proprietor to introduce him to the great Degas! 'Better not,' cautioned the proprietor, but as the young fellow insisted he presented him to Degas. Of course the youth was delighted, but after a few moments' conversation Degas turned to a picture which stood upon an easel and said 'Jeune homme, c'est vous qui avez fait ca?' (Young man, did you do that?) 'Mais oui, monsieur,' replied the young fellow, delighted that Degas had noticed his canvas. 'Je vous plains' (I pity you) and he turned upon his heel and left the shop."

"He was indeed dreadful," I said sympathetically, but knowing Miss Cassatt was quite his equal in repartee I led her on to tell me more by asking: "How could you get on with him?"

"Oh," she answered, "I am independent! I can live alone and I love to work. Sometimes it made him furious that he could not find a chink in my armor, and there would be months when we just could not see each other, and then something I painted would bring us together again and he would go to Durand-Ruel's and say something nice about me, or come to see me himself. When he saw my *Boy Before the Mirror* he said to Durand-Ruel: 'Where is she? I must see her at once. It is the greatest picture of the century.' When I saw him he went over all the details of the picture with me and expressed great admiration for it, and then, as if regretting what he had said, he relentlessly added: 'It has all your qualities and all your faults—c'est l'Enfant Jésus et sa bonne anglaise.' "

COLORPLATE 91

"C'est l'Enfant Jesus et sa bonne anglaise"; It's the baby Jesus and his nanny.

"Did no one ever hit him back?" I asked.

"Oh! certainly," replied Miss Cassatt, "but Degas never cared. When criticism was at its worst, he said to me: 'Ils sont tous jaloux de nous. Ils veulent nous voler notre art' (They are all jealous of us, and wish to steal our art)."

"But," continued Miss Cassatt after a quiet moment, and I saw her face light up with a beautiful expression, "magnificent! and however dreadful he was, he always lived up to his ideals." Miss Cassatt folded her hands and I saw she had said all she cared to for the moment.

Yes, this great painter lived up to his ideals! He was a primitive of his own day, seeing things as they really were, depicting life in its terrible reality. Many things have been written and said about Degas, but the truest of all was said about him by Miss Cassatt. "He is a philosopher, and there it is," she said.

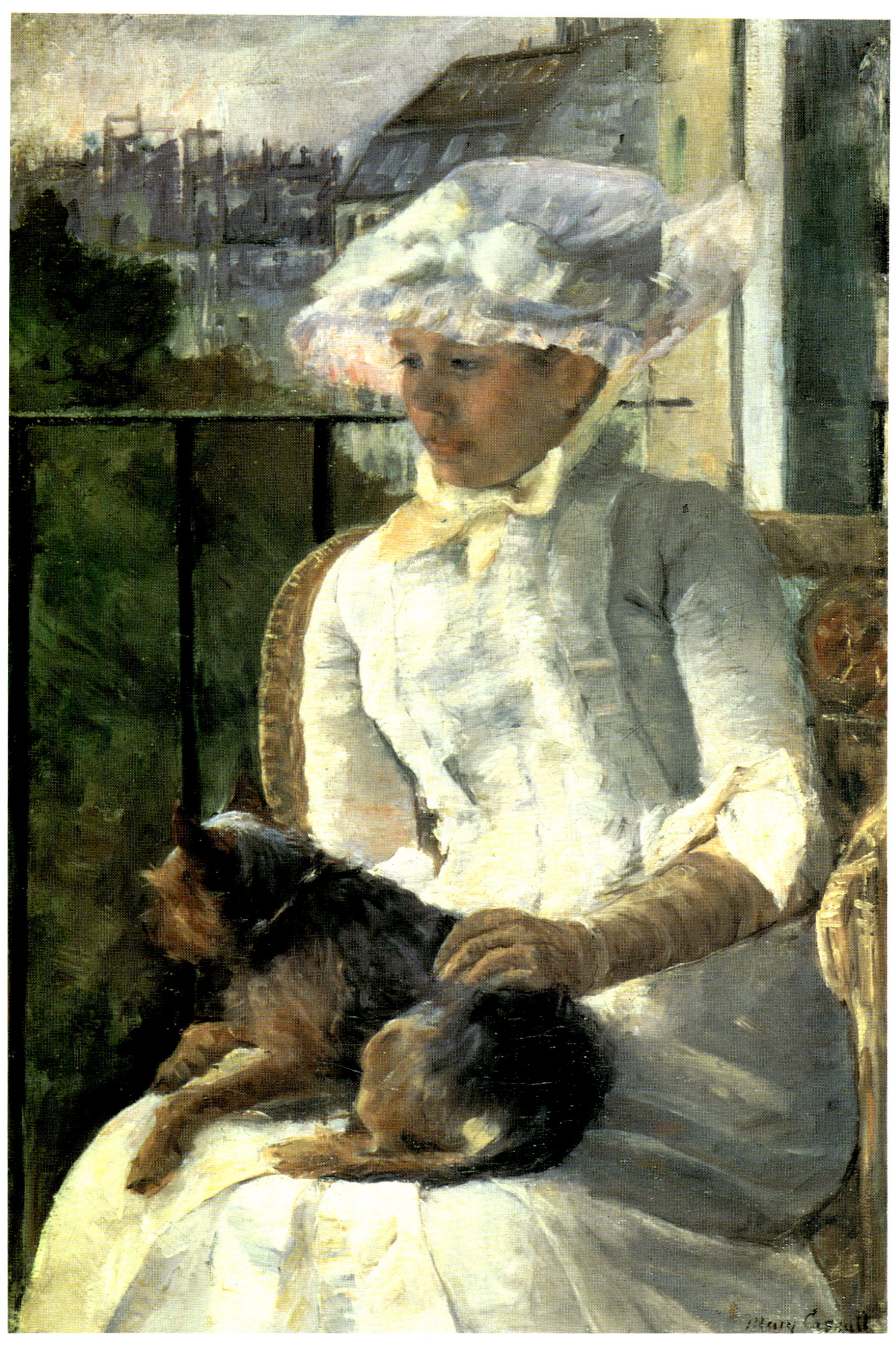

COLORPLATE 30. *Susan on a Balcony Holding a Dog.* c. 1880. Oil on canvas. 39 ½ × 25 ½ in. (100.3 × 64.7 cm). The Corcoran Gallery of Art, Museum Purchase, Gallery Fund.

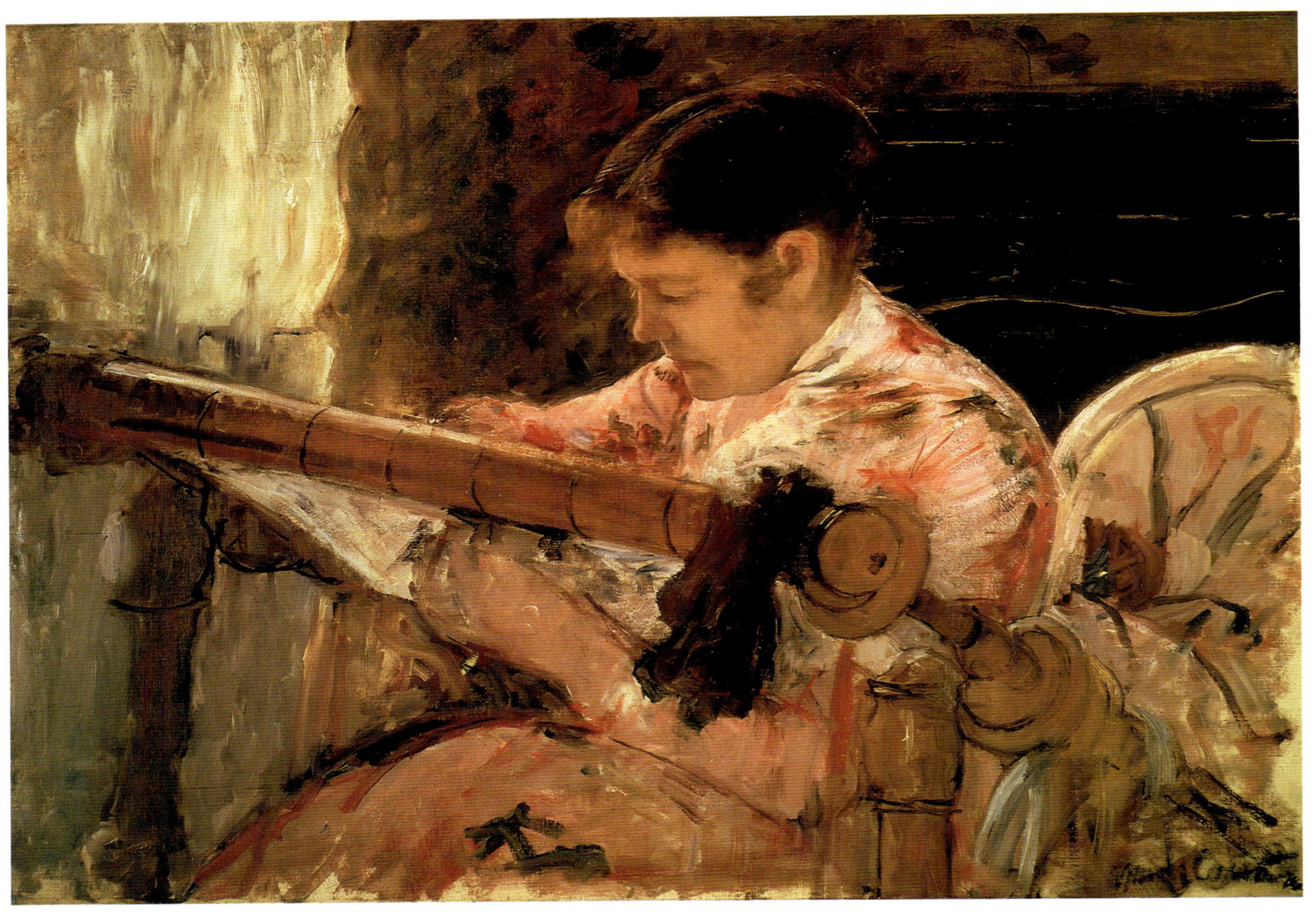

COLORPLATE 31. *Lydia at a Tapestry Frame.* c. 1881. Oil on canvas. 25 5/8 × 36 3/8 in. (65 × 92.4 cm). Courtesy of the Flint Institute of Arts. Gift of the Whiting Foundation.

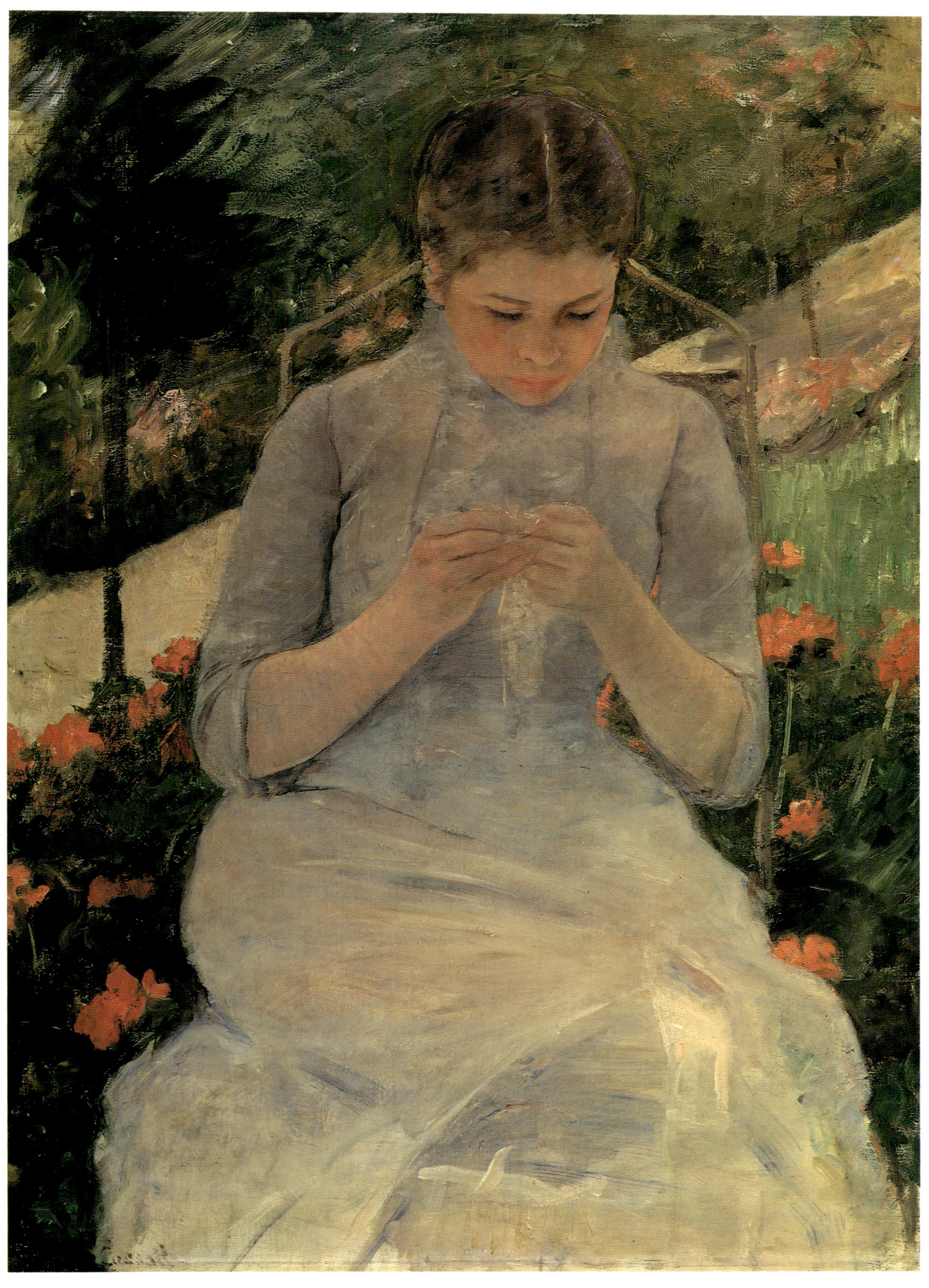

COLORPLATE 32. *Young Woman Sewing.* 1883–86. Oil on canvas. 36 × 25 ½ in. (91.4 × 64.7 cm). Musée d'Orsay, Paris. Photograph: Réunion des Musées Nationaux.

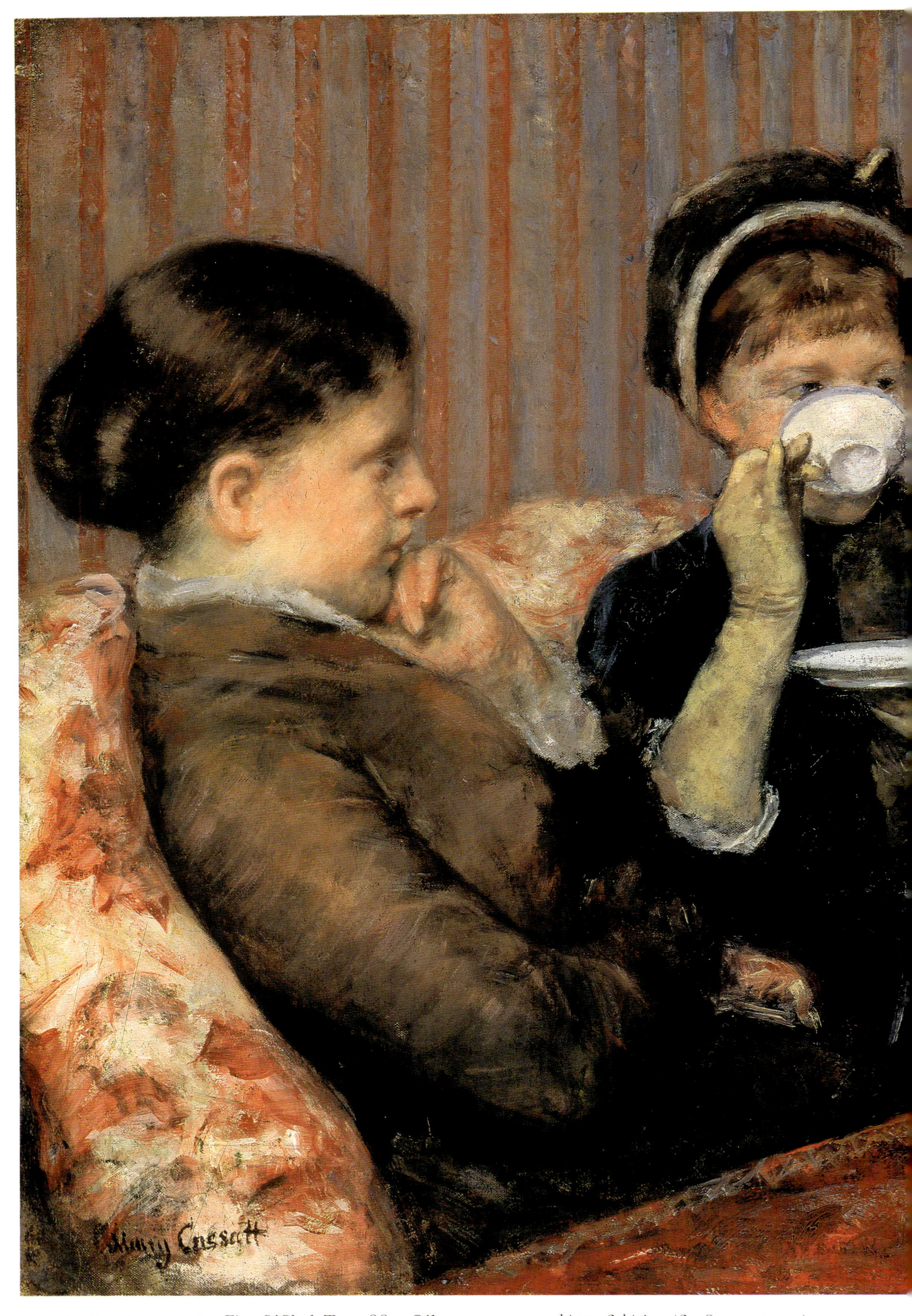

COLORPLATE 33. *Five O'Clock Tea.* 1880. Oil on canvas. 25 ½ × 36 ½ in. (64.8 × 92.7 cm).
Courtesy of Museum of Fine Arts, Boston. The M. Theresa B. Hopkins Fund.

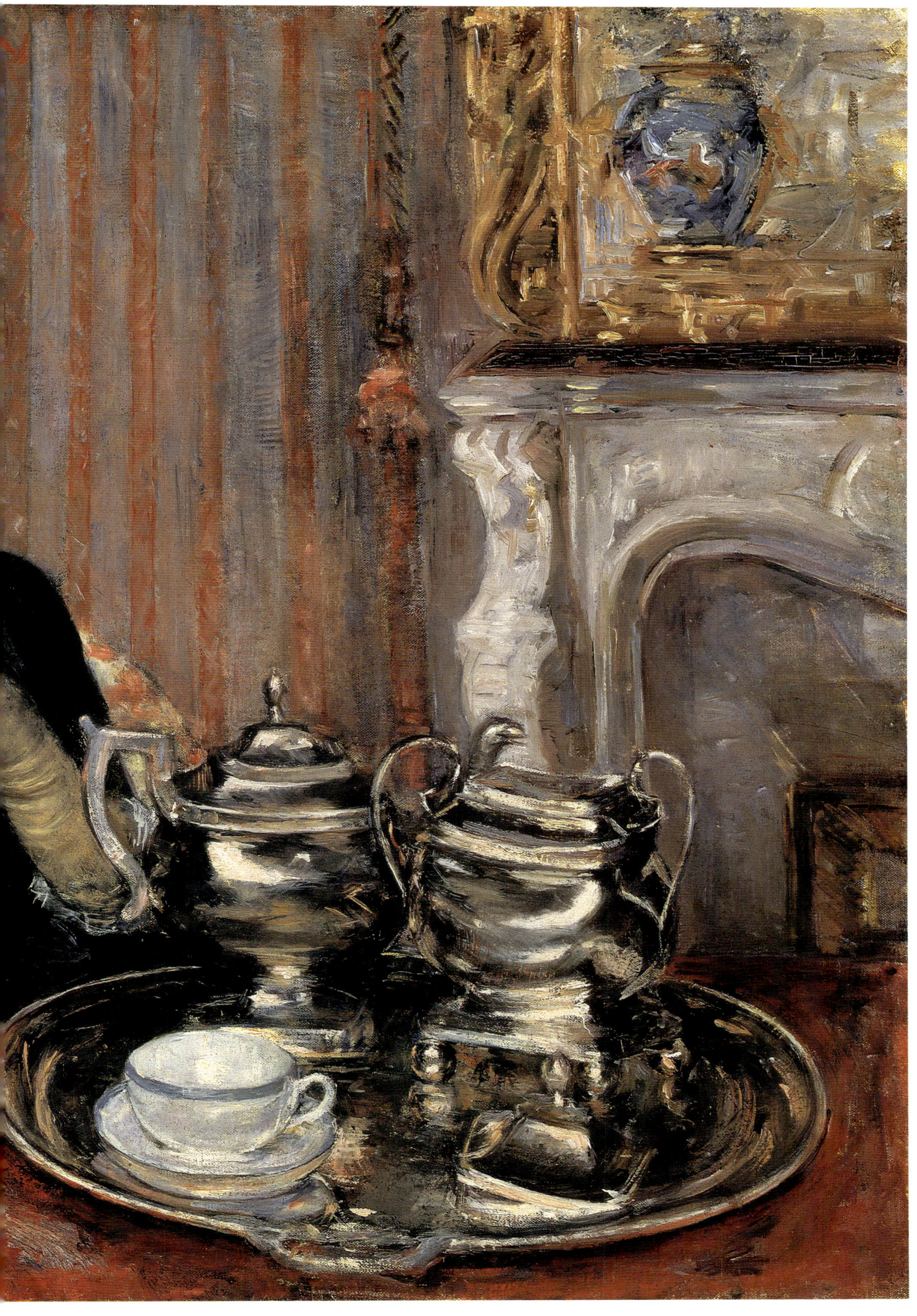

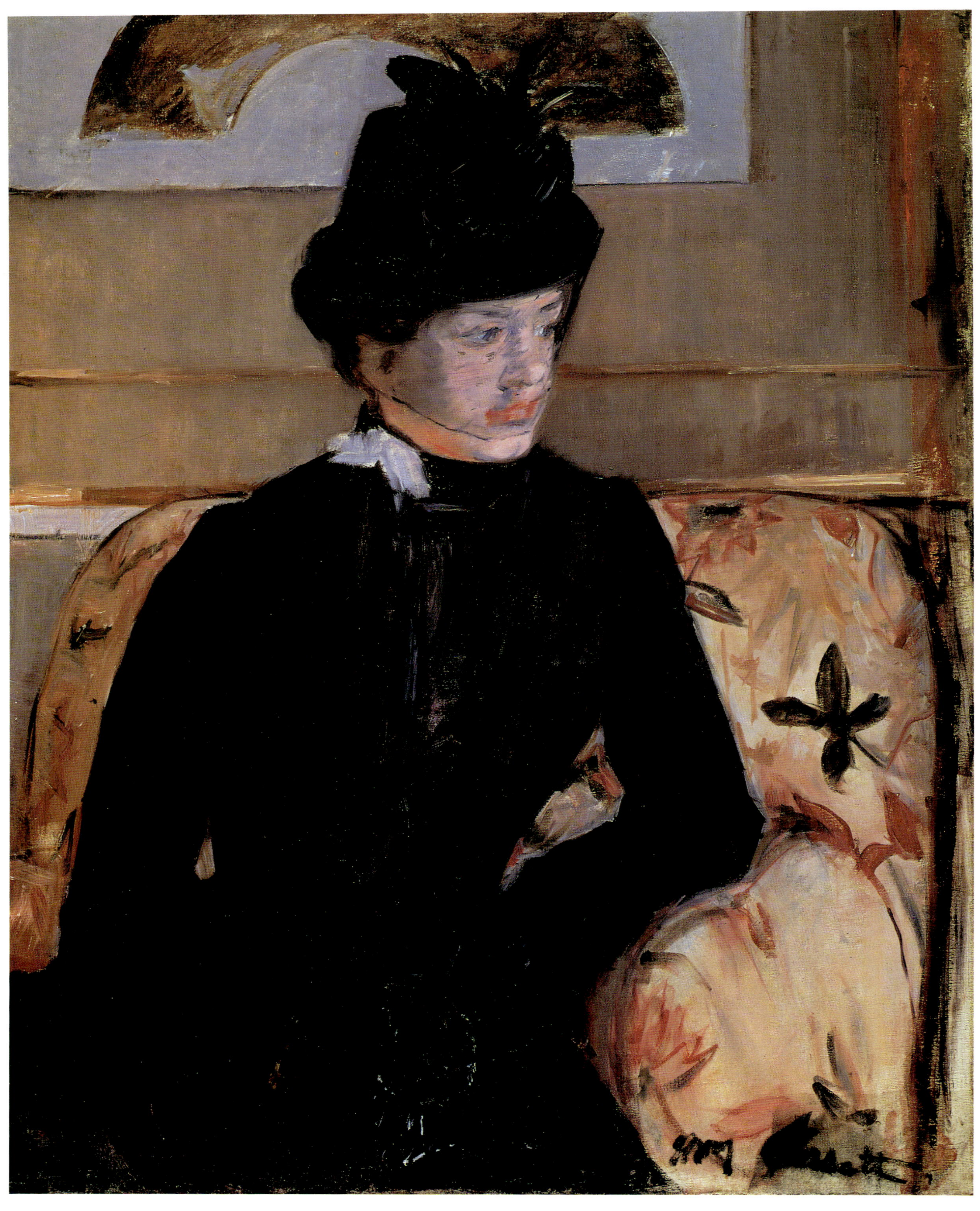

COLORPLATE 34. *Portrait of a Young Woman in Black.* 1883. Oil on canvas. 31 13/16 × 25 ½ in. (80.8 × 64.8 cm). The Peabody Institute of the City of Baltimore, on extended loan to The Baltimore Museum of Art.

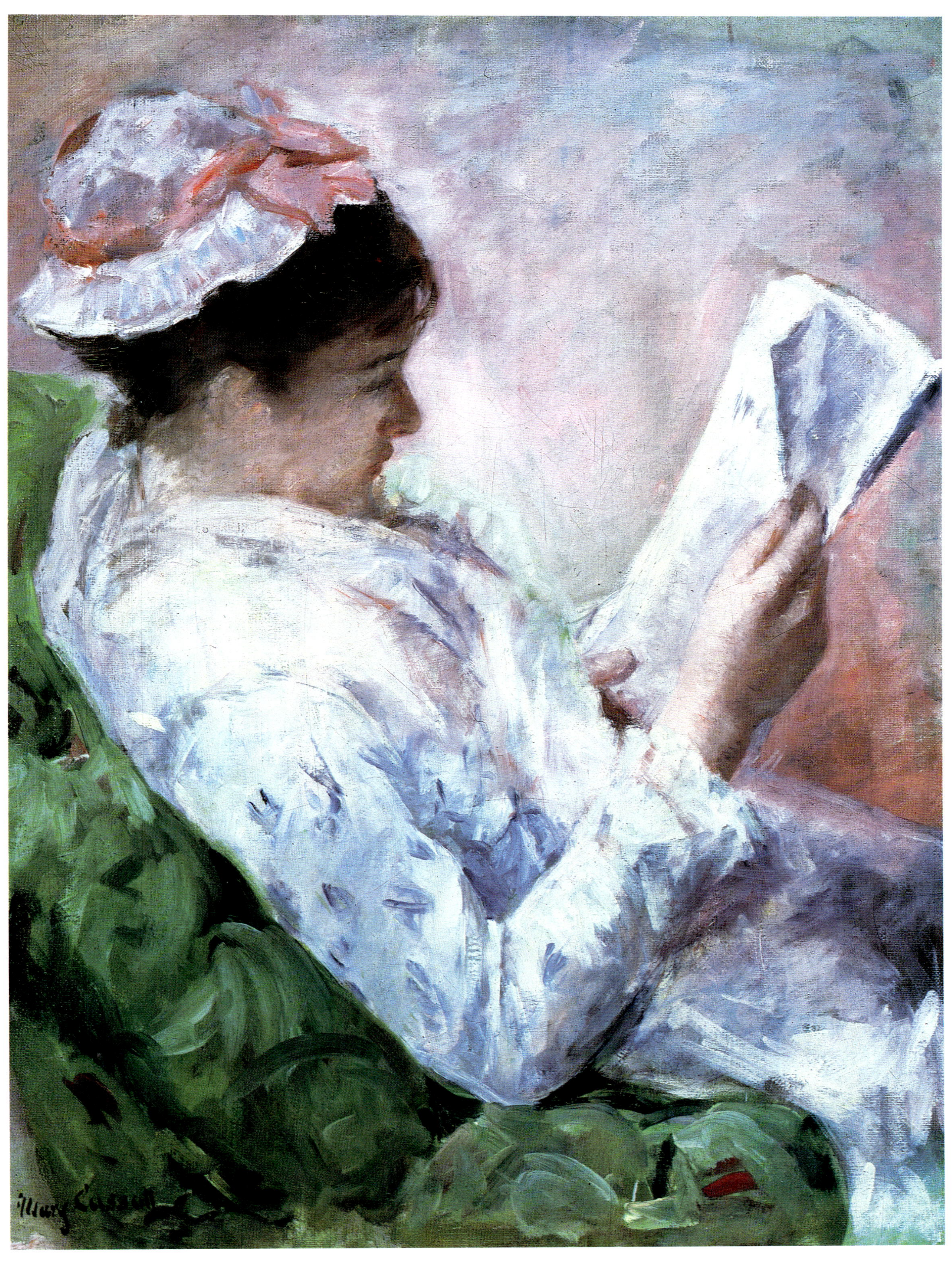

COLORPLATE 35. *Woman Reading (Portrait of Lydia Cassatt, the Artist's Sister).* 1878–79. Oil on canvas. 32 × 23 ½ in. (81.2 × 59.6 cm). Joslyn Art Museum, Omaha, Nebraska.

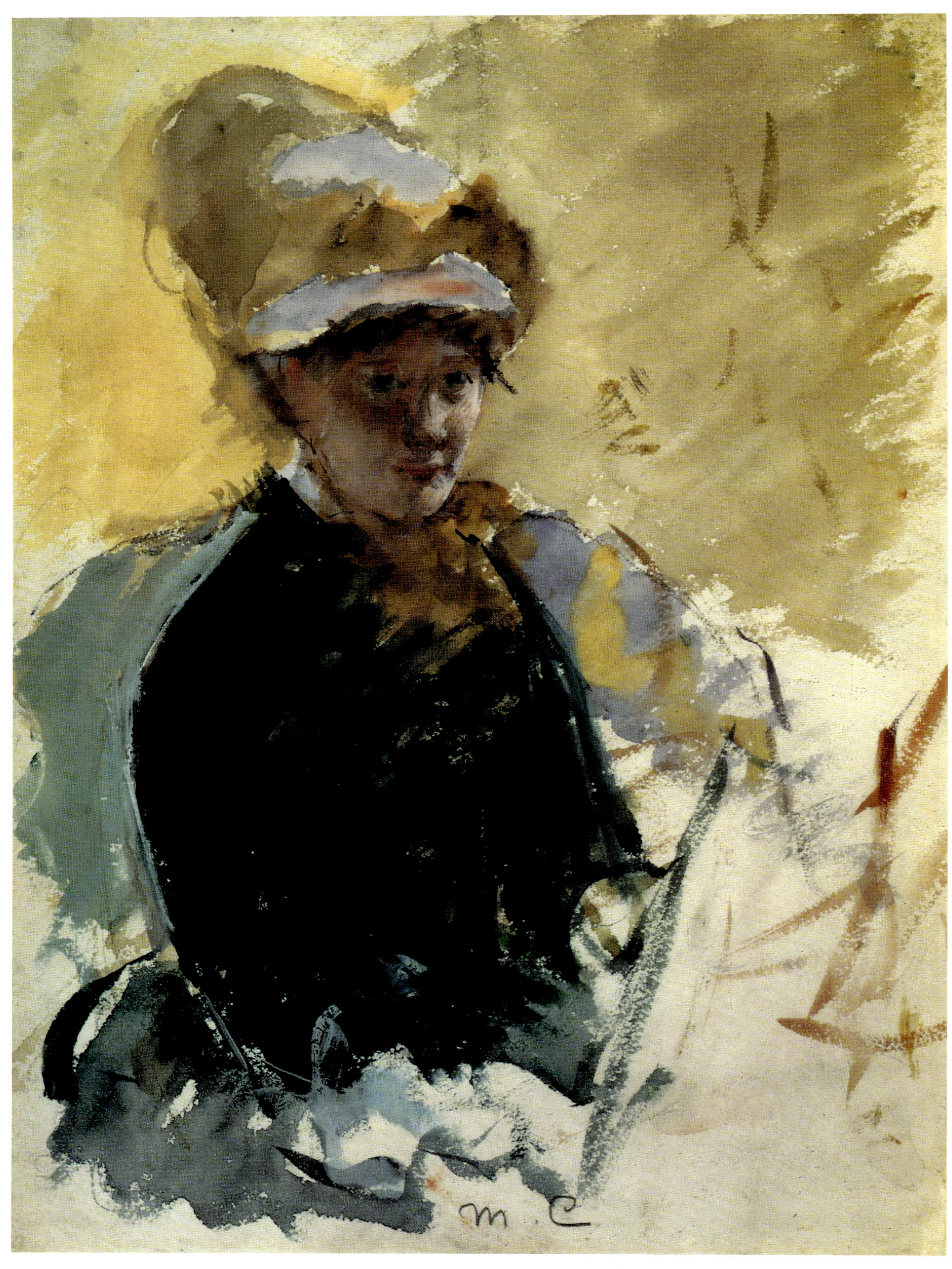

COLORPLATE 36. *Self-Portrait.* c. 1880. Watercolor on paper. 13 × 9 5/8 in. (33 × 24.4 cm). National Portrait Gallery, Smithsonian Institution. Photograph: Art Resource, New York.

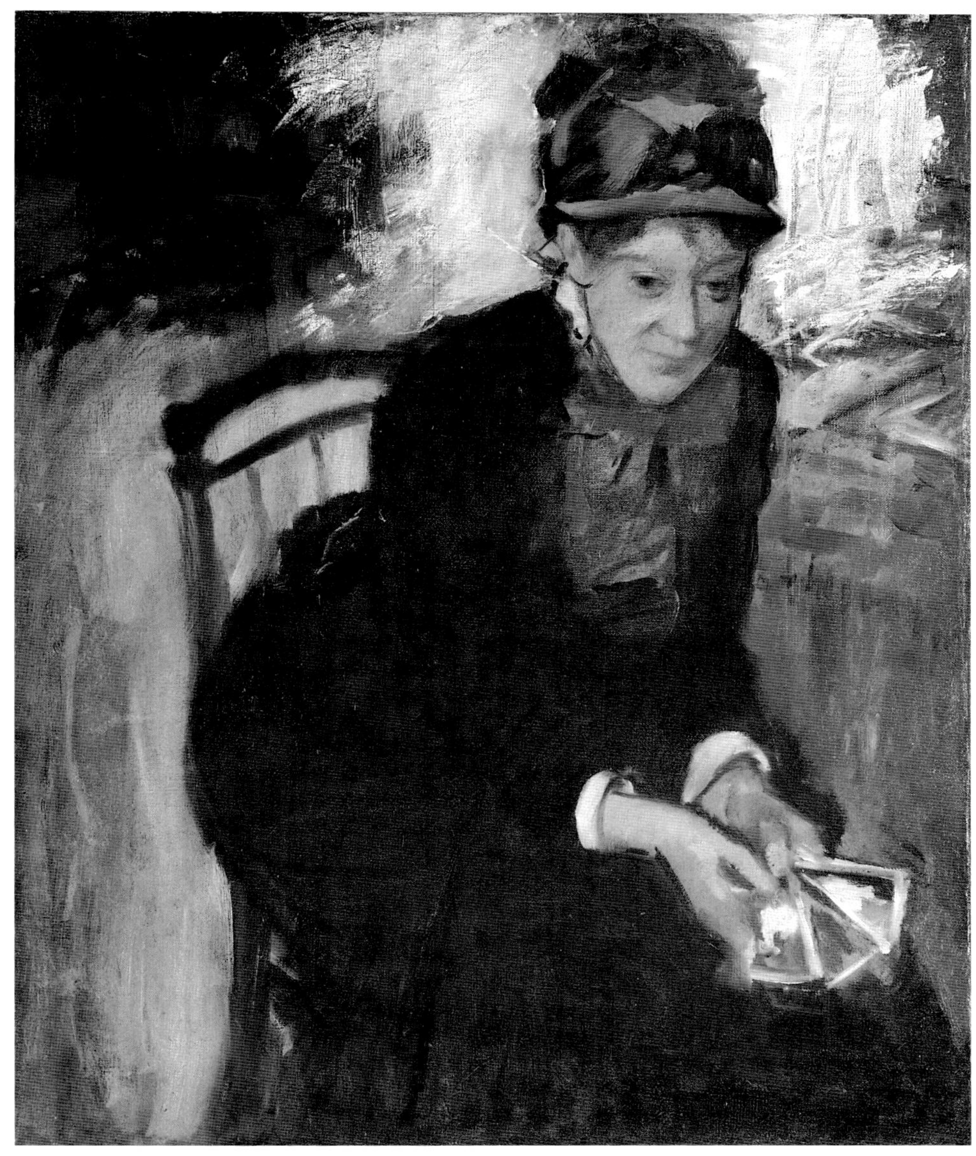

Edgar Degas. *Mary Cassatt.* c. 1880–84. Oil on canvas. 28 1/8 × 23 1/8 in. (71.4 × 58.7 cm). National Portrait Gallery, Smithsonian Institution. Gift of the Morris and Gwendolyn Cafritz Foundation and the Regents Major Acquisitions Fund.

Letter from Mary Cassatt to Paul Durand-Ruel

On Degas's Portrait of Cassatt

1912

Dear Sir,

What I chiefly wish to part with is the portrait Degas did of me, which is hanging in the room next to the drawing room (my studio).

The canvases you saw lying on the floor were left there accidentally. Those are things of mine that went wrong, and I should burn them.

As for the portrait by Degas, I especially desire not to leave it to my family as being me. It has artistic qualities, but is so painful and represents me as a person so repugnant that I would not wish it to be known that I posed for it. The picture is framed and there is a glass over it. The fan in my opinion is the prettiest thing that Degas painted. I suppose it is worth a certain price, I thought twenty-five thousand, as it dates from the period of the dancers at the rail . . . If you think my portrait saleable, I should like it to be sold abroad but without my name being attached to it.

Letter from Robert Cassatt to His Son, Alexander Cassatt

On Cassatt's First Reviews as an Impressionist

May 21, 1879

13, avenue Trudaine
Monday, May 21, 1879

My dear Son,

I have written you twice within the last six weeks, my last letter being on a very interesting subject to us all, an answer to which I am looking for with not a little anxiety!—We none of us have anything from you later than yours to your Mother 26th March—I expect certainly to have a letter from you by the mail which left New York 14th & which will probably be distributed here next Sunday—In addition to my letters I have also sent you a number of newspapers, art journals &c containing notices of Mame,—Her success has been more and more emphasized since I wrote and she even begins to tire of it—"The Artist" [*L'Artiste*] for May—edited by Arsène Houssaye—Alex Dumas etc. contains an extremely flattering notice of her—and the *Review des Deux Mondes* has an article entitled "Les Expositions d'art" page 478 very hard on the Independant artists generally—Makes an exception as to Mr Degas, & Mame, in terms that under the circumstances and the source must I think also be construed as very complimentary: The Philada Library takes the *Deux Mondes*—& you can of course get it from them. We hear also, almost daily of notices in other French & English papers which have escaped our notice—In short everybody says now that in future it dont matter what the papers say about her—She is now known to the Art world as well as to the general public in such a way as not to be forgotten again so long as she continues to paint!! Every one of the leading daily French papers mentioned the Exposition & nearly all named Mame—most of them in terms of praise, only one of the American papers noticed it and *it* named her rather disparagingly!!! . . .

Gard writes in good spirits about his business, but does not tell us of anything else—except that you are in the country—We are *all* very well for the moment Your mother as well as ever she was—I hope you too are all well, we all join in love—Kiss the children for me tell Eddie I am expecting a letter from him soon

Your aff Father
R.S.C.

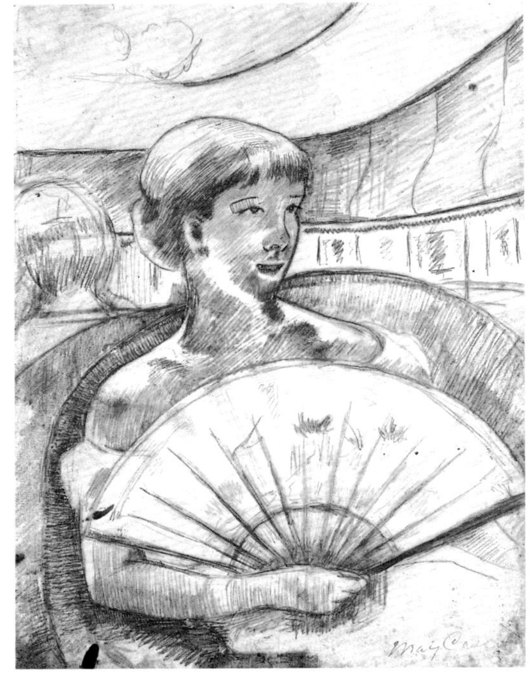

Drawing for *In the Opera Box* (No. 3). c. 1880. Pencil. 8 5/16 × 6 5/16 in. (21.2 × 16 cm). National Gallery of Art. The Rosenwald Collection. Photograph © Board of Trustees, National Gallery of Art, Washington, D.C.

Robert Simpson Cassatt (1806–1891), Mary Cassatt's father, began his career as a merchant in Pittsburgh and then established an investment firm in Philadelphia. Robert and his wife, Katherine, moved with their eldest daughter, Lydia, to Paris to live with Mary in 1877.

The "very interesting subject" possibly refers to Aleck's impending resignation from the Pennsylvania Railroad.

The American paper referred to here is possibly "The American Register."

From *The American Register*: "The Exhibition of Independent Artists"

American Attitudes Toward Impressionism

May 17, 1879

For a month past the vacant salons of an apartment on the Avenue de l'Opéra have been occupied by an exhibition of the works of the so-called

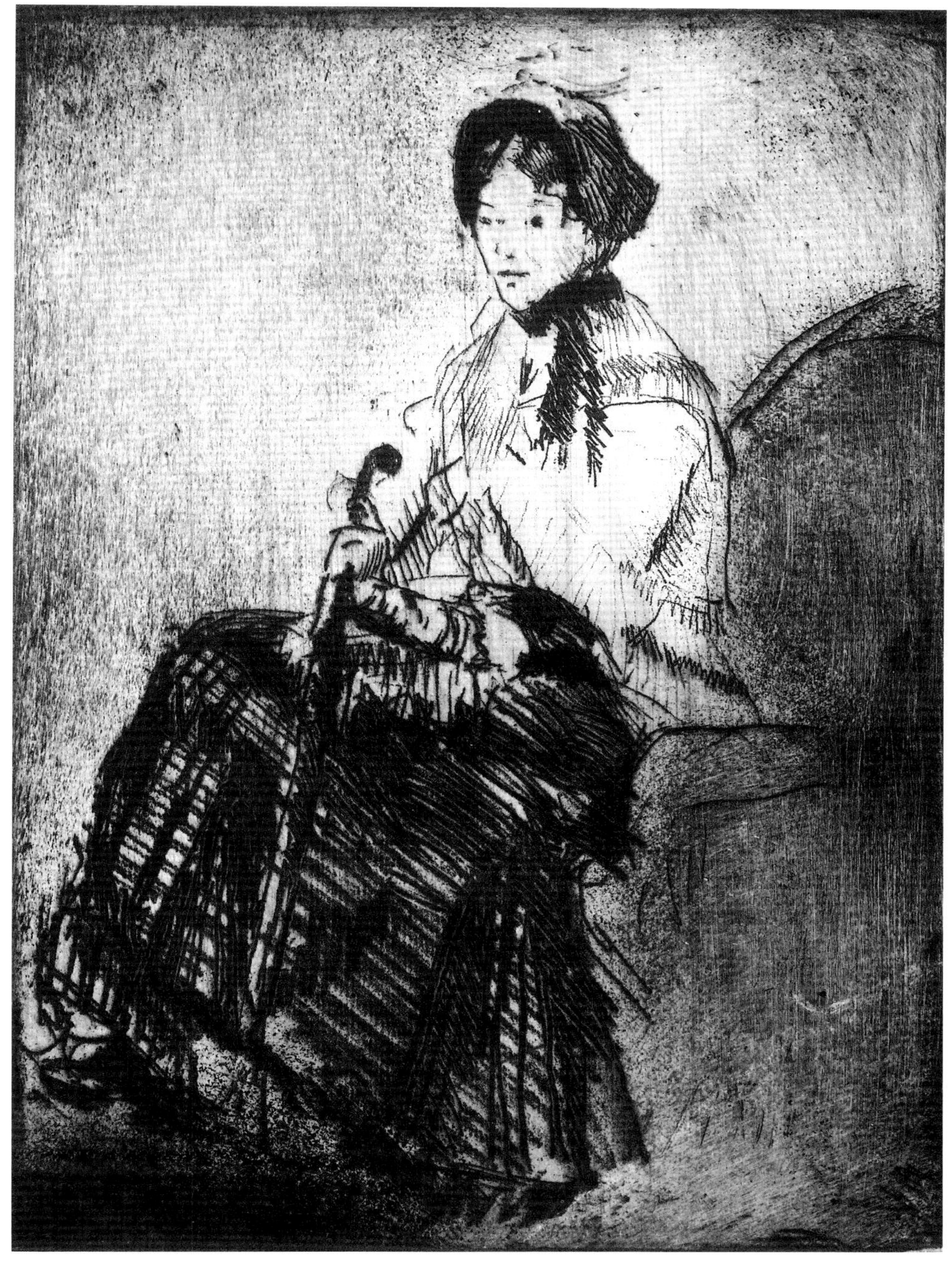

The Umbrella. 1879. Soft-ground etching (first state). 10 7/8 × 7 5/16 in. (27.6 × 18.5 cm). Philadelphia Museum of Art. Gift of R. Sturgis Ingersoll, Frederic Ballard, Alexander Cassatt, Staunton B. Peck, and Mrs. William Potter Wear.

"Independent artists." Independent of what, we should like to know. Of criticism? of purchasers? or of all ideas of perspective and of color? We pause for a reply.

In the landscapes, Nature seems to have abdicated all her rights. Pink skies overhang a lilac forest, the trees are blue in another picture, and the heavens are brown. The portraits in the exhibition were, however, the most wonderful objects of all. In one corner, a pea-green woman, evidently in the last stages of Asiatic cholera mooed at you from out of the shadows. . . . A poor young woman, very far gone with the Jaundice was shown wrestling with her fan in the depths of an opera-box. We cannot in fact understand the purpose of the new school. . . . We can see in it only the uneasy striving after notoriety of a restless vanity, that prefers celebrity for ill doing rather than an unnoted persistence in the path of true art.

LOUIS DURANTY

From *La Chronique des arts et de la curiosité*

"The Fourth Exhibition by a Group of Independent Artists"

April 19, 1879

Louis-Émile Edmond Duranty (1833–1880), French novelist and critic, edited the periodical "Le Réalisme" from 1856 to1857 and worked as an art critic for the "Gazette des Beaux Arts" beginning in 1872. In 1876 he published the book "La Nouvelle peinture," analyzing Realism and Impressionism.

As we are about to enter upon a somewhat burning subject, where one is in grave danger of not agreeing with popular opinion, we pray you to be willing to follow us, believe that we are loyal to no particular position, and allow that we have before us, at the least, a quite curious case in the history of contemporary art.

The title that these painters take on means that they are independent of the official organization. In order to be one of them, one must promise not to exhibit in the Salon. Thus, one finds not only *Impressionists* in the Avenue de l'Opéra, but artists of various stripes. . . .

That astonishing artist named M. Degas is there in the exhibition, in all his wit, whims, mordancy, and acuity, an exceptional man, who is beginning to be appreciated and who will be particularly esteemed in a few years, a man to whose influence twenty other painters owe their success, for one cannot approach him without his passing on sparks.

It is equally impossible to visit the exhibition without finding most interesting Mlle. Cassatt's portraits. An utterly remarkable and very English (she is American) sense of elegance and distinction marks these portraits. Mlle. Cassatt *deserves very special attention. . . .*

In short, we find that the Impressionists, at least such as MM. Monet and Pissarro, are serious people, gifted with a strong artistic feeling, which they translate very freely and broadly, too broadly and too freely sometimes, in the eyes of those who like things polished and precisely trimmed, and it is a great treat to see M. Degas's and Mlle. Cassatt's pictures.

Claude Monet (1840–1926), leader of the landscape faction of the Impressionist group.

Camille Pissarro (1830–1903), writer and French Impressionist painter. He welcomed many new artists into the Impressionist group and became especially close friends with Cassatt.

GEORGES LAFENESTRE

From *Revue des Deux Mondes*

Cassatt's Images of Parisian Life

May 15, 1879

Georges Lafenestre (1837–1919).

The republic of the arts is not the best arena for the exercise of freedom. There is no dearth of noisy voices denouncing the tyranny of the Academy and preaching insurrection against Government interference. Until now, this unrest has always dispersed into words. Despite the frequently invoked example of their British counterparts, who are able to organize into active groups, French artists have made only timid attempts to elude official protection and to ask the public directly to approve their talent. . . .

Nevertheless, for the last few years, a large number of individual exhibitions—whether at the École Nationale des Beaux-Arts, in the arts clubs, the general auction rooms, or at the dealers'—have shown artists and art-lovers alike other avenues than the Champs-Élysées. This is very welcome indeed. . . . At the moment, just as the Salon opens, more cluttered than ever, two privately mounted exhibitions of contemporary art have not yet closed their doors. One is by a *Group of Independent Artists,* in avenue de l'Opéra, the other, by the French Watercolorists' Society, in rue Laffitte. Though both exhibitions are mounted rather simply, a numerous enough public is attending to prove to the artists that the time of their liberation has come, if they will bring some strength of will to it.

Success, it goes without saying, will cleave only to those who deserve it. The group of so-called "Independents" must become more robust if they wish a long and prosperous life, even though they have already existed for four years. The group's exhibition, as was true of the legendary exhibition of the *refusés,* has been sustained by a certain fashion for hilarity, upon which it would be imprudent to depend. The Parisian enjoys a good laugh, and understands pranks, but he does not allow the laughter to be always at his expense, and he tires of a joke that is beaten to death. . . . In actual fact, the little troop of *Independents* is but the last remnants of the group of the *Impressionists,* which in turn was only a straggling rear guard of the battalion of the *Realists.* . . .

Our Independents are in fact just isolated laggards who are storming open doors, pleading cases that have already been won. They are not the only ones who know how to execute subtle analyses of the phenomena of light, who seek to place things in their proper surroundings, nor are they alone influenced by the honest, delicate charm of English art or able to capture the lively, whimsical poetry of Japanese art. The influences of England and Japan are visible in this school, but we owe this movement to neither M. Degas nor Mlle. Marie Cassatt. Yet, M. Degas and Mlle. Cassatt are the only artists who stand out in this group of obedient Independents, and who provide some attractive elements and some excuse for this pretentious display of preliminary sketches and childish daubs, in the midst of which we are almost surprised to encounter their neglected, but vividly observed paintings. Both of them have a marked sense of how light breaks down in Parisian interiors; both of them discover singularly refined colorations in order to render the complexions of women worn out from late nights and the weightless shimmer of fashionable ensembles. . . .

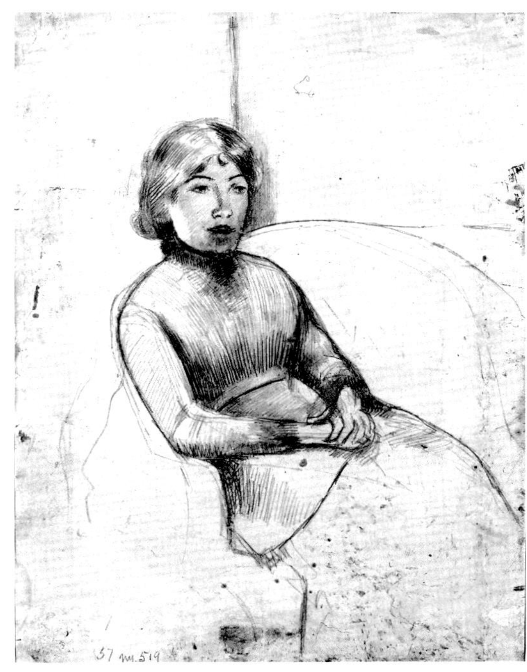

Drawing for *Corner of the Sofa* (No. 1). c. 1879. Pencil study for the soft-ground etching. 11 3/8 × 8 5/8 in. (28.8 × 22 cm). The Art Institute of Chicago. Gift of Tiffany and Margaret Blake. Photograph

Letter from Katherine Cassatt to Her Son, Alexander Cassatt

On the Impressionist Exhibition of 1880

April 9, 1880

Katherine Kelso Johnston Cassatt (1816–1895), Mary Cassatt's mother, came from a distinguished and well-educated family in western Pennsylvania. She visited her daughter often in Europe before she and her husband moved to Paris in 1877.

13, avenue Trudaine
April 9

My dear Aleck,

I suppose of course your father has written to you since the receipt of your last letter—since then we have several from the children which have all been answered. . . . They don't say anything more about coming over here and as Gard doesnt mention it either I am afraid you have abandoned the idea—I hope not, for I have been looking forward to the delight of seeing you all so long that it will be a severe disappointment if you don't come— . . .

I suppose your father has written or Gard has told you how ill Lydia has been—she doesn't often get alarmed about herself but this time she says

Lydia Simpson Cassatt, Mary's older sister, whose condition was diagnosed as Bright's Disease, an affliction of the kidneys. She died on November 7, 1882.

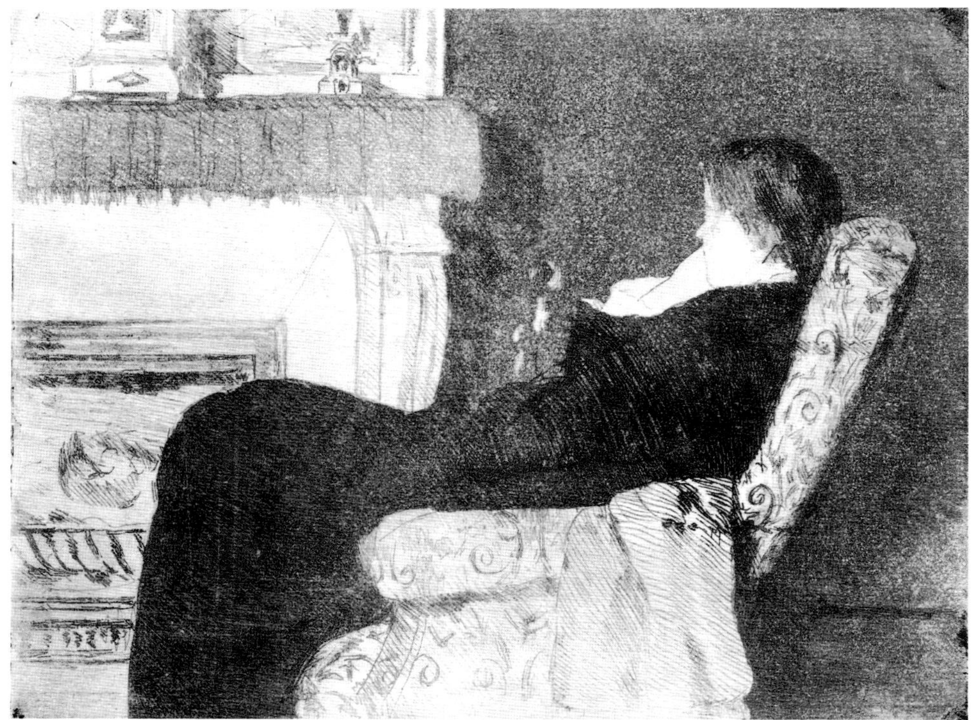

Before the Fireplace (No. 1). c. 1880. Soft-ground etching and aquatint. 6 7/16 × 8 1/16 in. (16.3 × 20.5 cm). National Gallery of Art. The Rosenwald Collection. Photograph © Board of Trustees, National Gallery of Art, Washington, D.C.

she thought it was going to be the last—neuralgia to the stomach is far worse than to the head and lasts much longer—it is now a month since she was attacked, and although she is able to go out & is getting some appetite she still has some uneasiness which doesn't however amount to pain—She is now taking Spa water & if it agrees with her it is likely we will go there this summer—that is she & I will go for your father will not consent to go where there [are] many people—in fact will not tie himself to any one place and Mary must stay with him—

The exhibition of the "Independants" is now open—it is not such a success financially as it was last year, but as the *Figaro* has opened on them this morning, it may do them good in that way—Mary had the success last year, but this one she has very few pictures, and is in the background—Degas who is the leader undertook to get up a journal of etchings and got them all to work for it so that Mary had no time for painting and as usual with Degas when the time arrived to appear, he wasn't ready—so that "Le jour et la nuit" (the name of the publication) which might have been a great success has not yet appeared—Degas never is ready for anything—This time he has thrown away an excellent chance for all of them—As I said they have not had such a success financially but nearly all of the exhibitors have sold, which shows that the school is beginning to succeed even with the public—

Degas, Pissarro, Cassatt, and other Impressionist artists were organizing a journal to be called "Le Jour et la nuit" (Day and Night), which would feature articles on the arts accompanied by original etchings. The journal was never published.

I suppose you don't see much of Gard. . . . Write to us soon dear Aleck and tell us if we may hope to see you soon—

With best love to all I am your affectionate

Mother—

Reviews from the Impressionist Exhibition of 1880

"Le Monde des Arts—Exposition de la rue des Pyramides," by Armand Silvestre. *La Vie Moderne,* April 24, 1880.

Armand Silvestre (1837–1901), French author and critic known for his early writings on the novelty of Impressionism.

As in previous years, M. Degas remains the incontestable and uncontested master. . . . I will mention immediately after him Mlle. Mary Cassatt, who proceeds directly from him. Her *Portrait of Mme. J* . . . in a black dress, seated against cushions with a floral pattern, is a full-flavored piece. I also very much like the woman reading on a balcony, where shrubs frame her blonde head with peonies—much like Japanese art, with its absence of deep space and the happy mix of colors in an entirely cheerful scale. The woman in a yellow dress on a red velvet chair, looks, from a distance, like a Degas; but, as one examines it more closely, one sees everything that it will take for the student to attain the master's sureness of execution and intensity of impression. This reservation aside, every one of Mlle. Cassatt's fifteen entries merits consideration for some felicity of movement or harmony.

COLORPLATE 34

"Expositions des artistes indépendants," by Charles Ephrussi. *Gazette des Beaux Arts,* May 1880.

Charles Éphrussi (1849–1905), author and French art historian. He worked on the staff of the "Gazette des Beaux Arts" beginning in 1875 and became director in 1894.

If one were willing to enter, with a somewhat open mind, the galleries in which the group of painters known as "independents" has installed its fifth exhibition; if one agreed to patiently seek out the good, which is rare, without becoming too indignant about the bad, which is not; if, for the violent criticisms that excite those with an unhealthy self-regard, one substituted a more careful and impartial appreciation; if, unfazed by the first impression that may be produced by a baroque subject, a disagreeable face, or excessive triviality, one went further into the heart of the work, one might discover certain qualities that initially escaped one, and, beneath the violently original intemperance, detect at times a painterly temperament; . . .

These relations between tones seem more marked in the experiments of Miss Cassatt, M. Degas's valuable pupil. Here, the larger figures receive the accidental light more fully. A red-haired woman, in a dress of yellow tulle (and what a yellow!), sits, in the dimness of a box in a theater, on a red chair, before a mirror; her bare shoulders and arms are lit by a purplish-blue light with yellow highlights, blended into a very daring harmony, by a hand that is, if not firm and skillful, at least light and delicate. The facture of *Thé* and *Jeune femme en blanc* are rather heavier; in them one feels more the English soil than M. Degas's counsels. We think we have encountered studies in this style, bright and done in free, broad brushstrokes, in many exhibitions of painting in London. . . .

COLORPLATE 17

COLORPLATE 33

"Courriers de Paris," by Albert Wolff. *Le Figaro,* April 10, 1881.

Albert Wolff (1835–1891), French novelist, critic, and playwright who wrote for "Le Figaro" in the 1870s and 1880s, and was known as a staunch opponent of Impressionism.

The intransigeants of boulevard des Capucines include more than one fine intelligence that suffers from one of these mysterious and terrible bees in their bonnet. Their work is like a conversation with one of those mentally ill persons I mentioned; they plead, some of them even very eloquently, a very clear and very well-founded artistic principle; they maintain rightly that the first condition for a work of art is that it preserve the living quality of nature, rather than immobilizing it in a conventional rendering, and when one is beginning to be interested in them, when one is just about to concede their point, that's when the illness suddenly explodes in some aspect of their work. I have no objection to the section of the troubled souls, whose brains are haunted by singular hallucinations; they see nature in their own way, with red soil, purple trees, and fairyland skies; they have

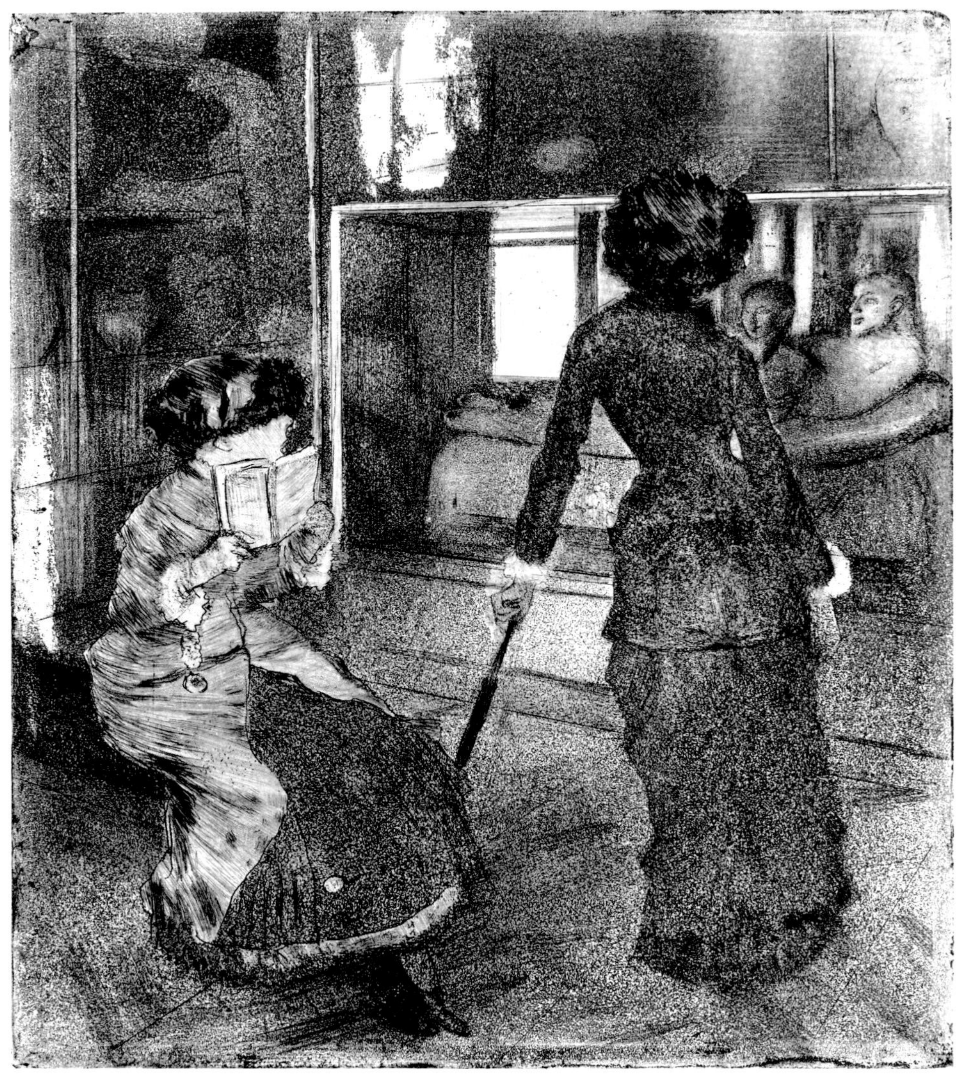

Edgar Degas. *At the Louvre: Mary Cassatt in the Etruscan Gallery* (seventh state). 1879–80. Soft-ground etching, drypoint, aquatint, and etching. 10 ½ × 9 ⅛ in. (26.7 × 23.2 cm). Courtesy of Museum of Fine Arts, Boston. Katherine E. Bullard Fund in memory of Francis Bullard and proceeds from the sale of duplicate prints.

arrived gradually at that state of exaltation for which there is no longer any remedy; they can only be pitied.

There is, though, the section of the merely ill, those who more or less make sense, and who, in repose, are quite lucid and full of talent, and who are, for that very reason, amazing for what a notable expenditure of very brilliant qualities is, alas! once more, embattled in some aspect of their work by that little bee. From this scientific point of view, Mlle. Cassatt is a true phenomenon; in more than one of her canvases, she is on the very brink of becoming a notable artist, with an extraordinary feeling for nature, a very penetrating capacity for observation, and a meditative subordination before the model that characterizes the unrivalled artists; then, just when this fine intelligence has labored well and while it is resting, the little bee takes up palette and brushes and makes its mark on the work, either in unlikely hands or a few utterly pointless areas of color, but always a deformed and monstrous aspect that makes one shiver, and say, "What a tragedy!"

What I have just said about Mlle. Cassatt, who adds some luster to the group of the Indépendants, is equally applicable to Mlle. Morisot, and most of all to M. Degas, the head of this league.

ACHILLE SEGARD

From *Mary Cassatt: Un Peintre des enfants et des mères*

On Cassatt's Place Among the Impressionists

1913

In the works of the great masters, there often merely appears to be a variety of subjects. The most profound, those most certain to survive as long as there are men and those men love painting, are those which have expressed perfectly a few sentiments that are common to many. To convey a general point of view from individual examples, to express an opinion of the society in which one lives (and on the world generally) by interpreting a particular category of subjects, to summarize and, as it were, to collect all their sensations, desires, and aspirations with regard to a single category of concrete motifs—all this is compatible with a variety of sentiments, an innumerable variety of pictorial sensations, a renewal of the means of expression, innovations in the palette, and new approaches to the execution.

Miss Mary Cassatt's choice implied a concern with psychological observation, comprehensive and generalized points of view concentrated in the faces of children, studies of movement in gestures and attitudes, and every kind of purely pictorial observation. Meanwhile, her choice of an order of sentiment earned her a unique place among the Impressionists. Strictly speaking, Degas was not a member of this group. In any case, his bitter irony, the terrible lucidity in his paintings of his judgements of men, the cruelty of his observations, and finally the incisive, striking quality of his whole oeuvre demonstrate that, where sentiment is concerned, he and Mary Cassatt have nothing in common.

The other members of the group were almost all landscape artists. So averse were they to anecdote, historical painting, and the painting of themes, that they eventually gave their attention entirely to the study and interpretation, through new means, of variations in atmospheric conditions. "The quality of the color of the air!": These words sum up Claude Monet's oeuvre fairly well. It was executed from an exclusively pictorial point of view. Barely cerebral, save unconsciously (for it is the property of genius to go beyond the limits that the will sets), [it is] even less intellectual. One can more or less summarize the essence of these works with two words: a gaze and a palette. Pissarro and Sisley also worked by approaching nature from a purely visual standpoint. Renoir was one of the few in this group to paint figures. He is one of the greatest painters of our age. Yet, one would be hard pressed to discern either subtleties of sentiment or psychological concerns among the many extraordinary qualities that cause us to consider him one of the greatest artists of the French school. He has been an extraordinary painter of the nude. He has been one of the greatest interpreters of the female body. He invented his palette and his draftsmanship; his personality and his originality are quick and passionate. He has painted three or four thousand pictures. Not one is unimportant. He has taken on every subject. He has painted in every circumstance and his whole life through. He is the demon of painting, incarnate for a century within a human being who has been driven entirely by this single preoccupation: the art of painting. Yet he seems to have had no other thought than to live through his eyes and to execute with virtuosity using beautiful materials. His feeling for the material is one of Renoir's greatest qualities. This material is wonderful, it is infinitely delicate, supple, thick, shining, and long-lasting. It is a delight. Yet, again, it must be noted that Renoir

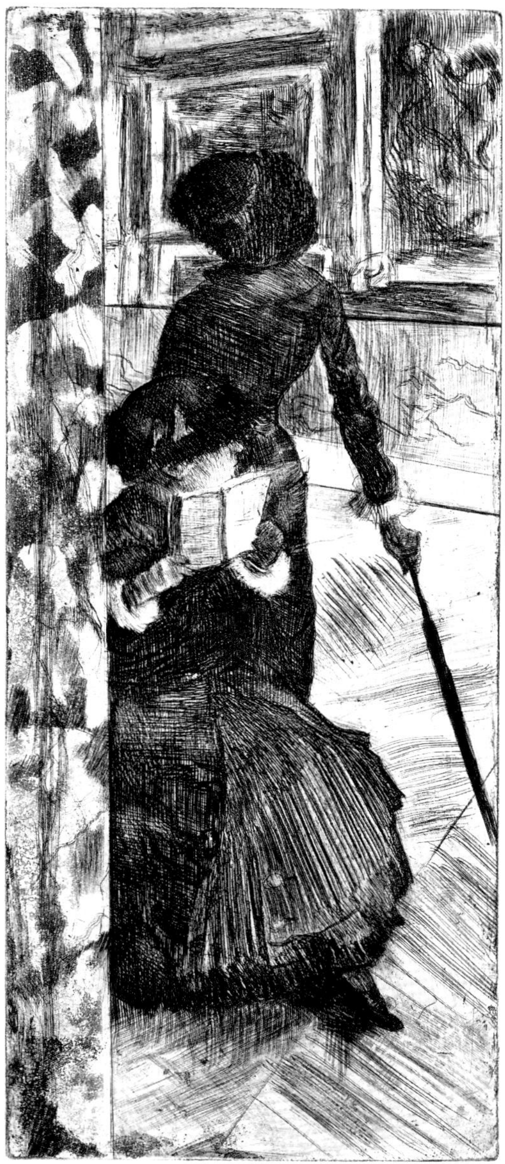

Edgar Degas. *At the Louvre: Mary Cassatt in the Paintings Gallery* (fifth state). 1879–80. Etching, drypoint, and aquatint. 12 × 5 in. (30.5 × 12.7 cm). Courtesy of Museum of Fine Arts, Boston. Katherine E. Bullard Fund in memory of Francis Bullard and proceeds from the sale of duplicate prints.

Alfred Sisley (1839–1899), Impressionist landscape painter. The "Mme. Sisley" that Cassatt painted in 1873 is believed to be a portrait of his wife (see COLORPLATE 11*).*

loves painting for its own sake and his materials for their own sake, and that his women's faces are magnificently but undeniably animal-like. The Impressionists in general were mad for the wonderland of atmospheric conditions, and the riches and brilliance of the palette. They remained strangers to the painting of individual expressions of the human soul. Within this group, Miss Mary Cassatt is an exception.

* * *

Perhaps hers was a more general and refined intellectual culture than that of her comrades in the 1879 Exposition. She was a friend of Mallarmé. Huysmans and Zola admired her, though they did not know her personally. She was ever a patient reader, passionate about history and archaeology. Looking at life's scenes, her feelings have been more than purely visual, she has been intellectual and emotional. One is aware that this artist has a painter's gaze, but also a questioning intelligence that is particularly dedicated to the problems surrounding the emotions, and that seeks to rise from the individual subject to general ideas.

Stéphane Mallarmé (1842–1898), a French poet, was an important member of the Symbolist literary movement, and a social friend of many Impressionist painters including Cassatt, Degas, and Morisot.

Joris-Karl Huysmans (1848–1907), French novelist who first worked under Émile Zola's influence and then developed an influential Symbolist style. His review of this and other Impressionist exhibitions appeared in his anthology of critical commentaries, "L'Art Moderne," in 1883.

Thus, she remains to some degree isolated within the group. She has had few personal dealings with Manet or Renoir, few, too, with Sisley. It was only because she happened to take a summer house near Pissarro's, in the region of the Oise, that there were neighborly relations between herself and Pissarro. They often worked from the same subject. "Pissarro," says Miss Mary Cassatt, "was such a teacher as might have taught the stones to draw accurately!" Yet she received no advice from him. Pissarro in the end is primarily a landscape artist, and Miss Mary Cassatt is exclusively a figure painter. There is nowhere in her oeuvre a landscape painted for its own sake. The gardens, parks, and greenery in her paintings are but backgrounds subordinated to the figures.

And there is not a single feature in these figures that could bring Pissarro to mind.

Let us add that, for the greater part of her career, Miss Mary Cassatt has not been a traveler. Her connection has always been Paris. This attachment to Paris, too, sets this artist apart from the other Impressionists, who almost all live in the country, carrying their easels from one picturesque spot to another, living the rustic life of the landscape artist, and maintaining some muted resentment or other against city life in general and Paris in particular. Miss Mary Cassatt loved Paris. She still loves it. She has never left it. When she goes to Egypt, returns to Italy or Spain, or visits the French provinces, these trips are for her a rest, or a distraction. They are occasions to see museums, to refine her cultural education, to pursue her interest in people and what they make, but these travels are not work. The atmosphere of the Ile de France has been necessary to her investigations. She has rarely worked outside of this atmosphere. Her models are almost always city-dwellers. When they are children or women of the countryside, a refinement in their coloring and a certain treatment of the facial expressions reveal that they have been seen through a city-woman's eyes.

Such is her place among the Impressionists. She agrees with all the others when it comes to the use of lively and brilliant tones; new and unpredictable harmonies of color; certain peculiarities of composition, or, properly speaking, of the *mise en toile;* the need to allow neither anecdote nor any conventional subject; the belief that realism is indispensable; a scrupulous conception of artistic conscience, which demands that one transcribe only emotions that one has experienced sincerely; the obligation to work only directly from nature. But Miss Mary Cassatt is set apart from all the others by the intellectual quality of her feelings, and by a sort of emotional lyricism that is revealed, in her work, through faces, gestures, and movements alone.

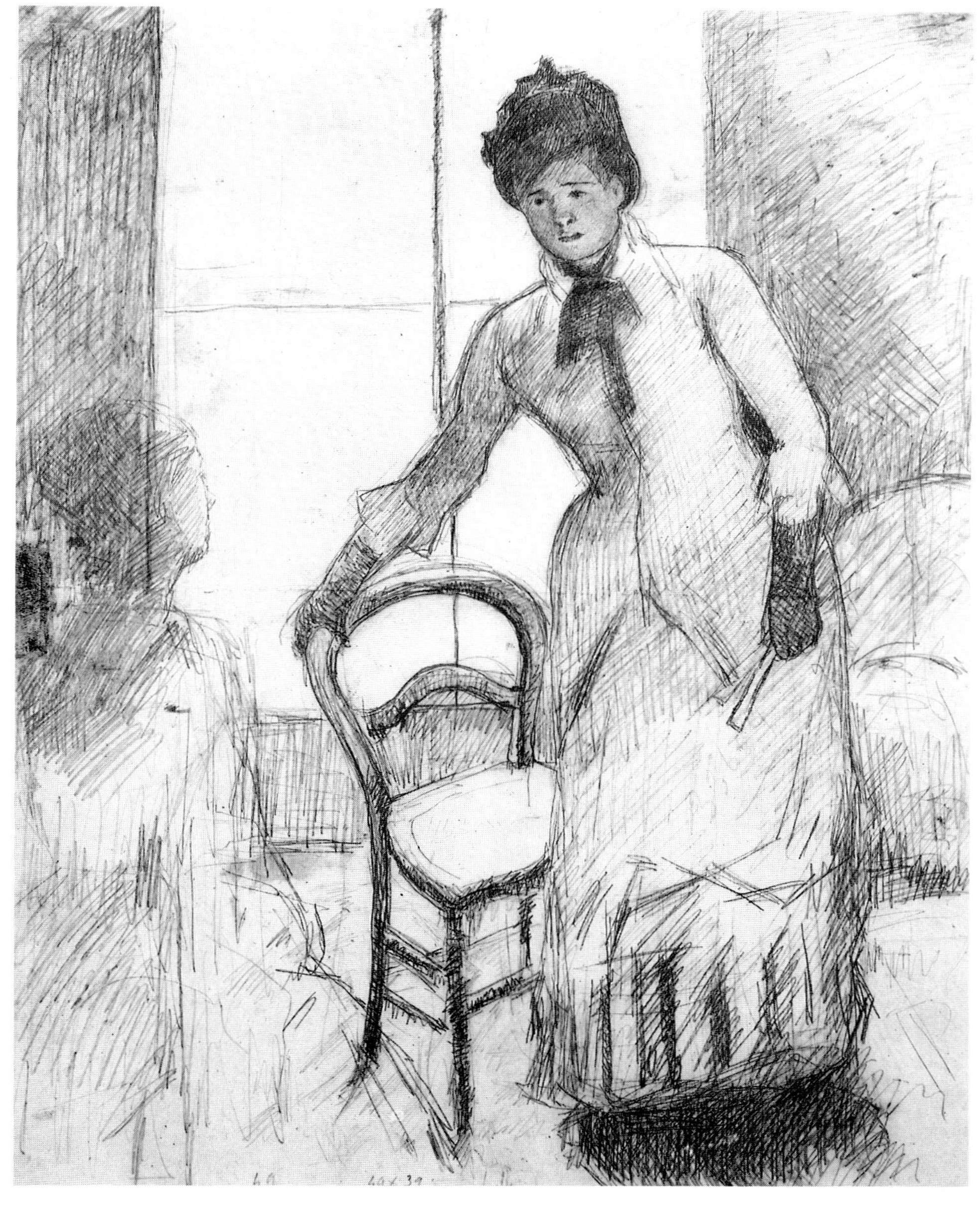

The Visitor. c. 1879–80. Graphite. 15 3/4 × 12 3/16 in. (40 × 30.9 cm). © The Cleveland Museum of Art. Gift of Fifty Members of The Print Club of Cleveland on the Occasion of the Fiftieth Anniversary.

JORIS-KARL HUYSMANS

From *L'Art Moderne:* "L'Exposition des Indépendants en 1881"

On Cassatt's Babies

1883

I wrote last year that most of Mlle. Cassatt's canvases recall M. Degas's pastels, and that one of them derived from the modern English masters.

From these two influences an artist has emerged who today is beholden to no one, an artist who is entirely spontaneous and personal.

Her exhibition consists of portraits of children, interiors, gardens, and it is a miracle how, in these subjects, beloved of the English painters, Mlle. Cassatt has been able to avoid the sentimentality that most of them have knocked up against in all their works, both written and painted.

Oh, my God! those babies! How those portraits have made my flesh crawl, time and again!—A whole passel of English and French smearers has painted them in such stupid, pretentious poses!—The moderns were still battening on the foolishness of dead painters, to the point where even

Henri IV playing horsy with kids became tolerable. For the first time, thanks to Mlle. Cassatt, I have seen effigies of enchanting tots, calm and bourgeois scenes, painted with an utterly charming sort of delicate tenderness. Besides, it must be repeated, only woman is qualified to paint childhood. There is a feeling there that a man could not render; unless they are singularly sensitive and nervous, his fingers are too thick and ungainly not to leave clumsy and brutal marks; only woman can pose a child, dress it, put in pins without sticking herself; unfortunately, she then turns to simpering or the teary eye, like Mlle. Élisa Koch in France and Mme. Ward in England; but Mlle. Cassatt, thank God, is neither one of these daubers, and the gallery in which her canvases hang contains a mother reading, surrounded by tykes, and another mother kissing her baby on the cheeks—they are irreproachable, softly lustrous pearls; they are family life painted with distinction, with love; one automatically thinks of those modest domestic scenes of Dickens's, those Esther Summersons, Florence Dombeys, Agnes Copperfields, little Dorritts, and Ruth Pinches, who so fondly dandle their children on their knees, while in the quiet room the copper kettle hums, and the low light on the table brings the teapot and cups to life, and cuts in two the farther plate on which slices of bread and butter are stacked. There is, in this series of Mlle. Cassatt's works, such an affective understanding of the good-tempered life, such an insightful sensation of intimacy, that to find their like one would have to go back to Everett Millais's painting *Les Trois Soeurs,* exhibited in 1878, in the English section.

Elisa Koch, nineteenth-century French painter, specialized in portraits in oil and pastel.

Henrietta Mary Ada Ward (1832–1924), English painter who, as a mother of eight, executed numerous portraits of children.

Sir John Everett Millais (1829–1896), English Pre-Raphaelite painter.

Two other paintings—one called *Le Jardin,* in which a woman in the foreground reads, while, slantwise behind her, green masses dotted with the red stars of geraniums and bordered with the deep purple of Chinese nettle rise up to the house, the lower part of which edges the canvas, and the other titled *Le Thé,* in which a lady dressed in pink is smiling in an armchair, holding a small cup in her gloved hands—add to this tender, private note a further delicate undertone of Parisian refinements.

COLORPLATE 21

COLORPLATE 20

And therein is an inherent mark peculiar to her talent: Mlle. Cassatt, who is American, I believe, paints French women for us; yet she brings to her very Parisian homes the benevolent smile of the "at home"; she elicits from Paris what none of our painters could express, the joyous quietude, the tranquil simplicity of an interior.

ACHILLE SEGARD

From *Mary Cassatt: Un Peintre des enfants et des mères*

Cassatt and Impressionist Printmaking

1913

They are all the more spontaneous for the immediacy of Miss Cassatt's working method. She engraves directly onto copper, from the model, with no preliminary study or drawing. She uses a point as others use a pencil. Now, since the process allows for neither retouching (which painters call pentimenti) nor corrections, it follows that she must obtain the desired result at the first attempt or abandon the plate. One infers that she achieved this mastery only through long preliminary efforts. This precision and sureness in the lines are the reward for countless exercises. It is surprising that she has been able to achieve, by this method, the synthetical

Cassatt actually used a drypoint process in which she used a diamond-tipped needle to scratch lines into the copper.

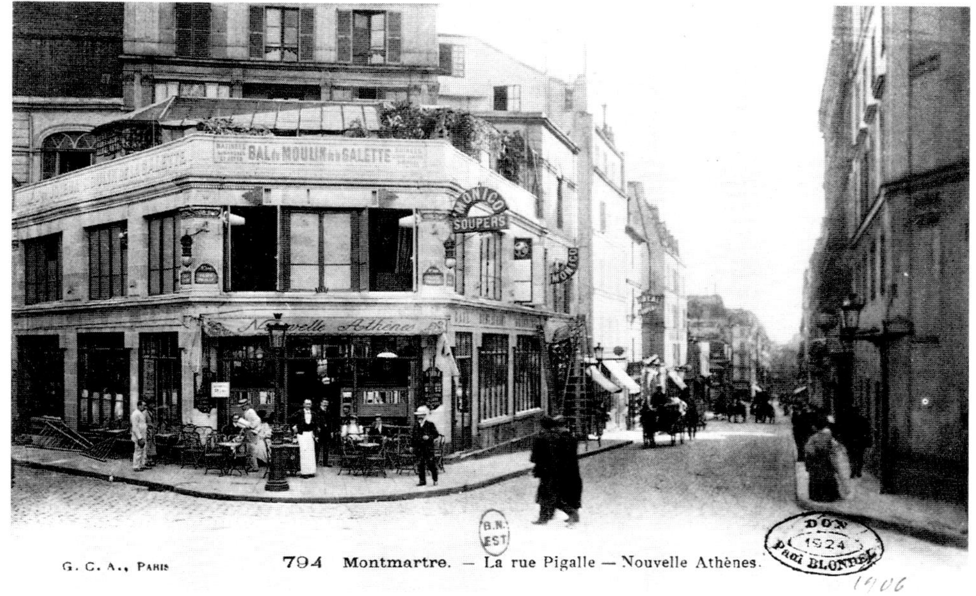

Photograph of the Café Nouvelle Athènes (c. 1906), Paris, a gathering place of the Impressionists. Cassatt's studio was only a few doors away. Photograph © Bibliothèque Nationale de France, Paris.

conciseness of certain foreshortenings. We can already see in the work the moral benefits that she has gained by this severe discipline. In front of the aquatint that represents the artist's mother and sister, the one reading, the other sewing, in the dimness of a cozy room, by the luminous globe of a table lamp that gathers all the light and projects a large,bright area, Miss Cassatt once exclaimed in my presence: "*That's* what teaches you to draw!" With these words, we grasp the aim that, willy-nilly, she has pursued. Printmaking has served as her drawing school.

CHRISTIAN BRINTON

Christian Brinton (1871–1942), American author and critic.

From *International Studio*

"Concerning Miss Cassatt and Certain Etchings"

November 1905

It is consoling to recall that the early struggles of the Impressionist painters in France were made less bitter and were in many ways brightened through the efforts of certain exceptional women. When Pissarro and Monet returned from London obscure and unregarded, the movement had few champions. The slender and often dubious little band used to meet nightly at the Café de la Nouvelle Athénée in order to discuss various theories of color. Zola helped them rigorously in "Mes Haines," and other recruits came forward, but for the most part they were compelled to bear alone the combined derision of press and public. What was even more rueful, they were scarcely able to exist on the proceeds of their sales, canvases by Sisley, Renoir and Pissarro bringing with difficulty $5.00, $10.00 and $20.00 apiece. Sharing from the outset their disappointments, and in several instances their poverty, were four of the only women who have ever contributed materially to a new phase of art. Of these, three were Frenchwomen. They were later joined by the fourth, an American. Any reference to Impressionism in France would be incomplete without the names of

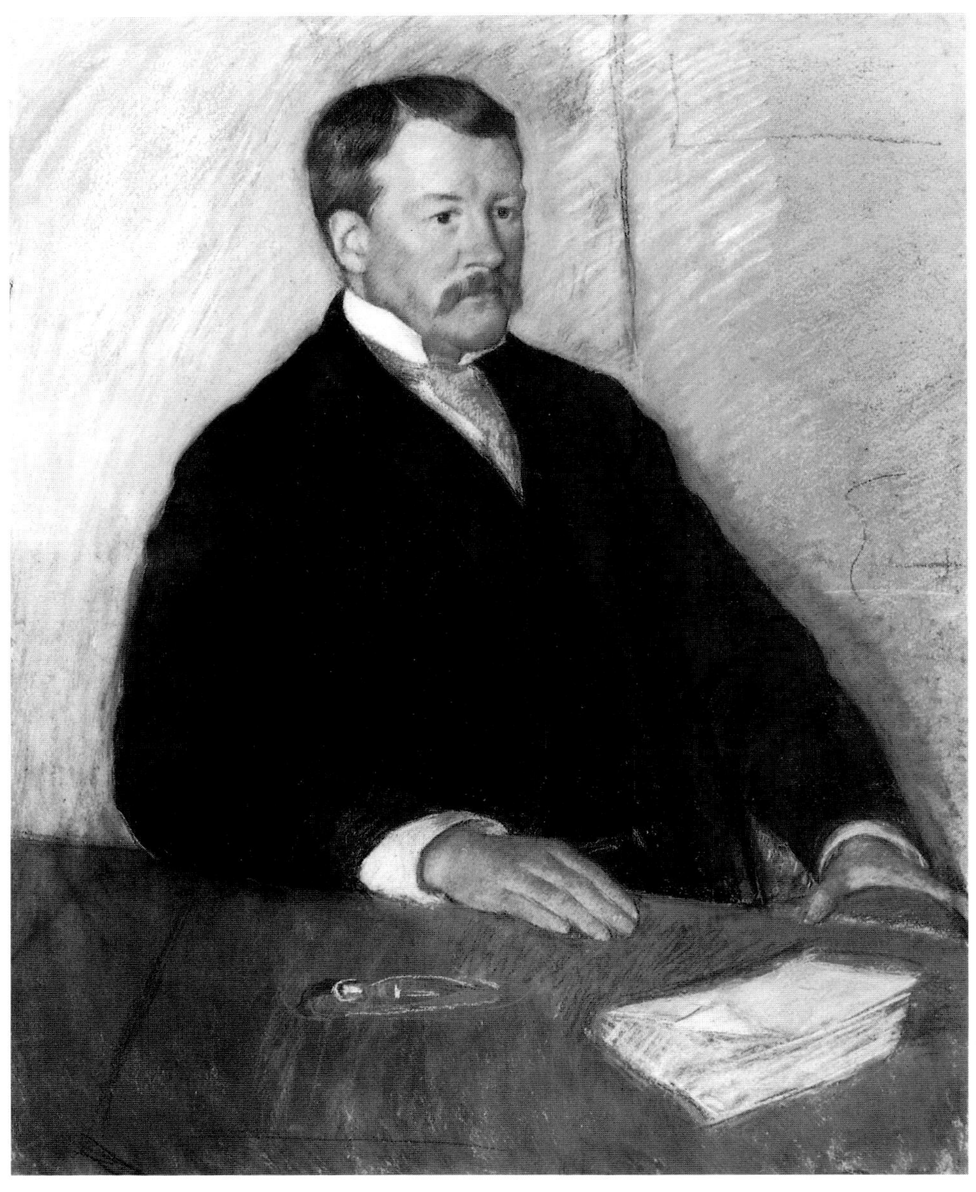

Portrait of Alexander J. Cassatt. 1888. Pastel. 35 1/2 × 27 3/4 in. (90.2 × 70.5 cm). The Seattle Art Museum. Gift of Mr. and Mrs. Louis Brechemin, by exchange. Photograph: Paul Macapia.

Mlle. Berthe Morisot, Mme. Marie Bracquemond, Mlle. Eva Gonzalès and Miss Mary Cassatt, for it was they who gave the movement that essential touch of humanity it might otherwise have lacked. While Monet and Sisley were painting so luminously along the coast or amid the summer radiance of the fields, Mlle. Berthe Morisot and Miss Mary Cassatt were studying that same undulant play of light in the boudoir, the library, or the green and gold of garden and orchard. The impersonality of haystack or strip of water they supplemented by the intimacy of the dressing room and the nursery. They were natural Impressionists, for painting with them was never divorced from the pervasive instincts of domesticity and of maternity.

Marie Bracquemond (1841–1916), French Impressionist painter and printmaker, married printmaker Félix Bracquemond in 1869.

Eva Gonzalès (1849–1883), French Impressionist figure painter and, like Cassatt, a student of Charles Chaplin.

Expressive and full of gracious allure as their art was, the work of Miss Cassatt for virility, for dignity and for serious intent frankly transcends that of her sister Impressionistes. In her numerous versions of mother and child, or of child and nurse, so penetrating, so tender, and yet so devoid of sentimentality, she has sounded the deepest note of the four. The others were sometimes absorbed by transient considerations; Miss Cassatt seldom forgets the inherent significance of her subject. The diffused glow of a quiet interior, or the sharper definition of an outdoor scene, have always meant less to her than a direct presentation of her main theme. She is, first and last, a figure painter; one who chooses natural, inevitable surroundings rather than the fictitious background of convention.

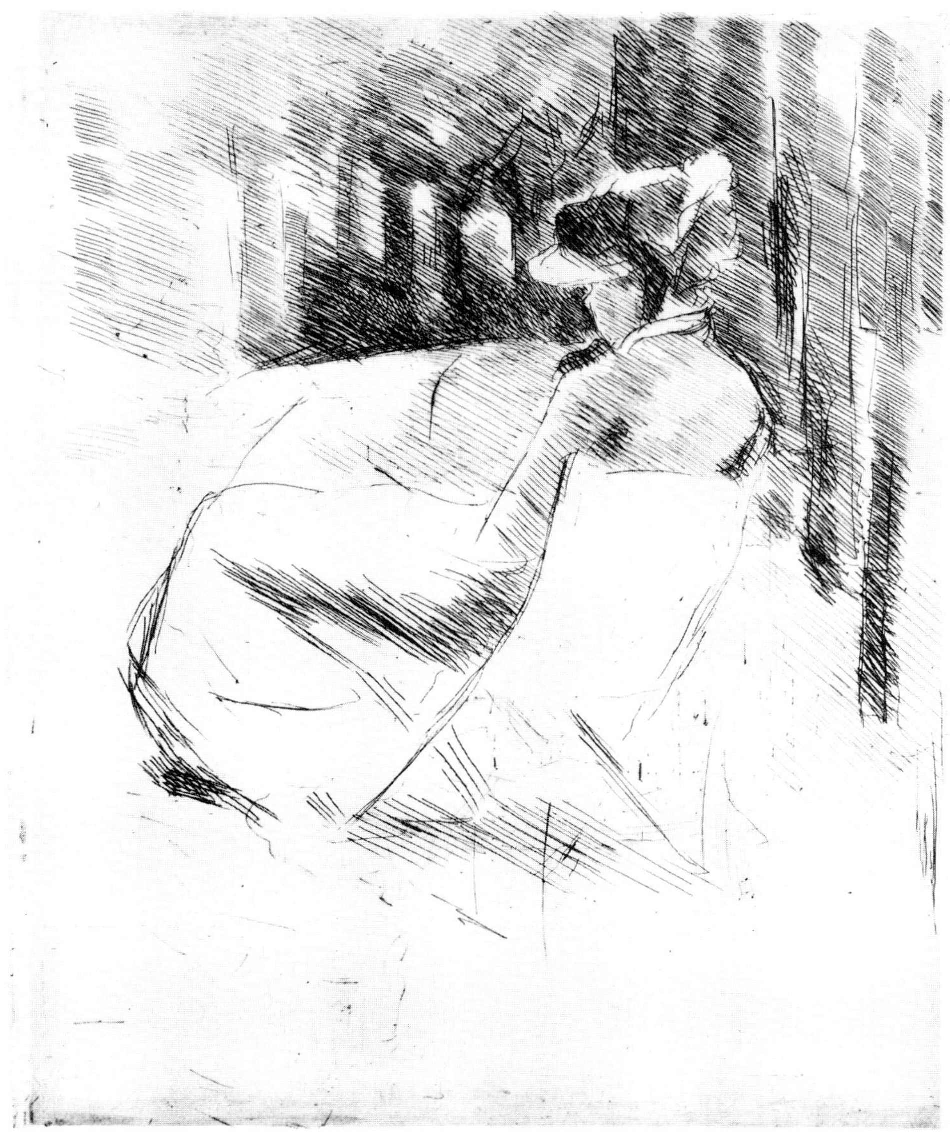

The Folding Chair. c. 1880. Etching. 7 7/8 × 6 1/8 in. (20 × 15.5 cm). The Metropolitan Museum of Art, New York. The Rogers Fund. Photograph © The Metropolitan Museum of Art.

GUSTAVE GEFFROY

From *La Vie artistique*

On Harmony in Cassatt's Paintings

1893

It is impossible not to surrender to the charm of many of these light-filled paintings, velvety pastels, and firm and supple engraved drawings. From the works of her earliest years of her time in Paris, to yesterday's works, the progression of her talent is apparent; the sureness of the drawing and the accuracy of the coloration are more in evidence, a particular expression is confirmed: a refined way of seeing women and children in the light of gardens, in light-filled rooms veiled by blinds.

En brodant is one such: a woman wrapped in a shawl, wearing a large white hat, sitting at the entrance to a flowered allée. Her face is faintly visible in the luminous air, and yet her expression is deep and languid. She is at the beginning of life's autumn, it is a gentle and melancholy feeling. Another such is *La Tasse de thé:* a woman in pink dress and hat, who holds a cup with gloved fingers. Her skin is delicate and wan, her delicate, prudent profile expresses the ceremonial of the visit, the armored politeness, the conversation listened to, the next reply. Another such is the *Jeune fille se coiffant,* all fresh from her morning ablutions—others such are other por-

COLORPLATE 21

COLORPLATE 20

COLORPLATE 41

traits of women, outdoors or at the theater; young girls; children glimpsed beneath trees, on lawns, in the sun, in the corners of windows, bathed in light. There is usually an explicit harmony among the healthy, breathing skin, the light-colored fabrics, and the tender greenery. The drawing bends to the softnesses of the fabrics, the nervousness of the hands, the inflections of the supple bodies. Her color blends the tones of objects and the degrees of light and shadow, in exact proportions.

There truly is, in these representations of children blossoming like flowers, young girls as lithe and fresh as sturdily growing plants, there is more than painting—a sort of emanation of life, made up of summer's temperature and the scent of flesh. That is, I believe, the essential character of this art of Mary Cassatt's, the aspect of beauty that captivates her. She rightfully loves the balance of bodies, the graceful movements of arms, the complexions of faces. She seeks out these external aspects, this fine health, this physiological tranquillity of human beings. But there is also an expression, and it is not here that one will find the quiverings and agonies of the maternal spirit, the silently suffering faces, the embraces that love the moment and fear the future. It is enough that the artist has seen exactly, in the gardens where she likes to find the surroundings for her art, the pink children, playing or frowning and trying out gestures, and the women with their freckled faces, hard rural countenances, and clearcut, serious, impassive faces, the nursery-maids from the villages, the correct governesses, and the peaceful mothers.

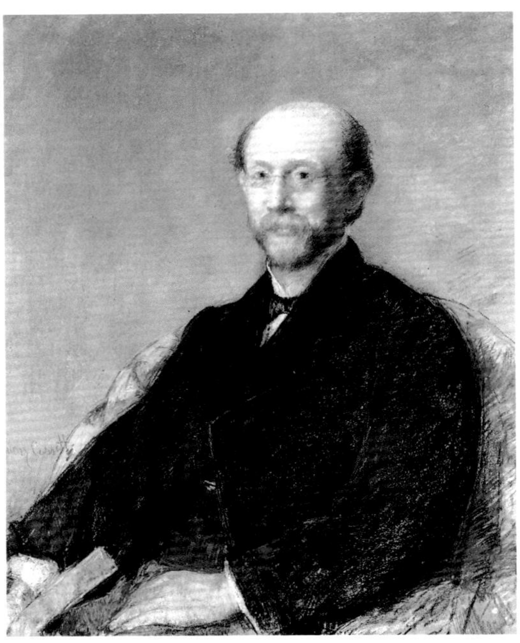

Moïse Dreyfus. 1879. Pastel on paper mounted on canvas. 32 × 25 5/8 in. (81.3 × 65 cm). Musée du Petit Palais, Paris. Gift of Justin Mayer in the name of Mme. Moïse Dreyfus, in memory of Moïse Dreyfus. Photograph © Photothèque des Musées de la Ville de Paris, SPADEM.

Letter from Katherine Cassatt to Her Granddaughter, Katharine Cassatt

On the Family Group

April 15, 1881

13, avenue Trudaine
April 15

My dear Katharine,

Your & Robbie's very nice letters which gave us all a great deal of pleasure were received some time ago . . . I hope you are all quite well & happy enjoying the mild spring weather which I hear you are having—I dare say you are galloping on your ponies all over the country. . . .

We are going out to Marly again on the 1st of May to that pretty old place that we missed getting last year—you would all have enjoyed the garden so much—there are so many places to play hide & seek in that we shall long to have you all with us & your Aunt Mary counts on painting out of doors & wishes she had you all there to put in her pictures—Do you remember the one she painted of you & Rob & Elsie listening to me reading fairy tales? She finished it after you left & it is now at the exhibition—A gentleman wants to buy it but I don't think your Aunt Mary will sell it—she could hardly sell her mother & nieces & nephew I think—

. . . When you write tell me how the music comes on. . . . Did Eddy get his postage stamps and were they of any value? . . .

All join in love to Mama & Papa & all the children—With best love & kisses all round I am your affectionate

Grandmother Cassatt

Katharine Cassatt (1871–1905), Mary Cassatt's niece, born July 30, 1871, was the second child and elder daughter of Aleck and Lois Cassatt.

Marly-le-Roi, a town outside of Paris where the Cassatts rented summer homes in 1880 and 1881. In 1880 Aleck and Lois brought their four children to stay with Mary and Mr. and Mrs. Cassatt at Marly.

COLORPLATE 26

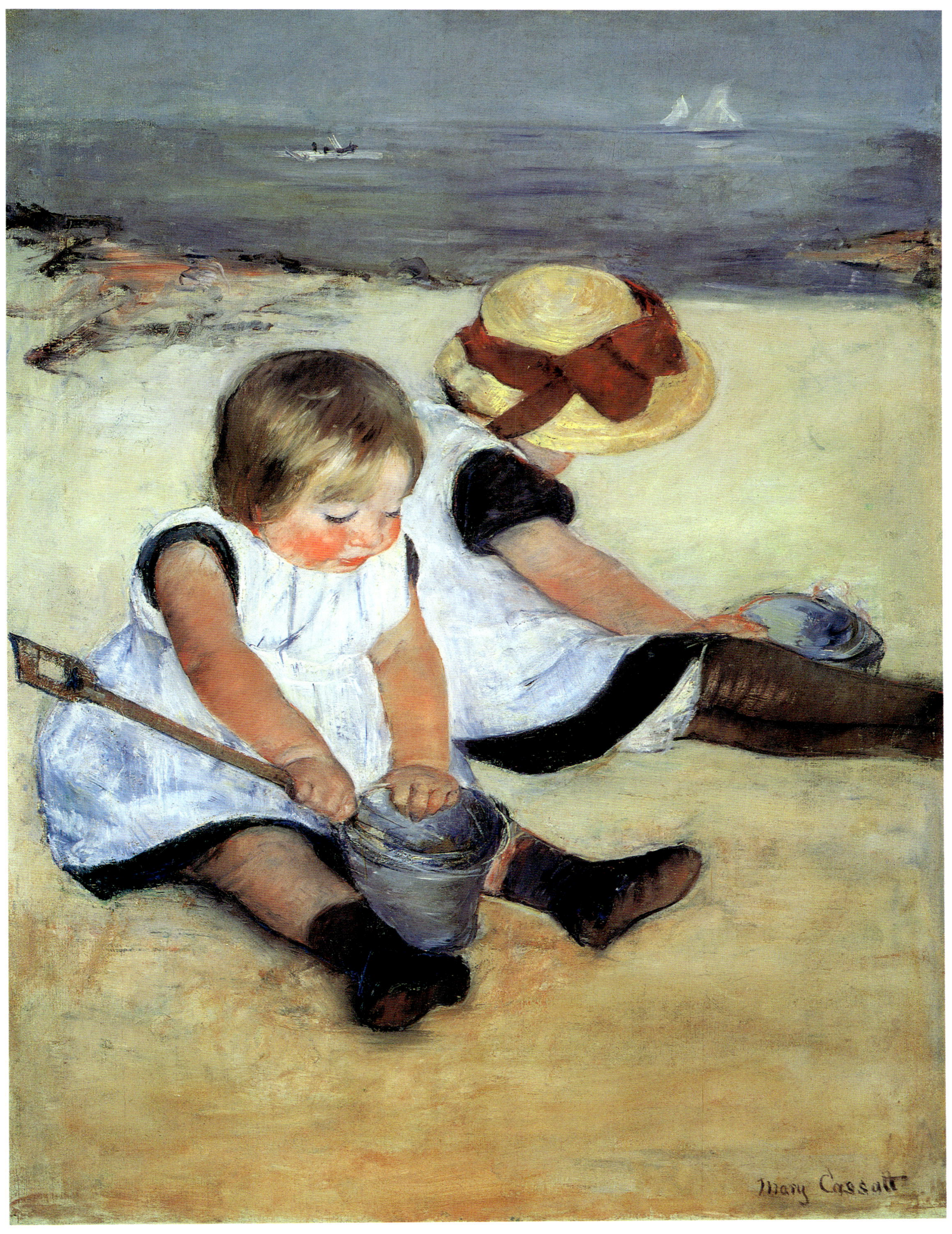

COLORPLATE 37. *Children Playing on the Beach.* 1884. Oil on canvas. 38 3/8 × 29 1/4 in. (97 × 74 cm).
National Gallery of Art. The Ailsa Mellon Bruce Collection.
Photograph © Board of Trustees, National Gallery of Art, Washington, D.C.

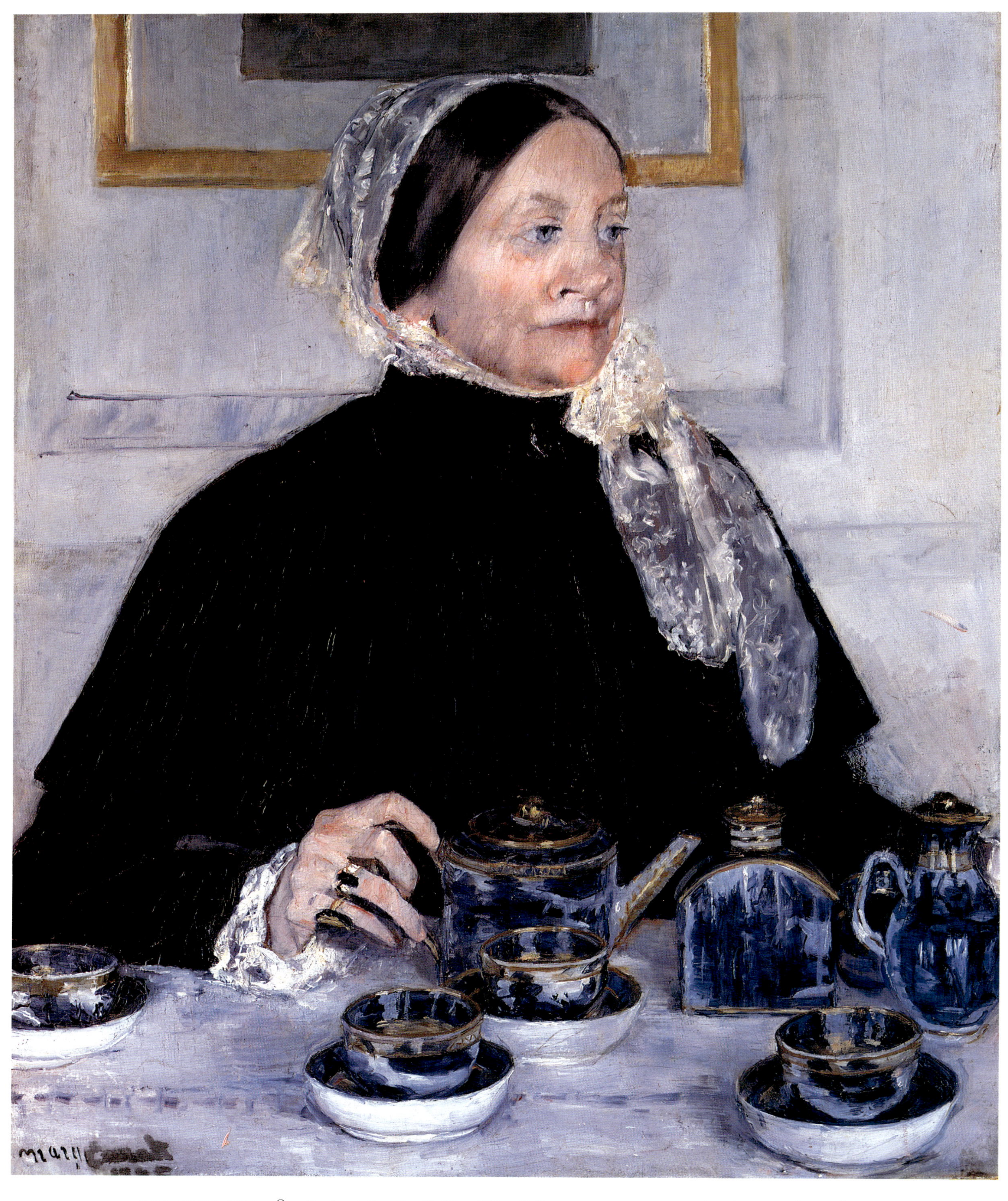

COLORPLATE 38. *Lady at the Tea Table.* 1883. Oil on canvas. 29 × 24 in. (73.4 × 61 cm). The Metropolitan Museum of Art, New York. Gift of the artist, 1923 (23.101).

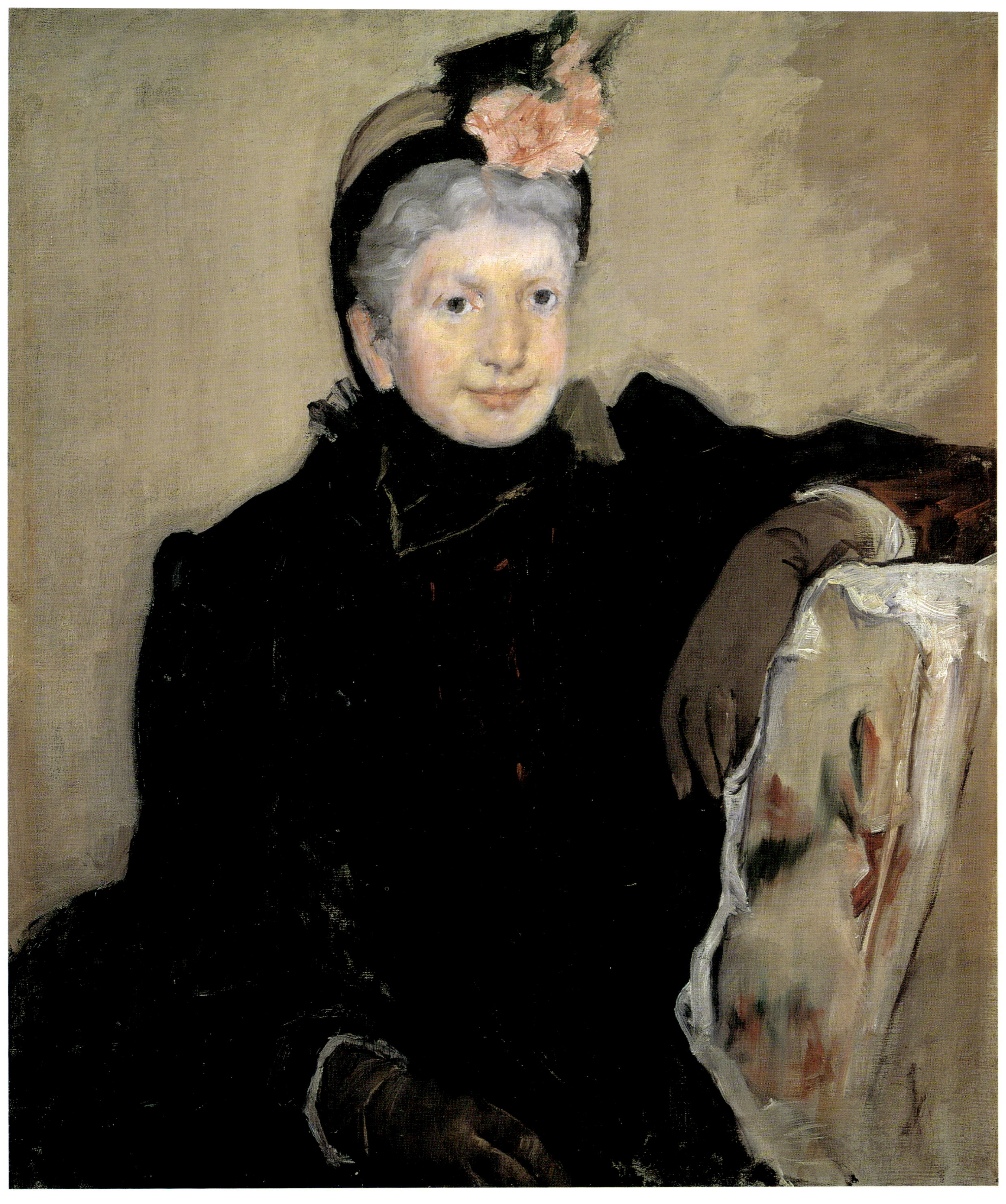

COLORPLATE 39. *Portrait of an Elderly Lady.* c. 1883. Oil on canvas. 28 ¾ × 23 ¾ in. (73 × 60.3 cm). National Gallery of Art. The Chester Dale Collection. Photograph © Board of Trustees, National Gallery of Art, Washington, D.C.

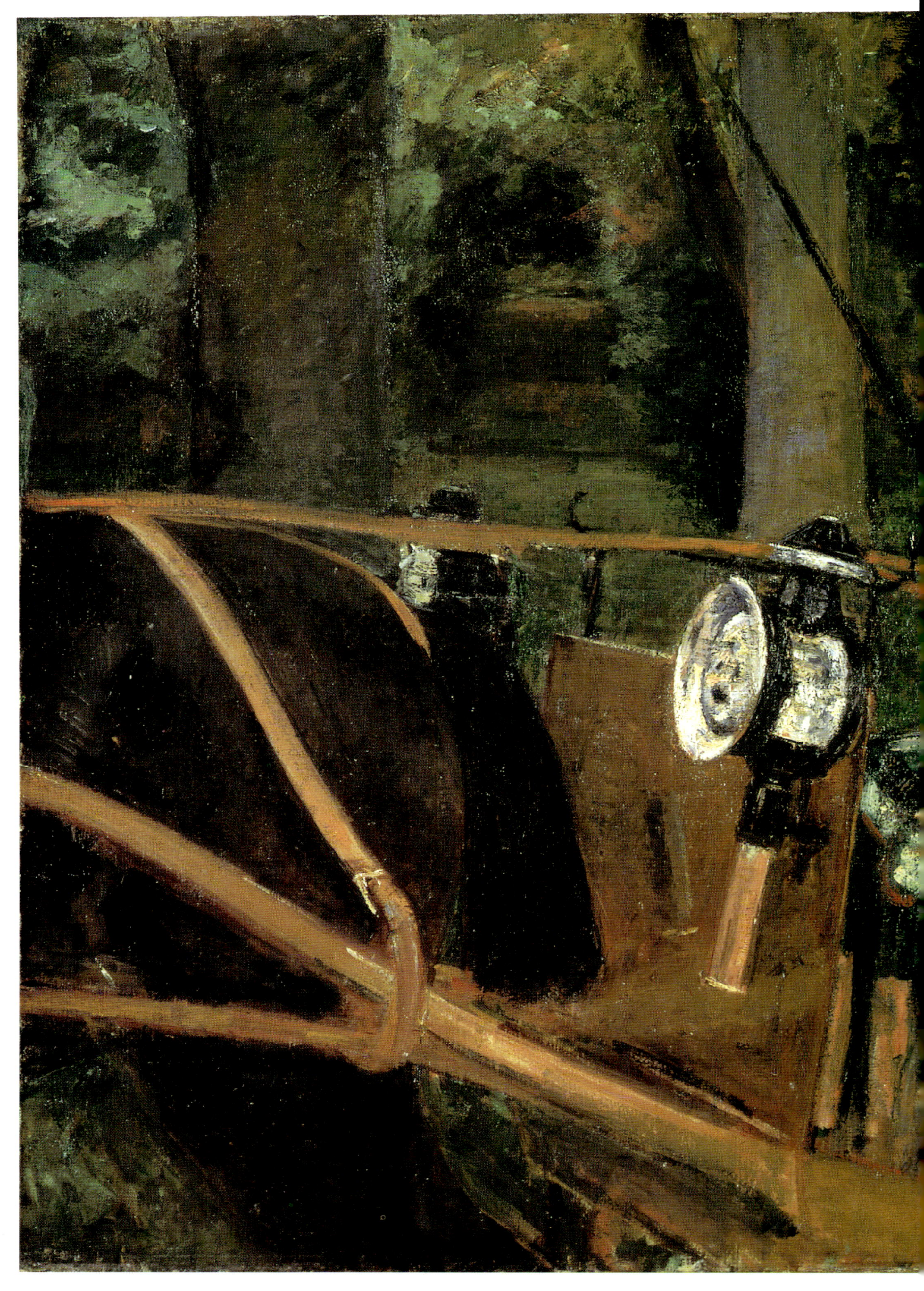

COLORPLATE 40. *Woman and Child Driving.* 1881. Oil on canvas. 35 ¼ × 51 ½ in. (89.5 × 130.8 cm). Philadelphia Museum of Art. The W.P. Wilstach Collection.

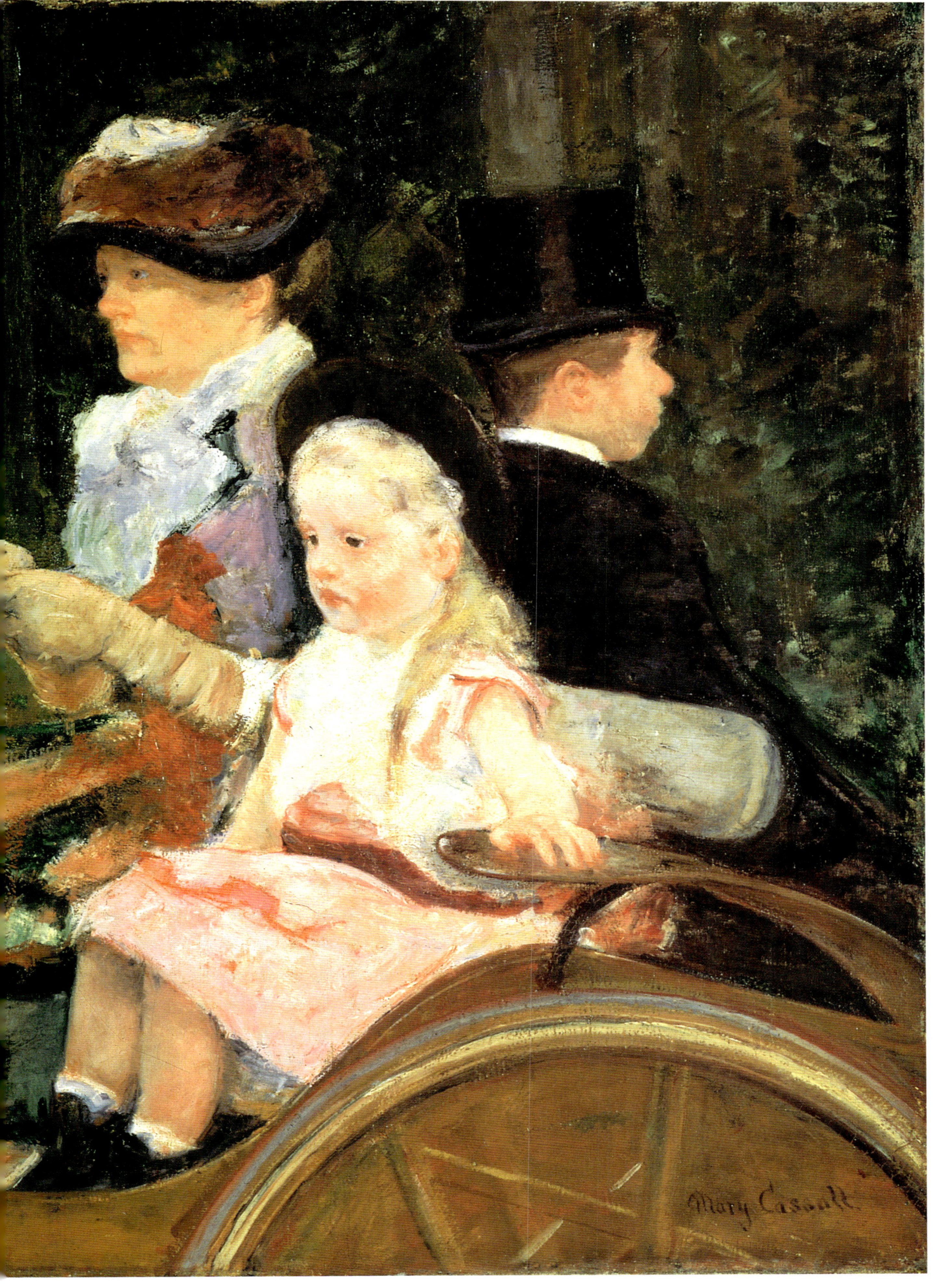
Mary Cassatt

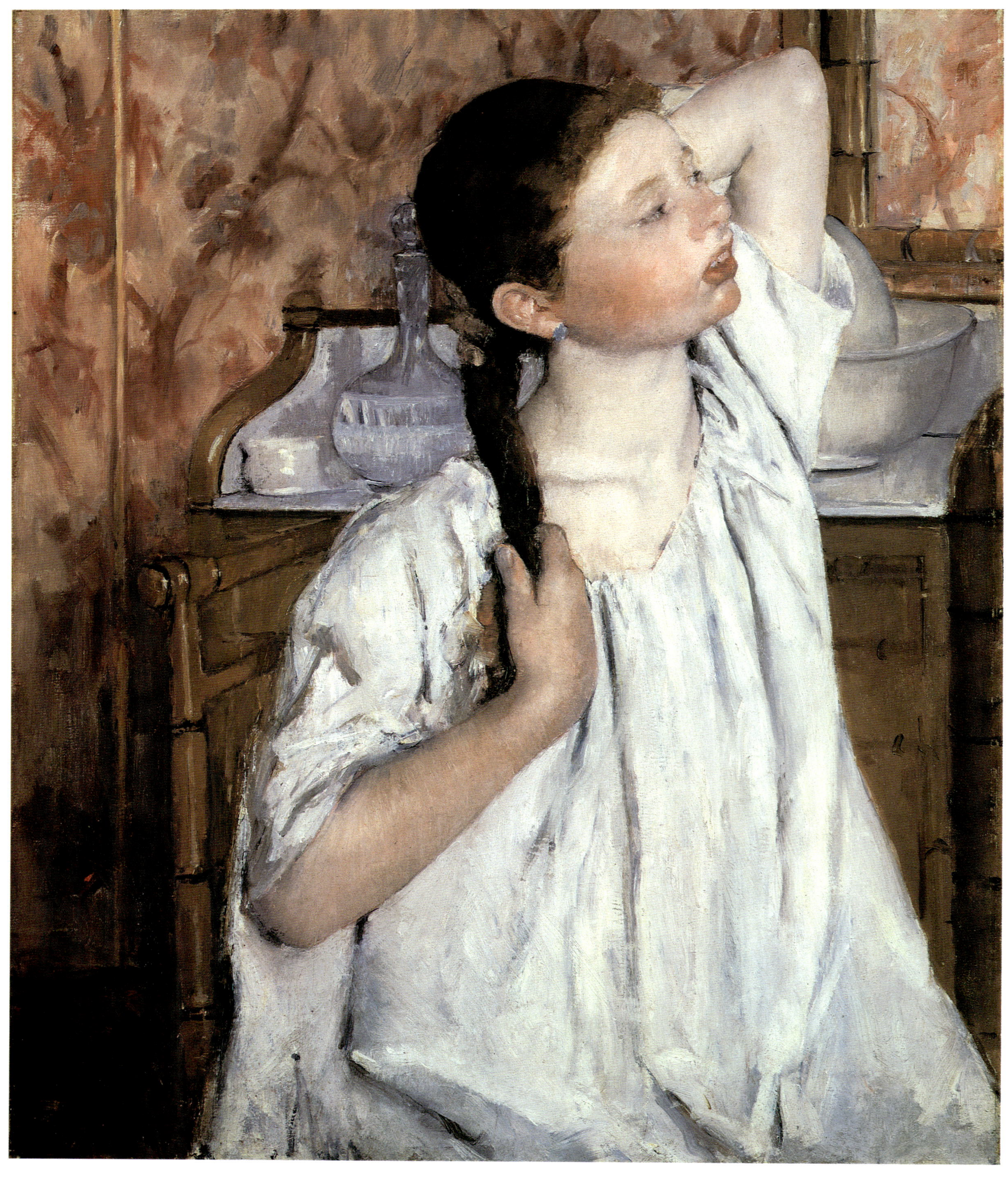

COLORPLATE 41. *Girl Arranging Her Hair.* 1886. Oil on canvas. 29 5/8 × 24 5/8 in. (75.2 × 62.5 cm).
National Gallery of Art. The Chester Dale Collection.
Photograph © Board of Trustees, National Gallery of Art, Washington, D.C.

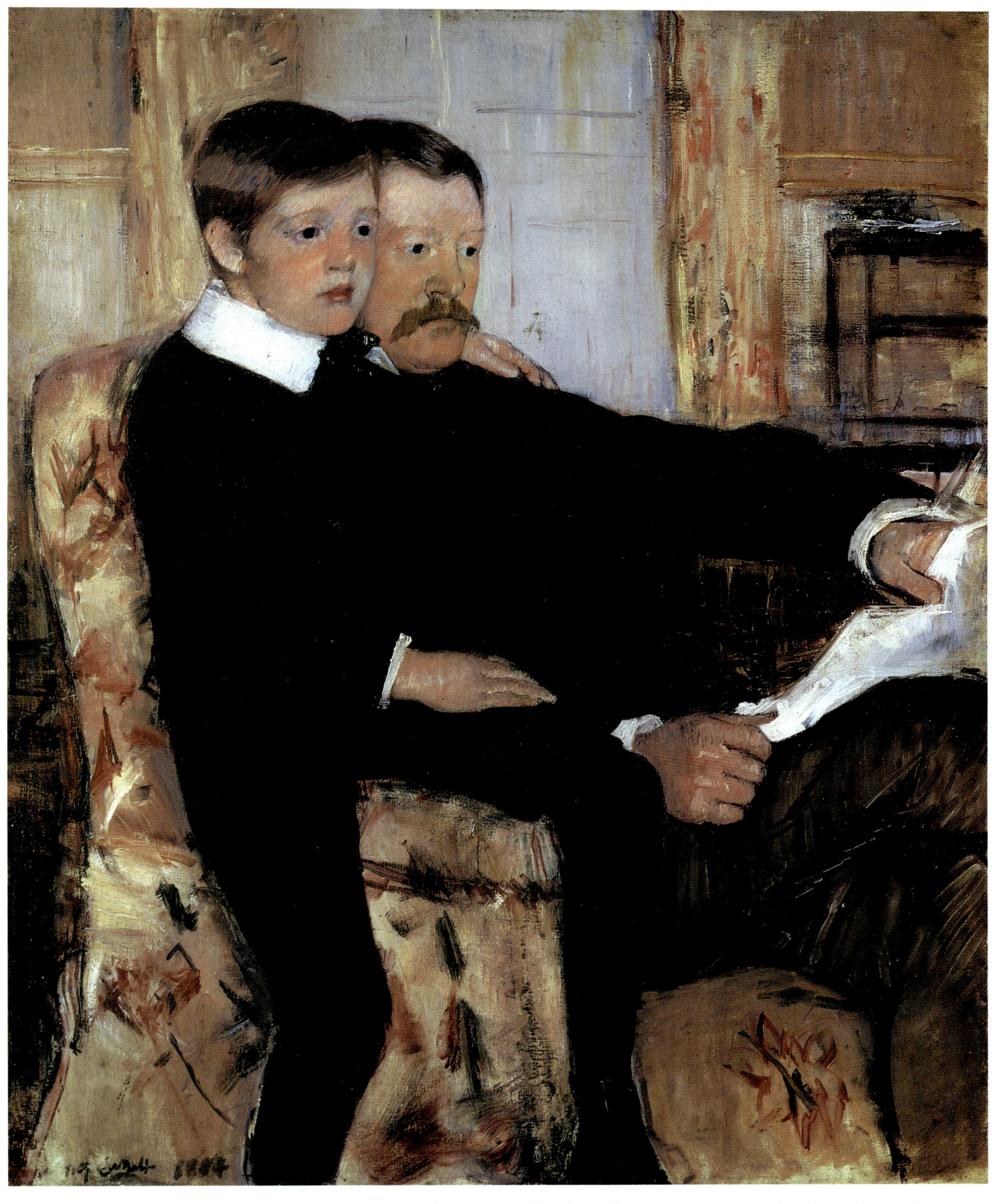

COLORPLATE 42. *Alexander Cassatt and His Son Robert.* 1884–85. Oil on canvas. 39 × 32 in. (99 × 81.2 cm). Philadelphia Museum of Art. The W.P. Wilstach Collection.

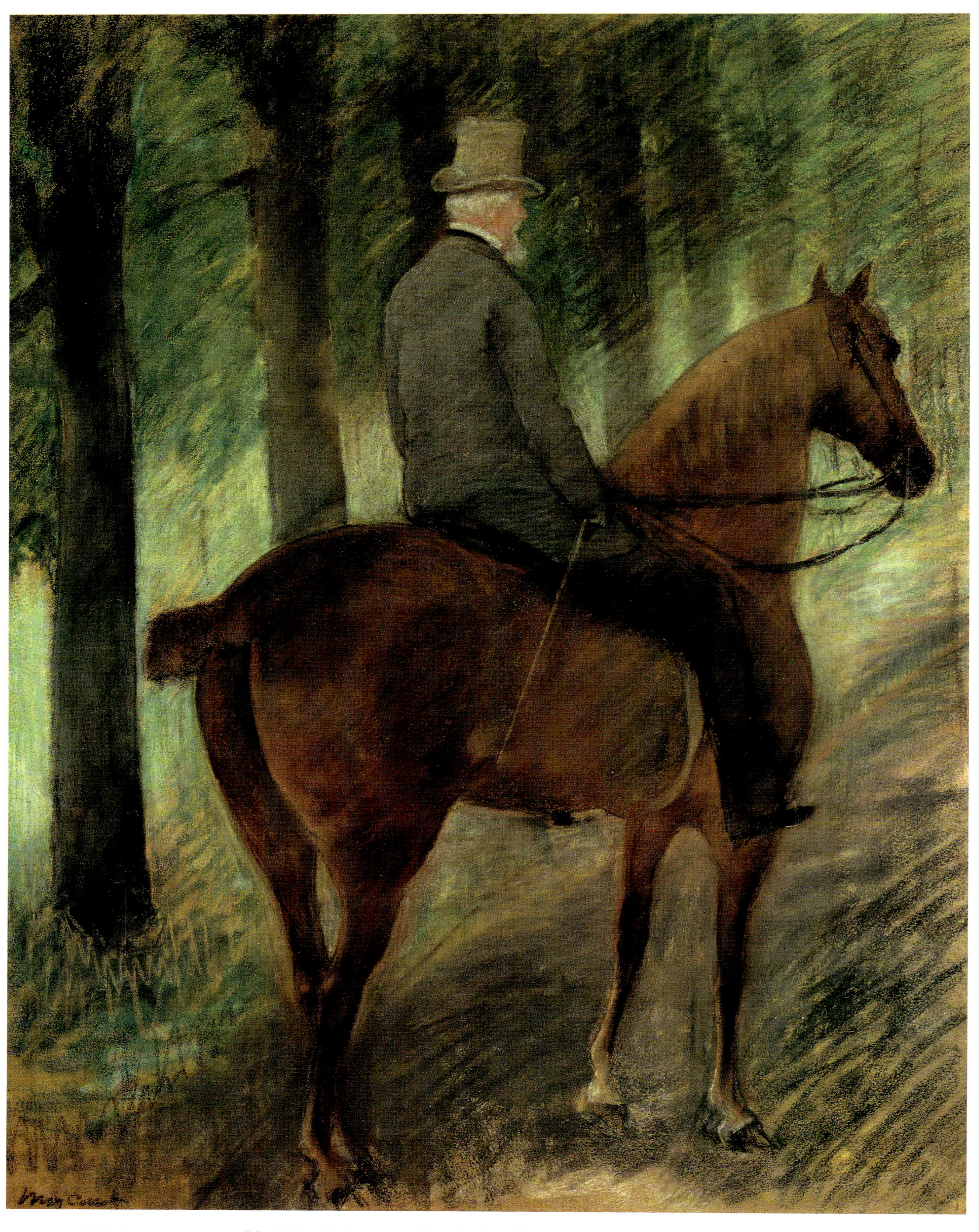

COLORPLATE 43. *Mr. Robert S. Cassatt on Horseback.* 1885. Pastel on paper. 36 × 28 in. (91.4 × 71 cm). Private collection, Toronto.

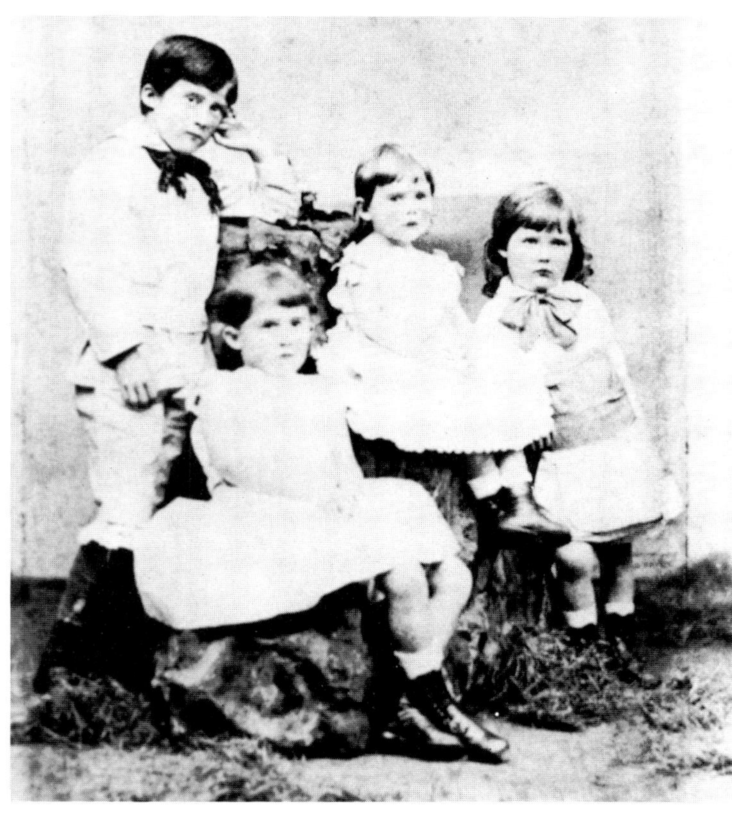

Photograph of the children of Alexander and Lois Cassatt. c. 1878. From left, Eddie, Katharine, Elsie, and Robert. Location of original unknown.

Letter from Mary Cassatt to Her Brother, Alexander Cassatt

On *Mrs. Cassatt Reading to Her Grandchildren*

June 22, 1883

13, avenue Trudaine
Friday, June 22

Dear Aleck,

I have a few minutes before the mail goes out to tell you about the picture business. Dreyfus told me finally that I might have the group of Mother & the children for you. I would rather keep it myself but I know he would not be pleased if I made him give it up to anyone but you. He won't take back the money for the picture, I am either to paint a portrait of his wife or if she won't consent to that I am to give them another picture; so as soon as the London exhibition is over I will send you Elsies portrait and the group. Please tell Lois I think the group will look well in a light room; that is light paper & perhaps over a door; it is painted to look as much like frescoe as possible so that it would be appropriate over a door as the Italian painters used to do, they are called "dessus de porte" here. About your portrait I am undecided, I am not satisfied with it, I think the one I did at Marly the best of the two; I will make up my mind when Gard comes, I am anxious to know whether he will think it like; whatever his opinion will be I know he wont conceal it, frankness is his virtue. . . . With much love to all

Moïse Dreyfus, a Frenchman, was both a patron and friend of Cassatt. Cassatt executed a pastel portrait of M. Dreyfus, which was exhibited in the Fourth Impressionist Exhibition in 1879.

COLORPLATE 26

Cassatt's younger brother, Joseph Gardner Cassatt (1849–1911).

Your affectionate sister
Mary Cassatt

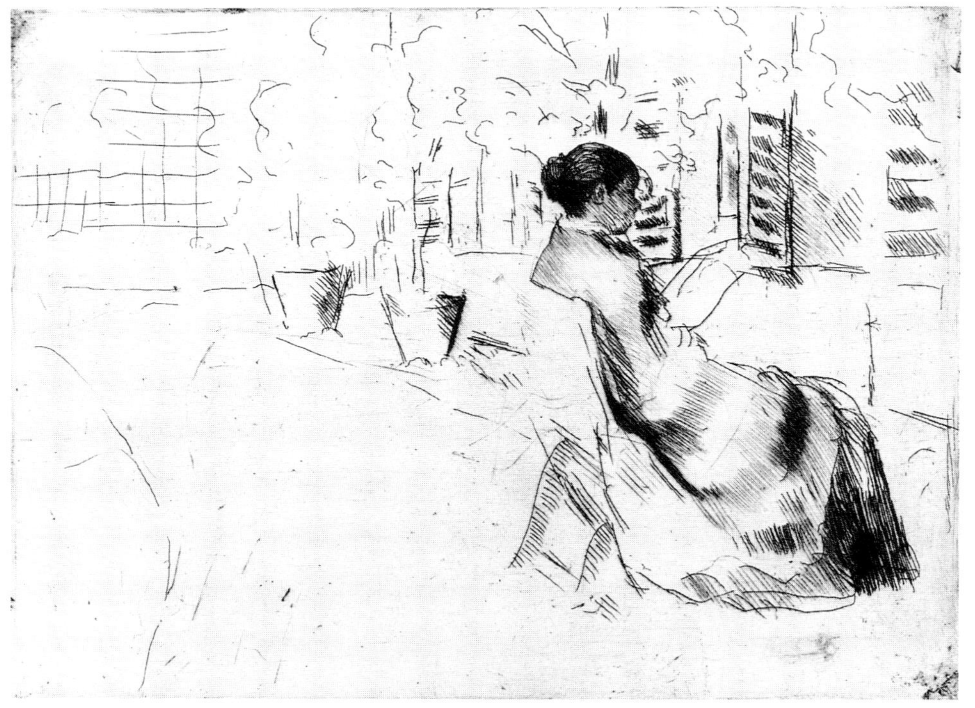

In the Garden at Marly. c. 1881. Etching and drypoint. 5 1/16 × 6 5/8 in. (12.9 × 16.8 cm). The New York Public Library. Astor, Lenox and Tilden Foundations. S.P. Avery Collection. Miriam and Ira D. Wallach Division of Art, Prints and Photographs.

ACHILLE SEGARD

From *Mary Cassatt: Un Peintre des enfants et des mères*

On Portraiture

1913

We will call a portraitist a painter who studies human faces, divines what states of mind certain traits reveal, how heredity or a profession has deformed or tainted a face. He observes facial expressions, divines the principal traits of the physical character and the moral character, forms a personal opinion of that particular model and of the environment in which he lives, and a general opinion of his origins and tendencies. The portraitist's gaze is a painter's gaze, that is, he sees modelling, depth, lines, and colors, but his gaze is also that of the psychologist who subordinates all his purely pictorial impressions to the interpretation of a character, a social sphere, and a state of mind.

If this is the definition of a portraitist, then we would designate as a picture and sometimes even a genre picture, rather than a portrait, those paintings that are done from a live model, but where the principal concern is not psychological divination and the desire to express a reasoned opinion of an individual character by pictorial means.

It is in this sense that the little girls sewing and the many "maternities" painted from specific models (moreover, as alike as they could possibly have been by chance) are not, strictly speaking, portraits. Miss Cassatt chose her models so that they might provide her with elements of comparison with her preconceived ideas of her pictures; she did not submit to the model in order to subordinate her work to the particular truth that the model bears within her. For example, wanting to express a certain nuance of maternal love, she has sought and found certain young mothers and certain children whose physical type and facial expressions agreed with the way she understands her subject and with her own pictorial means. Certain colors of skin and hair, certain facial expressions, certain gestures, and certain ways of dressing offered her in reality what she wanted to capture on

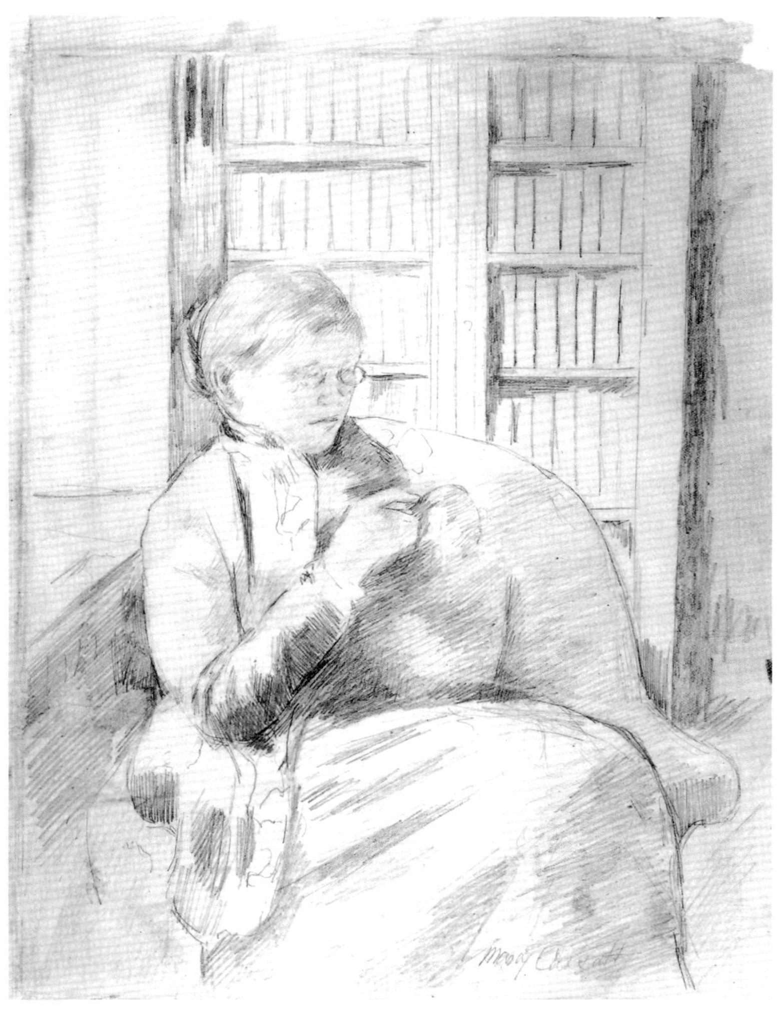

Drawing for *Knitting in the Library*. c. 1881. Graphite. 15 ¾ × 12 ⅜ in. (40.1 × 31.4 cm). The Cleveland Museum of Art. Bequest of Charles T. Brooks.

canvas, and it happened that the model corresponded to the painter's wishes so exactly that the latter believed in good faith that she had only to copy reality exactly to capture her interior dream in her work.

However perfect the resemblance, the difference in the starting points of a picture thus conceived and of a true portrait will always be such that there can be no possible confusion to perceptive eyes. For a portrait to be one, the idea of the picture must spring from the model's personality and take over the painter. It is the model who is the subject and, in a sense, the master of the work. The painter's role is to submit to the model and to place at the model's service all the psychological intuition he may have, and all the resources of his knowledge and skill. When the painter's only concern, relative to the model, is to express a preconceived idea or sentiment, which he renders specific by chance from a given model, but which he might have derived from another one as well, he is not, strictly speaking, making a portrait. Thus, from the same professional model, for example, each painter will draw effects that are specific and usual to himself. The results might be masterpieces, and yet not portraits.

The born portraitist understands all faces and loves them all. He is not discouraged by asymmetries or so-called homelinesses. These often reveal traits of character, and, in any case, they are part of the problem whose solution he seeks. He is like the born surveyor who finds before him a particularly freakish terrain, and who is all the more eager to mark and measure it perfectly exactly. The born landscape artist has a particular opinion on every region and almost every motif that meets his eyes. Likewise, on every space available for painted decoration, the born decorator sees great rhythms of wavy lines, shapes, and colors arranged over large areas. The figure painter who is not a born portraitist, however, understands only a certain category of human faces, and often, even in the case of subjective artists like lyric poets, for example, they understand but a single category of faces, only those in which they find reflected their own sensibility and their way of understanding the world.

When they are fortunate enough to encounter a face that bears the reflection of their own thought, how right they are to cling to it! Given this happy coincidence, if they are good painters, they succeed in making not only magnificent pictures, but also, *because of this coincidence,* magnificent portraits. They are "second-hand" portraitists.

This is the case with Miss Mary Cassatt.

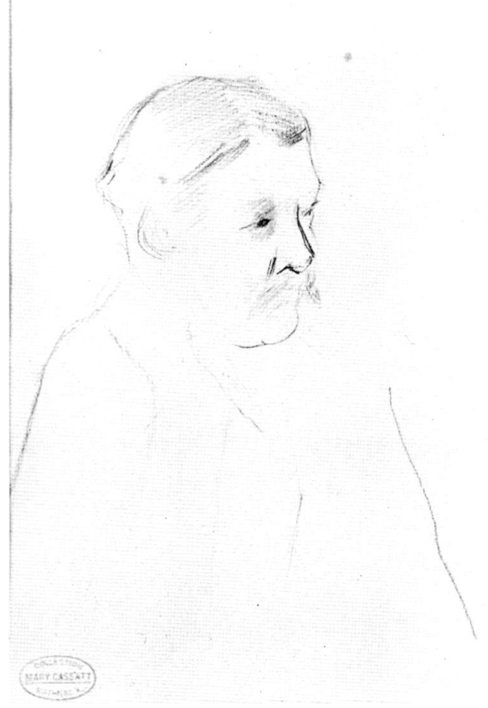

Portrait of the Artist's Brother, Alexander J. Cassatt. c. 1880. Chalk on paper. 9 3/16 × 5 13/16 in. (23.3 × 14.8 cm). The Nelson-Atkins Museum of Art, Kansas City, Missouri. Gift of Mr. and Mrs. Thomas K. Baker. Photograph © The Nelson Gallery Foundation.

Letter from Katherine Cassatt to Her Son, Alexander Cassatt

On *Lady at the Tea Table*

November 30, 1883

13, avenue Trudaine
November 30

My dear Aleck,

On Wednesday last the 28th I sent to Liverpool care of Richardson, Spence & Co. a box with some things for the children which I hope will arrive safely & not much behind time. . . . I send Elsie something for her doll & Robbie a toy thinking him not yet too big for one & Eddie some books which his Aunt Mary chose for him & one which she says she thinks you yourself will read with pleasure—the one by About—

I hope you have found the pictures by this time—it would be a great pity to lose Elsie's portrait for it really is nice—Your father kept saying & thinking it was the fault of the stupid Frenchman who shipped the box, but it turned out to our surprise that the English are in fault—Your father wrote you all about it of course—

You see we are not off yet as up to this time it has not been cold & as your father doesn't like the idea of leaving Paris & I don't think it just the right thing to leave him behind I have hesitated about deciding—just now I am trying daily frictions, but cannot judge yet if they will do good or not—if I get better I don't think we will leave Paris, but if not I must try something as I get a great deal worse—The other day I said I shall have to take to a cane & last evening there came a cane with a beautiful tortoiseshell handle tipped in gold from Mrs. Riddle & an exquisite black feather fan for Mary—I don't know if your father or Mary told you of the presents of porcelain Mrs. Scott sent us after we got home from England & you know she insisted on our being her guests at the Hotel in London—When they came here Mary asked Mrs. Riddle to sit for her portrait thinking it was the only way she could return their kindness & she consented at once & Annie seemed very much pleased—the picture is nearly done but Mary is waiting for a very handsome Louis seize frame to be cut down to suit, before showing it to them—As they are not very artistic in their likes & dislikes of pictures & as a likeness is a hard thing to make to please the nearest friends I don't know what the result will be—Annie ought to like it in one respect for both Degas & Raffaelli said it was "la distinction même" and Annie goes in for that kind of thing—Lois wrote from London that Mrs. Riddle enjoyed buying pretty things for presents beyond anything & I

COLORPLATE 38

Elizabeth Foster Cassatt (born August 14, 1875) and Robert Kelso Cassatt (born September 28, 1873) were Aleck and Lois's two youngest children.

Edmond François Valentin About (1828–1885), a popular French author.

Mary Dickinson Riddle, Mrs. (Katherine) Cassatt's first cousin.

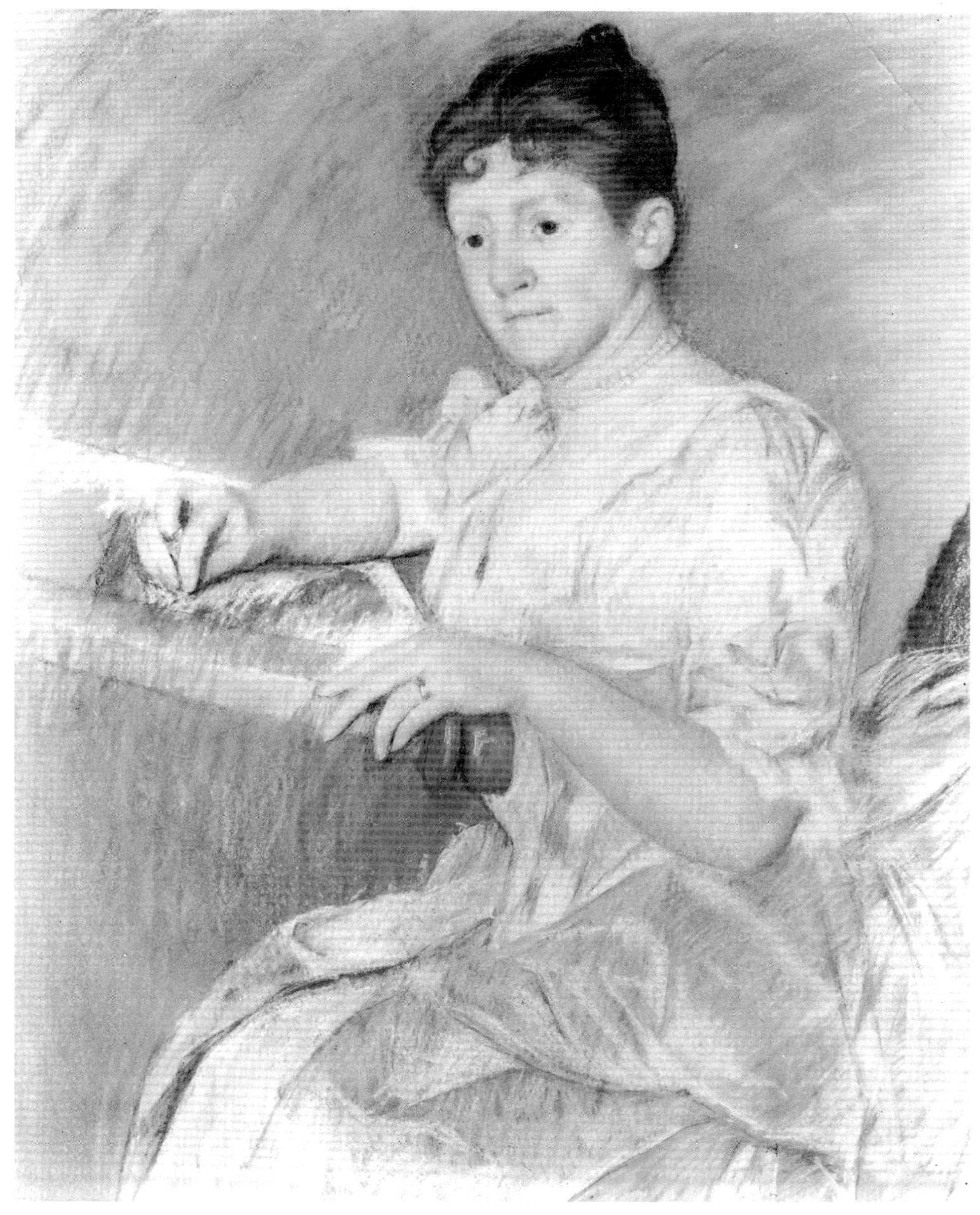

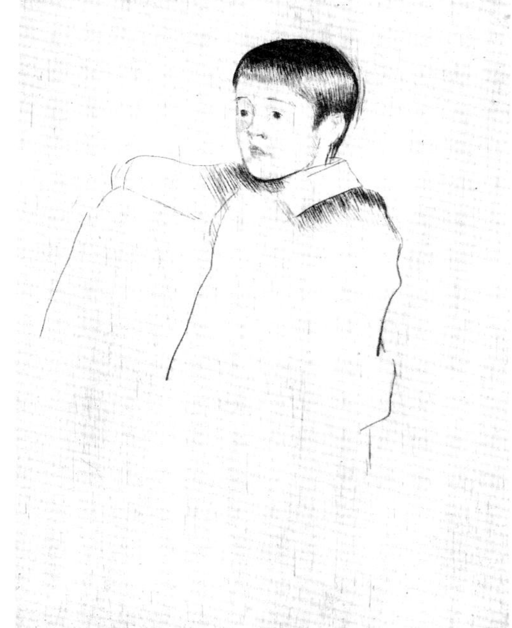

Robert Seated, Facing Left. 1885. Drypoint. 6 1/4 × 4 5/8 in. (15.9 × 11.8 cm). The Metropolitan Museum of Art, New York. Gift of Mrs. Emory DuVey. Photograph © The Metropolitan Museum of Art.

Mrs. Alexander J. Cassatt Seated at a Tapestry Frame. 1888. Pastel. 32 × 25 in. (81.3 × 63.5 cm). Private collection.

suppose Annie does also, otherwise one would & indeed does feel overwhelmed— . . .

Your father is anxious to know if any of your friends appreciate the Monets you took home—We have one here now which Mary admires immensely—it is a view of Amsterdam—Your father has allowed Mary to change our "Trouville" for a sea piece—it is certainly one of those which it would take an artist to appreciate or maybe a sailor—it is a boat tossing on a great wave tipped with foam—the contrast of the white foam & the very dark blue of the water is tremendous—Manet's pictures are to be exposed at the Academie des Beaux Arts in a month or two & then sold—as the executors have managed the whole thing badly it is thought some things may be picked up cheap—By the way Annie went to Durand Ruel's the other day & bought a picture by Mary—perhaps you may remember it—two young girls at the theatre—She also seemed inclined to buy one by Renoir, but she says all her ideas of art are upset & she won't buy much until she knows exactly what she likes—at present she is somewhat in the dark— . . .

Memorial exhibition and auction of the works of Édouard Manet, who died on April 30, 1883.

By the time you get this you will be busy preparing for Christmas & the children will be happy—Give them all my love—Also to Lois and yourself from your father & Mary and your affectionate

Mother

Letter from Mary Cassatt to Louisine Havemeyer

On *Lady at the Tea Table*

February 4, 1915

COLORPLATE 38

Villa Angeletto
February 4

Dearest Louie,

George D.R. has just written to me about Mrs R's portrait. My dear I would give it to you at once, (of course to be left to a Museum.) only I have more than half promised it to the Petit Palais.

On no account shall Bessie Fisher ever own it. She sent me the most decided messages regretting that there was so little likeness to her Mother! The line of the back & the hand & that is all. Even the worm will turn, & I see no excuse for her too evident desire to snub me. Well let her rejoice in Miss Beaux portraits & leave me alone. Jennie wrote that she was told Edgar Scott was crazy to get the picture. He or Brothers children are the only one's who could have even the shadow of a claim to it. I wonder if any one will care for it at the Exhibition. I doubt it, its home ought to be in Paris where I painted it. . . .

ever affectionately yours.
Mary Cassatt

George Durand-Ruel, son of Paul Durand-Ruel.

Bessie Fisher was Mary Dickinson Riddle's daughter.

Cecilia Beaux (1855–1942), a prominent portraitist working in Philadelphia and New York from the 1890s to the 1920s. Frequent comparisons between Cassatt and Beaux forced them into an uncomfortable rivalry.

Edgar Scott, Mrs. Riddle's grandson.

ACHILLE SEGARD

From *Mary Cassatt: Un Peintre des enfants et des mères*

On Cassatt's Use of Unattractive Models

1913

[Miss Cassatt] is constantly seeking to simplify, desiring to transfigure, pursuing the effect to be produced, with purely pictorial means (and in this sense one might say with scrupulous integrity); she reaches a certain depth of sentiment and through that sentiment to a certain grandeur, she achieves a style.

They say that one day, in front of Degas, Miss Cassatt, judging a great painter, a friend of theirs, dared to say, "He has no style." And Degas began to laugh, shrugging his shoulders, with a movement that meant: Who are these women who presume to judge! Do they even know what style is?

At that, Miss Cassatt took offense. She chose as her model a very ugly woman, a sort of typically vulgar servant-girl. She posed her in a nightdress, by her dressing table, in the movement of a woman preparing for bed, her left hand holding up at the nape of her neck her thin braid, while the other hand pulled up the braid to tie it up. The girl is seen almost entirely in profile. Her mouth hangs open. Her expression is stupid and weary.

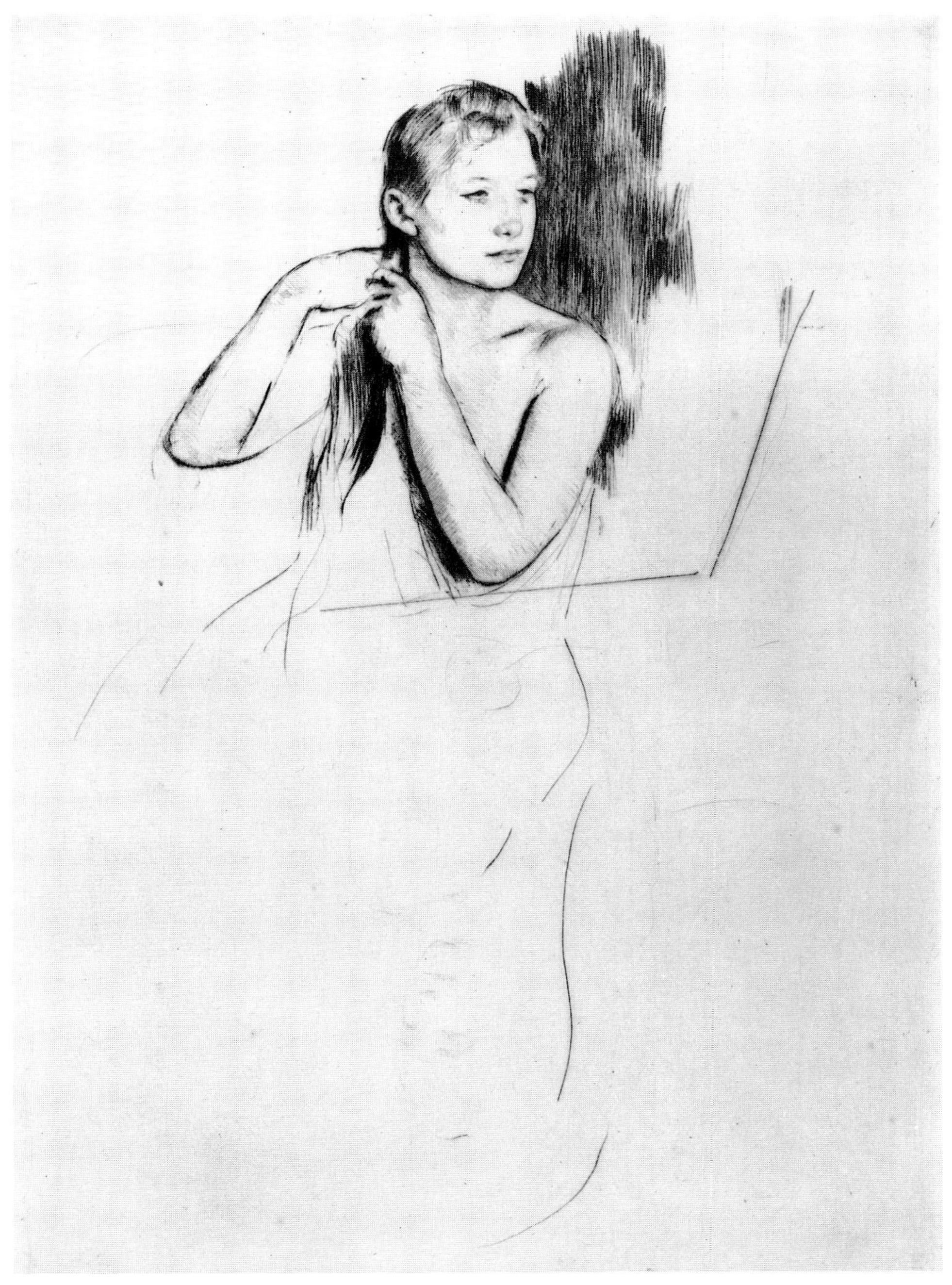

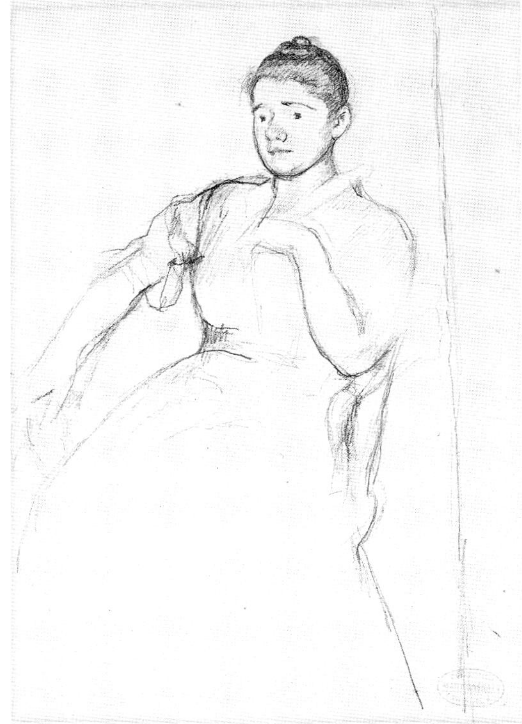

Sketch of Katharine Kelso Cassatt Seated in an Armchair. c. 1888. Pencil. 9 ¼ × 6 ¼ in. (23.5 × 15.9 cm). Museum of Fine Arts, Springfield, Massachusetts. Membership Collection.

Young Girl Fixing Her Hair (third state). c. 1889. Drypoint. 8 ⅜ × 6 ¼ in. (21.3 × 15.9 cm). Photograph courtesy of the Library of Congress.

COLORPLATE 41

When Degas saw the picture, he wrote Miss Cassatt: What drawing! What style!

And indeed the work is superb. It has style. Firstly, because all useless details have been eliminated, and all essential details graduated with discernment, these last contributing to an impression of the whole that is clean and vigorous, secondly because of the tone of deep sincerity and life that animates the entire work, then because of the felicitous combination of lines that converge precisely and harmoniously, demonstrating the truth that the painter wishes to demonstrate, finally, because of the felicitous balancing of masses and areas of color, which, in perfect proportion, are also subordinated to the impression of the whole, so that one could change nothing in it, nor add, nor subtract, without diminishing its order, stability, tranquillity, and, so to speak, the mathematics of the work. These are the qualities that make up its style. It in no way depends upon the subject nor its so-called nobility. The most pretentious historical paintings, though they be made according to all the international canonical rules, can be utterly without style.

NANCY MOWLL MATHEWS

"Beauty, Truth, and the Artist's Mirror: A Drypoint by Mary Cassatt"

The Aesthetics of Ugliness

1985

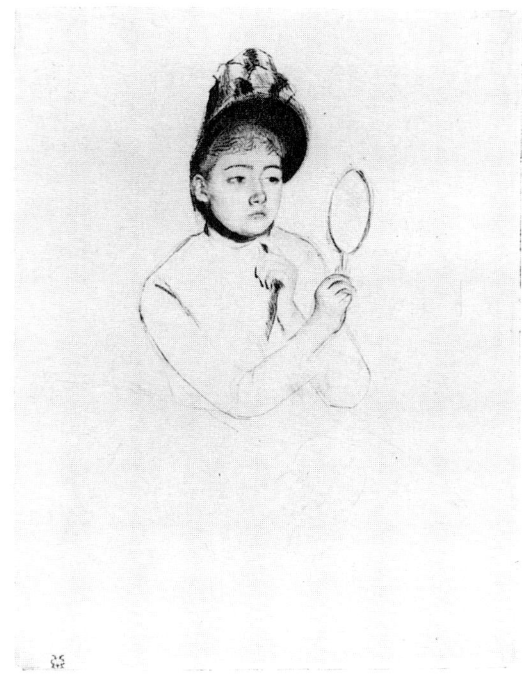

The Bonnet. 1889–90. Drypoint. 7 3/8 × 5 1/2 in. (18.6 × 13.9 cm). National Academy of Design, New York. Samuel Colman Collection.

Only the woman in *The Bonnet* confronts herself in the mirror, and in spite of a very stylish hat, she, unlike Courbet's Jo, has no reason to luxuriate in the image reflected there. Her hair is hidden, her modest figure barely sketched in. Her face shows concentration rather than pleasure.

Thus, for Cassatt's model, who is intentionally not a great beauty, the mirror has a more practical function. Rather than revealing the woman's sensuality, it serves to guide her in the small but necessary decisions that rule everyday life. Cassatt's use of the mirror as a reflection not of beauty, but of ordinariness, and as an aid to human decision making and self-improvement (even if it's only the banal choice of the right hat) is a fresh and accurate application of a traditional theme to modern life. Given Cassatt's great knowledge and appreciation of Courbet, this could be a modest but deliberate reprise of *Portrait of Jo*, his earlier emblematic work, or a general reinterpretation of the woman and the hand mirror.

Cassatt's interpretation owes a great deal to her association with Degas and her sympathy for his own twisting of traditional concepts of beauty, as explained by his friend Diego Martelli: "The relationship between the study of the beautiful and that of the ugly is intimate, and Degas, through his own genius, had to wed and harmonize these two sentiments in an originality all his own, by means of which the feeling for truth of the primitives is invested with the light and phosphorescent scintillations of our times."

In fact, *The Bonnet* owes a great deal to a work that vividly illustrates Martelli's statement: Degas's *At the Milliner's* (c. 1882). Not only are the works linked by subject (Degas's woman stares intently into an unseen mirror as she ties the hat under her chin), but by Degas's unprepossessing model, who has been traditionally identified as Mary Cassatt herself. Although *At the Milliner's* is not in the same tradition as Courbet's and Cassatt's images of a woman's private contemplation of her own reflection, it is clearly a stepping stone in the evolution of Cassatt's drypoint and her dramatic reversal of Courbet.

When we realize that in *The Bonnet* Cassatt hired a model to duplicate her own pose of seven years before in *At the Milliner's* and put her own round mirror into the model's hand, the work takes on an unexpected autobiographical dimension. Cassatt was well aware of her own lack of beauty and resented the pressures she endured because of it. She wrote with some feeling to Havemeyer: "I think sometimes a girl's first duty is to be handsome and parents feel it when she isn't, I am sure my Father did, it wasn't my fault though." Consequently, her confrontation of issues of female beauty in her art must have taken a measure of personal courage and self-assessment. If we see the model in *The Bonnet* as a stand-in for Cassatt, we see the artist coming to terms with her own appearance in a no-nonsense way and using the mirror to help her in decisions of personal enhancement. On the simplest level, this refers to a plain woman's ability to improve her appearance through fashion, as Cassatt herself had done.

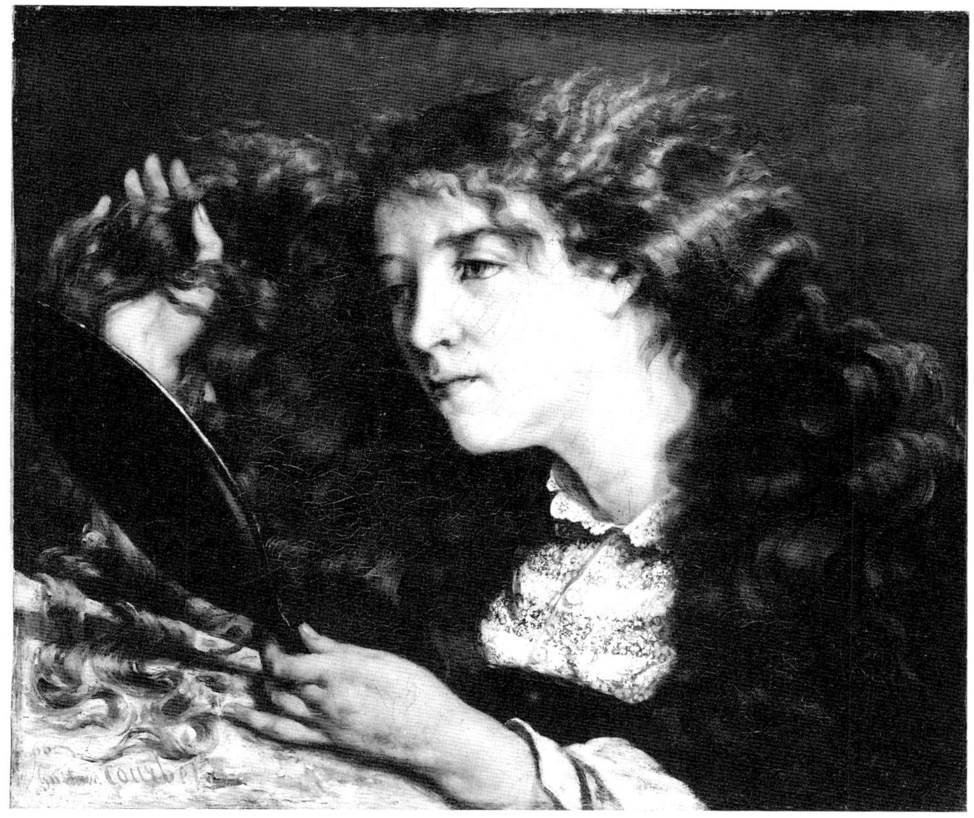

Gustave Courbet. *Portrait of Jo (La Belle Irlandaise).* 1866. Oil on canvas. 22 × 26 in. (55.9 × 66 cm). The Metropolitan Museum of Art, New York. Bequest of Mrs. H.O. Havemeyer, The H.O. Havemeyer Collection. Photograph © The Metropolitan Museum of Art.

YVELING RAMBAUD

From *L'Art dans les Deux Mondes*

Cassatt's Vision

November 1890

"L'Art dans les Deux Mondes" was published by the Durand-Ruel galleries in Paris and New York.

Few women do sincere painting.

Despite their studies, despite a sincere intention to paint realistically, it seems as if they cannot help surrendering to an imperious need for convention, which follows as an inevitable consequence upon their temperament, education, and their role in society.

Therefore, we are happy to salute, in this first issue of a magazine devoted to Art, the vigorous personality of Miss Mary Cassatt.

Her works are known by only a small number of artists, and yet they have already won an important place among the works of the painters of the realistic school.

It is not our intention today to write a review, we will merely publish a simple biographical account.

Miss Cassatt belongs to a family of business people.

It must be admitted that there was little in her early education that oriented her toward a career in the arts.

She was born in Pittsburgh, Pennsylvania. She studied first at the Philadelphia Academy, but rather dissatisfied with the models she had in front of her, she made up her mind, with an entirely American independence, to study in lands more fertile in art, and undertook a voyage to Italy, Spain, and Holland.

Invigorated by serious studies, exposure to the chef d'oeuvres of the great masters of these different schools, Miss Cassatt arrived in Paris.

She was immediately struck by the talent of M. Degas. She became his pupil for fifteen years, was inspired by his opinions, and ended by becoming a master in her own right.

How often we have heard her say that she considered M. Degas the most classic and skilled of painters!

In every case, she has been, with a few of her compatriots, the first to appreciate the works of Millet, Manet, and Claude Monet, well before France did.

Do not seek to find in her preferences, which many might denounce as odd, any pretention to being an original.

We said at the beginning that she was eminently sincere.

This sincerity is so much her chief characteristic that it has come to endow her with the gift of second sight, of an altogether singular and unknown *impression*. In fact, and we hope she will forgive this detail, which will make the reader privy to an area of her private life, *Miss Cassatt has dedicated herself to Art as other women have to religion.* Miss Cassatt has not married.

Now, it is impossible for those who follow her work closely, who have admired, in their utterly simple and natural graces, those wonderful children whom her brush or burin has brought into the world, not to recognize the sentiment of maternal charity, that feeling arising from experience that would seem to be the monopoly of motherhood in the psychological sense of the word.

Miss Cassatt's mothers and children are the result of this kind of double sight so often observed by those engaged with psychic investigations.

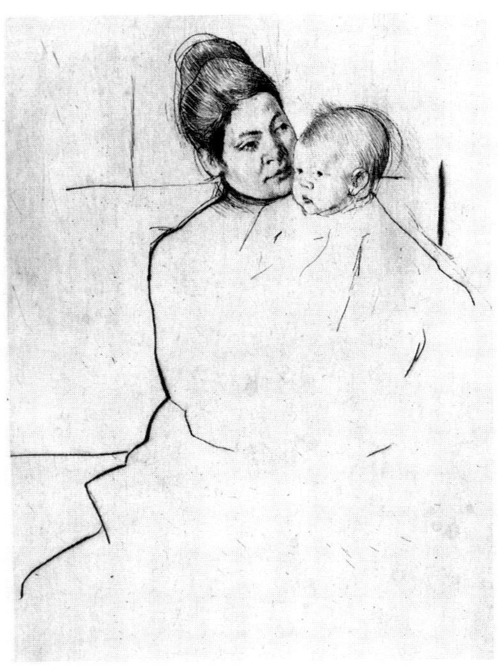

Gardner Held by His Mother. 1888. Drypoint. 8 1/4 × 5 7/16 in. (21 × 13.8 cm). The New York Public Library. Astor, Lenox and Tilden Foundations. S.P. Avery Collection. Miriam and Ira D. Wallach Division of Art, Prints and Photographs.

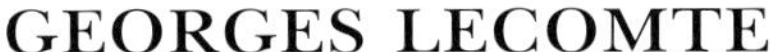

GEORGES LECOMTE

Georges Lecomte (1867–1958).

From *L'Art Impressioniste d'après la collection privée de M. Durand-Ruel*

The "Modern Holy Family"

1892

Miss Mary Cassatt's very distinguished art also rises beyond living realities by the breadth of its Idea. She has extracted their characteristic aspects from the momentariness and randomness of things. Ostensibly painting mamas and babies joined in various entwinings, she has achieved the portrayal of mother Love. The gestures and faces are accurately observed and rendered: everything comes together to define the mother's tender care and the child's quietude.

There was reason to fear that her concern for so vast an expression might lead this painter either to excesses of sentimentality or to mannerisms in the execution. But Miss Mary Cassatt, enamored of truth, conveyed only instinctive attitudes that she had observed around her in their unconscious spontaneity and expressions of normal tenderness. She refrained from those embraces that are spoiled by the intentional exaggeration that always results from a model's immobility and the deliberate protraction of an attitude.

The sincerity of her vision thus saved her from inexpressive generalizations. Indeed, her syntheses of emotions are not obtained by methodical abstractions to the detriment of reality. They emanate from very precise studies and are all the greater for the distinctiveness and liveliness of the drawing.

When Miss Cassatt portrays children and mothers, her compositions are ennobled by the very exalted quality of a Holy Family, but a modern

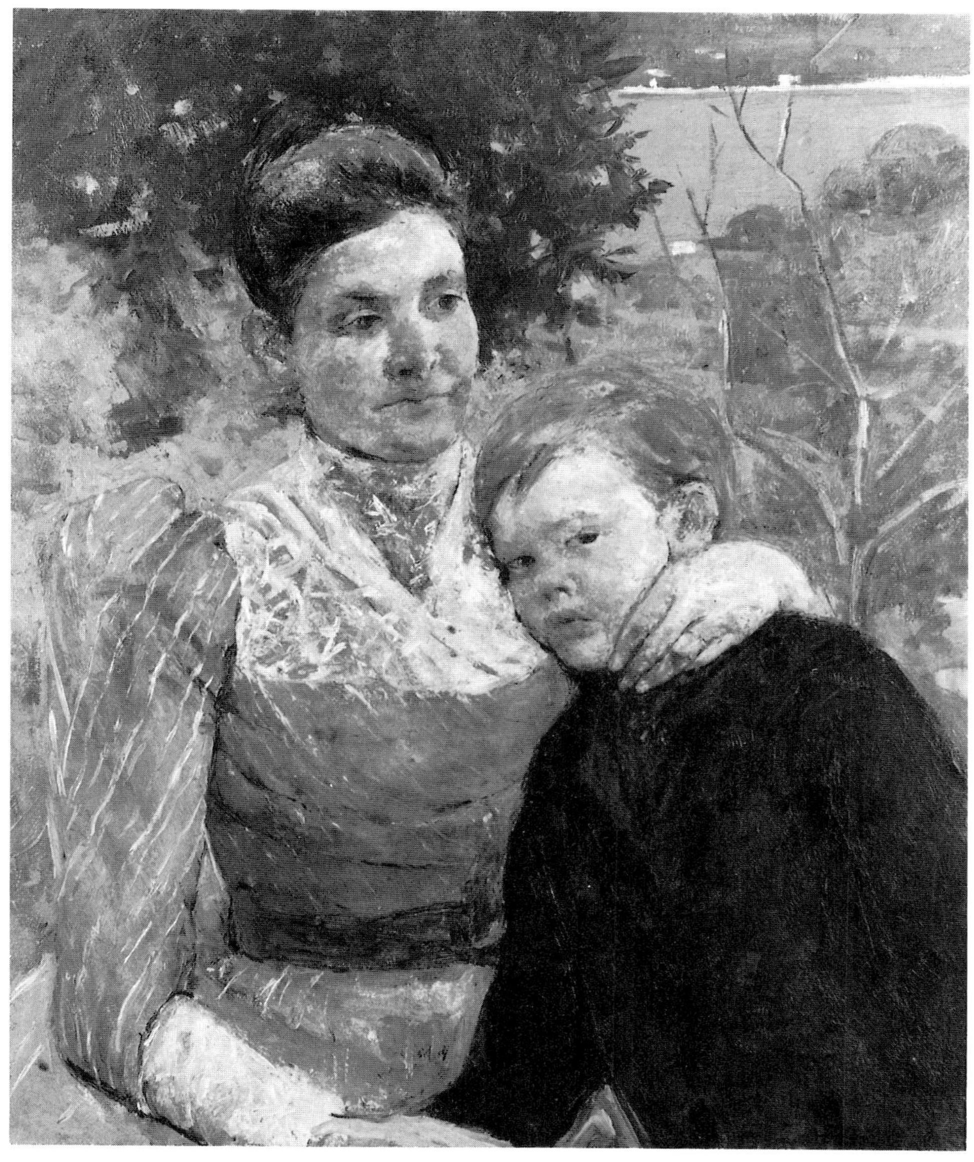

Jenny Cassatt with Her Son Gardner. 1895–96. Oil on canvas. 28 3/4 × 23 3/4 in. (73 × 60.3 cm). Collection of The Newark Museum, Newark, New Jersey. Purchase 1931, Felix Fuld Bequest Fund.

Holy Family. Indeed, no longer are they ecstatic virgins, holding, on stiff knees and with no tenderness, a child conscious of his destiny and who is already in flight. These are infinitely human and loving mothers who clasp to their bosom pink-skinned babies who are well and truly alive and have no thought for anything but their mother's caresses.

An intimate, necessary bond joins human beings: they live through each other. Their facial expressions are related. This tenderness, at first of the flesh, then completed by a moral affection, becomes graced by an austere gravity. Miss Cassatt endows her mothers with the rounded brow of certain Primitive virgins: it is full of thoughts of a purely human order, not at all supernatural. The mother is thinking about her duties, about the future. Her brow is highlighted, signifying the intelligence of her love, not ecstasy. The eyes, soft and slow, have no uneasy gaze when they contemplate the child.

This serene tenderness and emotional simplicity are expressed magnificently in the canvas that graces M. Durand-Ruel's showroom.

A woman with her dress slightly undone, as if for ready nursings, strolls down a garden path with her little baby, whom her large motherly hands, skillful and good, clasp to her bosom. She cannot yet talk to him, but it is of him that she is thinking. She is conscious of her duty, and, too, has a solemn pride in her maternity. The child, all pink with fresh life, snuggles into this embrace that is all the world to him. He knows perfect quietude and security.

What graceful, supple movements Miss Cassatt has realized! Her babies' gestures are exquisitely fidgety and awkward. Their eyes, astonished and naive, stare solemnly. The folds of fat in their pink, milky flesh and their plump softnesses show them to be in fine health. The babies' attitudes are spiritual and remain true to life. Always, Miss Cassatt avoids compromising their sincerity with conventional prettinesses, that of agile kittens playing in yarn, with which so many painters saddle childhood. Her art maintains its distinction as well as its truth.

Miss Cassatt is related to the Impressionist development in the skill with which she captures the precise emotions of her very fresh vision with expressive and broad drawing, and by the freedom of her colorations.

GARDNER TEALL

Gardner Teall (1878–1956), American painter and illustrator.

From *Good Housekeeping Magazine*

On the "American" Mother and Child

February 1910

The mother and child in painting is art's supreme subject. It has humanized the world's greatest religion and it has spiritualized the world's greatest art. Giotto was the first great painter to cast aside the formal style of the conventional Byzantines. He painted natural pictures which appealed to the heart. In the fourteenth century he painted a mother and child that revolutionized all art up to then. This splendid work may be seen in Florence today. It has not lost its interest.

The early Renaissance painter Giotto di Bondone (c. 1267–1337) was being rediscovered by modernist artists and writers.

Through all the centuries that followed this record of Giotto's inspiration, art has become more real and more beautiful. Esthetic qualities alone do not make a work of art great. Whether it is a picture or a statue it must be human to live.

The art of Mary Cassatt is great art because it is the work of a true and of a gifted humanist who perfectly expresses her humanism. One may not compare it to the painting of Andrea del Sarto, or Raphael, or Titian, to Correggio, or to Rubens—it is itself strikingly individual, though it has in it just that which makes these masters loved—a humanity speaking by art's voice to a man's ear of beautiful things he comprehends. Mary Cassatt's art does not devise fascinating intricacies to enmesh the admiration of the esthete. Like Sorolla she puts health into the beautiful souls she suggests, from infancy to maternity, and she never leaves us feeling sorry for mankind, as we do when we stand before the pictures of even so marvelous a painter as Zuloaga.

That this American girl should have gone to a foreign land to study and to live and yet should have remained typically American in all that makes us proud of American womanhood, is a note of the strength of her personality . . .

In Paris Mary Cassatt settled. There she worked long and faithfully under Degas. Just as he and Manet, or Sisley, Renoir, Monet or any of that group which used to gather at the Cafe Guerbois, were born impressionists, so too was Mary Cassatt, whose vision always has been measured by a dignified virility that easily would seem to place her ahead of her sister impressionists—Berthe Morisot, Marie Bracquemond, or Eva Gonzales.

However, one must not be frightened away by this talk of impressionism. There are no perversely blue cows, pink sheep or purple faces

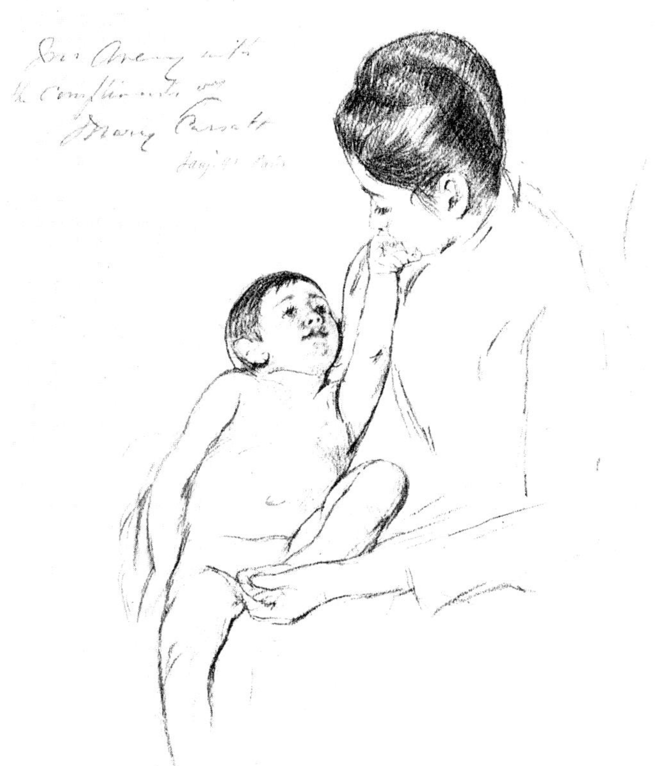

The First Caress. 1891. Crayon. 10 ½ × 7 ½ in. (26.7 × 19 cm). The New York Public Library. Astor, Lenox and Tilden Foundations. S.P. Avery Collection. Miriam and Ira D. Wallach Division of Art, Prints and Photographs.

devised for spectric contortionists by Mary Cassatt's brain. In common with that of Renoir, her art is a sane art. The obviousness of the merely pretty in life concerns her little, or not at all; yet the soulfulness of beauty is a thing she marvelously well suggests in her subdued whites and grays and in quiet but lovely fresh spring colors, spread on her canvases in solid but fine unobtrusive impasto, and again with her pastels, in the luminosity of well-chosen pigments. Her technique makes a strong appeal to the layman.

A little house just off the Champs Élysées is where Mary Cassatt lives during the winters in Paris, and summer finds her at her country place, the delightful Château de Beaufresne, at Mesnil, Oise. But her comings and goings are unheralded. She works quietly and happily. I doubt if there exists a photograph of her, and yet I feel, as everyone must feel who knows her and who studies her work, that so much of herself is embodied in each of her pictures that they, perhaps, are almost themselves portraits of the soul of this great artist who paints with perfect fidelity that nobility of womanhood which is the American ideal.

FRANK WEITENKAMPF

Frank Weitenkampf (1866–1962), author of "American Graphic Art" (1924) and curator of prints at the New York Public Library.

From *Scribner's Magazine*

On Cassatt's Mother and Child Prints

December 1909

The woman etcher of serious achievement is in the main and essentially a product of the late nineteenth century. She is not numerously represented, this type of artist who happens to be a woman, with which fact her art has not *per se* anything to do, and who makes no appeal on the score of sex nor

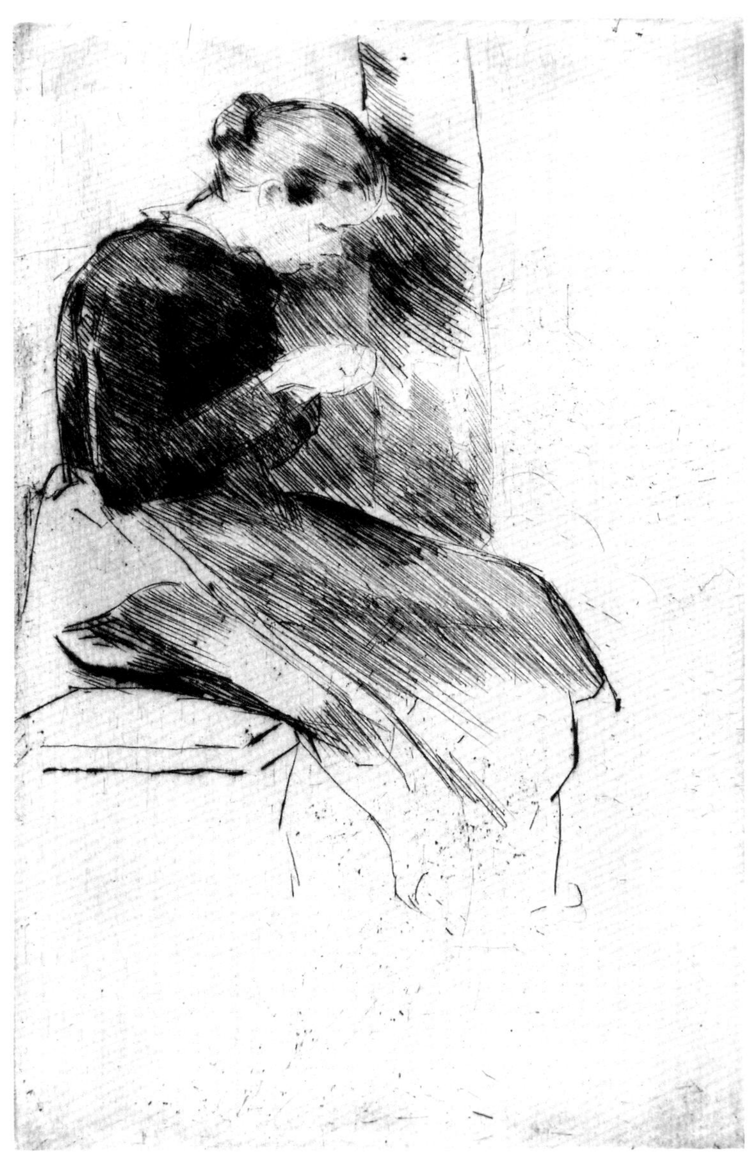

Susan Looking Down at Her Hands. c. 1882. Drypoint. 8 ¾ × 3 ⅜ in. (22.2 × 8.6 cm). The New York Public Library. Astor, Lenox and Tilden Foundations. S.P. Avery Collection. Miriam and Ira D. Wallach Division of Art, Prints and Photographs.

by choice of sentimental subjects or manner. There are a few striking and particularly noteworthy examples of this quasi-sexless attitude, and a somewhat larger number who come in a good second. All of which does not imply that few women have etched. On the contrary, the list is long and extends far back in time. . . .

Once or twice, in the catalogues of the Etching Club exhibits in the old Academy building on twenty-third street, in New York City, there appeared the name of Mary Cassatt. Since then, she has placed many plates to her credit, mostly drypoints.

Miss Cassatt's etchings and dry-points show the not too common quality which marks the best work accomplished with the needle and the copper plate—a full appreciation (sensitive, notwithstanding a robustness often emphasized by the models used by her) of the nature of the medium, a recognition of its possibilities and its limits. This adaptation of manner to process is one of the most important factors in any art. Miss Cassatt's work shows a wise reticence in linear expression, the "tact of omission" as Walter Pater, speaking of Watteau, happily characterizes it in his "Imaginary Portraits." The secret of compressed statement is hers, of condensed significance. The synthesis which, consciously or unconsciously, we look for in the painter etching. (I remember meeting a man who, knowing nothing about etchings, never having heard of Whistler, immediately appreciated the latter's etchings because they "told so much with such few lines.") In its forceful technic, its firmness, its spontaneous vitality, its succinct straightforward manner of statement, its judicious and effective economy of line, her work forms an admirable model in the art of etching. With all their apparent robust vigor in subject and execution, these plates on closer study, reveal a sensitive suavity of line, which, while never sweet for the sake of sweetness, deftly caresses the form which it indicates. Her subjects in black and white (as in painting) are usually women and children. There are not wanting those who wonder why she selects homely models. One has but to get a little below the uncompromising realism of this absolute truthfulness in presentation to see the beautiful expression of relationship under this homely exterior. Her sympathy with her subject, free from the weak sentimentality that pervades so many "mother and child" pictures, is shown in deft and subtle records of fleeting expression of face and quickly shifting pose or characteristic gesture. She reveals the beauty of the relation between mother and child without calling in the aid of a superficially pleasing prettiness which, after all, has nothing to do with the matter. Perfectly natural caresses, instinctive movements of childhood, changing expressions of the eye, attitudes and movements full of significance are observed with a complete understanding of child nature; noted with a penetrating insight into its different manifestations of character and temperament and mood. Here are babies feeding (little gluttons), in the bath, accepting caresses with the lordly air that their plump highnesses not infrequently display. We who study these pictures enter into full enjoyment of the intimacy, the simple tenderness of these scenes of home life. And the appeal to our human sympathies is stronger and deeper and fuller by reason of the knowledge which makes this appeal solely on the merits of the case.

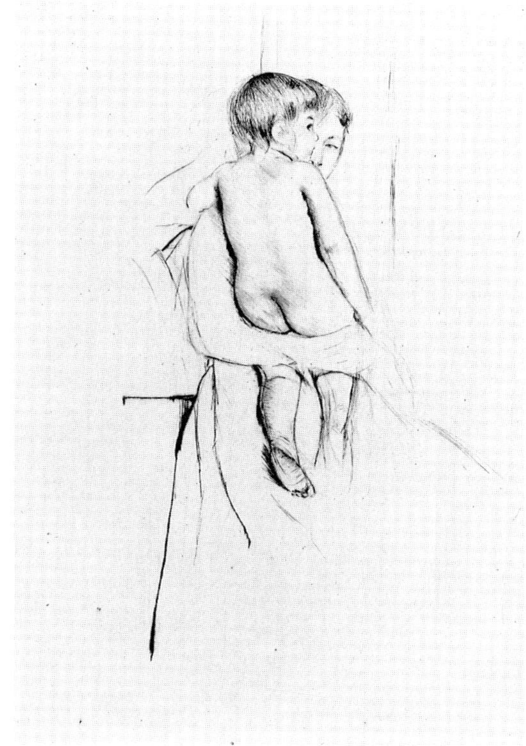

Baby's Back. 1889–90. Drypoint in brown ink. 9 1/4 × 6 1/2 in. (23.4 × 16.5 cm). National Academy of Design, New York. Samuel Colman Collection.

FRANK WEITENKAMPF

From *Print Collector's Quarterly*

"The Dry-Points of Mary Cassatt"

1916

To call Mary Cassatt a depicter of childhood and motherhood is to do so without any reference to the spirit and methods which such a descriptive phrase would be only too apt to recall. Her work is entirely lacking in the smirking sentimentality so often connected with this subject. One need by no means descend to the most elementary taste in such matters to find Miss Cassatt's art not exactly an open book. It is conceivable and a fact that well-intentioned people of taste may not be attracted at first sight by her dry-points. Their vigor, their uncompromising directness must be overcome and appreciated before the discriminating and absolute truthfulness in these pictures of every-day plain women and ordinary babies makes its appeal. And again, the homely exterior of the models must be overcome in order to get at the delightfully felt and expressed sense of maternal and filial relationship. Her work is compelling,—after it has been sympathetically studied. . . .

Miss Cassatt tells no story in the sense that she is a dispenser of illustrated anecdote. She draws for us, in dozens of *nuances,* women and babies just as she sees them. Not only "just as *she* sees them," that is, with an implied absence of prettifying touches and alluring frills, but also "just as she *sees* them," that is, going below the surface. It is all so simple and so subtle. Simple in effect, subtle in import. Subtle in perception, not with the subtlety of hyper-preciosity, of a painful seeking for something apart. Her attitude and work are eminently sincere and sane. I should even hesitate to attribute to her a volitional psychological analysis of her models. All the better. We get the thing without the accompaniment of irritating intention. Suppose we assume that our artist was concerned only with the depiction of what was before her. Then we still have to deal with the difference between a soulless setting down of obvious facts and the deepseeing sympathetic setting forth of souls within bodies. . . .

There are some studies of women alone, which somehow look as though they had been posed for and executed with a certain self-conscious directness, a posy stiffness one might say, that eliminated all possible grace. Among these—woman with a parrot, woman trying on her hat before a hand mirror, young woman playing the mandolin—the most pleasing is perhaps that full-length of a young woman in street costume and hat, seated, with hands crossed on knee, showing the play of shadows on the face.

"Freedom of handling" has been attributed to her, but it never degenerates into looseness. Her line is, with rare exceptions, direct and firm. Incisive is perhaps not quite the word. The line is clean cut and yet does not cut its way, but is of a remarkable pliancy. There are subtle indication and suggestion in the hardly perceptible variations from the straight line. The thing's done before you really see how. Of course, here, as everywhere in art, the medium plays its part: the richness of the scratched dry-point line, though never so fine, is in palpitating evidence. . . .

Conservative estimate will place her in the front rank of those who have depicted the child. It is an open question whether, in her own special sphere, she has ever been surpassed.

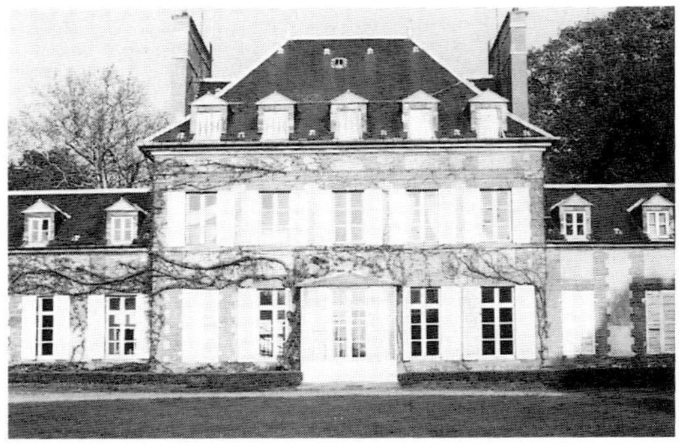

Photograph of the Château de Bachivillers, the country house outside of Paris that Cassatt rented from 1891 to 1893.

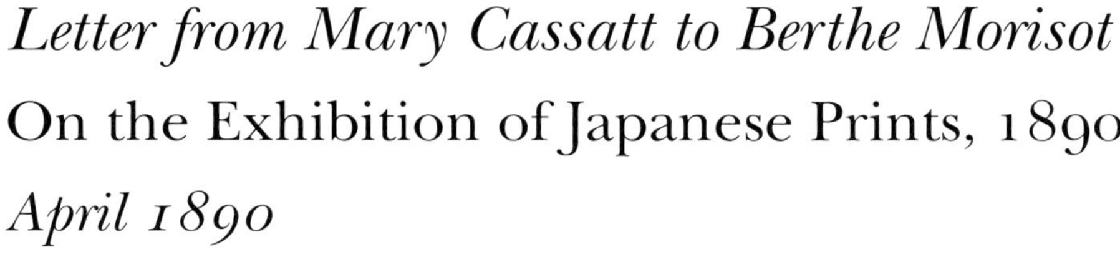

Letter from Mary Cassatt to Berthe Morisot

On the Exhibition of Japanese Prints, 1890

April 1890

10, rue de Marignan
Tuesday

Dear Madame Manet,

Thank you very much for your letter and for your offer to look for a retreat for us for this summer, but we have Septeuil. At any rate we will be neighbors and I promise you I am not sorry to be returning there and to be spared the trouble of investigating other estates. We have rented it from the first of June and I hope that we will be able to move in on that day, I am eager to be in the country. A thousand thanks for your kind invitation. I haven't seen "la belle Louise" to deliver it for you but I know that for the moment she is making a dress for the wedding and she is completely absorbed in this occupation, and doesn't even have the time to see her friends; also I think she is vexed with me because Melle Germaine repeated to her that I believed she would *never marry*!

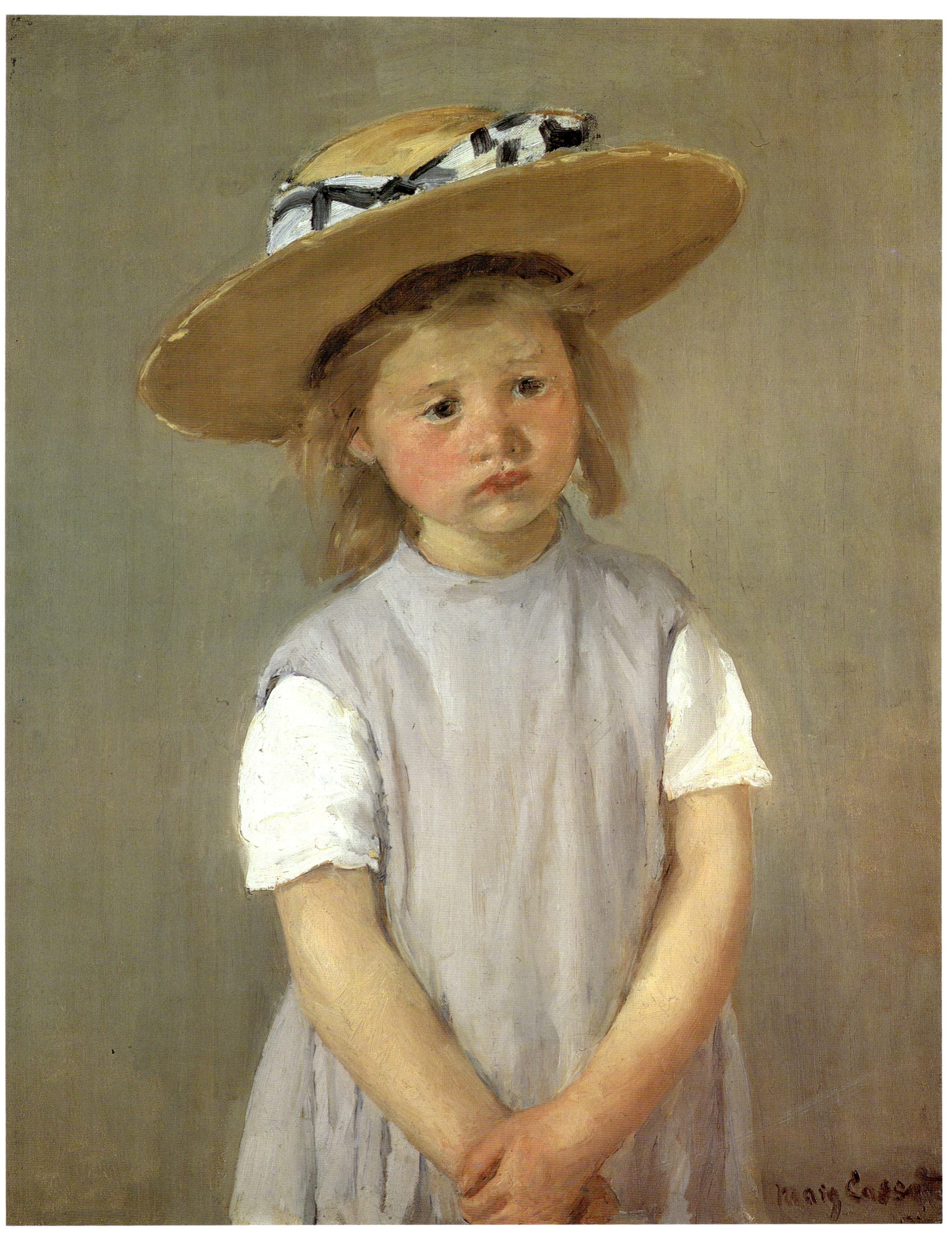

COLORPLATE 44. *Child in a Straw Hat.* c. 1886. Oil on canvas. 25 ¾ × 19 ½ in. (65.4 × 49.5 cm). National Gallery of Art. Collection of Mr. and Mrs. Paul Mellon. Photograph © Board of Trustees, National Gallery of Art, Washington, D.C.

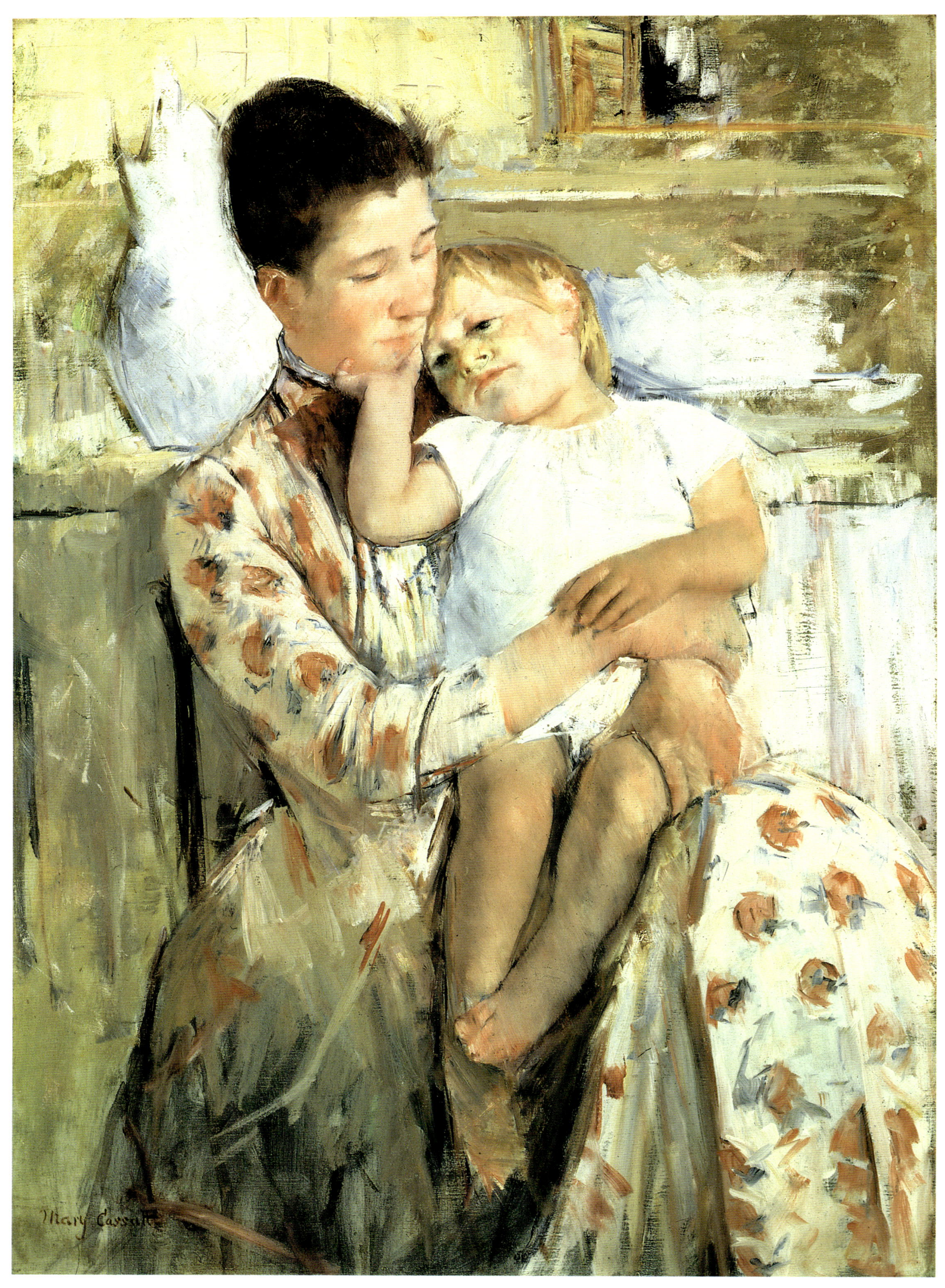

COLORPLATE 45. *Mother and Child.* c. 1890. Oil on canvas. 35 3/8 × 25 3/8 in. (89.8 × 64.4 cm). Wichita Art Museum. The Roland P. Murdock Collection.

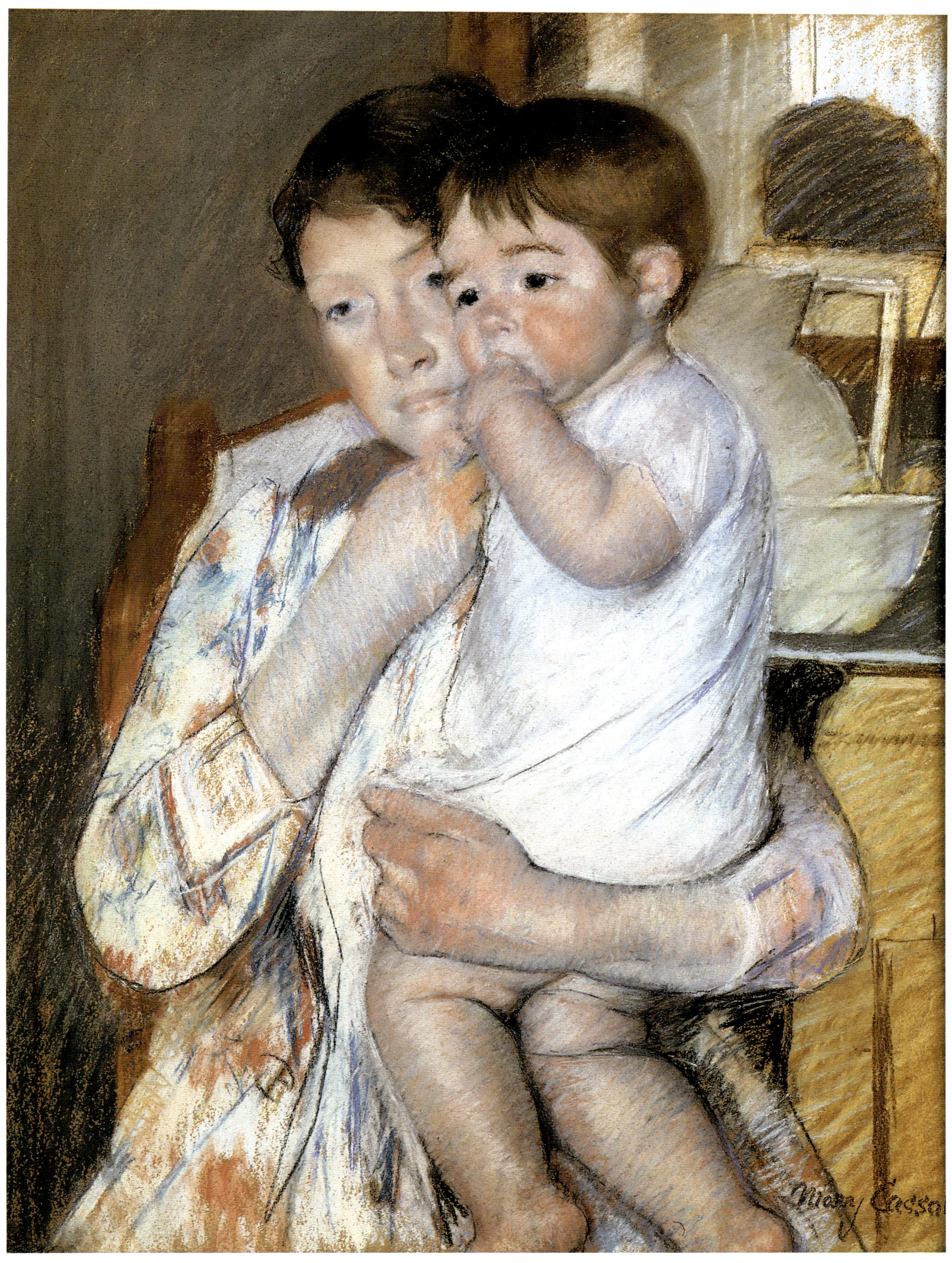

COLORPLATE 46. *Baby in His Mother's Arms.* 1889. Pastel on paper. 25 × 19 in. (63.5 × 48.2 cm). Musée du Louvre, Paris. Photograph: Réunion des Musées Nationaux.

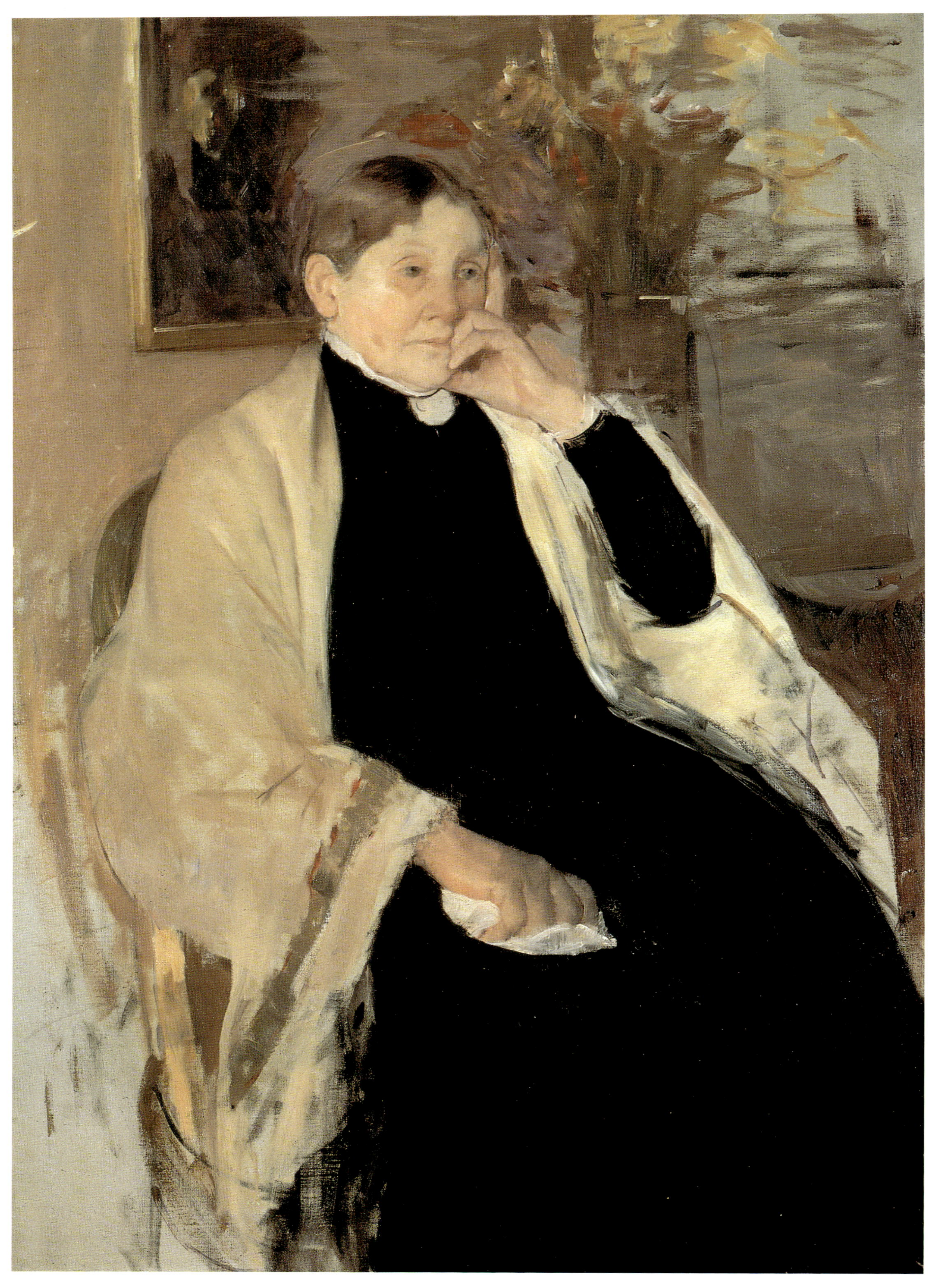

COLORPLATE 47. *Mrs. Robert S. Cassatt, the Artist's Mother (Katherine Kelso Johnston Cassatt)*. c. 1889. Oil on canvas. 38 × 27 in. (96.5 × 68.5 cm). The Fine Arts Museums of San Francisco. The William H. Noble Bequest Fund.

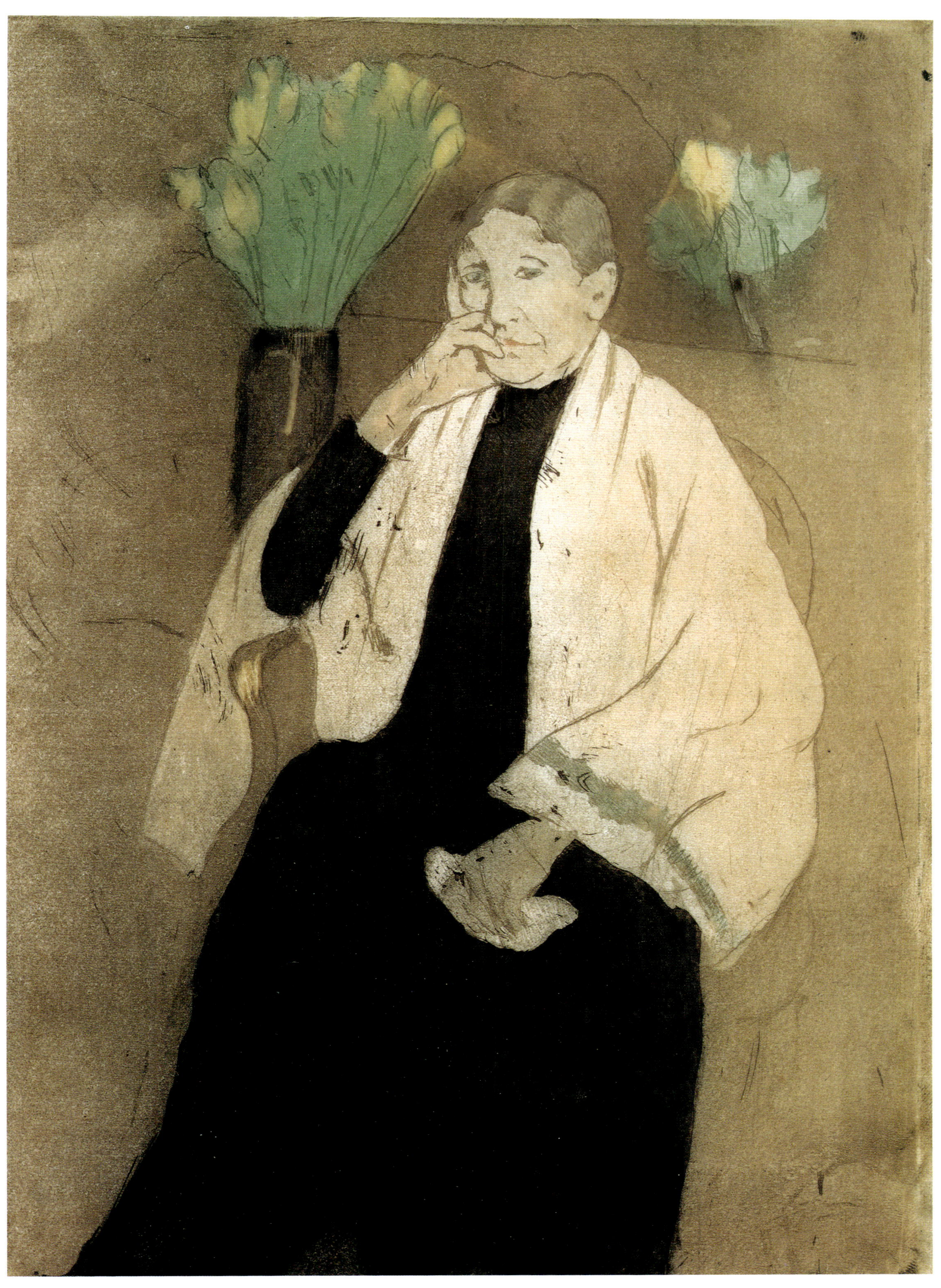

COLORPLATE 48. *Portrait of the Artist's Mother.* c. 1889–90. Soft-ground etching and aquatint. 13 7/8 × 8 1/2 in. (35.2 × 21.5 cm). National Gallery of Art. The Rosenwald Collection. Photograph © Board of Trustees, National Gallery of Art, Washington, D.C.

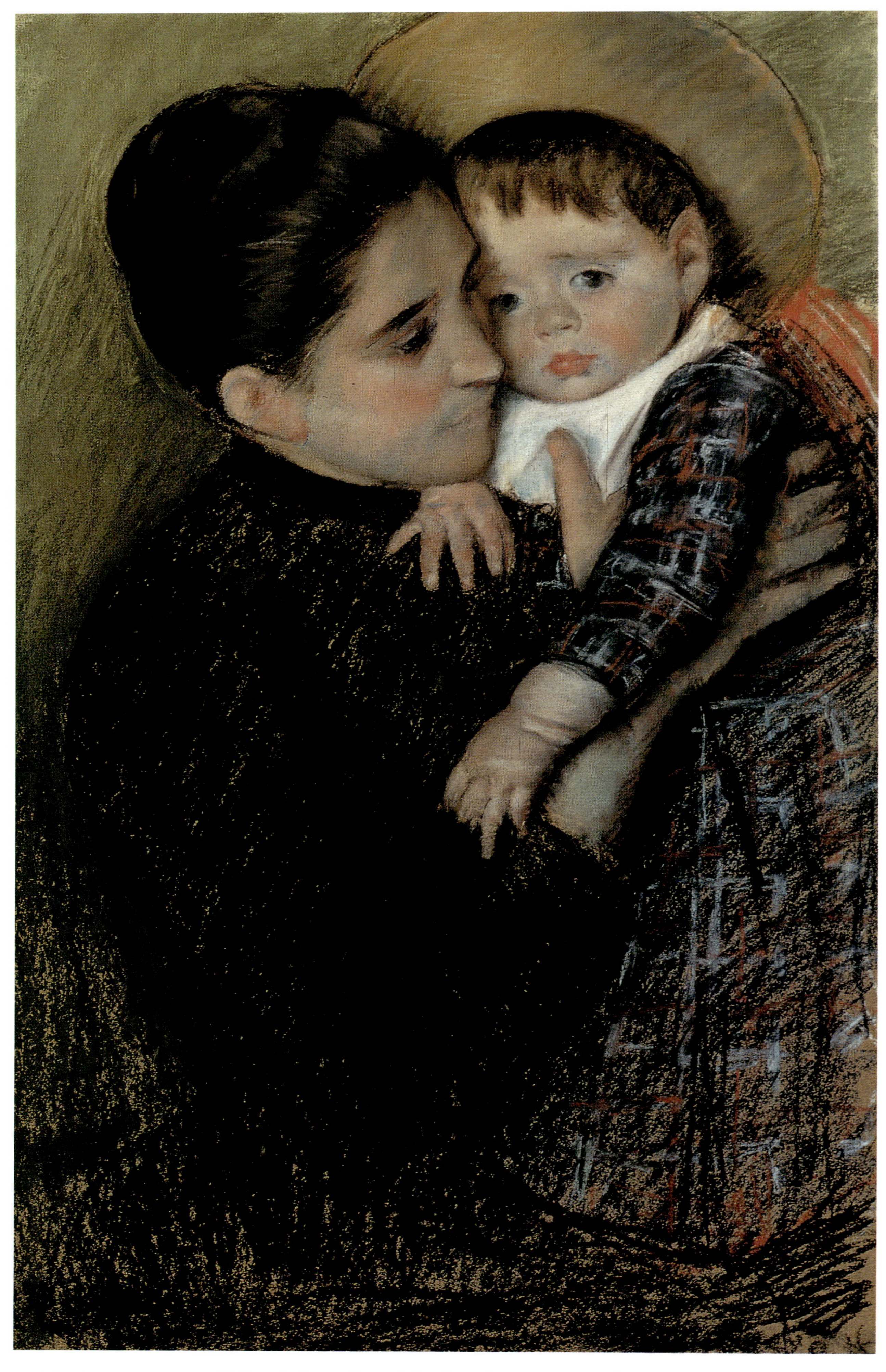

COLORPLATE 49. *Hélène de Septeuil.* c. 1889. Pastel on paper. 25 ¼ × 16 in. (64 × 40.6 cm). The William Benton Museum of Art, The University of Connecticut. The Louise Crombie Beach Memorial Collection.

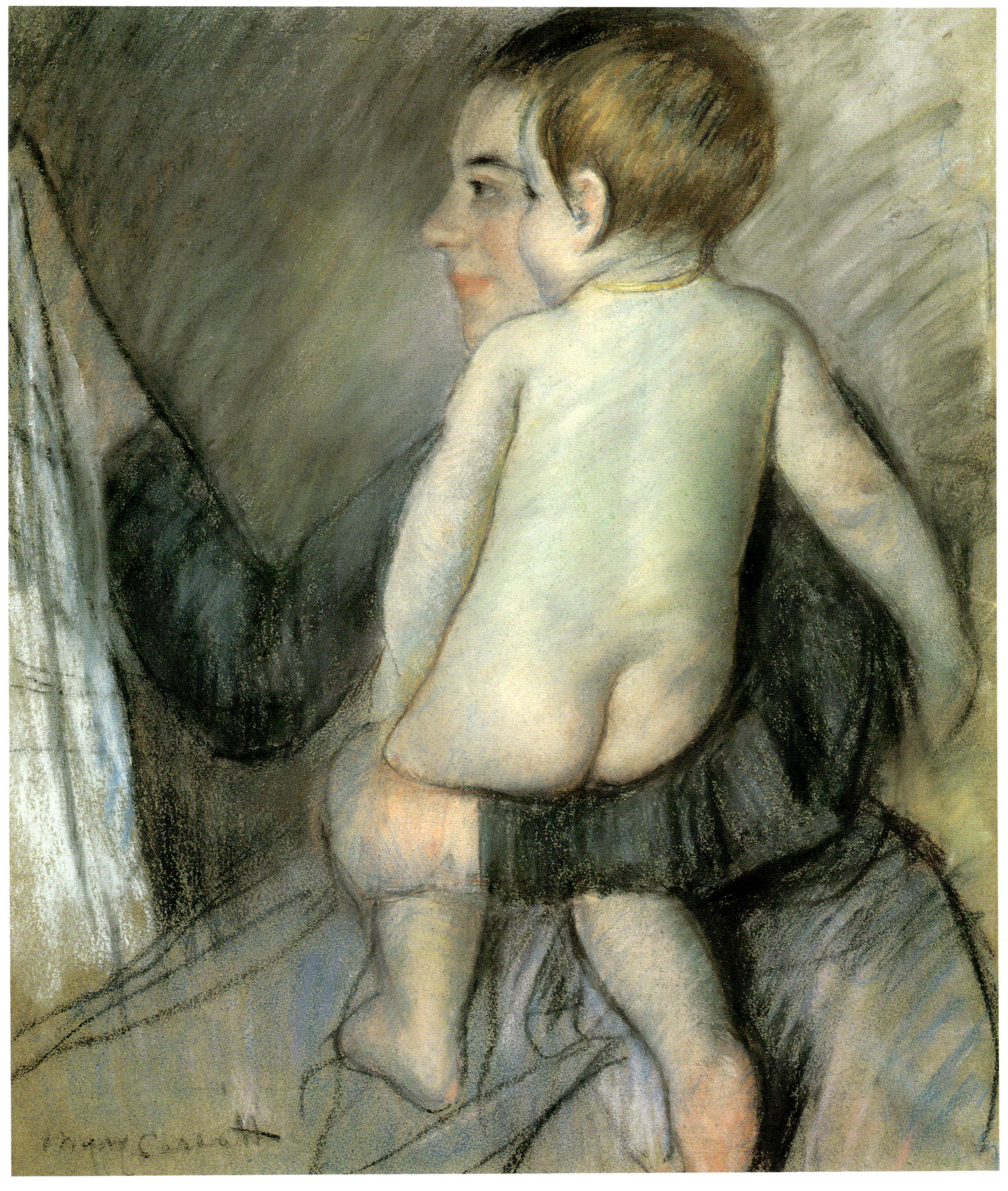

COLORPLATE 50. *At the Window.* 1889. Pastel and charcoal on paper. 29 3/4 × 24 1/2 in. (75.5 × 62.2 cm). Musée du Louvre, Paris. Photograph: Réunion des Musées Nationaux.

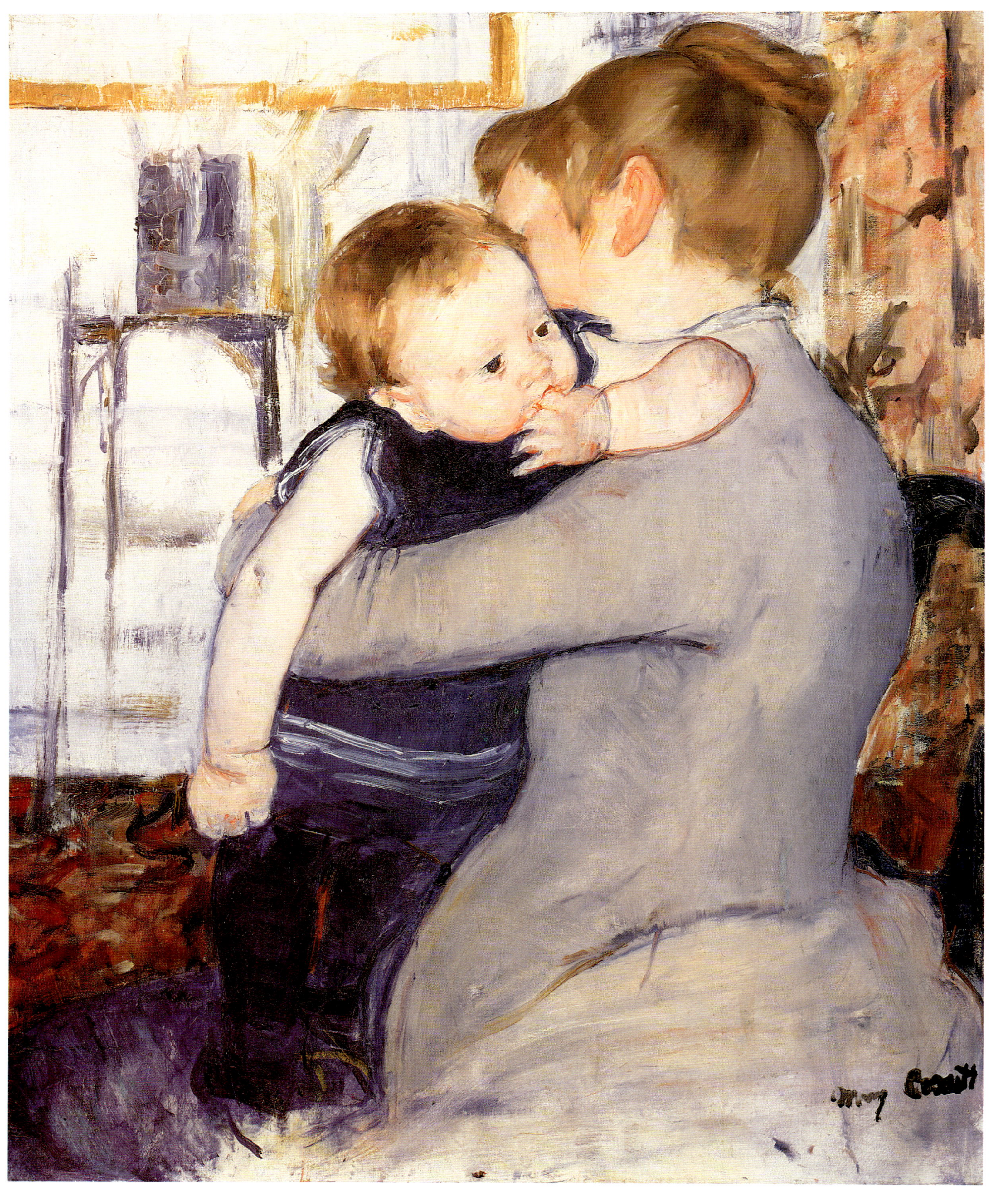

COLORPLATE 51. *Mother and Child (Baby in a Dark Blue Suit)*. c. 1889. Oil on canvas. 29 × 23 ½ in. (73.7 × 59.7 cm). Cincinnati Art Museum. John J. Emery Fund.

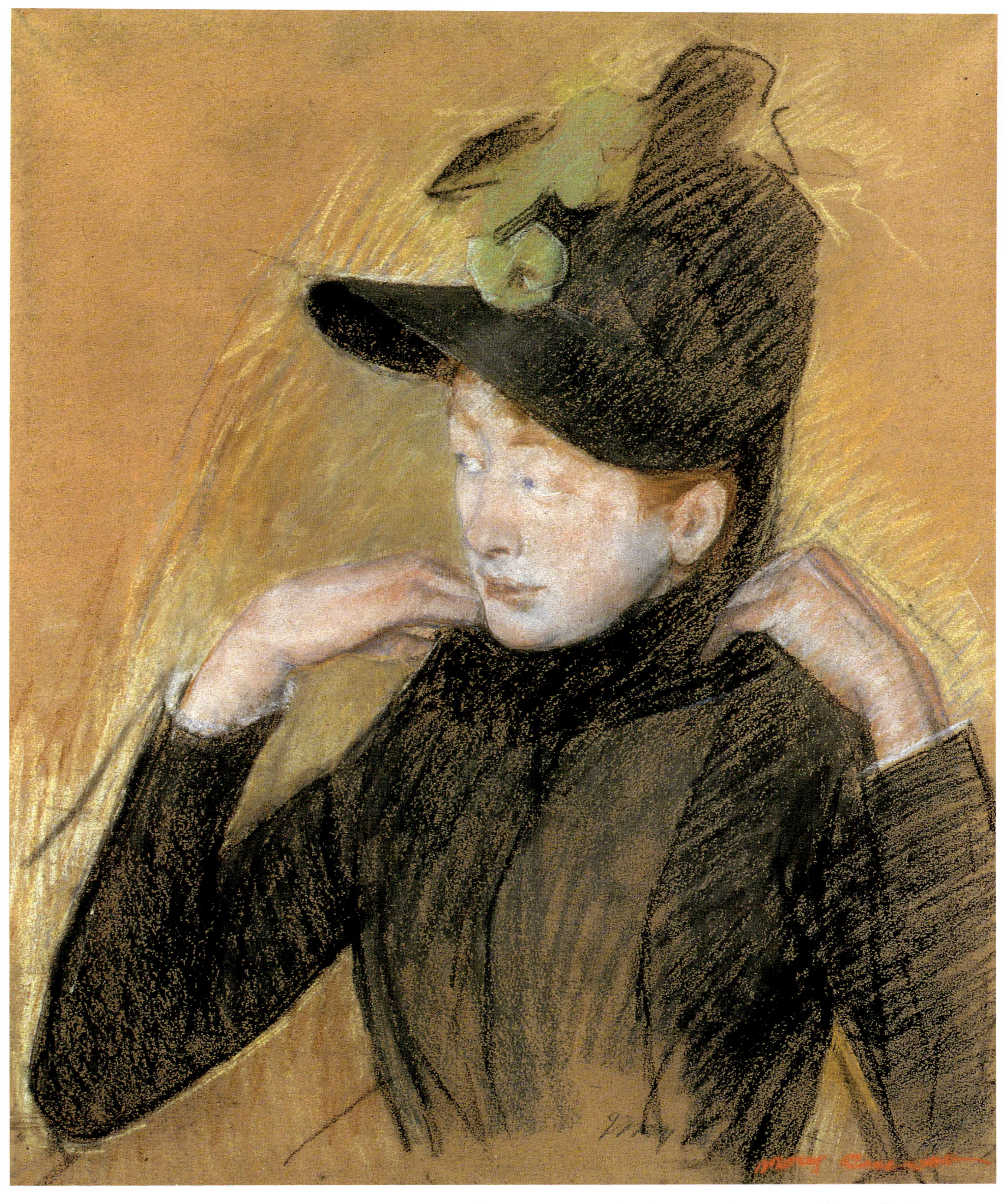

COLORPLATE 52. *Woman Arranging Her Veil.* c. 1890. Pastel on buff-colored wool paper. 25 7/8 × 21 7/16 in. (65.7 × 54.4 cm). Philadelphia Museum of Art. Bequest of Lisa Norris Elkins.

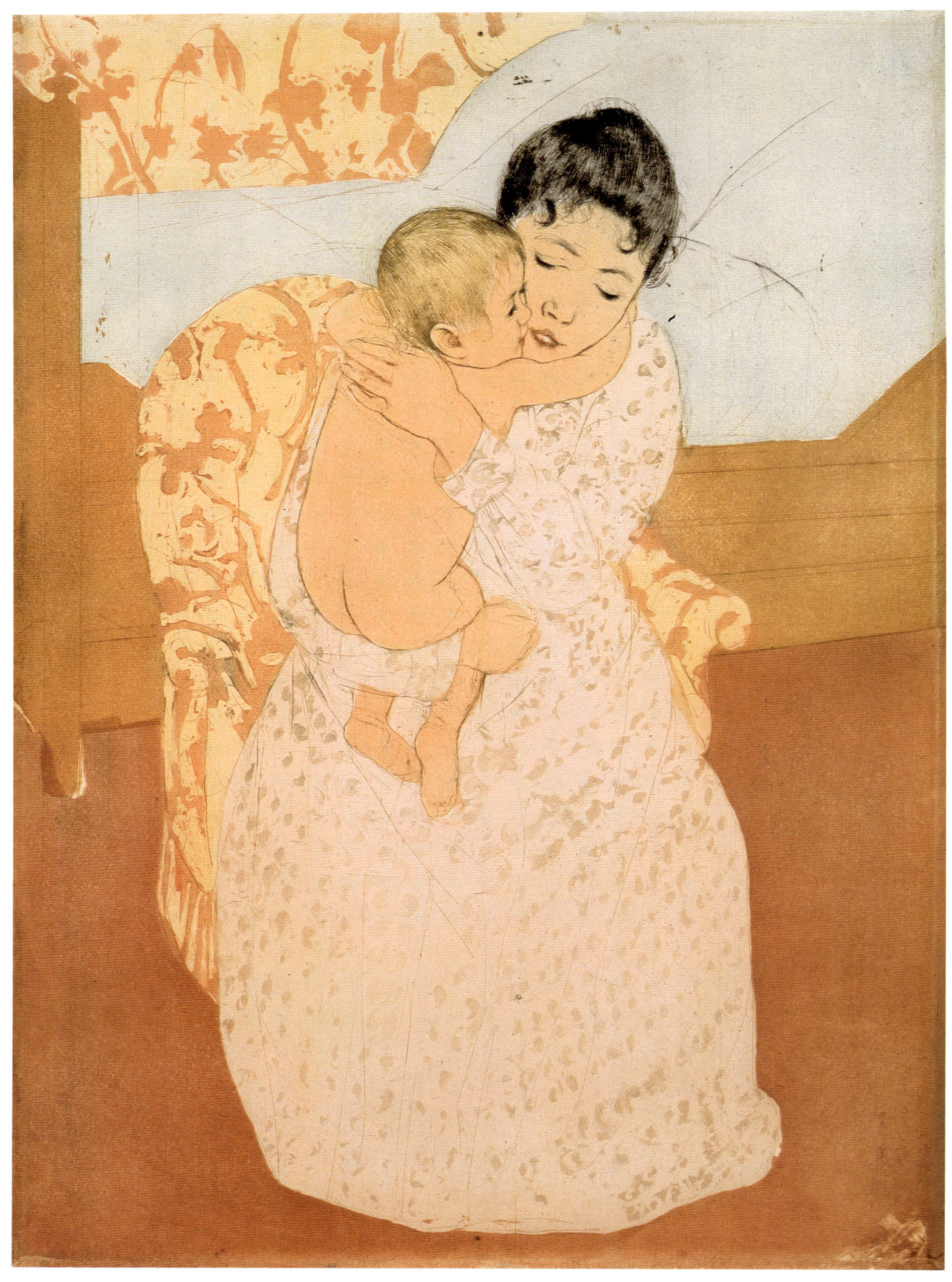

COLORPLATE 53. *Maternal Caress* (sixth state). c. 1891. Drypoint and soft-ground etching. 16 13/16 × 12 5/16 in. (42.7 × 31.2 cm). National Gallery of Art. The Rosenwald Collection. Photograph © Board of Trustees, National Gallery of Art, Washington, D.C.

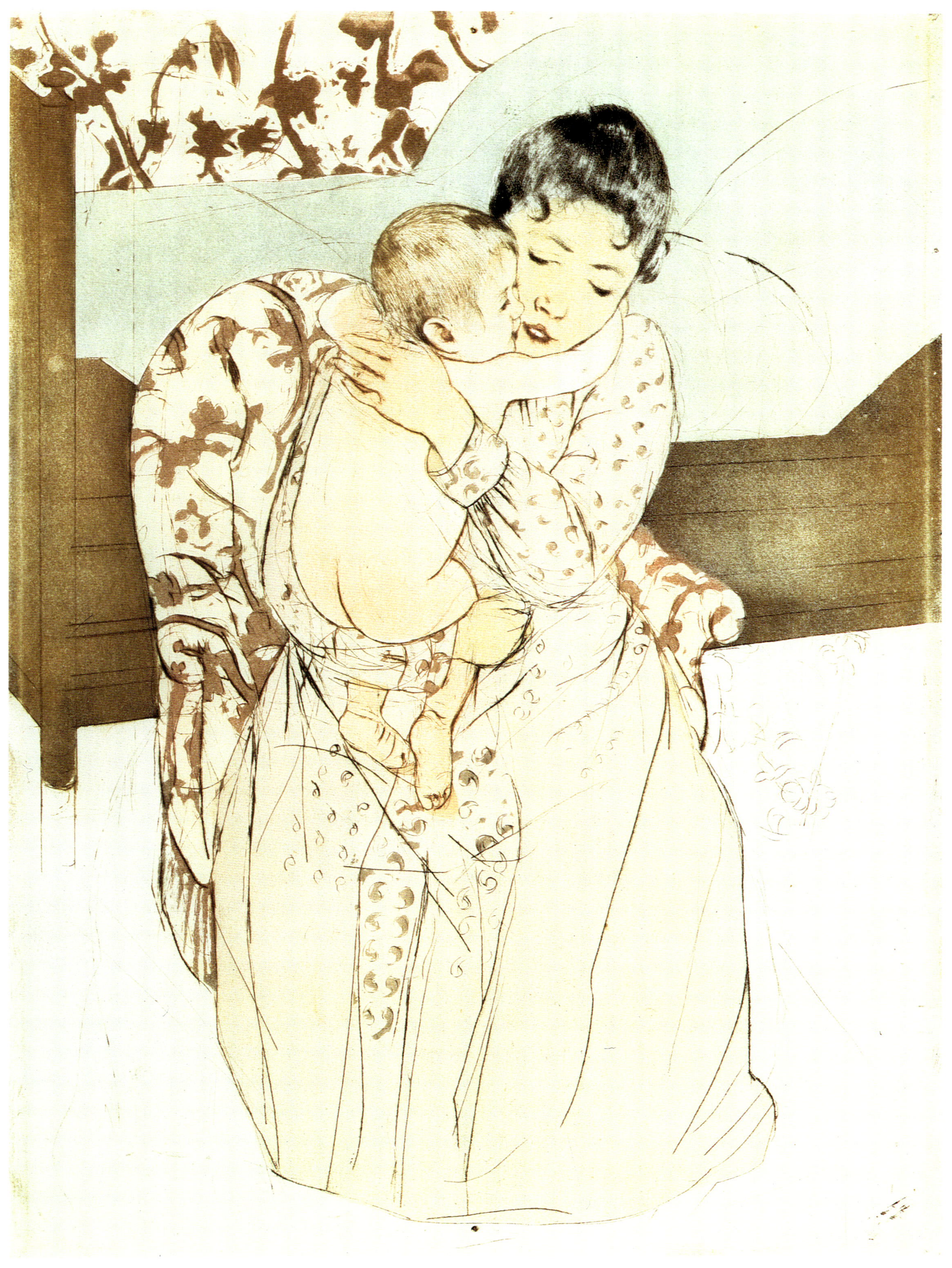

COLORPLATE 54. *Maternal Caress* (fifth state). 1891. Drypoint and aquatint. 14 ½ × 10 9⁄16 in. (36.8 × 26.8 cm). The Miriam and Ira D. Wallach Division of Art, Prints and Photographs. The New York Public Library Astor, Lenox and Tilden Foundations.

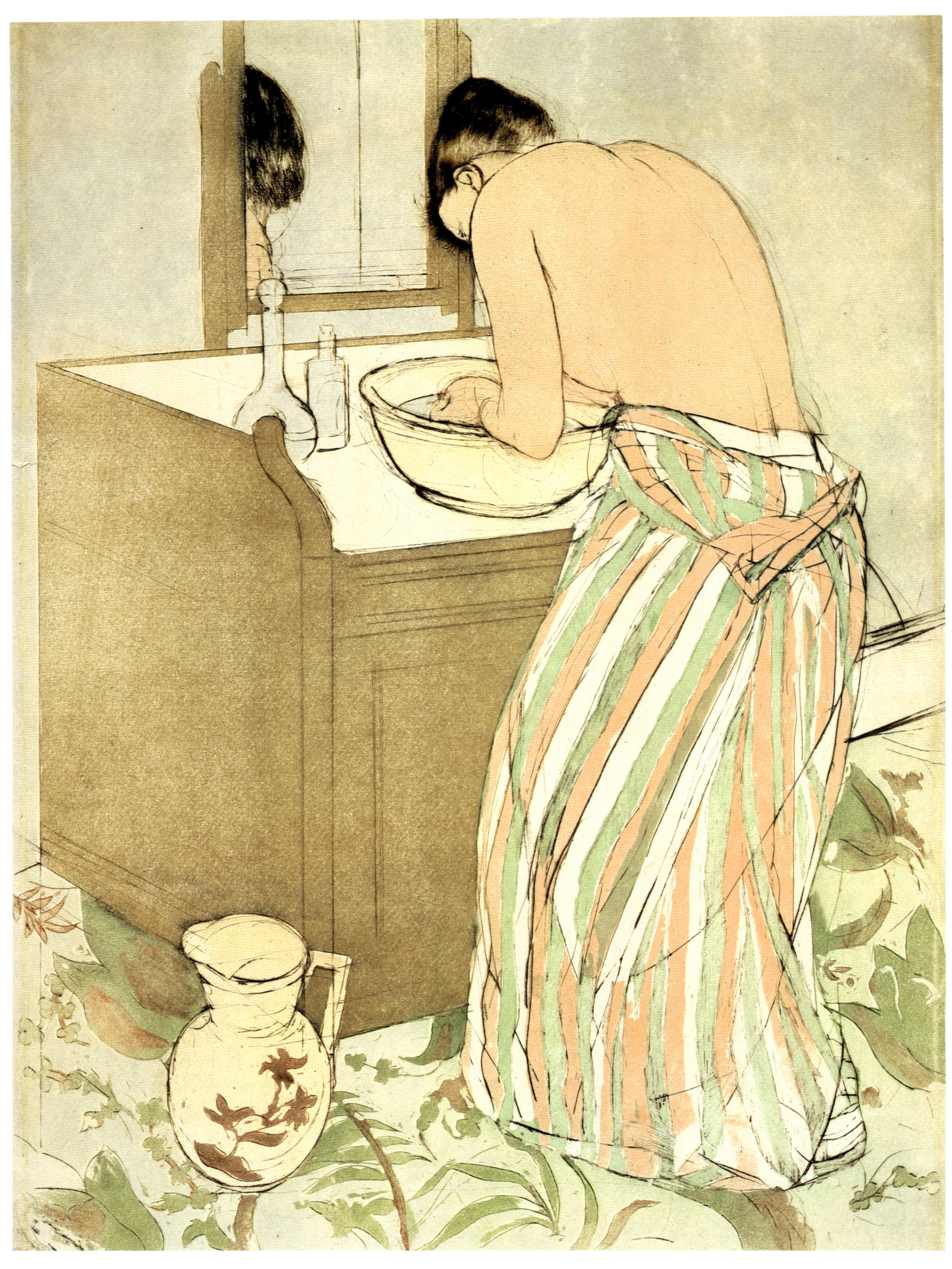

COLORPLATE 55. *Woman Bathing* (third state). 1890–91. Color drypoint and aquatint. 16 11/16 × 12 in. (42.3 × 30.4 cm). National Gallery of Art. The Rosenwald Collection. Photograph © Board of Trustees, National Gallery of Art, Washington, D.C.

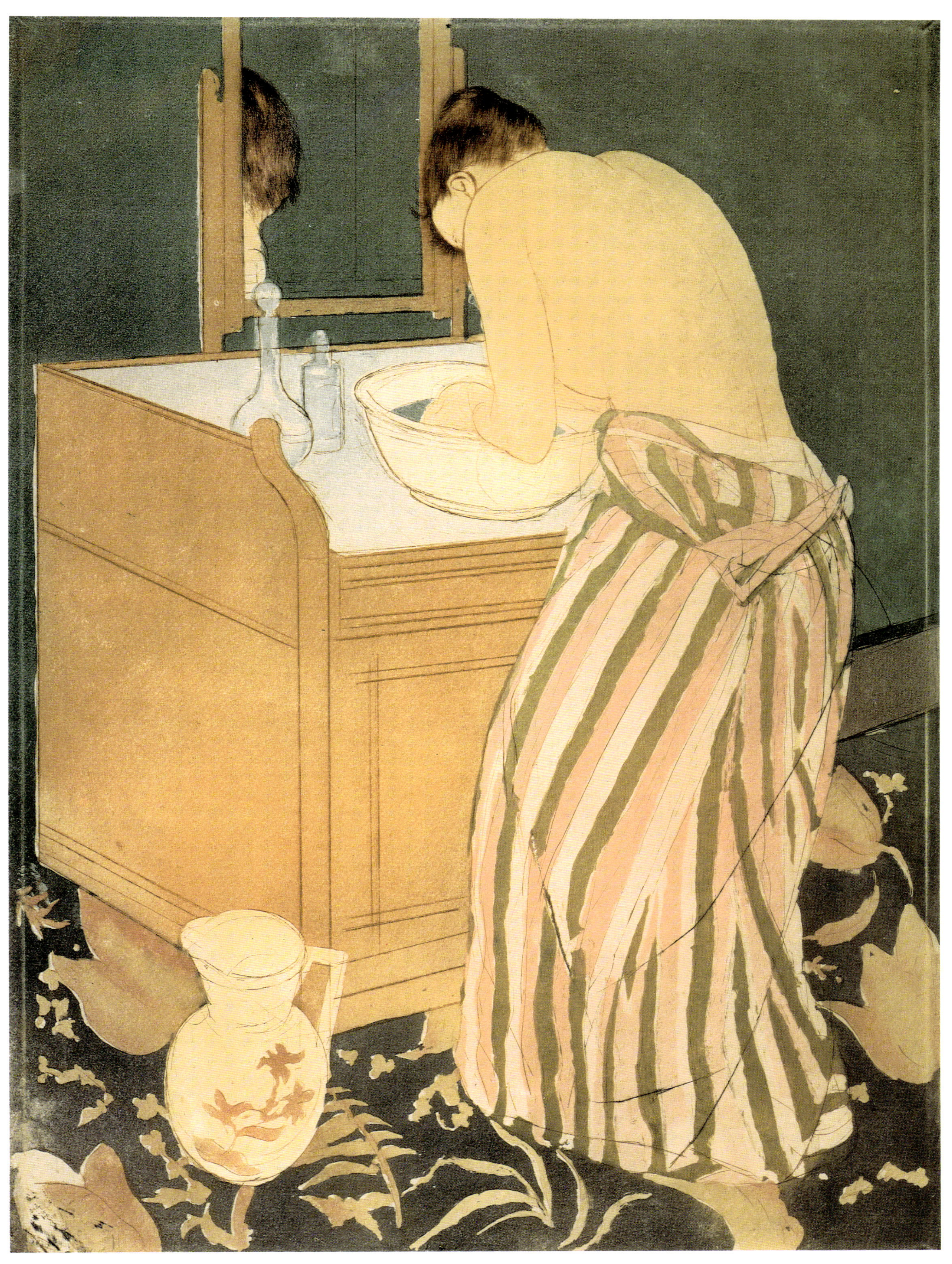

COLORPLATE 56. *Woman Bathing.* 1890–91. Color drypoint and aquatint. 16 11/16 × 12 in. (42.3 × 30.4 cm). National Gallery of Art. The Rosenwald Collection. Photograph © Board of Trustees, National Gallery of Art, Washington, D.C.

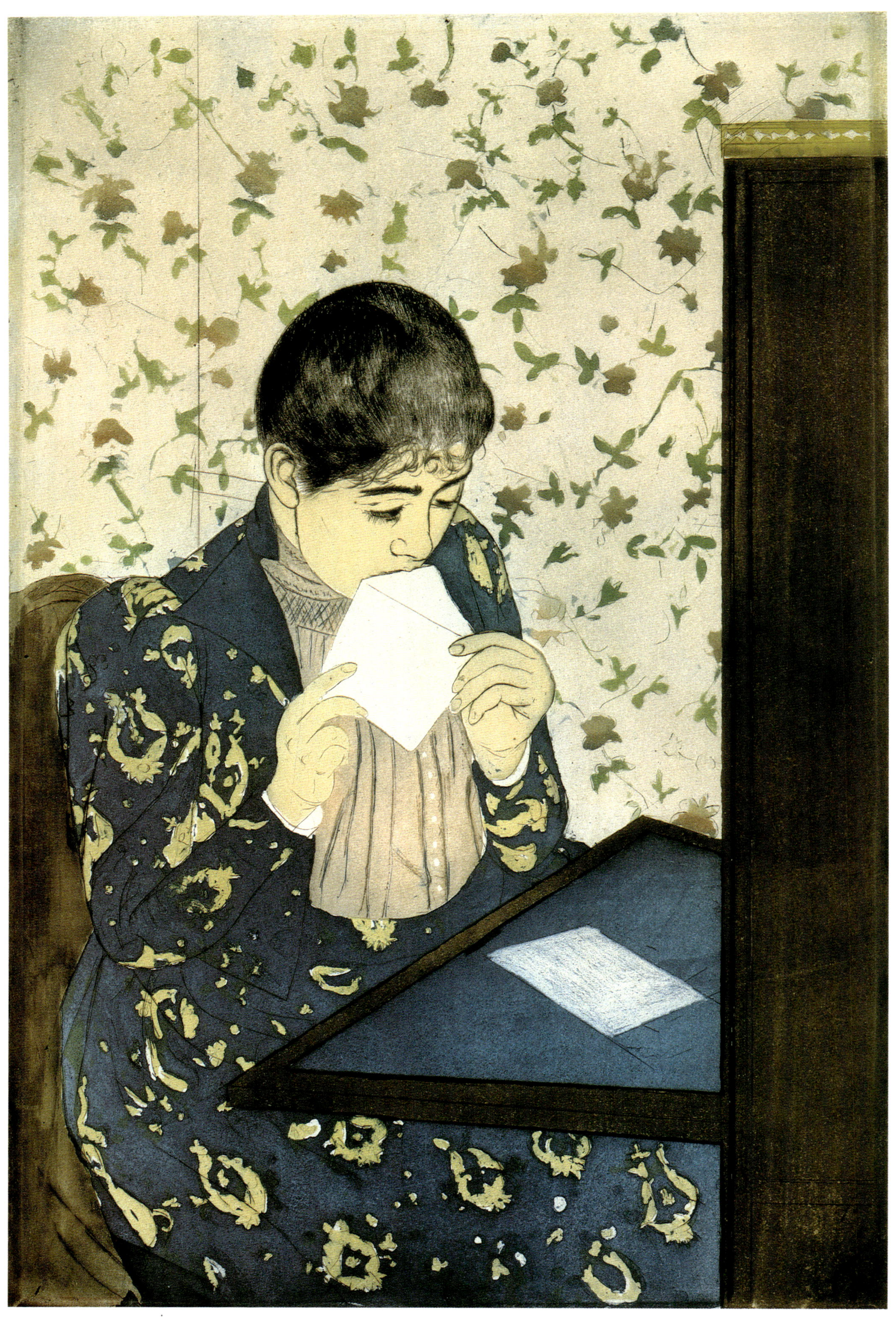

COLORPLATE 57. *The Letter.* 1890–91. Color drypoint and aquatint. 17 × 11 15⁄16 in. (43.2 × 30.3 cm). National Gallery of Canada, Ottawa. Bequest of Guy M. Drummond, Montreal.

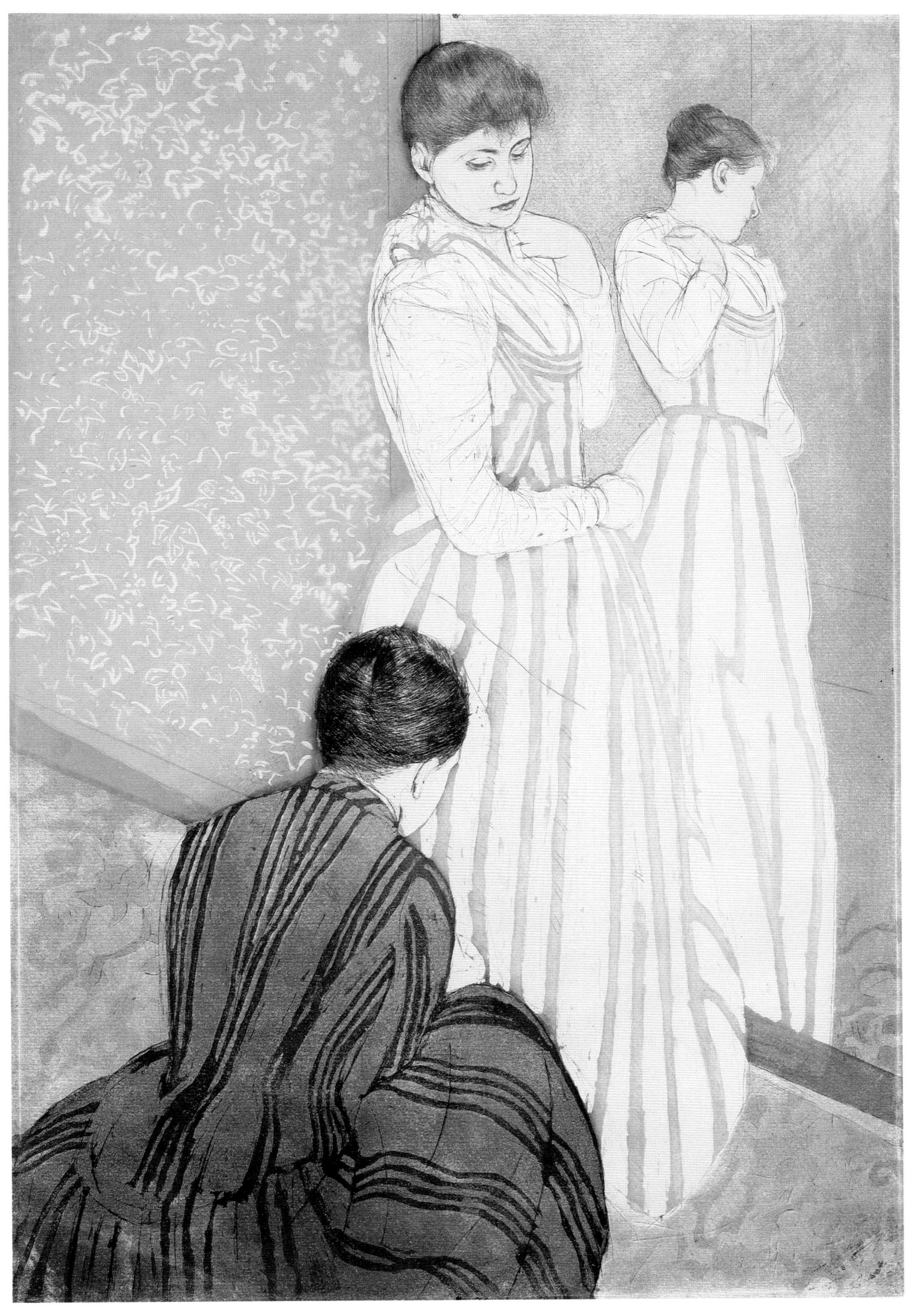

COLORPLATE 58. *The Fittng* (final state). 1891. Color drypoint and aquatint. 14 ¾ × 10 ⅛ in. (37.5 × 25.7 cm). Worcester Art Museum, Worcester, Massachusetts. Bequest of Mrs. Kingsmill Marrs.

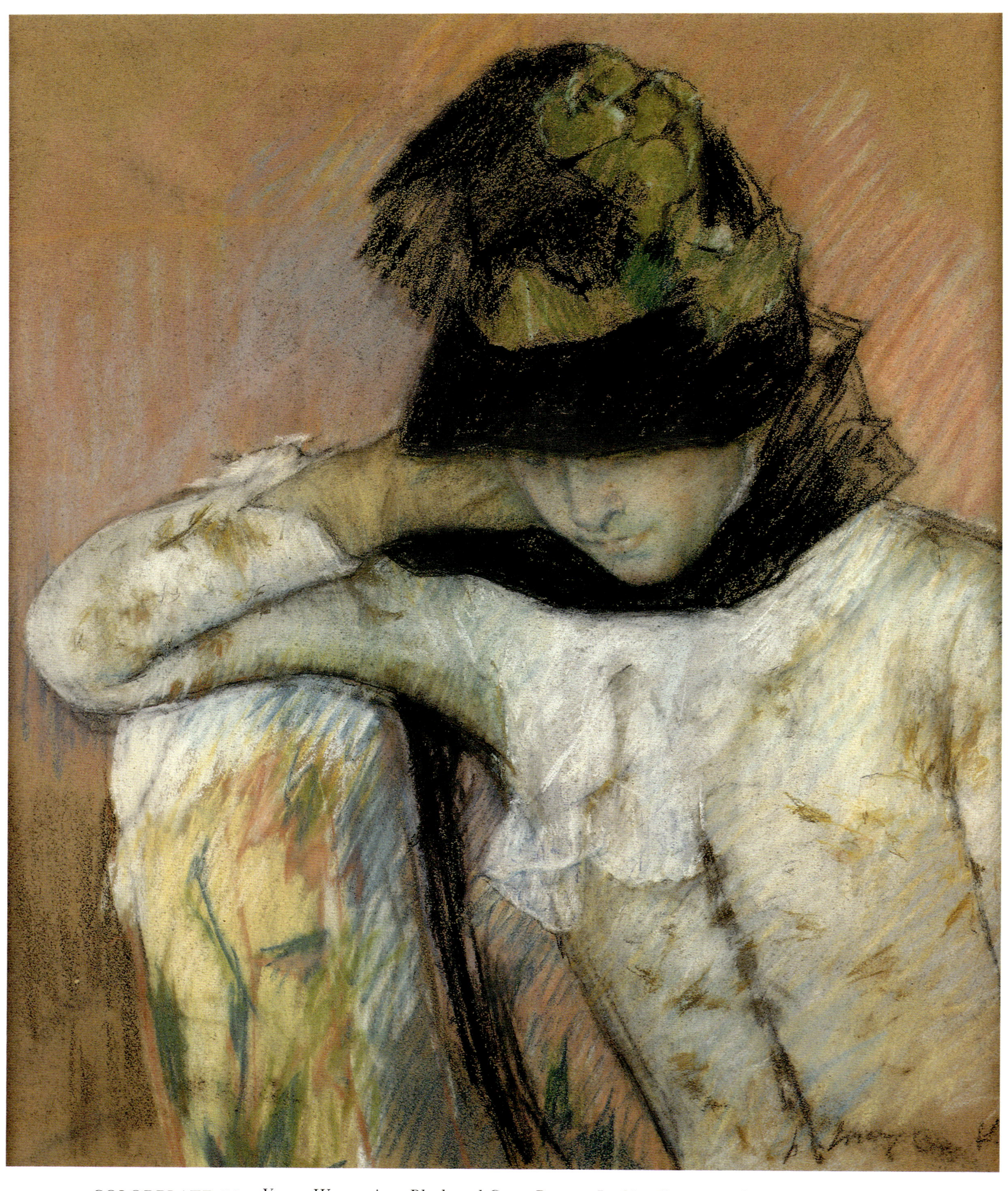

COLORPLATE 59. *Young Woman in a Black and Green Bonnet, Looking Down.* c. 1890. Pastel on paper. 25 ½ × 20 ½ in. (65 × 52 cm). The Art Museum, Princeton University. Gift of Mrs. Sally Sample Ely. Photograph: Bruce M. White

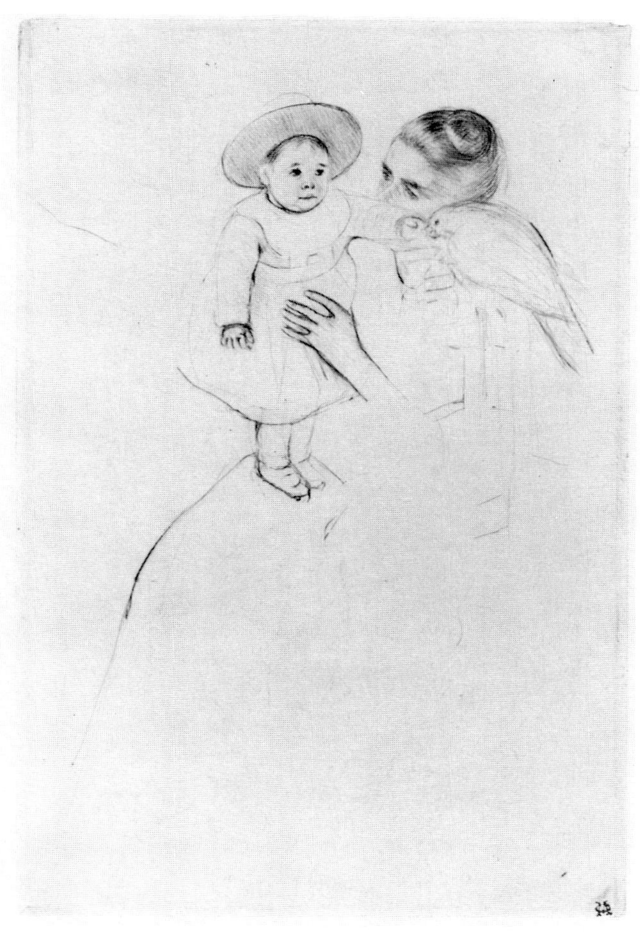

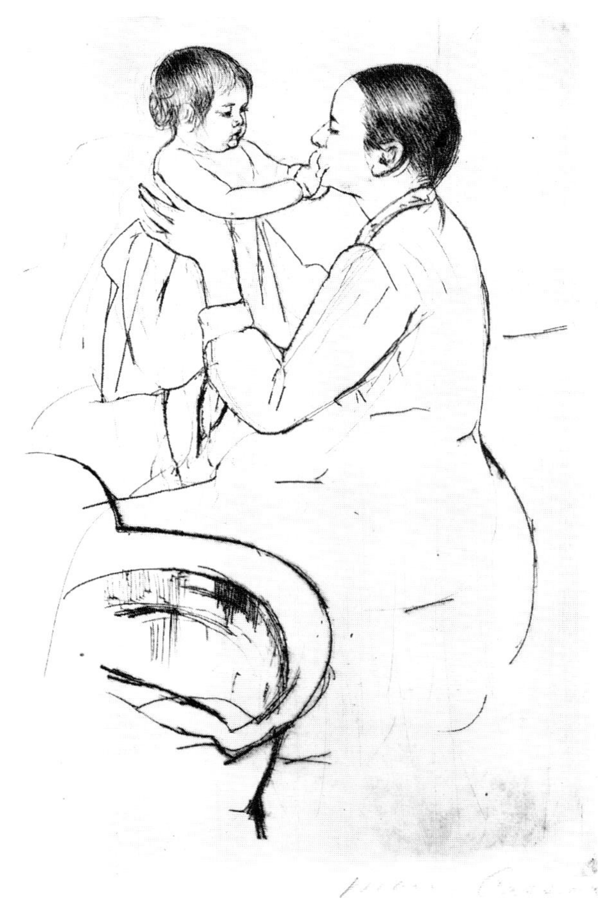

I think that for the time being I am not able to go and have lunch at Mezy, but if you would like, you could come and dine here with us and afterwards we could go to see the Japanese prints at the Beaux-Arts. Seriously, *you must not* miss that. You who want to make color prints you couldn't dream of anything more beautiful. I dream of it and don't think of anything else but color on copper. Fantin was there the 1st day I went and was in ecstasy. I saw Tissot there who also is occupied with the problem of making color prints. Couldn't you come the day of the wedding, Monday, and then afterwards we could go to the Beaux-Arts? If not that day then another and just drop me a line beforehand. My mother sends her compliments and I send a kiss to Julie and my best regards to Monsieur Manet.

Yours affectionately
Mary Cassatt

P.S. You *must* see the Japanese—*come as soon as you can.*

(Left) *Hélène de Septeuil.* 1889–90. Drypoint. 9 1/2 × 6 3/16 in. (24.1 × 15.7 cm). National Academy of Design, New York. Samuel Colman Collection.

(Right) *Mother Marie Dressing Her Baby After its Bath.* c. 1890. Drypoint. 9 3/4 × 6 5/8 in. (24.8 × 16.8 cm). Photograph courtesy of the Library of Congress.

Large exhibition of Japanese prints which opened at the École des Beaux-Arts on April 15, 1890.

Henri Fantin-Latour (1836–1904), French painter who studied with Courbet and became a member of the Realist movement in the 1850s and 1860s in Paris. Though he did not exhibit with them, he was a friend of many of the Impressionist artists.

James Joseph Jacques Tissot (1836–1902), French painter, etcher, and friend of Degas who spent most of his career (between 1871 and 1902) working in England.

GRACE GASSETTE

From *The Art Review*

"How Miss Cassatt Happened to do Colored Etching"

December 1908

Grace Gassette, American painter and sculptor, made contact with Cassatt while studying in Paris in 1906.

Only rarely has the public an opportunity to see the works of Mary Cassatt, that American woman of rare and original talent who ranks with the foremost painters of her time. There are some fifty canvases exhibited (most of them loaned), and they represent the various periods of her work. . . .

Miss Cassatt seems to be less known in America as an etcher than as a painter or pastellist. While having etched for many years, her most notable set of etchings was shown for the first time in 1892 [*sic*] at Durand-Ruels, Paris, galleries. They were colored etchings and were a rediscovery of the art of colored etching, opening a new field for experimenting. Since then she has had many imitators. There were twenty-five sets of these etchings and they were immediately disposed of.

Exhibition of color prints April–May, 1891 (not 1892).

It may be interesting to know how Miss Cassatt happened to do colored etching. The year previous she had attended at Beaux Arts with Philippe Burty, the art critic, the first official exhibition of Japanese pictorial art ever held in France, which was a recognition of oriental art and a decided breaking down of official feeling.

Philippe Burty (1830–1890), French art critic.

Burty called her attention to the superimposed line and color in a print which represented beautifully clothed women seen through a netting and enthusiastically remarked that no European could do that.

Miss Cassatt, with true American grit, made up her mind that she would at least make an effort to do so and prove the fallacy of his statement. This she did, and one of her greatest regrets was that Burty died before she had accomplished her task.

In spite of this achievement by which American etchers have benefited, I read not long ago what was supposed to be a comprehensive article on American etchers in which Miss Cassatt was not even mentioned. Whether she was willfully or ignorantly omitted by the author I do not know, but I know that we have no American figure etcher that can approach her dry points.

From *L'Art Moderne*

Pissarro and Cassatt at Durand-Ruel's

April 26, 1891

Paul Durand-Ruel (1828–1922), French art dealer, took over his father's business in 1855. He was known for his support of the Barbizon School and then, after 1871, the Impressionists. Durand-Ruel first began handling Cassatt's work in 1881, but did not have an exclusive contract with her until 1890.

M. Camille Pissarro and Mlle. Cassatt also exhibit with Durand-Ruel, in two small adjoining galleries, which one enters upon leaving the engravers' arena.

With twelve etchings (peasant women, markets, landscapes), two gouaches (one masterpiece, his *Marché dans la Grande-Rue à Gisors*), five color drawings, and three pastels, as well as in five graceful fans and some bucolic scenes, fresh summer mornings, and sunsets in which snowy fields

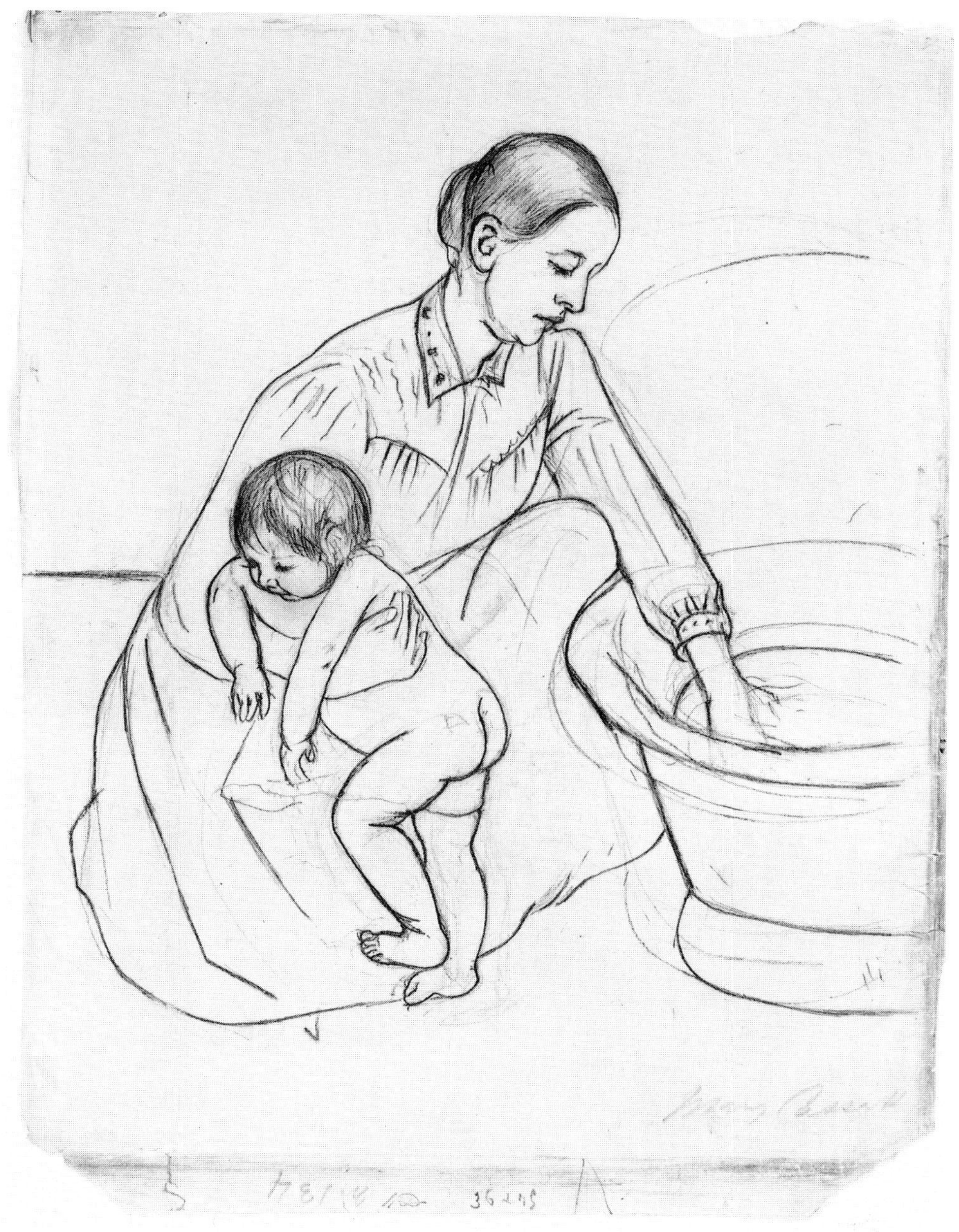

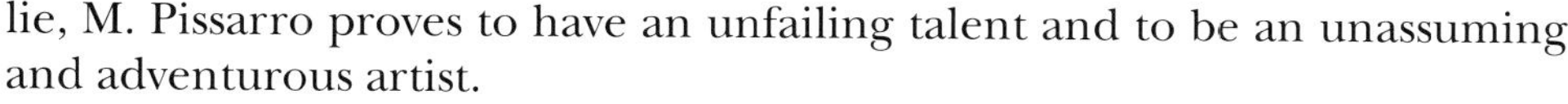

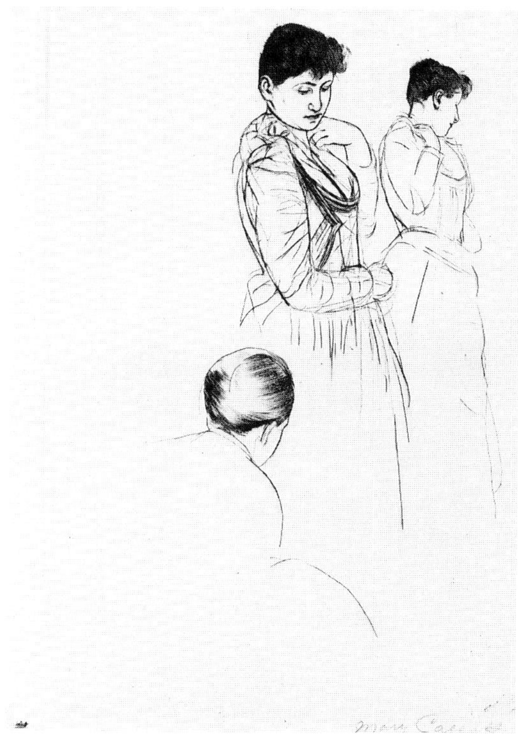

(Left) Drawing for *The Bath.* 1890–91. Graphite and black crayon. 13 ½ × 10 13/16 in. (34.2 × 27.4 cm). National Gallery of Art. The Rosenwald Collection. Photograph © Board of Trustees, National Gallery of Art, Washington, D.C.

(Right) *The Fitting* (first state). 1890–91. Drypoint. 14 ¾ × 10 in. (37.5 × 25.4 cm). National Gallery of Art. The Rosenwald Collection. Photograph © Board of Trustees, National Gallery of Art, Washington, D.C.

lie, M. Pissarro proves to have an unfailing talent and to be an unassuming and adventurous artist.

In her oils and pastels, Mlle. Cassatt is not very concerned with clear or brilliant painting; she is principally a draftsman, and Degas's only student. A master in her own right, she has given us variations on the theme of a mother and her child. But beyond the marvelous style of these honest works, which can bring to mind Ghirlandaio himself, there is the exquisite, unexpected grace of childish gestures that only a woman's soul could so subtly observe and express.

Domenico Ghirlandaio (c. 1448–1494), Italian Renaissance painter.

In eight engraved plates (drypoint and aquatint), Mlle. Cassatt breaks new ground. Scenes both intimate and worldly, these engravings, like the Japanese plates, are printed in color. If the first, her *Bain d'enfant,* is, in its attention to the process, a deliberate European translation of Utamaro (indeed, the artist titles it *Essai d'imitation de l'estampe japonaise*), *La Lettre,* the *Jeune femme essayant une robe* promise thoroughly personal works of charming artistic innovation.

COLORPLATE 57
COLORPLATE 58

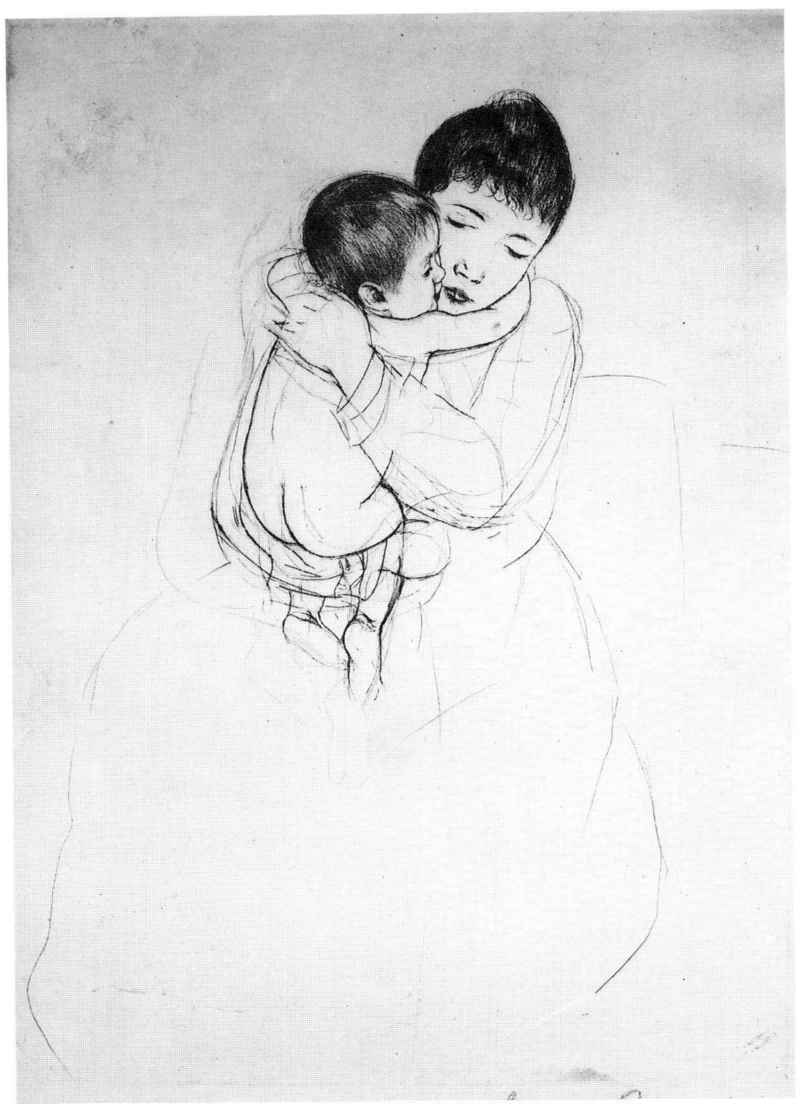

Maternal Caress (first state). 1890–91.
Drypoint. 14 ½ × 10 9/16 in. (36.8 × 26.8 cm).
Yale University Art Gallery. Gift of
Ivy Lee Callender, Walter R. Callender
Memorial Collection.

CECILIA WAERN

Cecilia Waern (1853–?), American author and art critic.

From *Atlantic Monthly*
"Some Notes on French Impressionism"
April 1892

Synthesis, too, has its heroes, artists to whom it has been a vital principle, not a mere formula, and who have won great and deserved success outside the narrow confines of the coterie; and I should delight to linger on the powerful qualities of the art of M. Degas, on M. Forain's penetratingly clever and artistic interpretations of some phases of contemporary life, on Miss Mary Cassatt's truly womanly studies of mothers and children, or felicitous, free translations of the exquisite synthetic art of the Japanese. . . .

Jean-Louis Forain (1852–1931), French painter, illustrator, and caricaturist.

This formula of synthesis, or the reduction of drawing to the necessary, the vital lines of the movement, cannot lay claim to the same originality as that of the décomposition du ton. Not to mention the Japanese, who have carried the synthetic treatment of line to such high and singular excellence, or the Greek vase-painters, or Giotto, or countless others, all children and primitive artists are synthesists after their fashion,—a fashion that seems to meet the high approval of some of the present synthétistes, to judge by specimens of their work. In others, you perceive landscape, with the element of light left almost entirely aside, synthetized down to the dusky dull sign-painting of our grandfathers' times, or scenes from contemporary life to grotesque caricatures. There is a good deal of affectation and coterie fashion in this, and of that curious allegiance to definite formulas, no matter how cramping, which mingles so strangely with the true artistic faculty in many French minds. But there are also, in many painters, the most undoubted sincerity, a profound feeling for the charm of mystery, and that longing for and reaching after the deeper spiritual truths of life that are thrilling through many a corner of Paris, undreamt of by the foreigners on the boulevards and the frequenters of the light theatres. Many an imaginative truth or curious suggestion looks out at you from among the exaggerations or mannerisms of products of *l'art hiératique* or *l'art symbolique,* whether enveloped in dusky mystery or wedded to luminism in visions of splendor.

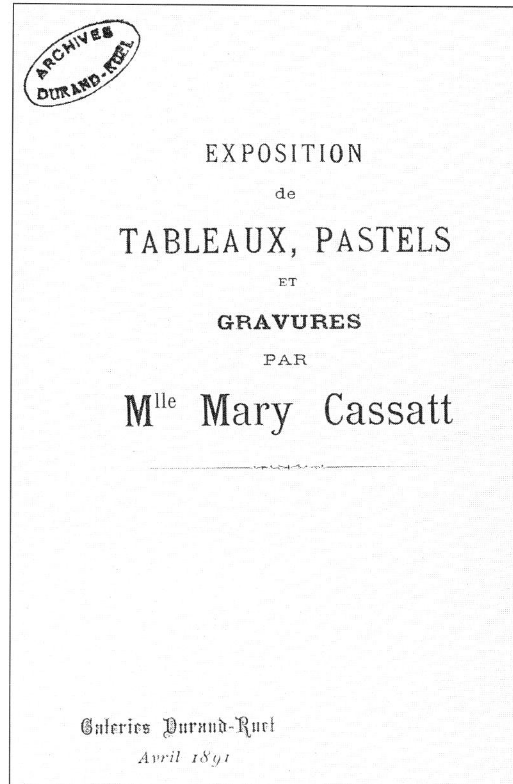

ARCHIVES DURAND-RUEL

EXPOSITION

de

TABLEAUX, PASTELS

ET

GRAVURES

PAR

Mlle Mary Cassatt

Galeries Durand-Ruel

Avril 1891

Photograph of the cover page of the Mary Cassatt Exhibition catalogue, Cassatt's first individual exhibition consisting of color prints, pastels, and paintings, held at the Galerie Durand-Ruel, Paris, in April 1891. Photograph courtesy of the Durand-Ruel Archives, Paris.

Félix Fénéon (1861–1944), French magazine editor and art critic, wrote on Seurat and other Post-Impressionists. During his career he was deeply involved in several movements that focused on social and artistic change—Symbolist literature, Post-Impressionist art, and anarchist agitation for workers' rights. Fénéon co-founded two Symbolist periodicals: "La Revue Indépendante" and "La Vogue."

FÉLIX FÉNÉON

From *Le Chat Noir*

On Cassatt's Exhibition of Color Prints, 1891

April 11, 1891

Besides the exhibition of the Peintres-Graveurs, at 11, rue Peletier, there are two solo exhibitions opening at 12, rue Lafitte: M. Camille Pissarro's and Miss Mary Cassatt's.

* * *

By the former: A child in its mother's arms. Their two heads touch, side by side, or else the tot, its arm outstretched, caresses the mummy's mouth, and we are not looking at a cute, quaint, or overly sentimental scene, the casual whim of a precarious tenderness; the figures remain normal, and a feeling of permanent maternity gently emanates from the group. Although Miss Cassatt's two paintings and two pastels illustrating the single theme are equally noble in conception, the execution of the pastels is one hundred times more attractive than that of the paintings: it is supple and active, portrays to perfection this naked child's body, these lilac, plaid, and white floral fabrics; the other tarnishes the faces with dull shadows, and freezes and immobilizes the country background.

Ten other numbers, in a layout that loses them in vast empty spaces, present familiar subjects, gracefully chosen, their arrangements more decorative than descriptive, and these unshaded, unmodelled, unmodulated compositions are colored in light tints that, retreating to their rings, stagnate there in their purity. In these figures, and more especially in certain details—the hair of a woman, the role of a mirror, the decoration of a carpet—this series conforms to the program announced in the catalogue: to attempt an "Imitation of the Japanese Print." What Cassatt has left the Japanese is any oversimplified formula for heads and hands, as well as their "dropped-out" white: her women's bodies, unlike the practice in the Far East, are tinted; though paler, it is the coffee color of the effigies of men in their albums. No matter what she wishes to adopt of the fundamental conventions of Japanese art, as legitimate as our own, her works in that course will maintain their originality intact, as long as she generalizes her sympathy for the masters from out there, rather than allowing [that sympathy] to be monopolized by any one of them. Today, the lace-like way she treats arms, shoulders, and generally all the lines of a nude recall too clearly dear Outamaro, but here [the] lines are more inflated than in Outamaro, and, therefore, influenced by Kiyonaga, with his fat napes, yet without a trace of what is a little facile, a little vulgar in Kiyonaga's naturalism.

Her stroke does not presume to the calligraphic bravura of Japanese colored woodcuts, cut like a brushstroke: hers, done with a dry point, is a slender stroke. The stroke seeks to render the enveloping lines clean, and often succeeds; it makes the interior ones sinuous; and, to close examination of proofs done with so light a hand, reveals its hesitations in spidery scrawls: there is nothing displeasing there. The copies of these "dry-point and aquatints" in the exhibition were well printed "by the artist and M. Leroy": only the faintest areas mar tints that are, by definition, flat. Faces whose cheekbones, eyes, and base of the nose are drawn in black have a bistre drawing for the nose and lips: and this contrast renders the features of the upper part of the face hard, and the whole discordant and, at times, almost baroque.

The observation of these women's faces and of these children is refined and calm. Lightly, the letter-writer expresses an effort to compose what she wishes to say in her letter, and her hesitation to close, and that the "Young woman trying on a dress" records a fleeting disquiet and curiosity. And, always, the large hands, those fine masculine hands that Cassatt likes to give her women, have a decorative function, especially when, contrasting with the bodies of naked children, they disrupt the lines, then rejoin them in unexpectedly created arabesques.

COLORPLATE 57
COLORPLATE 58

ACHILLE SEGARD

From *Mary Cassatt: Un Peintre des enfants et des mères*

Cassatt's Color Print Exhibition of 1891

1913

In order to force herself to an all but absolute precision in her drawing from the model, Miss Cassatt forced upon herself a working method that allows for no cheating or inaccuracy whatever. She was not satisfied to draw in pencil. She wanted to etch the copper with an iron point, so that the plate would retain the traces of her mistakes and pentimenti.

What a magnificent discipline! There is none more severe, none that gives finer results.

This etching in black rendered her an inestimable service. She began to practice this difficult art very early on. The public was unaware of this outstandingly conscientious artist's experiments and results until her April 1891 exhibition.

The exhibition was sparse. [At the Galerie Durand-Ruel. Until 1891, Miss Cassatt had shown with other engravers. In 1890, under the presidency of Henri Guérard, they formed the Society of French Painters and Engravers. The name excluded Miss Mary Cassatt. At first she felt it very deeply. Regaining heart, she obtained from MM. Durand-Ruel a room apart in which to show thirteen prints, while her rivals showed theirs in the large gallery.

Henri-Charles Guérard (1846–1897), French engraver and painter married to Eva Gonzalès.

The public's enthusiasm proved her right. One infers, however, that her success gave rise to a certain animosity against her. The artist recalls a dinner that took place the day after the opening of the painter and sculptor Bartholomé. Her fellow-guests teased her, at times with such

Albert Bartholomé (1848–1928), French painter and sculptor, and a good friend of Degas.

malice that she left the gathering extremely upset, almost in tears. This example suggests that her beginnings were sometimes difficult.] It was made up of only four—albeit magnificent—oil paintings and a series of ten color engravings, one of an edition of ten, pulled by the artist herself. The printing had been done in a sort of feverish haste, with materials hastily assembled, in collaboration with a skilled artisan, whom the artist, with scrupulous delicacy, wished to ally to her success by including his name in the catalogue. This caused Degas to say, "Why this man?. . ."

Today, this series is virtually unobtainable. [The author owns one complete series, MM. Durand-Ruel have another, and M. Vollard has a third.] It was simultaneously a point of departure and a culmination. Even at the time it was a culmination, because its creator had been exercising her art conscientiously for some years. It was a point of departure as well, because many times later on she surpassed herself in this area.

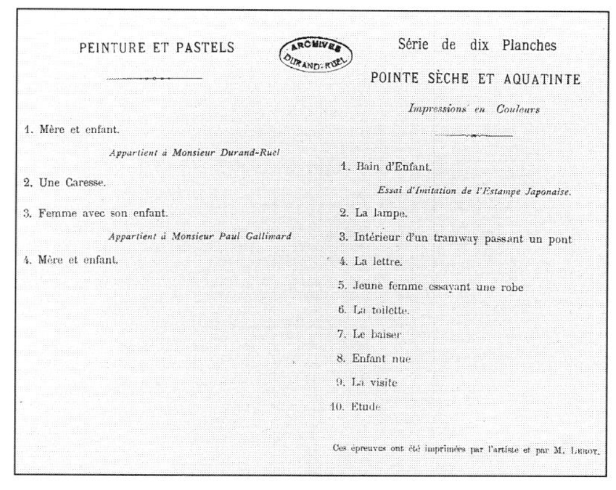

PEINTURE ET PASTELS

1. Mère et enfant.
Appartient à Monsieur Durand-Ruel
2. Une Caresse.
3. Femme avec son enfant.
Appartient à Monsieur Paul Gallimard
4. Mère et enfant.

Série de dix Planches

POINTE SÈCHE ET AQUATINTE

Impressions en Couleurs

1. Bain d'Enfant.
Essai d'Imitation de l'Estampe Japonaise.
2. La lampe.
3. Intérieur d'un tramway passant un pont
4. La lettre.
5. Jeune femme essayant une robe
6. La toilette.
7. Le baiser
8. Enfant nue
9. La visite
10. Etude

Ces épreuves ont été imprimées par l'artiste et par M. Leroy.

Photograph of the list of works in the Mary Cassatt Exhibition catalogue. April 1891. Photograph courtesy of the Durand-Ruel Archives, Paris.

"Why this man" refers to Louis Leroy, see photo page 186.

Lucien Pissarro (1863–1944), French painter and printmaker, and the eldest son of Camille Pissarro.

CAMILLE PISSARRO

From *Letters to His Son Lucien*
In Praise of Cassatt's Color Prints
April 3, 1891

Paris
April 3, 1891

My dear Lucien,

It is absolutely necessary, while what I saw yesterday at Miss Cassatt's is still fresh in mind, to tell you about the colored engravings she is to show at

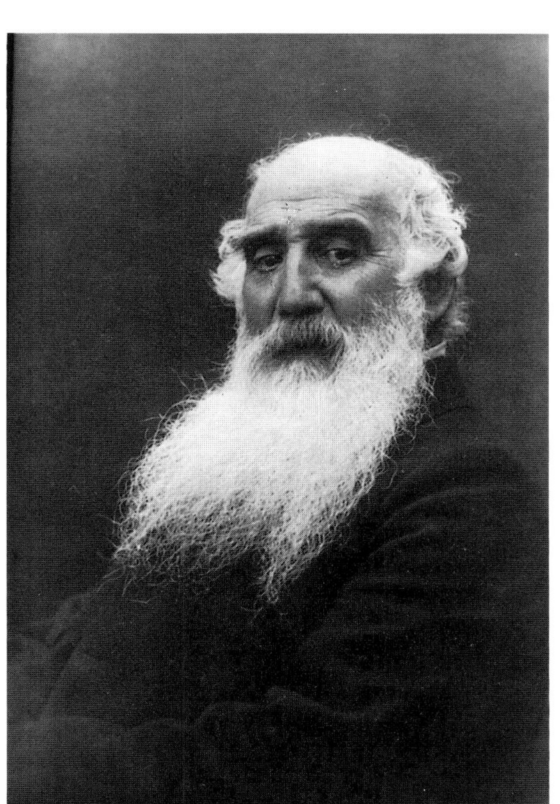

Photograph of Camille Pissarro. c. 1893. Photograph courtesy of the Durand-Ruel Archives, Paris.

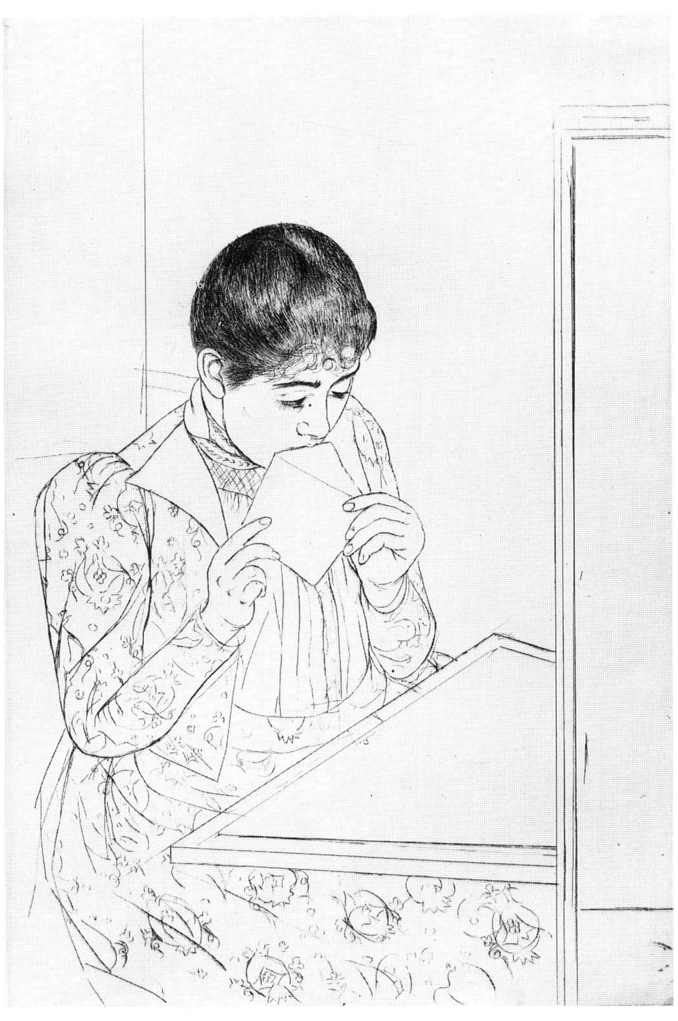

The Letter (first state). 1890–91. Drypoint. 13 5/8 × 8 5/16 in. (34.6 × 21.1 cm). The Metropolitan Museum of Art, New York. Gift of Arthur Sachs. Photograph © The Metropolitan Museum of Art.

Durand-Ruel's at the same time as I. We open Saturday, the same day as the patriots, who, between the two of us, are going to be furious when they discover right next to their exhibition a show of rare and exquisite works.

You remember the effects you strove for at Eragny? Well, Miss Cassatt has realized just such effects, and admirably: the tone even, subtle, delicate, without stains on seams: adorable blues, fresh rose, etc. Then, what must we have to succeed? . . . money, yes, just a little money. We had to have copper-plates, a *boîte à grain,* this was a bit of a nuisance but it is absolutely necessary to have uniform and imperceptible grains and a good printer. But the result is admirable, as beautiful as Japanese work, and it's done with printer's ink! When I get some prints I will send you some; incidentally I have agreed to do a series with Miss Cassatt; I will do some *Markets, Peasant Women in the Fields,* and—this is really wonderful—I will be able to try to put to the proof some of the principles of neo-impressionism. What do you think? If we could make some beautiful engravings, that would really be something.

Camille Pissarro's home at Eragny, near Gisors, about fifty miles northwest of Paris.

This series was never realized.

I have seen attempts at color engraving which will appear in the exhibition of the patriots, but the work is ugly, heavy, lusterless and commercial. I am certain that Miss Cassatt's effort will be taken up by all the tricksters who will make empty and pretty things. We have to act before the idea is seized by people without aesthetic principle.

This is a bad moment for me, Durand doesn't take my paintings. Miss Cassatt was much surprised to hear that he no longer buys my work, it seems that he sells a great deal.—But for the moment people want nothing but Monets, apparently he can't paint enough pictures to meet the demand. Worst of all they all want *Sheaves in the Setting Sun*! always the same story, everything he does goes to America at prices of four, five and six thousand francs. All this comes, as Durand remarked to me, from not shocking the collectors! True enough! What do you want, I replied, one has to be built that way, advice is useless. But while waiting we have to eat and pay our debts. Life is hard!

Letter from Mary Cassatt to Frank Weitenkampf

On Printing

May 18, 1906

10, Rue de Marignan
Paris

Dear M. Weitenkampf,

In reply to your's of May the 9th asking about the printing of my colored etchings, my system was as follows—I drew the outlines in dry-point and laid on a grain where color was to be applied, then colored "à la poupée"—I was entirely ignorant of the method when I began, and as all the plates were colored by me, I varied sometimes the manner of applying the color—The set of ten plates was done with the intention of attempting an imitation of Japanese methods—of course I abandoned that somewhat after the first plate, and tried more for atmosphere—

Believe me very sincerely yours,

Mary Cassatt

LOUISINE HAVEMEYER

From *Sixteen to Sixty: Memoirs of a Collector*

Cassatt at the Printing Press

1930

I recall the time when she was interested in etching. Eight o'clock in the morning would find her in her gray blouse in the small pavilion over the dam that fed her *pièce d'eau* and where she had installed her printing press. There she would work while daylight lasted with the aid of a printer. She did her own coloring and wiping of the plates. It was at the cost of much physical strain for she actually did the manual work.

"I wonder all etchers do not do their own printing!" she said to me. "It makes a great difference, for no two impressions are exactly alike." Then she continued, "I love to do the colored prints, and I hope the Durand-Ruels will put mine on the market at reasonable prices. For nothing, I believe, will inspire a taste for art more than the possibility of having it in the home. I should like to feel that amateurs in America could have an

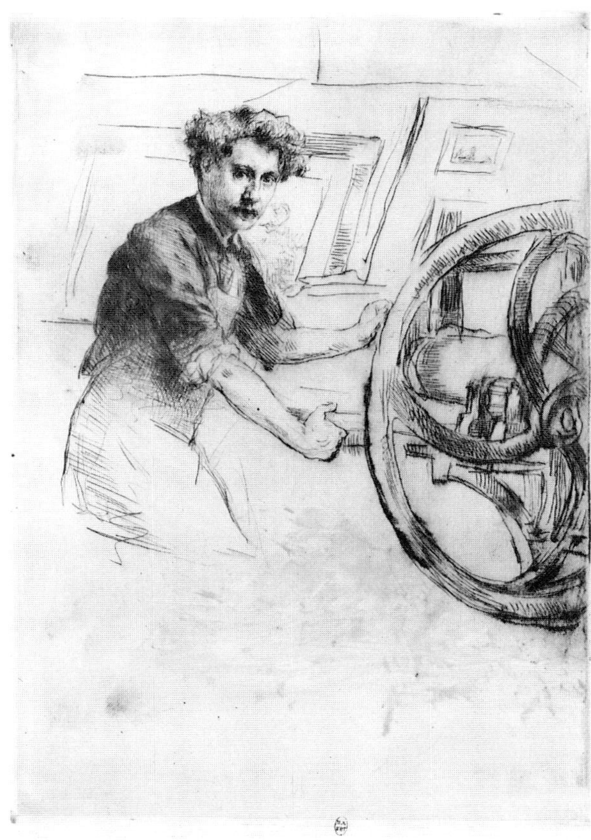

Marcellin Desboutin. *Portrait of the Printer, Leroy* (third state). 1875. Drypoint. 11 ⅝ × 8 ¼ in. (29.5 × 21 cm). Photograph © Bibliothèque Nationale de France, Cabinet des Estampes, Paris.

example of my work, a print or an etching, for a few dollars. That is what they do in France. It is not left to the rich alone to buy art; the people—even the poor—have taste and buy according to their means. And here they can always find something they can afford."

Helas! Miss Cassatt did not continue etching! "The Durand-Ruels tell me there is not enough in it," she said to me rather bitterly. "They want me to go back to pastels." I bought an impression of her colored print of *The Girl with the Banjo*. The price was fifteen dollars.

COLORPLATE 72

Letters from Mary Cassatt to Bertha Palmer

On the *Modern Woman* Mural

1892

Bertha Honoré Palmer (1849–1918), Chicago society leader and supporter of social and economic reform. She was the wife of one of Chicago's most prominent businessmen, Potter Palmer. Cassatt met Palmer in Paris and advised her on purchasing works of the French Impressionists, thus introducing these works to America. Palmer served as chair of the Board of Lady Managers of the Woman's Building for the World's Columbian Exposition held in Chicago in 1893.

The "Modern Woman" mural was painted for the Hall of Honor of the Woman's Building. It was to fit the tympanum (the curved space under the barrel-vaulted roof) opposite the mural "Primitive Woman" by Mary Fairchild MacMonnies (1858–1946).

Bachivillers
October 11

My dear Mrs. Palmer,

Your letter of Sept. 27th only arrived this morning, so unfortunately this will not reach you by the 18th as you desired. Notwithstanding that my letter will be too late for the ladies of the committee, I should like very much to give you some account of the manner I have tried to carry out my idea of the decoration.

Mr. Avery sent me an article from one of the New York papers this summer, in which the writer, referring to the order given to me, said my subject was to be the "The Modern Woman as glorified by Worth"! That would hardly describe my idea, of course I have tried to express the

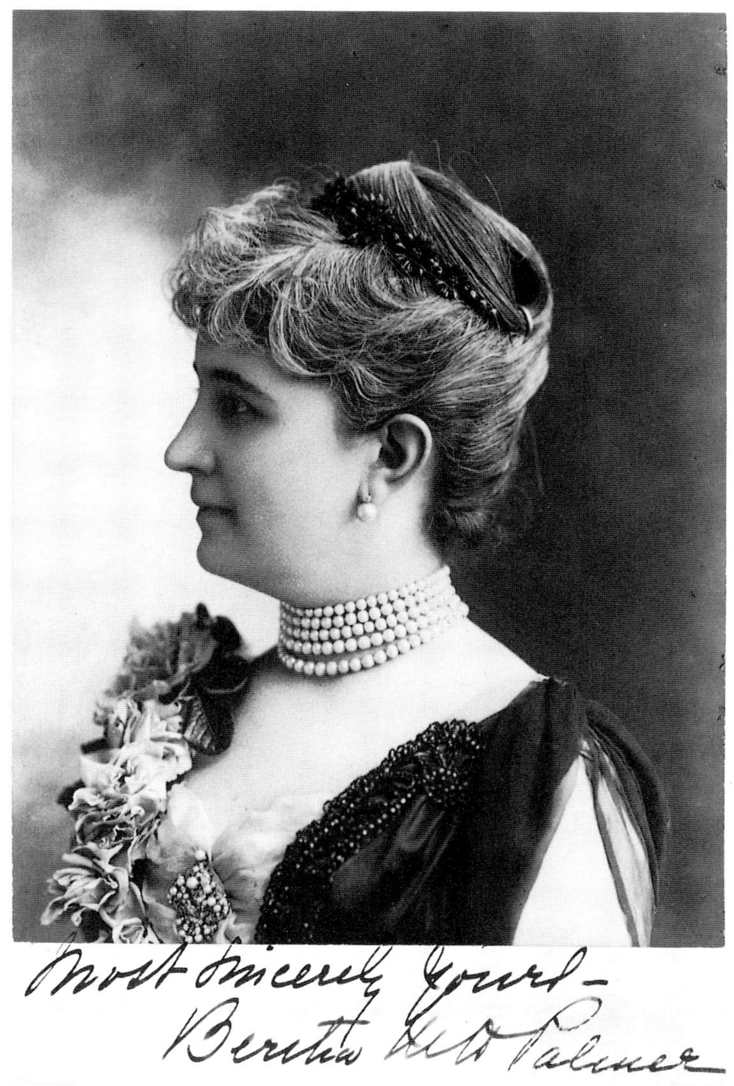

Photograph of Bertha Honoré Palmer (Mrs. Potter Palmer). 1892. Photograph courtesy of the Library of Congress.

modern woman in the fashions of our day and have tried to represent those fashions as accurately & as much in detail as possible. I took for the subject of the central & largest composition Young women plucking the fruits of knowledge or science &—that enabled me to place my figures out of doors & allowed of brilliancy of color. I have tried to make the general effect as bright, as gay, as amusing as possible. The occasion is one of rejoicing, a great national fête. I reserved all the seriousness for the execution, for the drawing & painting. My ideal would have been one of those admirable old tapestries brilliant yet soft. My figures are rather under life size although they seem as large as life. I could not imagine women in modern dress eight or nine feet high. An American friend asked me in rather a huffy tone the other day "Then this is woman apart from her relations to man?" I told him it was. Men I have no doubt, are painted in all their vigour on the walls of the other buildings; to us the sweetness of childhood, the charm of womanhood, if I have not conveyed some sense of that charm, in one word if I have not been absolutely feminine, then I have failed. My central canvass I hope to finish in a few days, I shall have some photographs taken & sent to you. I will still have place on the side panels for two compositions, one, which I shall begin immediately is, young girls pursuing fame. This seems to me very modern & besides will give me an opportunity for some figures in clinging draperies. The other panel will represent the Arts, Music (nothing of St. Cecelia) Dancing & all treated in the most modern way. The whole is surrounded by a border, wide below, narrower above, bands of color, the lower cut with circles containing naked babies tossing fruit, &&c. I think, my dear Mrs. Palmer, that if you were here & I could take you out to my studio & show you what I have done that

Charles Frederick Worth (1825–1895), English couturier who, after he came to Paris in 1845, established one of the most influential fashion houses in the world.

Theme of the Woman's Building.

you would be pleased indeed without too much vanity I may say I am almost sure you would.

When the work reaches Chicago, when it is dragged up 48 feet & you will have to stretch your neck to get sight of it all, whether you will like it then, is another question. Stillman, in a recent article, declares his belief that in the evolution of the race painting is no longer needed, the architects evidently are of that opinion. Painting was never intended to be put out of sight. This idea however has not troubled me too much, for I have passed a most enjoyable summer of hard work. If painting is no longer needed, it seems a pity that some of us are born into the world with such a passion for line and color. Better painters than I am have been put out of sight, Baudry spent years on *his* decorations. The only time we saw them was when they were exhibited in the Beaux-Arts, then they were buried in the ceiling of the Grand Opera. —After this grumbling I must get back to my work knowing that the sooner we get to Chicago the better.

You will be pleased, believe me, my dear Mrs. Palmer

Most sincerely yours
Mary Cassatt

Bachivillers
December 1

Cassatt built a glass studio outside the château at Bachivillers (north of Paris) in the summer of 1892 to accommodate the 58-foot-long mural.

My Dear Mrs. Palmer,

Your telegram received today gave me the greatest pleasure. I am infinitely obliged to you for the kind thought which prompted you to send it.

The fact is I am beginning to feel the strain a little & am apt to get a little blue & despondent. Your cable came just at the right moment to act as a stimulant. I have been shut up here so long now with one idea, that I am no longer capable of judging what I have done. I have been half a dozen times on the point of asking Degas and come and see my work, but if he happens to be in the mood he would demolish me so completely that I could never pick myself up in time to finish for the exposition. Still he is the only man I know whose judgment would be a help to me. M. Durand-Ruel, poor man, was here with his daughters a week ago, it was most kind of him to come, they are all broken-hearted over the death of poor Charles. M. Durand was very kind & encouraging, said he would buy it if it were for sale, & of course from his point of view that was very complimentary but it was not what I wanted. He seemed to be amazed at my thinking it necessary to strive for a high degree of finish; but I found that he had never seen the frescoes of the early Italian masters, in fact he has never been to Italy except to Florence for a day or two on business. I asked him if the border shocked him, he said not at all, so it may not look eccentric &, at the height it is to be placed, vivid coloring seems to me necessary.

I have one of the sides well under way & I hope to have the whole finished in time for you to have it up & out of the way by the end of February.

You must be feeling the strain too, with all the responsibility on your shoulders, I hope you will have strength & health to bear you through. With kindest regards & renewed thanks my dear Mrs. Palmer

Sincerely yours,
Mary Cassatt

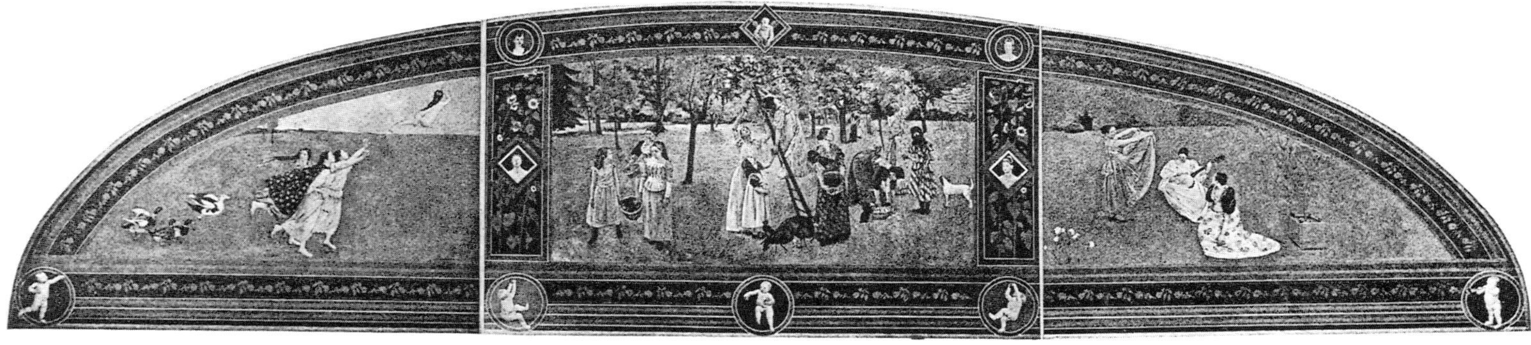

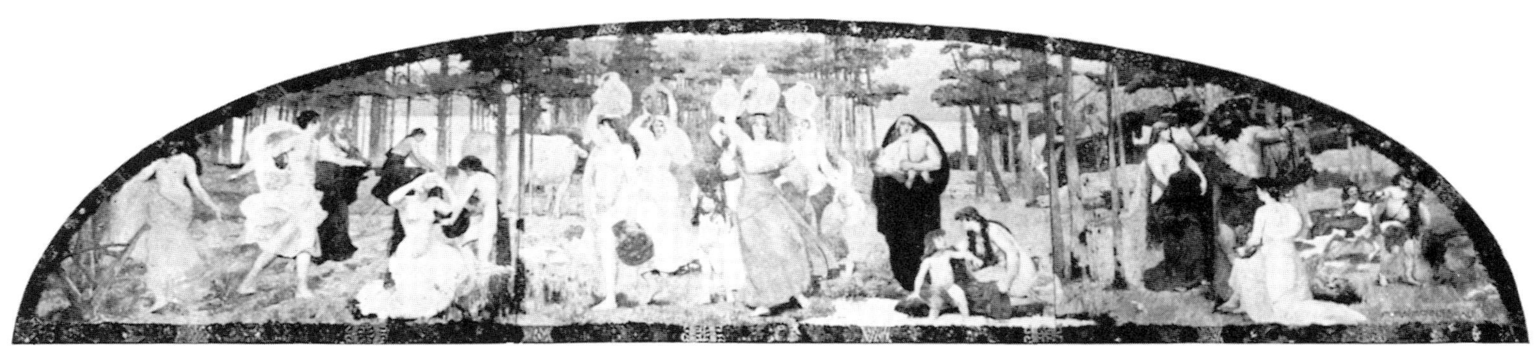

(Above) *Modern Woman.* 1892–93. Photograph taken from *Art and Handicraft in the Woman's Building of the World's Columbian Exposition*, ed. by Maud Howe Elliott. Photograph courtesy of the Chicago Historical Society.

(Below) Mary Fairchild MacMonnies. *Primitive Woman.* 1892–93. Photograph taken from *Art and Handicraft in the Woman's Building of the World's Columbian Exposition*, ed. by Maud Howe Elliott. Photograph courtesy of the Chicago Historical Society.

Letter from Bertha Palmer to Mary Cassatt

In Praise of the *Modern Woman* Mural

December 15, 1892

Chicago
December 15, 1892

My dear Miss Cassatt,

I have received your letter written after the arrival of my telegram of congratulation, and I need not tell you how pleased I am to have a further description of the charming decoration.

I consider your panel by far the most beautiful thing that has been done for the Exposition, and predict for it the most delightful success. It is simple, strong, and sincere, so modern and yet so primitive, so purely decorative in quality, and with still the possibility of having an allegory extracted if one wants to look for that sort of thing. It does seem a pity to torture such a lovely piece of decoration with any attempt at forcing a stilted meaning into it. I am enthusiastic over your success, and am making myself odious by my boasting to all the men who are doing decorations, for I feel sure that your color is to be just as charming as your strong modeling and lovely composition. I must congratulate you most sincerely on having accomplished so successfully the heavy task which you had to perform in a very limited time.

I hear from Miss Hallowell that she has secured a charming example of your work for the Exposition. I do not know the picture, but only know of her delight in obtaining it. I see from a notice sent me from New York, that a picture of yours is in an exhibition now going on there, a lady in white reading the *Figaro*, which seems much admired.

I am thoroughly delighted to have your things appearing in this country, and am very regretful that the Durand-Ruel exhibition of your work has not materialized.

COLORPLATE 15

May I not conclude, my dear Miss Cassatt, by asking a very special favor, that is, that you accept the position of juror on the New York Art Jury which has been or will be tendered you. I know your hatred of art jury service, and that your inclinations will be against this, and also that you will probably be in Paris at the time this jury acts. It nevertheless is a great point gained by women to have their names prominently mentioned on art juries, and this effort has been successful only after a long struggle. If it stands, therefore, even though you perform no service at all, it will help your sex who are generally entirely unrecognized in art matters. Pray do not refuse.

Cassatt declined. For her opinion on this subject, see Cassatt's letters to Harrison Morris and John W. Beatty (pp. 284–285).

Of course you will come over to place your panel. When may we expect you?

With kindest regards, believe me

Most cordially yours

MAUD HOWE ELLIOTT

Maud Howe Elliott (1854–1948), American author and daughter of writer Julia Ward Howe and Dr. Samuel Gridley Howe. While in her youth she studied painting in Rome, Paris, and Boston, she settled on writing as her career choice, first in fiction and later in art criticism and biography. She married painter John Elliott in 1887 and became a lecturer on art.

From *Art and Handicraft in the Woman's Building of the World's Columbian Exposition*

Celebrating the Art of Peace

1894

The great work of the world is carried on by those inseparable yoke-mates man and woman, but there are certain feminine touches in the spiritual architecture which each generation raises as a temple to its own genius, and it is as a record of this essentially feminine side of human effort that the Woman's Building is dedicated.

In the dread art of war the male element of the race asserts itself alone. In its antithesis, the art of peace, woman is paramount. We are yoke-fellows, equal and indivisible, tugging and straining at the load of humanity which we must drag a few paces onward ere our work is done. On the outskirts of the throng of tireless workers there are a few men and women who, when the heat and stress of the day are over, climb to the hill-tops, and looking into the mute heavens read the promise of the coming day. A generation ago the seers of our race foretold two great things: a material growth and prosperity, the like of which the world has never seen; a mastery of electricity, that most potent of man's friendly genii, and a great city through which the traffic of the world should roll, one of the strongholds of the earth—all this the voice of the male seer foretold from his tower, and much more.

A clearer, sweeter prophecy went forth from the tower where the wise women watched the signs of the times: "Woman the acknowledged equal of man; his true helpmate, honored and beloved, honoring and loving as never before since Adam cried, 'The woman tempted me and I did eat.' "

We have eaten of the fruit of the tree of knowledge and the Eden of idleness is hateful to us. We claim our inheritance, and are become workers, not cumberers of the earth.

Twenty years ago to be called strong-minded was a reproach which brought the blood to the cheek of many a woman. To-day there are few of

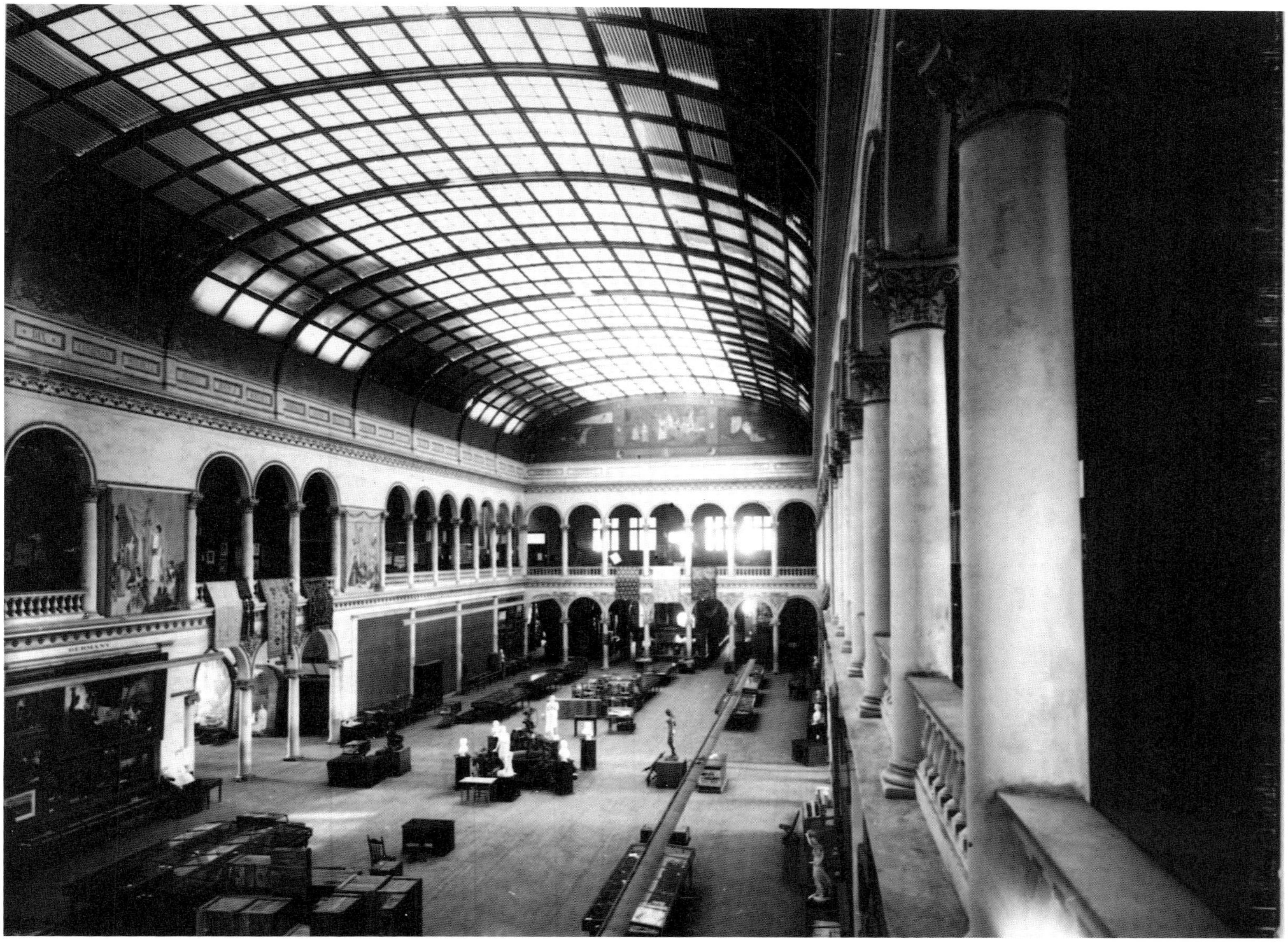

Photograph of the Hall of Honor, Woman's Building, World's Columbian Exposition, Chicago. 1893. Photograph courtesy of the Chicago Historical Society.

our sisters who do not prefer to be classed among strong-minded rather than among weak-minded women. The battle has been fought out, and the veterans who have been wounded and scarred with that cruelest weapon of ridicule, smile to see how easily we assume the position which they gave the glory of their youth to win for us. We honor these women and have written their names in golden letters for all the world to see and salute in our Hall of Honor.

To see the work of woman at the World's Fair we must go through every department of human ingenuity, for there is scarcely one of these where woman's hand has not done a share of the work. The work of man and woman, like their interests, is one and indivisible.

In welcoming the visitor to our building, we would say: "Enter here for a space; sit in our library and rest your eyes with its soft colors; pace through our Hall of Honor and understand the spirit in which it is raised; leave criticism upon the threshold as you enter. Our salutation is, 'Peace be with you.' May your answer be, 'And with you be peace.'". . .

The north tympanum of the hall is enriched by a decorative painting by Mrs. Frederick MacMonnies, representing the Primitive Woman. At the other end Miss Mary Cassatt presents her conception of Modern Woman. Mrs. MacMonnies' subject is well chosen and ably treated. On the extreme right we have a single male figure, a hunter clad in skins—he has just returned from the chase. A group of women and children bear away the game he has killed and minister to his wants. A kneeling girl crushes a bunch of grapes into a cup to refresh the tawny giant. In the middle

Mary Fairchild MacMonnies Lowe (1858–1946), American painter, pupil of Carolus-Duran in Paris, and friend of Puvis de Chavannes. She was one of the upcoming young Americans in Paris when she was awarded this commission. She later settled in Giverny.

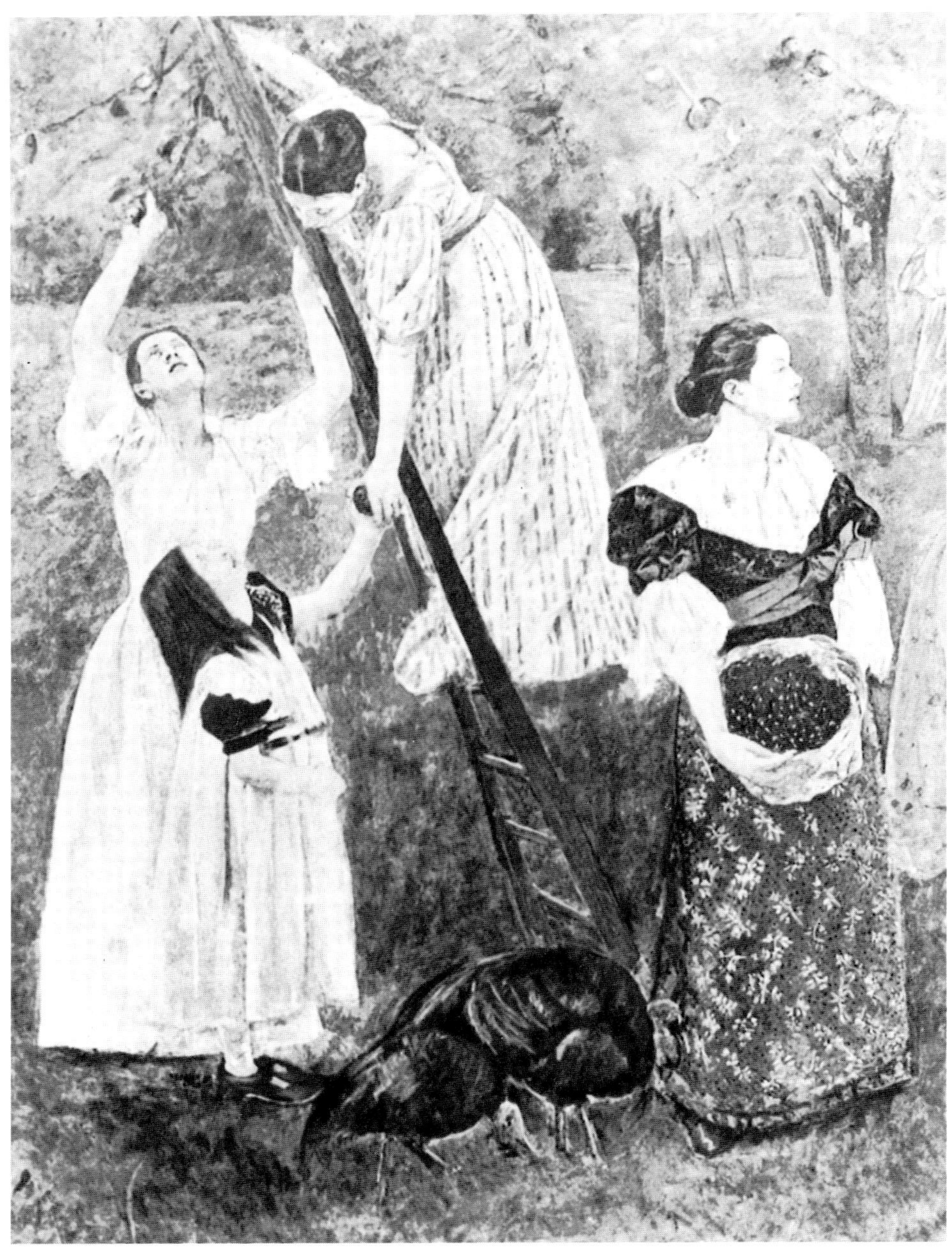

Detail of the central panel of *Modern Woman*. 1892–93. Photograph taken from *World's Columbian Exposition: Art and Architecture* by William Walton.

grouping we have woman, the bearer of burdens, typified by a band of girls carrying water-jars. In the foreground a maiden bathes a laughing child in a clear stream, while a mother advances toward the water bearing two children in her arms. On the extreme left we see the sturdy daughters of the plow driving a yoke of milk-white oxen. A band of sowers scatters the grain in the new-made furrows, while one tired girl, kneeling in the foreground, drinks from a vase. The background of trees and water and distant land is excellently treated. The dark figures of two horsemen are to be seen at the extreme right. Mrs. MacMonnies' work is of a high order; it shows a true decorative sense, a sure hand, and a fresh, joyous imagination. Artistically and intellectually it is a composition which commends itself to all those who understand and honor the idea for which our building stands.

The central portion of Miss Cassatt's panel shows us a group of young women gathering apples in a pleasant orchard. On the right is a band of ladies variously engaged. One is playing upon a stringed instrument, while another poses in one of the attitudes of the modern skirt-dance. On the left we have Fame, a flying figure, pursued by a flock of ducks and women. The border of the tympanum is very charming; the children quite beautifully painted. Both Mrs. MacMonnies and Miss Cassatt received orders for their work from the Executive Board of the Woman's Building. The two decorations were executed in Paris and sent to Chicago.

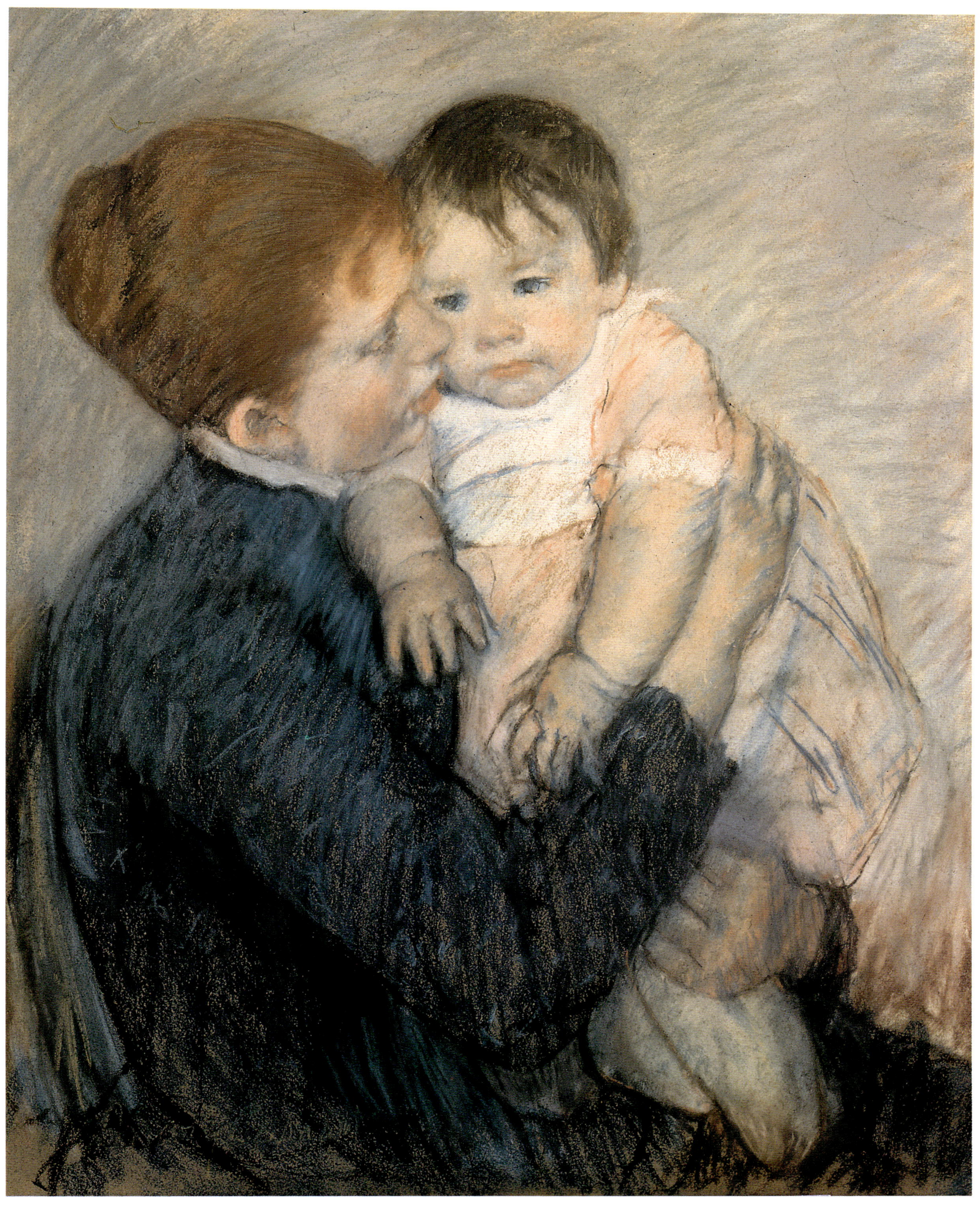

COLORPLATE 60. *Agatha and Her Child.* c. 1891. Pastel on paper. 26 × 22 in. (66 × 55.9 cm). The Butler Institute of American Art, Youngstown, Ohio.

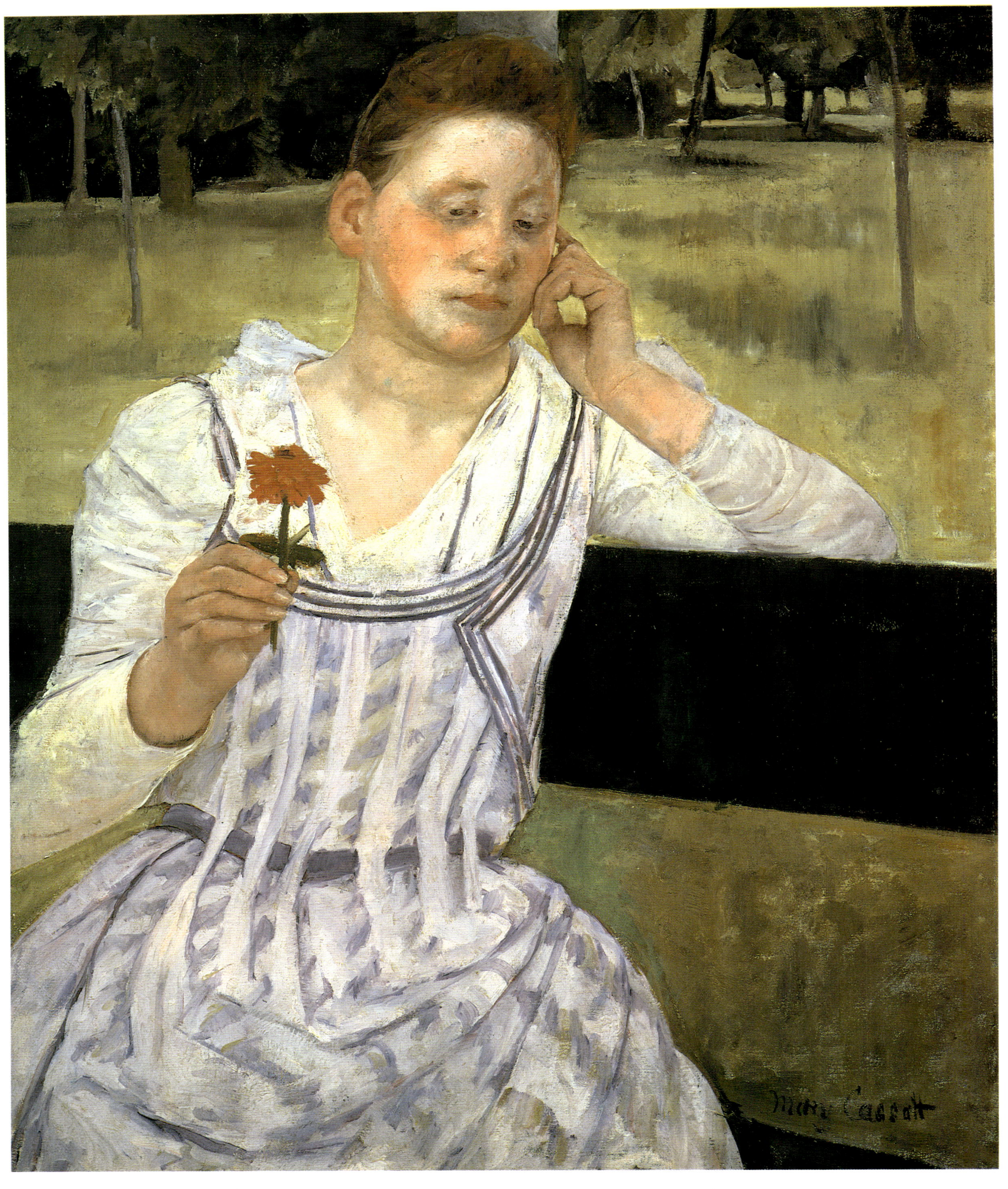

COLORPLATE 61. *Woman with a Red Zinnia.* 1891. Oil on canvas. 29 × 23 ¾ in. (73.6 × 60.3 cm).
National Gallery of Art. The Chester Dale Collection.
Photograph © Board of Trustees, National Gallery of Art, Washington, D.C.

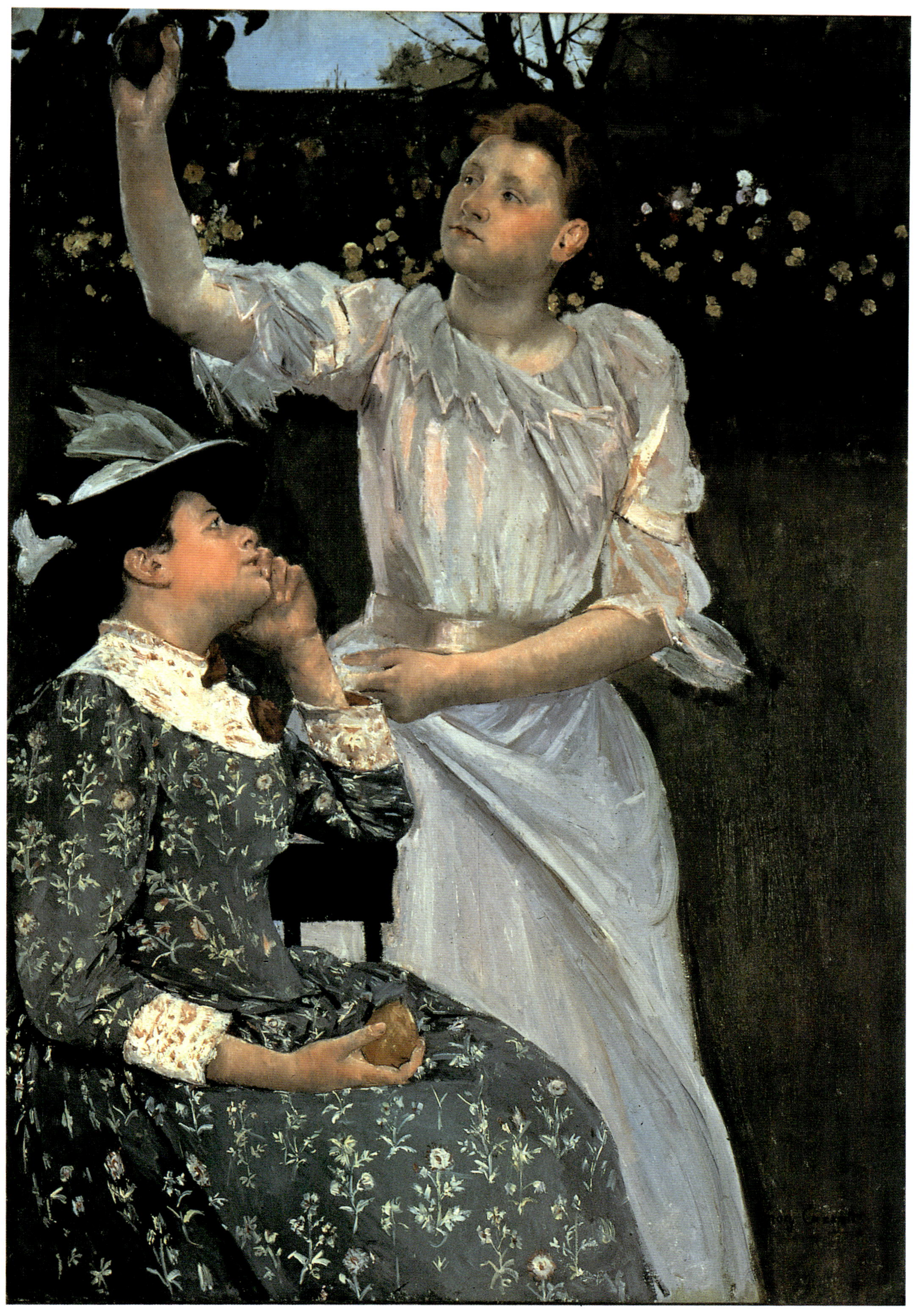

COLORPLATE 62. *Young Women Picking Fruit.* 1891. 51 ½ × 35 ½ in. (130.8 × 90 cm). The Carnegie Museum of Art, Pittsburgh. Patrons Art Fund.

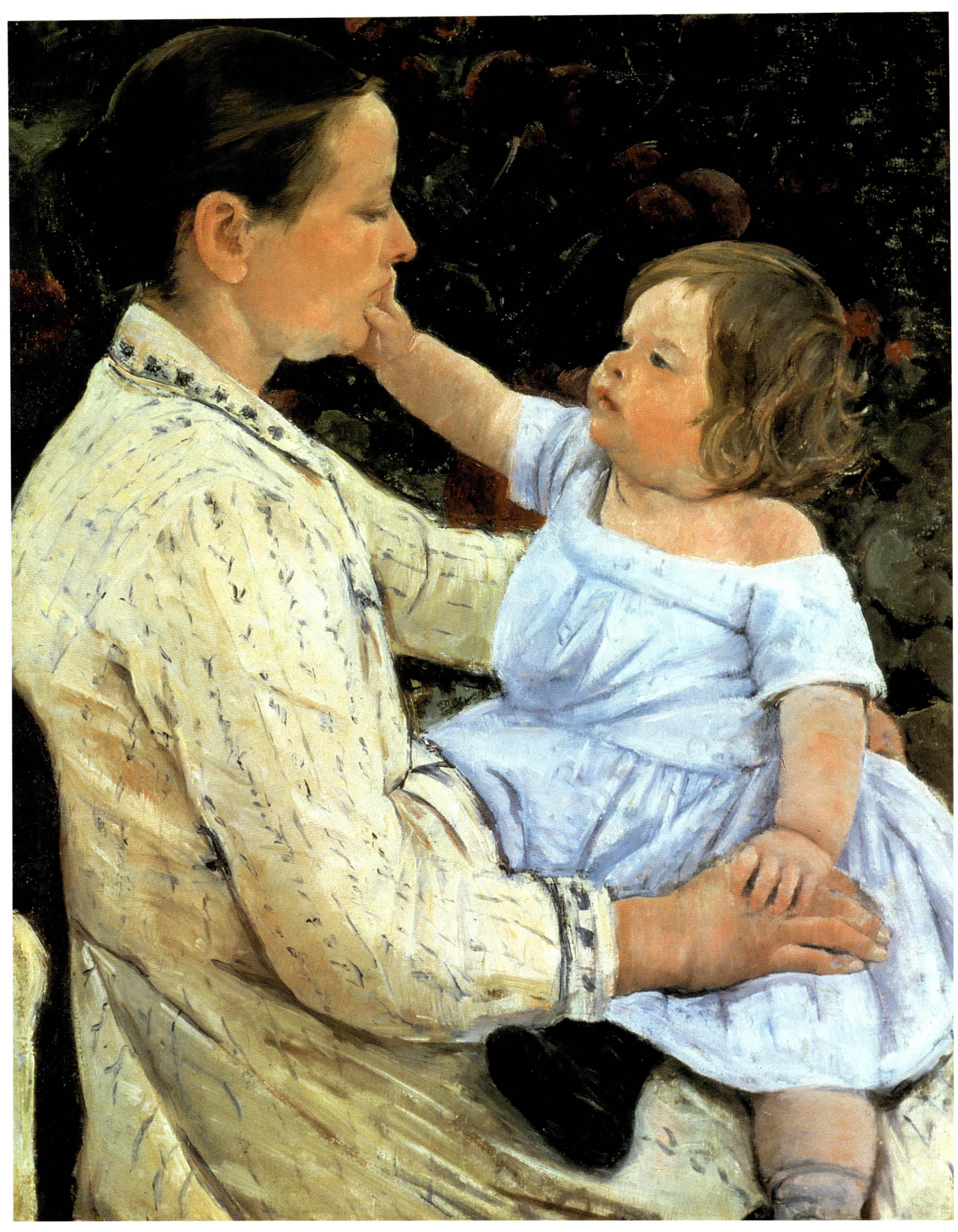

COLORPLATE 63. *The Child's Caress.* c. 1891. Oil on canvas. 26 × 21 in. (66 × 53.3 cm). Honolulu Academy of Arts. Gift in memory of Wilhelmina Tenney by a group of her friends.

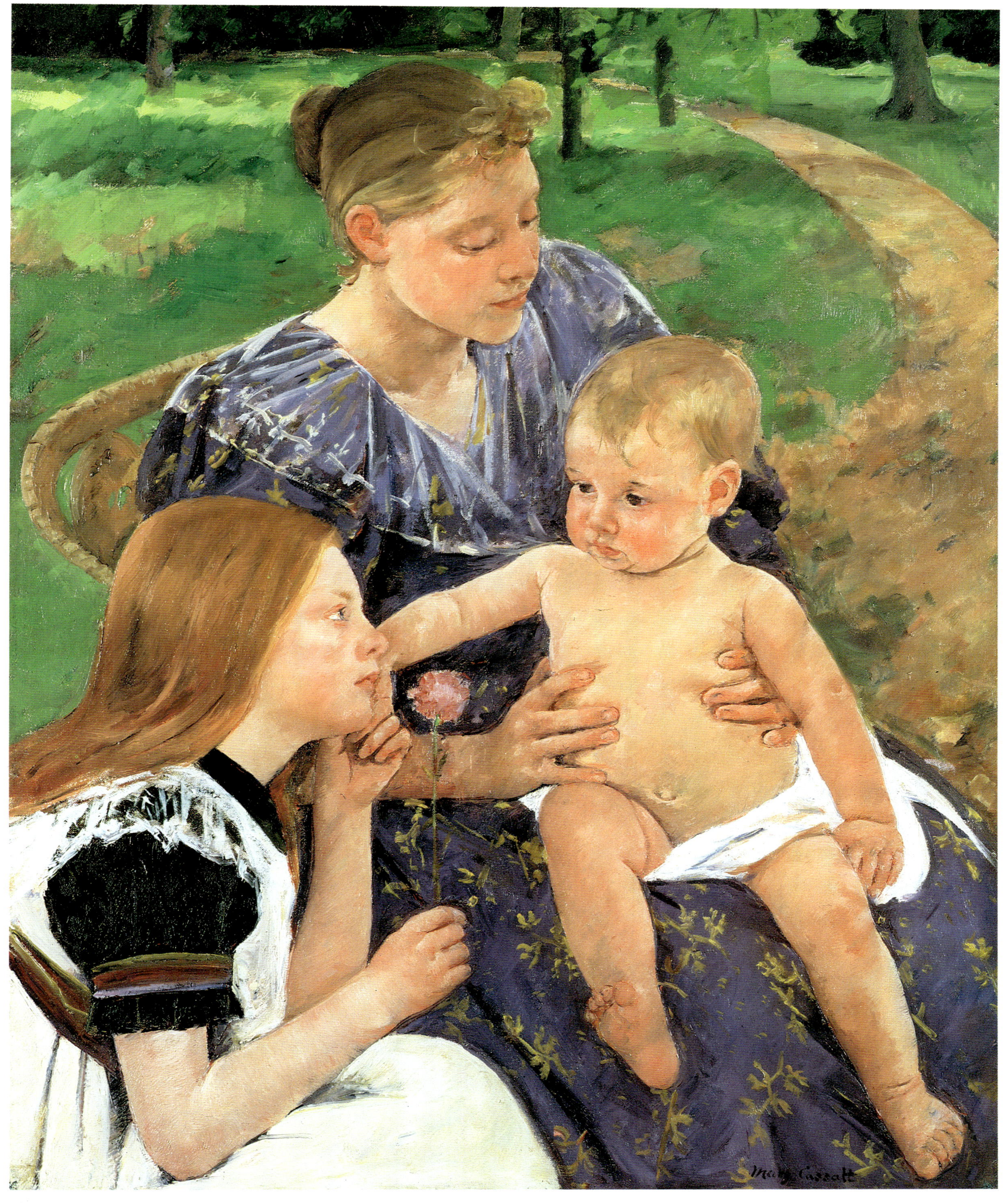

COLORPLATE 64. *The Family*. c. 1892. Oil on canvas. 32 ¼ × 26 ⅛ in. (81.9 × 66.3 cm). The Chrysler Museum, Norfolk, Virginia. Gift of Walter P. Chrysler, Jr.

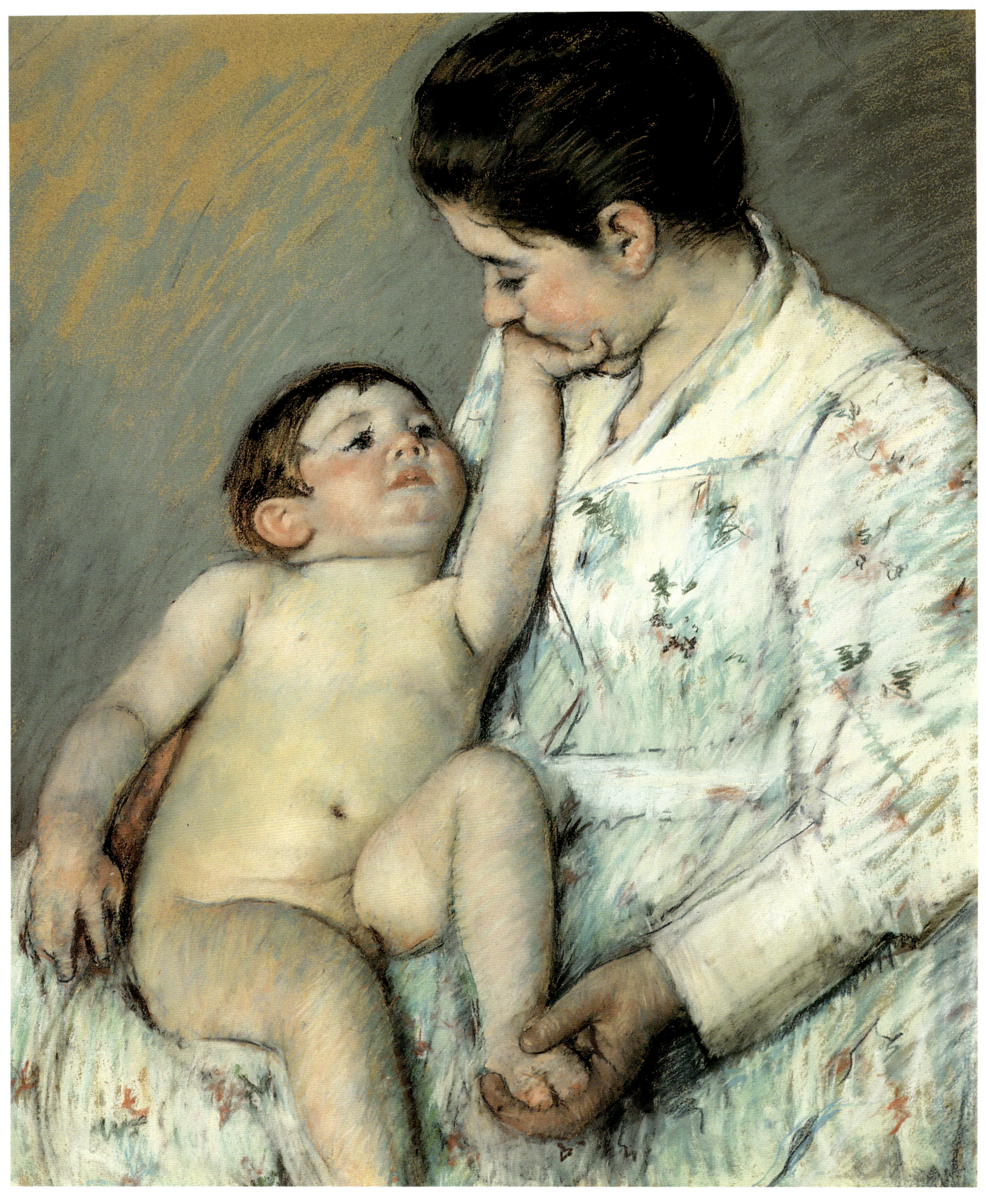

COLORPLATE 65. *Baby's First Caress.* 1891. Pastel on paper. 30 × 24 in. (76.2 × 61 cm).
New Britain Museum of American Art. Harriet Russell Stanley Fund. Photograph: E. Irving Blomstrann.

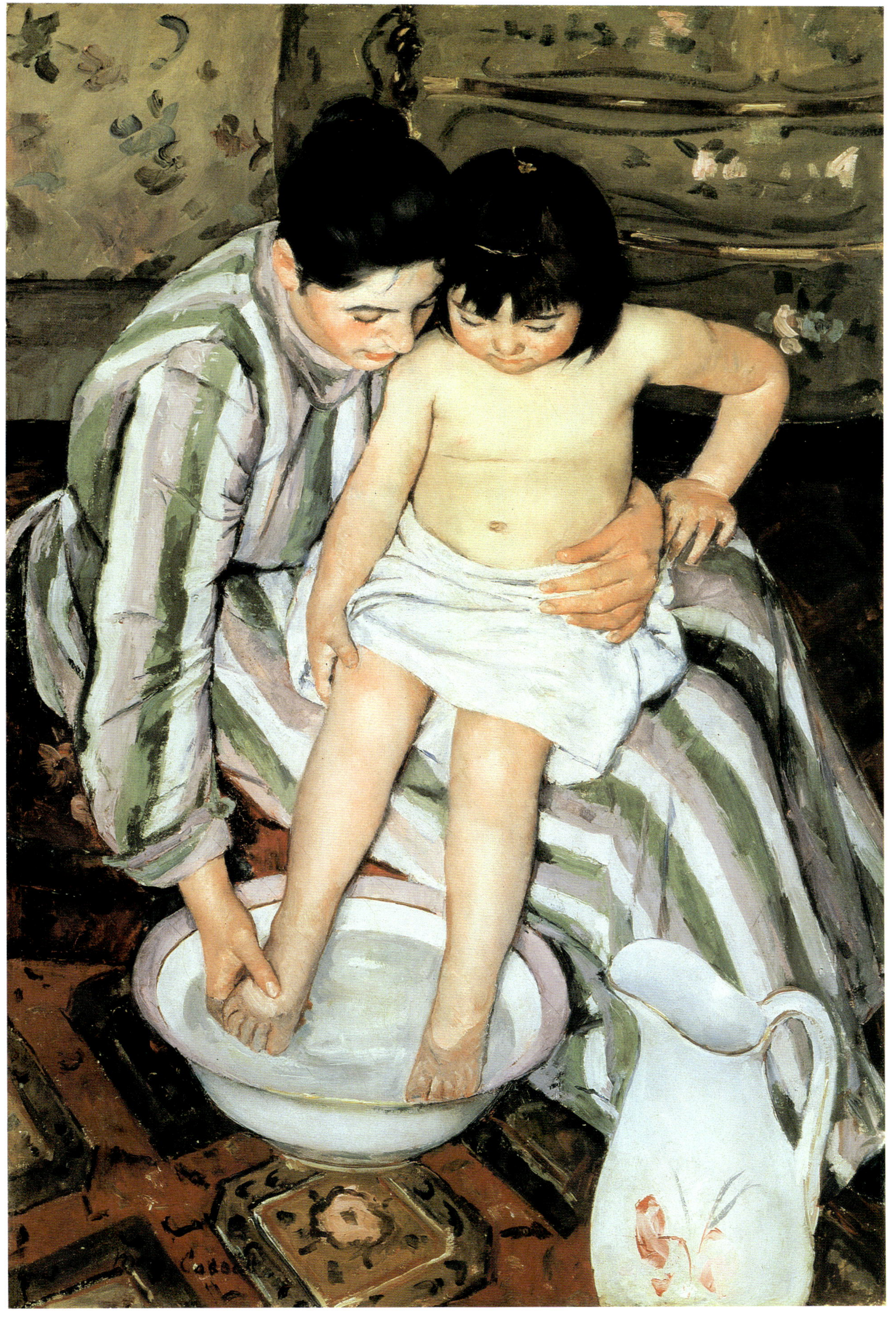

COLORPLATE 66. *The Bath.* 1891–92. Oil on canvas. 39 ½ × 26 in. (100.3 × 66 cm). The Art Institute of Chicago. The Robert A. Waller Fund. Photograph © The Art Institute of Chicago.

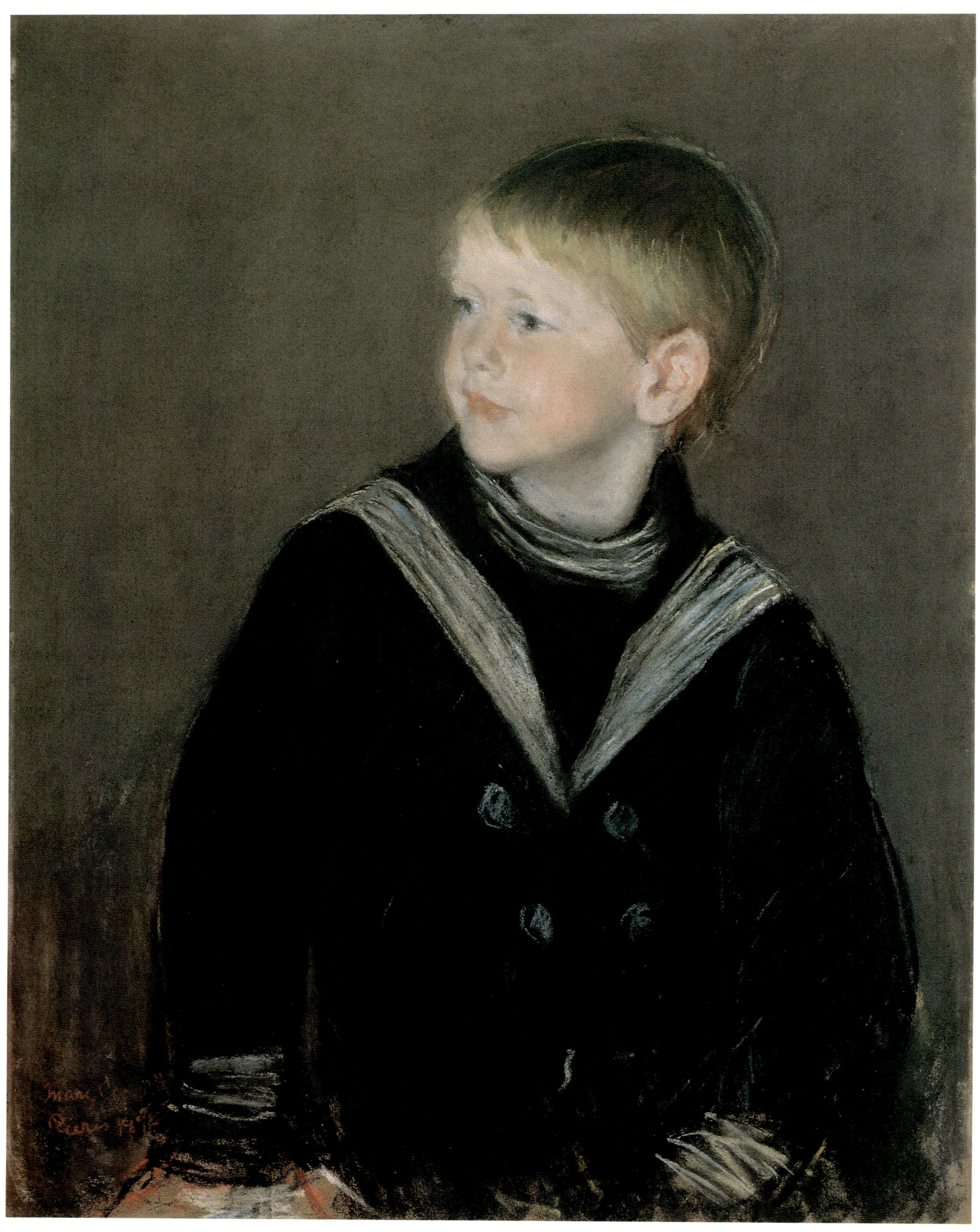

COLORPLATE 67. *Sailor Boy (Portrait of Gardner Cassatt as a Child).* 1892. Pastel on paper. 25 × 19 in. (63.5 × 48.2 cm). Philadelphia Museum of Art. Gift of Mrs. Gardner Cassatt.

Reviews of the *Modern Woman* Mural

"Chicago Letter," by Lucy Monroe. *The Critic,* April 15, 1893.

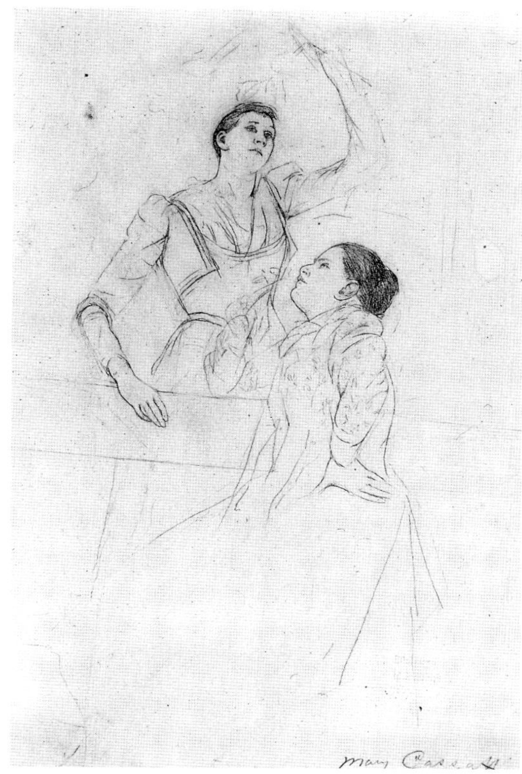

Study for *Young Women Picking Fruit.* 1892. Graphite. 17 ¼ × 11 in. (43.8 × 28 cm). Collection of Susan and Herbert Adler.

I was fortunate enough to see Miss Cassatt's painting the other day just after it was unpacked, and a striking thing it is. There is color enough in it to give character to the entire gallery, but it may focus one's attention too sharply upon itself. Were it possible, however, to lead up to it in the decoration, to give at some point an answering note of color, this difficulty would be obviated. In Miss Cassatt's scheme, a bright grass green is the prevailing tone of the pictures themselves, and in brilliant contrast with this she has used in the wide borders around each panel a deep, rich blue. The result is admirably decorative, varied as it is by notes of dull red and of many gay and sunny colors in the costumes of the women. Miss Cassatt's subject is "Modern Woman" in contradistinction to "Primitive Woman" which was chosen by Mrs. MacMonnies. The central panel represents an orchard, with the apples red upon the trees and a group of graceful women engaged in gathering them,—significant, of course, of the fruit of the tree of knowledge. A smaller panel at the right suggests the arts of music and dancing very charmingly, with its corn color and violet against the green. On the other side of the central picture several rustic maidens vainly pursue a flying figure,—of Fame perhaps, or the elusive unattainable Ideal. The borders are interrupted at the corners by medallions, and in these the babies are given place, and Miss Cassatt can paint most cherubic infants. Her entire work is conceived decoratively and painted flatly without shadows. The space is admirably filled, simply and naturally; but it is in the coloring after all that this impressionist has shown herself a true decorator. Her figures are some of them stiff, her ladder seems to have no branch to rest upon; but her color is superb—she understands the resources of her palette.

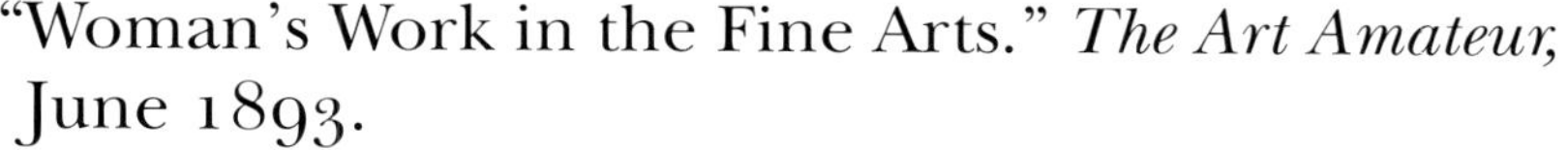

"Woman's Work in the Fine Arts." *The Art Amateur,* June 1893.

But the pictorial decorations of the hall, though not many, are important from their size and position, and one of the artists entrusted with them, Miss Cassatt, has chosen for her large elliptical lunette at one end of the hall a scheme in which dark blue and green predominate. This makes her painting unduly conspicuous, which is the more to be regretted as it is more pictorial than decorative in feeling. It is intended to represent Modern Woman, and is divided into three sections, in the first of which the pursuit of the ideal is typified by three barefooted lassies, who are running after an absconding nude female, who has taken the pathway of the skies, apparently because her legs were never made to walk upon the earth. The centre panel represents an orchard, in which girls are shaking down fruit, others are gathering it, and still others are carrying it away in baskets. This half score or so of figures are very well grouped for a purely pictorial composition, and are drawn and painted with that delightful verve for which Miss Cassatt has become celebrated. This must stand, we suppose, for Work, for the third panel evidently represents Play. In it one young woman in lilac is performing a skirt dance, to the music of a mandolin played by another young woman in yellow, while a third, seated upon the grass, appears to be occupied in seeing and hearing only. As all three are open-air subjects, the painter had an opportunity—which she has neglected—to secure unity by carrying the one landscape background behind all the figures. The dominance of greens, blues and purples and the frankly realistic character of the design so sharply separate the composition from the other decorations of the hall that it is difficult to regard the three portions of it separately. Nevertheless, it is essential that the visitor should do so, for the two end panels are more or less ridiculous. The central subject is, taken separately and as a picture, not a decoration, a very beautiful piece of work. A rich border of blue, green and orange, adapted from the Persian, and Italianized by the insertion of pretty medallions of babies and female heads in circular and lozenge-shaped compartments, completes the work.

ANDRÉ MELLÉRIO

From *Exposition Mary Cassatt*

On Cassatt's First One-Woman Exhibition, 1893

November–December 1893

André Mellério (1862–?), French writer and critic who frequented Symbolist art and literary circles in the 1890s.

The source of Miss Cassatt's inspiration is—Woman and Child.

She has studied them in depth, in their common existence, in all their moments. "An intimate, necessary bond unites these beings: they live through each other. Their facial expressions are related." What Miss Cassatt has sought in women is less their delicate grace, that fragile flower of fleeting sensuality, than the austere, yet ennobling aspect of maternity....

Miss Cassatt knows and understands the ladies of society—because she herself is one. She conveys them and renders them with rare felicity and perfect accuracy, because her nature is that of an artist as well. She has the self-respect and refined breeding of a lady, that care for her dignity and noble pride that command esteem. Of the artist, she has the spontaneous vision, and the free and frank execution. . . .

As we were saying, she has fixed upon maternity. She has not chosen its conventional, easily melodramatized aspects, nor has she exaggerated the purely material details. Her innate distinction never leaves her. Amid scrupulously maintained gardens and soberly yet tastefully decorated interiors, the artist unfolds the myriad scenes of this moving drama, which, in their simple and profound tenderness, child and mother never cease to perform for each other. She has captured the instinctual gestures of a life at its lisping beginnings, opening its naive, astonished pupils to the light. Glimmers of intelligence, harbingers of the future, appear in these brilliantly shining eyes, as yet unclouded by existence. Those tears that burn later on, merely brighten the sparkle of the child's gaze. Already the being of a higher order is breaking through the purely animal grace, innocent shamelessness, and unreasoned movements. Similarly, the humble pursuits to which mothers devote themselves take on dignity from the sense of duty that makes them seem necessary, even sacred. It has been well said that Miss Cassatt has painted only women "with quiet souls."

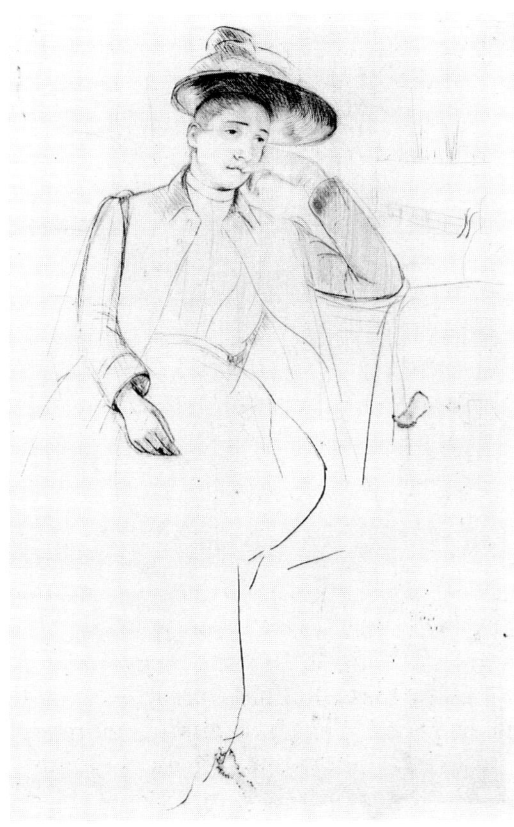

Celeste Seated on a Park Bench. c. 1899. Drypoint. 11 × 7 in. (28 × 17.8 cm). Philadelphia Museum of Art. Gift of R. Sturgis Ingersoll, Frederic Ballard, Alexander Cassatt, Staunton B. Peck, and Mrs. William Potter Wear.

Yet these women have an intimate and affecting charm, with nothing artificial about it, that derives from the harmony of their dress, their measured gestures, the honest environment of the homes in which they live—where they reign and thrive. Like their mothers, the children shine with fresh health. We feel a young race, maintaining its vigor with a rational upbringing, keeping the human body in balance by means of the proper exercise of its strength. These beings, with their open ways, expressing

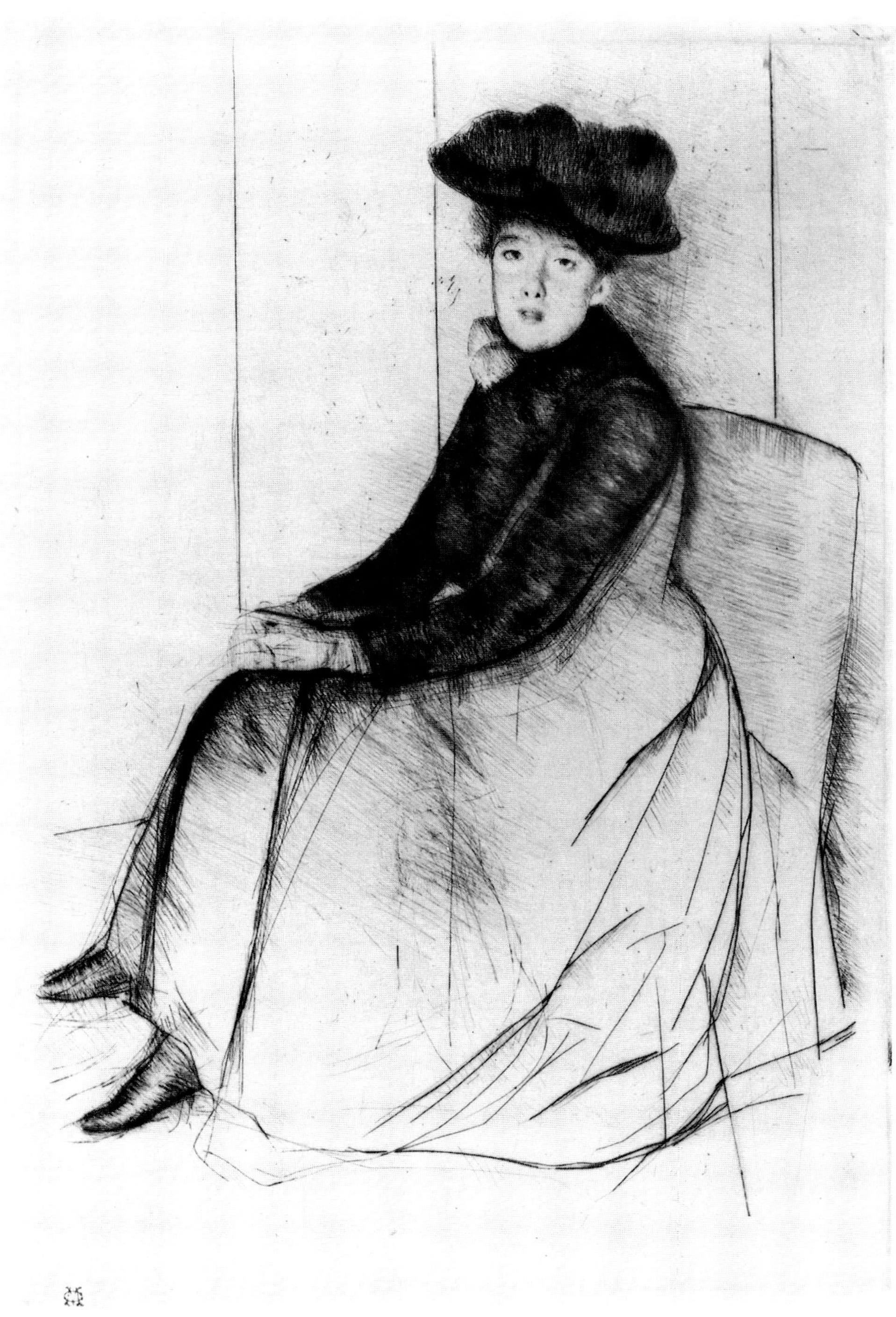

Reflection. 1889. Drypoint in brown ink. 10 1/4 × 6 7/8 in. (26 × 17.5 cm). National Academy of Design, New York. Samuel Colman Collection.

candor in their calm features, borrow their magical coloring from air and light. Air and light—these also endow Miss Cassatt's skill with its attraction and power!

How unfortunate that a work so characteristic of the artist could not appear in this exhibition: *Jeunes Filles cueillant des Fruits,* which she sent to Chicago. One of the girls stands on a ladder, bending in a graceful movement to toss what she has picked to her companions. A second girl, her head raised, her countenance expressive, reaches her arms out, at her side a tot who imitates her gesture. Finally, the gesture of the last girl, who carries a basket of fruit, is marked with the grandeur and simplicity of a young priestess in an antique procession. There is serenity in Miss Cassatt's choice of broad color, without impasto, while her characters move freely in a limpid atmosphere.

Here in France, we would have to go back to Puvis de Chavannes to find so masterly an understanding of large decorative scenes.

Pierre Puvis de Chavannes (1824–1898), French painter known for his simplified style in painting historical subjects. He was embraced by both conservatives and moderns.

Miss Cassatt has shown us woman in her true social functions, the mistress of her home, devoted to the concerns of maternity. She has expressed

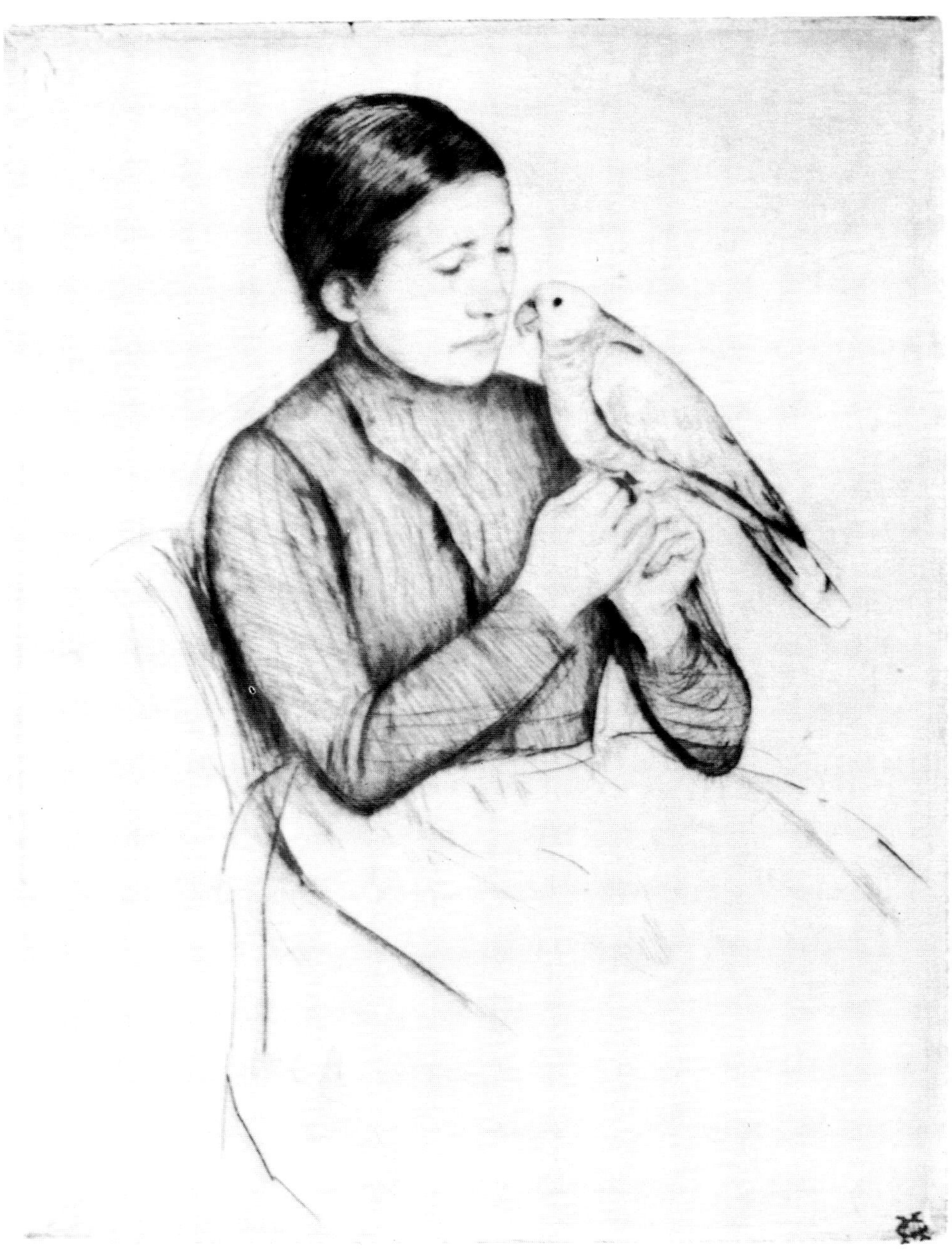

The Parrot. 1889. Drypoint in brown ink. 6 3/8 × 4 3/4 in. (16.2 × 12 cm). National Academy of Design, New York. The Samuel Colman Collection.

the spontaneous manifestations of children, and their early grace. She has marked her subjects with a high artistic feeling. At the same time, she has been able to turn the colors and lines of modern dress to advantage. This is her secret and her talent—as it is of the masters—to have preserved the solid foundation of humanity, the eternal warp and weft of all works of art, while weaving into it the myriad nuances of an age, a race, and a milieu.

We must cite as part of the artist's contribution her etchings, so intense with life, just as we must mention the curious series of compositions on intimate domestic life, in which drypoint is enhanced with colors. These works are absolutely original, and to produce them Miss Cassatt took the particular trouble to oversee their printing herself and in her own studio. And with these, we have reviewed a total oeuvre that is complete and distinctive, worthy of commanding the public's attention.

In all sincerity, it must be said that, at the present time, Miss Cassatt may be, with Whistler, America's only artist of lofty, personal, and distinguished talent.

James Abbott McNeill Whistler (1834–1903), American painter and printmaker who worked in London and Paris. He was a friend of Degas, Cassatt, and other Impressionists but never exhibited with the group.

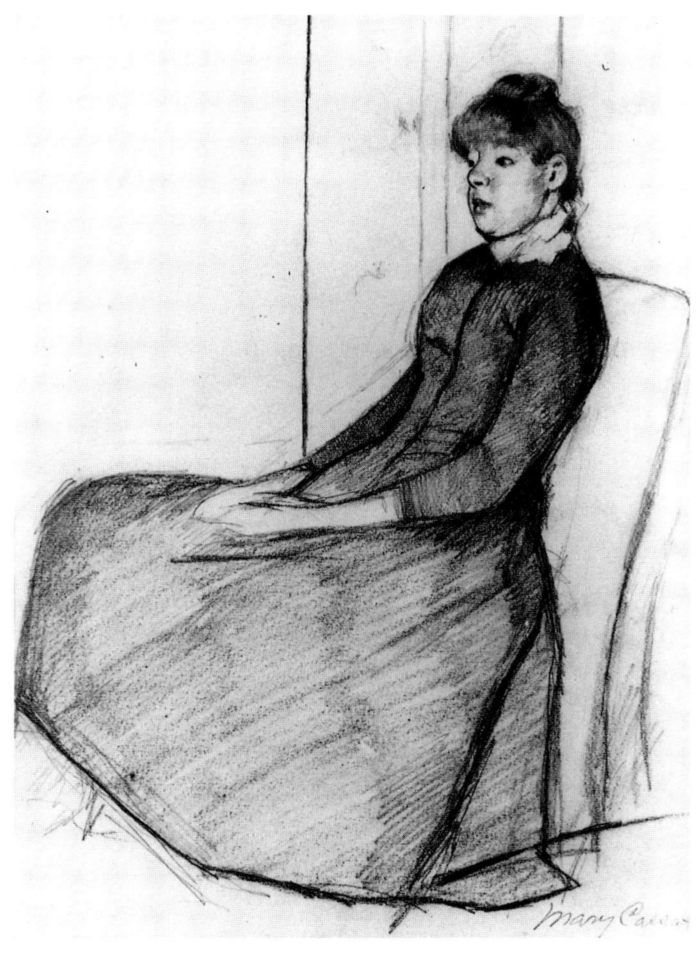

Drawing for *Sombre Figure*. c. 1889. Pencil and black crayon. 10 3/8 × 7 1/2 in. (26.5 × 19.1 cm). The Baltimore Museum of Art. Bequest of Wilmer Hoffman.

A. DE LOSTALOT

Alfred de Lostalot (1837–1909), French writer.

From *La Chronique des arts et de la curiosité*

Review of the 1893 Exhibition

December 9, 1893

We announced this Exhibition and we said that it was particularly remarkable. Indeed, one finds oneself in the presence of uncommon works, which reveal the artist's very strong personal feeling, an exquisite taste, and a great deal of talent.

Miss Cassatt is an American who settled among us some time ago; upon her arrival in Paris, she was strongly impressed by some of our painters who have become renowned outside the School: Manet, Pissarro, Renoir, and Degas. But it is especially with the latter two that we may compare her talent, whose originality, however, is in no way diminished by the comparison.

Miss Cassatt learned from M. Degas the art of emphasizing the drawing, underscoring it in the right places, and ignoring everything that could dilute the effect and weaken the expression of the artist's plastic thought.

In Renoir's work, she studied the colorist's craft; yet, one could say that she has not yet found her bearings in this area. By the variety of their appearance and the differences in the treatment—sometimes thick and heavily impastoed, sometimes fluid and melting into weightless layers—her paintings testify to a complete absence of preconceptions: that is the sure sign of a sincere and searching talent devoted to the constant observation of nature.

We prefer to the paintings, as captivating as they are, certain delightful drypoints, into which Miss Cassatt has put both all her art and all her soul. They are little poems, exquisite in their grace and feeling, wherein she tirelessly repeats her eternal subject: motherhood. A few lines barely emphasized with shading—she needs no more than this to express the child's artless miming and the mother's enveloping gestures and infinite caresses.

Finally, Miss Cassatt is showing color engravings, obviously inspired by Japanese art: here, we feel her success to be less complete, and, since the draftsman's abilities have not changed, we are led to attribute the inadequacy of the results to the choice of process. The edges of the drawings seem to us too sharp; the proportions are wrong between the contours and the colors they embrace. To tell the truth, we do not believe that an artist whose aesthetic sentiment finds its chief expressive resources in drawing can ever completely assimilate the techniques of an art in which the charm of color plays the principal part.

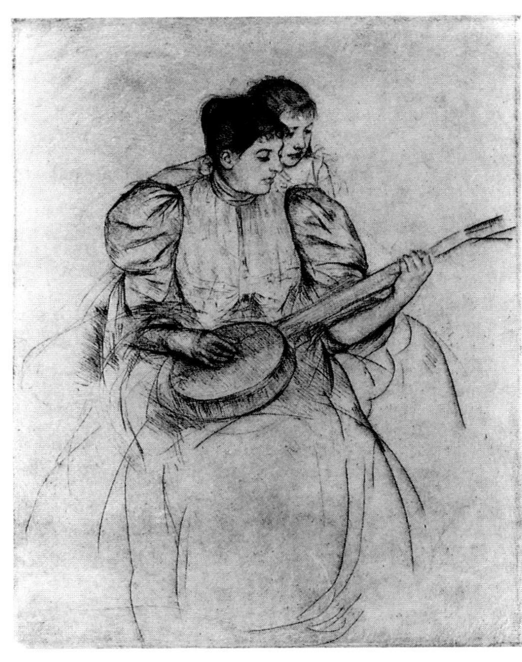

The Banjo Lesson (second state). c. 1893. Drypoint. 11 9/16 × 9 3/8 in. (29.4 × 23.8 cm). The Ursula and R. Stanley Johnson Collection.

Letter from Mary Cassatt to John H. Whittemore

Thoughts on Exhibiting

December 22, 1893

John H. Whittemore, an American art student who met Cassatt in 1892 when he was studying in Paris. He formed an important collection of Impressionist paintings.

10, rue de Marignan
December 22

(We are off to Cannes tomorrow but our address is the same)

Dear Mr. Whittemore,

. . . I am glad you are getting on so well with the Independents & am much obliged for your kindness in advancing my subscription, please have it refunded to you at Mess Durand-Ruels—Don't allow them to allot me any space in their exhibitions, my sympathy is with them, but I have no intention of sending anything. The advantage of such an exhibition is that one has space to develop oneself, & it would be much against my interests if only one or two of my pictures were sent, & yours would be the only ones—I am almost sure that there will be an exhibition of my pictures & etchings in New York this winter or spring, if it is only half as well received as the one just closed in the rue Lafitte I will be satisfied—I can hardly imagine though, that the Metropolitan Museum will propose, to buy one of the pictures as the Musée de Luxemburg has just made me the compliment of doing—

The Salons des Artistes Indépendents were juryless exhibitions held every year in Paris since 1884. Cassatt and most of the other Impressionists declined to show in these exhibitions.

This exhibition did not take place until April 1895.

The Luxembourg Museum was France's repository of the work of living artists. The collection was built as the museum purchased chosen works from the artists themselves. In this case the work requested did not belong to Cassatt but to Durand-Ruel, who would not relinquish it. Cassatt's work did not enter the French national collection until 1897.

I am glad you saw the Degas & admired it, I also think your Manets better than my brothers as I remember his—

Comantron was here the other day & I told him what I had written to you about the Degas, he says I am wrong, & that he would buy back the Degas you bought in the Spring at an advance—He seemed sincere—I don't think my friend in N.Y. would sell her pastel it would bring 20,000 fr. in Paris! Not a bad investment—

With kindest regards to both you & Mrs. Whittemore believe me with many thanks for your kind offer of service

yours most sincerely
Mary Cassatt

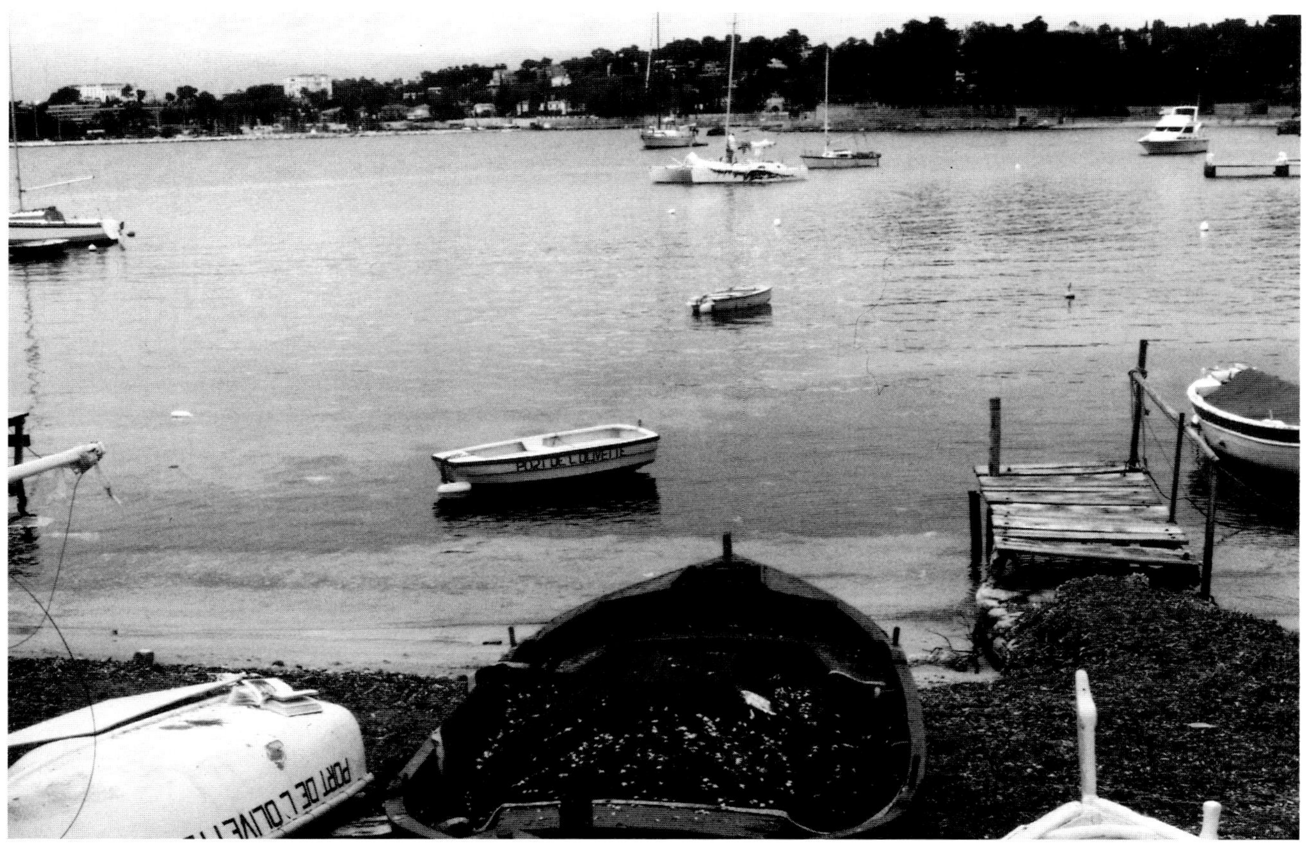

A view from the beach of Cap d'Antibes where *The Boating Party* was painted.

Letter from Mary Cassatt to Eugenie Heller

On the Cap d'Antibes Landscape

January 30, 1894

Villa "La Cigaronne," Cap d'Antibes
(Alpes-Maritimes)
January 30

My Dear Miss Heller,

I have often wondered, since I left Paris, how you were getting on. I hope you & Mrs. Sprague Smith escaped the [illegible]! I see that M. Guillaumin's exposition is opened, I hope you have seen him & are profiting by his conseils—I have an idea that he must be able to impart his knowledge with facility—

For anyone fond of the sea, & color & light, to say nothing of boats, this is a wonderful place—Our villa is on the sea with the snow capped mountains in the distance & below them the olive clad hills—I believe there are a number of American landscape painters here—It (the landscape), is rather too panoramic for my taste, but doubtless could be interpreted by a great man, in an artistic way; I have never yet seen it done to my satisfaction.

I content myself with a little bit as background to my figures, & ought to be thankful for the sun & the long days. We have had, though nearly a week of steady rain, such a downpour as one does not often have in the North—

With kindest regards to yourself & friend & sincere hopes that all is going well with you

very truly yours
Mary Cassatt

Eugenie M. Heller (1868–?), American artist and sculptor who studied with J. Alden Weir and Augustus Saint-Gaudens before going to Paris in 1893. She befriended Cassatt when she asked for advice on selecting a teacher in France.

Jean Baptiste Armand Guillaumin (1841–1927), French Impressionist painter and friend of Cézanne and Pissarro, he had a job with the city of Paris to supplement his income from painting.

COLORPLATE 75

FLORENCE FINCH KELLY

Florence Finch Kelly (1858–1939), American author and journalist.

From *The Hampton Magazine:* "Painters of Sea and Shore"

A Lighthearted View of *The Boating Party*

COLORPLATE 75

August 1907

The annual high-day of the seashore regions has arrived. At the touch of mid-summer suns the bare sands have blossomed into a garden of life. From Bar Harbor and the Maine coast southward, to Palm Beach; and on the Pacific Coast from Santa Cruz and Monterey to the gardens of San Diego—these hundreds of miles of beach, harbor and island shore are glowing and throbbing with the brilliance and gayety of summer throngs out for a holiday. Banners and flags flutter in the crisp breeze, lovely girls in pretty frocks are everywhere, gay parasols bloom like tropic flowers out of the gray sands.

Why has not all this brilliant display of color and of life at its most joyous expression attracted the American artist? The illustrators have made much of it, and the Sunday newspapers and the magazines have teemed with their drawings. But the artist, to whom it is given to put upon canvas a more permanent interpretation of the beauty of a land and the life of its people, has shunned the seashore when it is peopled. And yet among our painters are a number who are reckoned among the best shore and marine artists in the world. But the "rapture of the lonely shore" is the theme that appeals to them. The might of high waves breaking upon a rocky coast; the beauty of wavelets of surf upon a long stretch of sandy beach, with the ocean tossing restlessly from a far horizon; these and similar subjects they paint with masterly skill and with such poetry and imagination as make their canvases always delightful. . . .

Miss Mary Cassatt has painted, in *The Boat's Crew,* a charming little bit of summer life on the water. It is a French family, out for a day's boating. Miss Cassatt has lived in Paris for many years. Alexander J. Cassatt, long president of the Pennsylvania railroad, was her brother. But notwithstanding her ties in America, Miss Cassatt returns as rarely and makes her stay as short as her affairs will permit. She found, years ago, in the French capital the artistic atmosphere and fellowship in art matters that seemed to her necessary for her life work, and these things made the alien land more home to her than was her native country without them. But the pleasures of a summer day's outing have no nationality, and the athletic young fellow whose muscles are all alive with the delight of the rhythmic motion of his oars and the swift movement of the boat across the water, might be taking his little family for a Sunday spin along the shore waters of Staten Island.

Does the mind of the American artist harbor some vague conviction—offspring perhaps of that far-away Puritan time when pleasure was sinful—that pleasure is not artistic? If not, why does he eschew this lighter side of seashore life which girts the country with its midsummer brightness and gayety? The idleness and pleasure of summer life by the shore, as one phase of our many-sided American life, as scenes appealing because of their beauty or their picturesqueness, are surely as worthy of portrayal as are the toil and hardness of the workaday life.

ACHILLE SEGARD

From *Mary Cassatt: Un Peintre des enfants and des mères*

Cassatt As a Progressive

1913

For a long time, Degas was the judge of Miss Mary Cassatt's works.

The canvases in Miss Mary Cassatt's oeuvre in which one infers her concern with winning that arbiter's benevolent neutrality are the earliest. They are also the most concise and energetic. What eloquence in that nervous line that demarcates a contour, emphasizing its volume and suggesting an impression of modeling, while leaving the "envelope," that is, that atmospheric something that plays about everything in nature!

Miss Mary Cassatt has only gradually achieved this sureness of vision and conscious mastery of technique.

Manet had sent to the 1882 Salon a portrait of a young woman that he had titled *le Printemps,* the model for which had been a young actress, Mlle. Demarsy. It is also known as *la Femme à l'Ombrelle.* The portrait was a brilliant success. It is—as Huysmans said—a charming portrait, in which the oil takes on the softness of pastels. It was perhaps Manet's least controversial success. This occurred just before he died.

If we compare the photograph of this picture to the photograph of Miss Mary Cassatt's portrait of her sister, we sense a certain similarity between the two portraits. Now, Miss Mary Cassatt's portrait of her sister was painted in 1879. A comparison of the works, moreover, reveals fundamental differences in vision and feeling. The only reason, therefore, to dwell on this juxtaposition is to identify briefly the intellectual atmosphere within which Miss Mary Cassatt composed her first works. She loved Manet before he was fashionable and drew inspiration from his lessons, to the extent that his lessons were compatible with the particular qualities of her temperament and sensibility. His influence did not go very deep, and it was general rather than particular, but one might find traces in her constant care to eschew all conventional painting generally, and all historical painting in particular, in her concern with capturing the individual characteristics of her time and expressing them with new means, appropriate to the age; and lastly in certain modes of *mise en toile.* In support of this last observation, one could compare Miss Cassatt's *la Barque* of 1894, painted at Antibes, and Manet's famous picture *En Bateau.* The latter picture had been shown at the 1879 Salon, and had been accepted by neither public opinion nor by the critics. It shocked the habits of the time. Miss Mary Cassatt loved it, and after the picture passed from hand to hand, she had the pleasure of advising its purchase to one of her friends, Mme. Havemeyer of New York, who gave it pride of place in her collection.

COLORPLATE 75

One must remember Miss Cassatt's *la Barque* when one wishes to examine the painter's technique, the way she distributes the masses of color to achieve an overall effect, and we will find in this picture an opportunity to identify what makes her execution "decorative." It is already interesting to note, in the *mise en toile* of these figures, in the way the boat, cut in two by the frame, moves toward the center of the picture and stands out against the blue-green of the water, as well as in the way the principal figure is placed in the foreground, a certain similarity with Manet's *En Bateau.* It is to Miss Mary Cassatt's credit that she was one of the first to appreciate Manet's very important qualities, and it is to her honor that she has so preserved her own personality that this comparison points up only affinities of mind and similarities that do not go to the heart of the work.

With respect to some of the early works and especially to a portrait of her sister seated in an interior, wearing a dress of a very delicate, tender, and lustrous pink, a few people have attempted to establish a comparison with the works of Berthe Morisot. Mme. Morisot and Miss Cassatt did indeed show with the same group and breathed the same atmosphere. If one were to insist absolutely upon establishing a likeness between them, one would have to note that they both demonstrated a preference for certain masters who were, moreover, unappreciated at the time. Yet the differences in temperament and character quickly revealed themselves. Chatting with another painter at the 1879 Exposition in front of the works of the two rivals, Gauguin—so sensitive to color and so passionate a partisan of originality—made a determination: "Miss Cassatt is equally charming, but she is more forceful."

Paul Gauguin (1848–1903), self-taught painter who entered the Impressionist group through Camille Pissarro and then went on to become a leader among the Post-Impressionists in Paris. Before he gave up his employment in the financial district of Paris, he acquired an important collection of Impressionist works, including a pastel by Mary Cassatt.

Letter from Mary Cassatt to Paul Durand-Ruel

On Renovating Her Country House

Summer 1894

Cassatt purchased her country home, Mesnil-Beaufresne, in 1894 with proceeds from recent sales of her works.

Mesnil-Beaufresne, par Fresneaux
Montchevreuil (Oise)

Dear Sir,

I am writing to ask you if you would please tell Madame Aude that I have a favor to ask of her. We are finally settled here and, even before we came, I had had enough of my role as landlord; I have given nearly three months of my time and I know that I still have a part of the summer to devote to giving orders, and I ask myself when will I find the time to do a bit of painting! Madame Aude knows the landowners of Trie, would she be so kind as to tell them I am putting Mesnil-Beaufresne up for sale?

Mme. Marie Aude, Paul Durand-Ruel's daughter and Cassatt's neighbor at Bachivillers.

The house is very good, very sound. I had water, &c put in. Indeed I cannot say that everything is not well, but I do not want to give any more orders to workmen, who don't follow them anyway.

We got the property for a good price, 39,000 frs. and 4 hectares of meadow are leased at 80 frs per hectare. We have incurred some expenses, but I do not yet know the figure.

What I want is the freedom to work. My mother is no longer of the age or the strength to concern herself with the outdoors, and I don't have the interest.

My brothers will surely laugh at me, but I won't say anything until I have sold it and won back my freedom. Certainly it is the best thing in the world.

I am completely fed up with the trouble I had to get a bit of work done.

Pray accept, dear Sir, my best compliments for you and yours. You don't know how lucky you are to be just a tenant!

M. Degas declares that architects are the lowest class of society!

Mary Cassatt

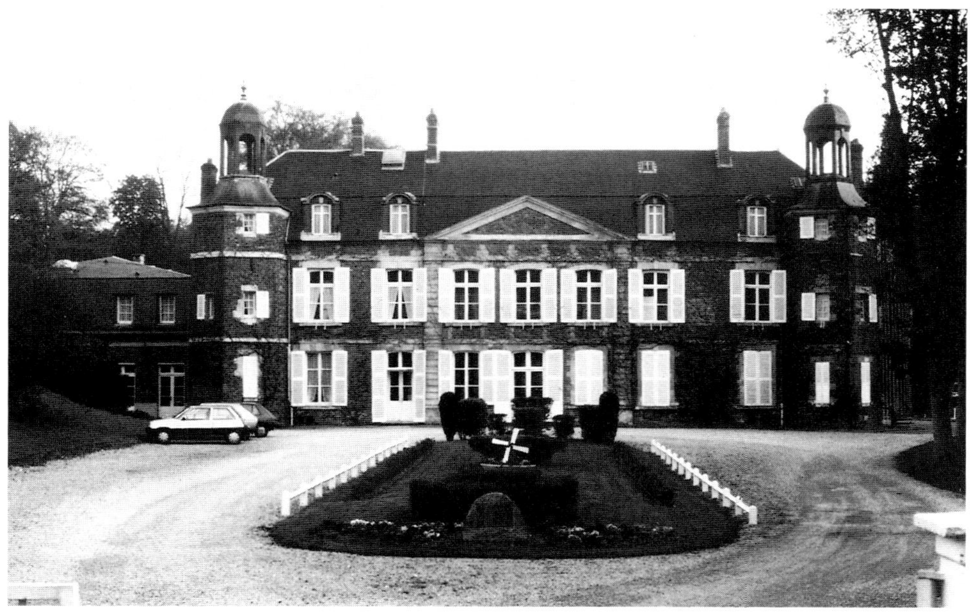

Photograph of the front view of Château Beaufresne in Mesnil-Théribus (fifty miles northwest of Paris), as it appears today. Cassatt purchased and renovated the property in 1894, and it remained her country house until her death.

Letter from Mary Cassatt to Rose Lamb

On Her Mother's Illness

April 26, 1895

Rose Lamb (1843–1927), American portrait painter and teacher who studied with William Morris Hunt and H. Knowlton. Lamb went to Paris to study in 1881 and 1890, and is believed to have met Cassatt in 1892.

10, rue de Marignan
April 26, 1895

My Dear Miss Lamb,

Your letter gave me a most pleasant surprise this morning, & as you see I answer it at once, first because it is mail day & secondly because I don't know if I may have an opportunity soon again—I did receive a letter from you two years ago & not having answered it at once I mislaid your address—& have thought of you with remorse ever since.

Since I saw you last we, my mother and I have been here & in Italy in the South & again at Bachivillers & then in our own country place. My mother has been often ill & I often nurse for weeks at a time, & this last winter ever since 10th of Dec she has been a victim to grippe. [illegible]. She is now up & goes out but is still very ill, she says to tell you that the woman you knew as my Mother is no more, that only a poor creature is left! Which proves that her head is not quite so affected as she thinks, But there is no doubt that her head *is* affected & the depression is at times very great. In fact life seems very dark to me just now; three weeks ago I was exchanging cables with my brother Gard & they were all including my sister in law & the baby (sister to the boy you remember) & the boy himself on the point of sailing. You who have taken care of old people know what it is—We bought a country house in the neighbourhood of Bachivillers a year ago. We were turned out of the latter place by the marriage of our fat landlord to a young woman desirous of living in a "chateau," so we bought one of our own—Last summer was spent in getting the workmen out of the house & getting it in order, & I now wonder if ever I shall take my mother to be there after all our trouble to make it comfortable for her. Our address in the country is Chateau du Mesnil Beaufresne, par Fresneaux Mt Chevreuil (Oise)—& a letter here will always find us. If things go better with us, won't you when you do come over, come & make us a visit, my Mother wishes to see you again as much as I do. I am afraid there is no place I know of where you would be comfortable, Pissarro is getting old & his advice would not be so good as it was—We lost Mme Manet (Berthe

Morisot died March 2, 1895.

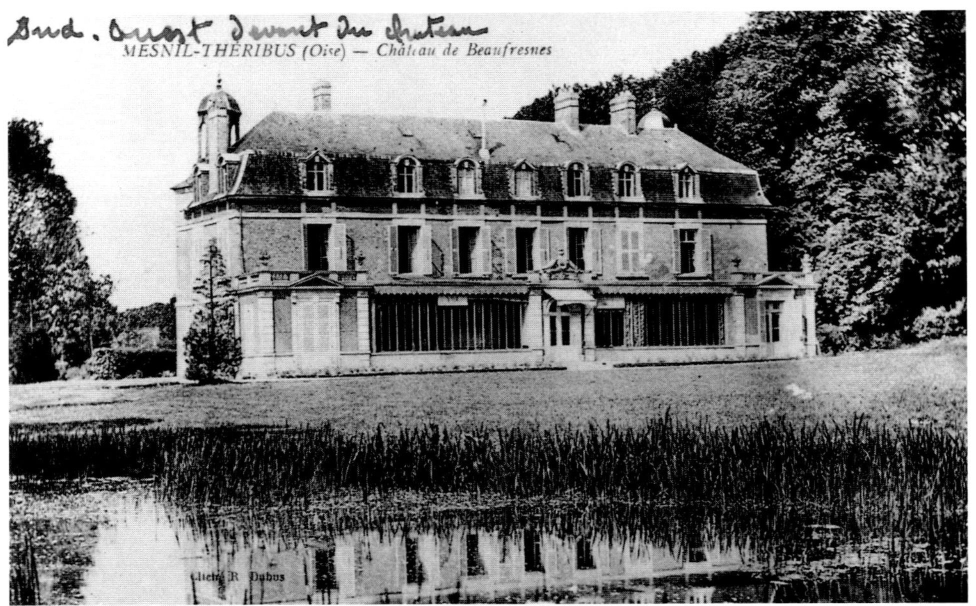

Historical photograph of the back view of Château Beaufresne.

Morisot) this winter carried off in five days by grippe. Degas works as much as ever Bartholome is still at tombs, I never see him.

I am much pleased at your liking my little pastel. I worked amid distraction this last winter & would have preferred putting off the exhibition, hoping to see you over here soon & with much love from my mother & from me.

Cassatt's exhibition at Durand-Ruel's gallery in New York in 1895.

Yours affectionately
Mary Cassatt

FREDERICK SWEET

Frederick A. Sweet (1903–1984), American author, museum curator, and author of the first modern, full-length biography of Mary Cassatt in 1966.

From *Miss Mary Cassatt: Impressionist from Pennsylvania*

"A Château in the Country"

1966

From the road, Beaufresne is seen across a long grassy forecourt on either side of which is a driveway and masses of trees. Built of mellowed pinkish-red brick, the house has three stories, each of which is separated by a band of chalky-white marble. The façade has a pediment spanning the central three windows, and at each side are hexagonal towers surmounted by open belfries. All the windows in the first two stories have gray-white blinds. This was once a hunting lodge, a dependency of a much larger establishment in the neighborhood, and was built at the time of Louis XIII, but the left tower is said to be even older. The entrance is not, as one would expect, in the center of the symmetrical façade but towards the left, leading to a rather small stair hall, with the kitchen to the left, and at the right a large dining room, with a circular drawing room beyond, and at the end of the house what Mary Cassatt called her "painting room." Across the garden side a nineteenth-century addition with a glassed in gallery served as an informal living room and had a beautiful view out over the wide lawn. Here

Mary Cassatt used to serve coffee after lunch and enjoyed discussing art and politics with her frequent guests. Along the inner wall of the gallery were massed many of her Japanese prints and on tables were pieces of Venetian glass. Upstairs there are six bedrooms—one of the smallest of which was Miss Cassatt's—and two primitive bathrooms with tin tubs. The servants had rooms under the third-floor mansard roof. Much of the furniture, especially in the drawing room and bedrooms was Empire, left there by the De Grasse family, from whom Mary Cassatt bought Beaufresne. The simple lines of this style, very unfashionable at the time, appealed to her taste and she liked to paint the bedroom pieces apple-green. Furniture held in such general disfavor was most inexpensive; therefore, in painting it, there was no thought that valuable antiques were being defaced.

There were about forty-five acres in the estate, much of it in the wide expanse of garden and lawns. Great chestnut trees grew about the grounds, and Lombardy poplars bordered the long, narrow pool. Outside the gallery were enormous rosebushes. There were fruit trees and a vegetable garden where Mary Cassatt enjoyed growing unusual things such as American corn and eggplant. At one side of the house and scarcely visible were the farm buildings, hot frames for tomatoes and strawberries, stables, a carriage house, and, after 1906, a garage for the Renault limousine.

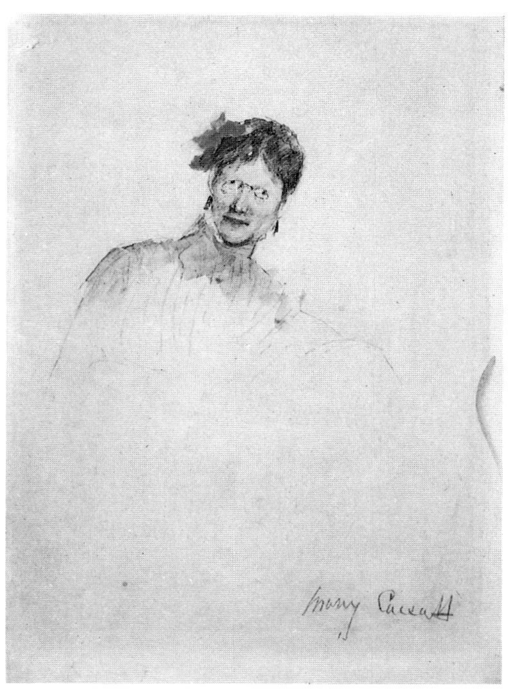

Sketch of Vernon Lee. 1895. Watercolor. 9 ½ × 6 ¾ in. (24.1 × 17.1 cm).

Whether Mary Cassatt was in the "gallerie" of Beaufresne or in her salon on the Rue de Marignan, she enjoyed brilliant conversation and knew many people who were good foils for her. Although she was capable of annihilating argument, she could not stand up to Degas, who did at times, she said, "demolish" her. He was the most intellectual of the painters she knew and, despite their many tiffs, offered her the greatest stimulation. She entertained Clemenceau, Marcel Cachin, Jacques-Émile Blanche, George Moore, Stéphane Mallarmé, Ambroise Vollard, Berthe Morisot, who was a sort of friendly rival, and Violet Paget, the English friend of Sargent who wrote under the pseudonym Vernon Lee.

Vernon Lee is the pen name for Violet Paget (1856–1935), the expatriate American writer who focused on aesthetic and literary matters.

After a visit to Beaufresne, Vernon Lee wrote to her friend Kit Anstruther Thomson, July 28, 1895:

> I liked immensely being at Mesnil. That high-lying, monotonous, not at all beautiful French country, crude or dingy in colour, composed of blunt lines, without romance or suavity of village or old house, moreover apparently depopulate, has yet a charm of breadth, of belonging to an endless continent—no island or semi-island like England or Italy—there being *enough land*, and enough sky especially, leagues of cloud and air; a certain charm to me, of unusualness, of a back of beyond, due to its lines *leading nowhere* (do you know what I mean?). The complete scheme of the eternal story told by mountains and rivers, the story of watersheds and sea, of perpetually becoming and going. And I liked the Louis XVI Château and the sort of white bareness of the rooms, making me feel almost like Corobbia. Poor old Mrs. Cassatt is, I fear, slowly dying. Her daughter will probably write to you to find her an English nurse for she seems to know no one in London, and I ventured to tell her she might.
>
> Miss Cassatt is very nice, simple, an odd mixture of a self-recognising artist, with passionate appreciation in literature, and the almost childish garrulous American provincial. She wants to make art cheap, to bring it within reach of the comparatively poor, and projects a series of coloured etchings, for which she wants me to write a little preface. She wants other artists to do something similar, suggested Sargent—do you think he would? She has most generously given me one of her new and most beautiful etchings, a mother and baby, green on green, quite lovely.

ANNA ROBESON BURR

From *The Portrait of a Banker: James Stillman*

A Visit to Beaufresne

1928

Anna Robeson Burr (1873–1941), American author.

James Stillman (1850–1918), American businessman who was president and subsequently chair of the board of the National City Bank of New York. Stillman, a friend of Cassatt and collector of her work, owned an apartment in Paris from the 1890s but did not move there until 1909.

The other day-trip was to Beaufresne, the home of Mary Cassatt. Her old brick house had originally been a hunting lodge, belonging to some château—one of those delightful rambling buildings with more picturesqueness than convenience. I remember especially a sort of long, glassed room, like a sun porch, and the lovely pond with willows hanging into the very water, beside which many of her pictures were painted. As those who know her work know, Miss Cassatt usually painted out of doors in bright sun-light. Much of her best work was done at Beaufresne, where the models were neighboring peasant women and their children. Critics have sometimes objected to the homely faces of her women. But as Miss Cassatt wrote to me later when I sent her a photograph of my first baby "Most mothers with nurses do not know how to hold their children." This great painter of maternity wanted the rhythm of the constantly curving arm—the constantly bending back. She found it in those French women of the soil, and stooping over their firm-bodied children.

Miss Cassatt herself was tall and gaunt, dressed in a shirt waist and black skirt. But her strong face and her rapid intelligent conversation gave me little time to notice externals. We had delicious curried chicken for lunch, a *specialité de la maison,* and looking forward to my first housekeeping I asked for the recipe. Miss Cassatt expressed surprise that I was interested in cooking, and then I received one of the only two direct compliments my father-in-law ever gave me. After all, it was chiefly negative. "She isn't a spoiled New York girl," he said.

Miss Cassatt wanted to paint Mr. Stillman's portrait and I wish that he had given her the opportunity. I do not know that she ever had painted a man, but she knew her old friend, and knew what expressions to watch for in his often mask-like face. Kaulbach, who is said to have told the Kaiser that, "he painted men, not buttons," did make a fairly good portrait of

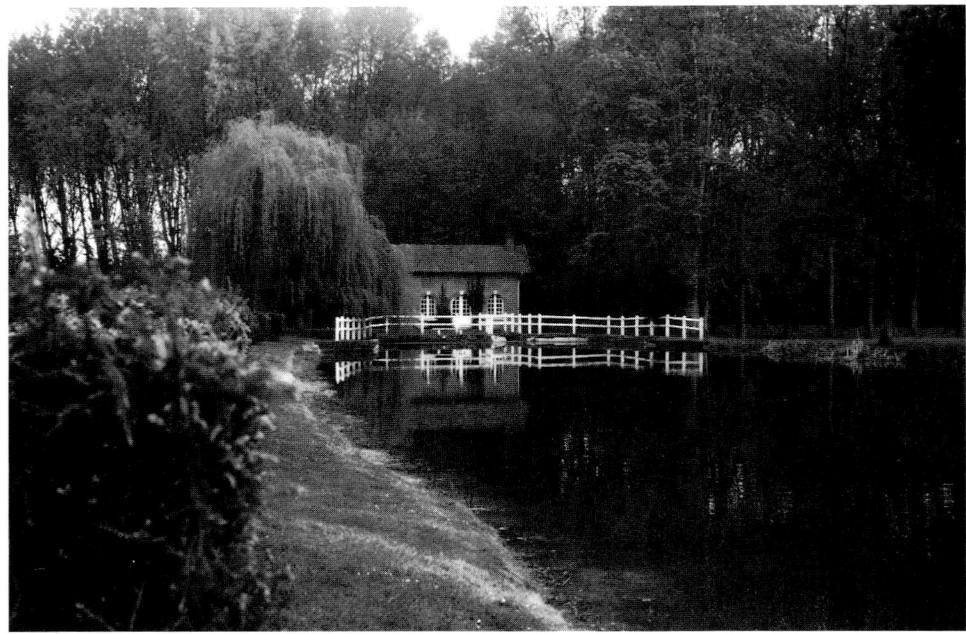

Photograph of the pond at Château Beaufresne, as it appears today. This view inspired Cassatt's *Feeding the Ducks,* found on page 236.

James Stillman the banker—but I think Miss Cassatt would have painted the father and the friend.

Miss Cassatt was heart and soul a modern. She abhorred the sentimental. She prevented Mr. Stillman from buying two small heads of Greuze, with their pastoral sweetness; and when I mentioned the beauty of Mme. Vigée le Brun, she dismissed her with this comment. "She painted herself."

Jean-Baptiste Greuze (1725–1805), French genre and portrait painter.

Reviews of Cassatt's First New York Exhibition, 1895

"Pictures by Mary Cassatt." *The New York Times,* April 18, 1895.

Fugitive sketches, an occasional painting and some etchings by Miss Cassatt have been shown now and then in this city, and at the World's Columbian Fair visitors to the Woman's Building had the opportunity to see her large decoration. It is possible now, however, to see her work under the best of conditions at the gallery of Durand-Ruel, on Fifth Avenue, where there are on exhibition fifty or more important examples from her first success of 1878 to the present day.

Without doubt the collection will attract much attention to a woman whose reputation in Paris is of a high order among the latter-day painters, and who, though following in the train of the impressionists and being greatly influenced by many of the pleinairists, manages to preserve a powerful personality and a strong originality that are extremely attractive.

It is curiously interesting to observe the unmistakable sympathy that Miss Cassatt has for the work of Manet, Degas, and others of their school, and to perceive how forcibly they have appealed to her, yet she has gone at her pictures in her own way, obtained her results in quite a different manner and has in no wise imitated them.

The work here shown is quite uneven, though rarely, if ever, uninteresting, and it is confined principally to portrait studies out of doors of women and children. The mother and child seem to have had peculiar fascination for this artist, and have afforded her the theme for many canvases. In her earlier studies there seems to be a greater harmony of color and a softer envelopment of atmosphere, which is lacking in the more recent work. These last are frequently hard, crude, and have a tendency toward the brutal. Inharmonious masses of uncomplimentary color are brought side by side and shock the eye. A rude strength, at times out of keeping with the subject, is noticeable, and takes away in a measure from the charm of femininity.

Perhaps no picture in the collection is so full of power and of the unctiousness of luscious, rich color as is the picture painted some years ago, *Dans la Loge,* and which first called public attention to Miss Cassatt. It is an unusually distinguished canvas and at the time was a remarkable departure from conventional methods. A portrait of Mrs. C. is also a most attractive work and is quiet, refined, and brushed in with great freedom. Others in the same vein are a portrait group of an old lady and three children, a lady knitting, the cup of tea, and two or three pastels. A woman with a fan, however, is clumsy, and a Spanish scene, suggestive of Manet, is extremely low in key and not agreeable in color. There is pleasant tone in a portrait, painted in 1877, the head being delicate and having great refinement.

The canvases of later years find the artist working in a new color direction and with a change of technique. Here is apparent a certain hardness, a quality of dryness, and a curious constraint in handling. It is difficult to characterize, but we miss the freedom of the brush work, the work lacks spontaneity, and the pigment is no longer fresh and luscious. Disagreeable reds and yellows occur in the flesh, and the women look hard and coarse.

Young Women Gathering Fruit is an example of this, and, though the canvas contains many fine qualities of textures, of drawing, and of arrangement of light, it is difficult not to regret the absence of a certain purity of flesh tones, of more feminine quality of grace, of beauty, and of what may be called daintiness, all of which could have been added without the loss either of dignity, strength, or force. COLORPLATE 62

Unevenness is apparent more in the studies of mothers and children than in other work. Many of these are delightfully naive, and some of the latter have been caught in astonishingly characteristic poses.

Most of the little ones are painted with a faithfulness that gives evidence of great study, intimate knowledge, and loving interest in the subject. Occasionally, however, as in a child gathering fruit, painted in 1892, and which is hard and unsympathetic, and in a pastel, *The Young Mother*, painted in 1890, and which is quite the reverse, the difference is apparent and it is difficult to realize the same touch in both. COLORPLATE 74

A group of pastels, dated 1895, each a variation on the same theme, is marked by a quality of hardness and a lack of purity of color, and these are faults that are absent in *Mère et Enfant*, which is a delightful study of child life.

A Portrait of Miss S., one of the last that Miss Cassatt has painted, has curious defects in the drawing of the face, and the ear of the young lady is most unfortunate in its careless construction. A portrait of a man is included in the collection, which, though vigorous, does not call for special comment, and the large portrait of the child with a dog develops a tendency to heaviness and is not as agreeable as work in a higher key.

Besides the paintings, there are many etchings in dry point and some few printed in colors. These have all a very personal touch, are Japanesque in feeling, and highly decorative in character. They are also in the new movement, popular in Paris, but they lack the grace and delicacy of their Oriental prototypes. Our Eastern civilization, represented in these methods, somehow seems clumsy and awkward. The occidental face and dress do not conventionalize with equal readiness.

The exhibition may be seen daily until the 30th of April.

The Collector, May 1, 1895.

The recent death of Mme. Berthe Morizot leaves Miss Mary Cassatt, as far as her sex is concerned, practically in undisputed possession of the field both have cultivated so long. Miss Cassatt, who is a native of Pittsburgh, and was originally a student of the Academy of Fine Arts, in Philadelphia, settled in Europe about twenty-five years ago, and for some twenty years has frankly and industriously applied herself to working out the artistic gospel laid down by Edouard Manet, and adopted or adapted by his successors. That Miss Cassatt is a strong and original woman, such an exhibition of her as has been made at the Durand-Ruel Galleries, in this city, abundantly proves. How much stronger might have been the results she is capable of one can pretty clearly infer from those which she now achieves. That I do not agree with Miss Cassatt in viewing the antithesis of merely pretty art as the only cogent protest against artificiality and conventionalism, is because I believe that while beauty of form and grace of line are to be found in nature, they are to be preferred to coarser and less lovely themes. But I like

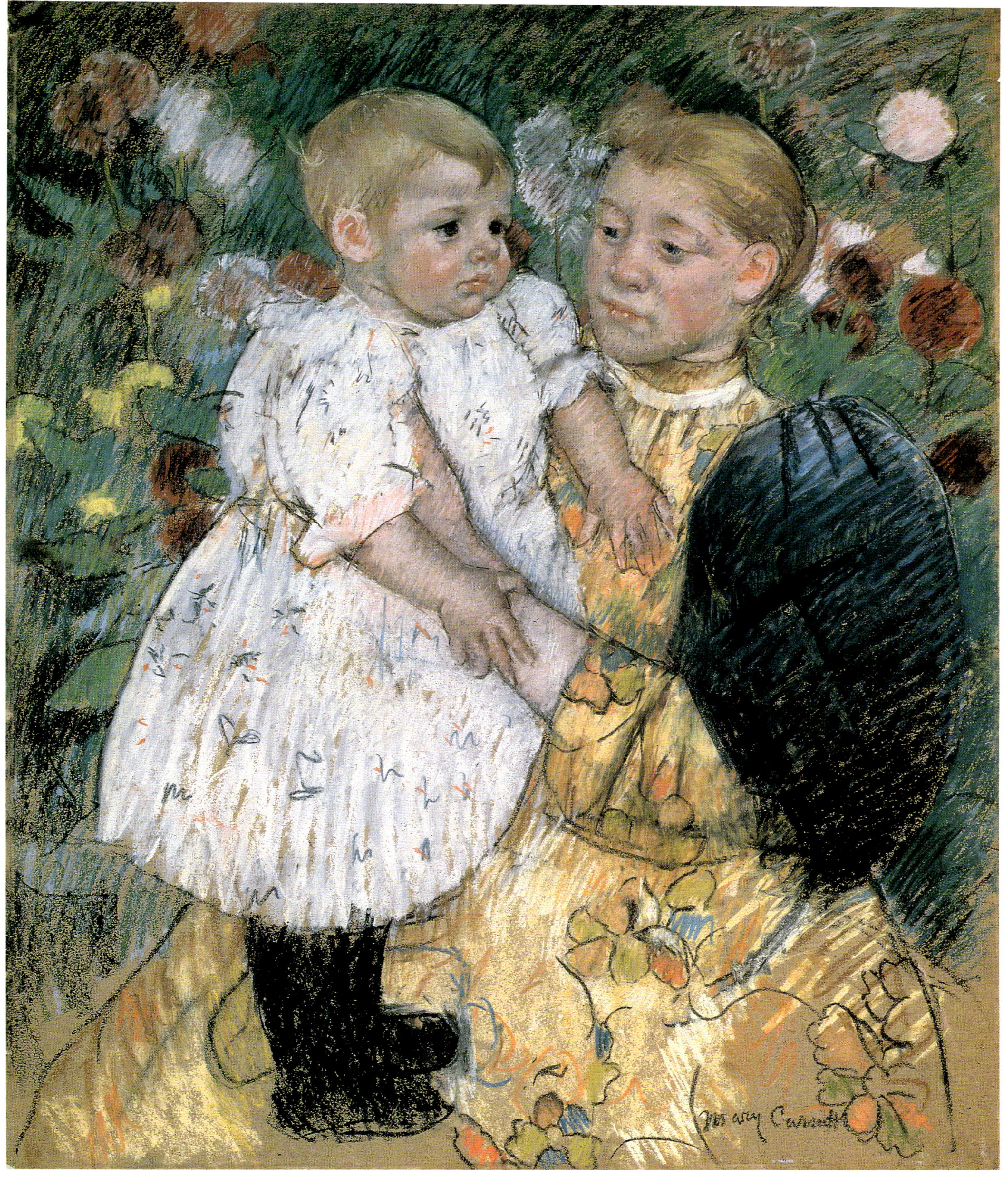

COLORPLATE 68. *In the Garden.* 1893. Pastel on paper. 28 ¾ × 23 ⅝ in. (73 × 60 cm). The Baltimore Museum of Art. The Cone Collection, formed by Dr. Claribel Cone and Miss Etta Cone of Baltimore, Maryland.

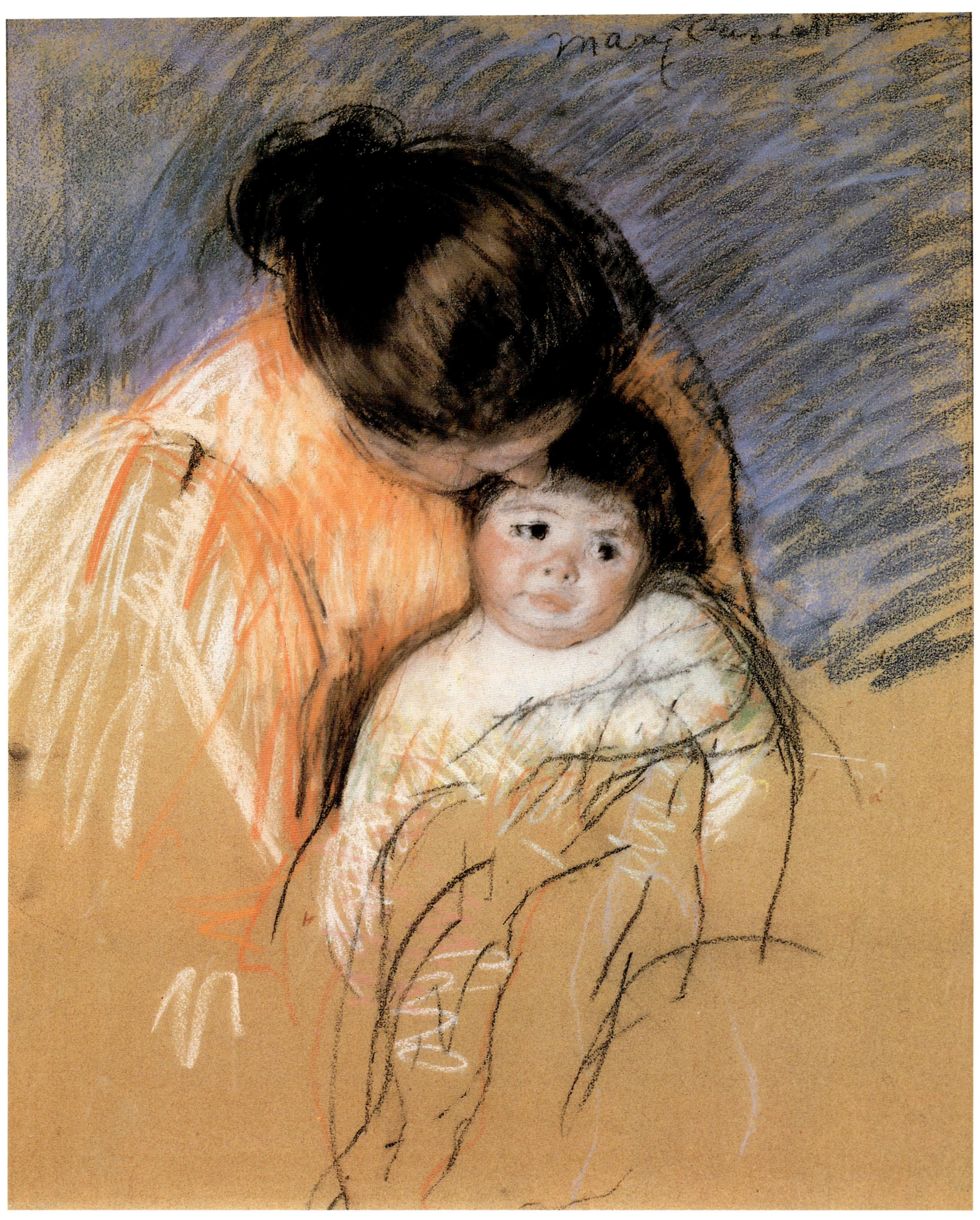

COLORPLATE 69. *Sketch of a Mother Looking Down at Thomas.* c. 1893. Pastel on paper. 27 × 22 ½ in. (68.5 × 57 cm). Collection of Jacqueline and Matt Friedlander; on extended loan to the High Museum of Art, Atlanta (EL 44.1985).

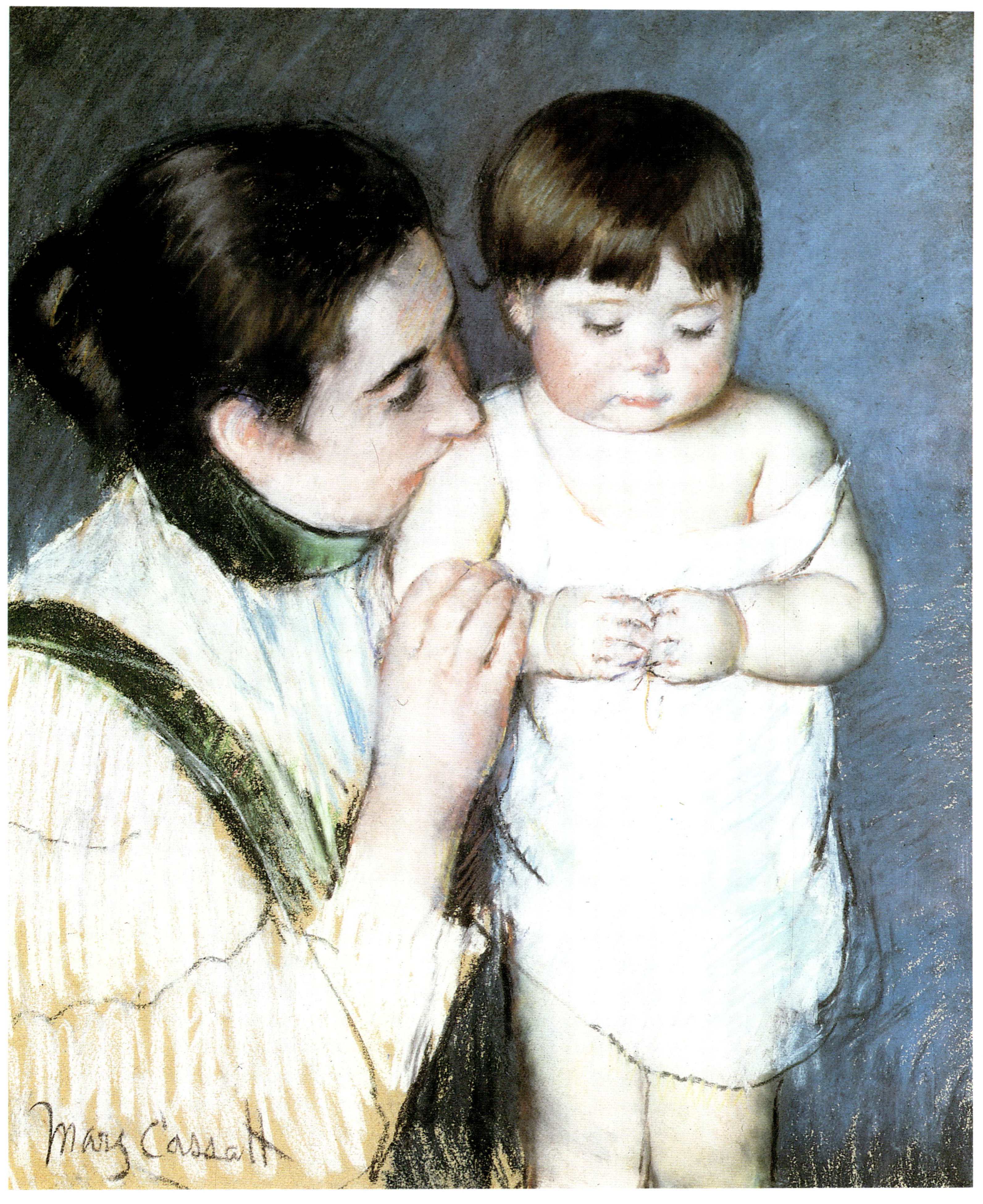

COLORPLATE 70. *Young Thomas and His Mother.* 1893. Pastel on paper. 23 ⅝ × 19 ¾ in. (60 × 50 cm). The Pennsylvania Academy of the Fine Arts.

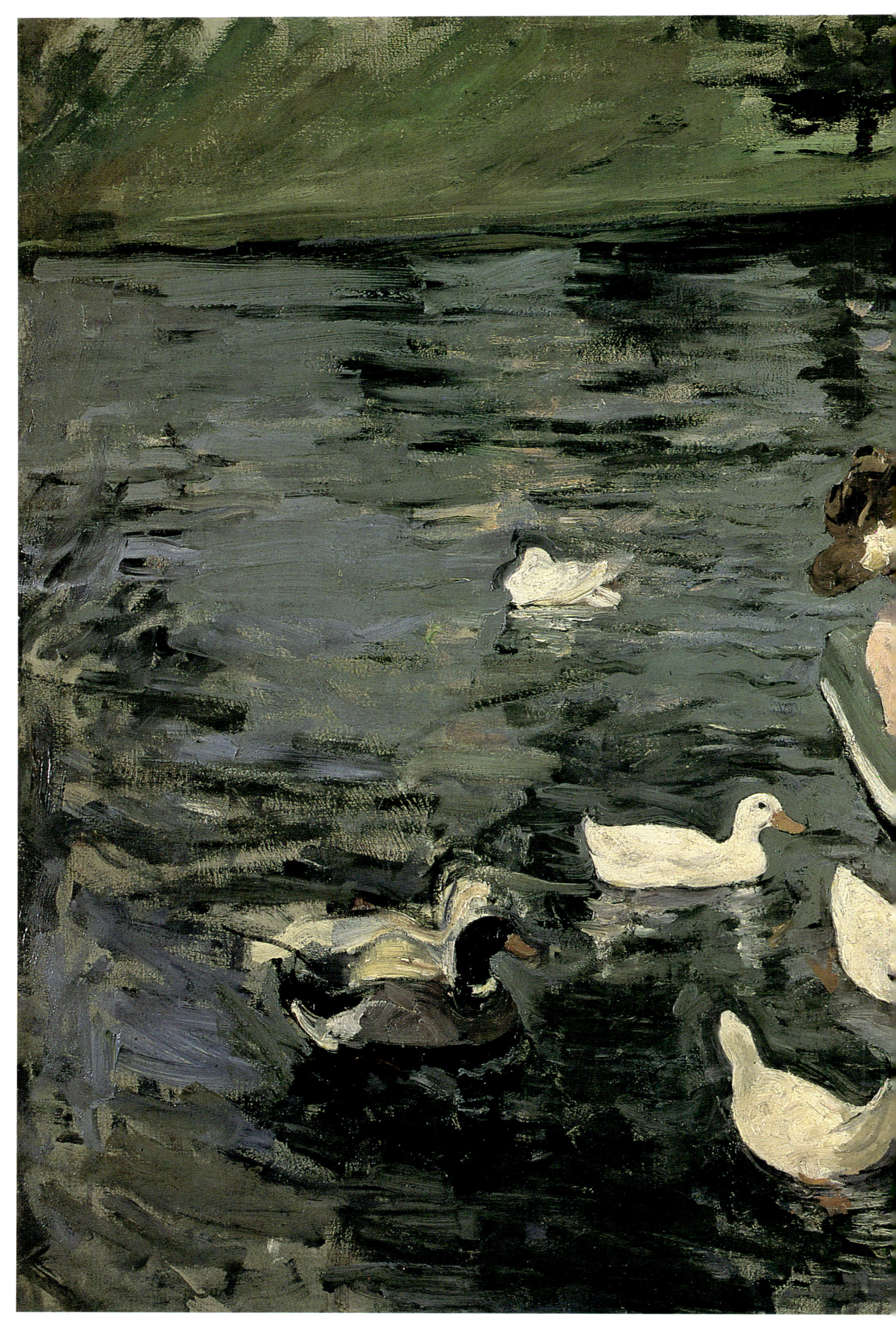

COLORPLATE 71. *Summertime.* 1894. Oil on canvas. 28 7/8 × 39 1/2 in. (73.4 × 100.3 cm). The Armand Hammer Collection, UCLA at the Armand Hammer Museum of Art and Cultural Center, Los Angeles.

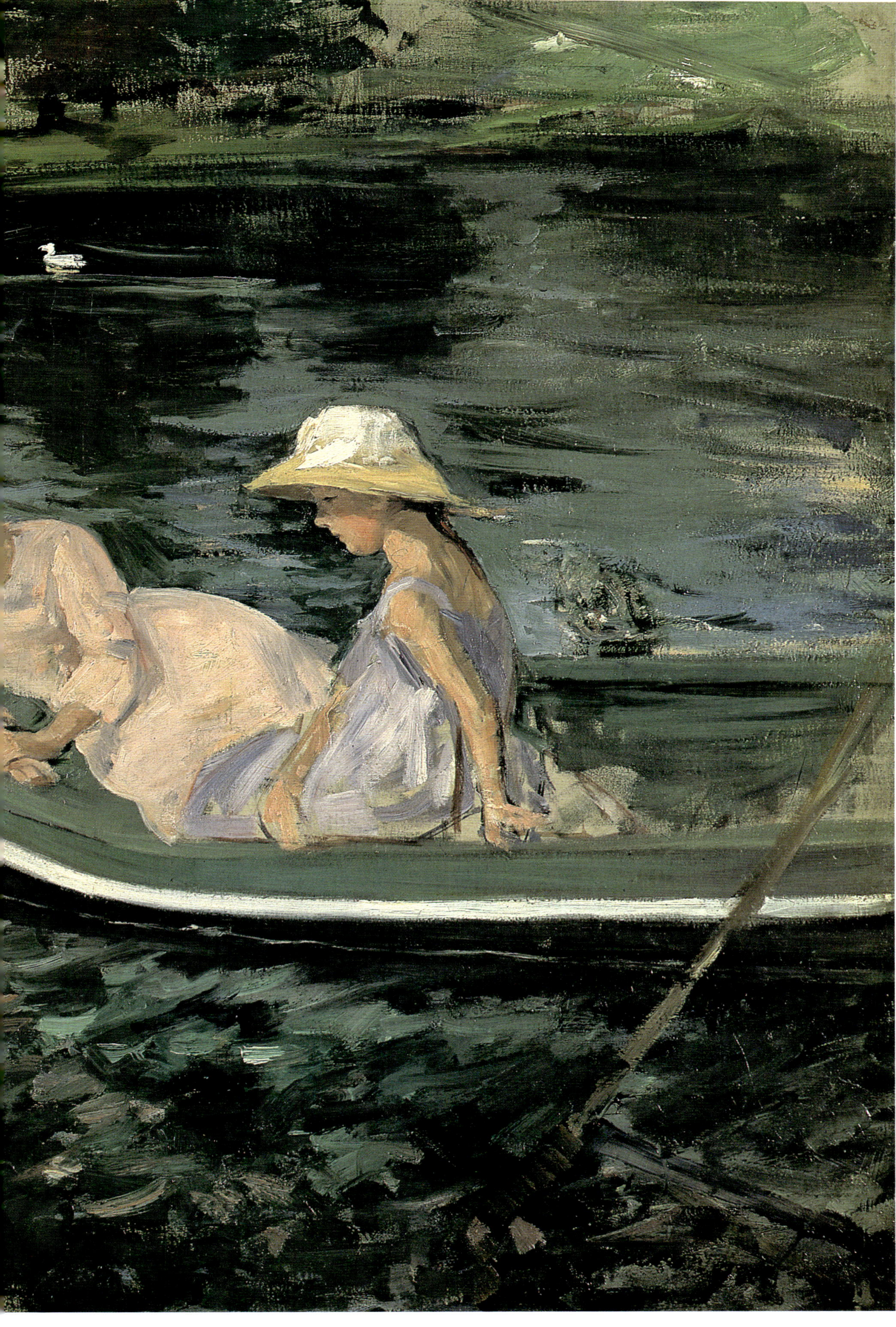

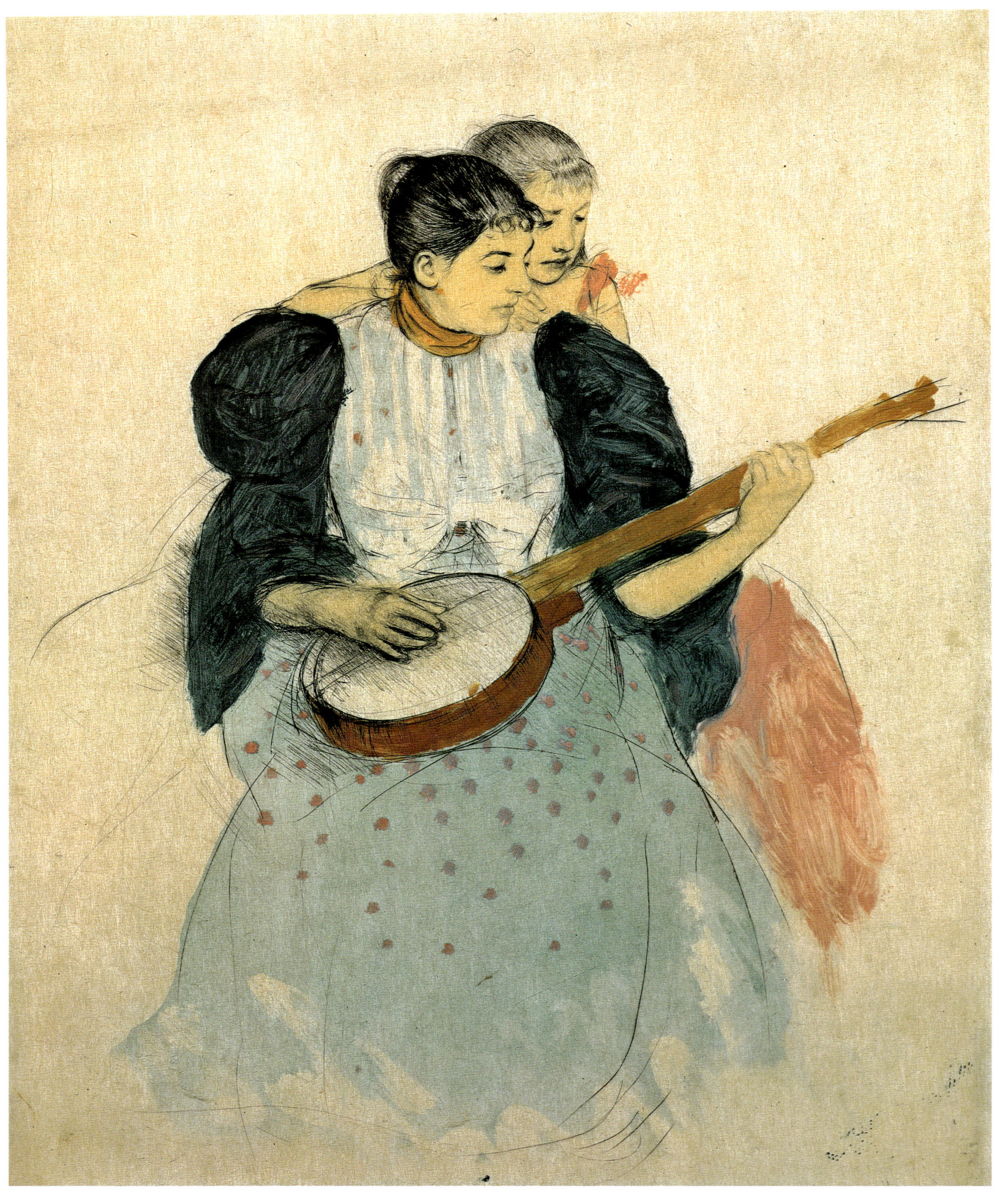

COLORPLATE 72. *The Banjo Lesson*. c. 1893. Drypoint and soft-ground etching. 16 ½ × 11 ½ in. (42 × 29.2 cm). National Gallery of Art. Gift of Mrs. Jane C. Carey as an addition to the Addie Burr Clark Memorial Collection. Photograph © Board of Trustees, National Gallery of Art, Washington, D.C.

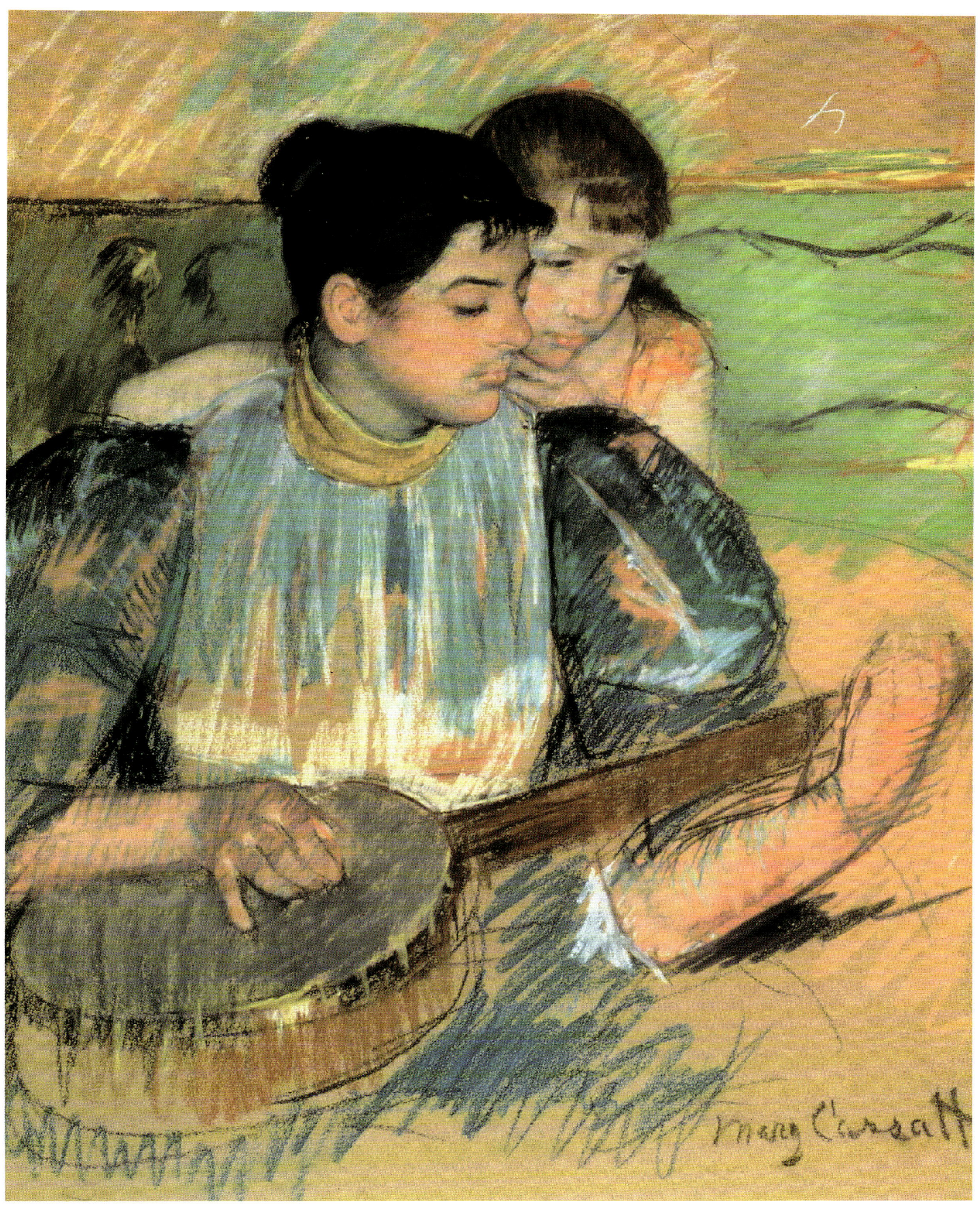

COLORPLATE 73. *The Banjo Lesson.* 1894. Pastel on paper. 28 × 22 ½ in. (71.1 × 57.2 cm). Virginia Museum of Fine Arts, Richmond. The Adolph D. and Wilkins C. Williams Fund. Photograph © Virginia Museum of Fine Arts.

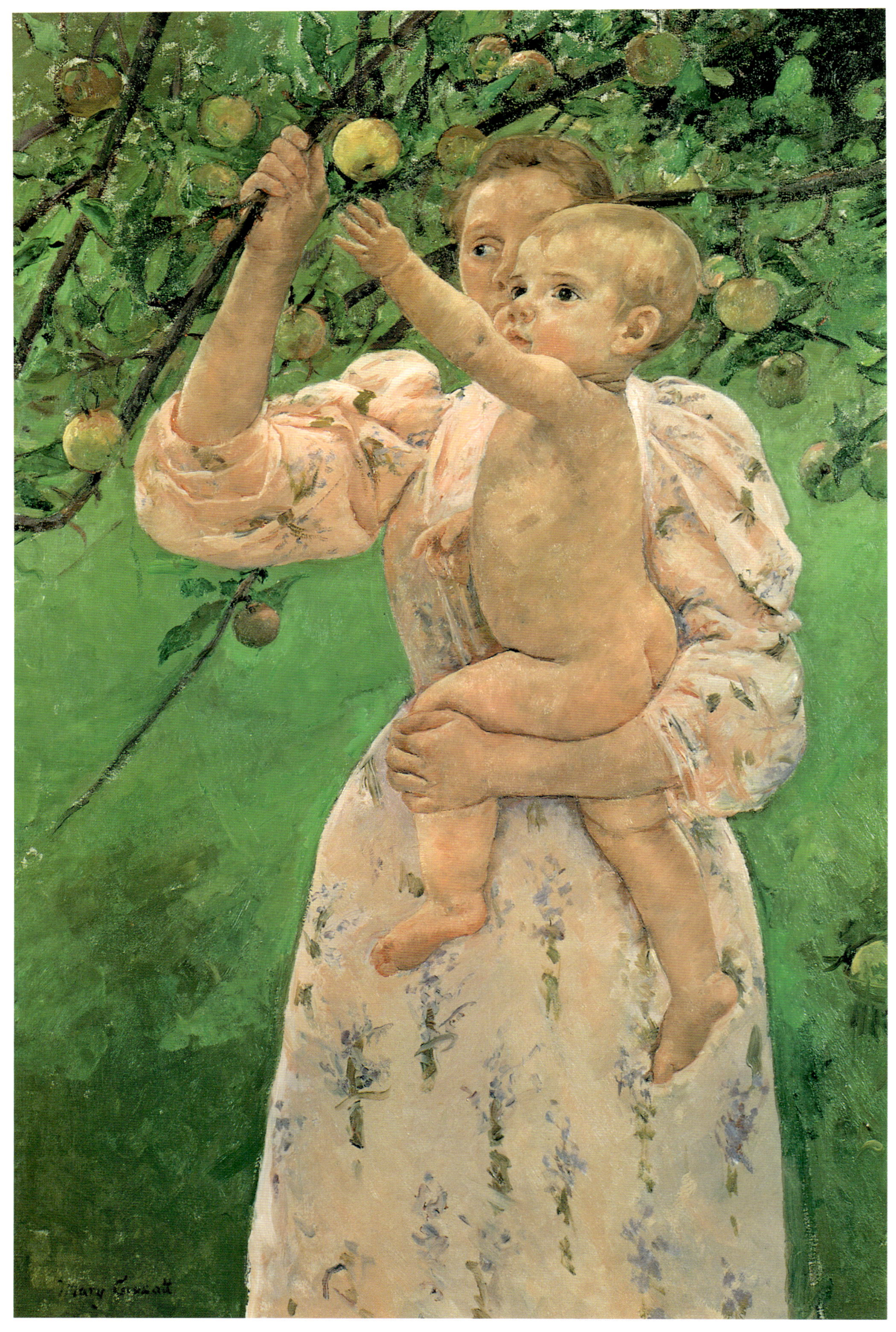

COLORPLATE 74. *Baby Reaching for an Apple.* 1893. Oil on canvas. 39 ½ × 25 ¾ in. (100.3 × 65.4 cm).
Virginia Museum of Fine Arts, Richmond. Gift of Ivor and Anne Massey.
Photograph: Grace Wen Hwa T'sao, © Virginia Museum of Fine Arts.

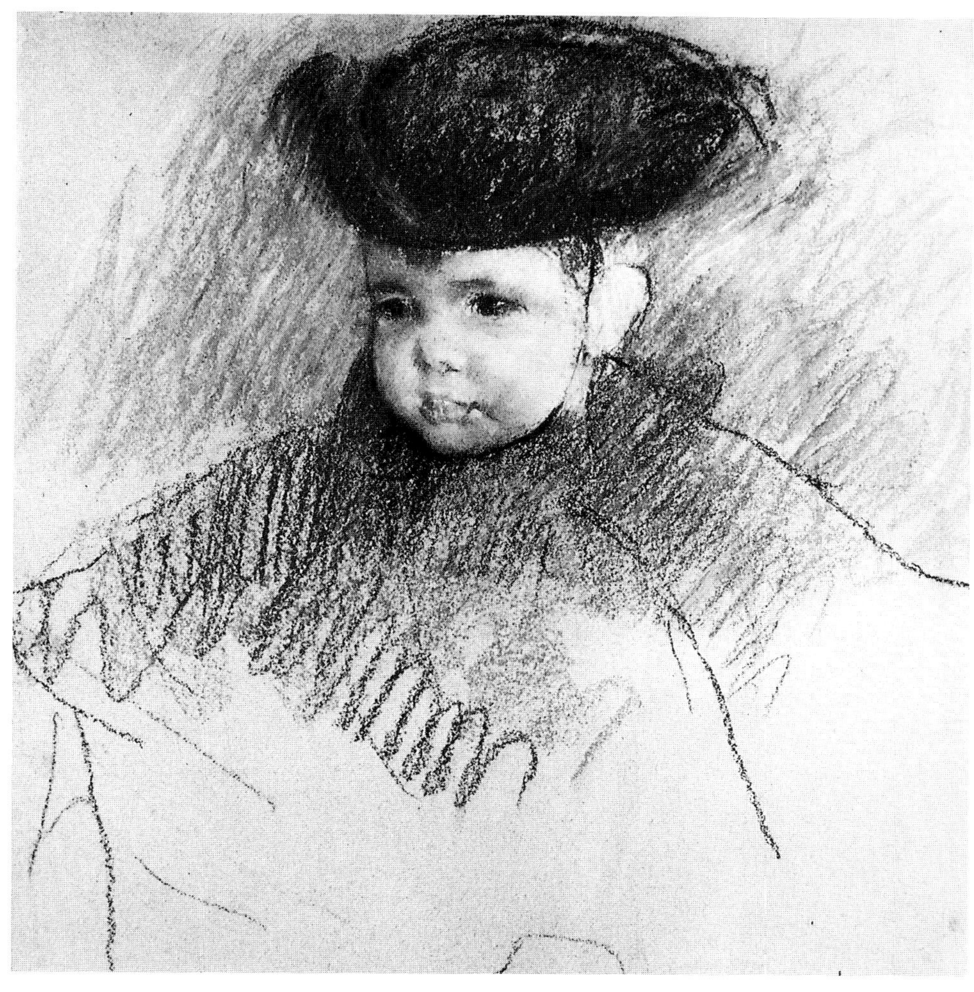

Head of a Small Boy (Master Gardiner Green Hammond, Jr.). 1898. Pastel on paper. 20 × 19 ½ in. (50.8 × 49.5 cm). Phoenix Art Museum. The Harrington Collection.

to look at Miss Cassatt's works, all the same, for those individual qualities which no defects or weaknesses of the motives to which they are applied can hide. To praise her as lavishly and unreservedly as her admirers do, is not in me, but to deride her, as others have done, is equally impossible. She exercises her right to express herself in her own way. That her way is not the best way I firmly believe, and I believe also that this will be the verdict of posterity.

The Art Amateur, May 1895.

Miss Mary Cassatt, one of the best known of living women painters, though a native of Philadelphia has been a resident of Paris for the last fourteen years; and though she has been deeply influenced by Manet and Degas, has developed a highly personal manner of her own. At the exhibition of her works at the Durand-Ruel Galleries on Fifth Avenue, Manet's influence was most strikingly shown in *La Loge,* a portrait of a lady in her box at the opera, low in tone and broadly but sympathetically handled. Another portrait, *Enfant et Chien,* bears a more superficial resemblance to Manet's work, and a *Scène Espagnole, Seville,* two pretty girls flirting with a cavalier in a balcony, is much of the same character. These three works were painted between 1873 and 1886. In more recent works, such as *Les Canotiers,* a woman and child in a yellow boat on a very blue lake, with a boatman attired in indigo, Manet's influence is again apparent in the broad and firm touch and the excellent sense of construction displayed. But quite a series of paintings show a morbidezza of color and a leaning to a treatment for effect more likely to have been learned from Degas and the later Impressionists. Of these are the charming *Femme a l'éventail,* painted in

COLORPLATE 18

COLORPLATE 7

COLORPLATE 75

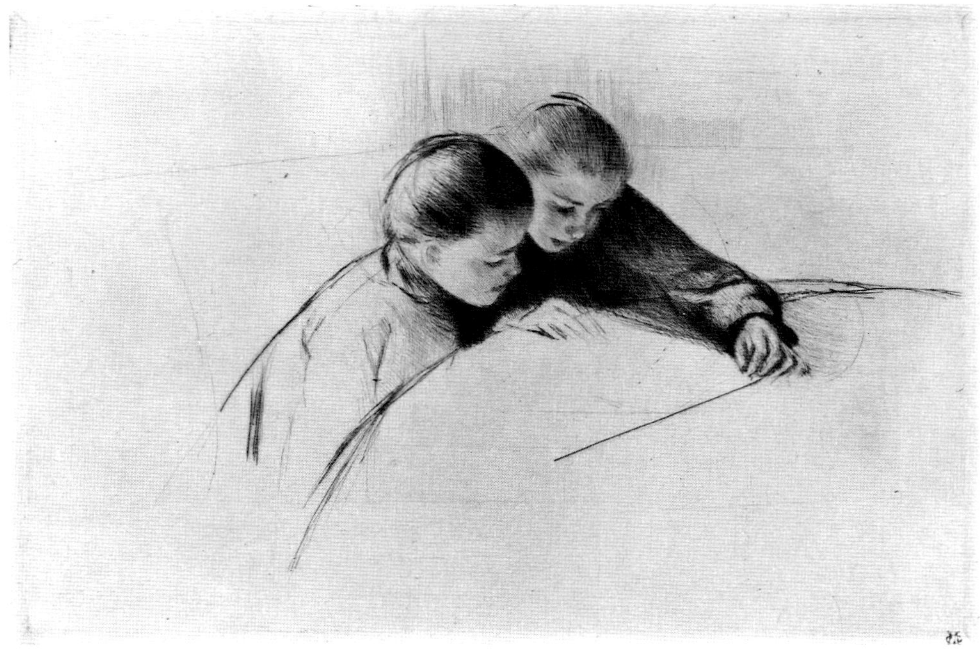

The Map. c. 1890–91. Drypoint in brown ink. 6 1/4 × 9 1/4 in. (15.8 × 23.4 cm). National Academy of Design, New York. Samuel Colman Collection.

1878, and two portrait groups, *Nourrice et Enfant,* and *Au Théâtre,* painted probably at about the same date. That the Japanese color print has attracted Miss Cassatt's notice there is evidence in the charming series of dry points, which next to Whistler's paintings are the most distinguished work visibly affected by Japanese art. The subjects are her usual scenes of home life and portraits, drawn with a free and pure outline and colored with a few flat tints printed from separate blocks or plates. We do not hesitate to say that these prints will be reckoned among the most artistic of the century. In a few of her recent oil paintings a very flat modelling, bright color, and a firm, precise outline produce an effect now Japanese, now more closely approaching the manner of the Italian pre-Raphaelite painters. *Jeune Femme cueillant un Fruit,* a garden scene with two figures, and *La Toilette d'Enfant,* are of this sort. In the latter, the mother's striped wrapper, pink, green, and white, is painted as frankly as it would be by Botticelli, but there is no sense of crudity in the tones. We have thought that it would be of interest to point out Miss Cassatt's affiliations. It would be difficult if not impossible to give an adequate account of the individual charm of her work, which, nevertheless, is most striking. In other words, it is easy to class Miss Cassatt among the Impressionists, but not so easy to determine her proper place among them, except to say that it is an important one.

COLORPLATE 16

COLORPLATE 62
COLORPLATE 66

"Miss Mary Cassatt," by William Walton. *Scribner's Magazine,* March 1896.

William Walton (1843–1915), American author, painter, and craftsman who specialized in designs for stained glass. A longtime admirer of Cassatt, Walton wrote for "Scribner's Magazine" and is the author of "Art and Architecture, World's Columbian Exposition, 1893."

The number of picture exhibitions in New York City, in the winter season of 1894–95, was very considerable, but, as among other institutions, those only of these displays make durable impressions which are endowed with strongly marked characteristics, and there are only a limited number that are worthy of permanent record. One of these in this case was undoubtedly that of a certain number of the works of Miss Cassatt, in which the strong individuality of the artist seemed to move and live, as it were, behind the mask of her works, and the spectator was impressed by a new personality with which he was brought almost into contact. The technical problems of their art, which have so great an importance in the eyes of the painters, interest only in slight degree, as everybody knows, the larger body of laymen, and it is the characteristics of the painter himself, as he makes them manifest, that lend their value in the eyes of the public to these technical processes. Miss Cassatt's works, oils, pastels, and dry points, seemed to have so much a style of their own as to at once attract attention—even among those more conventional or more timid who preferred milder methods of painting pictures. So many things are required in the successful practice of this art, that the translation of impalpable qualities by tangible and material applications assumes all sorts of interests to different appreciations, and this little exhibition, somewhat peculiar in this respect, while appealing most strongly to the visitor with a certain amount of information, was yet interesting to everyone. The subjects were mostly simple studies of women, or of women and children, frequently of the same sitters; a certain superficial family resemblance characterizing the very important group of pastels and paintings executed within the last five years, and a similar bond uniting the very different series of dry points printed in colors, somewhat better known to the ordinary New York picture-seer. Of still different methods were the earlier pictures in oils, some of them painted as far back as twenty years ago. . . .

From these urban and somewhat conventional themes, Miss Cassatt seems to have turned in later years to the consideration of the simplest domestic and rural subjects, mothers with babies, or without their babies, seated on the grass, or on garden benches. Many of these are midsummer scenes, set in the greenest of landscapes. In all of them may be felt that directness and vigor of presentation which has caused this lady to be claimed by the impressionists; but hers is scarcely impressionistic painting as generally understood, vague as is that term. In all of them may be felt a certain sentiment, or charm, or poetry—something much more than mere good painting. The feeling of nature, of summer air and space, of the charm of green apple orchards, or parks, and, very frequently, the mystery of mother love and the pulchritude of the Baby. But seldom indeed has that inefficient but most valuable of potentates been more carefully studied and faithfully rendered, in many of his various moods, and in his relations with the mother that bore him or the nurse that tends him. In this little exhibition alone might be seen a dozen variations on that old, old group of the Madonna—posing only as "Mother and Child," or "The Young Mother," or "Nurse and Child," with a fine affectation of being only painter's studies, with that aversion to the appearance of being sentimental so characteristic of the works of the artist of the day. In one painting only, the *Maternal Solicitude*, has the painter ventured to give the real title of her work—the wonderful, infinite motherly yearning over the queer little unresponsive, responsive being of which she knows so little. The mystery, real and fictitious, of these small, naked infants counts for even more in the obsession of the painter than the thorny technical problem of presenting their bodies—and she seems to render it even more truly. That later prophet, Nordau, in his character as general scold, could never say of her infants as he does of those of Miss Kate Greenaway, that they are the disordered products of an unfortunately diverted love of children. Miss Cassatt seems to have two of these youthful sitters, one dark-haired, dark-eyed, and the other with scant yellowish hair, but also very effective dark eyes. The latter appears in the important painting reproduced in the frontispiece, and also in the *In the Garden* of the smaller illustration. For both of them she renders most sympathetically that imposing air of infancy, that putting-on of strangeness and unutterable knowledge, which no consciousness on our part of its unreliability deprives of its power over us. In art, as in real life, a first-rate make-believe is frequently just as good as the real thing.

COLORPLATE 68

In her rendering of the adults that hover round these infants, or occasionally occupy themselves without them, there is the same search for character and truthfulness, with even less regard for that mere prettiness of expression that was once thought so requisite in similar subjects. The old doctrine of "Beauty" has been superseded among the moderns by a haunting fear of falling into the pretty-pretty. Miss Cassatt is probably too conscious of her strength to be much troubled by this dread, but the unregenerate spectator will sometimes wish for a little more pandering to his prejudices in this matter. To adopt his point of view for the moment, we may say that there was a fine sentimental picture among these, in which the blonde sitter who appears so frequently is represented on a bench under the trees, and looking at a pink or a geranium which she holds somewhat stiffly before her. Her physical beauty in this instance is even less than usual; of that youthful charm and grace, which were formerly considered indispensable under these circumstances, there is scarcely a trace. The probabilities are, however, that by avoiding the conventional and the pretty the painter has evolved a better and more artistic situation—the suggestion perhaps of the upspringing of all these tender, youthful, feminine longings and aspirations, and half formed ideas in some soul more worthy of our interest than the usual one. A sort of variation on Hegel's theory of the beautiful—"the presence of the idea in limited phenomenon." This replacing of the pretty by something better is also very noticeable in *The Caress*, suggesting the old renderings of the mystic marriage of Saint Catherine, and, like them, apparently meaning much more than it says. The baby's head is quite dignified and noble, and quite baby-like; and the settling of his fat, little shapeless body, creased by the mother's fingers in the mother's lap is excellently given. The thoughtfulness behind the good painting gives all these pictures their human interest.

COLORPLATE 65

In the technical rendering, the painter has apparently addressed herself, as the important thing, to the solution of the unsolvable problem of painting flesh. In this great problem even those are now beginning to be interested who, despite their interest in pictures, considered flesh as something unprofitable. Something ugly, meaty, and indecent, to be covered up on all occasions and not mentioned outside the bath-room. They are not yet converted to the artist's belief that it is the most beautiful substance in nature, and one of the most wonderful; that neither the Japanese, Barbedienne, nor Thiébaut frères can make such bronze as the clear, translucent brown of a young negro. The nature of the pigments supplied to the painter by his dealer is such that he is able, approximately, to render either the superficial color and form of this integument or something of its texture, but not both, and he is immediately called upon to decide. Many, and some of them of great renown, elect to try for the beautiful, smooth, delicately tinted surface; the more analyzing and tormented souls resolve, at all hazards, to give the substance and qualities of this baffling epidermis. The method of the intransigeants is well known—to construct, as it were, the substance with varying and violently colored pigments, and then leave the putting on of the finishing and smoothing outer cuticle to the judicious spectator and his duly elongated point of view. The solution of this problem by some of the masters, three or four hundred years ago, has been accepted as very nearly satisfactory without anyone's being able to discover just how they did it; at least one distinguished American painter devoted a large part of his working life to the attempt to solve the problem of "Titian's flesh," and is said to have died in the belief that he had succeeded, without convincing his fellows. An experiment made upon a Rembrandt in the Louvre, a few years ago, seemed to determine, what had been suspected, that the yellow and golden glow of the picture was due in great measure to time, Spanish licorice, and many coats of varnish; but the new Rembrandt underneath was thought to be even finer. The qualities of this admirable substance with which we are clothed are such that it is difficult even to describe it; Fuseli's apparently idiotic phrase for Rubens's flesh, "the brawny pulp of slaughtermen," is not to be despised. The conscientious painter thinks he must at least suggest all the qualities of this "brawny pulp"—its color and form, contexture, resilience and other properties, even to its muffled resonance when struck. And his pigments and chalks naturally abandon at once any such unequal contest.

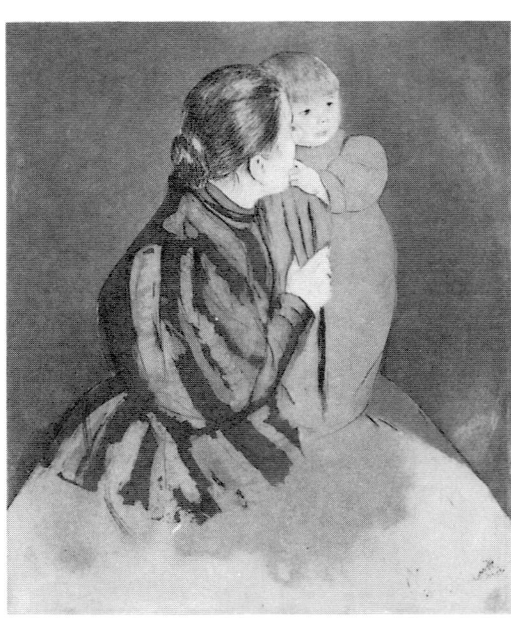

Peasant Mother and Child. c. 1894. Drypoint. 18 1/4 × 13 in. (46.3 × 33 cm). Courtesy of Museum of Fine Arts, Boston. Gift of Denham W. Ross.

Miss Cassatt's selections and compromises, among the various methods of flesh-painting known, constitute one of the most interesting features of her work. She cannot reconcile herself to the painting of a beautiful, smooth, hard substance like tinted ivory, and she is not satisfied with the coarsely hatched structure of many of her contemporaries, which at least suggests the depth of the fleshly integument, if not the finish. By wise and vigorous painting, with the full strength of her palette and a careful observance of the local variations, she secures the intrinsic quality of her fleshly tones—so that you can well imagine that her rendering would feel under your fingers much as the naked body does in life—and she is much aided in securing this desirable effect by a free use of that hard outline which the impressionists so generally disregard. In her etchings, also, this skilful use of the outline is of the greatest service in securing this truthfulness—an almost flat rendering of a baby's torso is made at once to seem both pulpy and solid by the strong folds of the lower part of his body when seated on his mother's arm, or the creases and dimples which her fingers make in his sides. In her painting, to supplement this rendering of the structure, she contrives, by a certain care in blending and finishing, to invest it with more of that smooth and pleasant outer surface than do generally the practitioners of the newer schools; but her main care is, evidently, to make sure of the pulpy and kneadable quality rather than of that pinkness and whiteness and exquisite smooth coolness which make a baby's or a young girl's cheek such a delight to the touch. There is much to be said on both sides of this question—the delight of the eye is to be considered by the artist, and it may be doubted whether such flesh as sailors and laborers wear, and many painters paint, would ever have led civilized man to the invention of caresses and kisses. Something more than usual of this care for the outer finish may be seen in the beautiful pastel study of the child with the orange. This little maid's countenance, her round, white forehead, are so truly and beautifully rendered as to furnish a permanent joy—even her little nose is gently fleshly and compressible, instead of being hard and osseous in structure.

The modelling of the flesh in the dry points is generally summarily done by fine lines running in one direction, frequently diagonally, with none of the regular etcher's care for the individual black line. For the curious, decorative dry-point plates printed in colors, a flat, conventional grayish flesh tone generally does duty for all exposed portions, both of mother and infant, and the careful and sometimes eccentric outline finishes the rendering. The hair, on the contrary, is carefully done in detail, generally giving the light and shade and the contour of the head. The outline drawing of the infants, and sometimes of the adults, is a species of compromise between nature and Japanese methods. In her neglect of these structural qualities for the elaborate repetition of pattern on wall or drapery, Miss Cassatt also follows the traditions of the Japanese artist, who wreaks himself on the infinite detail of the *kimono* to the total neglect of the body it covers, because he is so constituted. The color is pleasant, decorative, and cool, running to grays and keeping within a reasonable distance of nature. Occasionally on tea-pots or other important substances, as well as on the human head, it breaks into a little modelling and roundness.

The color in the later pastels and paintings ranges through a long scale, sometimes very rich and decorative, and at others much quieter and simpler. In the *Child with the Orange*, one of the most sumptuous, the fruit makes a sudden and brilliant spot of color in the centre of the shining, beautiful greenish-blue of the dress, the silky yellow hair is crossed with a red ribbon, the vase behind has strong blue accents, and the background has apparently been constructed by striking a luminous green across a solid, rich reddish-brown. The advancing and receding planes are sometimes carefully attended to and sometimes neglected in these works, as the painter thought them important in her scheme or not, but the solidity of

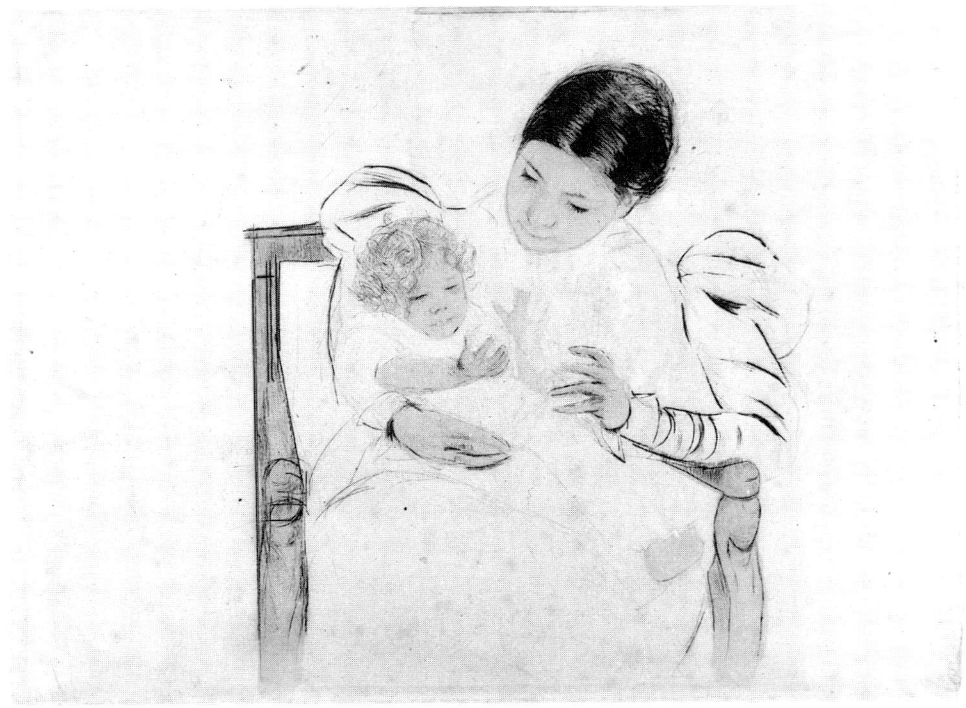

The Barefooted Child. 1898. Color drypoint and aquatint. 9 5/16 × 12 3/4 in. (23.6 × 32.4 cm). Philadelphia Museum of Art. Gift of Mrs. Horace Binney Hare.

the figure is always taken care of; and the roundness, generally. There is also no hampering by definite rules about "finish"—in the lower part of the skirt of our little orange girl the gray pastel paper has been left almost wholly uncovered, because the painter found she had given enough of the luminous satiny color of the gown. The *Maternal Solicitude* and the mother and child in the garden are also very handsome and pompous; in the latter, the large, dark-red flowers in the background, which perhaps, keep their places, and perhaps do not, are all but dominated by the brilliant spots of orange, green, and yellow in the mother's dress. The bodice of the lady who stoops so tenderly over her black-headed little son, is in yellows and oranges, very rich in color, and her skirt is pale pink with dark-greenish spots. In the large painting in oil reproduced for the frontispiece of this number—which the French Government vainly desired for the Luxembourg—the sturdy naked body of the baby is very delicately relieved against the nurse's pink dress, of almost similar value and color. The heavily laden boughs come down very solidly over their heads, and the stretch of grassy lawn behind them is painted almost flat—this painter believing that we see much less aerial perspective than we think we do.

COLORPLATE 68

COLORPLATE 74

Among the paintings shown in this exhibition was a large one, representing a section of a boating party, the back of the rower in the foreground, nearly life-size, being clothed in flat, very dark blue, pure color, and his sash of a paler blue, much like the flat water beyond. At the top of the picture was a strip of landscape of about the same value as the water; the corner of sail shown was distinctly greenish in hue, and the boat was painted in green and white, amidst all of which the baby in the stern sheets was of a species of shrimp pink. As a contrast to this cheerful navigation there was a little marine very like a Manet, a flat, grayish-yellowish expanse of sea spotted with three or four little black boats. Miss Cassatt's large painting for the decoration of the north tympanum of the Woman's Building at Chicago, two years ago, will be remembered by many visitors notwithstanding the very inconvenient height at which it was placed. In this she had worked in the methods exemplified in the later pictures shown in the New York exhibition, and her theme was not dissimilar—carefully selected but not idealized figures of women and children gathering fruit in a long, green orchard. It may also be remembered that some of the Western "Lady Managers" thought this conception of "Modern Woman"—her theme—somewhat inaccurate.

To the first exhibition of the impressionists in Paris, in 1878, Miss Cassatt was an important contributor, and her works have appeared in the Salons both before and since that date and in this country—as in the galleries of the Society of American Artists and at the Loan Exhibition of Portraits of Women in New York, November, 1894—but in general she seems to have attained to that desirable condition, coveted of artists, of being able to dispense with the annual exhibitions. An art so learned, so well-inspired as hers, which so well combines the letter and the spirit, and knows how to present the prettiest and most popular of themes in a large and comprehensive way, preserving all the tenderness and avoiding all of the little and the commonplace, is sufficiently rare even in this age of over-production, and any knowledge of it is to be accounted as gain.

The First Impressionist Exhibition was held in 1874; Cassatt did not begin to exhibit with the group until 1879, which was their fourth exhibition.

Letter from Mary Cassatt to Eugenie Heller

Advice to an Art Student

c. February 1, 1896

10, rue de Marignan
Sunday

Dear Miss Heller,

After I left you yesterday, it seemed to me I might have given you an impression of want of interest, & want of appreciation of your work—I can only say I did not mean to do so, I saw that you had studied & improved, I merely wished to give you if possible another direction, much more severe things have been said to me & I am thankful for it now. When I came to live in Paris after having painted in Rome & other places, the sight of the annual exhibitions, quite led me astray. I thought I must be wrong & the painters admired of the public right—It was then I fell in with our band & took quite another direction—

Cassatt attempted to become a fashionable portraitist in Paris between 1875 and 1877.

My sister-in-law, Miss Hallowell, & I are going this week to St Quentin for the day. In the Musée of St Quentin are eighty pastels of Latour which I very much wish to see. Wont you go with us? We are going 2nd class, & will leave in the morning early & if possible stop over two hours at Compiègne to see the Hotel de Ville in that place & then go on to St Quentin where we will have 4 hours & back to Paris in time for dinner.

Maurice-Quentin de La Tour (1704–1788), French painter and pastel portraitist.

There are Latour's in the Louvre, but the St Quentin ones are celebrated. He was an artist, most simple most sincere, no "brio," no facility of execution, but his portraits are living & full of character—

I should like you to meet Miss Hallowell, she may be useful to you & you may be to her; I will explain to you my ideas of decoration which she is to help to execute besides having much taste of her own in that way. Your firm might find such correspondence over here useful—I want to help in that sort of thing & personally don't wish to make anything out of it—

We have not yet fixed on a day for St Quentin, but not Wednesday or Thursday—If the weather changes perhaps Tuesday, in the meantime I should be glad to see you soon if you come this way.

Yours sincerely,
Mary Cassatt

LOUISINE HAVEMEYER

From *Sixteen to Sixty: Memoirs of a Collector*

Cassatt and Her Work Ethic

1930

When her family came abroad to live with her, they finally made their home in the rue Marignan, and there she lives today in a charming apartment with windows both on the rue Marignan and on the rue François I. It was all cheerful and light and had an excellent exposure for painting.

How well I recall the little room she used as a studio! It was not half as large as the studio at Beaufresne, and tiny in comparison to the glass gallery where she worked in Grasse, but many and many a pastel was done there and the "placard" was full of canvases of pictures that were never finished, portraits that she kept for herself, sketches for compositions, or studies of children. It was a simple room and without any artistique effects. She selected it because it had good light. It contained little furniture but her easels and a few fine Empire and Louis XVI chairs which are familiar to any one who knows her work. I recall her drawing room and the tender green of the soft silk curtains, the rich brocades she had collected when in Italy or Spain. Several [works by] Degas and a still life of Cézanne were upon the walls, and a gesso of Donatello was on an easel in a corner.

How many pictures of ours at one time or another were placed in that salon or in the hall, waiting to be sent to America, or to be seen and passed upon by friends and critics. Goyas and Grecos, Courbets and [works by] Degas, Ingres, and Chardin, all went to the rue Marignan, where Miss Cassatt could see and pass judgment upon them.

In the dining room was a little cabinet of exquisite silver and a fine Courbet upon the wall. Wonderful times we had in that dining room, true symposiums of intellectual refinement and free from any taint of bohemianism, wonderful evenings when Miss Cassatt and a few friends conversed and the rest of us were delighted to listen.

It was in the rue Marignan that Miss Cassatt developed her remarkable capacity for work. She inherited her energy from her mother, but its application to her work was all her own. I remember she said to me one day: "Why do these young girls come to me for advice? They have not the slightest notion of giving to art the devotion it requires. I say to them, 'Do you ever go to the Louvre and copy some of the great masters?' And they invariably answer, 'Oh, no, we can't, we are working in a studio, we have no time.'

" 'Degas does,' I answer. 'He will go to Lille for weeks or to St. Quentin for months.' But what good does it do to talk to them? They will never arrive! Mme. Morisot was right when she said a young student should go to some provincial town where there are a few good pictures and avoid the distractions and the snares of the studios of Paris." Miss Cassatt was silent a moment and then continued: "I went to Seville when I was a young girl. It was horrid and I was alone, but I braved it out for a year. Then I felt I needed Correggio and I went to Parma. A friend went with me; she did not remain, but I stayed there for two years, lonely as it was. I had my work and the few friends I made. I was so tired when my day was done I had little desire for pleasure. Even now I work eight hours a day and afterward take my walk with Matilde, and in the evenings after reading a little I am quite ready to go to bed."

Mathilde Valet was Cassatt's housekeeper and companion from about 1882 until Cassatt's death in 1926.

Miss Cassatt seemed inclined to talk and continued: "I doubt if you know the effort it is to paint! The concentration it requires, to compose your picture, the difficulty of posing the models, of choosing the color scheme, of expressing the sentiment and telling your story! The trying and

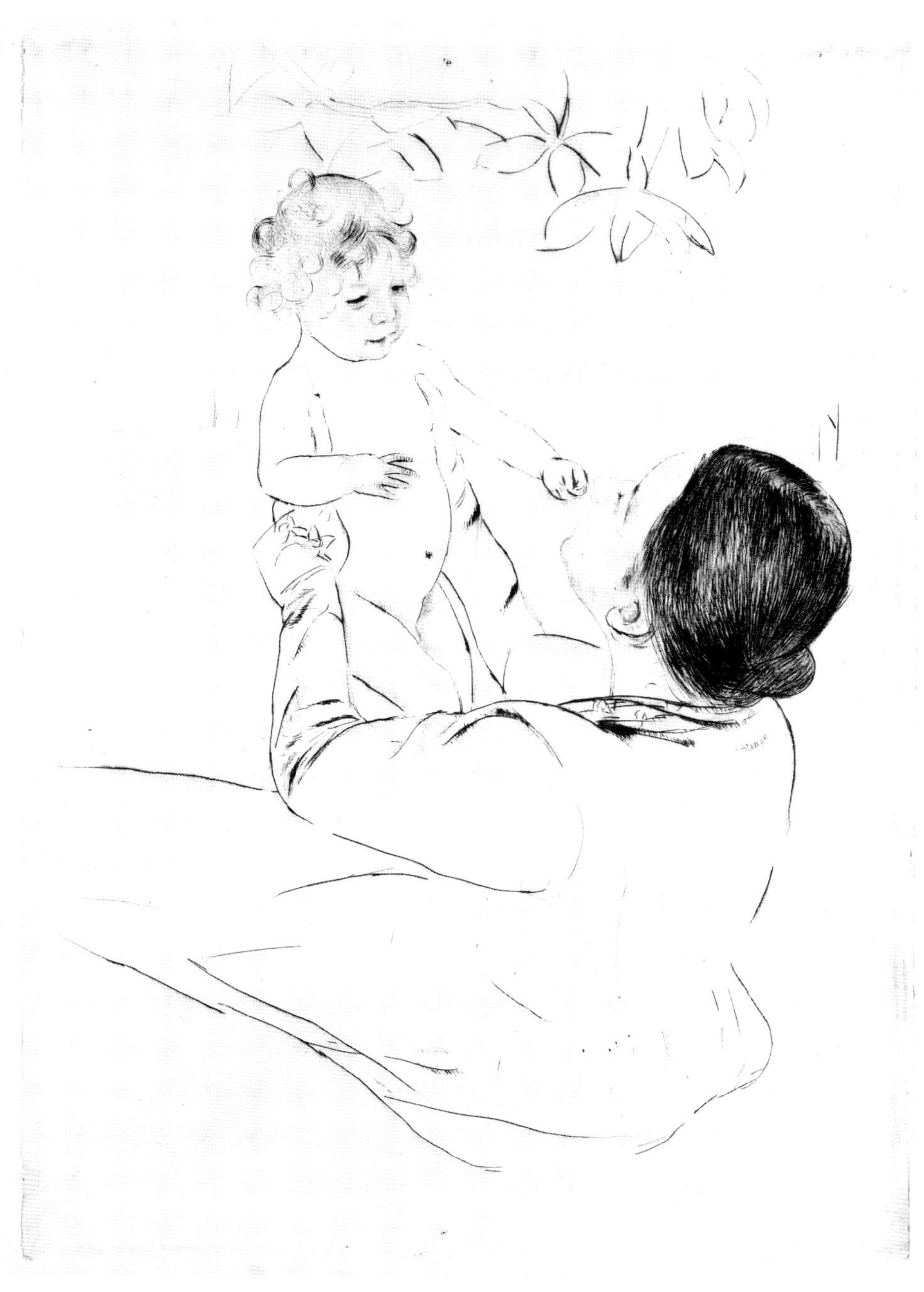

Under the Horse Chestnut Tree (first state). 1896–97. Drypoint. 15 7/8 × 11 1/4 in. (40.3 × 28.6 cm). Private collection.

trying again and again and oh, the failures, when you have to begin all over again! The long months spent in effort upon effort, making sketch after sketch. Oh, my dear! No one but those who have painted a picture know what it costs in time and strength!

"After a time, you get keyed up and it 'goes,' you paint quickly and do more in a few weeks than in the preceding weary months. When I am *en train*, nothing can stop me and it seems easy to paint, but I know very well it is the result of my previous efforts."

I have tried to repeat Miss Cassatt's words as nearly as I can remember them, for it is interesting to know how a painter works, and it may help some young student who is really serious and knows there is no royal road to fame.

Miss Cassatt always deplored the invasion of the French studios by Americans, who were lured to Paris by the fata morgana of thinking that a disposition for art meant a talent for art, and who were sure to fail after years of useless labor, or be lost in the contamination of the Latin Quarter. "How much better for them to find something to do at home," she would say to me. "I have worked for forty years and I feel I need forty more. Few have the courage to stand the strain."

ARTHUR HOEBER

From *The Century Magazine*

On Cassatt's Second New York Exhibition, 1898

March 1899

Arthur Hoeber (1854–1915), American landscape painter, illustrator, critic, and author. He studied with Gérôme in Paris and exhibited at the Paris Salon from 1882 to 1885.

There are few things more interesting to study in art than the development of individuality. As a rule, the artist passes through many stages of experiment, and shows traces of influence all the way along the career. From the very beginning at the schools, in the preference for certain casts, through the painting classes, biased by clever comrades, to the final choice of subject material and the inclination toward certain technical methods, there are few painters who are not seriously affected by the work of others.

Admitting this, however, the artist's profession is, after all, a lonely one, and the end must be attained with little outside aid. The law student has the benefit of numberless volumes to which reference may be made; the embryo physician can rely on the experience of his professional brethren, carefully set down in comprehensible print; while the other callings to which men and women find themselves drawn all have their libraries of books and their traditions to guide the novice. But in matters artistic the worker walks virtually alone, or, frankly admitting himself an imitator, forfeits claim to serious recognition.

No one may give a formula for painting, for it is impossible to make rules applicable to color, or to have every eye see nature in the same way. Tone is so delicate and fugitive, so affected by circumstances, time, and surrounding conditions, that its diagnosis is hopeless. Drawing is more or less a matter of feeling; it is impossible to describe, and has no known laws by which to establish precedence.

But if the artist, though fascinated by the methods of a Velasquez or a Rembrandt, of Manet or Whistler, may not copy servilely, it is still comprehensible that the works of these men may have a deep and lasting impression, and their influence may shape a career that, but for them, might have found its vent in totally different directions.

Nevertheless, it is for the painter, accepting the good in the canvases he is privileged to study and rejecting the bad, yet to retain his own originality, and so to translate nature as to give the absolute personal impression. Otherwise the picture is relegated to the great majority of commonplaces that annually fill the galleries, to the despair of the critic and the apathy of the public.

Of the colony of American painters who for a decade or two past have made Paris their home, few have been more interesting, and none more serious, than Miss Cassatt. From her canvas *Dans la loge*, sent to the exhibition of the Society of American Artists some years ago, to her more recent contributions to the Durand-Ruel galleries in New York winter before last, this artist has gone through various stages of experiment and study that have all been entertaining, and have all, in the end, conduced to her advancement in art.

COLORPLATE 16

The influence of the impressionists has been scarcely less apparent than that of the art of Japan. Time was when Miss Cassatt gave strong evidence of her predilection for the curious group of Frenchmen who, sacrificing line and form, composition and harmony of arrangement, even beauty itself, concerned themselves solely with problems of light, air, and the effort to produce scintillating color. Then came her leaning toward those Oriental workers in the land of chrysanthemums, and Miss Cassatt produced many delicately conceived etchings, drawings, and paintings,

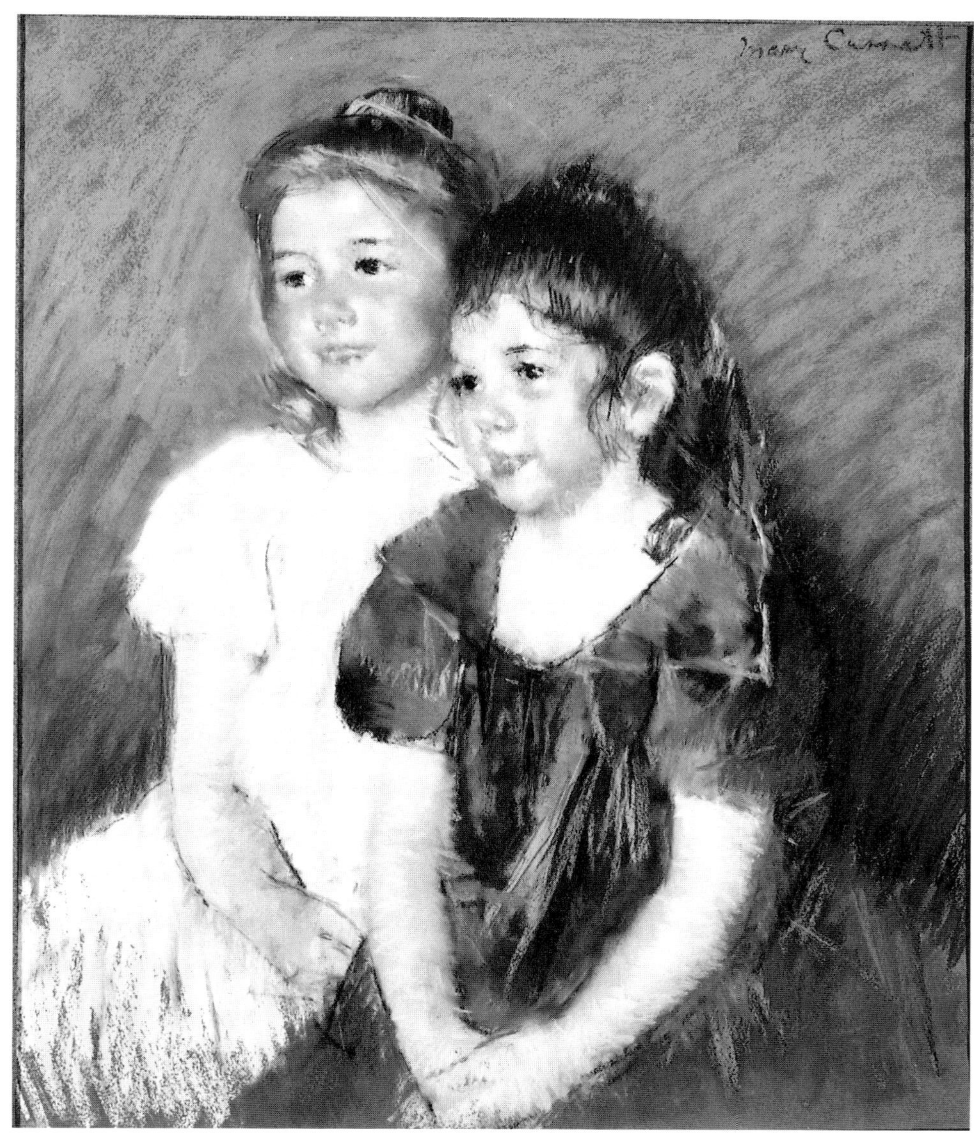

Young Girls. c. 1897. Pastel on paper. 25 × 20 3/4 in. (63.5 × 52.7 cm). Photograph © Indianapolis Museum of Art. The James E. Roberts Fund.

betraying her affiliations with a wonderfully decorative race. Through all the efforts, however, there were seriousness, intelligent searching, and always individuality.

It would seem, however, that Miss Cassatt has found her true bent in her recent pictures of children and in the delineation of happy maternity. Here she has caught with great fidelity the beauty of child life and the dignity of motherhood, fitting subjects for the artist's brush, ennobling material for intellectual investigation. These she has portrayed with delicacy, refinement, and sentiment. Her technic appeals equally to the layman and the artist, and her color has all the tenderness and charm that accompanies so engaging a motif.

From *The Art Amateur*
On Cassatt's Women and Children
May 1898

Women, children, young girls, in the house and in the garden, are the source of Miss Cassatt's inspiration; she rarely paints anything else. The

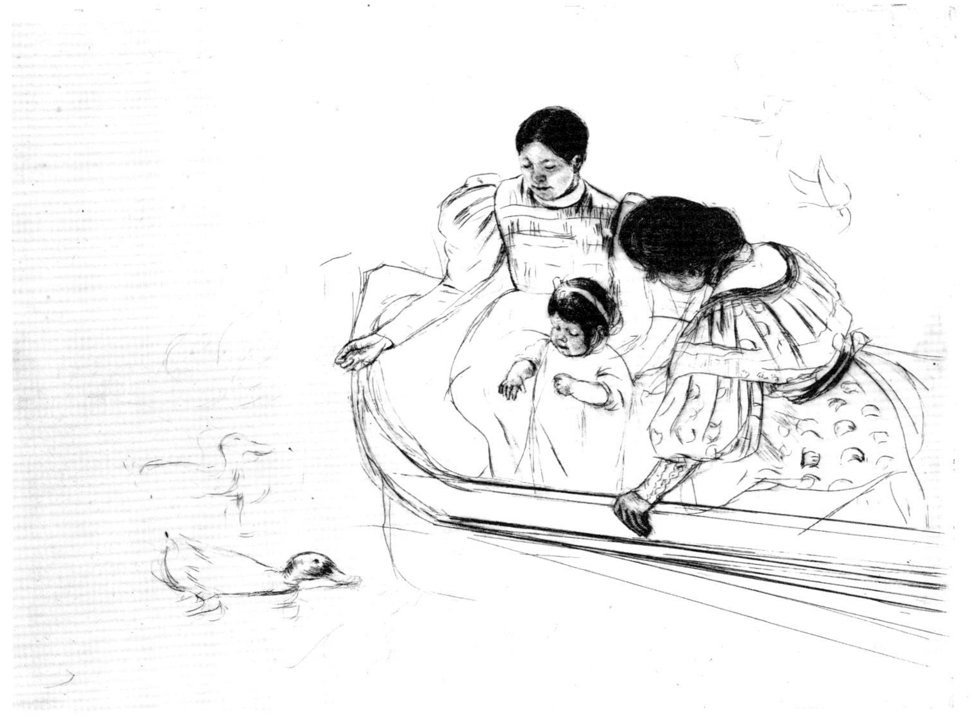

Feeding the Ducks (first state). c. 1895. Drypoint. 11 5/8 × 15 5/8 in. (29.5 × 39.7 cm). The Metropolitan Museum of Art, New York. Bequest of Mrs. H.O. Havemeyer, The Havemeyer Collection. Photograph © The Metropolitan Museum of Art.

children are at the morning bath, or taking the air in the arms of their nurse, or holding court among admiring elder sisters. The woman of society is shown in her box at the theatre, receiving the visit of a friend, returning from a promenade, trying on a dress, writing, embroidering, sipping tea, thrumming on a banjo. Girls not yet of an age for those serious occupations are shown plucking fruit, or whispering, with heads close together, or learning their lessons. But the almost purely physical beatitude of babyhood attracts her most. Baby is shown pleased with an orange, or content to suck her fat finger; planted in a fauteuil, or seated on her mother's knee; dressed in rose color or in blue, or—supremely indifferent to the fashions of today—arrayed like Eve in Paradise. The conventional woman, elegant, sickly, and insipid, and the conventional infant are nowise to Miss Cassatt's taste. She likes them strong, lusty, brown or rosy, alive and glad of it.

EDGAR P. RICHARDSON

From *Art News*

"Sophisticates and Innocents Abroad"

April 1954

Edgar P. Richardson (1902–1985), American art historian, administrator, editor, and author who served as director of the Detroit Institute of Fine Arts, Michigan, from 1945 to 1962. He is particularly known for his book "Painting in America: The Story of Four Hundred Fifty Years."

I dare say that fifty years ago, at the time of the Whistler memorial exhibitions and of Sargent's great success as a portrait painter, if one were to name the American painters outstanding in popular reputation, Whistler and Sargent would have come first; and after them, probably the landscape painters, Inness, Wyant and Martin. The landscape triumvirate fell from its high place long ago. Eakins, Homer and Ryder, artists by no means considered among the first rank then, have proved to wear better. How do Whistler and Sargent stand up after fifty years of changing opinion? And what of Mary Cassatt, the newcomer to this triumvirate, who has been elected largely, so far, by European votes? She has been one of the few Americans always mentioned in European histories of art. Is she an illustration of the French partiality for those foreigners living in France who become more French than the French themselves? Or is she really a great artist? . . .

They are entertaining to look at together, these three artists, full of contrasts and reflecting vivid lights cast upon their age. Yet history is ironic, too. How the artists would have hated this grouping! Whistler and Sargent disliked each other in life and Mary Cassatt detested both of them. She once refused to receive Sargent when he called, because she so much disliked the portrait he had done of her brother, and she looked with nineteenth-century disapproval on Whistler's irregular life.

The obvious link between them is that all were expatriates. Yet expatriates is a word loaded with many dangerous, razor-sharp overtones that are apt to give a savage cut. We tend to forget, also, that we have had expatriate artists for two centuries and that they differ among themselves as much as artists who stayed home. For a moment let us pass over the fact that these three painters worked in Europe; what then?

All one can ask of artists is that they find their own material and do something personal and memorable with it.

By this standard, Whistler is, to my eye, the most original and distinguished of the three. He had great style, a personal vision, and he was always completely himself. Sargent had his own vision of scientific naturalism but many flaws in style. Cassatt had style but, except for a brief period in the 'nineties, less to say with it than either of the others. No doubt many will disagree with my judgment at this point. Today the pictorial manner of French Impressionism is so pleasing to the eye that an artist like Cassatt, who uses it charmingly, is automatically preferred to artists who do not use it. Let me, therefore, try to give my reasons. . . .

Cassatt achieved a bold, strong, Impressionist style that is her best quality. The fresh, clear harmonies of her canvases and the lovely luminosity of her flesh tones are admirable. She achieves, also, in a pastel like *The Long Gloves* or *Woman Arranging her Veil,* a dry elegance, halfway COLORPLATE 52
between the charm of an eighteenth-century pastel and the wry beauty of a modern fashion model, that is a delight to the eye. Degas did it first, but she occasionally comes very close to him.

What robs her of the important rank to which her vigorous style ought to entitle her is lack of individuality of mind. This exhibition shows her as more varied than we usually think. Yet all her early work follows in someone else's footsteps: she does a very good Degas, nearly as good as the original; she follows Renoir, also, and Manet less successfully. The merits of these pictures, both in style and choice of subject, are those of the school to which she belonged; and until about 1890 she seems to have been no more than a fair, second-string Impressionist.

About 1890, under the influence of Japanese prints, she entered a period that seems more of her own. Her color prints, though very Japanese, are acute and original work. Oils like *The Bath,* ca. 1892, in COLORPLATE 66
Chicago and the *Mother and Child,* from Wichita, are much more personal COLORPLATE 45
than anything that went before. In other words, although Mr. Sweet hoped to prove, I believe, that she was much more than a painter of mothers and children, that remains her one great and characteristic achievement. It was a very narrow territory, but she made it her own, both in feeling and style. Then, after a brief space, her eyesight began to fail and, although she continued to paint, the crispness and precision of touch faded.

She offers us a circumscribed Jamesian world of well-bred ladies living lives of leisure, delighting in their dresses, their company and their well-behaved children. There is an odd contrast between the boldness of her style and the world of perpetual afternoon tea it serves to record. Did she exhaust her sense of discovery in becoming an artist at all, over the furious protests of her family ("I would rather see you dead," said her father)? For all its distinction, her art is that of a very conventional person living in the very conventional world of the 'nineties. As a recorder of the female side of that little circle of wealth and privilege, she will always have a place. But—tea, clothes and nursery; nursery, clothes and tea.

Letter from Mary Cassatt to Paul Durand-Ruel

On Women's Art Exhibitions

January 22, c. 1898

Mesnil-Beaufresne
January 22

Dear Sir,

I have just received a letter from a lady secretary of the Ladies Art League, telling me that you promised her a choice of my pictures belonging to you to show in the exhibition that these ladies are going to have, subject to my consent. I refuse absolutely and I believe that you will not profit at all in showing my work in this exhibition. I know that my works have been sent even to the most amateur exhibitions of women artists in America. I doubt that this practice will do me any good, nor you. I would have thought that for selling, there would have been more opportunity last year in London.

Pray accept, dear Sir, my most sincere regards,

Mary Cassatt

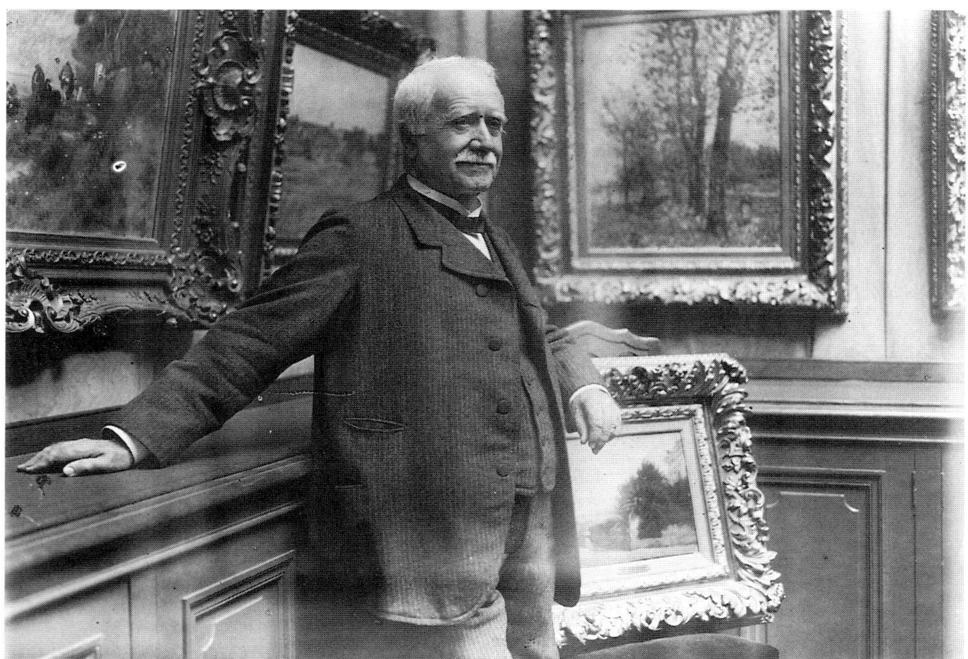

Photograph of art dealer Paul Durand-Ruel. c. 1910. Photograph courtesy of the Durand-Ruel Archives, Paris.

LOUISINE HAVEMEYER

From *Sixteen to Sixty: Memoirs of a Collector*

The Dreyfus Affair

1930

During that celebrated affair, Dreyfus did not have a more ardent or more able defender than Mary Cassatt. From first to last she fearlessly expressed her firm conviction of his innocence. And when his vindication came, no one rejoiced more sincerely than she did, for she felt, as she expressed it, France's honor was at stake.

She brought tears to my eyes one day as she glowingly related the following incident: "I was returning from town one evening just after Dreyfus was vindicated, but I did not know that Madame Dreyfus, who lived near me, was on the same train. As we pulled into the station, I noticed something unusual was happening, for every employee, high or low, appeared to be on the platform, and every passenger as they descended from the train joined the waiting line. Of course, I did the same, not knowing what it was all about. I soon found out, however. It was known that Madame Dreyfus was expected to return from Paris, and as she stepped out of the rear car every hat was taken off and not one word was spoken as the valiant woman, almost overcome, walked silently and erect down the platform, looking neither to the right nor to the left." I wiped my eyes and Miss Cassatt added, "I have never witnessed anything so touching in my life as that silent token of sympathy and respect for that brave and noble wife."

It is no wonder she quarreled with Degas over the Dreyfus affair, although on other occasions she would stand valiantly by and defend his work, a fact Degas appreciated even if he could not resist a little dart in his words of praise, as when he said of one of her compositions: "I won't admit a woman can draw like that!"

To appreciate how that remark could hurt, one must know that Miss Cassatt never admitted sex in art, and could never be persuaded to exhibit in any exhibition for women's work only. I have often, out of deference to her views, refused to lend her pictures on such occasions.

ANNA LEA MERRITT

From *Lippincott's Magazine*

"A Letter to Artists: Especially Women Artists"

March 1900

Anna Lea Merritt (1844–1930), American painter living in England who specialized in allegorical and literary figures. This article sums up many of the issues important to women artists at the turn of the century.

In America the patronage of native art used to be so exceedingly timid, though enormous prices were given for French pictures, that formerly young American artists had either to live abroad, so as to enter their native land under foreign colors, or open a studio to teach amateurs—almost exclusively lady amateurs. Perhaps this may ultimately evolve an appreciative purchasing class, but at present, like other painters, the amateurs are mainly interested in their own efforts, with a remarkable predilection for looseness of handling and whatever may be the newest fashion in color. The misfortune is we flatter them by involuntarily adopting a different standard of criticism in regard to their work. An artist of European distinction travelling recently in America remarked that everywhere he was supposed to feel deep interest in the works of amateurs. On every hand it was said to him, "My daughter would like to show you her painting; she could be a great artist if she chose." Very seldom was it asked, "Where can we see your works nearer than the Luxembourg?" We should really take our amateur painters seriously and tell them painful truths, as though they were of ourselves.

Is it possible that women are differently from men affected by all these modern circumstances?

Women artists have been fairly treated in the exhibitions; there was never any exclusion.

Recent attempts to make separate exhibitions of women's work were in opposition to the views of the artists concerned, who knew that it would lower their standard and risk the place they already occupied. What we so strongly desire is a place in the large field: the kind ladies who wish to distinguish us as women would unthinkingly work us harm.

The only complaint we have in England, and we never speak of it, is that no one of us has been elected to the Academy, even in an honorary degree, but when a lady comes whose art is unmistakably deserving of this distinction I do not believe it will be withheld. It would be a great encouragement to us all. It may be partly for want of this recognition and encouragement that women often fall short of the expectations formed for them.

But the inequality observed in women's work is more probably the result of untoward domestic accidents. Some near relative may be ill, and a woman will give her care and thought where a man would not dream of so doing, where no one would expect it from him. By many smaller things a woman's thoughts are distracted when a man's more easily keep on the course. Women who work must harden their hearts, and not be at the beck and call of affections or duties or trivial domestic cares. And if they can make themselves so far unfeminine, their work will lose that charm which belongs to their nature, and which ought to be its distinction.

The chief obstacle to a woman's success is that she can never have a wife. Just reflect what a wife does for an artist:

Darns the stockings;
Keeps his house;
Writes his letters;
Visits for his benefit;
Wards off intruders;
Is personally suggestive of beautiful pictures;
Always an encouraging and partial critic.

It is exceedingly difficult to be an artist without this time-saving help. A husband would be quite useless. He would never do any of those disagreeable things.

Another feminine defect is a tendency to over-thriftiness and over industry. For instance, in the spring, when our pictures are sent in, when the birds are singing, when "a young man's fancy (we are told) lightly turns to thoughts of love," to what does every true woman turn? To spring cleaning, of course. A man does not: he goes away.

We working women do not amuse ourselves, we are apt to be working always. Constant industry becomes plodding and monotonous. Some of us even make a dress occasionally. But this thriftiness is a great mistake, for ideas are begotten—and observation is acute in moments of leisure—far from the tools of craft. Only look how incessant industry has injured one class of little people whom it has been too much the habit to extol: I allude to the busy bee. When we were children we all learned that little hymn about the busy bee and how she improves the shining hours. What a mistake to improve it! Well, for hundreds of years, even thousands, the busy

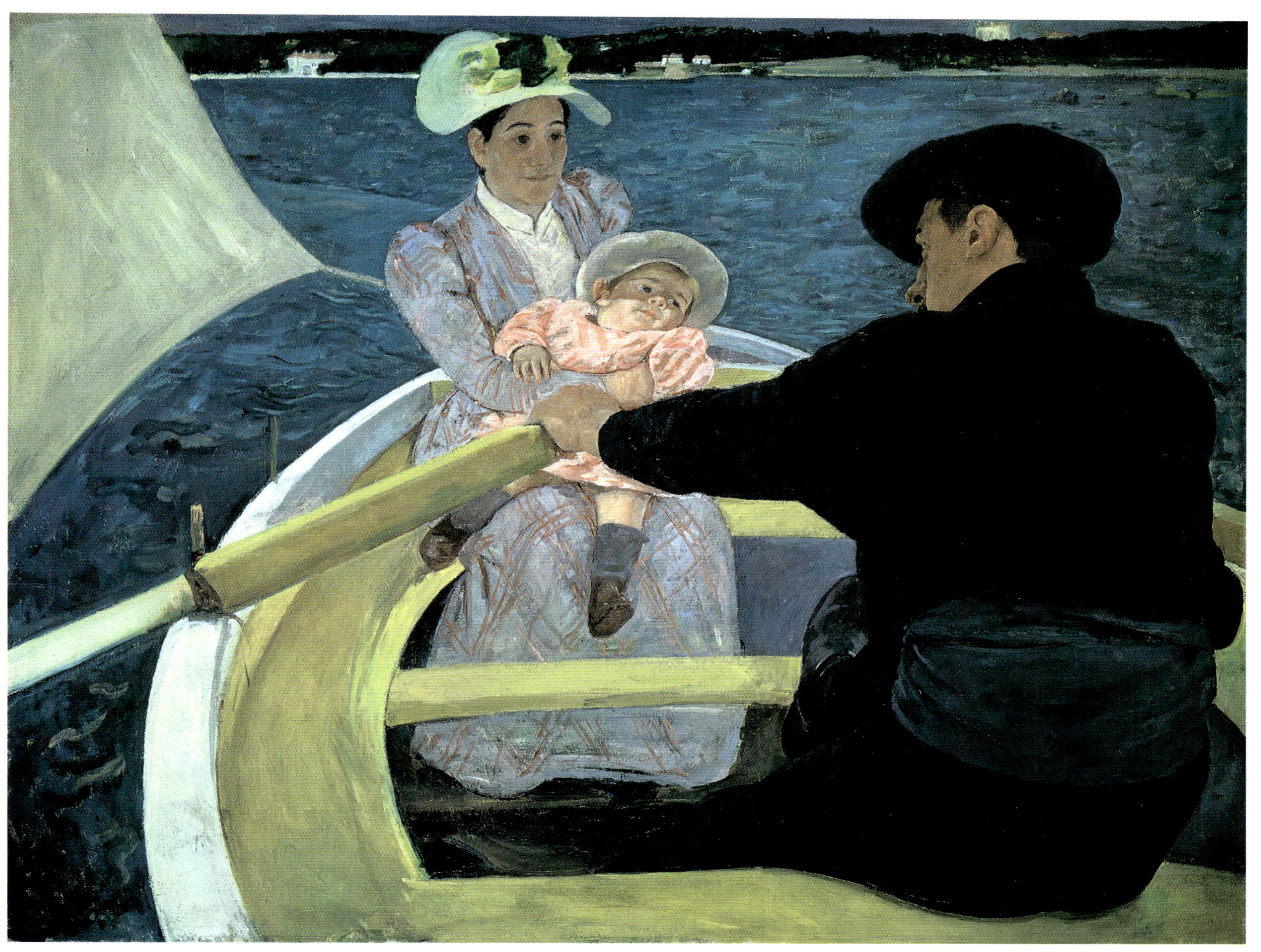

COLORPLATE 75. *The Boating Party.* 1893–94. Oil on canvas. 35 7/16 × 46 1/8 in. (90 × 117 cm).
The National Gallery of Art. The Chester Dale Collection.
Photograph © Board of Trustees, National Gallery of Art, Washington, D.C.

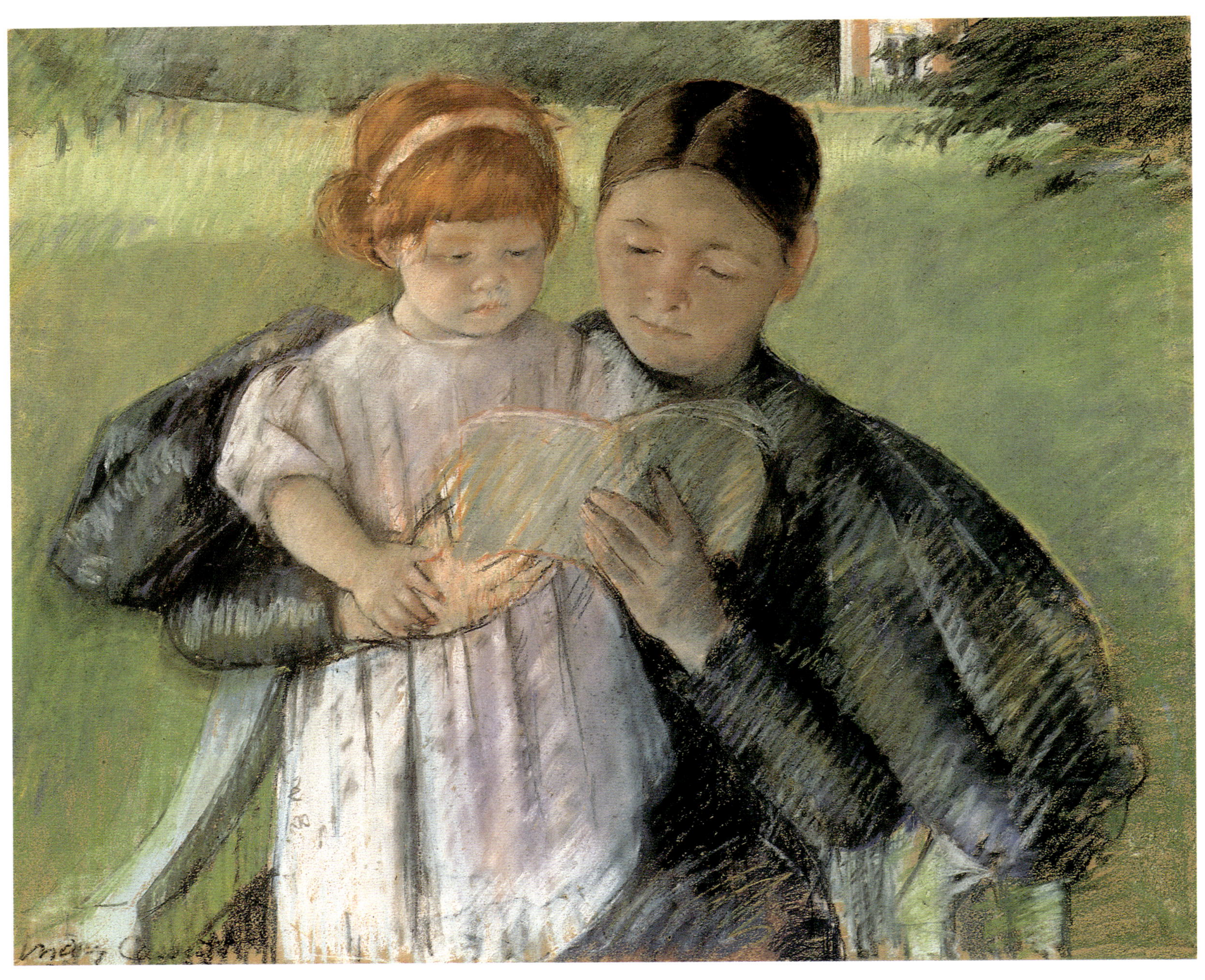

COLORPLATE 76. *Nurse Reading to a Little Girl.* 1895. Pastel on paper. 23 ¾ × 28 ⅞ in. (60.3 × 73.3 cm).
The Metropolitan Museum of Art, New York. Gift of Mrs. Hope Williams Read, 1962 (62.72).

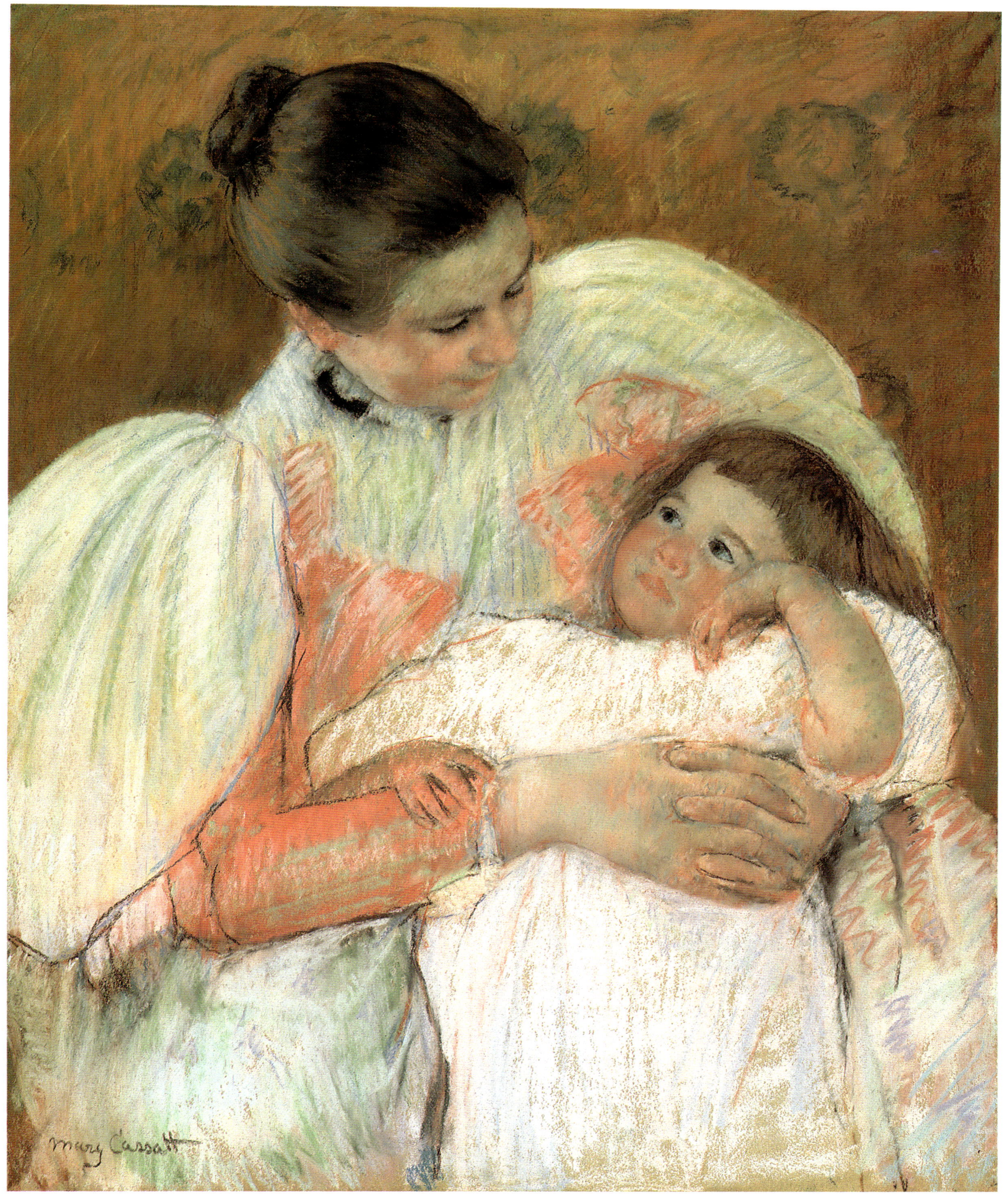

COLORPLATE 77. *Nurse and Child.* 1896–97. Pastel on paper. 31 ½ × 26 ¼ in. (80 × 66.7 cm). The Metropolitan Museum of Art, New York. Gift of Mrs. Ralph J. Hines, 1960 (60.181). © 1984 The Metropolitan Museum of Art.

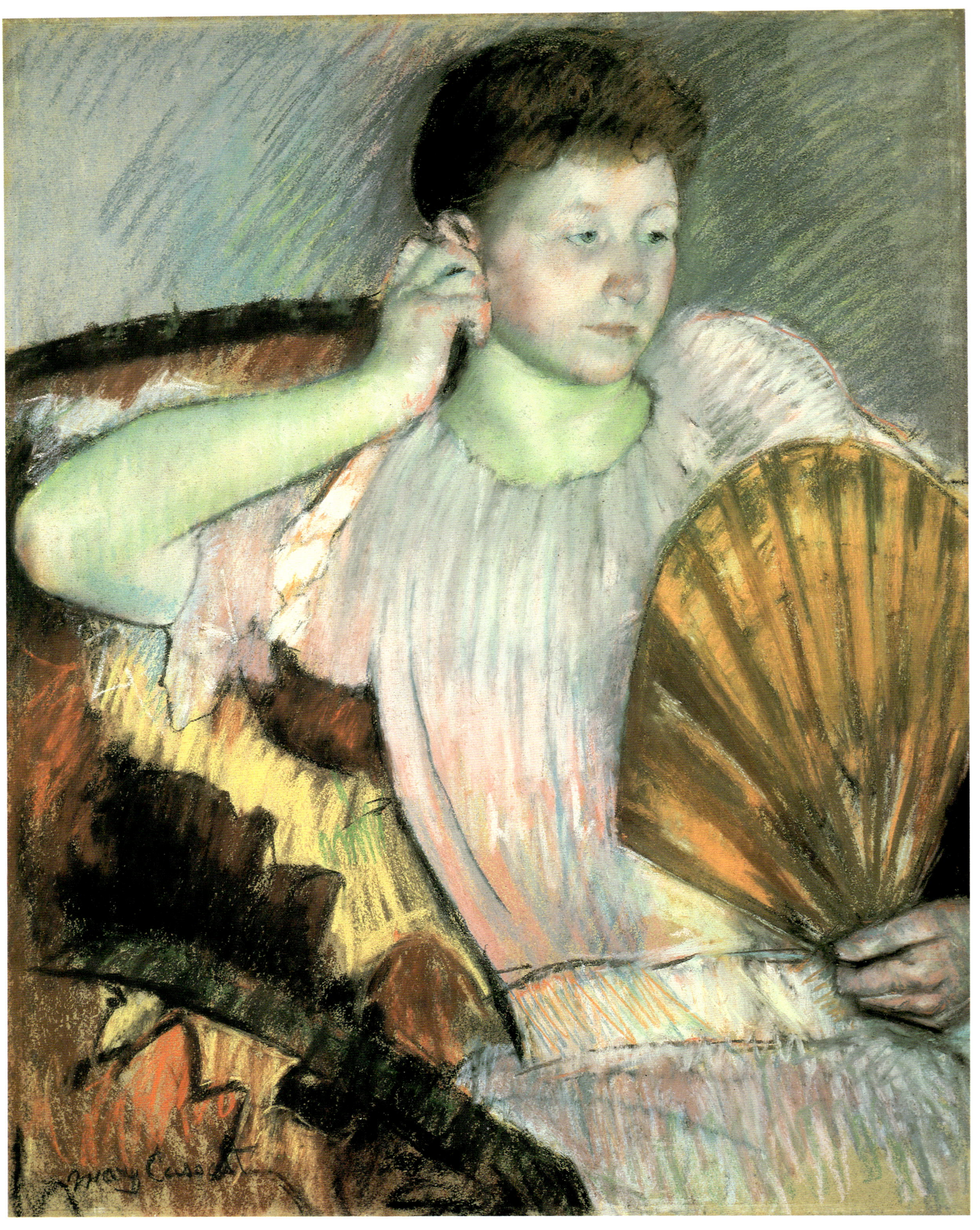

COLORPLATE 78. *Clarissa Turned Right with Her Hand to Her Ear.* 1893. Pastel on paper. 26 × 20 in. (66 × 51 cm). Private collection. Photograph: Bridgeman/Art Resource, New York.

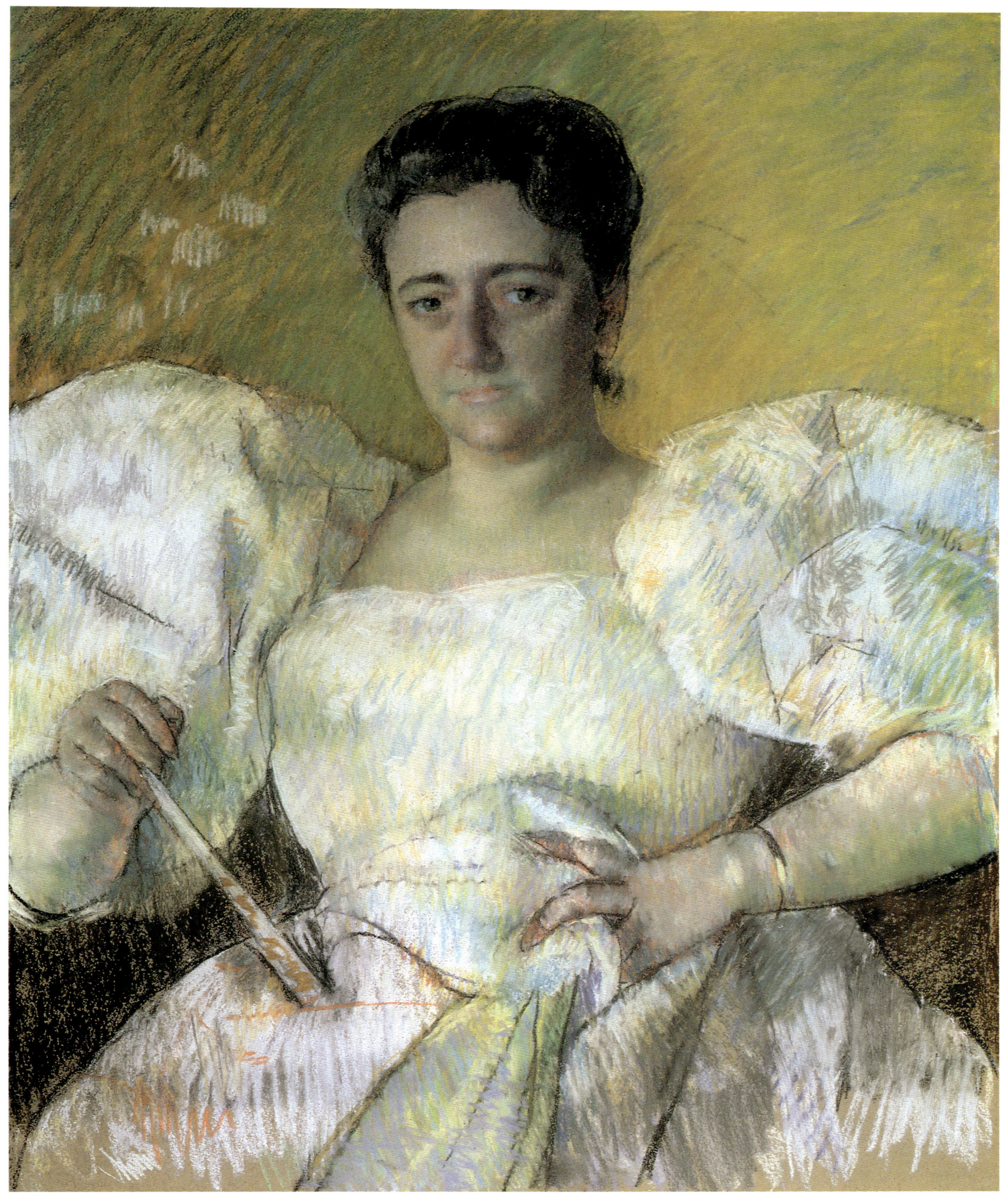

COLORPLATE 79. *Portrait of Mrs. H.O. Havemeyer.* 1896. Pastel on paper. 29 × 24 in. (73.6 × 61 cm). Shelburne Museum, Shelburne, Vermont. Photograph: Ken Burris.

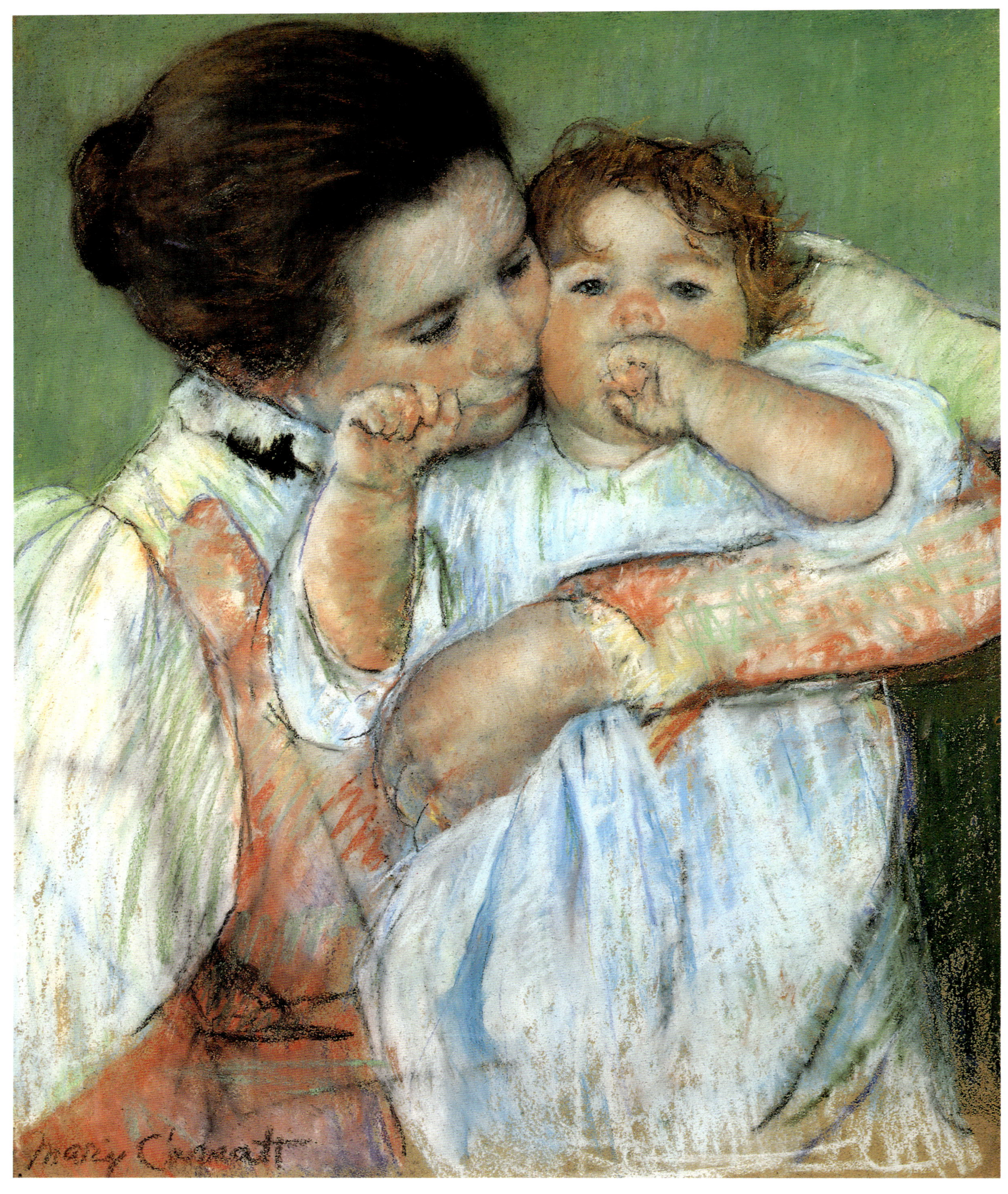

COLORPLATE 80. *Mother and Child (Little Anne Sucking Her Finger)*. 1896–97. Pastel on paper. 21 ¾ × 17 in. (55.2 × 43 cm). Musée d'Orsay, Paris. Gift of the artist. Photograph: Réunion des Musées Nationaux, Paris.

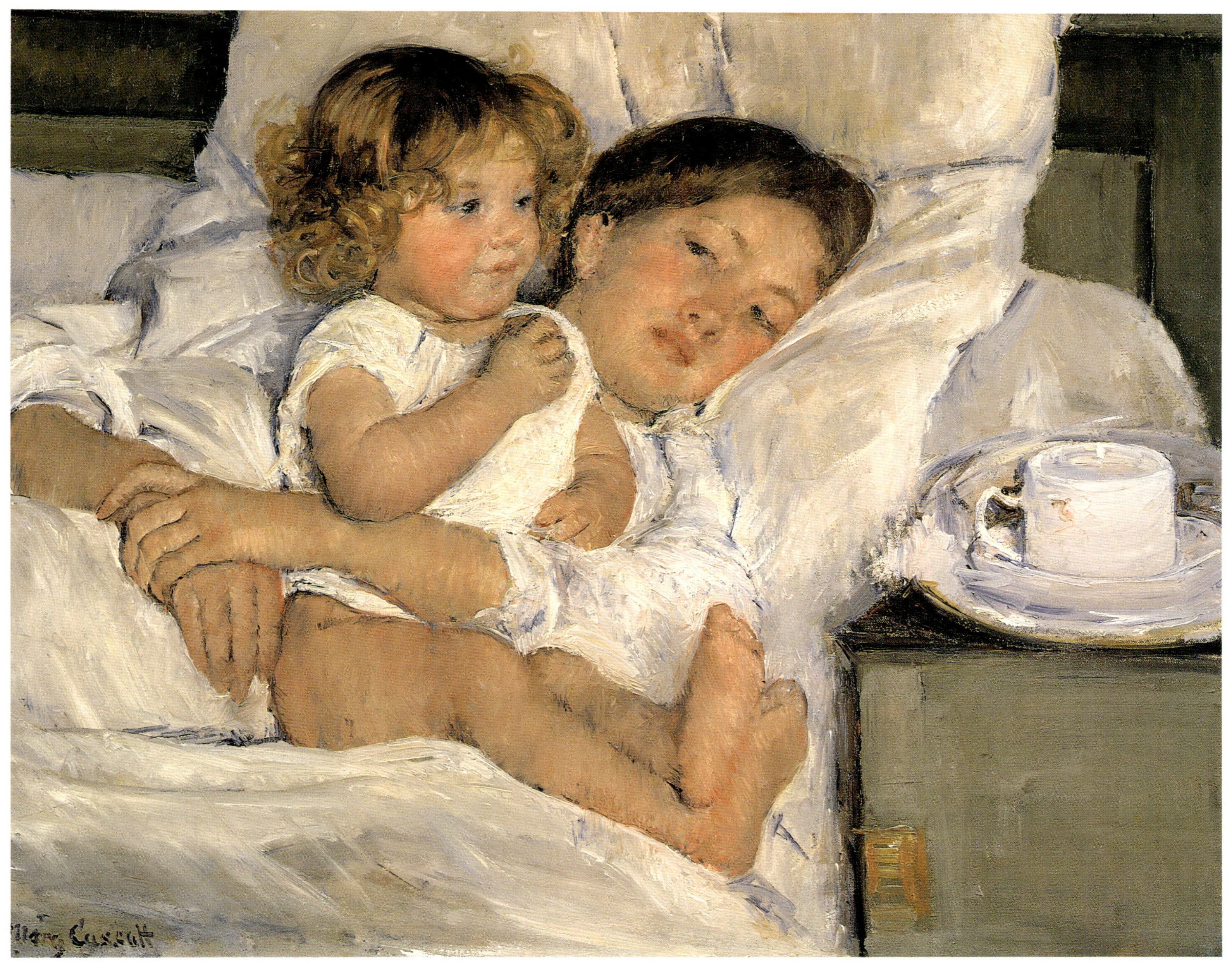

COLORPLATE 81. *Breakfast in Bed.* 1897. Oil on canvas. 23 × 29 in. (58.4 × 73.6 cm).
The Henry E. Huntington Library and Art Gallery, San Marino, California. Gift of the Virginia Steele Scott Foundation.

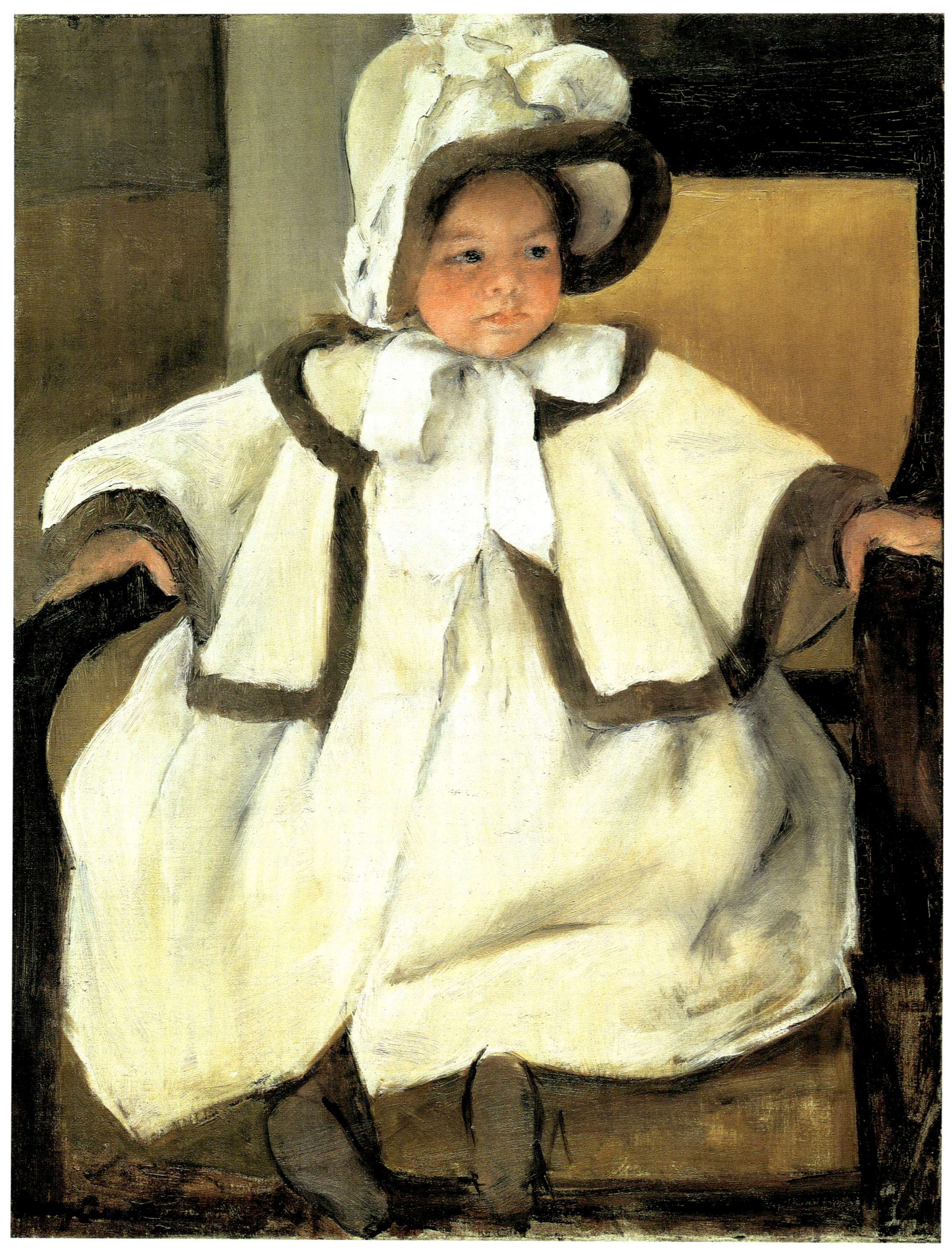

COLORPLATE 82. *Ellen Mary Cassatt in a White Coat.* 1896. Oil on canvas. 32 ¼ × 24 in. (82 × 61 cm). Courtesy of Museum of Fine Arts, Boston. Anonymous fractional gift in honor of Ellen Mary Cassatt.

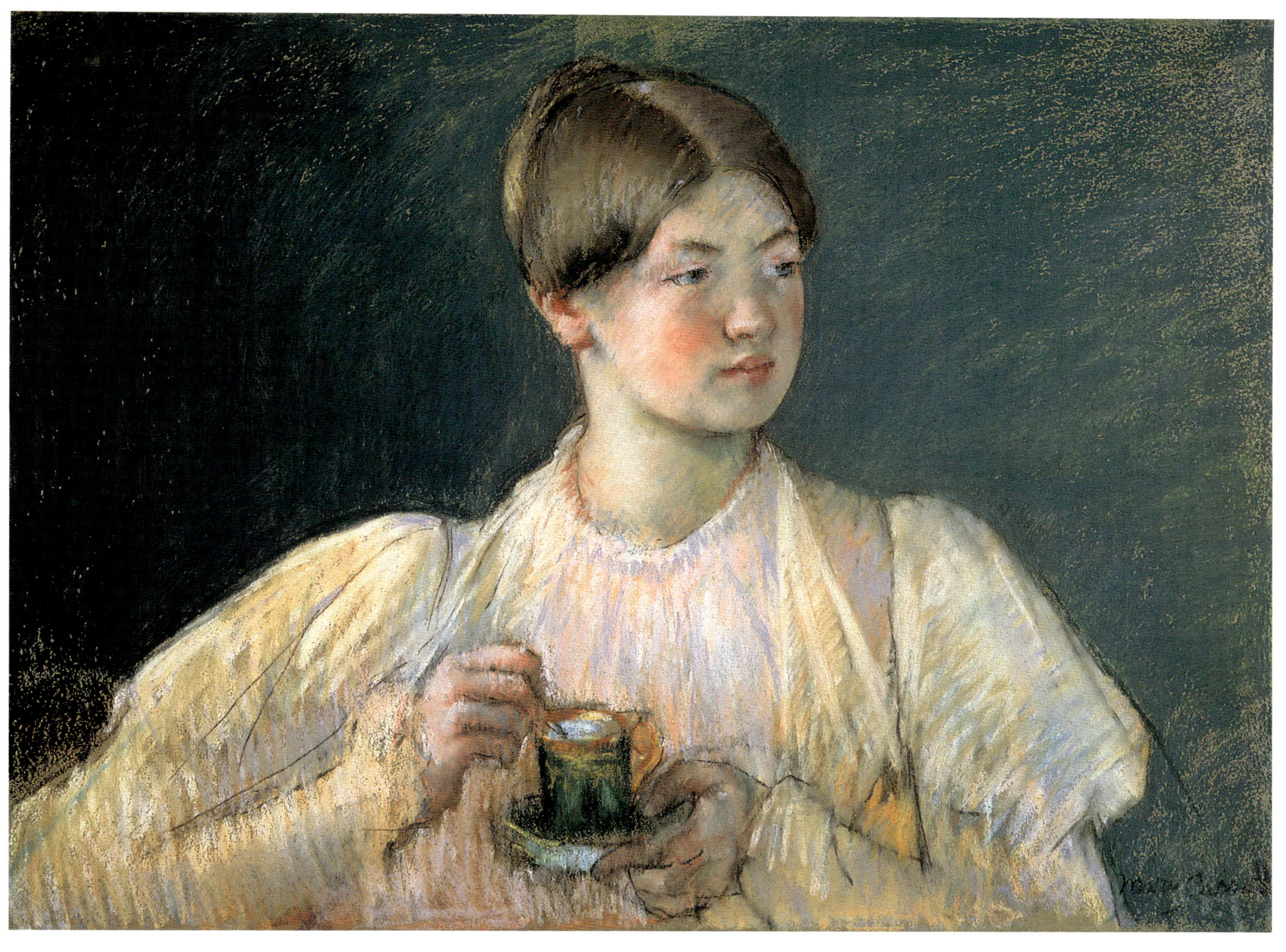

COLORPLATE 83. *The Cup of Chocolate.* 1897. Pastel on paper. 21 ¼ × 28 ¾ in. (54 × 73 cm). Daniel J. Terra Collection. Photograph © Terra Museum of American Art, Chicago.

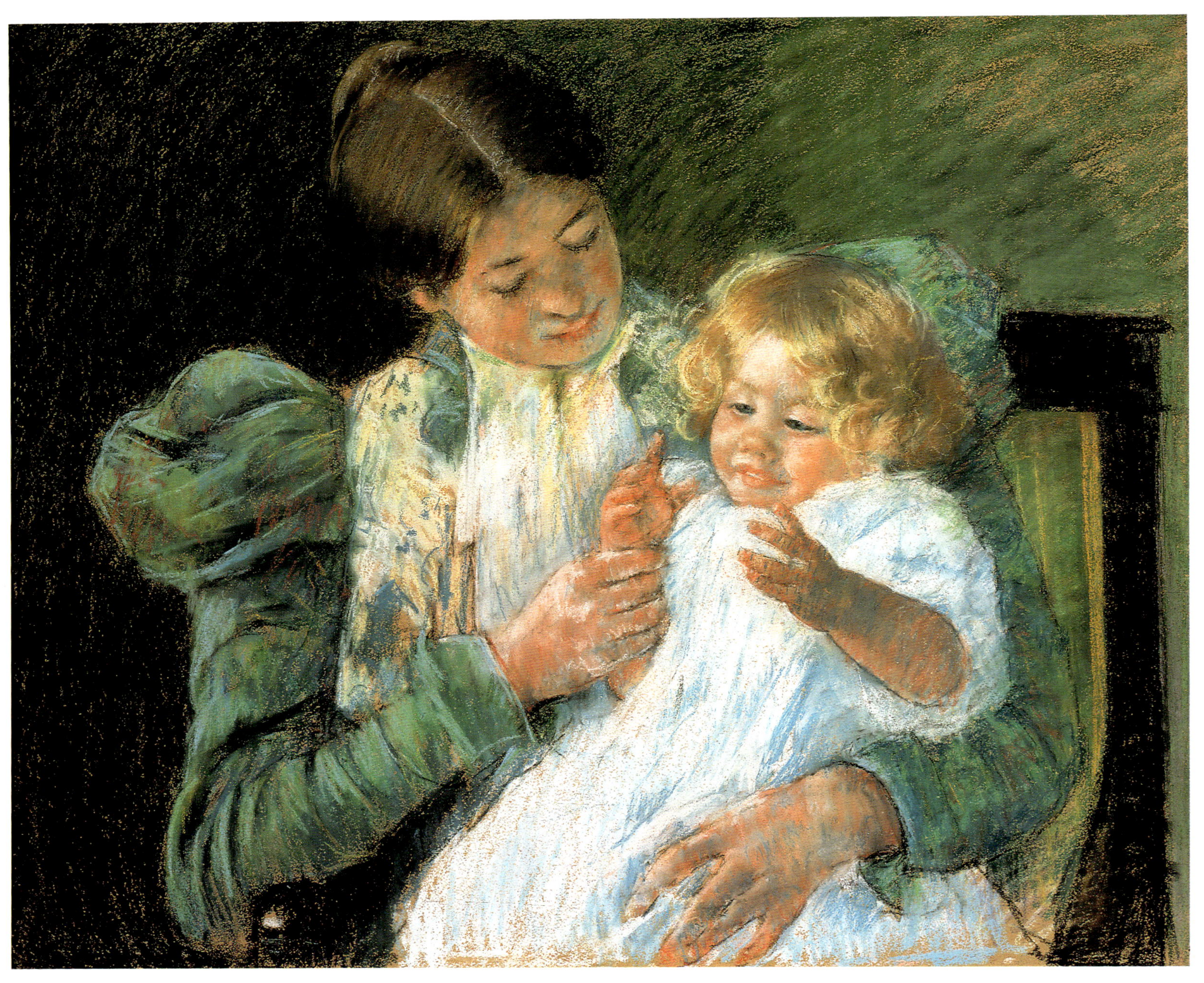

COLORPLATE 84. *Pattycake.* 1897. Pastel on paper. 23 ¾ × 28 ¼ in. (60.3 × 71.7 cm). Denver Art Museum.

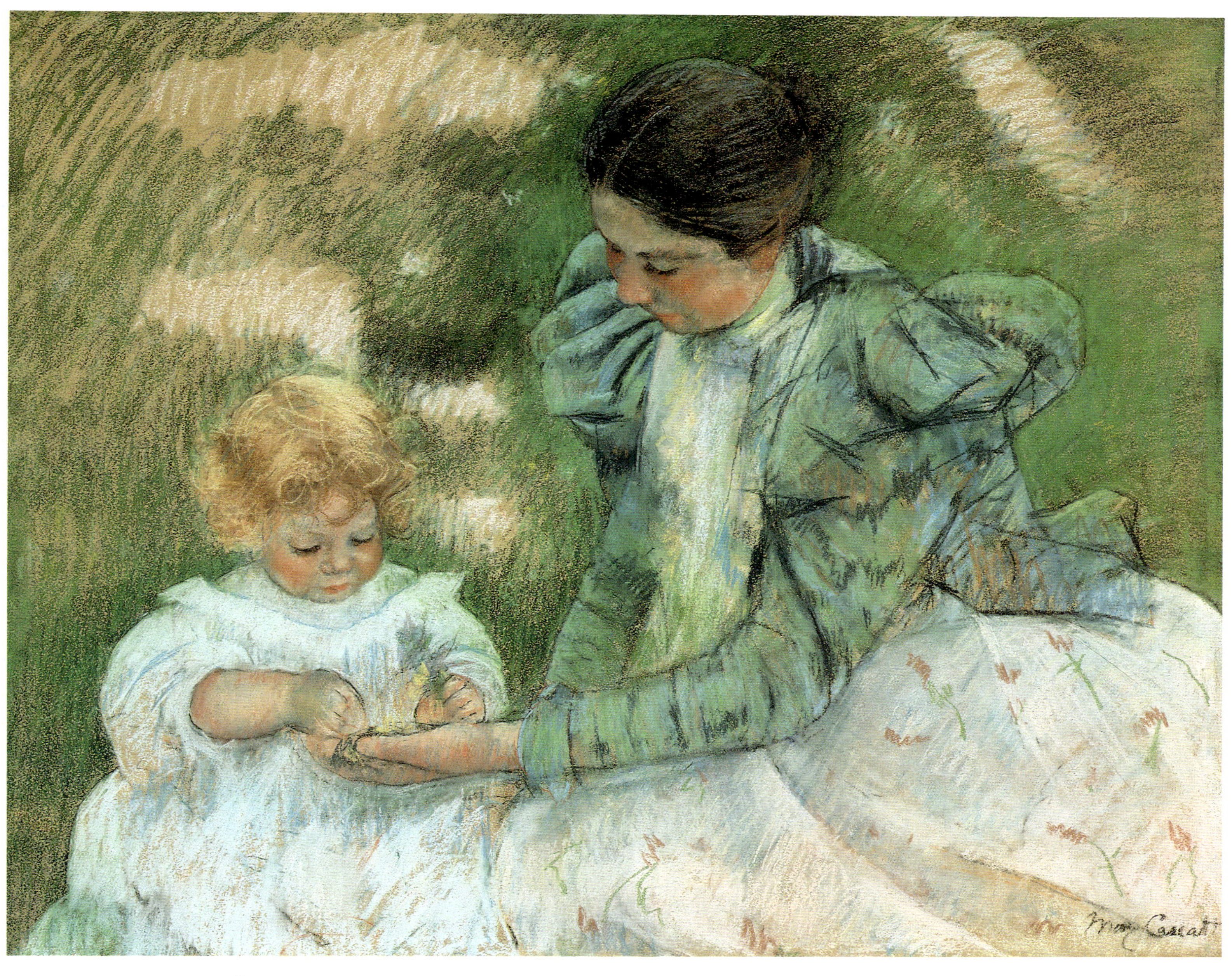

COLORPLATE 85. *Mother Playing with Her Child.* c. 1897. Pastel on paper. 25 ½ × 31 ½ in. (64.8 × 80 cm). The Metropolitan Museum of Art, New York. From the collection of James Stillman, gift of Dr. Ernest J. Stillman, 1922 (22.16.23). © 1984 The Metropolitan Museum of Art.

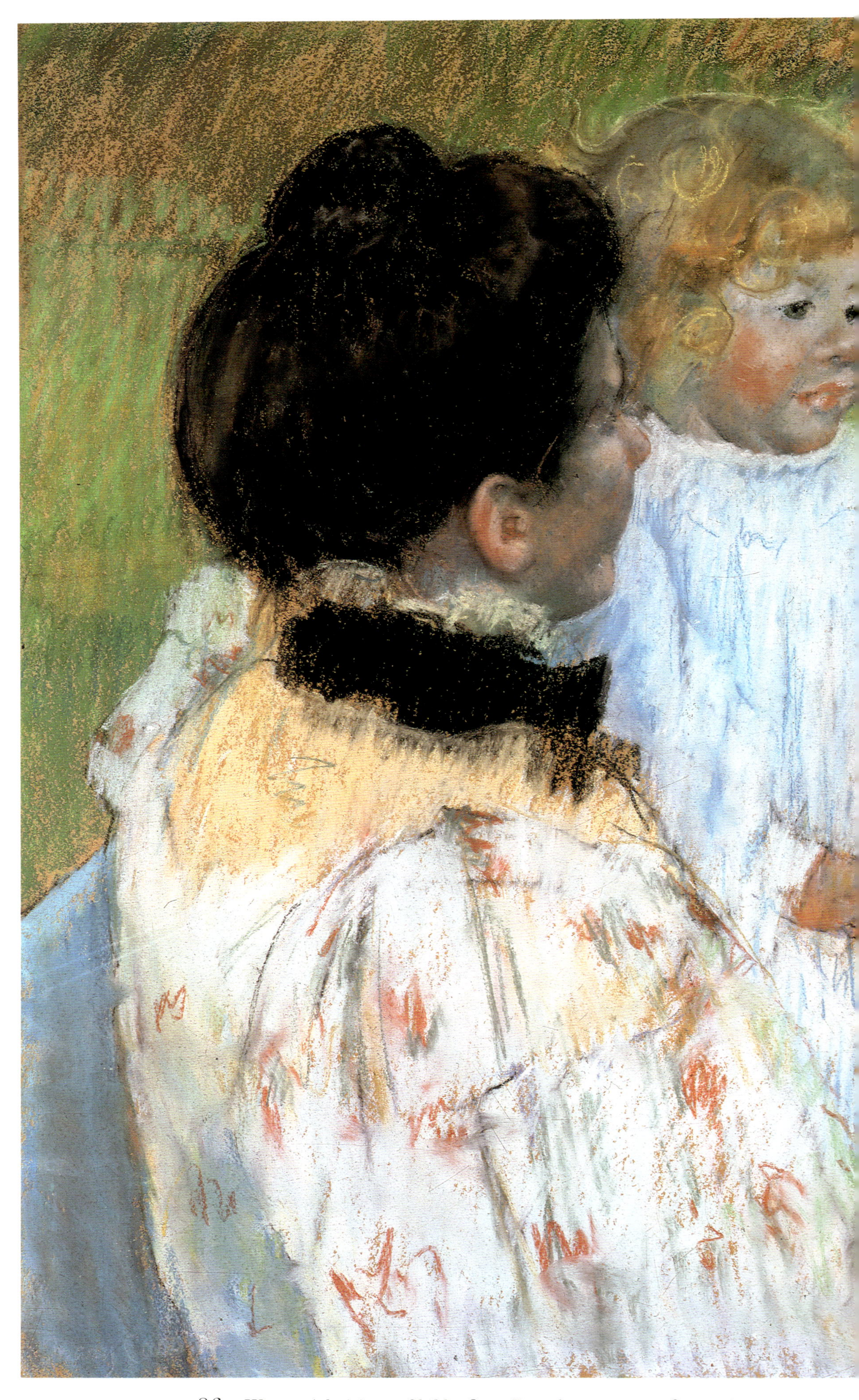

COLORPLATE 86. *Women Admiring a Child.* 1897. Pastel on paper. 26 × 32 in. (66 × 81.3 cm). The Detroit Institute of Arts. Gift of Edward Chandler Walker. Photograph © The Detroit Institute of Arts.

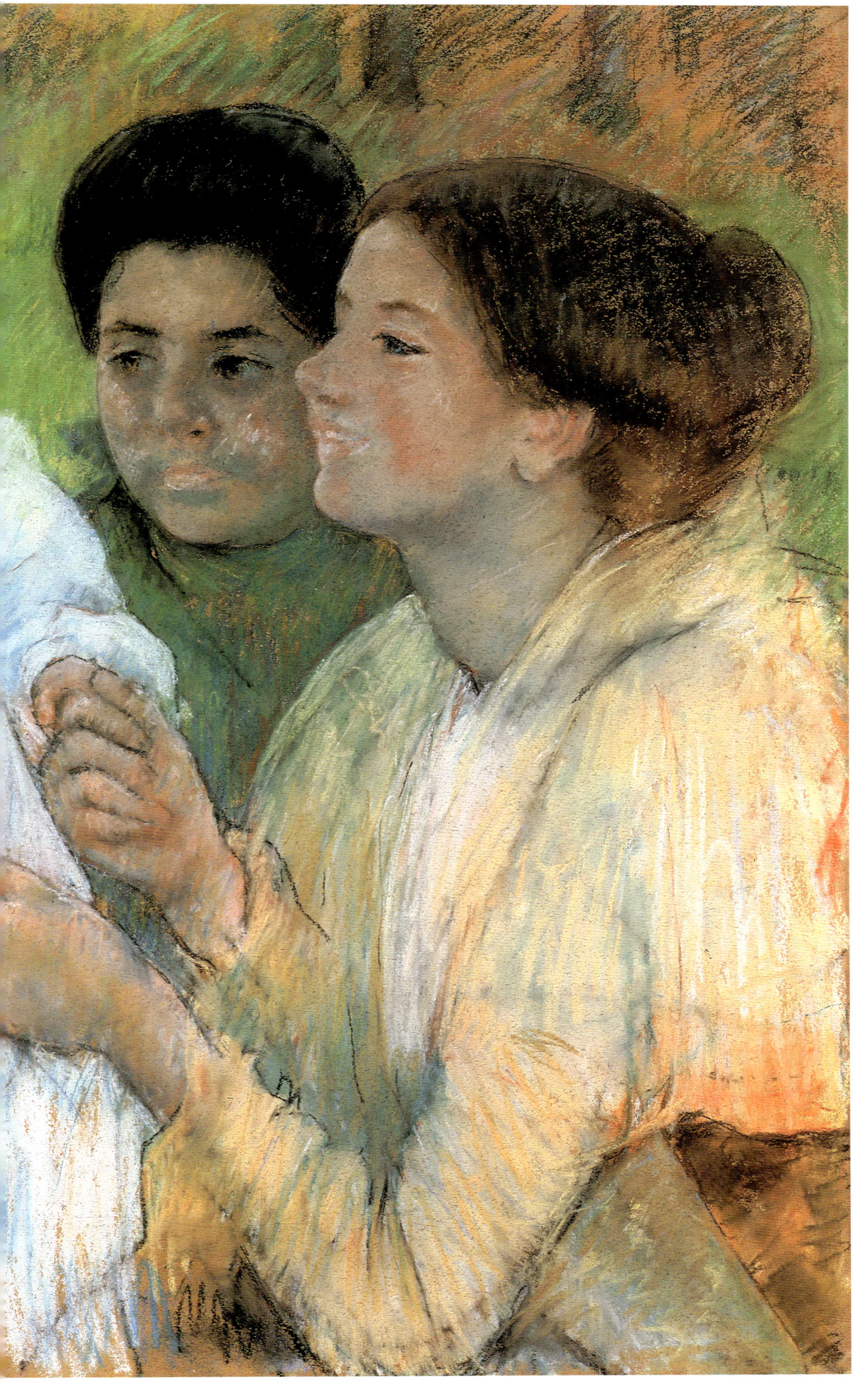

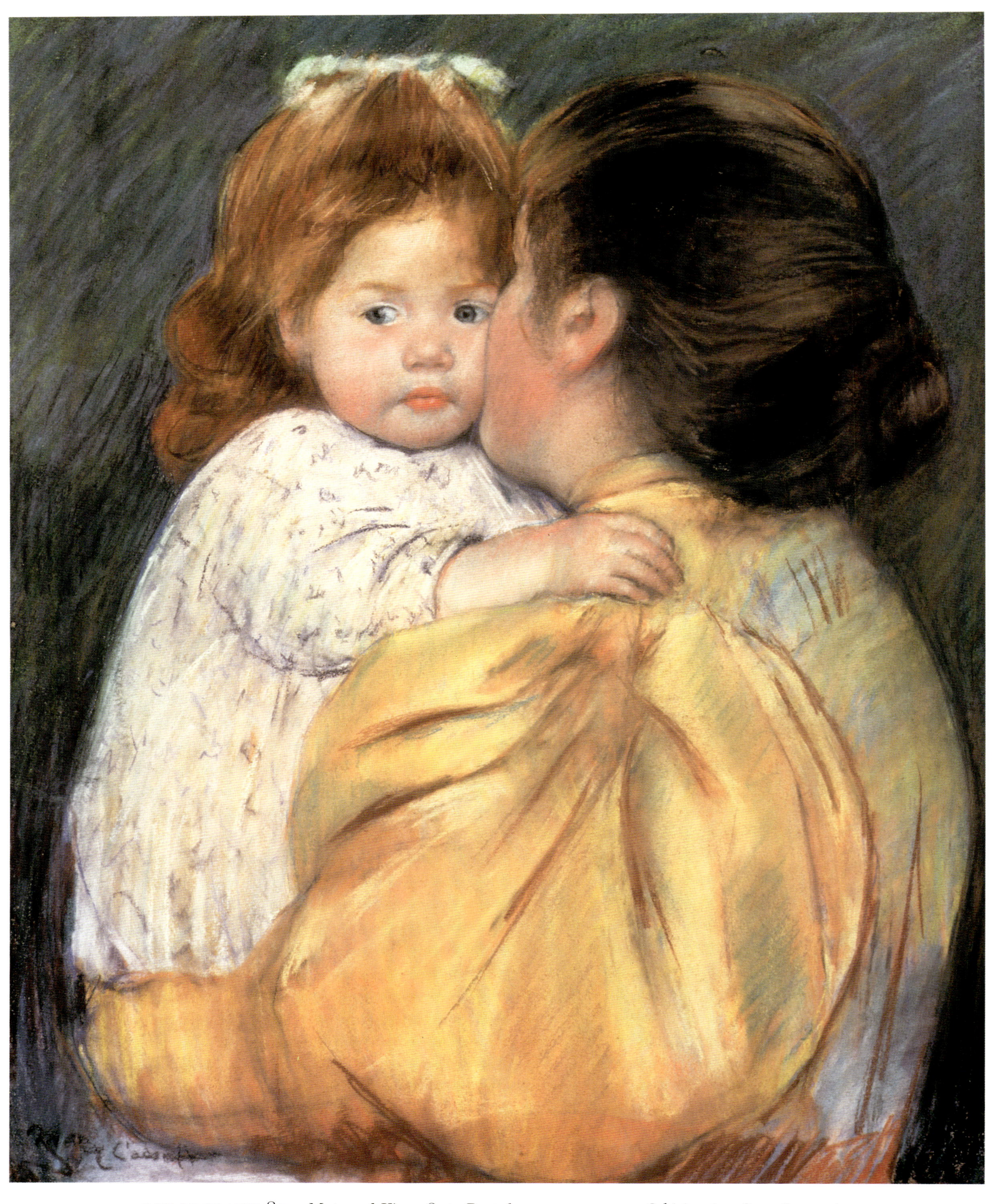

COLORPLATE 87. *Maternal Kiss.* 1897. Pastel on paper. 22 × 18 ¼ in. (55.8 × 46.3 cm). Philadelphia Museum of Art. Bequest of Anne Hinchman.

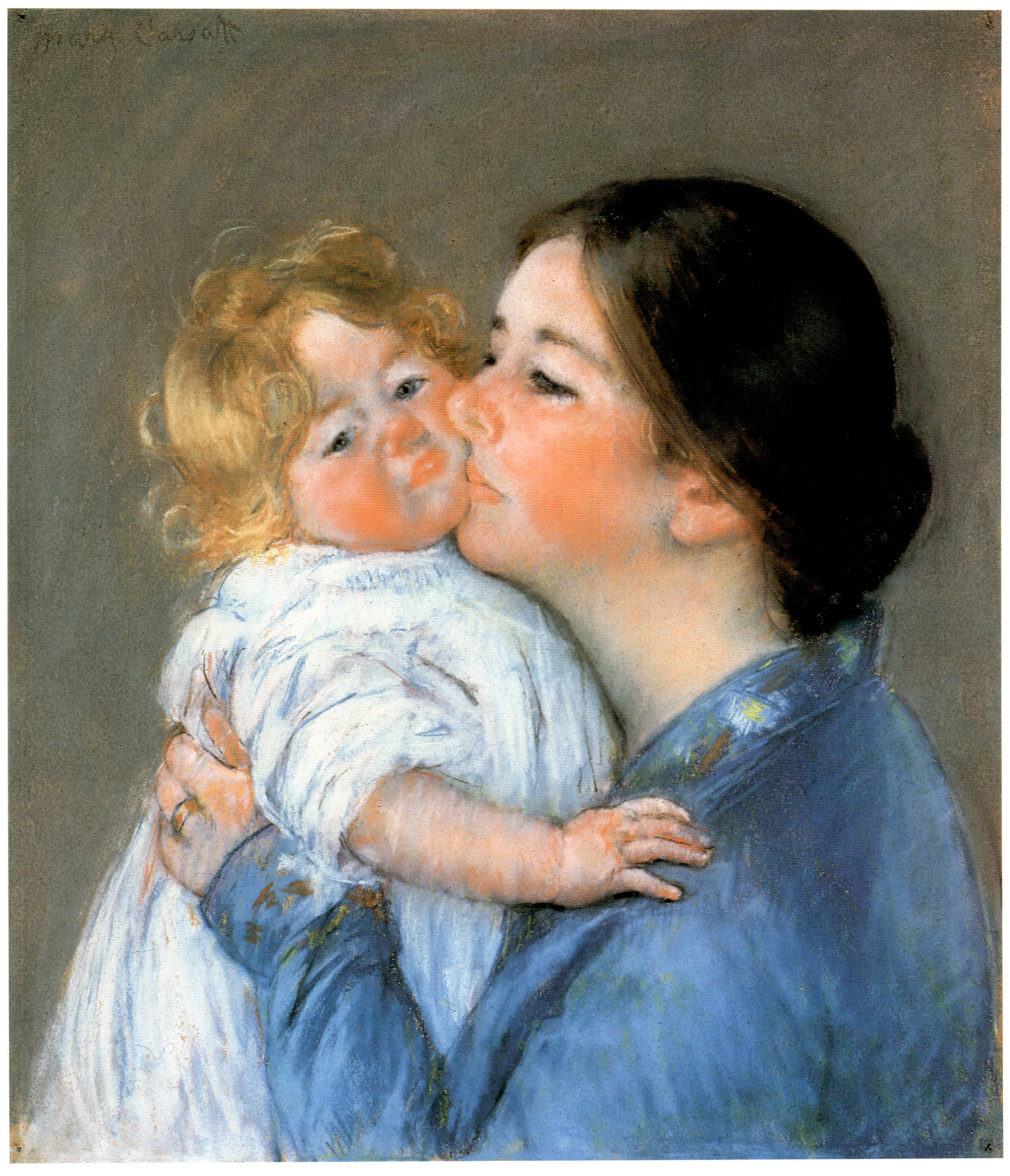

COLORPLATE 88. *A Kiss for Baby Anne.* c. 1897. Pastel on paper. 21 ½ × 18 ¼ in. (54.6 × 46.4 cm). The Baltimore Museum of Art. The Helen and Abram Eisenberg Collection.

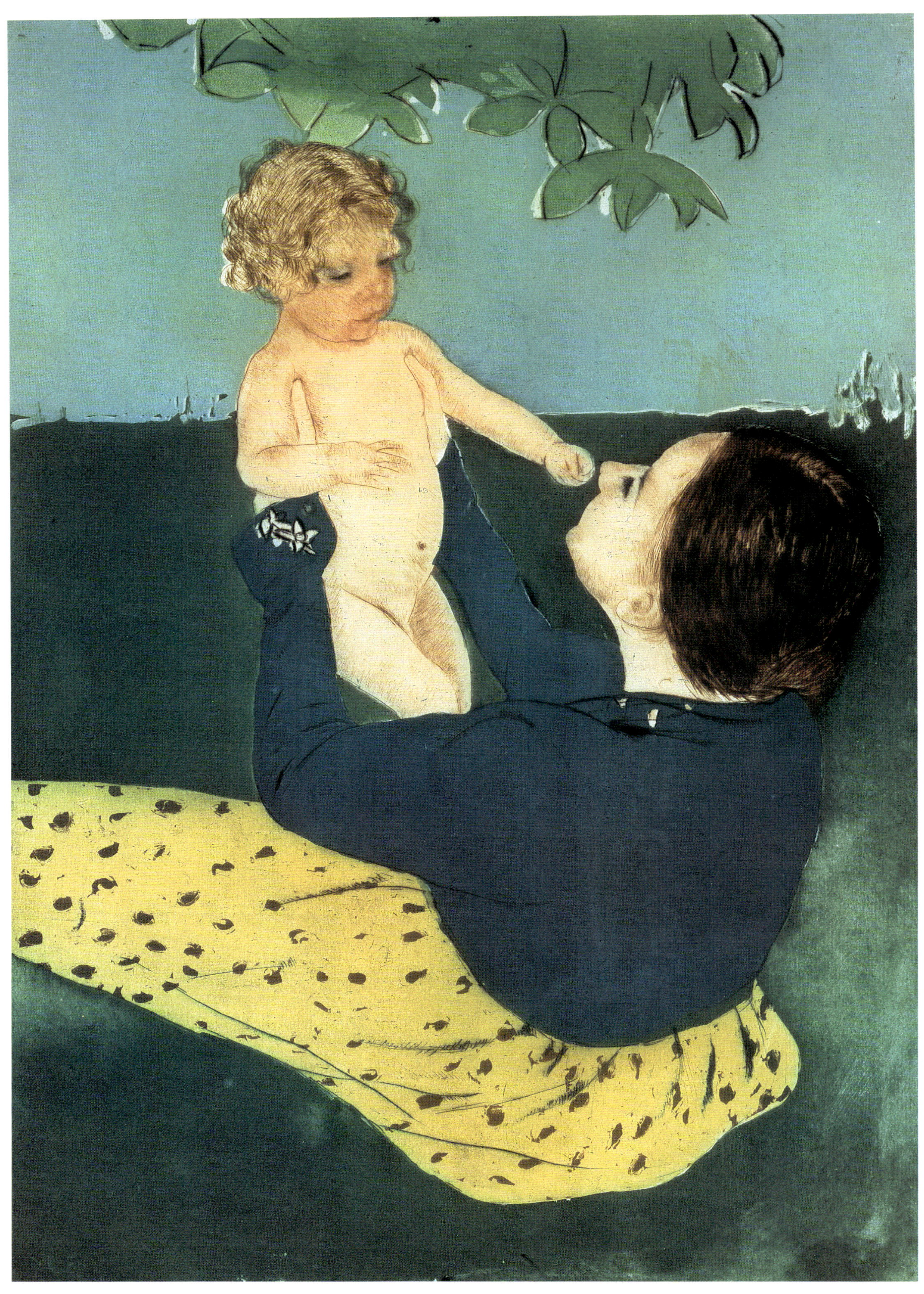

COLORPLATE 89. *Under the Horse Chestnut.* 1896–97. Color print with drypoint and aquatint. 18 ¾ × 14 ⅝ in. (47.6 × 37.1 cm). Courtesy of Museum of Fine Arts, Boston. Bequest of W.G. Russell Allen.

bee has been drudging all day long, buzzing with self-adulation over its virtuous business,—with what injury to its art? In all these years it has made no improvement in the architecture of its waxen house; every cell is made exactly as it was in the beginning. There is no novelty, no invention. If it would only loaf about sometimes it might get a new idea: but bees are governed by a matron with a profound belief in organizing industry for others. Save us from the modern tendency to turn art into an organized industry. This is woman's tendency—to deny herself frivolity or rest, to work overhard, to lose in consequence freshness and spontaneity, and to become like the miserable bee.

Art should be really all play—all recreation.

Re-creation is the truest description of art, which shares the joy of the universe and tries to re-create little portions of it, just to show her understanding of the Creator, and in this effort knows only joy and refreshment, never toil.

Not imitation but re-creation is genius.

Art in all its branches is a profession as open to women as to men. For women of exceptional ability there have always been interest and employment. In painting and in sculpture, in enamelling, in house decoration, bookbinding, and that most enchanting art, landscape gardening, many succeed and gain cordial recognition. There ought to be a lady member in every firm of domestic architects, for mere men have a way of forgetting coal cellars and linen cupboards. Doubtless women would think of many improvements in domestic convenience while not overlooking the beautiful. Home-making is their specialty.

The characteristic virtues of women are the greatest obstacles to their success. Thriftiness, industry, altruism—these qualities are not art qualities. While there is a field for the truly gifted in every branch of art, young people simply wanting a respectable business should look to something else where competition is less keen. Organization of art study and exhibitions tending to destroy individuality work great injury and finally the needed reward of high attainment is the opportunity of designing sculpture or picture in association with architecture or for special places. Without such association art lapses from the epic and can only fling out her thousand little lyrics to fly at random in a windy world.

FREDERICK SWEET

From *Miss Mary Cassatt: Impressionist from Pennsylvania*

On Life in the Country

1966

Mary Cassatt had a love of animals and kept a horse until her vision became impaired, around 1914. Although not able to ride after her accident in 1888, she continued to drive horses and retained her devoted coachman, Pierre. She had a passion for small dogs and raised Belgian griffons, some of which she brought to America to present to relatives. Mary Cassatt's last photograph, taken in the gallery at Château de Beaufresne at eighty-one, shows her holding her favorite griffon, Gamin.

Her first experience with these tiny dogs had been somewhat dismaying. In Brussels she purchased from a famous kennel a puppy

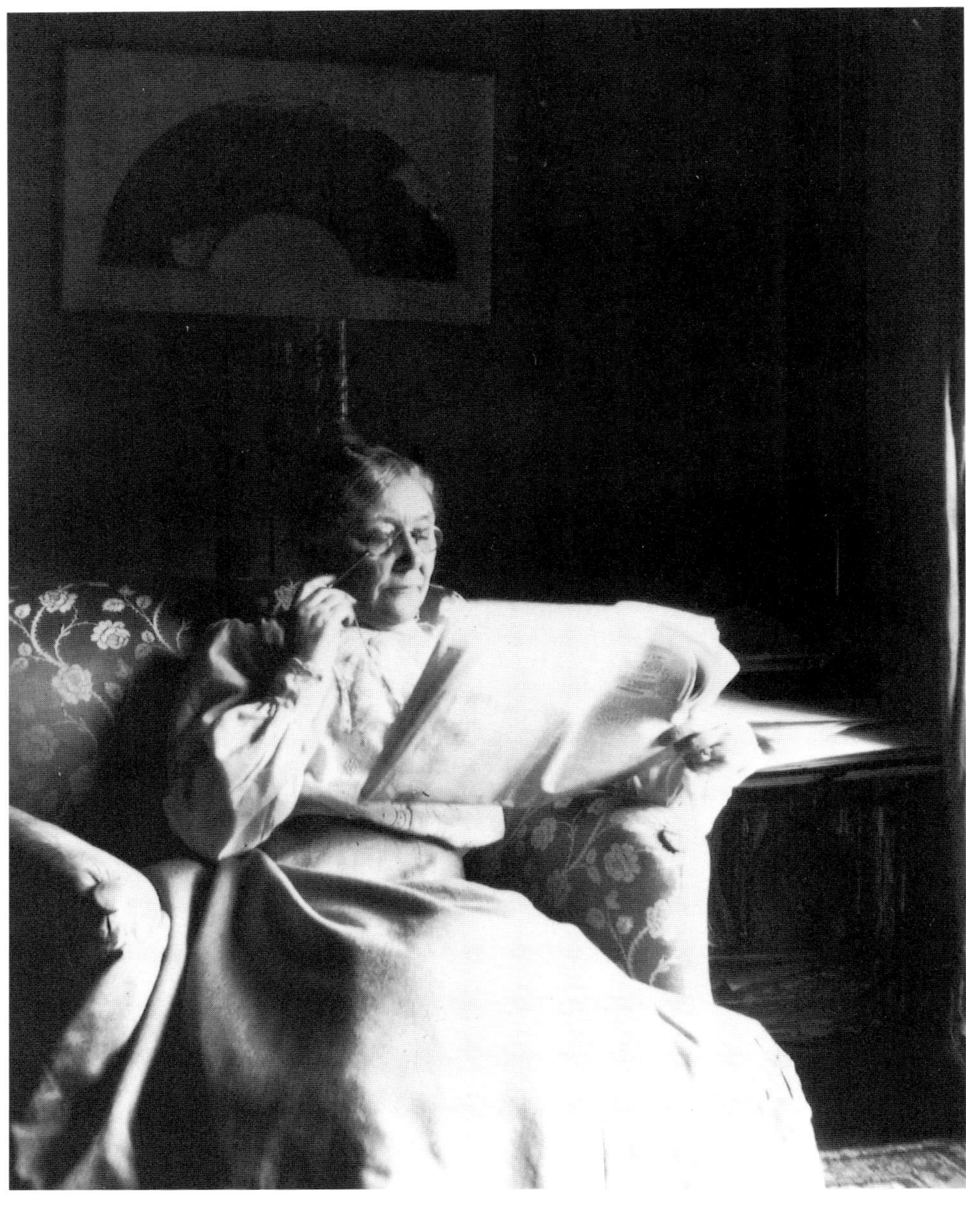

Theodate Pope photograph of Mary Cassatt at Beaufresne. 1903. Photograph courtesy of the Hill-Stead Museum, Farmington, Connecticut.

purporting to be a prize griffon, but as time went on it grew to strange proportions and turned out to be a King Charles spaniel. Undaunted, she tried again with more success, for to appease her, the kennel sent a truly choice griffon with his own brush and comb, a raincoat, an overcoat, and a pocket handkerchief. She later gave this elegantly equipped specimen, Nippo or Napoleon Bonaparte, to her young niece, Ellen Mary, daughter of her brother Gardner.

Miss Cassatt lived comfortably in a well-staffed house, and yet for that day her retinue was modest according to those of big French houses or to those of her two brothers in Philadelphia. Mathilde did her hair every morning and helped her dress; Mathilde was also the general supervisor of the household, what the French call the "*gouvernante.*" There was also a cook, a housemaid, a chambermaid, three gardeners, and the coachman, Pierre, who after 1906 became chauffeur. For all her comforts and service, Mary Cassatt never allowed her devotion to her art to lag, working eight hours a day in her studio and spending many evenings at drawing. Although she could not paint by artificial light, much of her finest draftsmanship was achieved in the evenings, as one can see from the many prints which show people under lamplight. Her ability to accomplish the seemingly impossible was due to the fact that she was truly dedicated to the work of a serious artist, and yet lived the life of a well-to-do, cultivated American and kept up all the appurtenances of gracious living. George Biddle, the well-known Philadelphia painter, who was a close, yet much younger friend,

George Biddle (1885–1973), American painter, sculptor, author, and critic from Philadelphia who was a frequent contributor to many national magazines. His book "An American Artist's Story," includes recollections of Cassatt from the perspective of a younger American artist abroad. Biddle became acquainted with Cassatt through her niece, Ellen Mary.

said of her, "She drew that almost impossible line between her social life and her art, and never sacrificed an iota to either. Socially and emotionally she remained the prim Philadelphia spinster of her generation." Any deviation from good manners or the slightest failure to meet her standards aroused her indignation, yet on growing older she became more and more opinionated and was capable of the broadest profanity when certain subjects were mentioned. One of these was Woodrow Wilson, whom she would, in any case, have disliked for his being a Democrat, as she adhered strictly to a Philadelphia "Main Line" Republican point of view. George Biddle also remarked, "She was one of the most vital, high-minded, dedicated and prejudiced human beings I have ever known, and had a strong influence on me as a student."

Mary Cassatt enjoyed good food and served the best of wines. In the country she kept trout in the pond and guests fished for those that would be served to them. While in Paris she enjoyed fine restaurants, and when she discovered an especially pleasing dish, sent Mathilde to the restaurant to sample the specialty and had her teach the cook how to make it. She held her servants to a strict routine and was easily angered by any lapse. She never smoked and no women ever smoked in her house.

Home remedies and odd cures fascinated her, and in this she was like an old fashioned country woman. Mallarmé wrote to Berthe Morisot in 1891:

> If either one of you has hayfever, I recommend that you have M. Dejouy bring you the "Corbelic smoke ball," of Miss Cassatt (whatever that is, I can hear him say), Geneviève finds it a marvel.

She dressed extremely well in a tailored manner, went to the best Paris dressmakers, such as Doucet, Redfern, or La Ferrière, and to Reboux for big hats with plumes and aigrettes, and often bought dresses at Paquin sales for her models, as she liked the flowing lines. William Ivins recalled that she both stood and sat very erect and that she was no doubt well corseted. Her shoes were made in England since she considered French footgear too frivolous. She liked to wear long amethyst chains with a lorgnette and had a passion for old jewelry. Very aristocratic in bearing, she was once mistaken by two young Royalists for the Comtesse de Paris.

William Ivins (1881–1961) was the first print curator of the Metropolitan Museum of Art and had many encounters with Cassatt over the years.

Armand Delaporte, her chauffeur in later years, said of her:

> Mlle. Cassatt was strong willed in character, voice strong, dry and at the same time sympathetic. In manner very very elegant and distinguished, impeccable in dress and in the best taste, very charitable, kind hearted, one never extended a hand to her in vain, especially for the blind to whom she gave a great deal. I myself distributed a great deal of money on her behalf to the blind. The poor and beggars of whom there were a lot at that time were lavishly fed at Miss Cassatt's at her Château de Beaufresne. The servants both indoor and outdoor were happy with her and all loved her. Mlle. was very fond of animals, especially horses. Mlle. never drove a car but on the other hand in the period of horses she always drove her horse or her two horses in tandem, having with her her old coachman Pierre. She also loved flowers, above all roses. She always had two massive bushes in front of the Château of which she was very proud. No one ever had the right to cut a rose. She did this herself when she wished to make a gift and even though blind she knew the color.

Mary Cassatt had several neighbors in the country of whom she was especially fond. About three miles away was Villotran, an eighteenth-century château and beautiful park belonging to a French family, the Mellons. She used to take her nieces there in summer to tea, which was put in a donkey cart, escorted through the gardens, and served by two footmen in a *temple d'amour*. Another close friend was Octave de Sailly, who lived in Château de Pouilly, a short distance from Beaufresne. His children, Agnes and Jean de Sailly, posed for Mary Cassatt as children. They recall that, when she came to call on their parents, she insisted upon remaining in her car, which meant that they all had to stand around, but they were so fascinated by her personality that they did not mind. Posing for Mary Cassatt, they said, was fun as she kept them amused with books and toys, but they were driven to distraction by her Belgian griffons nipping at their ankles.

LOUISINE HAVEMEYER

From *Sixteen to Sixty: Memoirs of a Collector*

Collecting with Cassatt in Italy and Spain

1930

Cassatt was not the best adviser on Old Master paintings especially at this time, when many paintings were being optimistically attributed to artists such as Raphael, Veronese, and El Greco. Most of the works the Havemeyers bought on this trip were subsequently re-attributed to lesser-known artists.

We sailed into the harbor of Genoa after a miserable night, and in the bright sunlight of early morning, from the upper deck, I could see Miss Cassatt walking impatiently up and down the wharf. It was not long before we were together, talking so eagerly that Mr. Havemeyer jollied us and suggested that my sister was suffering from the cold and that we should go to the hotel, have breakfast, and determine our plans. Of course, we ladies said we had no definite desires, but I assure you we were greatly astonished at Mr. Havemeyer's next remark:

"If it will be agreeable to you ladies, I should like to run up to Turin, and see the 'black Rameses.' ". . .

We started the next day for Turin—oh, how cold it was. Everyone told us it was the coldest winter ever known in Italy, but we did not believe it then, nor do I believe it now, for I have spent several other winters there in that "sunny" land that were just as cold, and one can suffer from the cold in Italy, I assure you. In Turin, even in the hotel, our breath looked frosty as we huddled close to the porcelain stove in the dining room and tried to eat with chattering teeth. My sister was disgusted; she had come to visit the "sunny south," and was obliged to wear her fur-lined coat continually, declaring she had to sleep in her wraps and overshoes in order to keep warm. The museum was the most desolate place I ever saw. We were its only visitors, and the guardians, hugging their meager braziers, looked sullenly at us, as if we were responsible for their misery in having to be there on such a day. When we asked our way, we received short answers but we soon found our statue in spite of their scanty instructions. There he sat, superbly grand, with an immense crown, and with but little raiment—just as he had sat centuries and centuries before upon the warm sands of Egypt. It was the work of a master; you wanted to look into the brain of the man who could have held a composition as great and intricate as that in his mind, to feel the hand of the workman who could have modeled the majestic repose of those calm features.

"Isn't it lifelike?" said Miss Cassatt softly. "You feel if you touched it, it must be soft like flesh."

"It was worth coming to see," said Mr. Havemeyer emphatically. . . .

Possessed of a melancholy that made our voices low, we slowly retraced our steps to the hotel, and were soon en route for Rome. Let him who takes the railroad to escape the miseries of the sea beware! The rocks and

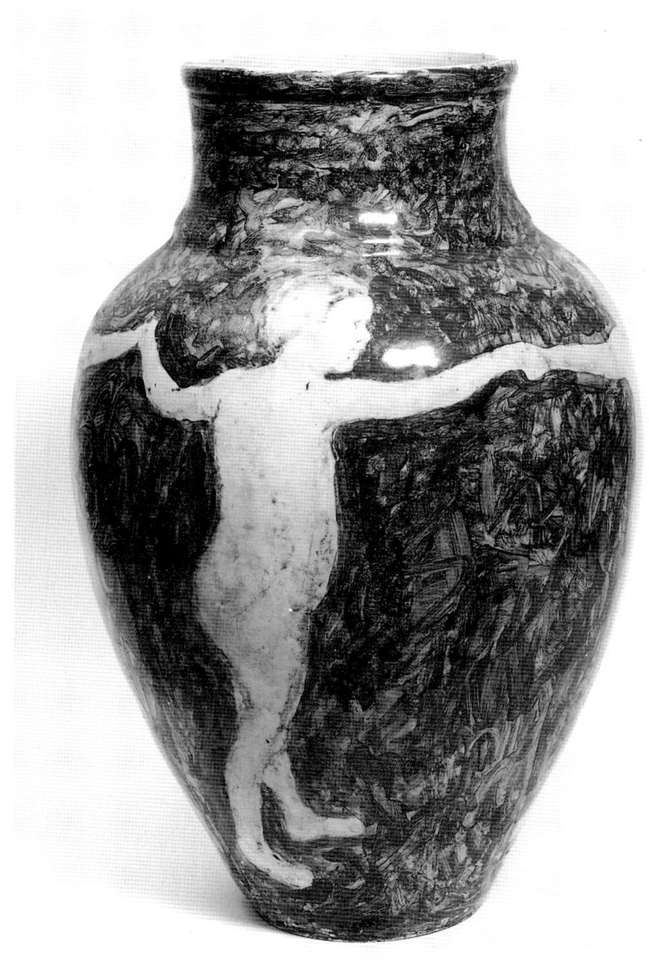

Ceramic Vase. c. 1903. Musée du Petit Palais, Paris. Gift of Ambroise Vollard. Photograph © Photothèque des Musées de la Ville de Paris, SPADEM.

the tide are not the only Scylla and Charybdis of Calabria, and in the choice of two evils, let him take care lest, like a pessimist, he choose them both. Miss Cassatt and I were both carsick and seasick, wretchedly miserable, capable of naught but a sense of suffering, until morning brought hope into our hearts—hope that Naples and a change to better cars would give us relief and bring us soon to Rome. I overheard my sister and my husband saying something in a low tone about the advantages of traveling by sea; I know they were disgusted, but I felt that my side of the argument was too weak just then to admit of discussion, and it required all my strength to aid Miss Cassatt and to collect my own hairpins for the speedy transfer to the Roman train.

What a delight it was after such a journey to find ourselves in a comfortable hotel salon with an interesting piazza beyond, the dome of Saint Peter's in sight, the consciousness of the Holy City, and hot coffee and rolls steaming upon the breakfast table. We forgot our journey and our guidebooks, and not even a reference to anything Roman, from the Punic Wars to the seven hills, was made during that delightful repast. If any voice of our social quadrangle had suggested a plan, it would have been voted down by the three remaining corners before utterance had reached our thoughts. Our hearts beat in thankful unison that this was not our first visit to Rome. If we did not care to know how many bricks were used in the original Baths of Caracalla, we could omit the addition, as we could the sight of the catacombs and Saint Clement's, and even pass the Forum without feeling obliged to crawl upon hands and knees under the big stone which a blinding flashlight showed us covered the grave of Romulus and his little brother.

The delicious coffee, the pleasant fire, and general sense of welfare soon restored us to normal. The afternoon was still bright when my sister announced that, providing a comfortable carriage could be found, she would watch the sunset from the Pincio. Mr. Havemeyer decided upon a brisk walk, while Miss Cassatt and I, with an unforgotten grudge against the previous night, remained together as companions in misery should do.

"They want to discuss the Boer War," said my sister to Mr. Havemeyer. "They had to stop last night, just as they began about 'the American mule'—you know, it means two hours at least. They will not miss us."

However, Miss Cassatt and I felt too peaceful for war, but we did discuss art and decided we must see Veronese's *Europa* at the Capitol, a picture whose beauty so captivated Mr. Havemeyer that it resulted in our placing four examples of the master in our gallery. Also, we determined to see all the Domenichinos in Rome, and even to go to Bologna and see still more of them if possible.

"Degas admires Domenichino so much and wonders he is so little known," said Miss Cassatt. "It upsets me terribly to see all this art," she continued. "It will be months before I can settle down to work again"—a paraphrase of the familiar words among the painters of France: "*J'ai perdu chemin.*" . . .

Cold, snow, frost, ice and wind!—that was the Florence we found in 1901. The cold was everywhere. It covered the plain, it mounted the hills, it grayed the Arno, it entered the hotels, it emptied the churches, it impudently sought our beds, it crept into the very marrow of our bones. We fussed and fumed and sent a malediction after the winds that swept and moaned about San Miniato. We crossly clung together as the wintry blast almost swept us from the Ponte Vecchio. We looked at the huge square walls of the Bargello, without the courage to enter. The Palazzo Vecchio made us shudder and even the pictures could not lure us within the cold galleries of the Uffizi. We felt a peevish disappointment that sunny Italy should prove so cold that wintry March. We huddled around the porcelain *stufa*, the scanty brazier of the hotel, and only when time pressed did we collectively find will power enough to make us face those March winds. However, there was a star rising on that bleak horizon that we little dreamed of and it was to point the way to many a work of art which eventually was added to our collection.

One afternoon Miss Cassatt and my husband agreed to go to a large dealer's, and at dinner that evening we learned the circumstances which had made their visit interesting. I listened eagerly to their tidbits of conversation.

"How ill he looked," said Mr. Havemeyer, "and altogether disgusted with his job. When he saw you he appeared embarrassed, as if he feared you would not care to recognize him."

"I knew him so many years ago," answered Miss Cassatt, "but his face puzzled me at first. He was an artist then, doing small things, *putti*, etc., and seemed rather successful. He married an Italian woman about the time I left Italy, and I never saw him again until today. He did indeed look ill and very poor, didn't he?"

Then there was an explanation. At the dealer's Miss Cassatt had met an old acquaintance who had evidently been forced to give up art and take a position as salesman at the dealer's.

Arthur Harnisch (1843– ?), an American artist Cassatt knew when they were both students. He acted as the Havemeyers' art agent in Italy from 1901 to 1913.

Suddenly Mr. Havemeyer said as if voicing a reflection:

"If he has lived so long in Florence, he should know something about art, and also where good things might be found."

Miss Cassatt gave Mr. Havemeyer a penetrating glance, for she caught his meaning at once.

"We can ask him when he calls this evening," she answered quietly.

I know Mr. Havemeyer and Miss Cassatt; they had caught a new scent and I was delighted when Mr. H. and his wife were announced. I saw a man past middle age, discouraged and weary, a wife much younger, courageous and merry—two human beings, one almost dead, the other very much alive. For the first time we met the man and the woman—for she did more than her share—who were to secure for us some of the finest pictures we ever owned. They were very ready to talk, and Miss Cassatt adroitly found out the circumstances of their life. They had lived all these years in Italy; he had traveled much, and was perfectly *au courant* in art matters and not only knew all the galleries, both public and private, but also was familiar with every inch of ground where a work of art could be found. The vivacious little wife could turn her hand to anything, was *persona grata* with the nobility of Florence, or wherever she could make herself useful to the *signori*. When many others would fail, she could wedge an opening with her twinkle and her smile. They lived in a miserable cupola, a sort of afterthought on the roof of a great high building, "suicide house" it was called, she told me cheerfully, on account of its height and because it stood upon the edge of the Arno. From time to time during our long friendship, I had glimpses into a brave little heart and learned to know of her struggles and of the good fight she had made: how useful to the Italian poor were the government-controlled *monte di pietà*, and how, on one occasion, her gold wedding ring had to be used to drive away the wolf who was howling at the door. I admired the valiant little black-eyed woman, who said naively:

"I could not let *il mio Arturo* starve."

It was not difficult for Mr. Havemeyer to examine and cross-examine them, and Miss Cassatt expressed her approval as he proceeded. By the pleasant glow of our fire the preliminaries were arranged. In due course of time, he was to give up his present position and to work for us alone, while his wife, who could express herself very well with the use of an occasional Italian word, told us she could take us to see something at once. She knew very well *palazzi* where pictures hung, which, if they could be allowed to depart in silence, would be given Godspeed as they left for the western world, while the ducats would be eagerly taken to fill the empty pockets and pay the pressing debts. Not later than the next day did La Signora appear to tell us that she would, with *molto piacere*, take us to see a collection and the pictures were all for sale.

A collection—"all the pictures were for sale"—you must remember this was many, many years ago. In the western world buyers were few and marketable pictures still fewer. Rembrandts could be counted on the fingers of one hand. So far as I know, great Italian pictures by even fewer digits still, and examples of Spanish art by almost none at all. We felt the keenest interest as we sallied forth into the bitter gray of that cold afternoon. I should blush to write what were my hopes, for only then did I begin my novitiate of picture hunting; visions of great finds haunted my thoughts and I was considering a choice of which masters I should select. When the *vettura* drew up before a shabby building, too far from Florence to be a palazzo and not far enough to be a villa, we followed La Signora and soon found ourselves in a large dark room, which, when some wooden shutters were thrown open, we found contained many pictures, most of them as dark as the room.

"I don't believe they could give them away," said my husband in disgust, turning to leave, but I caught his arm and, glancing at La Signora, I asked my husband just to make believe for a few minutes.

At an exclamation from Miss Cassatt, we turned around to see what she had found. From its hinges upon the wall she had swung a huge frame directly across the window and was looking at a portrait. As we gathered about her, La Signora said:

"That is by Paolo Veronese; it is a portrait of his wife."

It is no longer believed to be by Veronese.

We saw a middle-aged, portly woman, her yellow hair drawn back after the fashion of Veronese's time, and dressed in lilac and silver brocade; she sat holding her handkerchief in one hand and her dog in the other.

"See here," said Miss Cassatt. "This is very fine"; and she pushed the frame towards us a little to give us a better view.

My sister, who thought beauty essential in a portrait, did not like it and made fun of the full chest and tightly drawn bodice, while my husband seemed inclined to share her views; nevertheless, Miss Cassatt held firmly to her opinion and studied the picture carefully; she knew a work of art demanded truth as well as beauty. I fear we did not take Veronese seriously that afternoon, but the next morning at breakfast, Miss Cassatt began in her earnest manner:

"I've been thinking of that Veronese all night. My! my! my! the way that brocade is painted and the lace with the gold stars over the chest! Do you know, it is magnificent. The Venetians were full-busted, and *did* wear tight bodices. In all that rubbish I don't believe they know what a picture it is. If you don't like it, Mr. Havemeyer," she added, "I will take it myself, and sell something to pay for it when I return to Paris. What do you suppose they will take for it, ten thousand lire do you think?" Then turning to me, she added, "Let us go to the gallery at once and see if we can find any better portrait by Veronese, or any other painter there."

We spent a wonderful morning at the Uffizi. Miss Cassatt talked art to me as I have rarely heard her. She spoke of Veronese, of his composition, of his style, of his brilliant color and luminous shadows; she compared him favorably to Titian; she called him the father of modern art, and advised me to go to Treviso, probably in the Villa Manfrini, and see there another portrait of his wife, where he has painted her at the end of a gallery looking through a doorway. Then Miss Cassatt tried to find a Bronzino she could compare to ours.

"See how hard, how conventional they all are," she said.

"No, my dear, if Bronzino did your portrait he was a far greater painter than when he painted those."

Later Mr. Havemeyer joined us and at once we had to go and admire Botticelli. Mr. Havemeyer had seen the *Birth of Venus* for the first time.

"What a picture," he said emphatically. "It is worth the whole collection."

We smiled, for we very well knew what he meant. For the moment, it was the whole collection for him. He could see nothing else until he had absorbed it. He had to take it from the walls and press it close to his heart to stamp it upon his memory, in fact make it his own. It was pleasant to listen to him as he spoke his enthusiasm, to see his soul revealed in his eyes. It was singular that a man without technical knowledge could be so convincing in his appreciations, but he had an exceptionally keen and sensitive perception of truth and beauty. Many years after, in speaking of his love of art, Miss Cassatt said to me:

"He learned with leaps and bounds; there will never be another collector like him."

Mr. H. and La Signora took us again to see the "robust" Veronese, cautioning us as we entered to look at it all we pleased, but not to admire the picture openly. This time we saw it with other eyes, and Mr. Havemeyer listened with respect, if not with conviction, when Miss Cassatt said it ought to be in our gallery. With a sigh that it could not be his admired and coveted Botticelli, Mr. Havemeyer began negotiations. If he could not have Botticelli's *Birth of Venus*, why not consider a Veronese! Mr. H. was told to ask the price, and when he did so, his answer produced much amusement for the laugh was at Miss Cassatt's expense. No, it was not to be had for ten thousand lire; she would have to repeat her multiplication table nine times and more ere she reached the sum demanded.

"*Che, che, che*," said H., his favorite expression. "*Pazienza, molta pazienza;* wait; don't make any offer, you must leave it to me. I know these people and their ways."

Well, it required two years of "*pazienza*" before we owned that picture. In our letters we always referred to the portrait as "Venice" to conceal its identity, a precaution probably unnecessary, as at that time Veronese was not *à la mode*, even the galleria not caring to purchase it, which made it easy to take it out of Italy. When at last it reached Paris, Miss Cassatt wrote to congratulate us, and added: "I have taken H., who traveled with it to Paris, to the Louvre to show him some pictures there, in order that he may know what we want."

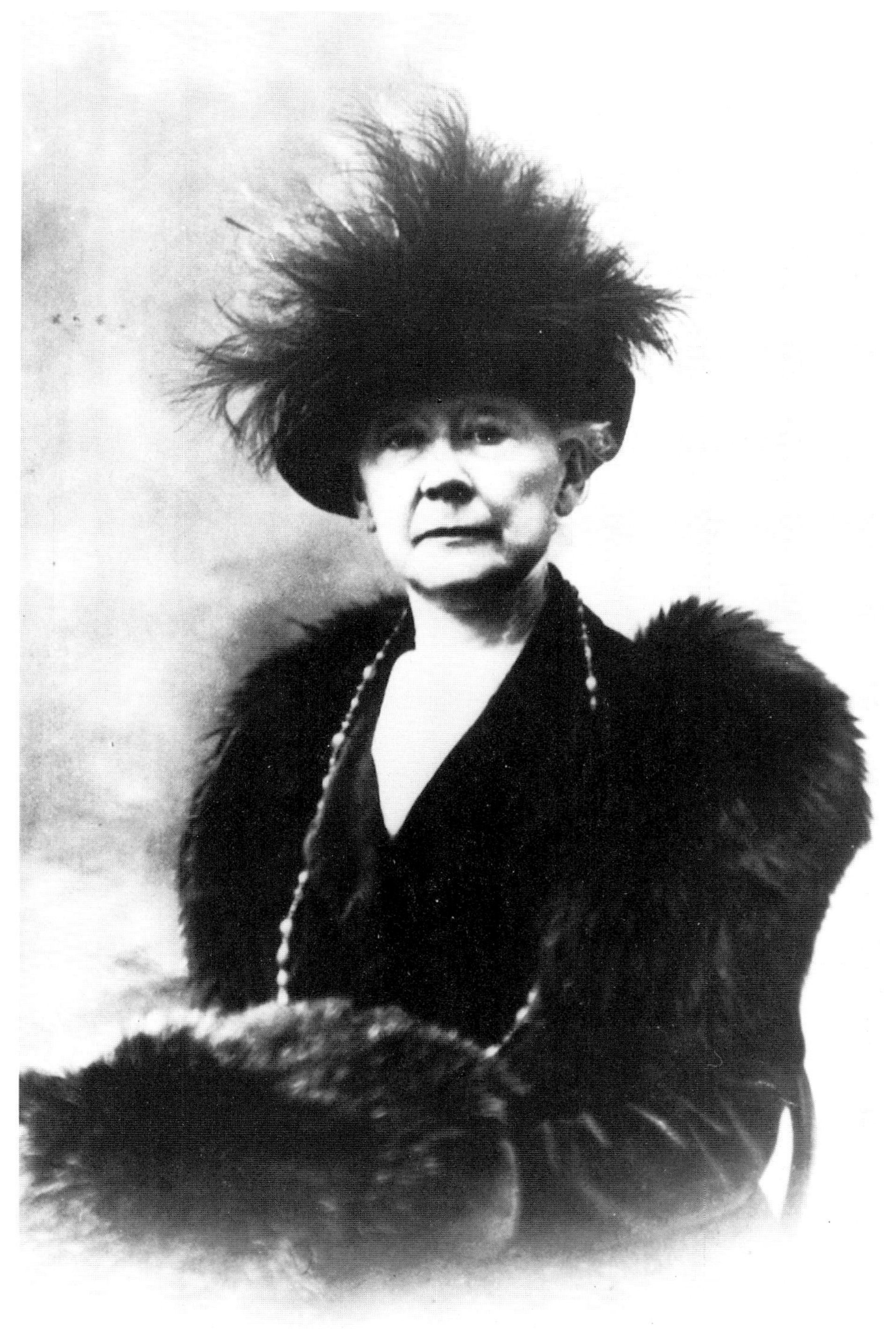

Photograph of Mary Cassatt, after 1900. Photograph courtesy of the Archives of American Art, Smithsonian Institution. The Frederick A. Sweet Papers. Location of original unknown.

Rather ambitious, was it not, but when one considers our Lippi, our Del Sarto, our Raphael and others, it must be conceded that she not only knew her agent but judged well of the opportunities that would offer.

* * *

Leaving my sister comfortably settled in Miss Cassatt's apartment in Paris, Miss Cassatt, Mr. Havemeyer and I started forth for Spain. It was a tiresome journey with a necessary change of carriages when one reaches the Spanish frontier, and we found we had to travel over a hot and dusty plain in order to reach Madrid. I became accustomed to Spanish ways, however, and thought nothing of the return trip, when I carried a small Greco in one arm and some Hispano-Moresque plates in the other, all of them done up in newspaper. There were no Ritz hotels there in those days, for which I am devoutly thankful, for if we had not gone to our comfortable hotel in the Puerta del Sol, Miss Cassatt would have perhaps missed meeting the Infanta's godson, through whom we were to find one very important picture. We settled in our hotel in Spain; we began at the beginning, and a good one it was, the Prado. Mr. Havemeyer always maintained that after the Spanish War we should have demanded the Prado as an indemnity instead of taking over the Phillippines, and he lived long enough to know that he was right. We did not need the Phillippines, and the Prado would have been inestimable to us as a young nation, young in an art sense. The gallery was a revelation of art; I think its contents the greatest and most creditable monument to the art-loving Charles V and his descendants, the many Philips. Is there any other gallery where you see so many masterpieces, and from so many different schools? Apart from Velasquez, who with his *Meniñas* and his *Hilanderas,* his portraits and his dwarfs, his "Don Baltazar" and *The Surrender at Breda,* would make it a gallery unique in the world, where can you find three out of his five full-length portraits by Titian, sixty Rubenses, including that marvel of portraiture, his *Marie de Médicis*—a painting so lovely in its transparency and in its charming grays that it seems fairly to have been blown upon the canvas—or another portrait that can rival it, *Queen Mary* by Sir Anthony Moro? Where will you find finer examples of Flemish art, or greater masterpieces of the Venetian school than those two gems of painting, *The Finding of Moses* by Paolo Veronese and Andrea Mantegna's *Death of the Virgin*? Can you think of a finer Zurbarán in any gallery than the *Vision of San Pedro*? Or of finer Murillos and Riberas than those in the gallery in Madrid? Goya has now added his fame to the Prado, and with his *Royal Family* and his *Majas* has lent new interest to that wonderful museum. One might well say, as Miss Cassatt did, that the resplendent gallery offered an "orgy of art."

We went there many times and my husband had the joy of discovering what was for us a new master—Greco. No great composition of Greco hangs in the Prado, but some of his best portraits are in the gallery and it was these portraits that first attracted Miss Cassatt and Mr. Havemeyer to Greco. Back and back we went, and always the fascination of that painter threw a spell over us. We could not resist his art; its intensity, its individuality, its freedom and its color attracted us with irresistible force. We determined to see every work of his in Spain, for we knew of few elsewhere, as the one in the National Gallery in London, or the very inferior one in the Louvre, gives no conception of Greco as a painter. As usual, Mr. Havemeyer wondered if we could not obtain one, and he appeared delighted when one morning Miss Cassatt and I said we were going out in quest of a Greco.

"You had better add a Goya while you are about it," said my husband.

"Perhaps we may, who knows," laughingly answered Miss Cassatt, and out we went. . . .

I recollect that on that morning, as we were returning to the Puerta del Sol, Miss Cassatt's quick eye caught sight of a painting that had been placed in the doorway of an "antiquity" shop. There were many such shops in the street and we knew the locality was a dangerous one for us. "There he is," said Miss Cassatt to me, and I, thinking she meant Mr. Havemeyer, looked quickly around and answered:

"I don't see him. Where is he?"

"There," replied Miss Cassatt. "That 'Christ' there, that small picture. It is Greco surely, no one else could have done those hands, look!"

I looked, and surely enough there was a small picture about twenty inches by twelve, a Christ holding the cross, a study probably for the painting called *El Espolio,* which we learned to know so well later in Toledo. The long slim fingers of the Christ were pressing the cross to his bosom, and the wan face, expressing intense pity, seemed human in its suffering. We stopped and examined it carefully. I waited for Miss Cassatt to pass judgment upon it, for I knew her knowledge and artistic sense would guide her, and I paid no attention to the voluble salesman who had come forward, having seen his line stir and knowing he had a nibble.

"Yes, my dear," said Miss Cassatt finally, and in the unmistakable way I knew so well. "That is a Greco, or I am mistaken, and a fine one. Do you suppose they are so plentiful that they can be found like this? I wonder how much he asks for it?"

"Shall we negotiate?" And as she nodded, I asked the price in French, and the salesman with consummate art answered in Spanish.

Inferentially, I judged it was too dear, so I shrugged my shoulders, shook my head, and made a motion to go, whereby I drew forth such a flow of Spanish that by the time he had finished, Miss Cassatt's previous knowledge of the language had gradually returned to her, and with the air of a true Castilian she concluded the bargain I had begun. Fifteen hundred pesetas; a peseta then was worth about seventeen cents, so my Greco cost me a little over two hundred and fifty dollars, and I carried it in my arms, frame and all, to the hotel to show it to Mr. Havemeyer. Apparently astonished that we should admire Greco, the dealer insisted upon showing us another, one more precious, hidden in a dark back room. It was a Saint Peter in a brilliant green robe, holding the keys upon his arms. Miss Cassatt greatly admired it also, but it would be so hard to carry, it was much larger, more important and to a dealer's mind worth a great deal more. Miss Cassatt decided she would not take it, as it might upset her in her work, and we let it pass. Eight years afterwards, when we were again traveling in Spain, my daughter Electra bought the picture in Vitoria, after it had gone around and about Spain until its wooden case was dark and travel-worn.

. . . we were, so to speak, to open the market for Grecos and Goyas, at least in the United States.

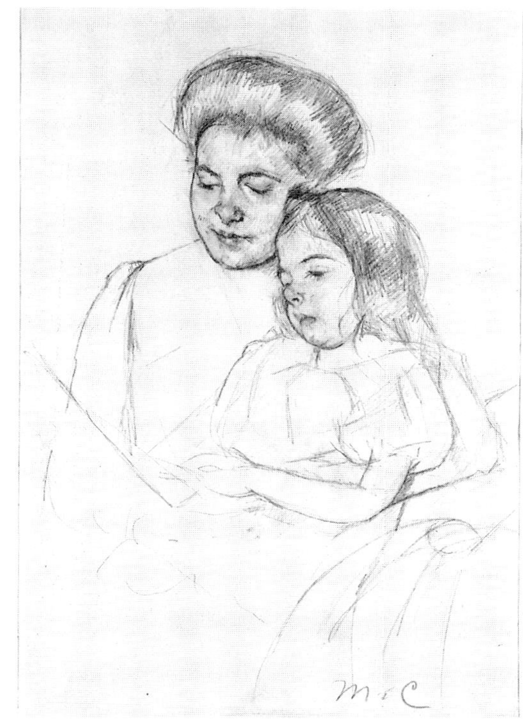

Drawing for *The Picture Book* (No. 1). c. 1901. Pencil. 12 5/16 × 8 in. (31.3 × 20.2 cm). National Gallery of Art. The Rosenwald Collection. Photograph © Board of Trustees, National Gallery of Art, Washington, D.C.

CAMILLE MAUCLAIR

From *L'Art Décoratif*

"A Painter of Childhood"

August 1902

Camille Mauclair (1872–1945), pseudonym of Camille L.C. Fausti, French Symbolist writer and art critic.

To paint an adult is to record a state of mind; to paint a child is to record the foreshadowing of a soul. To paint an adult is to sum up; to paint a child is to foresee. A man or a woman stands out, by a gesture or by beauty, against the background of life in the present; a child stands out against the background of the mysteries of the life before, recalled in its gestures. The gestures that the child attempts in its actual existence still cast their shadows against the wall of the unknown, which the child left in order to enter the phase of vitality made visible.

The mystery of a child is a smile made flesh; its tears are no longer of regret but they are not yet a rejection of what is to come. Sometimes an adult weeps, remembering the life of childhood, but a child cannot know yet that its life is better. A child moves forward, an adult looks back. Everything a child does prepares it for what it will do; what an adult does inclines him toward regret for that preexistence, or rather for the vast limpid night that is neither before nor after, but bathes life on all sides, and that we call past and future, for lack of better words, in order to believe in the truth of our fleeting stay on earth. In an adult, the gesture of meditation is that of contemplating one's origins; the adult leans forward, covering eyes and brow as if to go back down to whence he rose. But all a child's gestures rise, depart from him, aspire to embrace the unknown and the new; just so do those on board ship, as they sail from shore, if they are young and bold, keep their eyes fixed on the open sea that they would already have gained, and it is only much later that they turn back toward the indistinct line of the coast just as it is about to disappear from sight.

A child looks like a new tree, in the direction of gestures open to the sky and seeking, gestures that are nourished less by earthly sap than by the light that invigorates them. An adult refers to his roots; the older he becomes, the more he turns back toward the primordial earth. These are very simple schemas of life. The earliest attitude is that of aspiration, of expansive intoxication, separating from the shadows of birth and hurtling toward the future in order to traverse the vital phase and through it rejoin the posthumous time. The second attitude is that of the adolescent who puts hands to brow at the first sorrow; we recognize thereby that he has made his definitive contact with existence. Before then, he was either rapt or awkward, but once the first despair brings his hands to his temples, that is maturity declaring itself. And the third attitude is that of refusal, of withdrawing into oneself: arms crossed and hands hanging empty, and empty of the desire to hold anything, the man who has understood turns earthward every physical and mental course of his being. He no longer trusts anything but the press of his feet seeking to take root and taking possession, with a frightened wince, of the ground into which he will return. At this age, man casts the shadows of his gestures against the future, he is moving backward.

A child is moving forward, and this is its special beauty, reckless, radiant, irresistibly affecting, made to bring tears to older eyes. Its imprudence is disarming and enchanting. A laughing, singing, lisping, unselfconscious, naked child is extraordinarily, magnetically attractive. It is the eternal necessity of evolution through sorrow that is incarnated in this pink and happy flesh, it is the Unconscious made manifest. All is perpetual childbirth in the secret of an unknown womb, every birth is a death, and every death is reborn, and a child is the remarkable symbol of it all. Our time, a restless psychologist, has sought rather to advance this being's age, to decipher on its barely formed countenance the potential thoughts asleep there. Miss Mary Cassatt may be the only painter today to have given us an interpretation of childhood that is contained within the child itself. Faced with a being in process, she has not been anxious to divine its maturity. She stops her calm, sure contemplation at the very minute in which the creature she is studying appears before her; she captures the soul that is there, and that is all she needs to create a psychology that is new, fascinating, and powerfully inspired by nature.

Eugène Carrière's children are overloaded with precocious thoughts: the phosphorescent glow of the reflexive intellect shimmers across their tender skulls; their gazes are unfathomably solemn; they carry within them an entire program of suffering and dreams. The social struggles to come, the moral transformations, are written into these shadowed faces: these children are messengers from the people of the future, and a melancholy maturity wearies them, with the divine, mystical weariness that once hovered about the brows of Velásquez's infants. Renoir's and Besnard's children are but flowers and fruits; with their delicate animality, their life is all in the bloom of their downy flesh, its fresh pulp not yet saturated with the juice of consciousness. Mlle. Breslau's little girls are animated by a nervous liveliness, their eyes discriminating, their gestures already restrained and stylized by their upbringing. Their immediate shape of thought is obedience to the nicer conventions. Other painters try to sketch the adult in the child, or else, if they portray infants, wailing and almost shapeless, they are determined to use the child to suggest all the obscure terror of non-being, and evoke through this larva the pre-organic life; if they endow the child with a soul, that soul is either too old or smacks of spiritualism.

Eugène Carrière (1847–1906), French portrait painter specializing in portraits and religious pictures. Carrière was particularly interested in the theme of motherhood.

Paul Albert Besnard (1849–1934).

Marie-Louise-Catherine Breslau (1856–1927), German painter and lithographer who studied in Paris and is known for her portraits, particularly pastels of children.

Miss Mary Cassatt can claim the rare ability to observe a child's soul in its earliest stage, at two or three years old, and to show it neither premature nor unformed, relying only upon her keen painter's gaze, which makes no distinction between flesh and spirit. Also, because of her wonderful picto-

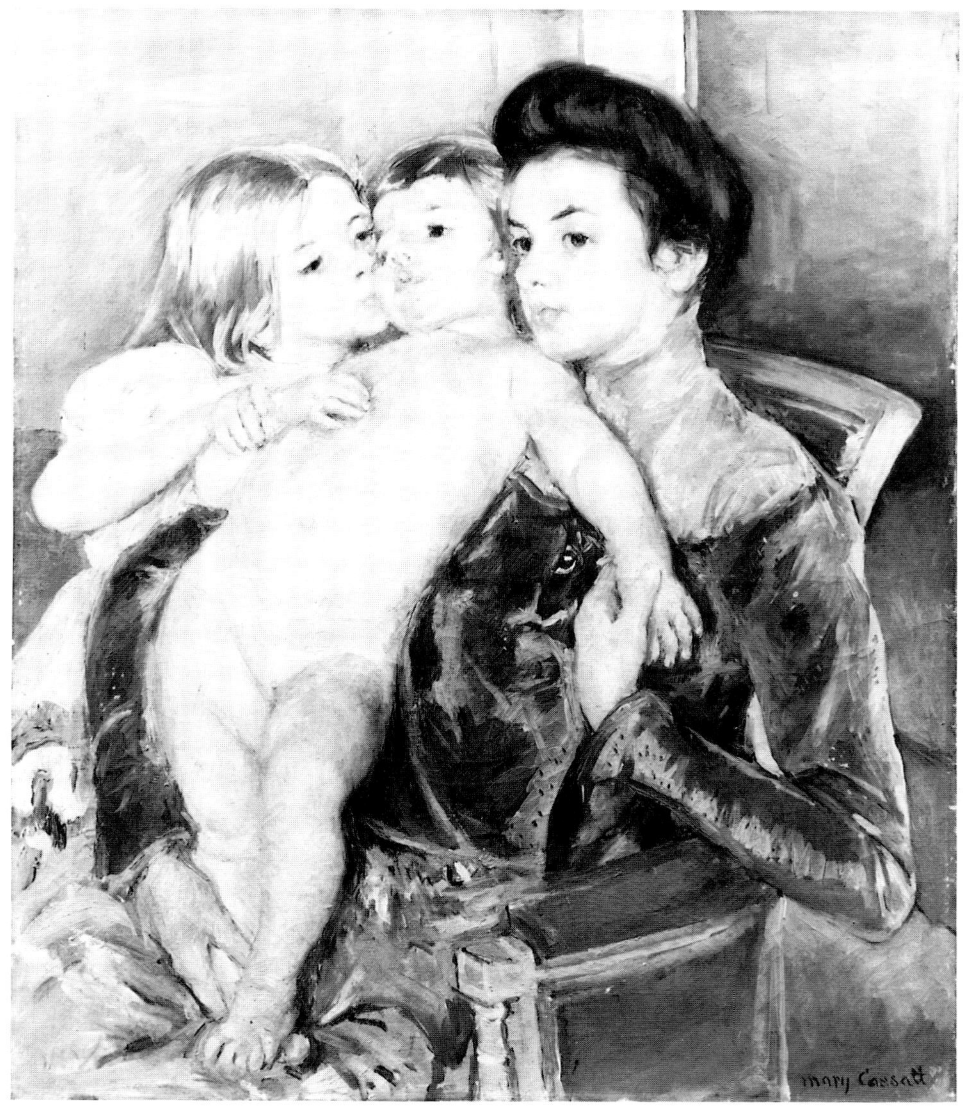

The Caress. 1902. Oil on canvas. 32 7/8 × 27 7/8 in. (83.5 × 70.8 cm). National Museum of American Art, Smithsonian Institution. Gift of William T. Evans.

rial sincerity, she is able to achieve such a difficult end without recourse to intellectual artifice. What she does is paint, nothing more; she represents what she sees. She uses no tricks, whether of shading, decor, or allegory, instead, she relies on the broad yet patient analysis of her precise draftsmanship; on lifelike gestures and the lively artlessness of pouts, laughter, and blinks; on the thought inherent in muscle formation. In the children she paints, the soul is exactly the same age as the skeleton and nervous system, the individual character partakes of the ethnographic character, and, because she has much observed, we have much to reflect upon.

MURIEL CIDLOKOWSKA

From *International Studio* "Painters' Ideals of Childhood" *March 1924*

Images of the Holy Infant excepted, children up to the end of the Sixteenth Century filled, largely, the parts of "supers" on the pictorial stage. They did not really begin to be starred until the Nature-worshippers, in England first, gathered them into the fold of their charming little Olympia of trees, flowers and animals, and the Impressionist painters, in France later, discovered in them qualities akin to sunshine and simplicity. The cult of the child was, indeed, the logical corollary of the theories of Jean Jacques Rousseau and the Lakists, and when, with the romantic school which paved the way for realism, Victor Hugo wrote his ode to *"L'Enfant"* he unconsciously composed the creed of a new religion in art.

To Rembrandt, rhapsodizing on the beauty of old age and seemingly oblivious to the pictorial possibilities provided by his own little ones, may be opposed Renoir and Carrière, whose children were their favorite models. Besides the host of paintings and pastels known to all, there are, by Renoir, that series of delicate pencil drawings of baby heads protruding from perambulators and fanned by a few leaves from an invisible tree and, by Carrière, in addition to his maternities, studies and sketches in charcoal of children eating soup, having their bath and in other familiar acts of their daily life. Although Renoir and Carrière were not, doubtless, the first artists to depict children *naturally*, it may be said that they were the first to depict them *intimately*. Even the most fluent English masters *studied* to be natural, and so they came near to forcing the charm, the lure and childishness of childhood. Their admiration for them verged on idolatry and, aided by the peculiar beauty of English children, they evolved a species of super-child who was less human than angelic. It wanted the realist Frenchmen, Renoir and Carrière, and Mary Cassatt to dare, moreover, and to have the capacity to seize the moods and gestures of children unobserved. Theirs was the human child once again, human as it was in the hands of the primitives; still also, in its stiff way, in Pourbus and Philippe de Champaigne, compared with whom little "Master Hare," were he not by the master hand of Reynolds, would be dangerously near being "mother's darling." More than any other artist, Miss Cassatt emancipated child art from the too theatrical interpretations of the past. Her absolute indifference to effect and conventional clichés, her extraordinary capacity for identifying herself with her subject, bringing it into pictorial life without superimposition or sacrifice of her own personality, have been the factors in her success in the portrayal of natural childhood.

From *American Childhood:* "Artists Every Child Should Know"

Cassatt's Studio

April 1927

Mary Cassatt's paintings of women and children are symbolic of motherhood today. Avoiding detail, using an amazingly flexible technic, and with a subtle grasp of the anatomy of childhood, she painted the joy and privilege of mothering as almost no other modern artist has seen it. She was a master draughtsman as shown in her etchings, with a feeling for the linear quality illustrated in Japanese art, but she could soften her line at will for holding a baby's flesh tints and the silken texture of a child's hair. Whether she worked in oil, pastel or dry point, she found a medium peculiarly adapted to her subject.

We may remember Mary Cassatt as a rather prim, dignified Philadelphia aristocrat, the mistress of a lovely chateau in the valley of the Oise not

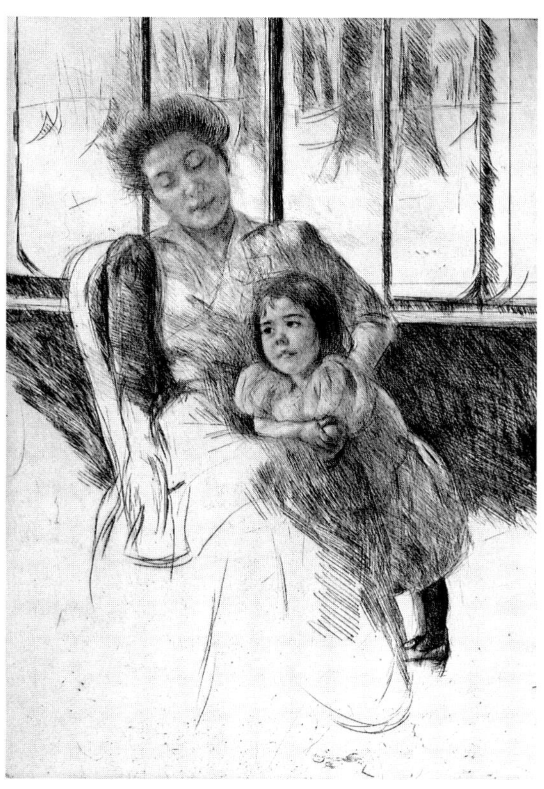

In the Conservatory. c. 1902. Drypoint. 15 1/4 × 10 5/8 in. (38.7 × 26.9 cm). The Cleveland Museum of Art. Bequest of Charles T. Brooks.

far from Paris. Surrounded by loved nieces and nephews from America and the group of children who were her favorite models, she had no desire to come home. France held everything she most loved. With grounds that included a miniature forest and a lake, shut from the world by great carved gates, Miss Cassatt spent the best years of a fruitful life with her garden, her farming, her hospitality and her painting. Her studio was a nursery, full of toys and picture books for charming the small models. She had many dogs, the piquant griffo breed most in evidence, as she liked to include these in her compositions. There were cats and a parrot to make the time pass more quickly for the children she was painting. Thus she was able to preserve, through natural play, the unaffected charm of childhood we find so appealing.

Hardly any painter but a woman would have been able to record so patiently and with so keen a vision the fleeting moods and poses of babyhood. This is one phase of Mary Cassatt's genius. Her ability was recognized by the public during her life. In 1904 she was made a chevalier of the Legion of Honor of France, and she was an associate of the National Academy. In 1914 she was awarded the gold medal of honor by the Pennsylvania Academy of Fine Arts.

From *Les Modes*

Cassatt's American Character

February 1904

What is Pittsburg, where the artist was born? It is a large city, Élisée Reclus tells us, the second most populous in Pennsylvania, and one of the most important cities in the Union in terms of industrial activity. It is a land of coal, oil, and fuel gas. It is a land of factories, the Fire City, the Smoky City.

Élisée Reclus (1830–1905), French geographer and revolutionary. His "Géographie Universelle" was published from 1875 to 1894.

It is a city "with a black sky, nearly unbreathable air, a hell." From the banks of the Ohio River, facing the confluence of the two rivers, the Alleghany and the Monongahela, one sees nothing but "two hazy avenues, and the bridges appear as if in a dream." It is pointless to leave the city in order to view it from a hilltop: one can see nothing, above the houses and monuments, but an opaque cloud of black smoke.

* * *

Needless, is it not, to add how many tons of coal the district produces, how many of pig iron, steel, and rolled iron the blast furnaces produce. It is quite certain that Miss Mary Cassatt's art expresses none of this, that it has fled the black clouds vomited by industrial flues, and every aspect of industrial machinery and work, to rejoice in blue skies, cool and verdant parks, gardens in flower, that it has chosen, instead of the energetic and rigid faces of the working world, the figures of young mothers in light colored fabrics and babies washed in running water.

If there exists a relationship between Miss Mary Cassatt's artistic intelligence and American society, that relationship is not apparent in Pittsburg.

What were her impressions of Philadelphia and what did she study there? There is industry there as well, but a whole current of general education, too: a university, an Academy of Natural Sciences, a Zoological Garden, a Historical Museum. The Museum developed, is sustained today, by European art, but this is a recent development. At the time Miss Cassatt was studying at the Philadelphia Academy, they had nothing but plaster casts of antique works. The antique, these were the artist's first models. It was undoubtedly before these perfect statues, these living fragments, that she derived her inherent sense of form. Her taste and her apprenticeship in painting would come to her later, but she had within herself the ability necessary to perceive the order in the scenes she beheld, and to arrange them on her canvas with their vital force, composition, and balance. She would travel the world when she left Philadelphia, she would learn every style of art that attempts to get closer to nature, the artless, persistent, patient endeavors of the Primitives, the confidence of the great artists of the fifteenth century, who had rediscovered antiquity and determined the movement of the Renaissance, then all the individual sentiments that would find expression in the increasing restlessness of the modern world.

Indeed, Miss Cassatt visited the museums and collections of Europe, and settled in Paris. I do believe her greatest affinities are with the Italian art of the fifteenth century, and Degas's teaching could only have confirmed her natural preference. At first, Degas, too, is close to the Italians; he places even the smallest parts of his work with the harmony of uninterrupted movements and the contrasting and logical colorations that give the Italian frescoes their beauty. But then he respects artistic individuality too much not to urge those who seek his counsel to pursue their own paths.

Miss Cassatt's individuality—she who was raised in Philadelphia, acquired her taste in form and drawing from the antique, visited Europe, became enamored of Italy, where she travelled, and of France, where she settled—this individuality is clearly a very simple, very logical compound. It begins, of course, with this woman artist's race, that overseas energy, that calm strength, that easy and forceful taking possession of things. She has a homeland, but it is a homeland without an artistic tradition, and because she is an artist, she must find herself ancestors. It is all well and good to declare that one is a student only of nature, that one can ignore monuments, museums, and all the examined, ardent and sensitive life of the old days, that one is a spontaneously generated being, with no ties of any kind, that one can create out of whole cloth an art that has absolutely nothing to do with yesterday's art. Not only has no one ever seen such an anomaly, but the conditions necessary for such an experiment have never been achieved. For there to be no trace of anything in the mind of a human being, this human being must have been kept away not only from monu-

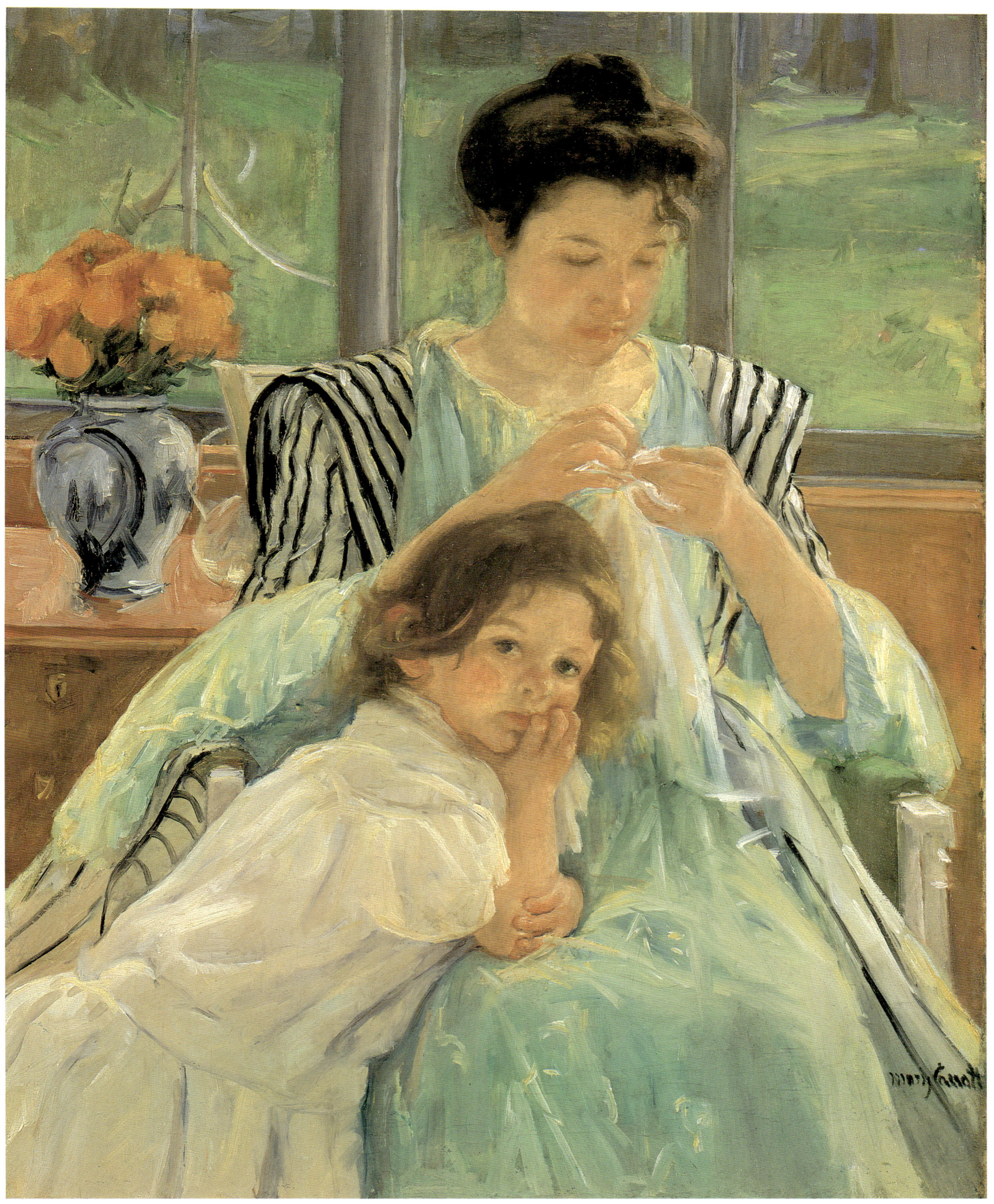

COLORPLATE 90. *Young Mother Sewing.* c. 1900. Oil on canvas. 36 3/8 × 29 in. (92.4 × 73.7 cm).
The Metropolitan Museum of Art, New York, H.O. Havemeyer Collection.
Bequest of Mrs. H.O. Havemeyer, 1929 (29.100.48). © 1982 The Metropolitan Museum of Art.

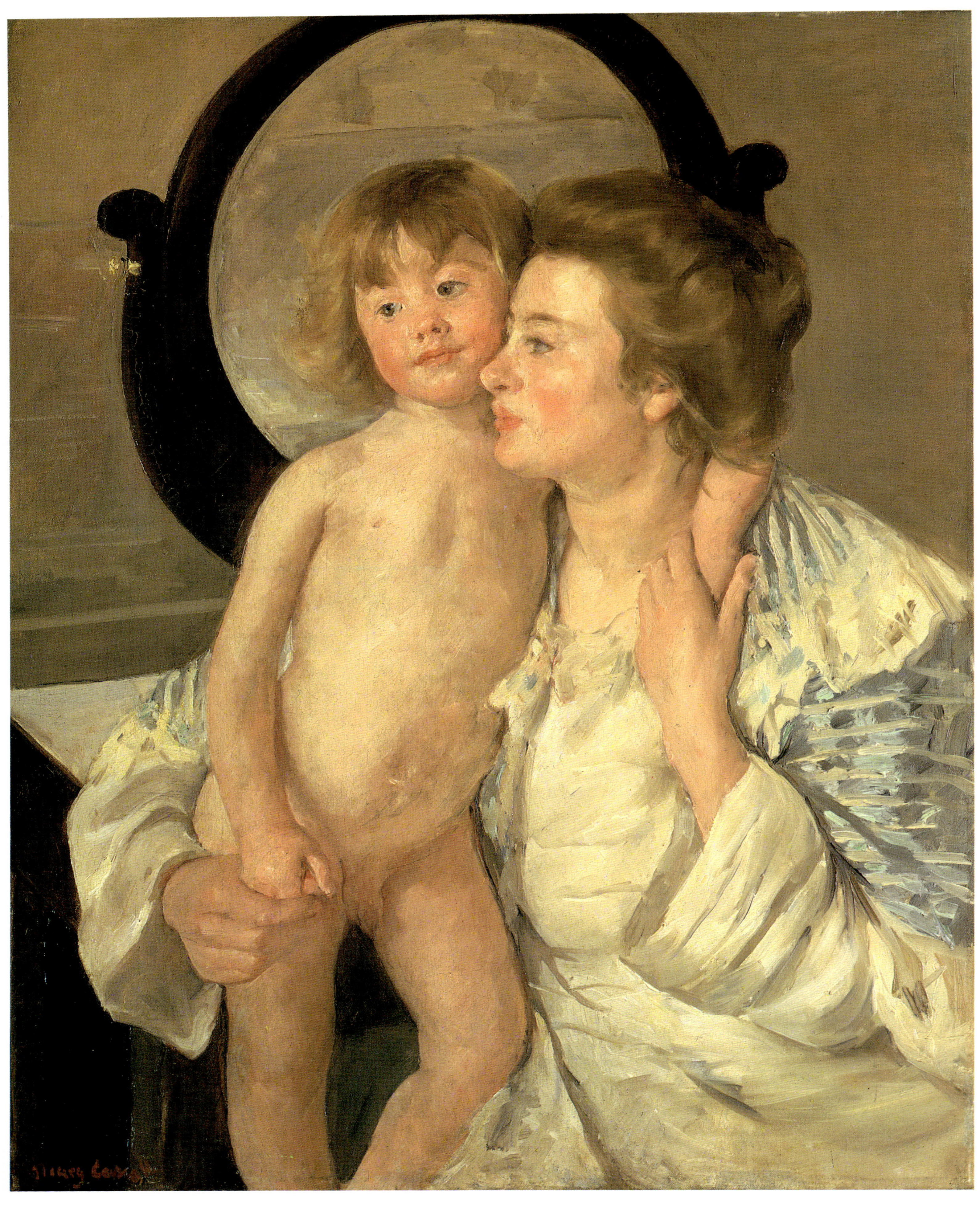

COLORPLATE 91. *Mother and Child (The Oval Mirror).* c. 1899. Oil on canvas. 32 1/8 × 25 7/8 in. (81.6 × 65.7 cm). The Metropolitan Museum of Art, New York, H.O. Havemeyer Collection. Bequest of Mrs. H.O. Havemeyer, 1929 (29.100.47). © 1984 The Metropolitan Museum of Art.

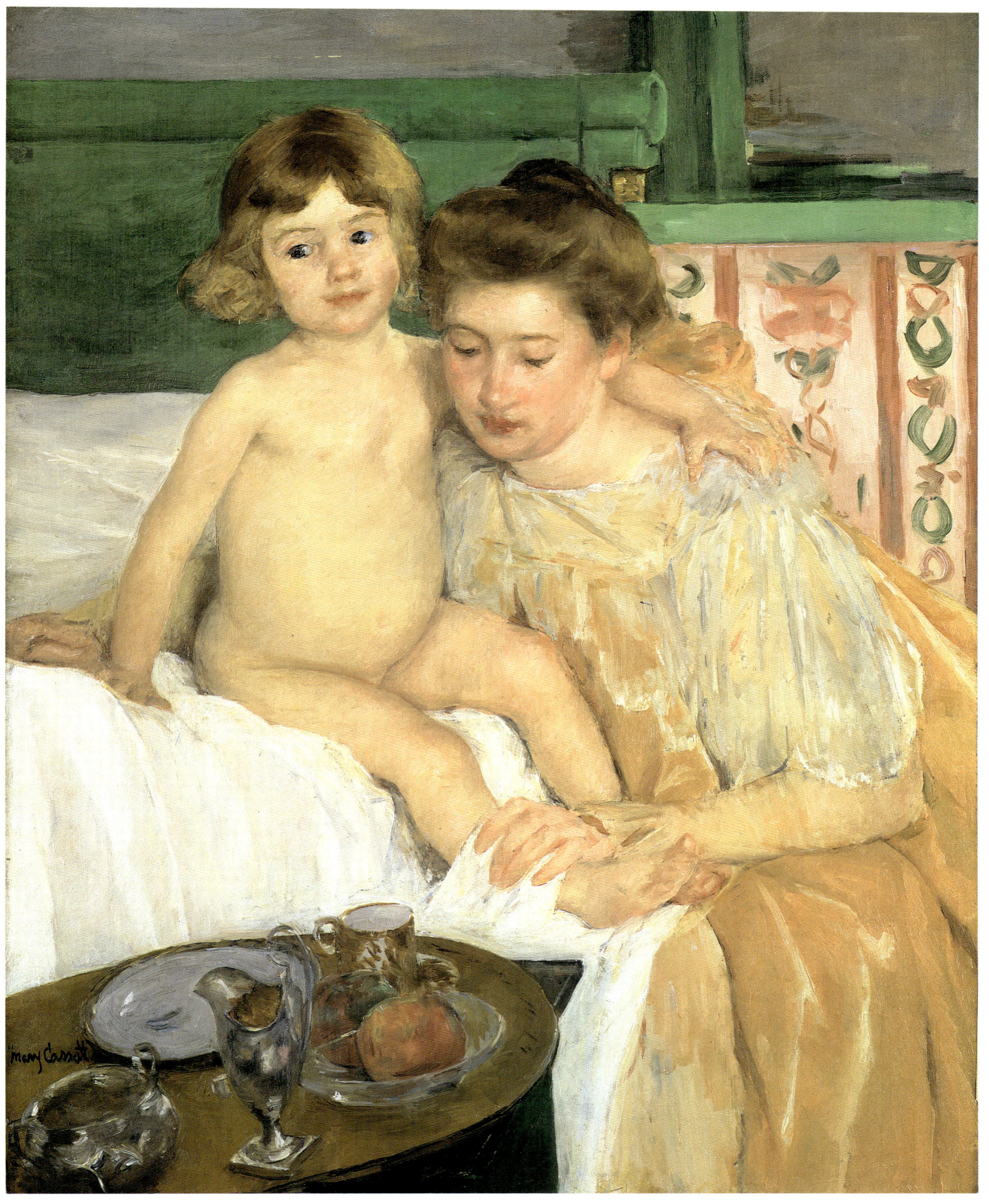

COLORPLATE 92. *Mother and Child (Baby Getting Up from His Nap).* c. 1899. Oil on canvas. 36 ½ × 29 in. (92.7 × 73.7 cm). The Metropolitan Museum of Art, New York, George A. Hearn Fund, 1909 (09.27). © 1996 The Metropolitan Museum of Art.

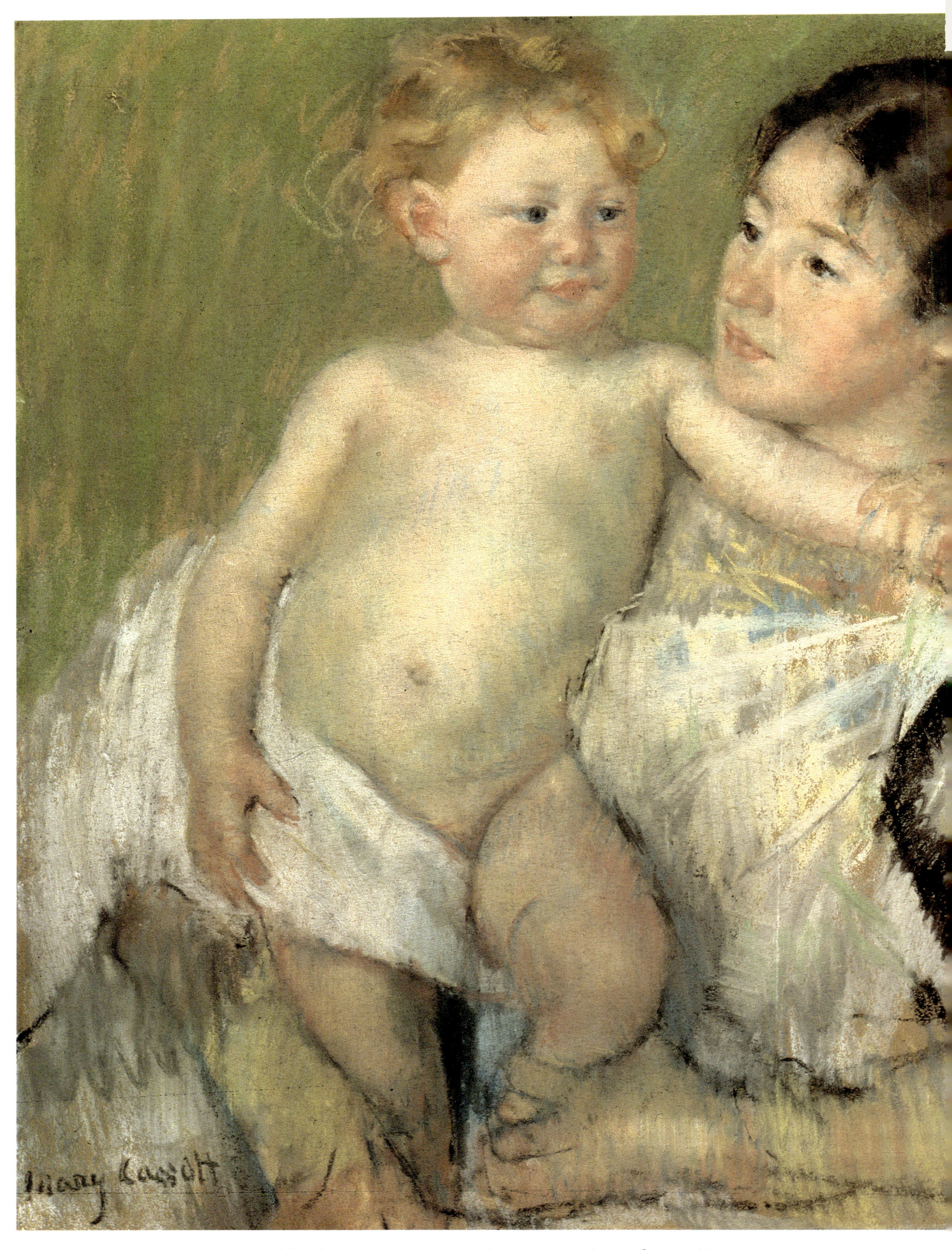

COLORPLATE 93. *After the Bath.* c. 1901. Pastel on paper. 26 × 39 3/8 in. (66 × 100 cm).
© The Cleveland Museum of Art. Gift of J. H. Wade (1920.379).

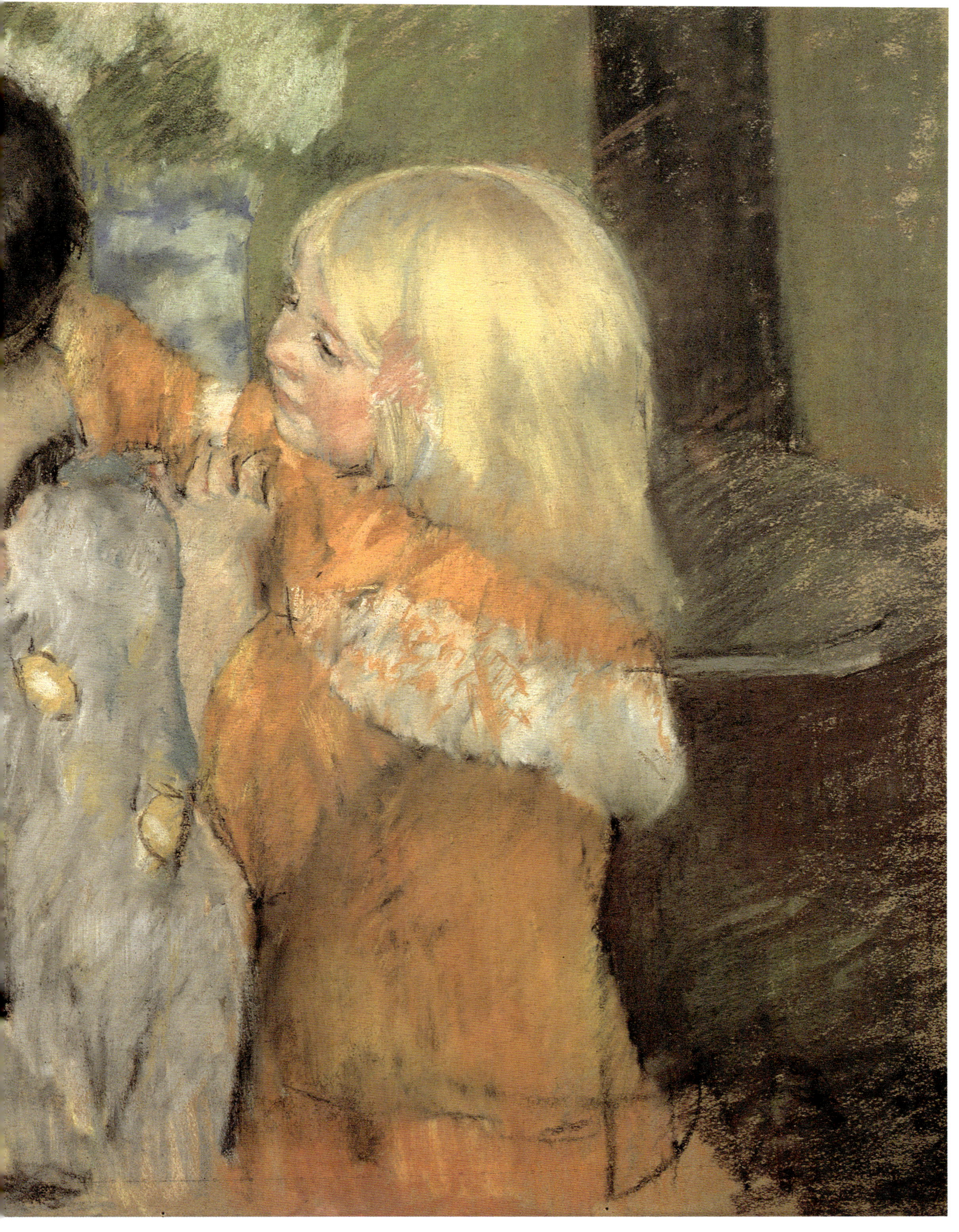

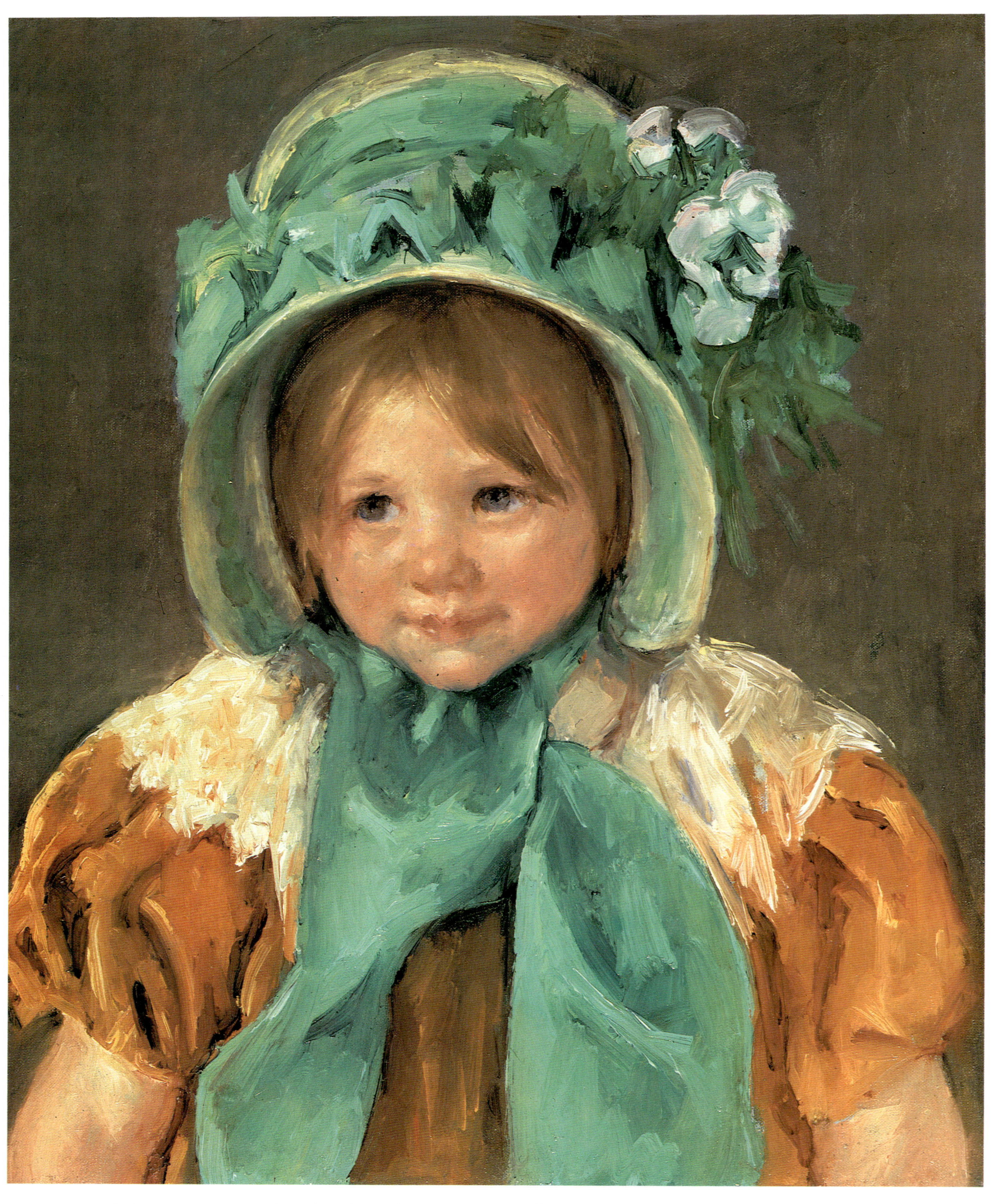

COLORPLATE 94. *Sara in a Green Bonnet.* c. 1901. Oil on canvas. 16 ⅜ × 13 ½ in. (42 × 34 cm). National Museum of American Art, Washington, D.C. Photograph: Art Resource, New York.

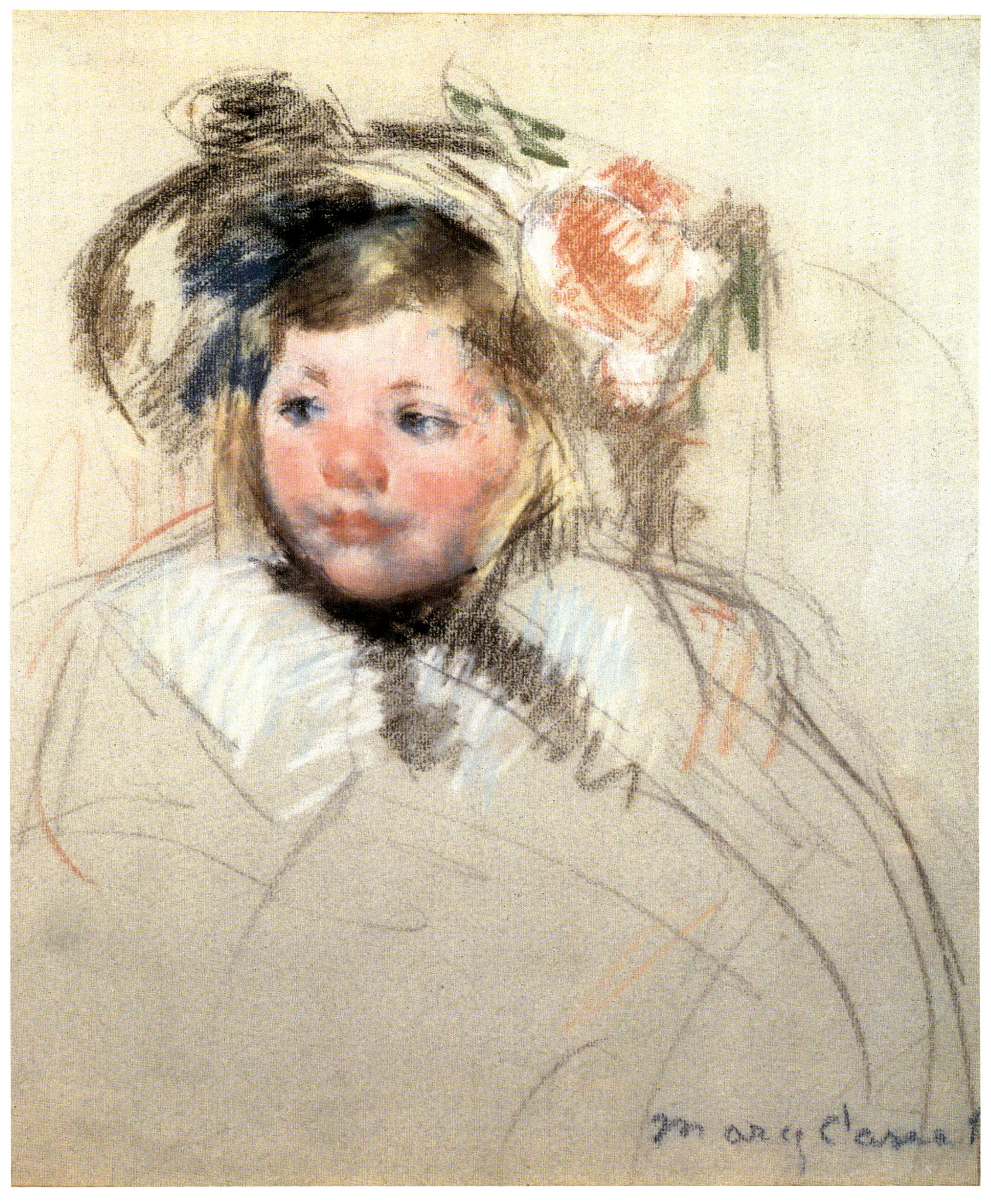

COLORPLATE 95. *Head of Sara in a Bonnet Looking to the Left.* 1901. Pastel on paper. 18 ¼ × 15 ¼ in. (46.3 × 38.7 cm). Private collection, Toronto.

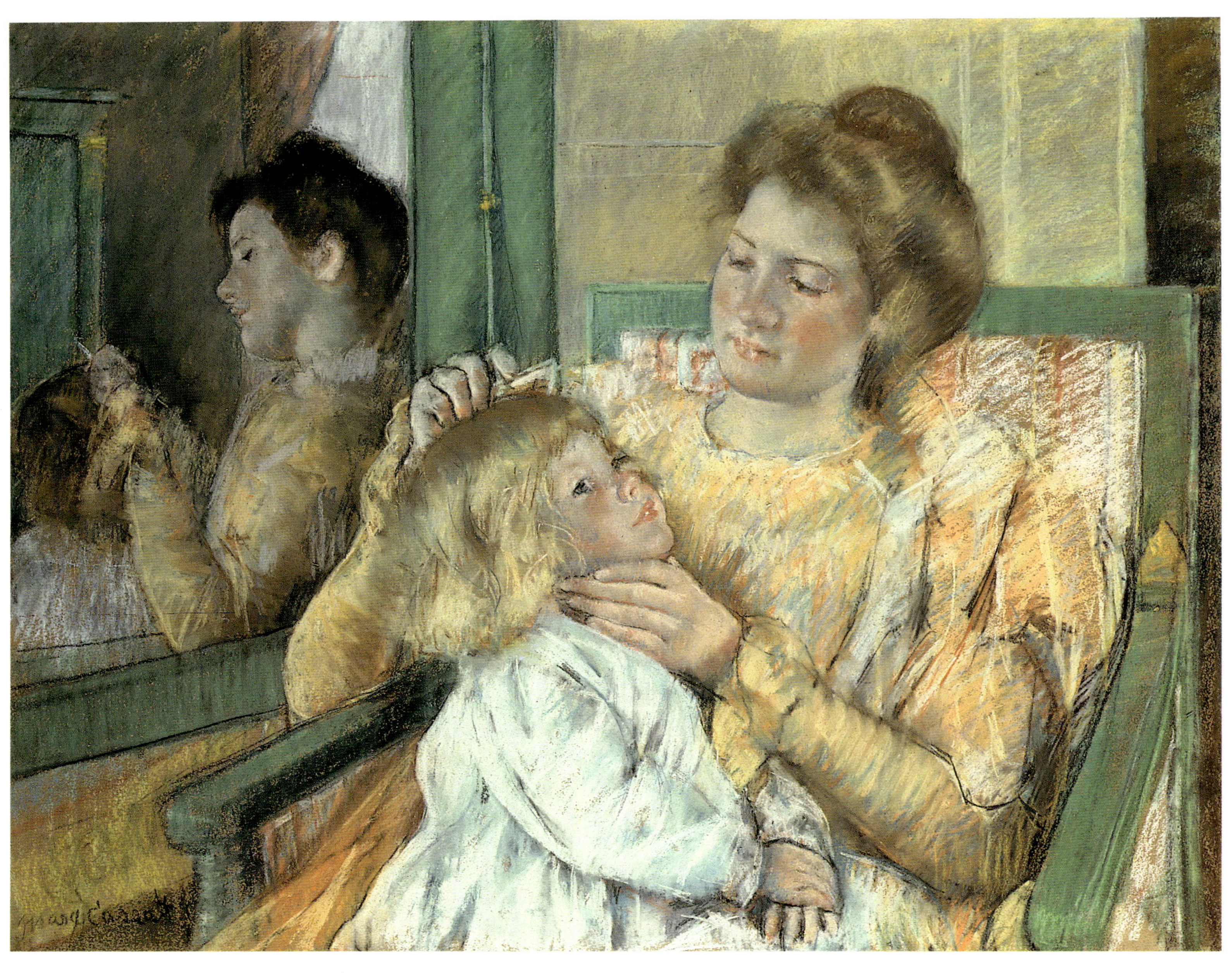

COLORPLATE 96. *Mother Combing Her Child's Hair.* c. 1898. Pastel and gouache on paper. 25 3/16 × 31 1/2 in. (63.9 × 80 cm). The Brooklyn Museum. Bequest of Mary T. Cockcroft.

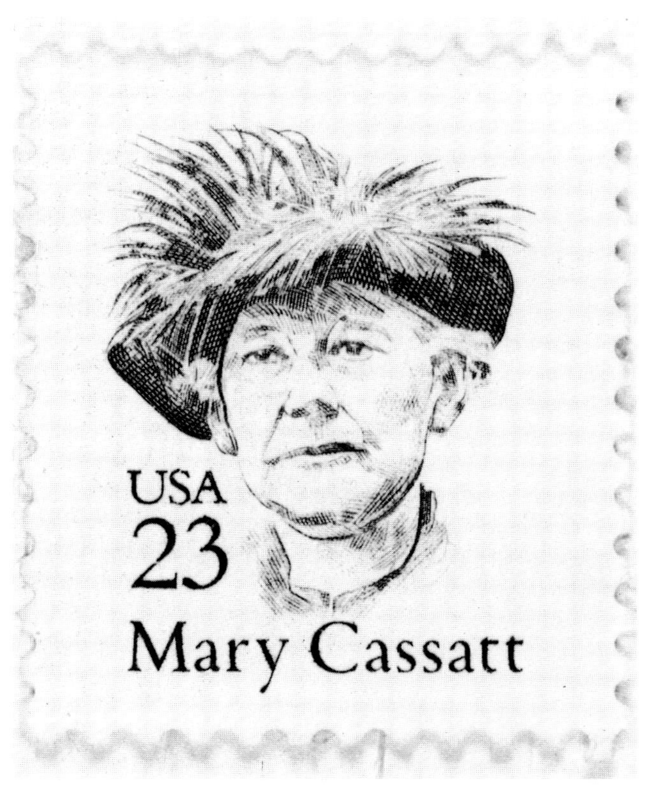

United States postage stamp. Great Americans series. Engraved. Issued November 4, 1988.

ments and museums, but even from anything that might instruct about the work of the centuries and humanity's present state. This person should not learn to read, so as not to come under the influence of any informative book. In fact, the person should not learn to speak, so as not to be instructed by a word. The student of nature would have to be put in a state of nature, nothing more. Then we would see what drawings, sculptures, constructions he would produce, if any. But why go on? He who would become a "primitive soul" achieves only a decadent and distressing imitation of naive and sincere endeavors, from which he wants to extract a system and a program.

Art today can no longer interpret nature with the forced simplicity and touching awkwardness of earlier times. [Nature] has been too scrutinized, too analyzed, and too interpreted, with ever more knowledge and infinite variety. Whether we would or no, we must pick up where our forebears left off. The new artist achieves originality on these terms: he will find it by going straight ahead, and not by trying to go back.

One should, therefore, not be surprised by the cosmopolitan sense that the Americans bring to their arts. America has barely a century of history. That is long enough to found the beginnings of a nation. It is not long enough to found an art. Who knows how many more years of action it will take this people—who already number so many individual scholars, historians, and sociologists, and can also pride themselves on a few poets and artists—to establish a tradition of national art? In the meantime, America seeks sustenance for its art in Europe. In this land of social bustle, if a museum is founded, if a shopkeeper wants to embellish his home with a gallery, they must go to nations with a past to find the art of the past. This is why a battle of buyers has been waged for close to half a century, to carry off from Europe the masterpieces of Italy and Flanders, Holland and France, Spain and England. This is why our nineteenth-century French school is better represented nowadays in America than in our public collections. This is also why America is ahead of our hesitant, stick-in-the mud, and bureaucratic judgment, and seizes works by our controversial artists, to which she confidently gives pride of place, while we lag behind, with our Salon successes and official acclaim.

I am also aware that she has somewhat hastily thrown herself upon anything that came her way from Europe and that she has received painting of every kind by the bale. There should be nothing surprising in this eagerness. It will all be sorted out later on; in fact, on certain points, the sorting has begun.

It has also happened that the young Americans who had the desire to become artists did what the shopkeepers and the art-lovers did. They came to seek their teaching from European art. Many immediately found themselves in the avant-garde of painting, in possession of recent methods, skilled at hodgepodge. We have seen them, rushed and capable, make every region, every formula their own, do Manet and Bastien-Lepage, found colonies in Paris and Brittany. This conquest was not undertaken only by the Americans. We have seen the same phenomenon of assimilation in artists from Northern lands with no artistic tradition.

Miss Mary Cassatt displays none of this indifferent facility. In her work, nothing is sacrificed to the brilliant exterior, to the show of surfaces. Once she had come to know her personality through her admiration for the works of past and present, once she had chosen her masters and her companions, then she dedicated herself to the patient, strenuous study of nature. And that is how she made her body of work, paintings, pastels, and engravings, in which are revealed the same delicate observation of scenes, the same strength, and the same refined execution.

Letter from Mary Cassatt to Theodate Pope
On The Importance of Art Collecting
September 1903

Theodate Pope Riddle (1868–1946), American architect and longtime friend of Mary Cassatt, was active in feminist and socialist causes. The two women shared an interest in spiritualism. She became an architect and designed schools, monuments, and houses between 1900 and 1930.

Mesnil-Beaufresne

Dear Miss Pope,

I ought to have answered your letter before this, but I have been very busy & I waited knowing you would soon be again in this part of the world—I had such a delightful letter from Miss Hillard & quite counted on answering it in person in Paris. I am very much disappointed to think I shall not see her again, & that she will be so busy with the new school she will not, probably, be able to come over to Europe very soon again—

Mary Robbins Hillard (18??–1932), close friend of Theodate Pope, who later became headmistress of Westover, a school for girls in Middlebury, Connecticut, which Hillard and Pope founded in 1909.

You must not discourage her about Art, I am sure she will derive great enjoyment from the effects in her surroundings, & also for herself. I am quite sure she will begin to feel pictures in a different way, you must remember that art is a great intellectual stimulus, & not reduce everything to a decorative plane—What you say about pictures being things alone, & standing for so much, & therefore the wickedness of private individuals owning them, is I assure you a very false way of seeing things, surely you would not have museums crowded with *undigested* efforts of everyone? Only in years after an artists death are his pictures admitted to the Louvre, I wish to goodness we had some sensible rule of that kind at home, instead of that everything can be crowded into public Museums, & no standard is possible in such a mess. I think it is very exhilirating to a painter to know he touches some individual enough for that person to want to own his work, & surely there is nothing wrong in a hard working lawyer or business man

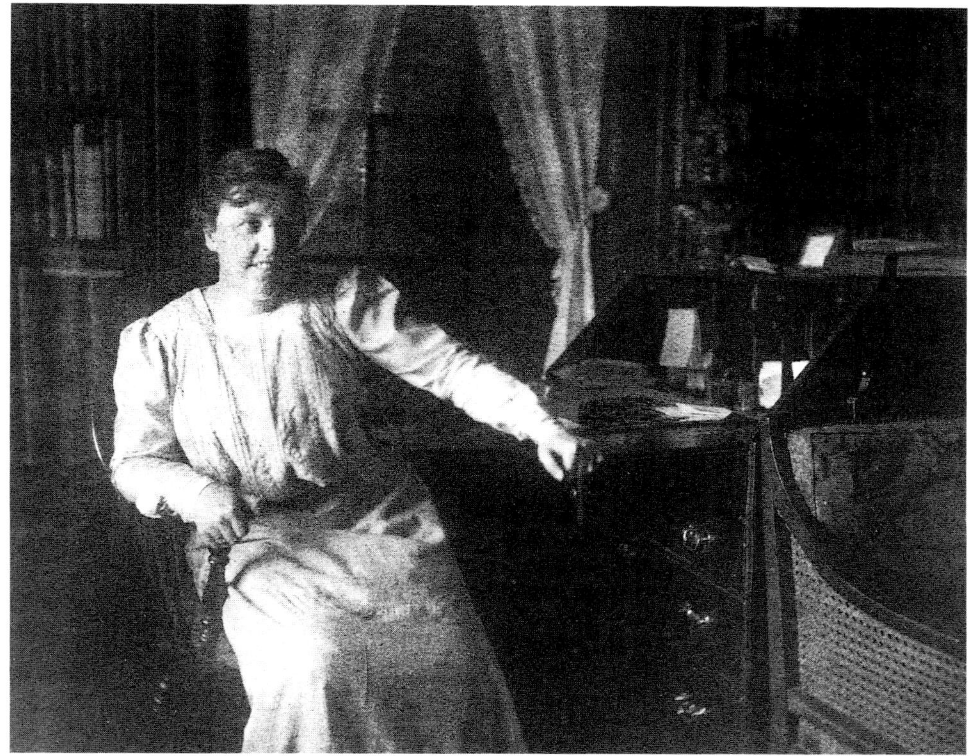

Gertrude Kasebier photograph of Theodate Pope. c. 1900. Photograph courtesy of the Hill-Stead Museum, Farmington, Connecticut.

putting some of his earnings in a work of art which appeals to him, when we must all work for the state may I no longer inhabit this planet—I assure you when I was in Boston & they took me to the Library & pointed with pride to all the young ones devouring books, & that without guidance, taking up all sorts of ideas of other people; I thought how much more stimulating a fine Museum would be, it would teach all those little boys who have to work for their living to admire good work, & give them the desire to be perfect in some one thing—I used to protest that all the wisdom of the World is not between the pages of books; & never did I meet any one in the Boston Museum, where the state the pictures are in is a disgrace to the Directors—As to the Havemeyer collection about which you feel so strongly, I consider they are doing a great work for the country in spending so much *time* & money in bringing together such works of art, all the great public collections were formed by private individuals—You say "no collection can be interesting as a whole"—There again you are thinking of decoration, but I know two Frenchmen who are thinking of a journey to New York, *solely* to see the Havemeyer collection because *only there* can they see what they consider the finest modern pictures in contact with the finest old Masters, pictures which time has consecrated & only there can they study the influences which went to form the Modern School, or at least only there see the result—You see how others look on collections.

Enough of this we can talk of art when we meet, I do hope you will come down here I shall be so happy to see you, come on a Saturday evening—spend Tuesday or if the weather does not tempt you I will go up & see you; at any rate we must meet, I had a young couple today to see the place who were enchanted. Kindest regards to all the party & hope you are all well ever yours most cordially

Mary Cassatt

HELEN W. HENDERSON

From *Brush and Pencil:* "Centenary Exhibition of the Pennsylvania Academy of the Fine Arts"

Cassatt Exhibits at Her Alma Mater

March 1905

The one hundredth anniversary exhibition of the Pennsylvania Academy of the Fine Arts holds, for the time, supreme sway in art interests throughout the country. The exhibition, as the most catholic and generous in its standards of admission, as well as the largest numerically by about three times the number shown by other institutions of importance, is in a sense the American salon. Any review of the exhibition, however adverse, must admit a certain great fundamental vigor in the management in producing so distinguished an aggregation of contemporary art, before which the inevitable injustices to the individual—the often unscrupulous disregard of personal rights and equity—fall away into the background of a result so satisfying in its entirety as to silence protest.

. . . The great pictures of the show are not the Sargents, not the Abbey, not the Whistlers, though these occupy the places of honor. The rarer and more lasting qualities of art are found in the quieter places, where their eloquence is the far more profound because unlooked for. . . .

Alfred Atmore Pope (1842–1913), American businessman and collector of Impressionist art; father of Theodate.

Mary Cassatt's *The Toilet: Mother and Two Children,* lent by Alfred Atmore Pope, presents the difficult problem of flesh painted in full light juxtaposed to strong color. The three figures are placed against a background of turquoise-blue. Of the same uncompromising hue is the drapery across the woman's shoulders, and the wicker and wood chair in which she sits. The baby is nude, seated upright upon the mother's arm, its well-constructed little back to the spectator, one arm thrown across his mother's shoulder and the other pressed against his side, the hand fingering the soap-dish, offered by the second child. The little sister is marvelously attired in a sort of matinée of saffron-yellow satin trimmed with lace. The lines of the composition run to diagonals, and are obviously disposed, the problem being felt first, and the working out to admiration purely mental process.

Letter from Mary Cassatt to Harrison Morris

On Prizes, Medals, and Juries

March 15, 1904

Harrison S. Morris (1856–1948), American author and museum director, and a contributor of articles and editorials to numerous periodicals. He was art editor of "Ladies Home Journal" from 1906 to 1907, and managing director of the Pennsylvania Academy of the Fine Arts.

10, rue de Marignan
March 15, 1904

My Dear Mr. Morris,

1904 Annual Exhibition at the Pennsylvania Academy of the Fine Arts.

I have received your very kind letter of Feb. 16th with the enclosed list of the different prizes awarded in the Exhibition. Of course it is very gratifying to know that a picture of mine was selected for a special honor and I hope the fact of my not accepting the award will not be misunderstood. I was not aware that Messrs Durand Ruel had sent a picture of mine to the Exhibition. The picture being their property they were at liberty to do as they pleased with it. I, however, who belong to the founders of the Independent Exhibition must stick to my principles, our principles, which were, no jury, no medals, no awards. Our first exhibition was held in 1879 and was a protest against official exhibitions and not a grouping of artists with the same art tendencies. We have been since dubbed "Impressionists" a name which might apply to Monet but can have no meaning when attached to Degas' name.

Liberty is the first good in this world and to escape the tyranny of a jury is worth fighting for, surely no profession is so enslaved as ours. Gérôme who all his life was on the Jury of every official exhibition said only a short time before his death that if Millet were then alive, he, Gérôme would refuse his pictures, that the world has consecrated Millet's genius made no difference to him. I think this is a good comment on the system. I have no hopes of converting any one, I even failed in getting the women students club here to try the effect of freedom for one year, I mean of course the American Students Club. When I was at home a few years ago it was one of the things that disheartened me the most to see that we were slavishly copying all the evils of the French system, evils which they deplore and are trying to remove. I will say though that if awards are given it is more sensible and practical to give them in money than in medals and to young and struggling artists such help would often be welcome, and personally I should feel wicked in depriving any one of such help, as in the present case.

Jean François Millet (1814–1875), painter of French peasant life, influenced many younger artists to abandon academic practices.

Cassatt served on the board of the American Students Club, an organization for American art students in Paris.

I hope you will excuse this long letter, but it was necessary for me to explain.

Thanking you again for your letter believe me, my dear Mr. Morris

Very sincerely yours
Mary Cassatt

Letter from Mary Cassatt to John W. Beatty

On Cassatt's Opposition to the Jury System

September 5, 1905

John W. Beatty (1850–1924), American painter, etcher, author, and museum director who served on the Advisory Art Committee for the Chicago Exposition of 1893, as well as other American world's fairs. He became director of fine arts of the Carnegie Institute in Pittsburgh.

Mesnil-Beaufresne
September 5

Dear Mr. Beatty,

I have long been wanting to write to you, & have hardly known how. It is so long ago that I had the pleasure of meeting you in Paris that you may have forgotten the conversation we had at that time. I then tried to explain to you my ideas, principles I ought to say, in regard to jurys of artists, I have never served because I could never reconcile it to my conscience to be the means of shutting the door in the face of a fellow painter. I think the jury system may lead, & in the case of the Exhibitions at the Carnegie Institute no doubt does lead to a high average, but in art what we want is the certainty that the one spark of original genius shall not be extinguished, that is better than average excellence, that is what will survive, what it is essential to foster—The "Indépendants" in Paris was originally started by one group, it was the idea of our exhibitions & since taken up by others, no jury, & most of the artists of original talent have made their début there in the last decade, they would never have had a chance in the official Salons. Ours is an enslaved profession, fancy a writer not being able to have an article published unless passed by a jury of authors, not to say rivals—

Pardon this long explanation, but the subject excites me, it seems to me a very serious question in our profession, these are my reasons for never having served on the jury of the Institute, if I could be of the least service in any other way I would most gladly. I would consider nothing a trouble to serve the Institute of which you are so devoted a Director.

As to sending pictures, this year I have none, they have been sold in Paris and I could not ask the owners to send them so far as it would seem to them.

With my sincere regrets & my renewed excuses, believe me, my dear Mr. Beatty most sincerely yours

Mary Cassatt

Letter From Mary Cassatt to Joseph Pennell
On Friction With Her Dealer, Durand-Ruel
November 17, [1905]

Joseph Pennell (1860–1926), American graphic artist and author, and friend and biographer of Whistler.

Mesnil-Beaufresne
Fresneaux-Montchevreuil
Mesnil-Théribus Oise
Nov. 17th

Dear Mr. Pennel,

Thanks very much for your very kind letter. I am late in answering it but it is not my fault. The trouble is I don't own any of my own pictures. I would have to borrow any I sent you and that I cannot do, even if the owners would lend. Up till this last affair my pictures went to the Durand-Ruels, and I have no power over them, and am angry at their not showing me with all my group, our group, last winter. That was a very shabby piece of work on their part. I haven't any etchings either. I know this sounds absurd but it is the simple truth. I sell the whole "tirage" [edition] at a time, and I have not etched for sometime. If it were not for the channel I would go over and see your exhibition. We are having the Salon d'Automne and Ingres' *Turkish Bath* is on view. I wonder if you have ever seen it, it is like nothing else in modern art, a thing by itself.

I hope I will have the pleasure of seeing you in Paris, and Mrs. Pennel also. With kindest regards to you both and regrets at not being able to accept your kind and flattering invitation, believe me

Most cordially yours
Mary Cassatt

If they had wanted to show by whom Whistler was influenced they could not have done it better, but I was surprised at the Rossetti note, it is evident he looked at that school. As for Courbet, his influence was the best. The head of the woman at the piano is full of him—

Dante Gabriel Rossetti (1828–82), British Pre-Raphaelite painter and poet.

The Durand-Ruels never even sent me a catalogue of your exhibition. I don't now know which of my etchings you showed!

SIDNEY ALLEN

From *Camera Work*

Cassatt as a Modern Artist

July 1903

Accuracy is the bane of art. There is no despotism so ghastly, so disastrous in its results. Slavery of observation and a too close discrimination of the actualities of life have foisted upon us a David and a Cornelius, the Dusseldorf and the Hudson River Schools, expressions of art which, according to the present codes of esthetics, are the very lowest imaginable. Modern Art has nothing to do with plumb-lines and mechanical props. It has taught every artist to delight in the report of his own eyes and to set it forth with all the eloquence he is capable of. His individual eloquence is generally more important to him than exact likenesses of form and color, and he would rather fail in conformity to truth than in eloquence. He recognizes that he can only master the general aspect of Truth, and that to copy nature slavishly is but to invite failure and to join hands with vulgarity.

Modern art, in its best examples, is the very antithesis of accuracy. Look at a Sargent or Boldini. What an apparent waste of accidental lights, passing shimmers, speckles, flashes, and other local impossibilities appear in all their pictures! And yet each of these embellishing touches lends its value to the variety and comprehensiveness of the total effect. As unimpor-

Giovanni Boldini (1842–1931), Italian painter who studied and worked in Paris for most of his career.

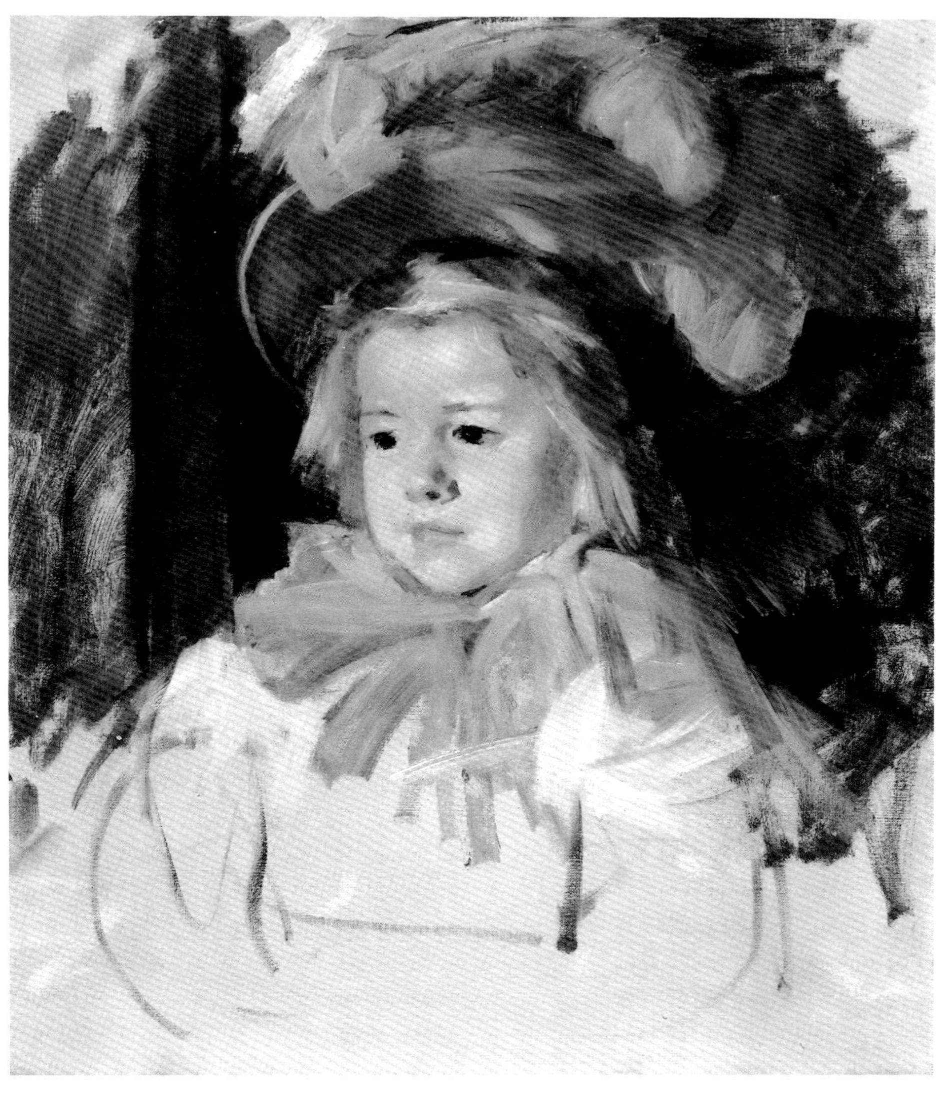

Simone in a Large Plumed Hat. c. 1901. Oil on canvas. 28 × 25 in. (71.1 × 63.5 cm). Museum of Art, Rhode Island School of Design. Gift of Mrs. Murray S. Danforth.

tant as these technical details may seem at the first glance, they are really the leading characteristics of modern art, for they lend virility to lines and masses. With their help the immobile becomes animated, the silent begins to speak, and the dull turns colorful.

The art-connoisseur of today wants to see subjects bathed in light and air, and wants an actual atmosphere to be interposed between his eyes and the representation of figures, flowers, fields, trees, etc. No matter if the arms and legs of a figure are rightly measured and located, if they only look like arms and legs he is satisfied.

Alma Tadema and Bouguereau have fallen in esthetic appreciation. Naturalness of effect in their pictures is invariably sacrificed to pedantic knowledge of form and line, and their groups of figures look cold, hard, and overstudied, like separate objects pitched together. Seen in fragments, each of their figures would affect one pleasantly, owing to their fine draughtsmanship; but when put together, one resents in them a too close discrimination of unessential facts and local tints.

Sir Lawrence Alma-Tadema (1836–1912), Dutch painter who assumed British nationality in 1873. He was known for scenes of classical antiquity.

Modern art has discarded the classic purity of the Greek line and substituted the rugged, picturesque line of the Japanese, which vibrates with the nervous touch of the artist's hand. A perfectly straight or clear line seems to us almost as offensive as the introduction of geometrical figures. We do not want the representation of facts, but of appearances, or merely the blurred suggestion of appearances and the swift reflections and subtle quivering of light do not permit any exact copyism. The natural result is a broader treatment, and as it is impossible to handle large masses successfully without breaking them up, the artist—each after his own fashion—has to find some technical device to lead him in the direction he desires.

Experiments will teach him to regard the eccentricities of brush-work, the apparently meaningless and inaccurate, as one of his safest helpmates. He may introduce, like Cecilia Beaux, red and blue color-daubs in the shadows, which are *apparently meaningless,* as they do not exist in reality, but which relieve the monotony of the actual local tints. Or, like Winslow Homer, he may accentuate his shadows in the foreground and render them inaccurate by painting them black, in order to give his objects more solidity and to heighten the impression of sunlight.

Peculiarities of style like these may easily deteriorate into trickery and mannerisms, but even then they are to be preferred to pure mimicry and imitation.

The love for exactitude is the lowest form of pictorial gratification—felt by the child, the savage, and the Philistine—it merely apprehends the likeness between the representation and the object represented. The unforeseen and unexpected effects are those which make the deepest impressions. Of course, the artist can not entirely rely on accidents—although accidental flourishes are apt to produce artistic and even remarkable effects at times—he must understand the underlying structures and keep enough force in reserve for the handling of the essential masses.

Take, for instance, Mary Cassatt, by no means a great artist, but on almost every one of her canvases, roughly, sometimes brutally composed, drawn, and painted, there is that touch, which by imparting to form and color some particular quality of effect, impossible to analyze, endows all her figures with the energy of life. How does she accomplish it?

Her style of painting consists primarily of a mosaic of irregular colored shapes. At close scrutiny we complain about bad drawing, wilful accentuation of detail (in particular in the boundary lines of shapes) and the unchromatic vehemence of her coloring. There are any amount of tiny, crisp, and angular lines and chaotic color-patches which apparently have nothing to say, and yet at a distance pull altogether and give a significance. A hand, represented by a few fragmentary scratches and scrawls of the brush and a juxtaposition of color, after all gives a more life-like impression than one which is faultlessly drawn and colored with all due observations of precise and pedantic realities.

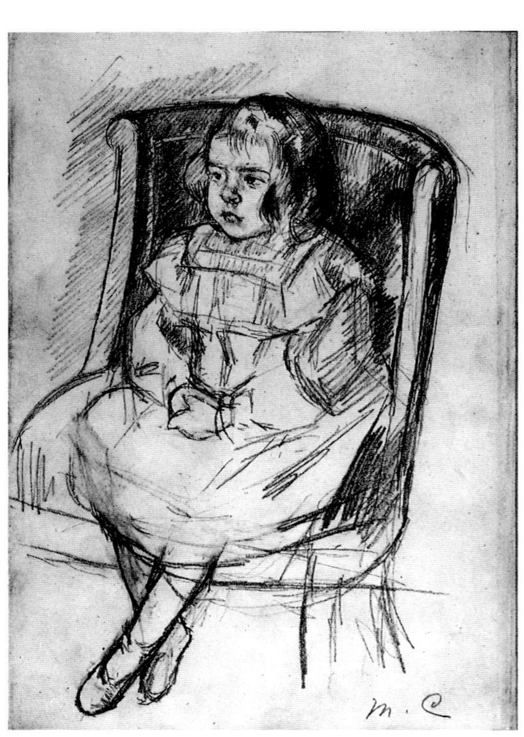

Simone Seated with Hands and Feet Crossed. c. 1903. Pencil. 8 5/8 × 6 3/16 in. (22 × 15.7 cm). The Cleveland Museum of Art. Gift of Leonard C. Hanna, Jr.

What does it matter if the rigging in Boudin's picture is nautically incorrect, if he gives his masts one yard too many or too little, as long as he suggests the peculiar charm and restlessness of seafaring vessels. He probably knows every stay and spar, but he feels that the eye of the spectator would be more satisfied with a few vital dashes than an accurate illustration. Also in the sky-line we notice many strokes and patches which do not resemble facts in accordance with the laws of perspective and the conventionalities of domestic architecture, but do they not as a whole give the impression of a little French harbor town, with its faint suggestion of the heavy ocean, of home-coming vessels and mutinous skies?

Eugène Boudin (1824–1898), French painter influential in the development of the Impressionist style.

Pictures like these the gum-workers should study in order to learn to eliminate facts and at the same time to subordinate the daubs and dashes which accomplish it, to the greater elements of composition, of proportion, and of dark and light. It would surely do no harm to cultivate that extraordinary acuteness of vision, which enables Monet and Whistler (the one in the prismatic colors of the rainbow and the other in grays and browns) to distinguish in one note of color twenty oppositions or more, each influencing the other by their tonal juxtaposition, like so many notes of music.

But may not too many inaccuracies be added at the expense of the general truth? Undoubtedly, nothing is more frequent with unskilful artists than to lose the swing of a line by separately accentuating particular indentations, or the character of a mass by over-modeling subordinate saliences. Any distraction of attention from the essential elements of a picture is apt to destroy the dignity and breadth of its view.

One must be a past-master of structural form before one can subordinate the means employed for an artistic attainment to the attainment itself. A technique affecting haphazard effects, misrepresenting natural vision and often merely clothing bad construction and other technical shortcomings, is affectation and foppery. Expression can not exist without character as its stamina, and character and stamina can be only given by those who feel them.

There is no set and definite mode of acquiring such faculties. It must be intuition, and as in the case of the artist's own affections, inspirations, and ideals, the result and the expression of his own spontaneous spirit and individuality. Thus, alone, it will have flavor, freshness, and suggestion.

Letter from Mary Cassatt to Her Niece, Ellen Mary Cassatt

On Matisse and the Steins

March 26, 1913

Ellen Mary Cassatt (1894–1978), Cassatt's niece and namesake, was the elder daughter of Gardner and Eugenia Cassatt.

Henri Matisse (1869–1954), French painter, graphic artist, and designer. He was a member of the "Fauves," the first avant-garde movement in Europe between 1900 and World War I, whose style was characterized by the bold use of color. Gertrude Stein was one of Matisse's most influential patrons.

Gertrude Stein (1874–1946), American author and art patron and collector. Her writing was heavily influenced by the work of philosopher William James. With her brother Leo, Stein moved to Paris in 1903 and established herself in intellectual circles as a proponent of Matisse and Picasso. Their brother Michael and his wife Sarah also had a fashionable "salon."

Villa Angeletto
March 26, 1913

Dearest Brown,

Yours of the 17th is just here; and as the weather is storming and a pouring rain has been our portion all night and likely to be all day, I have plenty of time before me to answer some of your questions about cubists and others. No Frenchman of any standing in the art world has ever taken any of these things seriously. As to Matisse, one has only to see his early work to understand him. His pictures were extremely feeble in execution

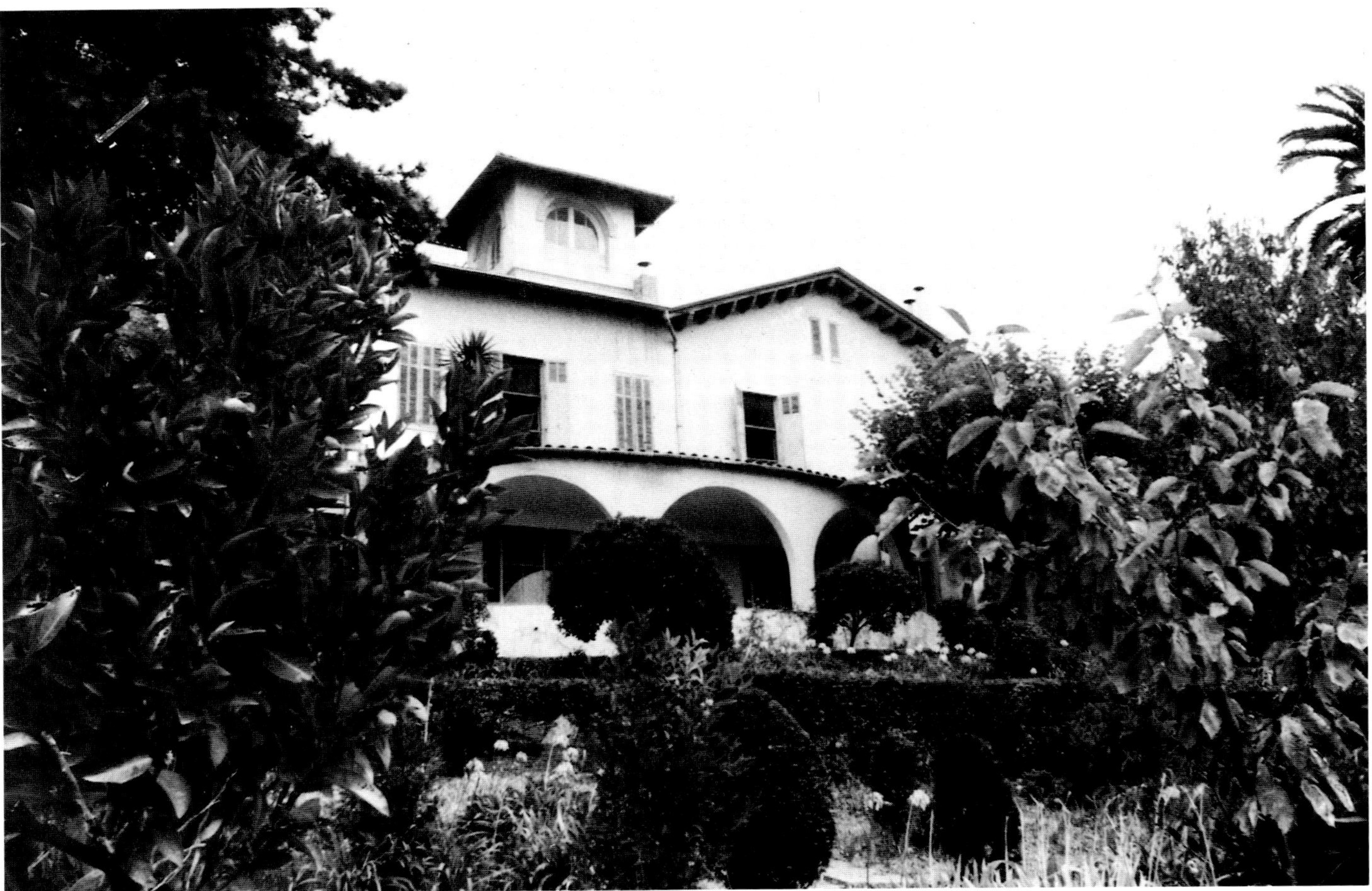

Photograph of the Villa Angeletto, Grasse.

and very commonplace in vision. As he is intelligent he saw that real excellence, which would bring him consideration, was not for him on that line. He shut himself up for years and evolved these things; he knew that in the present anarchical state of things—not only in the art world but everywhere—he would achieve notoriety—and he has. At his exhibition in Paris you never hear French spoken, only German, Scandinavian and other Germanic languages; and then people think notoriety is fame and even buy these pictures or daubs. Of course all this has only "un temps"; it will die out. Only really good work survives. As to this Gertrude Stein, she is one of a family of California Jews who came to Paris poor and unknown; but they are not Jews for nothing. They—two of the brothers—started a studio, bought Matisse's pictures cheap and began to pose as amateurs of the only real art. Little by little people who want to be amused went to these receptions where Stein received in sandals and his wife in one garment fastened by a broach, which if it gave way might disclose the costume of Eve. Of course the curiosity was aroused and the anxiety as to whether it *would* give way; and the pose was, if you don't admire these daubs I am sorry for you; you are not of the chosen few. Lots of people went, Mrs. Sears amongst them and Helen; but I never would, being to old a bird to be caught by chaff. The misunderstanding in art has arisen from the fact that forty years ago—to be exact thirty nine years ago—when Degas and Monet, Renoir and I first exhibited, the public did not understand, only the "élite" bought and time has proved their knowledge. Though the Public in those days did not understand, the *artists* did. Henner told me that he considered Degas one of the two or three artists then living. Now the Public say—the foreign public—Degas and the others were laughed at; well, we will be wiser than they. We will show we know; not knowing that the art world of those days did accept these men; only, as they held "L'assiette de beurre," they would not divide it with outsiders. No sound artist ever looked except with scorn at these cubists and Matisse.

Sarah Choate Sears (1858–1935), American artist and collector who became a member of the New York Photo Secession, led by Alfred Stieglitz. Helen Sears Bradley was her daughter.

Jean Jacques Henner (1829–1905), French academic painter and friend of Degas.

ELISABETH LUTHER CARY

"The Art of Mary Cassatt"

Cassatt's Later Style

1909

Some fifteen years ago, on the occasion of an exhibition in Paris of Miss Cassatt's work a French critic suggested that she was then, perhaps, with the exception of Whistler, "the only artist of an elevated, personal and distinguished talent actually possessed by America." The suggestion no doubt was a rash one, since, as much personal and distinguished work by American artists never leaves this country, the data for comparison must be lacking to a French critic; but it is certainly true that, like Whistler, Miss Cassatt early struck an individual note, looked at life with her own eyes, and respected her intellectual instrument sufficiently to master it to the extent, at least, of creating a style for herself. Born at Pittsburgh, Pennsylvania, she studied first at the Philadelphia Academy, and later traveled through Spain, Italy, and Holland in search of artistic knowledge and direction. In France she came to know the group of painters including Monet, Renoir, Pissarro and Degas, and especially influenced by the work of Degas, she turned to him for the counsel she needed, receiving it in generous measure. It was a fortunate choice, the most fortunate possible, if she wished to combine in her art the detached observation characteristic in general of the Impressionist school with a passionate pursuit of all the subtlety, eloquence and precision possible to pure line. The fruit of his influence is to be found in the technical excellence of her representations of life, and firmness and candor of her drawing, her competent management of planes and surfaces, and the audacity with which she attacks difficult problems of color and tone. The extreme gravity of her method is the natural result of working under a master whose intensity and austerity in the pursuit of artistic truth are perhaps unequaled in the history of modern art.

Her choice of subject is not, however, the inspiration of any mind other than her own. She has taken for the special field in which to exercise her vigorous talent that provided by the various phases of the maternal relation. Her wholesome young mothers with their animated children, comely and strong, unite the charm of great expressiveness with that of profoundly scientific execution. The attentive student of art is well aware how easily the former quality unsupported by the latter may degenerate into the cloying exhibition of sentiment, and is equally aware of the sterility of the latter practised for itself alone. With expressiveness for her goal and the means of rendering technical problems for her preoccupation, Miss Cassatt has arrived at hard-earned triumphs of accomplishment. One has only to turn from one of her recently exhibited pictures to another painted ten or twelve years ago to appreciate the length of the way she has come. The earlier painting, an oil color, is of a woman in a striped purple, white, and green gown, holding a half-naked child, who is engaged in bathing its own feet, with the absorbed expression on its face common to children occupied with such responsible tasks. The bricky flesh tints of the faces and hands, and the greenish half-tones of the square little body are too highly emphasized, but a keen perception of facts of surface and construction is obvious in the well-defined planes of the child's anatomy, in the foreshortened, thin little arm pressing firmly on the woman's knee and in the stout little legs, hard and round and simply modeled. There is plenty of truth in the picture, but in spite of an almost effective effort toward harmony of color, it lacks what the critics call "totality of effect." The annotation of the

COLORPLATE 66

various phenomena is too explicit, the values are not finely related, and there is little suggestion of atmosphere.

In the later picture this crudity is replaced by a beautiful fluent handling and the mystery of tone. The subject is again a woman and child, the latter just out of its bath, its flesh bright and glowing, its limbs instinct with life and ready to spring with uncontrollable vivacity. The modeling of the figures is as elusive as it is sure, and in the warm, golden air by which they seem to be enveloped, the well-understood forms lose all suggestion of the hardness and dryness conspicuous in the early work. Another recent painting of a kindred subject, *Le lever de bébé*, shows the same synthesis of detail, the same warmth and richness of tone, the same free and learned use of line. Obviously, Miss Cassatt has come into the full possession of her art and is no longer constrained by the struggle, sharp and hard as it must have been, with her exacting method—a method that has not at any time permitted the sacrifice of truth to charm. Since art is both truth and charm, record and poetry, there is a great satisfaction in watching the flowering of a positive talent, after the inevitable stages of literalism are passed, into the beauty of intelligent generalization. In all the later work there is the important element of ease, a certain graciousness of style, that enhances to a very great degree the beauty of the serious, dignified canvases. And from the beginning these have shown the admirable qualities of serenity and poise. There is no superficiality or pettiness about these homely women with their deep chests and calm faces, peacefully occupying themselves with their sound, agreeable children. The air of health, of fresh and normal vigor, is the characteristic of the chosen type, and lends a suggestion of the Hellenic spirit to the modern physiognomies.

LULA MERRICK

Lula Merrick (1878–1931), American art critic and one of the first people to advocate and direct travelling art exhibitions.

From *Delineator*

"The Art of Mary Cassatt"

August 1909

More than ten years have passed since a great French painter remarked: "There are only two American artists—Whistler and Mary Cassatt." Since then America has produced a number of real artists, men and women. Although art has advanced with us until it has gained serious recognition by all other nations, Mary Cassatt still holds her place as the most eminent of American women painters. In her portrayal of motherhood and childhood she stands alone. "No one else," it has been well said, "ever portrayed childhood as she. No one else has observed and made his own the thousand and one little gestures of babyhood."

Miss Cassatt was born in Pittsburg, and is the daughter and sister of well-known Pennsylvania Railroad magnates. The possessor of an independent fortune, and therefore free from those financial worries which are so often the inheritance of the art student, she found no obstacles in the pursuit of her life-work when she decided to travel and study abroad rather than to live in "commercial America." This was thirty years ago, when only the cultured few rather than the unlearned many had time or inclination to devote to the study of esthetics.

That her work is gaining recognition in this country as in France (where she is better known) is evident from the decided interest felt in her

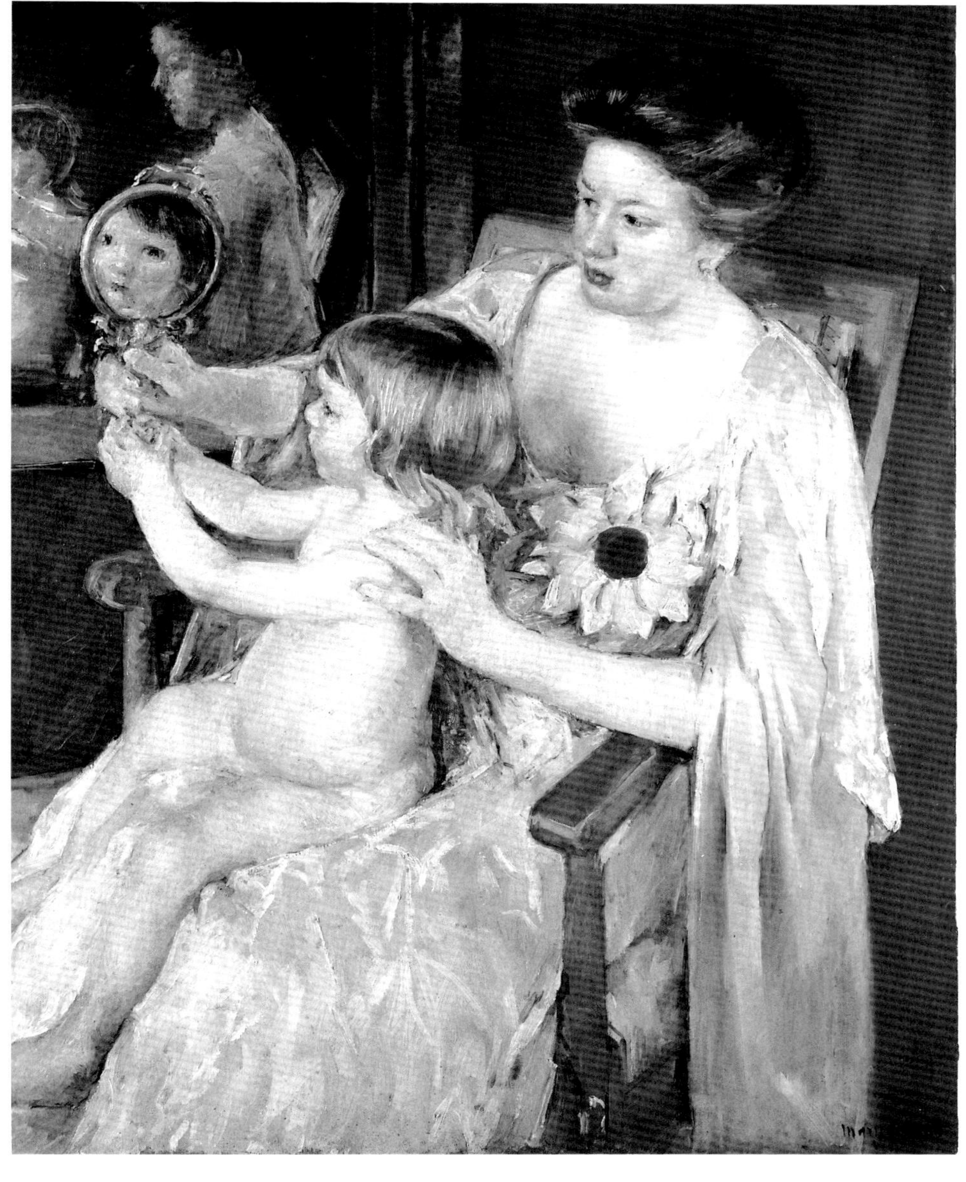

Mother and Child (Mother Wearing a Sunflower on Her Dress). 1905. Oil on canvas. 36 1/4 × 29 in. (92.1 × 73.7 cm). National Gallery of Art. The Chester Dale Collection. Photograph © Board of Trustees, National Gallery of Art, Washington, D.C.

recent visit to America, the first in twelve years, and the second since she left here about 1879. It was the welcoming of a celebrity.

Miss Cassatt has lived in Holland, Spain and Italy. It was in Italy, however, that she received her most profound art impressions, which have influenced her art throughout her career. This is noticeable in her choice of subjects, their arrangement and in her sentiment. Her mothers are Madonnas, "simple, unassuming and unmoved."

At the conclusion of her European travels she settled in Paris, where she made the acquaintance of Degas, the great French impressionist, who early recognized the young painter's ability and from whom she received much encouragement.

Although accepting advice from this master and appreciating his friendship, her art is nevertheless a personal one. This individuality is soon recognized. Her favorite subjects, as said above, are mothers and children, painted with a tender sincerity that never fails to awaken sympathy.

If "an artist's characteristics may be known by his work," one might gain the impression that Miss Cassatt was a tender, gentle, motherly little woman, while the contrary is true. In appearance she is tall and rather large of frame, her manner is decided, she knows what she is about at all times.

The only conventional teaching she ever had was obtained at the Pennsylvania Academy Schools in Philadelphia. She does not think that art, in its true meaning, can be taught. She knows that drawing and the mixing of pigments require a certain amount of training, but she thinks that great art, that power to make the subject live in the canvas, is one that comes not from teachers, but from intimate knowledge, understanding, and love of the work. She recommends that students make copies of the great masters, studying them carefully, and associating only with the best art the world affords.

Very little of Miss Cassatt's time is spent at her apartment in Paris. It is at her château near Chantilly that she loves to paint, where she finds the types that interest her most. Here she is often seen on pleasant mornings driving to fetch her models—peasant women and children—and again at sundown taking them home. She takes little interest in painting the up-to-date society mother. Although at all times she has held aloof from mere prettiness in art, her mothers are triumphs of maternal tenderness, and her children irresistible in their naturalness. It is this naturalness that appeals to Miss Cassatt, and this is why she prefers living in the country. There she has easy access to the types she loves, rather than in the city, where, owing to conventional education which makes them self-conscious and therefore not picturesque as models, she can not find that exquisite charm of utter abandon in children.

Her subjects are not always beautiful, as the layman sees beauty, but are at any rate real and human, just the kind of mothers and children that one knows. Their subtle charm of expression, combined with a masterly handling of draperies brought together in exquisite harmonies of tone, compels admiration from even the severest critics.

In all of Miss Cassatt's work are vigor and directness. For this reason she is often called an impressionist. She is not that, however, in its strictest meaning, as her works have more form and modeling than is usually present in what is generally understood as impressionism.

"In all of her works," says William Walton, "may be felt a certain sentiment, or charm or poetry—something much more than mere good painting—the feeling of nature, of Summer, air and space, of the charm of green apple-orchards or parks and very frequently the mystery of mother love and the pulchritude of the baby."

It is true that she can not reconcile herself to smooth, hard painting of beautifully tinted flesh, as in her large grasp of the subject she must delve below surface effects. She is not satisfied with the coarse treatment, but by that innate feeling for flesh-texture and judicious brushwork, gained by years of careful study, she portrays flesh, the health and vigor of which can as easily be imagined by an observation of her canvas as by a study of the subject in real life. This is where her art is individual, where, though preserving all the tenderness, she leaves out the "little things.". . .

Oil is not the only medium in which Miss Cassatt has distinguished herself. Many of her most important works are painted in pastel, which is her favorite mode of expression, as in it she is able to obtain beautiful harmony of line, to which she devotes great attention. Her success with dry-point etchings has won for her a place in the ranks with the best etchers of modern times. Some years ago she amused herself by producing dry-point etchings combined with color-prints and obtained interesting results. It was a slow and expensive process, as she sometimes devoted as much as two years to one subject. In line and composition this branch of her art shows the influence of Japanese masters.

Two of her canvases hang in the Luxembourg Galleries in Paris, and thus far she is the only American woman who has received this coveted honor. Many of her works are in collections of the best connoisseurs. Three years ago she accepted the decoration of the Legion d'Honneur in Paris, but other honors she has persistently refused. Her feeling in this matter was shown in this country during her recent visit when she refused to accept one which was offered her.

When the French Prime Minister, M. Clemenceau, in a recent speech referred to her as *"une de nos gloires artistiques"* he undoubtedly voiced the sentiment of the art public of France. Although Miss Cassatt's art is essen-

Georges Eugène Benjamin Clemenceau (1841–1929), French statesman, physician, publisher, and writer, was premier of France from 1906 to 1909 and again from 1917 to 1920. He founded the radical newspaper "La Justice" in 1881.

"une de nos gloires artistiques"; one of our artistic glories.

tially French, and it has been said so often that she is better known and appreciated in France than in this country, still the greater number of her pictures are owned by Americans either here or in Europe.

ANDRÉ MELLÉRIO

From *L'Art et les artistes*

Cassatt's American Character

November 1910

Whenever innovative spirits meet in a certain age, and form an art movement, their effect is doubled. On the one hand, they themselves work together in the direction they envisage, on the other, they influence a number of their artist contemporaries. Among the latter, some imitate slavishly, from either weakness or fashion. But there are others as well—they are the best—who, understanding the true lesson of the endeavor they admire, achieve a greater self-knowledge and a total liberation of their own personality.

Such were the consequences of that important movement in painting that flourished at the end of the nineteenth century, and to which was given the name, one it did not devise itself, of *Impressionism*. It was first and foremost a protest waged against the tyrannical yoke of the reigning Academism. In its most positively creative aspect, it appears to be—especially in Monet's works, which are a very significant expression of it—the advent of a brighter painting, as well as a keen study of atmospheric plays of light.

Mary Cassatt came, one might say naturally, to the group of the Impressionists, because her vision already predisposed her to a brightness of the palette, and because ultimately she was impatient with pointless obstacles and fervent about the freedom of art. But when she decided to educate herself seriously, to give her personality a more grounded and defined quality, the Master whose works interested her deeply, whose advice she sought—usually sparing, but lavished upon her—was Degas.

Because her temperament was entirely different, and she had no need to be concerned about preserving her own originality, so spontaneous and lively was she, Mary Cassatt was able to profit from that always formidable closeness with an artist of great talent, as well as of harsh character and unyielding will. To be sure, she never seemed a docile satellite, either in her choice of subjects or in the overall appearance of her painting, any more than in her sentiment and its expression. But she was a conscientious disciple, and learned from Degas an attention to form and movement, a horror of approximation and useless detail. She shared his deep and respectful admiration for nature, and also his tireless determination to fight nature in order to express it better, the double secret of those who have endured as masters. May we also add, and this is worthy of note, the artist's passionate enthusiasm for Ingres's deliberate and incisive work, her fellow-feeling for Courbet's robust painting and sincere realism?

We have noted the important points that one needs to know in order to understand Mary Cassatt; now let us look more closely at her and her work.

Mary Cassatt is American, part and distantly French in her family background. She was born in Pittsburgh, Pennsylvania. She first studied in Philadelphia. But the inadequacy of the instruction urged her to seek an

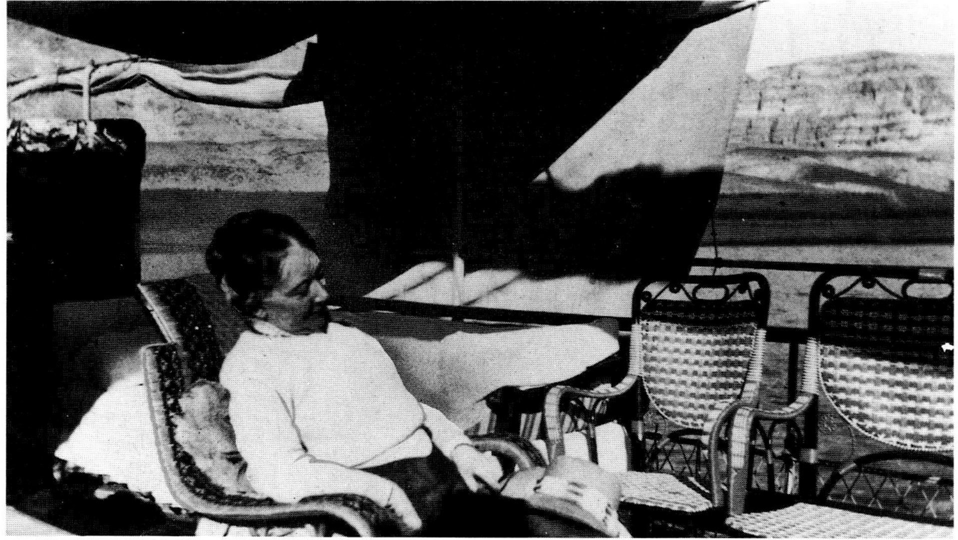

Photograph of Mary Cassatt asleep on the Cassatts' dahabeah (houseboat) on the Nile, Egypt. 1911. Photograph courtesy of the Archives of American Art, Smithsonian Institution. The Frederick A. Sweet Papers. Location of original unknown.

artistic direction elsewhere. She traveled successively in Italy, Spain, and Holland. It was in France that she met and frequented Monet, Renoir, Pissarro, and especially Degas.

Along with the Impressionist group, she showed her work publicly in special exhibitions, misunderstood and disparaged at the time, and which have since become watersheds in the development of French painting in the final years of the last century.

It was not until 1893, however, when an important collection of Mary Cassatt's works were presented in the Durand-Ruel galleries, that one was truly able to appreciate the artist's worth and the true place she held.

At the time, we had the opportunity to evaluate her work in some depth: "The source of Miss Cassatt's inspiration—we said—is women and children.

"She has studied them in depth, in their common existence, in all their moments. An intimate, necessary bond unites these beings: they live through each other. Their facial expressions are related. . . . What Miss Cassatt has sought in women is less their delicate grace, that fragile flower of fleeting sensuality, than the austere, yet ennobling aspect of motherhood. . . .

"She has not chosen its conventional, easily melodramatized aspects, nor has she exaggerated the purely material details. . . . Amid scrupulously maintained gardens and soberly yet tastefully decorated interiors, the artist unfolds the myriad scenes of this moving drama, which, in their simple and profound tenderness, child and mother never cease to perform for each other. She has captured the instinctual gestures of a life at its lisping beginnings, opening its naive, astonished pupils to the light. Glimmers of intelligence, harbingers of the future, appear in these brilliantly shining eyes, as yet unclouded by life. Those tears that burn later on, merely brighten the sparkle of the child's gaze. Already the being of a higher order is breaking through its purely animal grace, innocent shamelessness, and unreasoned movements. Similarly, the humble pursuits to which mothers devote themselves take on dignity from the sense of duty that makes them seem necessary, I might even say sacred. It has been well said that Miss Cassatt has painted only women 'with steady souls.' "

Whenever the artist escapes the nursery, she is able to give her figures an ease that is both simple and elegant, without conceit or affectation. "Miss Cassatt knows and understands the ladies of society—because she herself is one. She conveys them and renders them with rare felicity and perfect accuracy, because her nature is that of an artist as well. She has the self-respect and refined breeding of a lady, that care for her dignity and noble pride that command esteem." Young girls, too, so difficult to fathom

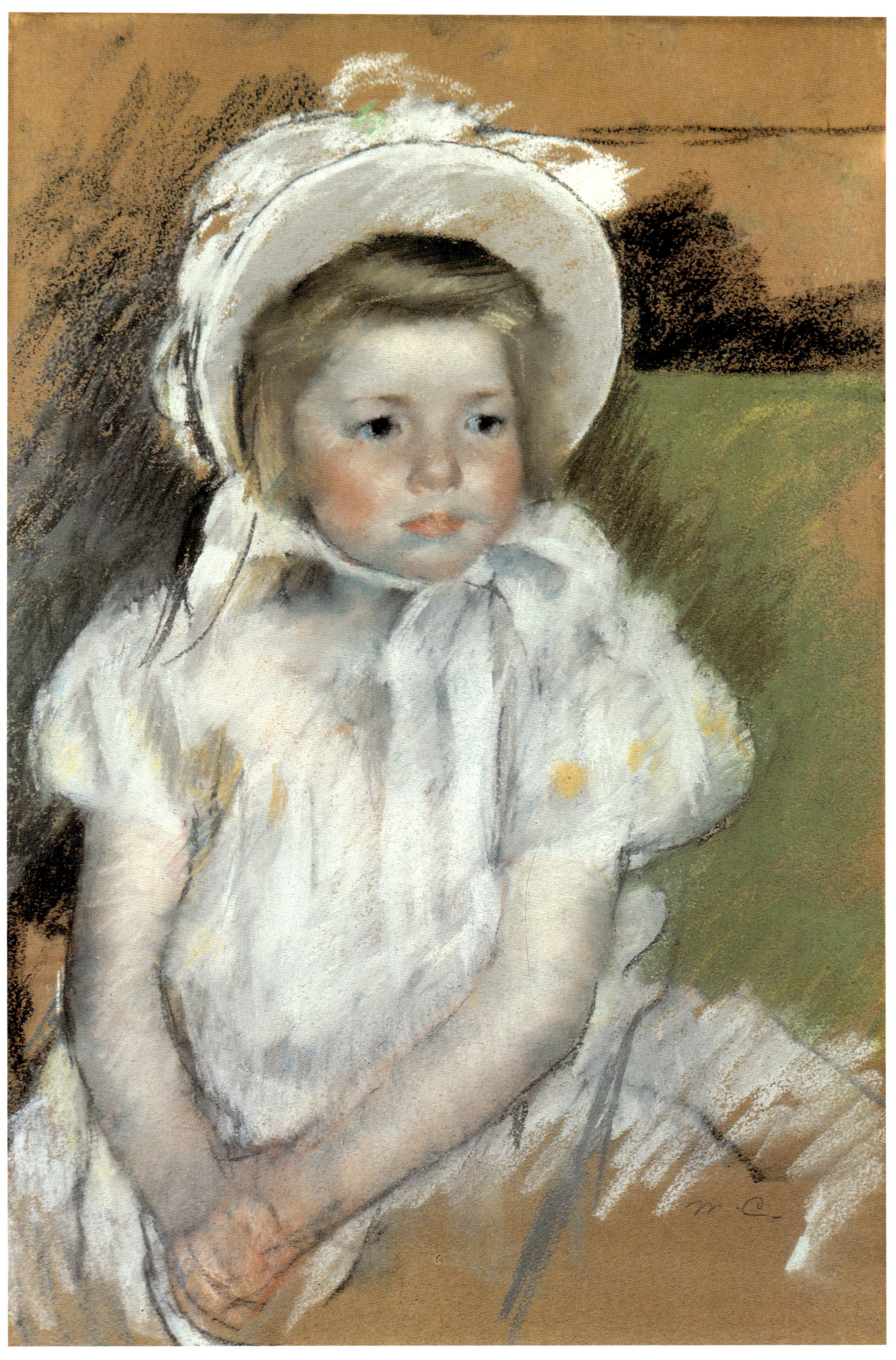

COLORPLATE 97. *Simone in a White Bonnet.* 1901. Pastel on paper. 25 ½ × 16 ½ in. (64.7 × 41.9 cm). Private collection. Photograph courtesy of Richard York Gallery, New York.

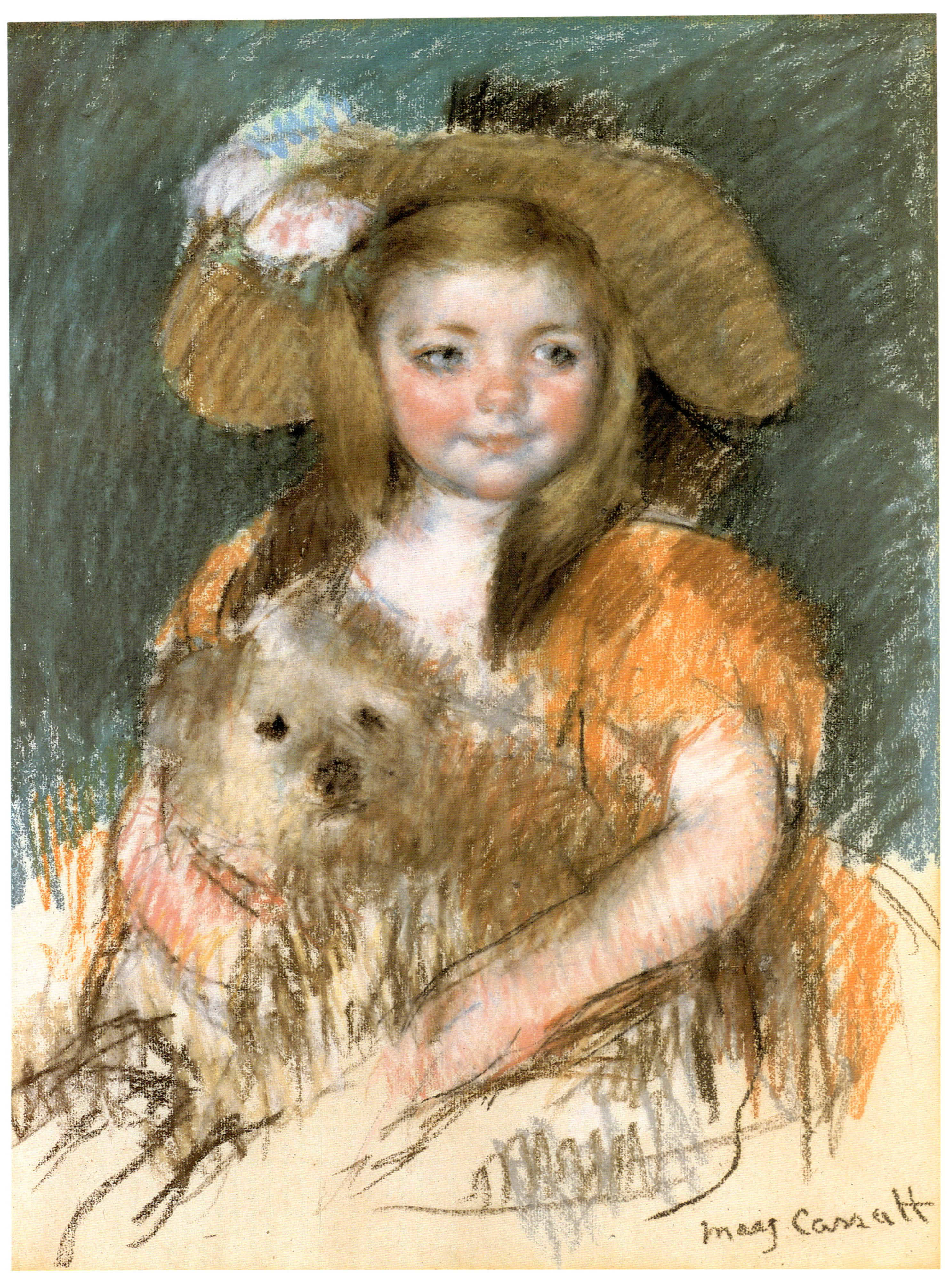

COLORPLATE 98. *Child Holding a Dog.* c. 1901. Pastel on paper. 25 ½ × 19 ½ in. (64.7 × 49.5 cm). Wadsworth Atheneum, Hartford. Gift of James Junius Goodwin.

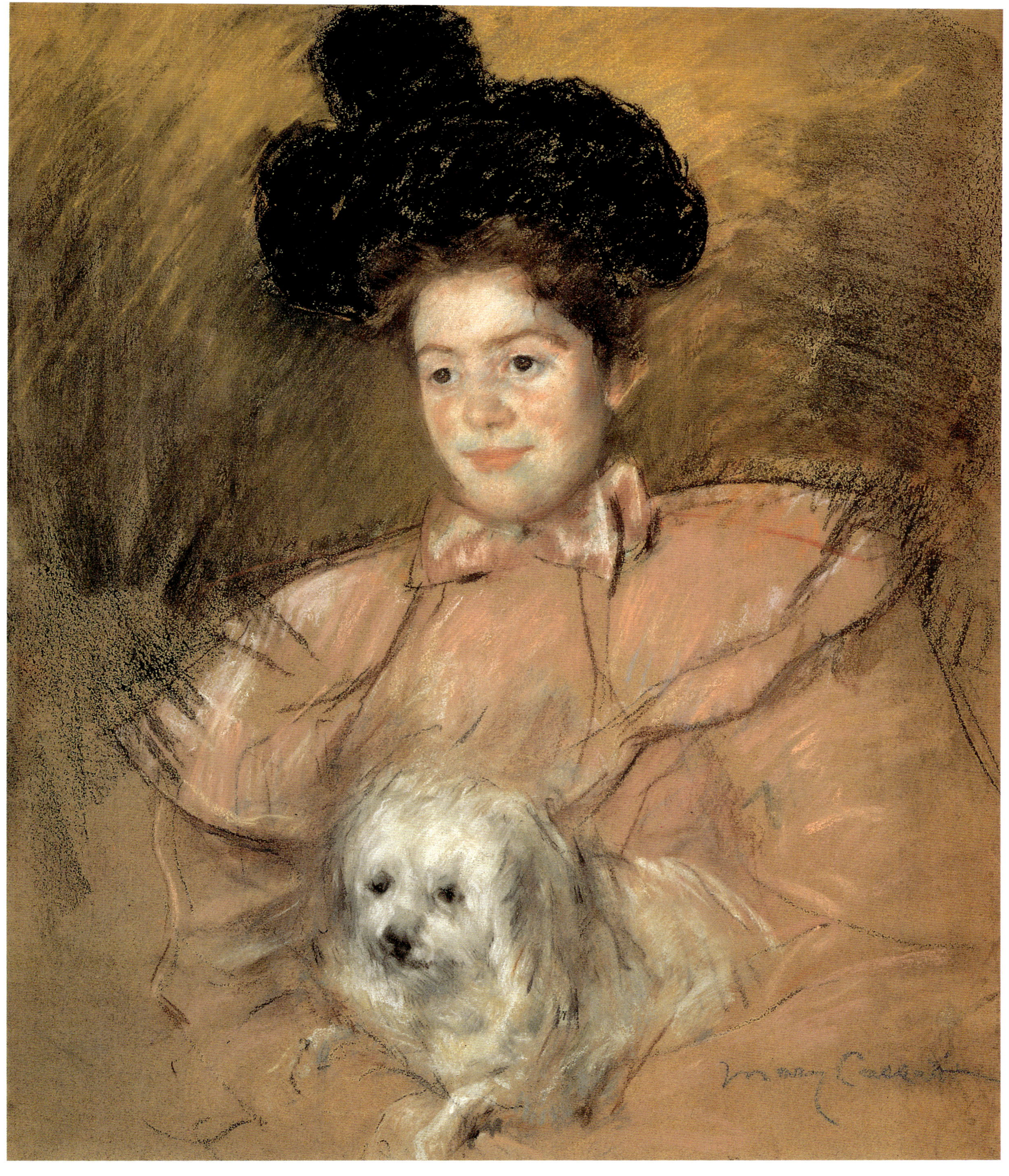

COLORPLATE 99. *Woman in Raspberry Costume Holding a Dog.* c. 1901. Pastel on paper. 28 ⅞ × 23 ½ in. (72.7 × 59.6 cm). Hirshhorn Museum and Sculpture Garden, Smithsonian Institution. Gift of Joseph H. Hirshhorn. Photograph: Lee Stalsworth.

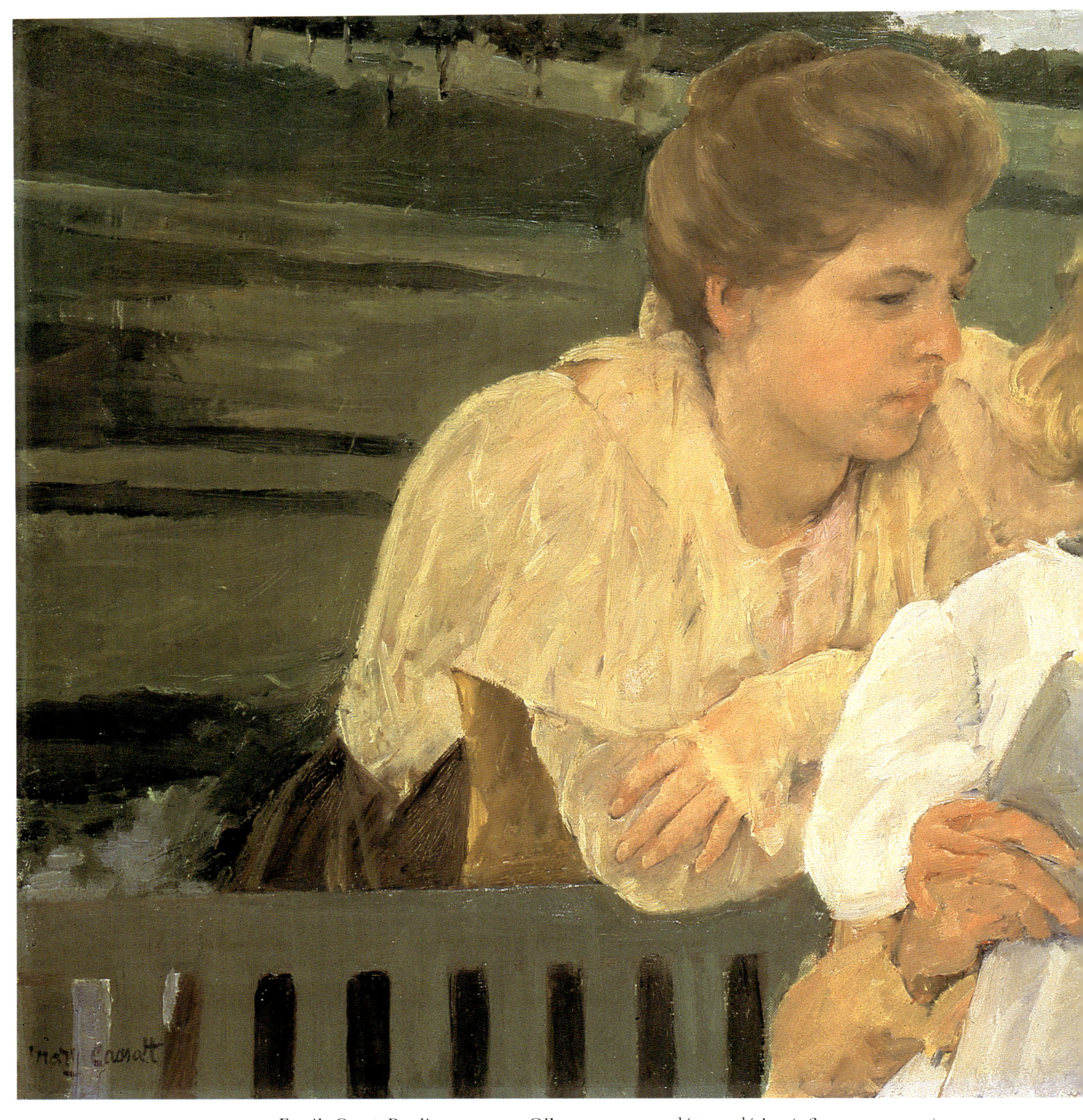

COLORPLATE 100. *Family Group Reading*. c. 1901. Oil on canvas. 22 ¼ × 44 ¼ in. (56.5 × 112.4 cm). Philadelphia Museum of Art. Given by Mr. and Mrs. J. Watson Webb.

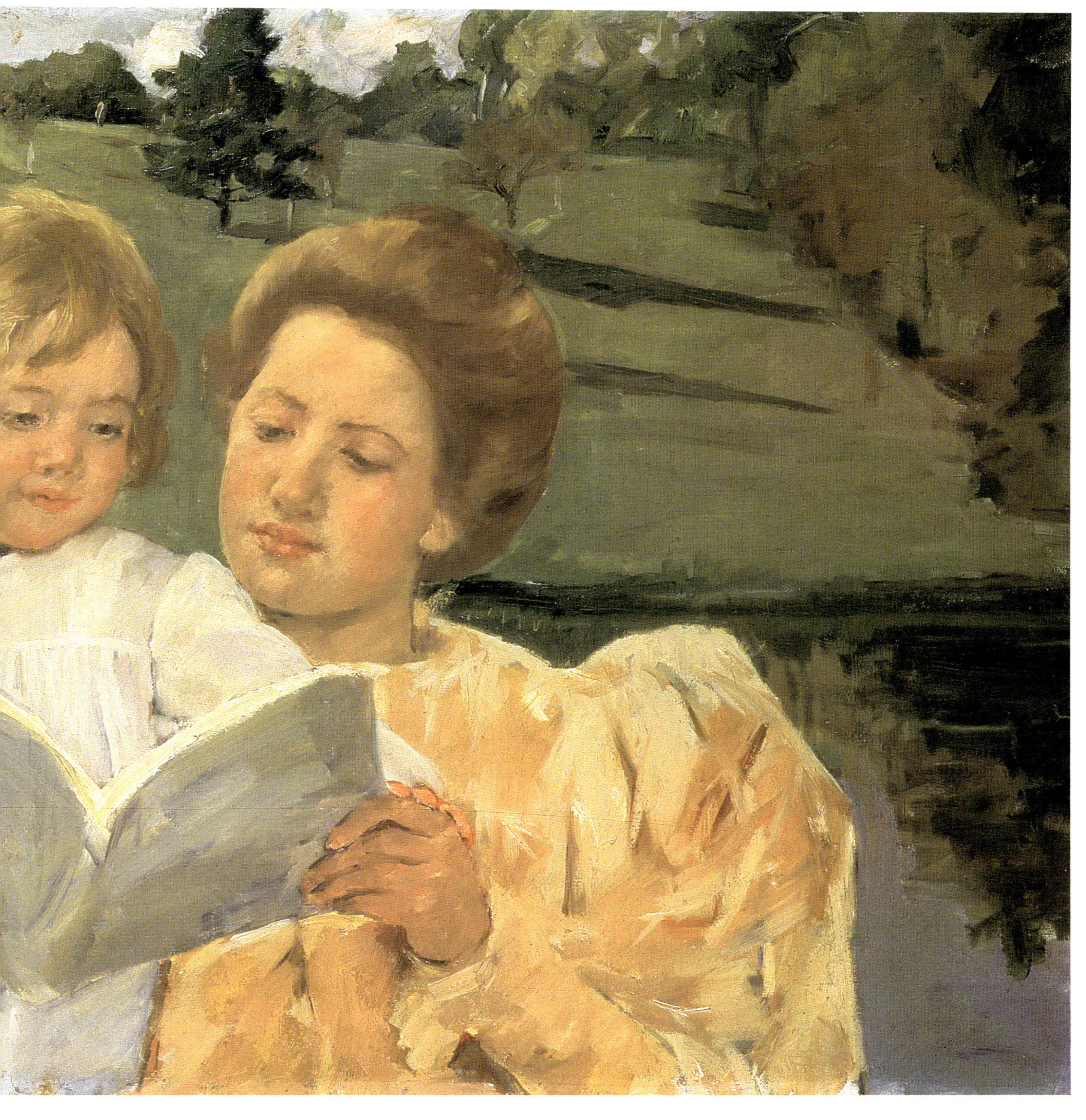

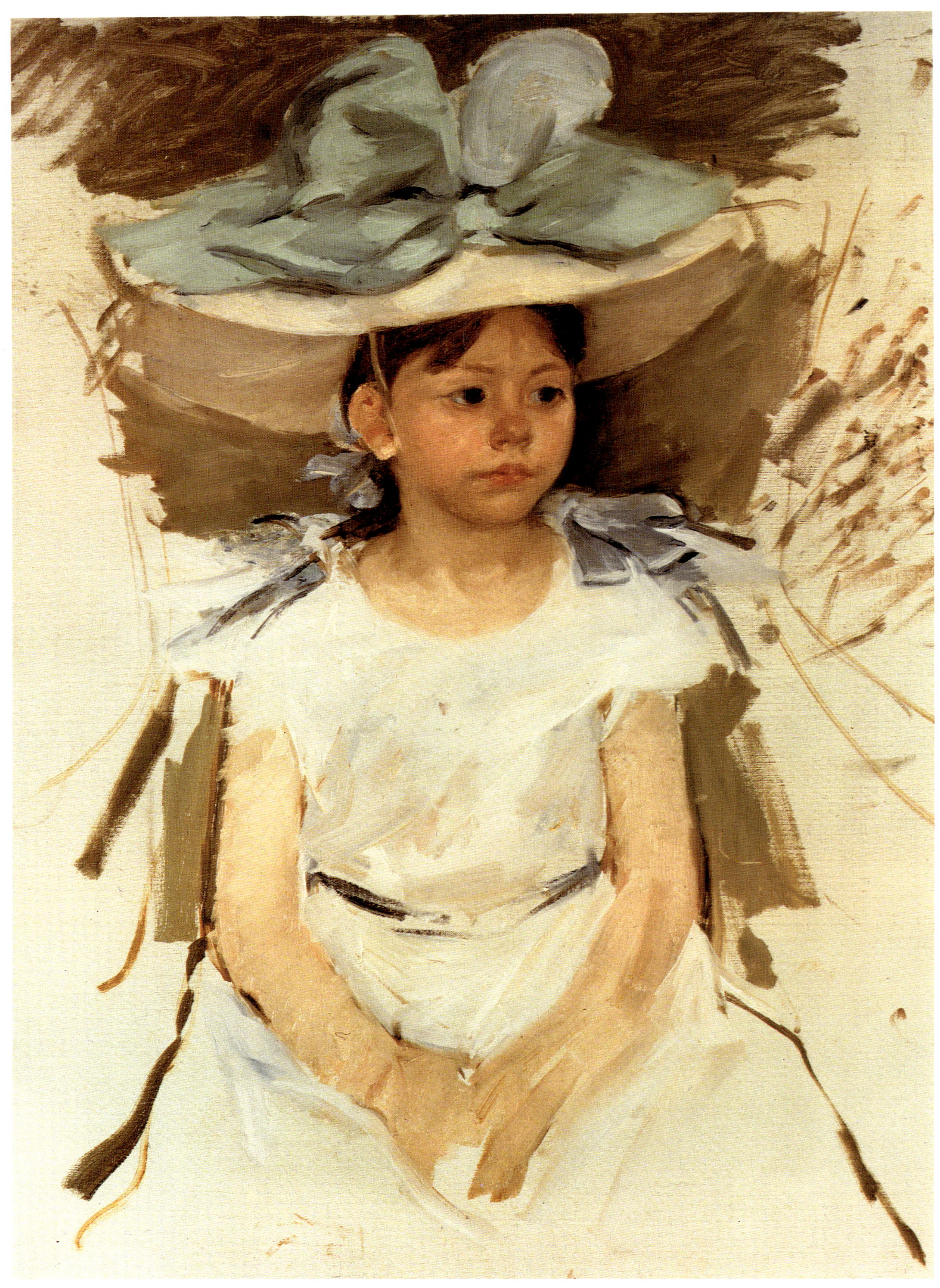

COLORPLATE 101. *Ellen Mary Cassatt in a Big Blue Hat.* c. 1905. 32 × 24 in. (81.2 × 61 cm). Williams College Museum of Art, Williamstown, Massachusetts. On extended loan from Dr. Herchel Smith.

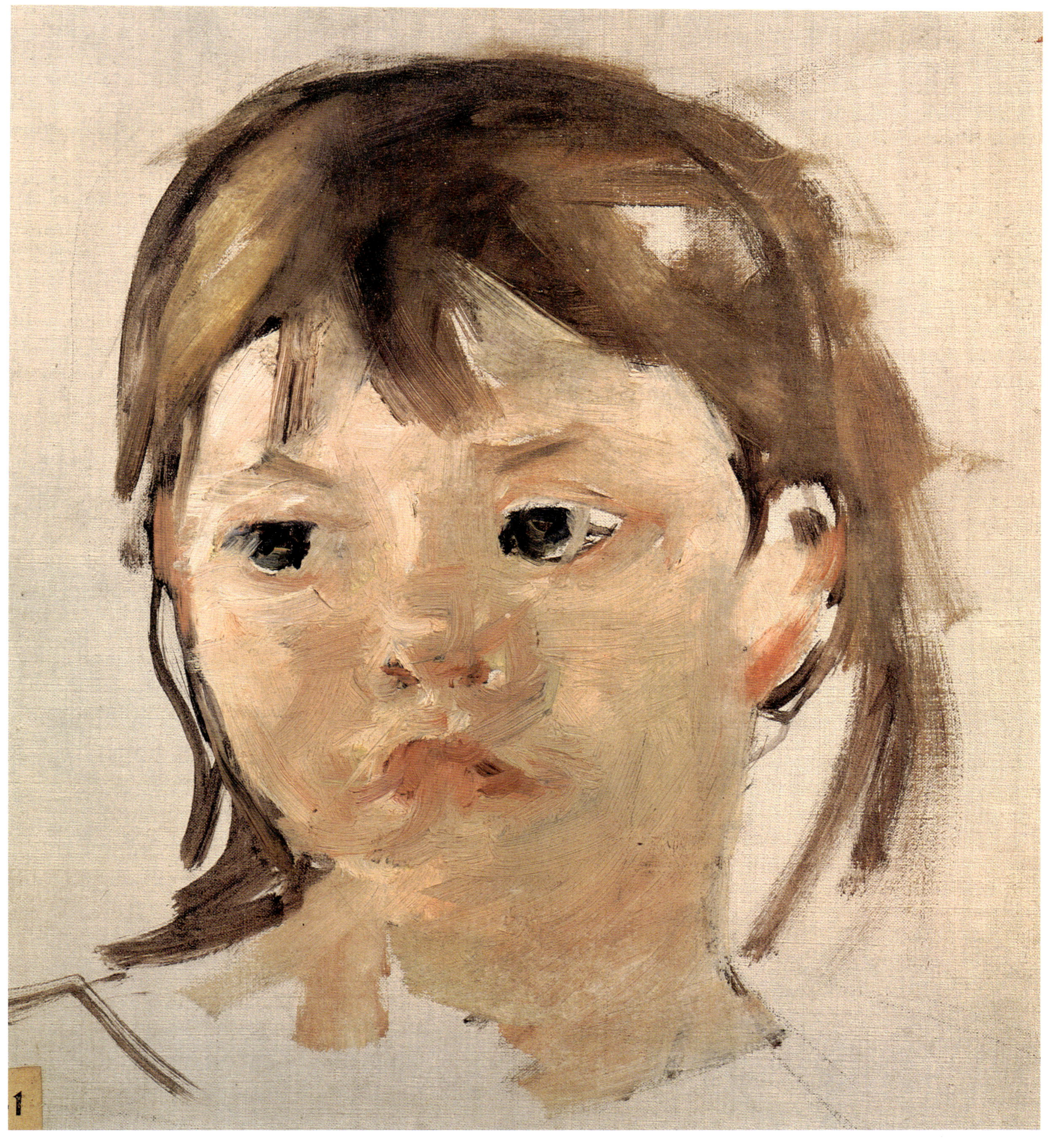

COLORPLATE 102. *Head of a Young Girl (Sketch of Ellen Mary Cassatt).* c. 1899. Oil on canvas. 8 ¾ × 8 in. (22.5 × 20.5 cm). Private collection, Paris. Photograph: Giraudon/Art Resource, New York.

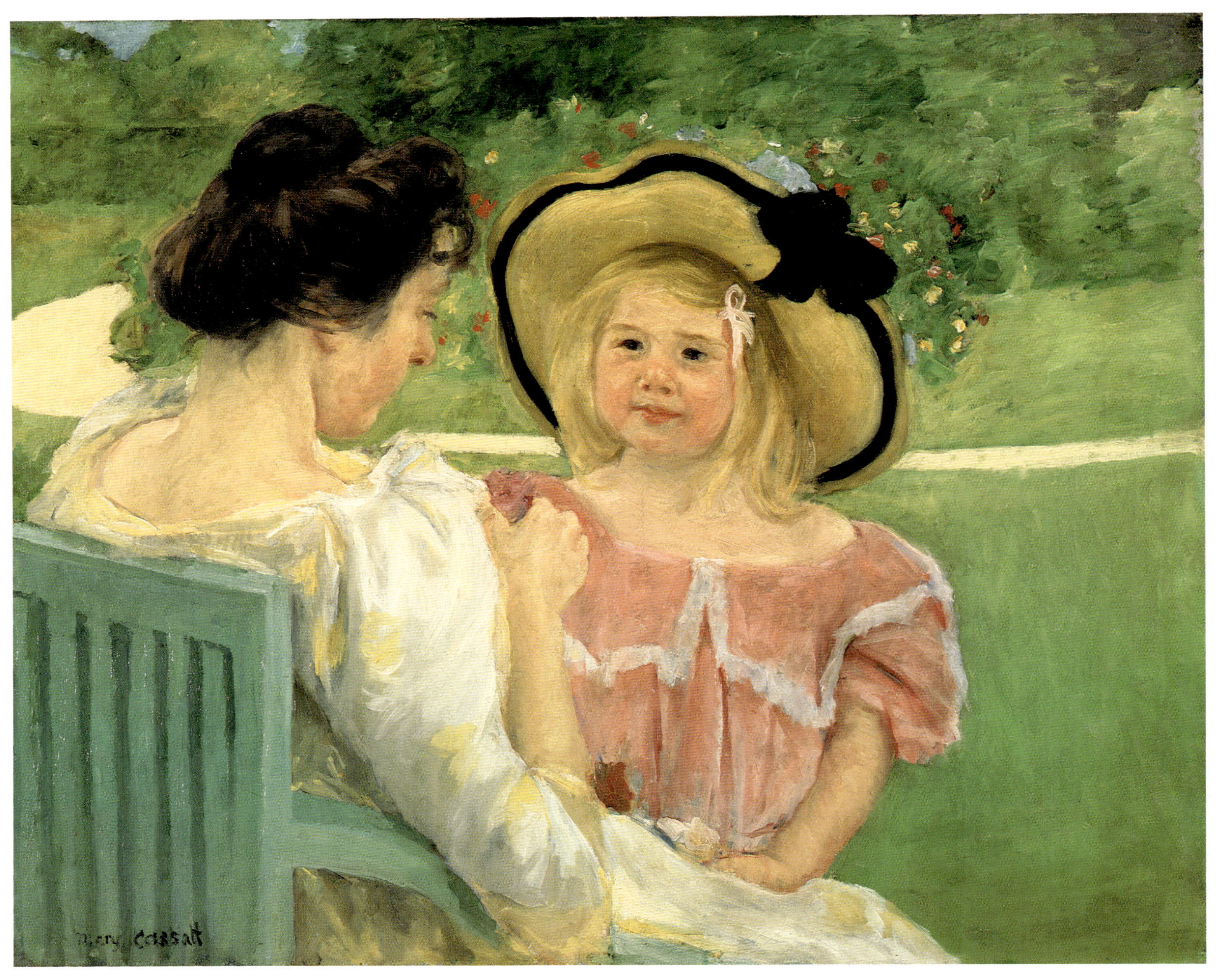

COLORPLATE 103. *Simone and Her Mother in the Garden.* c. 1904. Oil on canvas. 26 ¾ × 32 ½ in. (67.9 × 82.6 cm). The Detroit Institute of Arts. Gift of Dr. Ernest G. Stillman. Photograph © The Detroit Institute of Arts.

and to render in their entirety, appear in her work with an observed truth and in a natural style.

But whatever individuals are portrayed, in Mary Cassatt's work they always exude the fresh, full health that derives from an unblemished and robust heredity. This native vigor preserves itself further by means of "a rational education, whose goal is to maintain the human body's equilibrium by the lawful exercise of its powers." The artist advances instinctively, one might almost say without suspecting the existence of anything else, toward what is healthy, frank, open—absolutely in the same way that she loves a limpid atmosphere, and a decent and cheerful background.

The material means used are always suited to her manner of seeing and feeling. The paintings, like the pastels, look broadly drawn, with no empty affectations, or overworkings of the trade; the simplicity of the deliberate effects is set off by accuracy alone. One finds all these qualities as well in two means of expression that the artist used, when she saw fit to take them on, with a very personal acuity: drypoint and color engraving . . .

Mary Cassatt is a truly original artist, and an eminent member of her race.

These are the two essential traits that we feel sum her up. Aside from those considerations that we have revealed, they raise a problem of a higher order that we must point out.

North America is a young country, a new power. In its barely more than century-old career as a nation, it has nevertheless already lived an extremely eventful existence, and displayed intense activity. Composed of diverse elements, and often bringing in ethnically and historically distinct types, it recast them again in its melting pot. Knowing and frequenting old Europe, it has no intention of reallying itself with it—but on the contrary, to leave it behind in its surging progress, and to amaze it with the abundance of its productive resources.

While, in its beginnings, its efforts overall were concentrated especially in the industrial and commercial domain, the lucid spirit of the Americans soon realized that there were forces of another order that must be studied and fathomed—in order to possess them, as well.

And among those powers of the intelligence, there was Art. Across the Ocean, it might be considered without serious respect, as an amusing accessory, a refined, superfluous, and elegant ornament, or just another imported article. Or else, on the contrary, when their eyes opened to the light, they might confine themselves modestly to an astonished but fruitless admiration for the past. Pressing their boldness to the utmost, they might even attempt to produce something, after the fashion of still intrinsically fruitful modern peoples, such as France today.

Between these two reefs, easily recognized and equally to be avoided, there was yet a way. This one, attractive, to be sure, led to a noble purpose: to express by one's own means, the sense and emotions of a personal life, endowed with clearly defined traits. But though a specific direction and persevering energies are—perhaps!—enough to create a burgeoning industry, that was not at all true of Art. A sincere and truly fruitful artistic movement does not emerge on demand: it only flourishes if the spirit—that spirit that, it has been said, blows whither it will—comes in to give life to a creation that without it is pointless and dead.

And that is why Mary Cassatt's oeuvre is not only important in itself, but also opens up a horizon of possibility. This artist possesses an original inspiration that is representative of her time and race. Here is possibility materialized, already the realization of a direct and significant expression of the American character. From it, a great people, avid for every sphere of activity, may rightfully hope to add its part of artistic creation to the long past of the old nations, a glorious patrimony that humanity is called upon to ceaselessly increase.

From *The Craftsman*

"Mary Cassatt's Achievement"

March 1911

Love, absolute, complete, that vital creative quality which builds towering cathedrals, bridges Nature's chasms with fairy iron structures, that pours, through song, up to the edge of the infinite, that cherishes and nourishes little children—to portray this in art, to cover canvas with so beautiful a message of the supreme emotion, is indeed splendid accomplishment for artist and humanity.

To depict love, in its tenderest expression—contented mother and happy child—to reveal it in a mother's eyes, in the kind curves of her gracious body, to express the unutterable peace of accomplished maternity, and its response in the absolute confidence, joy and abandon of the child nestled eagerly to the warm encompassing heart, to do this with clarity of vision and surety of stroke and richness of tone, this is the art of Mary Cassatt, American born, French trained, wholly impersonal in the breadth of work, strikingly individual, yet national in the source of her inspiration.

It is an American mother and child whom Mary Cassatt paints, though her technique is of Paris, the free, fearless, forceful French technique of a decade ago. It is never the dramatic mother or the picturesque child she seeks, but the universal bond between mother and child. You feel how tenderly, how profoundly these mothers love their babies, and how adoringly the babies turn and cling to the mothers. It is beautiful because romance is there. The feet of the little children are treading the first days of life in holy places.

How can one paint love? Joy, easily; fear, with a few black strokes—but love which seems an ineffable light revealing the joy of the spirit, how can it be painted in the smile of a mother and the tender response in the faces of the young?

Oddly enough Miss Cassatt seems to accomplish this mystery of art with the boldest, most audacious methods. Her color is vigorous, at a first glance flamboyant (not in tone, but in handling), there is no seeking aid from her tools. She does not bring to her subject a lyrical brush, wearing vague poetical tints; none of the usual symbols for youth or love are employed. Apparently, to her, maternal love is not a pale blue emotion, to be draped with clouds and expressed with anaemic physique.

Life is richer than that. To one who knows, motherhood cannot be circled by a halo or made nobler by the attenuation of a Mediaeval saint. It is the incomparably greatest experience of womankind, the final joy, compounded of the keenest sorrow the world holds. It is this that Mary Cassatt's wonderful art portrays, with all the force, virility and freedom that her great gift, trained to rare skill places at her command. She has apprehended through her clear vision the spiritual height and human breadth of motherhood, the greatest miracle, often revealed to the least deserving.

If art is to portray life, and it is only of lasting value as it sincerely expresses the realities of life, then Mary Cassatt has established her preeminence beyond recall, for she reveals with intimate understanding the great romance of life.

Although her first experience in art influence lay in Italy, that land of pictured mothers and babes, Miss Cassatt's art is remote from the Mediaeval Madonna of tradition. It is not the deification of motherhood, one feels on these canvases, rather, the great possibilities of human achievement.

After Italy, Miss Cassatt traveled through Spain and Holland, interested, curious, alert, responsive, adding to her store of knowledge and appreciation, but without finding the call to stay and work in close companion-

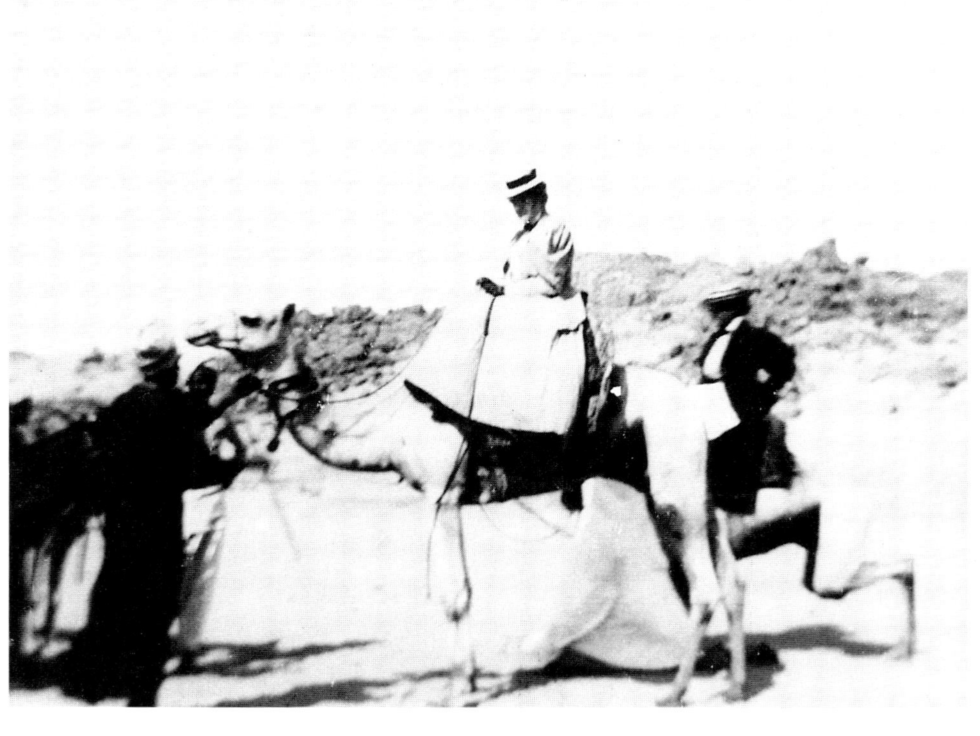

Photograph of Mary Cassatt on a camel during her trip to Egypt. 1911. Photograph courtesy of the Estate of Lois B. Thayer.

ship—a call which reached her ultimately in Paris, where she met and worked with Monet, Renoir, Pissarro and Degas. Of this group of liberal thinkers and enlightened artists, it was Degas, with his splendid humanity and forceful personality, who most influenced Mary Cassatt's work, and who recognized in her a spirit open to the big forces, a personality absolutely sincere, possessing a gift at once original in inspiration and universal in scope.

Although Mary Cassatt has made France her home, has accepted Paris as her standard of execution, strangely enough she has retained a personality definitely and staunchly American. The French artists with whom she has worked, count her one of themselves in attainment, yet recognize the inevitable difference of her point of view. Mellério writing of her achievement in *L'Art et les Artists* says, "She is wholly original, and belongs to her own race. Her art expresses her nation, young, full of new force; she is without prejudice, vital; although she is familiar with the culture of the old world, there is the freshness of a new nation in her art. Her inspiration is from her own epoch, her own race. She expresses the character of the American people, a people awakening to all that is best in art and eager to possess it in abundance."

Miss Cassatt has lived so long away from us and has worked so quietly, purposely avoiding the superficial popularity which comes from self-exploitation that outside the world of artists and lovers of art, her achievement in the progress of art history in America has not been fully understood.

Thus while appreciating the fine freedom to be gained from the methods of the true impressionist, she has remained consistently, if unconsciously, American. Her art belongs to us, and is a possession to treasure. In a recent exhibition of her work at the Durand-Ruel Galleries in New York a rare opportunity was afforded to study her painting of mothers and children. . . .

In *The Family* . . . we have a picture of a mother with her babe; the little girl who is seated to the left holds a carnation in her hand with which she had caught the baby's wondering attention. Yet this little girl is not looking at the flower,—she is not thinking of it as a plaything; instead, she seems almost wistfully conscious of mother-love within her own little soul, obliv-

COLORPLATE 64

ious to everything but an unconscious impression of that, fleeting as perhaps it may be. It is this very power to arrest such fleeting moments and make them live forever that adds to Miss Cassatt's extraordinary gifts.

There is a more conscious type of motherhood depicted in *The Mother's Caress,* and a more conscious type of childhood. In this picture we see only a part of the mother's face—we feel *sure* it *is* the mother!—for the child's chubby hand hides its features from us. The mother here is more a type of a woman of the people, and the child, too, has the suggestion of a sweet plebeianism about him. One of Miss Cassatt's loveliest paintings is *The Breakfast in Bed,* which . . . reveals one of her happiest choices of subject. COLORPLATE 81

Perhaps no painting in the retrospective exhibition of Miss Cassatt's work received more attention than *Children Playing with a Cat.* This canvas reveals completely Miss Cassatt's skill with light limpid quality.

The[se] pictures . . . illustrate Miss Cassatt's freedom from the convention of detail in accessories. All the backgrounds are luminous with atmospheric suggestion, even definiteness, but detail never obtrudes. This has always been noticeable in her pastels, for it must not be forgotten that Miss Cassatt has achieved work of supreme excellence in this medium.

But with all her acknowledged incomparable technique, what ranks Mary Cassatt's work with the great masters of painting, with Monet, Degas, Whistler is her power to penetrate into the supreme truths of life and bring them to light through her art for the world to better understand.

From *Current Literature*

Clemenceau on Cassatt

February 1909

When the French Prime Minister, M. Clemenceau, referred in a recent speech to Miss Mary Cassatt as "one of our artistic glories," he undoubtedly voiced the sentiment prevailing in France with regard to the gifted lady who is conceded, in artistic circles, to be the greatest woman-painter of American birth now living. Miss Cassatt was born in Pittsburg, but chose for artistic reasons to live in France. She has lately visited America for the first time in twelve years, and an exhibition of her pictures, soon to be held in Boston, promises to bring her work prominently before the public.

ACHILLE SEGARD

From *Mary Cassatt: Un Peintre des enfants et des mères*

Cassatt's Legacy

1913

From among so many Schools and so many artists who sought her distinction, she chose the French. Her example will long be persuasive.

By her work and her personal influence, she helped to guide her compatriots onto the best path for them. When the American School has become fully individualized, this period of transition will be seen to have been indispensable, and credit will be given those who will have helped avoid errors of orientation.

Miss Mary Cassatt will have had another virtue, and a fundamental one. She has given her compatriots an example of an aristocratic art that stands in distinct contrast to the rough tendencies of certain recent Schools that one could call democratic.

Miss Mary Cassatt occupies an important place in the French School, where she won her rank, and in particular in the group of the Impressionists.

It may be that she has devised nothing new technically. The great pioneers were Manet and Courbet. The great analyzer of the variations in outdoor light was Manet.

Miss Cassatt received from Manet, Courbet, and Degas the tradition that she has enriched with works that are entirely her own. From the collective endeavor of the group to which she belonged, she also received her palette, that is, the particular scale of tones that, by excluding certain colors, give certain others their predominance. She is counted among the first followers of the new doctrine. She has discovered applications of its general principles that are her own.

Her identity as a painter of figures—among so many landscape artists—and her specialization in a particular order of sentiments tend to give her a particular profile within the group. Her novel qualities as draftsman and colorist, her nuanced sensitivity, the often amazing mastery of her execution, or, in a word, the personal accent and the beauty of these pictures assure her one of the first places in the history of this period of French art. Preferring solitude for reasons of taste as much as temperament, she made the most of the great collective endeavor called "Impressionism," and anyone who would write the history of this group must study her work. She has been one of the painters of modern life. Her pictures have captured for a long time hence—if not forever—moments of our artistic history. Served by an instinct that she has consistently subordinated to reason's control, with an intellectual culture all the more remarkable because it has become increasingly rare among contemporary painters, she has observed as a painter, she has felt as a painter, and she has executed as a virtuoso. Her work is powerful and original, and its sentiments are very fresh. It contributes to the glorification of the great impulses of the human soul and in particular of motherly feeling. Intuition and will achieve harmony. In her work, visual emotion is coupled with intellectual emotion and a sentimental impulse. She portrays feminine grace touched with manly energy, in a group with no pretensions to charm. If she had been less modest, she could have been, very early on, the connection between the great pioneers and the public that is more sensitive to grace and gentleness than to rough force and the harshness of reality. She did not wish to allow a misunderstanding to arise. She preferred to keep her place, which is not first place, but very close to first. In her life and in her work, she has been delicate, energetic, and scrupulous. She leaves behind fine pictures and a fine example.

From *The Evening Post Saturday Magazine*
"At the Loan Exhibition for Woman Suffrage"
April 3, 1915

The accompanying reproductions of pictures by Edgar Degas and Mary Cassatt give only a hint of what the fortunate visitor will see at the loan exhibition to be held for the benefit of woman suffrage at the Knoedler Galleries, 556 Fifth Avenue, from April 7 to April 24, inclusive. Both of these artists will be exceptionally represented, for many collectors of their works have come forward generously to make the exhibition notable. There will also be, in addition to the works by the two modern masters, a number of famous old masters. No free tickets are to be issued for the exhibition, but as it will be of great importance to students to see it, a number of patrons of the arts have bought tickets to be distributed in certain schools and organizations. Checks for this purpose, as well as for the private view, can be sent to Mrs. H.O. Havemeyer, 1 East 66th Street, or to the Knoedler Galleries.

On April 6, at the private view, Mrs. Havemeyer will speak briefly on Miss Cassatt and Degas, and, as she has known them both for many years, her intimate and informal talk will be most illuminating. The admission fee for the private view is five dollars and for subsequent days one dollar, the proceeds to be devoted to the cause of woman suffrage.

In this connection it may be remembered that Mary Cassatt is a firm believer in woman suffrage and is all the more interested, for this reason, in the coming exhibition. It has even been said that she has refused to have her pictures shown except for this cause. Among the museums which have acquired her paintings are the Metropolitan Museum, the Luxembourg Gallery, the Corcoran Gallery, the Wilstach Gallery, the Worcester Museum, the Rhode Island School of Design, and the Art Institute in Chicago. In 1904 she was made a Chevalier of the Legion of Honor of France. The exhibition will show the development of her art over a period of fully thirty years.

Her pictures will be seen together with those by Degas in the large gallery at Knoedler's, the other two galleries being reserved for the carefully selected group of old masters. There will be approximately fifty pictures in the large gallery, and Degas, as well as Miss Cassatt, will be presented in an unequalled manner, which will illustrate the different periods of his development. In spite of the universal fame which Degas has long had, the general public is not as familiar with his work as it is with that of many of his contemporaries. Monet, Manet, and Renoir are seen here in regularly recurring exhibitions, but the same is not true of Degas. One has to go into private collections to see those extraordinary examples of his genius for drawing that have placed him, in the opinion of so many, at the very head of the late nineteenth-century artists. Our museums, too, have shown little enough foresight in acquiring his work, and, looking back, it seems remarkable that they did not have the wisdom years ago to appeal to Mary Cassatt's judgment, as so many private collectors have done.

The exhibition will include about eighteen old masters, all of them works of importance. Five are by Rembrandt, while rare examples of the work of Vermeer, Terborch, Rubens, Bronzino, Peter de Hooche, Holbein, Coello, and others are to be shown. It has been requested that no mention be made of the collectors who have made this remarkable exhibition possible, but the public can express gratitude and appreciation of the opportunity by going to the exhibition.

Jan Vermeer (1632–1675); Gerard Terborch (1617–1681); Sir Peter Paul Rubens (1577–1640); Agnolo Tori di Cosimo di Moriano Bronzino (1503–1572); Pieter de Hooch (1629–1684); Hans Holbein the Younger (1497/8–1543); Claudio Coello (1642–1693).

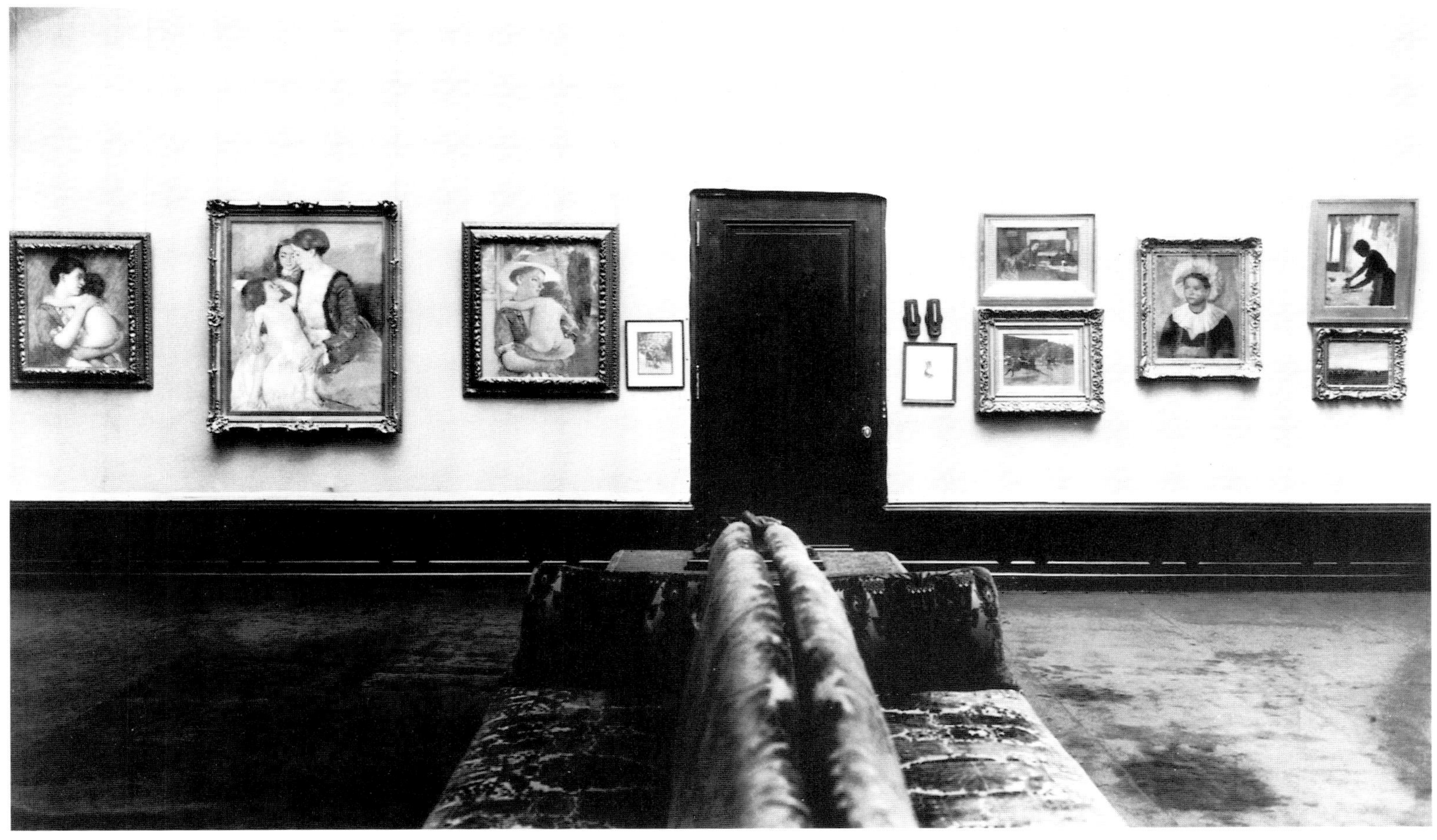

Photograph of the "Loan Exhibition of Masterpieces by Old and Modern Painters" at Knoedler Gallery, 1915. This view of the installation shows works by Mary Cassatt to the left of the doorway and works by Edgar Degas to the right. Photograph courtesy of Knoedler & Company, New York.

LOUISINE HAVEMEYER

A Tribute to Degas and Cassatt

April 6, 1915

Ladies and Gentlemen: When an inferior officer receives an order from a superior officer, if he is a good soldier, he touches his cap and obeys. I have touched my cap and am speaking to you to-day.

It seems to me that I have always known and admired the two painters to whom I now call your attention. I bought with my pin money the first work of Degas that came to America. It hangs upon the wall beside you, and as a matter of curiosity, I may add that I paid the large sum of five hundred francs for it, a sum, which materially reduced the balance of my pin money, and evidently helped to swell Degas' bank account, for he graciously thanked Miss Cassatt, who acted as our broker, saying he "sadly needed the money." Alas, poor artists! They pour their life blood into the furrows that others may reap the harvest.

Miss Cassatt and I have been life long friends. She has been my inspiration and my guide. I call her the fairy godmother of my collection, for the best things I own have been bought upon her judgment and advice. A trip to Italy or one to Spain in those early days when traveling there meant dirt, dust and discomfort was as nothing to her if there were a good picture for us at the end of the journey, or even the scent of a good one that could be followed up with results. I have to smile to-day as I think of her many adventures in our behalf. If ever there was a true artist, it is Mary Cassatt. Always steering toward the highest ideals undaunted and unflinching, her hand upon the tiller, she has kept true to her course through all the storms of adverse criticism, of raillery and of discouragement. "There are two ways

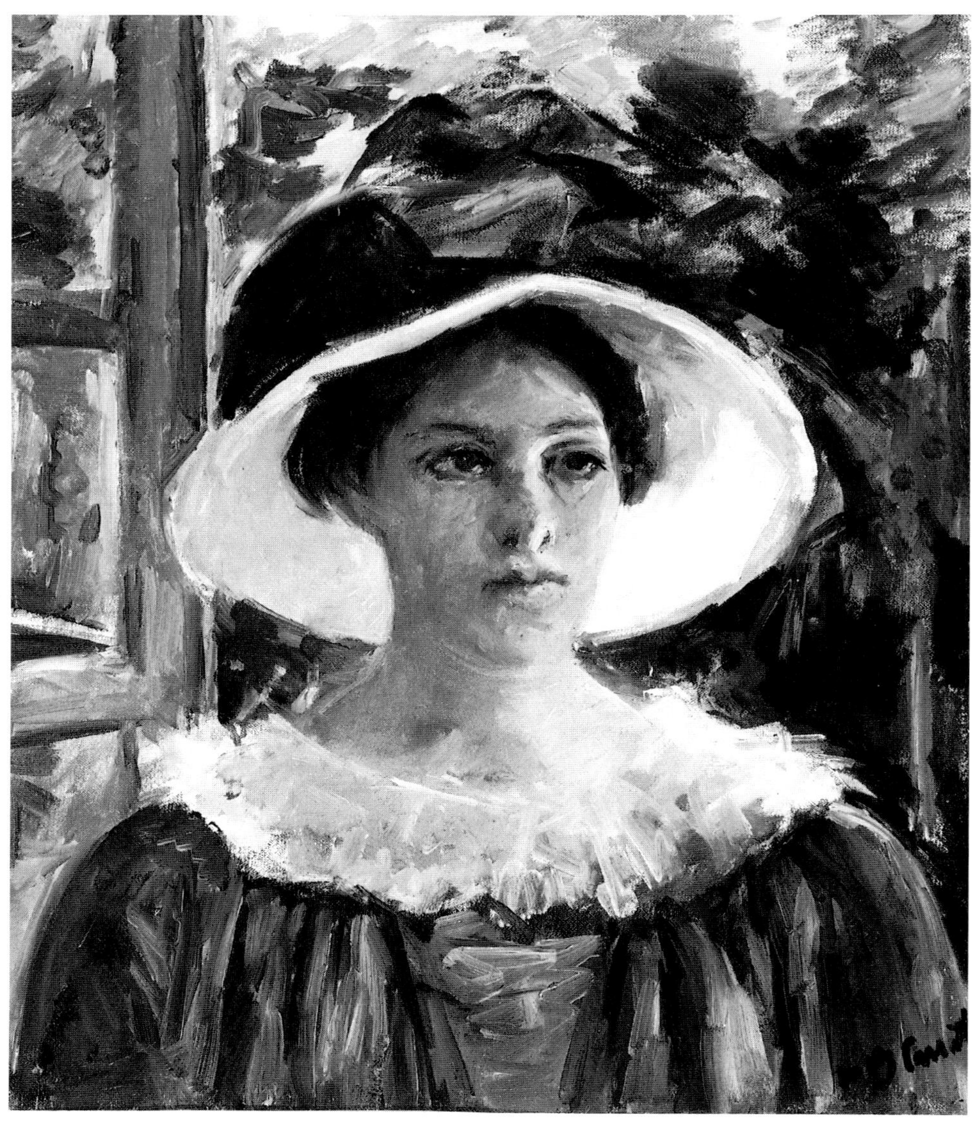

Young Woman in Green, Outdoors in the Sun. 1913–14. Oil on canvas. 21 11/16 × 18 1/4 in. (55 × 46.3 cm). The Worcester Art Museum, Worcester, Massachusetts. Gift of Dr. Ernest G. Stillman.

for a painter," she has often said to me, "the broad and easy one or the narrow and hard one."

It is a great gratification to me that at the sunset of their career, these two great painters should be so fully and completely revealed to the American public. I doubt if such a collection as you now see here could be made even in France, where they have always lived and worked. And now, right here I must make two statements which will probably cause surprise. Miss Cassatt was not a pupil of Degas, nor did either of them belong to that group of painters known as the Impressionists.

Unappreciated in that highly respectable institution known as the Salon, they exhibited with the Impressionists in their modest room on the Boulevard, but Degas and Miss Cassatt are not to be classified with Manet, Monet, Pissarro and the rest. As for Miss Cassatt being a pupil of Degas, it is not true, for she did not even meet him until she had known his works and felt their influence for several years. I will let her tell you so herself. She wrote me only a few weeks ago, and said:

"How well I remember, nearly forty years ago, seeing for the first time Degas' pastels in the window of a picture dealer on the Boulevard Haussmann. I used to go and flatten my nose against that window and absorb all I could of his art. It changed my life. I saw art then as I wanted to see it."

After they met, some time later, long years of friendship ensued, of mutual criticism, and, I must frankly add, of spicy estrangements, for Degas was addicted to the habit of throwing verbal vitriol, as the French call it, upon his friends, and Miss Cassatt would not have been the daughter of the

Cassatts if she had not been equal to parrying his thrusts. She could do without him, while he needed her honest criticism and her generous admiration. I have been amused during the long years I have known them at the little luncheons or dinners planned by friends in order to effect a pleasant reconciliation. In certain of Degas's pictures one can recognize Miss Cassatt as she helped him out of a difficulty by posing for a turn of the head or a movement of the hand. She can be easily seen in one of *The Milliners* series. Degas's admiration for Miss Cassatt was unbounded, but there was always a little dart in his remarks. "I will not admit a woman can draw like that!" he exclaimed, as he stood before one of her pictures. And again he said of that picture of the boy standing by the mirror, which now hangs before you: "The greatest picture of the nineteenth century," and added sarcastically: "It is the little Jesus and his English nurse." COLORPLATE 91

I have not time to begin to tell you of the many incidents of bygone years, of Degas' dinners and his beefsteak pies, of Miss Cassatt's evenings at home, where so many interesting people listened to her brilliant conversation, nor of her luncheons, where State and Church met and it took a Clemenceau to calm the resulting agitation. I must hurry on and say a word or two about their art, and I shall try to say it as simply as possible.

Miss Cassatt has often said that to make a great collection it is necessary to have the modern note. To be a great painter you must be classic as well as modern. . . .

I want to say a word to those who are to listen to me to-day and honestly wish to learn something about art. Let me tell you that this exhibition will give you an opportunity such as may not occur again in a long, long time, and, as far as I know, has never been offered before—that of comparing the old with the new, of seeing the masters of the Flemish school beside those of the French modern school. When I asked Miss Cassatt for advice about this exhibition she at once answered: "I advise you to put a Ver Meer of Delft near the Degas and let the public look first at the one and then at the other. It may give them something to think about." Through the generosity of a kind collector I have been able to accomplish this, and in the adjoining gallery you will find one of the best examples of Ver Meer's works. He was perhaps the greatest genre painter of the Dutch school and painted with such painstaking care that I believe he left only about forty pictures, and some of these are disputed. Nearly all are small, and the subjects are homely and very simple in character. You see a woman weighing her pearls, another filling a glass from a pitcher, but the sunlight and atmosphere which the painter imparts to his subjects astonish us. He, too, was a painter of contemporaneous subjects, and possibly was found fault with on that account in his day. I beg of you to look, as Hamlet said, first on this picture and then on that, and to observe and to consider. . . .

Reluctantly I must go on, and how much more could be said about Degas, about his wonderful nudes, his milliners, his horses, with their jockeys! I have only time for a few words about Miss Cassatt.

Think of it, a few words to describe the work of a long life! of hours that began at 8 in the morning and lasted until dark. Well knowing I cannot say the "half of it all," I am going to begin at the end and speak of her latest works first, of those she did last winter especially for this exhibition and that have not been exhibited here until to-day. I want to point them out to you. First there is the pastel *Mother Holding a Child Asleep in Her Arms*, a naughty little child was posed so badly that the kind-hearted painter let it climb into that position, put its head down upon its mother's shoulder and go to sleep, while she put the tenderness she felt for the little one on the canvas before her. It is clearly in her latest manner, strong drawing, great freedom of technique and a supreme mastery of color, which is one of Miss Cassatt's artistic assets. Then there is the oil painting COLORPLATE 117
of the mother in a hat holding her baby in her arms, remarkable for atmosphere and light and with a beautiful bit of outdoor background, including a classic cedar that stood close by the villa at Grasse. Perhaps of the five the

pastel of the peasant with her kerchief on her head and her child in her lap is the most appealing as well as the most masterly work. The child is so beautifully drawn and modelled and the movement so naive and childlike that you feel it is the success, even in a series of remarkable achievements. Miss Cassatt, the painter of maternity, has given a new note in the painting of children, namely, their infinite variety of movement. Look at that little child that has just thrown herself against her mother's knee, regardless of the result and oblivious to the fact that she could disturb "her mamma." And she is quite right, she does not disturb her mother. Mamma simply draws back a bit and continues to sew, while little daughter rests her elbows upon mamma's knee. Such a movement never could have been except just between mother and little daughter, and Miss Cassatt has caught and expressed it with all the beautiful accessories of flowers and of color and of light. How often have friends said to me: "Won't you ask Miss Cassatt to paint my little girl? I would like to have her painted just like that." Well, the "just like that" means years of study and observation and a large proportion of artistic insight added to the recipe.

COLORPLATE 118

COLORPLATE 90

Of her color I need say little. She long ago won the right to be considered a great colorist. She feels and expresses it as a gifted musician expresses harmonies when his fingers wander over the keys. With all her brilliance, she maintains a balance of tone. It is a natural expression of her art just as the maternal sentiment is interwoven with the formula of every new composition. Let me tell you, I, who have lived with her and know the method of her labors, that it is an exhausting process to compose a picture, to combine your colors, to remember the very strokes and hatchings, from sitting to sitting, to say nothing of the infusion of your own soul into the work you undertake. I will conclude with just one little story about a much talked of portrait. Miss Cassatt refused to let the Luxembourg or the Petit Palais have that portrait, anyway, not until after it had been exhibited here. I mean the *Lady at the Tea Table*. Last spring, when she left the Riviera and returned to Paris, I suggested that she should go through all the store closets in her apartment and into the big chest in the corridor where she kept her drawings and the studies for her pictures and see what would come forth. Mathilde, the faithful, was given the task, and faithfully did she accomplish it. I can tell you artistic Paris was very happy over the result. You can see some of these drawings and some of her colored etchings now at the Durand Ruel Galleries. I should like to tell you about those etchings, but I have not the time.

COLORPLATE 38

When I entered her apartment one afternoon, Miss Cassatt showed me The *Lady at the Tea Table* and said: "Tell me what you think of that." I looked and answered: "Very fine. An early work. Why have you never shown it before?" "The family did not like it, and I was so disappointed. I felt I never wanted to see it again. I did it so carefully and you may be sure it was like her—but—no one cared for it," she added sadly. "Well, I care for it," I said hotly, "and so will others if they know anything," and I insisted that it should be shown.

I was quite right. It was the sensation of the exhibition in the rue Laffitte last June. With the result, as I have said, that both the Luxembourg and the Petit Palais were anxious to have it. But through the kindness of Miss Cassatt it is your privilege to see it here to-day.

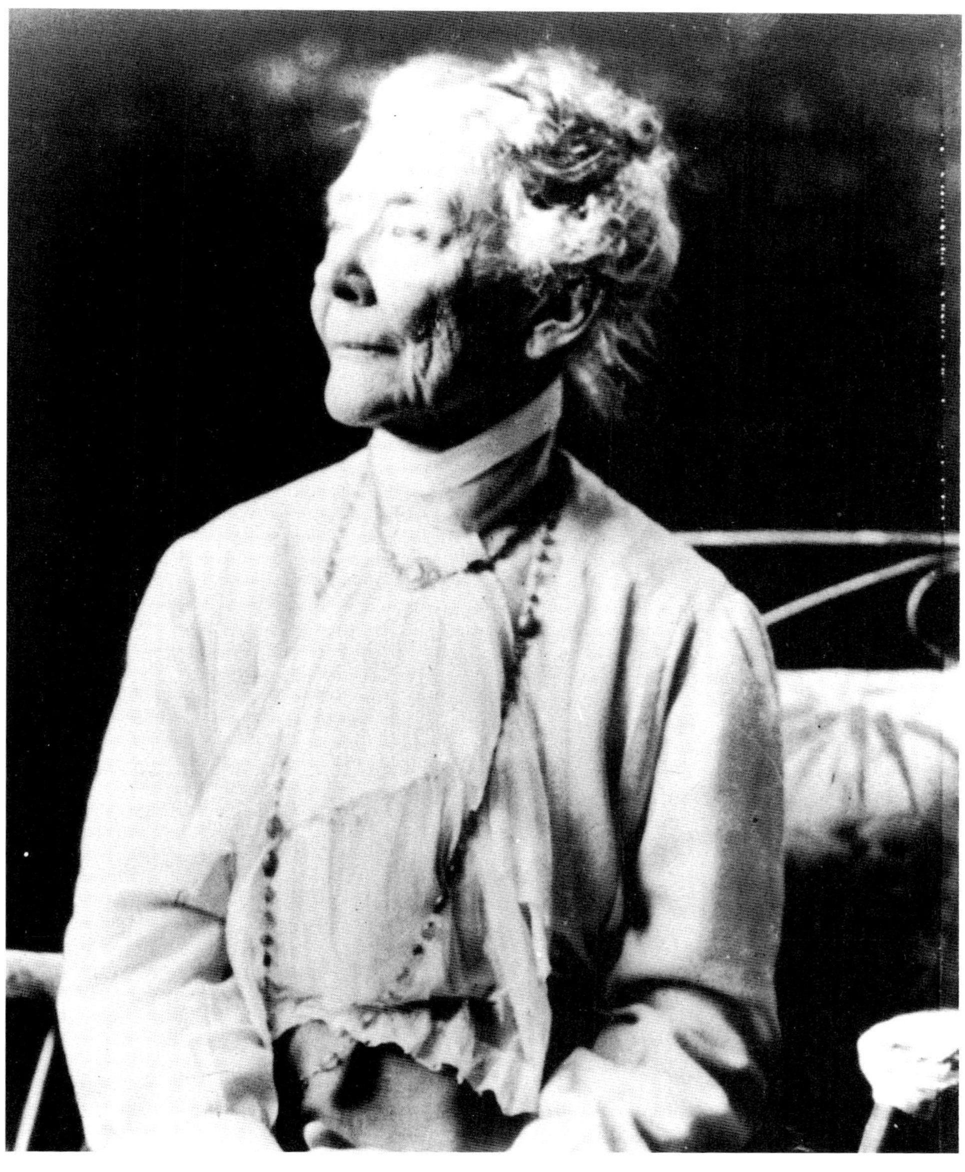

Photograph of Mary Cassatt at Villa Angeletto, Grasse. c. 1914. Photograph courtesy of the Estate of Lois B. Thayer.

ANNA LOUISE THORNE

"My Afternoon with Mary Cassatt"

May 1960

Anna Louise Thorne (1866–1965), American painter, etcher, and lecturer, whose painting "Boats at Harbor" was exhibited at the 1926 Paris Salon and won several awards. She visited Cassatt probably sometime after 1913.

My sister Isabelle was always meeting somebody important. On this particular day, she had traveled over to Roen to meet the Prince of Greece. The Saturday before that, she bragged about shaking hands with Queen Mary. My sister could make your eyes bubble with her glamorous tales about celebrities. I found it rather dull talk. I would put one over on her! I would go out toward Beauvais and visit my idol, artist Mary Cassatt. Even though I had never once tried to paint like her, it seemed that women rebels in the field of art were very rare. And we were both rebels, she growing old and I still young.

At this time of my life, my sister and I were "living it up" in Paris. She bought fancy feather hats and I spent my allowance on paints. But, on this particular day, there was enough money in my handbag for a binge in the country. I dressed in Sunday best, doffed one of my sister's fine hats, put my sketch book under my arm, bought a bouquet of violets and was off on the train for Chateau Beaufresne. Now, where was that? Did I really know? To tell the truth, I had no map. A guide at the Louvre had tried to explain the route. But, maybe, I was just another dumb American girl. Unfortunately, I was never good at following directions. But I tried. With my eyes glued to the train window, gloating in the lovely green landscape and feeling perfectly elegant in my sister's choice hat, what did I do but ride too far. I had not stopped in the right town. The train had taken me miles beyond. So, I asked my way to the chateau of the celebrated lady painter and decided to walk back.

It was a long walk. My feet were tired and the little Parma violets had almost withered. However, I blew breath into their petals and the blossoms seemed fresh again. Suddenly, before me, was the right place. It was a glorious sort of chateau, all formal and elegant, neat and precise as a wedding cake. A row of clipped chestnut trees ran down a long front walk up to a high, bronze-like, embellished door. Before gathering the courage to knock, I sat down on one of the stone benches that skirted the steps. Everything was so quiet, except toward one side of the house, from which I could hear a man singing a French tune. A liveried chauffeur was busy cleaning an odd-looking Renault. Brushing back my long hat plumes, I knocked at the great door. Quickly, it was opened by a "motion picture" sort of French maid.

"Does Madamoiselle have a card?" she asked. "No. No," I answered, "I'm studying art in Paris and am an American. I know that Miss Cassatt is from Philadelphia. I'm Doctor Sam S. Thorne's daughter from Toledo, Ohio and would like to have a short visit." Slowly, the door closed. There I stood, clutching the wilting violets. But, I waited. Then, the door opened again, this time with a wider view. A rather lovely woman stood in the shadowed interior. "I am Mademoiselle Mathilde," she said graciously, "companion and maid to Miss Cassatt. Will you come this way?" The inside of the chateau was glorious. It was like walking through some grand, unknown castle, filled with elegant beauty. I was all eyes. At the door of the parlor, we stopped. Mathilde turned and quietly spoke in soft English. "Miss Cassatt would love to see you. But, I must inform you, she's not been well. Last week, she had a severe fall and is confined to her chair."

We walked over the soft carpet. Sunlight was picking up the designs as it glistened through the tall chateau windows. I was so proud, clutching the violets, raising my head high, the feathers wiggling about like soft branches. Suddenly, we were inside a long avenue of windows. It was rather like a hall of mellifluous sunshine. There, at the far end, where the shades were drawn, sitting almost as one on a throne, I saw her, my idol; the painter of *La Loge* and *A Cup of Tea*—Mary Cassatt! We came closer. She did not smile, only sat there, arrogantly proud, austere; her white hair done in a precise, little, bright embroidered French cap; her thin hands folded in her lap. Then, suddenly, her proud head lowered and her eyes caught mine. Nervously, I clutched the violets. "How do you do," she said with a Pennsylvania accent, "So, you're an American? I don't like Americans. I've been in France too long. But sit down. You've come a long way to see me and we'll talk."

Mathilde pulled up a low French encrusted chair and I sat down. "Oh, these are for you," I said softly, handing her the violets. Her thin fingers took away the paper and she looked at the flowers. A smile caught upon her lips. "Somehow, I think it's my favorite flower," she said, "I've been where they grow." She bent down, looking close. I could tell then, that somehow, she did not see very well. Her eyes squinted up to look at me and then, with a harsh nervous note, she called for her companion to arrange her shawl. "You must excuse me, if I seem cross today," she said, "But, I've had a bad fall. When I can't go with Armande for my daily ride, it makes me feel miserable."

Then, she spied my sketch book. "So you're an artist, are you? Let me see." She reached out her hand. The fine lace at her cuff fell over her fingers. I handed her the notebook. Her eyes came close to the sketch lines. Nervously, I watched her turn the pages. Then, she handed the book back to me. "Pretty good," she said, "But not good enough. It takes almost a hundred years. Look at me. I'm old now and I hardly know what art is all about." "Oh, but everyone loves your paintings!" "Humph," she said with a sort of procrastination. Then, with an emotion of hatred, or grievous resentment, she spoke on; "I sold my soul to the dealers, that's all. It was the dealers who stole my life!"

Suddenly, my eyes caught sight of a grouping of beautiful prints. They looked almost Japanese with their block-like patterns, flat in two-dimensional space. "Oh, so you like my prints?" she said with a softer, sweeter voice. "Yes. Yes," I exclaimed, going closer to look at the row of colored aquatints and drypoints, "I didn't know you'd made them." Then, like a dream coming into her eyes, her hand brushed her flowered bonnet and she said softly; "It was with Degas, I first went to the Japanese exhibition. Oh, I learned so much. That's what you must get into your work, that flowing line. You have to learn from those true artists of the long ago." Then, she pointed to a table. "You see that Persian miniature. It's very, very old. I collect them. Take a look at it. It has a special, curious line that evolves into that magnificent pattern."

"Yes. Yes, I see!" I said with wide open eyes as the hat plumes fell over my face. "That's a fine hat," she said. "It's not mine," I answered, somewhat embarrassed, "It belongs to my sister." "Well, you tell your sister that she has good taste. I could recognize a Reboux, the minute I saw one. It's a very beautiful hat." For the first time, her eyes lit up and she smiled. But, at the same time, a sort of pain caught at her and she called for her nurse. "Maybe someday, you'll come back to America and visit us in Toledo?" I asked. "No. No," she rather grumbled, "I don't like Americans. I've been in France too long," she said, adding "Besides, I don't like to ride on the water. If ever I get well and able to ride again into Paris, you bring your sister to see me at my apartment on Rue Marignan."

Mathilde came close and gathered the shawl about the artist's shoulders. "She's grown very tired," said her companion. "Maybe, Amanda would drive the girl to the station?" said Miss Cassatt. "No. No," I exclaimed, "I'd rather walk." "You're so American," she grumbled. "I don't like Americans." That was the third time she had said it. Raising my hand, I placed it on hers and stroked her fingers. How soft and how great these artist's hands that would not work much longer. Then, the nurse led me from the room. "You must forgive Miss Cassatt," she said, "For seeming so cross, so irritable. But, she's not been at all well and even the children she always loved so much seem to annoy her." "But, she is very beautiful," I said, "And it was kind of you to let me see her."

I could hardly wait for the great front door to close. I wanted to cry. I sat down on the stone bench. My eyes filled up with tears. I was so American. Why was it, that anyone who had been born in Philadelphia and first studied painting at the Pennsylvania Academy, now disliked Americans so much? Or was it me she disliked? Or was she envious of my sister's fine hat? Always, even today, it seemed my sister who found the limelight. Now, Isabelle would wear this hat down to the Cafe for dinner and tell everyone that Mary Cassatt had loved it. Quickly, I took off the plumed hat and hurried out the gate. Looking back, I saw Armande still polishing the outdated Renault that Mary Cassatt would not be using much longer.

FORBES WATSON

From *The Arts*

"Philadelphia Pays Tribute to Mary Cassatt"

June 1927

Forbes Watson (1880–1960), American critic.

She had enjoyed in France as great a success as a sincere artist from the United States could expect. She knew Degas, though not until some years after she had bought pictures by him. (He met her first when he went to invite her to take part in the exhibition of 1879.) She knew Pissarro, Renoir and Manet. She knew Clemenceau, Mallarmé and many other eminent men. She had studied in Spain, in Italy, in Antwerp. Her house in Mesnil Théribus was a retreat of infinite charm and her apartment in Paris reflected a rare sense of living.

Her material situation would have made it possible for her to ignore official compromise but in fact her whole nature was ferociously opposed to half-beliefs. Mary Cassatt had a strong will and an ardor for painting that overcame as far as possible the obstacles of expatriotism. To visit her was to become warmed by her intellectual and aesthetic fire. Her cultivation in art was boundless. Her passion for an idea was unconquerable. She had to the end a sense of elegance that encompassed both her art and her living. Yet from no lips have I heard less ingratiating language when her passionately-held artistic beliefs were threatened.

The elegance that was Mary Cassatt's had its limitations. This was due to a fierce love of truth which made it impossible for her to say a gracious word to the conniving or to flatter the painter who had been untrue to himself. Miss Cassatt sent more than one inelegant message to those of her contemporaries who allowed their gifts to become tainted by worldliness. And upon stupid visitors who came to see her from idle curiosity, she could exercise a bitter tongue.

It is hard to believe nowadays that some of the people who came into contact with Mary Cassatt in the natural course of her social life remained for years unconvinced that she was anything greater than a lady amateur favored with a solid financial background. Such people naturally committed in her presence stupidities they were unaware of. They were left to wonder why it was that Mary Cassatt never saw them again. She was, of course, an egoist, but she would forgive those who did not appreciate the seriousness of her purpose, unless that lack of appreciation implied a stupid attitude toward art in general. Such people she cast out of her presence. Art was her life. She hated all who thought of it softly and sentimentally. She believed in hard labor. As she grew older she came more and more to look like a woman who had worked, and since painting, to be at all accomplished, requires long hours of physical strain, Miss Cassatt not surprisingly had the appearance of a woman trained to the bone by hard physical effort.

Possibly this sense that she gave out of a life devoted to work was unpleasant to those softer women who would like to be famous if it were not too much trouble. Possibly her ferocity for the truth and her almost violent intellectual activity frightened many women away from her. Nor are these attributes very famous as magnets to attract men. Her ferocity implied and hid a warmth which she gave to her friends and to art. In many cases she helped those friends to secure masterpieces of painting long before the rest of the world appreciated them, pictures which now enrich American collections.

ADELYN DOHME BREESKIN

From *Mary Cassatt: A Catalogue Raisonné of the Graphic Work*

The Incident of the Reprinted Drypoints

1979

Adelyn Dohme Breeskin (1896–1986), American art historian and museum director. An authority on Mary Cassatt, she mounted several exhibitions and published the catalogue raisonné of Cassatt's paintings and prints. She was director of the Baltimore Museum of Art from 1947 to 1962.

The story of the twenty-five prints reprinted in 1923 is a most interesting one, and I shall therefore present it here in detail.

At this time, Miss Cassatt was quite blind and Mathilde Vallet took complete charge of the household. Miss Cassatt wrote to Harris Whittemore on May 12, 1924, describing the story thus:

> These plates representing states were found put away in the closet of my painting room—found there by Mathilde—were shown to an artist friend [George Biddle], an engraver, taken to Delâtre, son of Whistler's printer, who was also mine and Degas'. The proofs were shown to artists and amateurs and generally admired. They were all dry points except two, one being an aquatint of my mother; that one I knew had already been printed, the others had never been seen. I sent the sets to Mrs. Havemeyer to show to Mr. Ivins with a request that he might exhibit them or rather one set and that if the Museum wished to buy a set the price was to be $2,000. I based the price on what my etchings are sold for here, at auction. My surprise and anger were great when I was confronted with an accusation of fraud! Mrs. Havemeyer immediately sided with Ivins and advanced the excuse that my sight had so dimmed that no blame was to be attached to me, but to Mathilde, using her as a scapegoat! She then wrote that "they", Ivins, herself and a collector who boasts of having all my etchings [this was Richard Hartshorne, who then had the largest collection in existence] were so jealous of my reputation they were going to save me. I answered that I could take care of my reputation and she of hers. I at once cabled to send the etchings to Georges Durand-Ruel. She cabled that my etchings were in the hands of Durand-Ruel, but they were not, only one set had been sent, as Joseph D-R wrote to me. She had kept the others to show to you and others to sell them! There was only one set for sale, three I keep. [Nine were printed] As to the price Ivins most impertinently fixed and what you know—and I was to sign every proof with the date of 1923 frankly accepting the fact that there were a series of plates previously printed. They have sent me photos of my drypoints to prove this. I took them to my printer and he said, "What does this prove?" I know there may be one or even two proofs of them but I defy them to show a series.

Eugène Delâtre (1864– ?), French printer, son of printer Auguste Delâtre (1822-1907).

To my mind, the advice of Mrs. Havemeyer and Mr. Ivins was right. It would have saved much confusion if the reprints had been so marked. As they now stand, it is very difficult to describe the differences between the early prints and the reprints. In many cases, the reprints show a weakening of the lines and in most cases vital lines have been reinforced and redrawn. So far, early prints of sixteen of the twenty-five subjects have been found. There are probably more. The paper used for the reprints is varied—the same types of paper such as Vanderley, Porcabeuf, and Van Gelder, which Miss Cassatt always favored. Therefore, one cannot differentiate the reprints by this means. There were nine sets printed of each of the twenty-

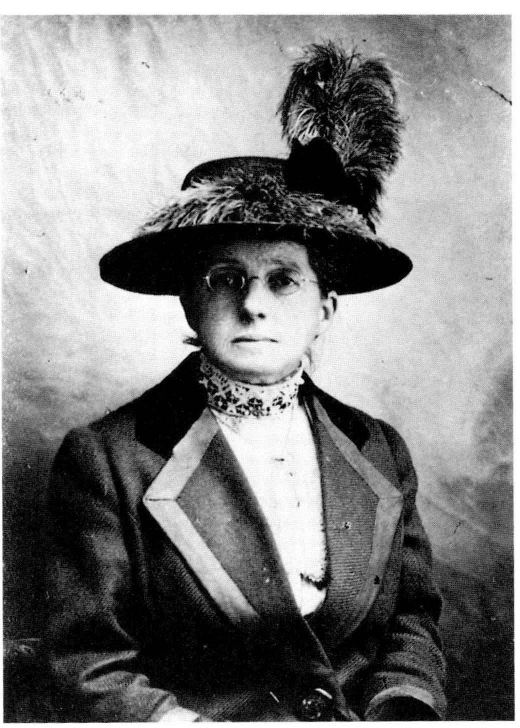

Photograph of Mathilde Valet, Cassatt's loyal maid and companion. 1914. Photograph courtesy of the Archives of American Art, Smithsonian Institution. The Frederick A. Sweet Papers. Location of original unknown.

five subjects in the series of these so-called reprints published by Delâtre in a cloth-covered portfolio in 1923. Four or five sets were inherited by members of Miss Cassatt's family. Twenty subjects from one of the sets were presented to the Philadelphia Museum. The remaining sets have been scattered and sold. Some prints from these are still in the hands of dealers. The quality of the prints is not equal to that of Miss Cassatt's best work. She was always very particular about the printing of her plates and would accept only clear, rich impressions. Certainly if she had retained her sight, she would have been the first to criticize the lack of sharpness and evenness of line in the reprints. As it was, her dander was aroused by the criticism of Mrs. Havemeyer and Mr. Ivins, and she made an issue of the matter and had her way. At the age of seventy-eight years, the high standard which she always maintained throughout her active years of work suddenly failed her. Temperament and blindness were to blame. She shows her attitude in another letter to Mr. Whittemore, as she writes:

> I have a good many proofs (of my work) more than enough to prove Mr. Ivins wrong. It is not for myself alone I am making this fight, but for those who may be treated as I have been and who need the money, for I don't need it. I could not sign the proofs 1923 for that would be acknowledging that Ivins is right which, of course, I never would. Therefore I won't sell. When I have made Ivins acknowledge his error it will be time enough to think of that.

She kept her word and did not sell any of the sets during her lifetime. They have come on the market only since her death. Any impression of these subjects obtained before 1928 or 1929 is therefore sure to be an early impression (with the exception of the set presented to the Petit Palais).

GEORGE BIDDLE

From *The Arts*

"Some Memories of Mary Cassatt"

August 1926

I saw Mary Cassatt for the last time late in January. It was bitterly cold and rained all day. I had received a letter in a trembling and uncertain hand, asking me to lunch with her at her chateau at Beaufresne, Mesnil-Théribus, near Beauvais. An accompanying note from the faithful Mathilde explained that several months before she had fallen from bed; since then she could not walk alone, but was carried almost daily to her automobile, for she was still fond of driving. Often she had serious attacks and at such times her memory failed her. She looked forward to seeing me but I must not be shocked by her altered condition.

Mathilde met me at the gate. She had telegraphed at the last moment not to come. Miss Cassatt had had a bad relapse the previous day. Perhaps she could see me later.

After lunch I went up to her room. There she lay, quite blind, on the green painted bed which I knew so well from the painting in the Metropolitan Museum and other paintings I had seen at Durand's. She was terribly emaciated. Her hands, which used to be such big, knuckled,

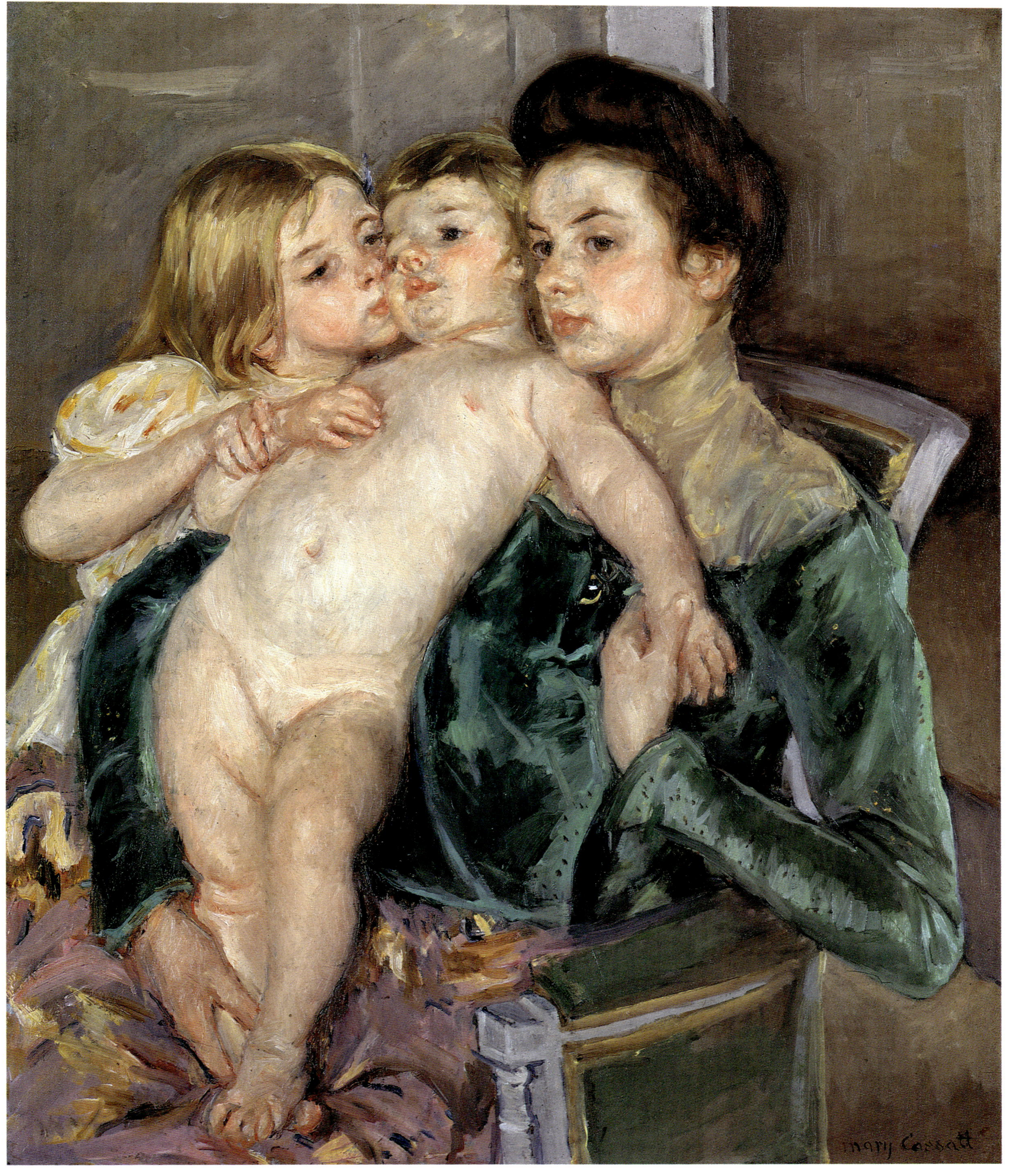

COLORPLATE 104. *The Caress.* 1902. Oil on canvas. 32 ⅞ × 27 ⅜ in. (83.4 × 69.4 cm). National Museum of American Art, Smithsonian Institution. Gift of William T. Evans. Photograph: Art Resource, New York.

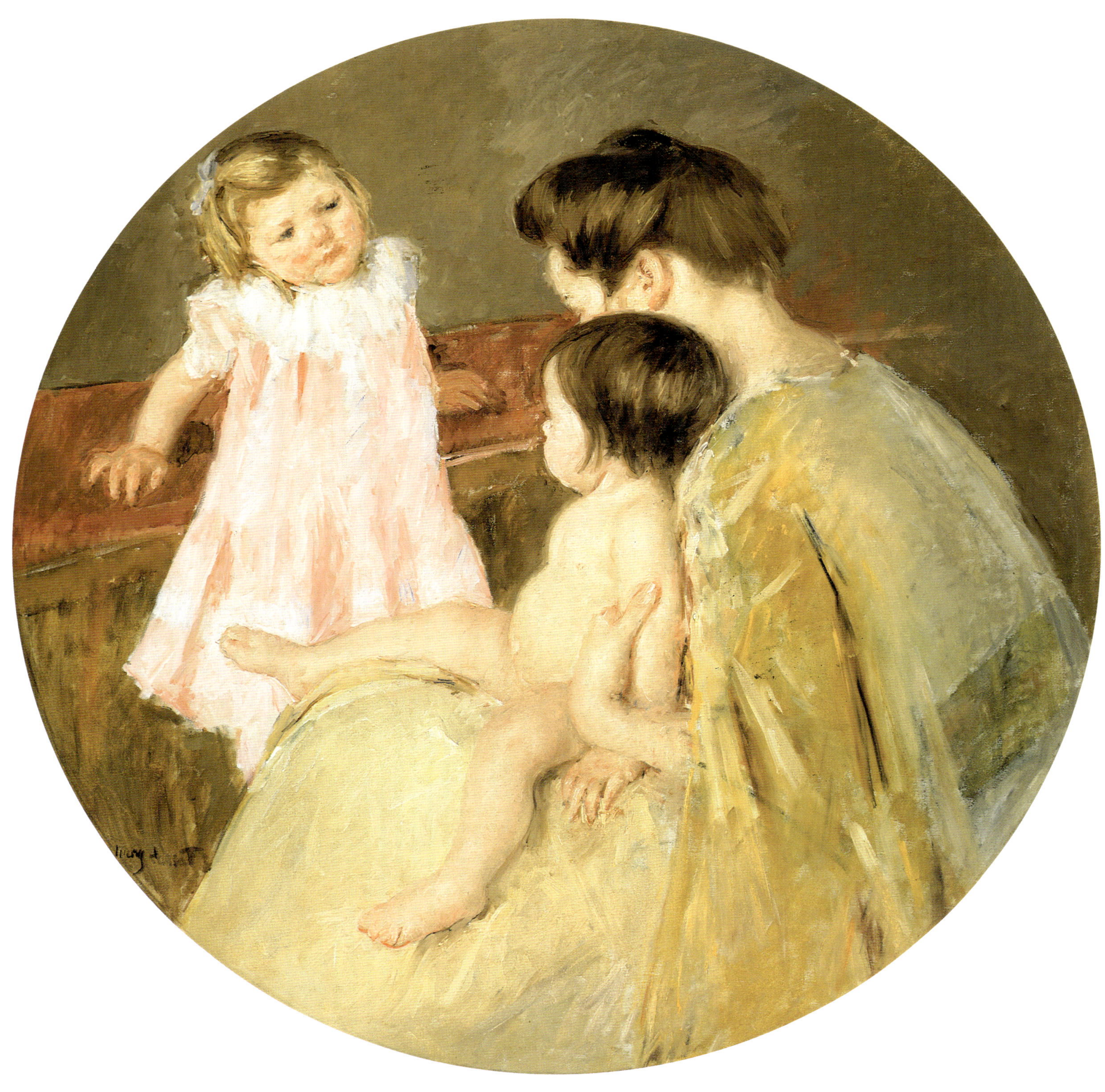

COLORPLATE 105. *Mother and Two Children* (tondo mural for Capitol Building, Commonwealth of Pennsylvania, Harrisburg). c. 1905. Oil on canvas. 37 ½ inches in diameter. (95.2 cm). Westmoreland Museum of Art, Greensburg, Pennsylvania. Anonymous gift.

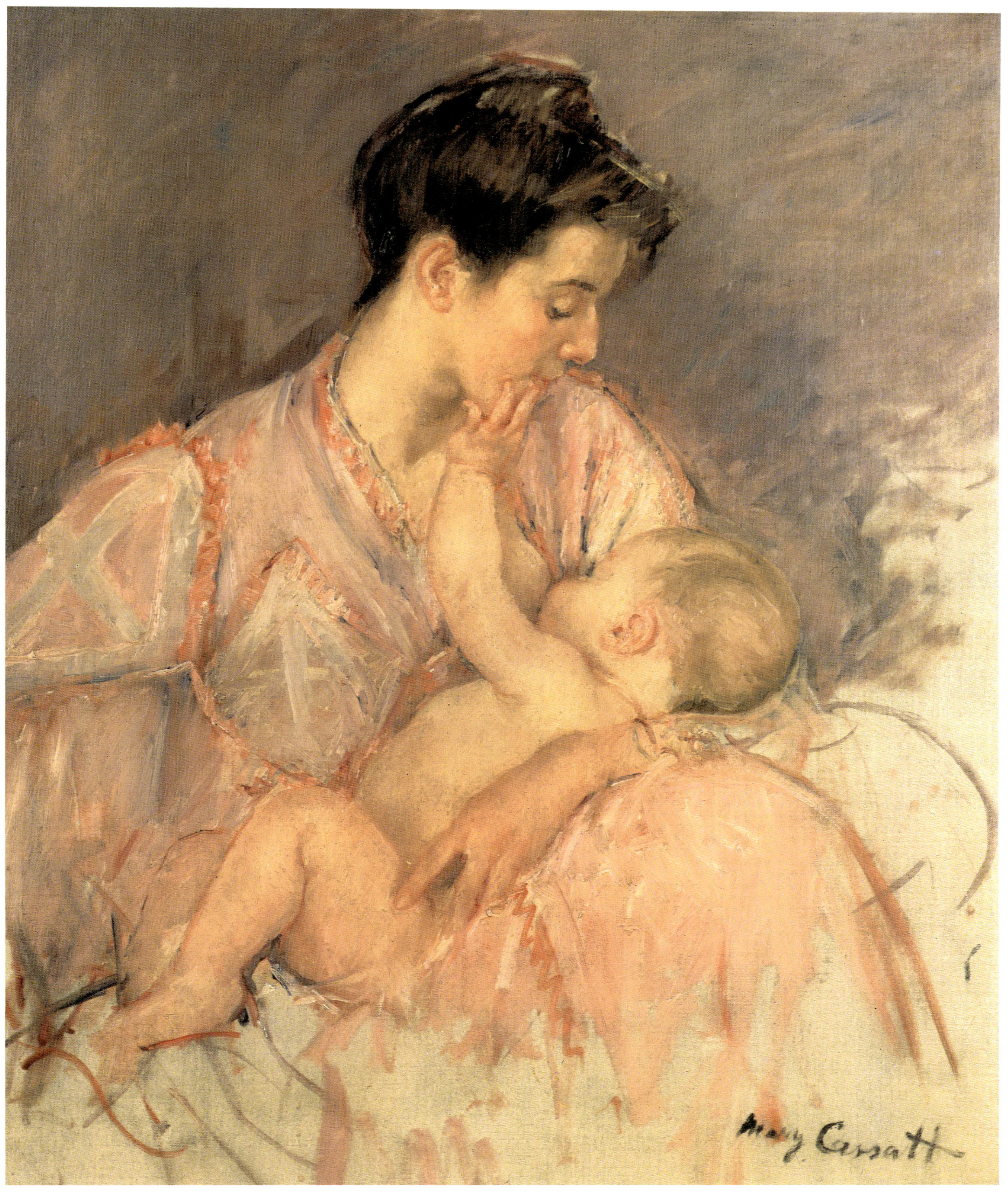

COLORPLATE 106. *Sketch of Mother Jeanne Nursing Her Baby.* c. 1906. Oil on canvas. 35 × 29 ½ in. (89 × 75 cm). Mitchell Museum at Cedarhurst, Mount Vernon, Illinois. Gift of John R. and Eleanor A. Mitchell.

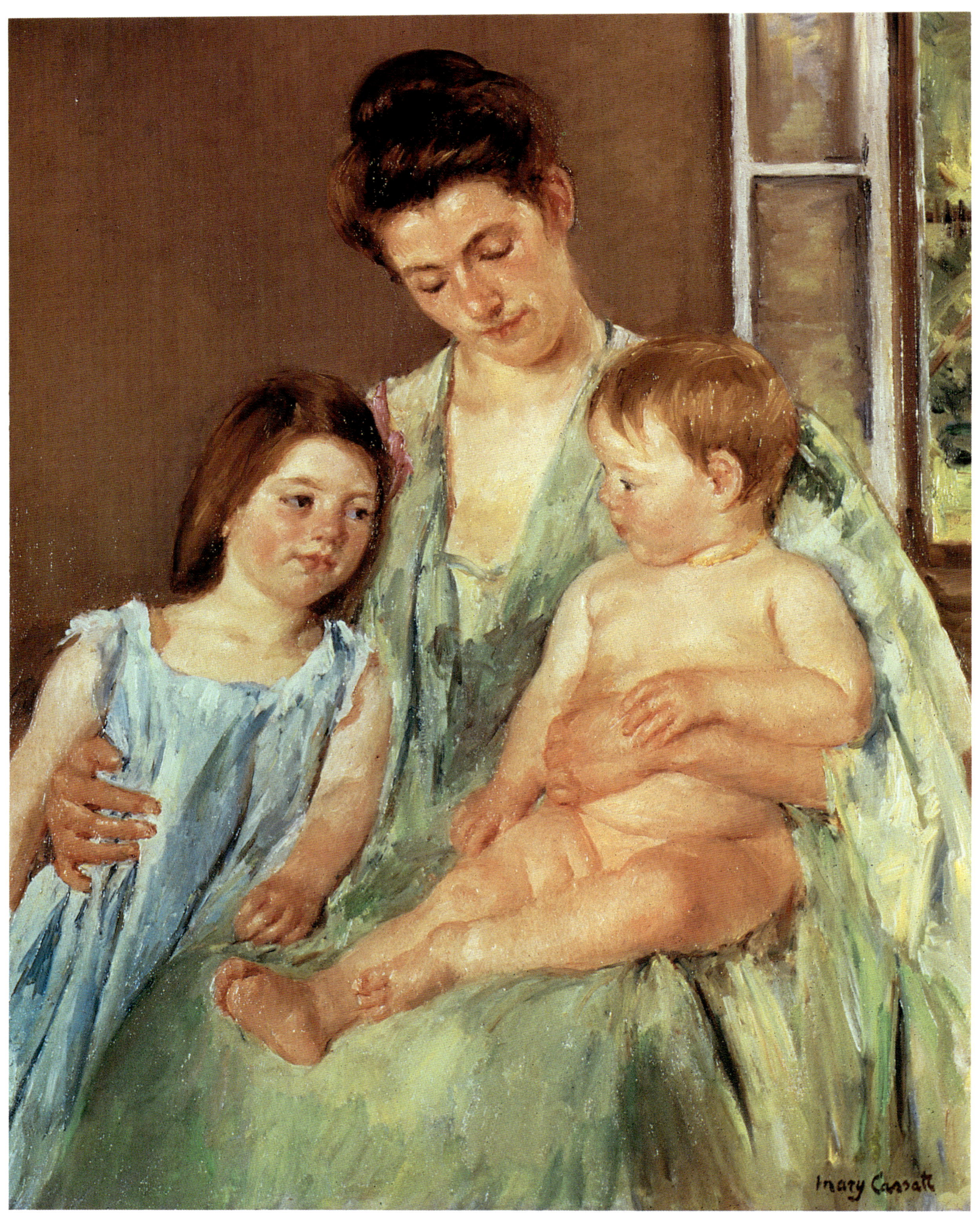

COLORPLATE 107. *Young Mother and Two Children.* 1905. Oil on canvas. 36 ⅜ × 29 in. (92.4 × 73.6 cm). The White House Collection, Washington D.C. Photograph © White House Historical Association.

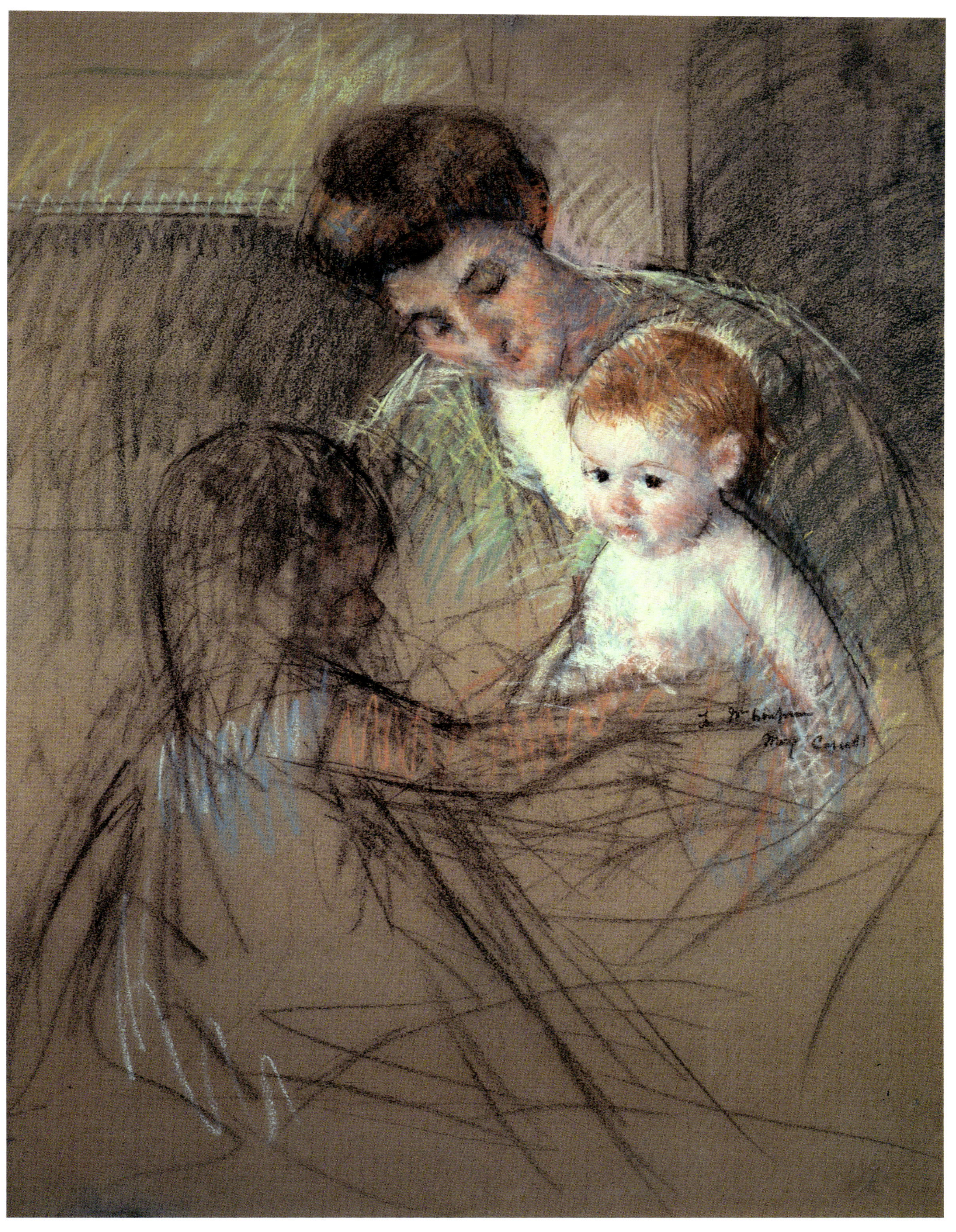

COLORPLATE 108. *Sketch of Mother and Daughter Looking at the Baby.* c. 1905. Pastel on paper. 36 ½ × 29 in. (92.7 × 73.6 cm). Maier Museum of Art, Randolph Macon Women's College, Lynchburg, Virginia.

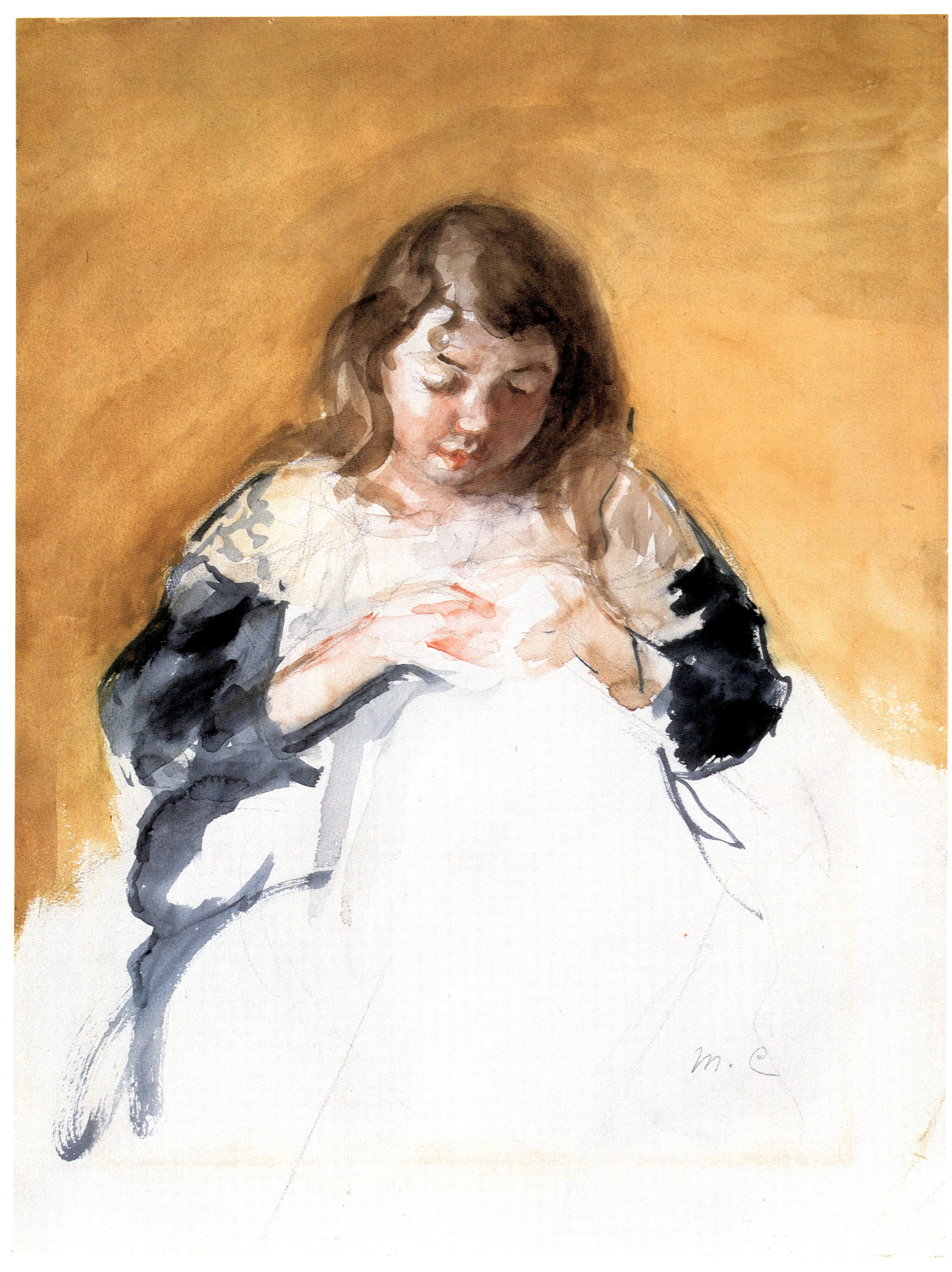

COLORPLATE 109. *Young Girl in Blue (Francoise Sewing,* no. 1). c. 1908. Watercolor and pencil on paper. 18 15/16 × 13 15/16 in. (48.1 × 35.4 cm). Hirshhorn Museum and Sculpture Garden, Smithsonian Institution. The Joseph H. Hirshhorn Bequest. Photograph: Ricardo Blanc.

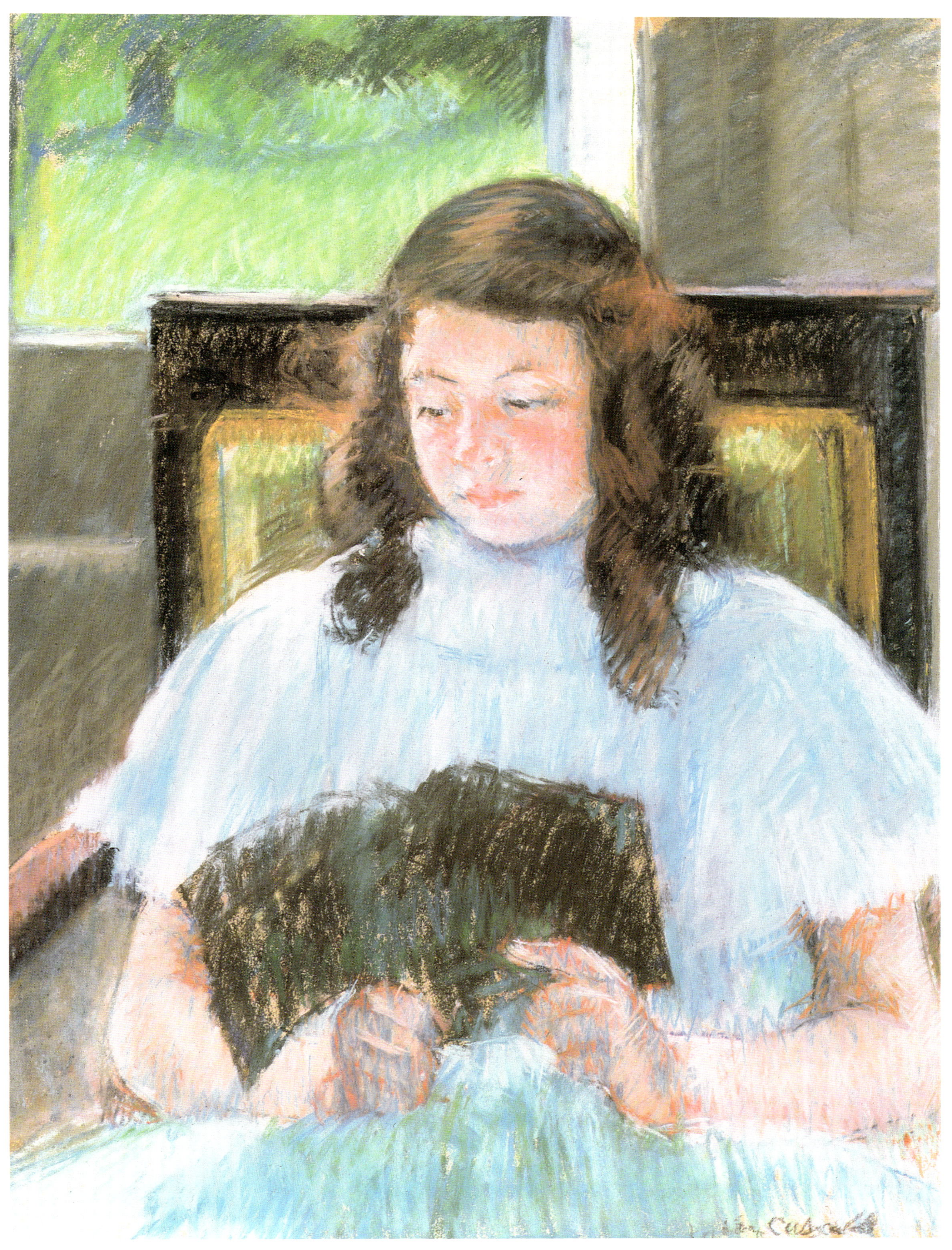

COLORPLATE 110. *Young Girl Reading*. c. 1908. Pastel on paper. 25 5/8 × 19 3/4 in. (65 × 50.1 cm). Seattle Art Museum. Gift of Mr. and Mrs. Louis Brechemin.

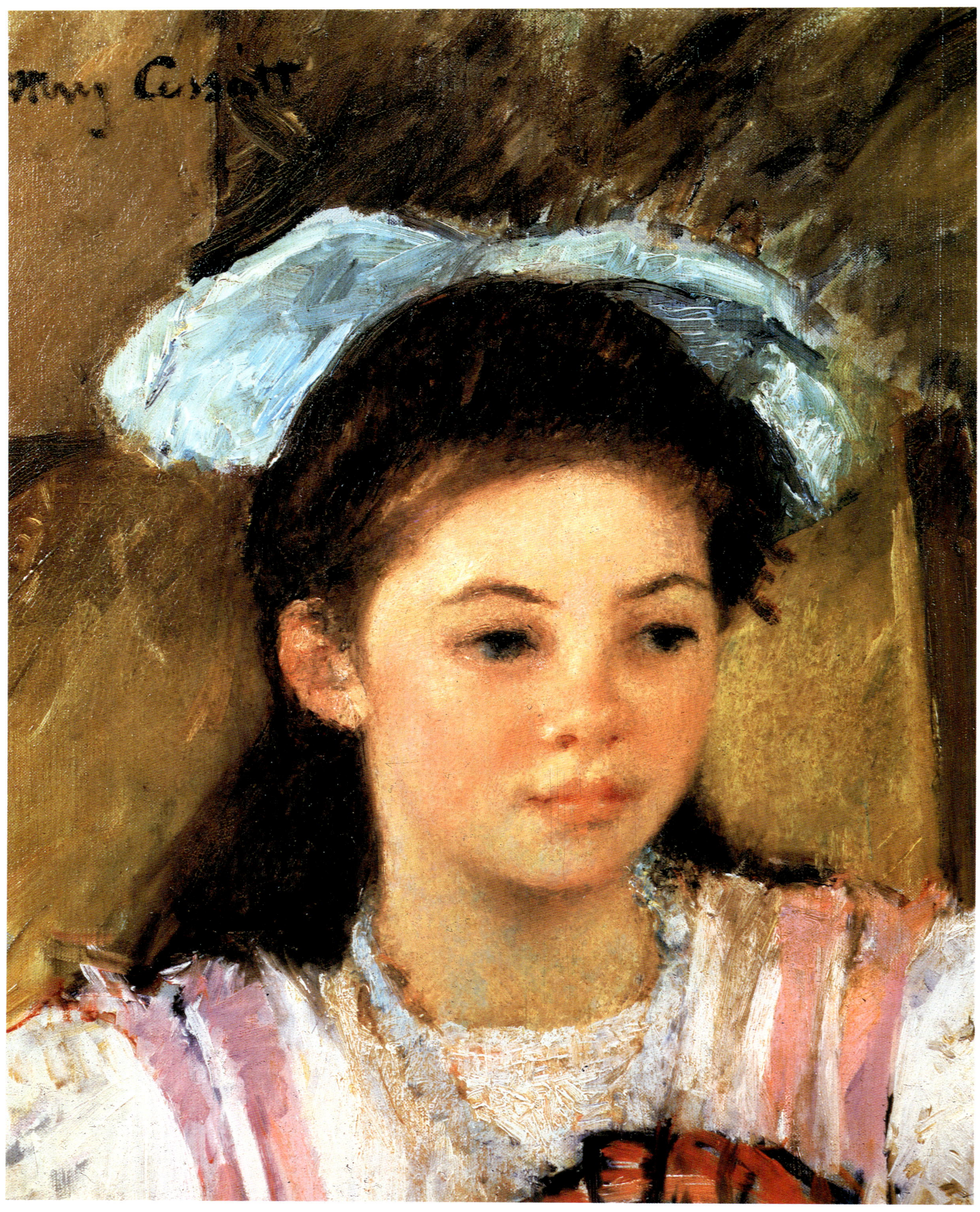

COLORPLATE 111. *Ellen Mary Cassatt with a Large Bow in Her Hair.* c. 1908. Oil on canvas. 16 ⅛ × 13 in. (41 × 33 cm). Private collection, Toronto.

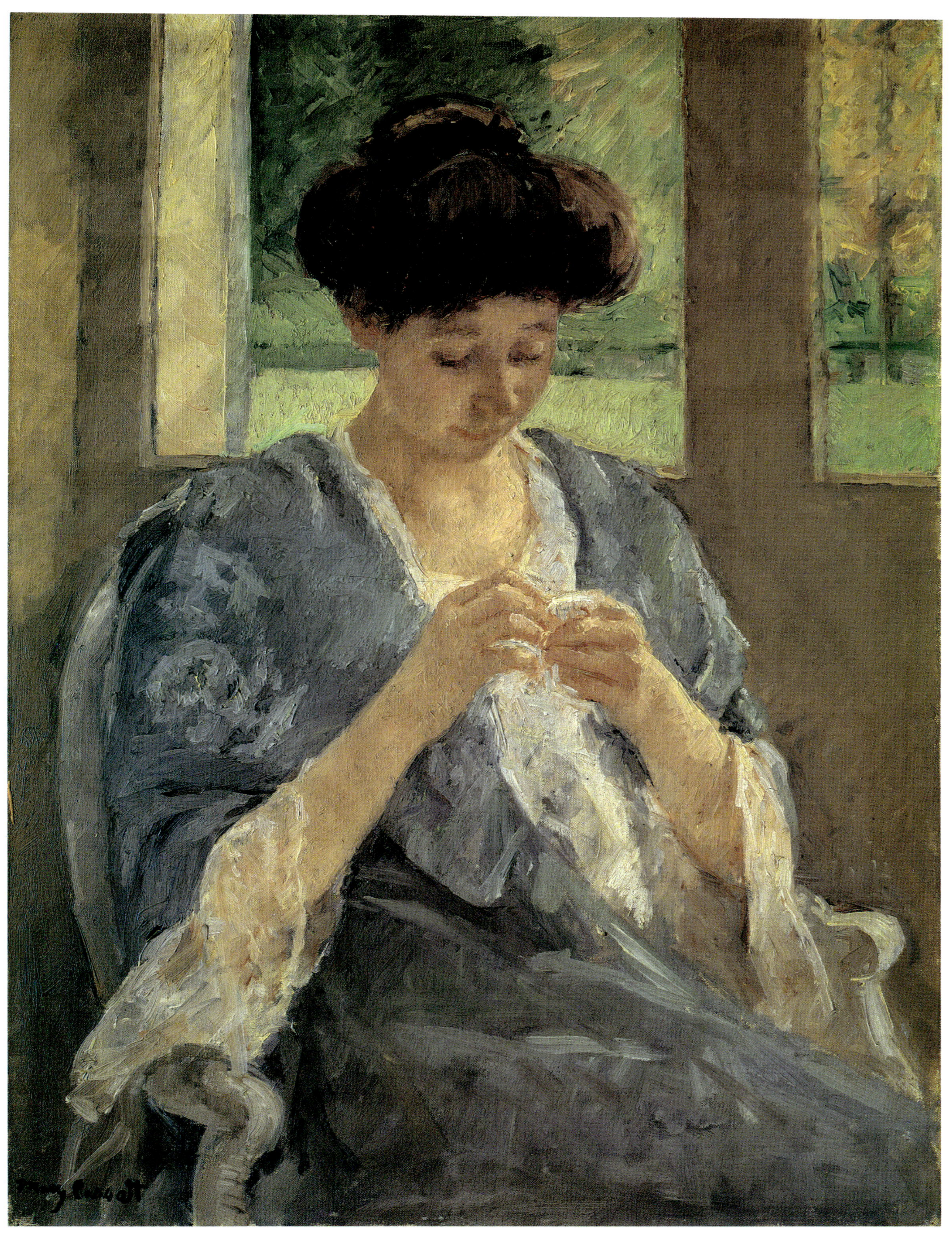

COLORPLATE 112. *Augusta Sewing Before a Window.* c. 1905–1910. Oil on canvas. 31 ¾ × 23 ¾ in. (80.6 × 60.3 cm). The Metropolitan Museum of Art, New York. From the collection of James Stillman, gift of Dr. Ernest G. Stillman, 1922 (22.16.19).

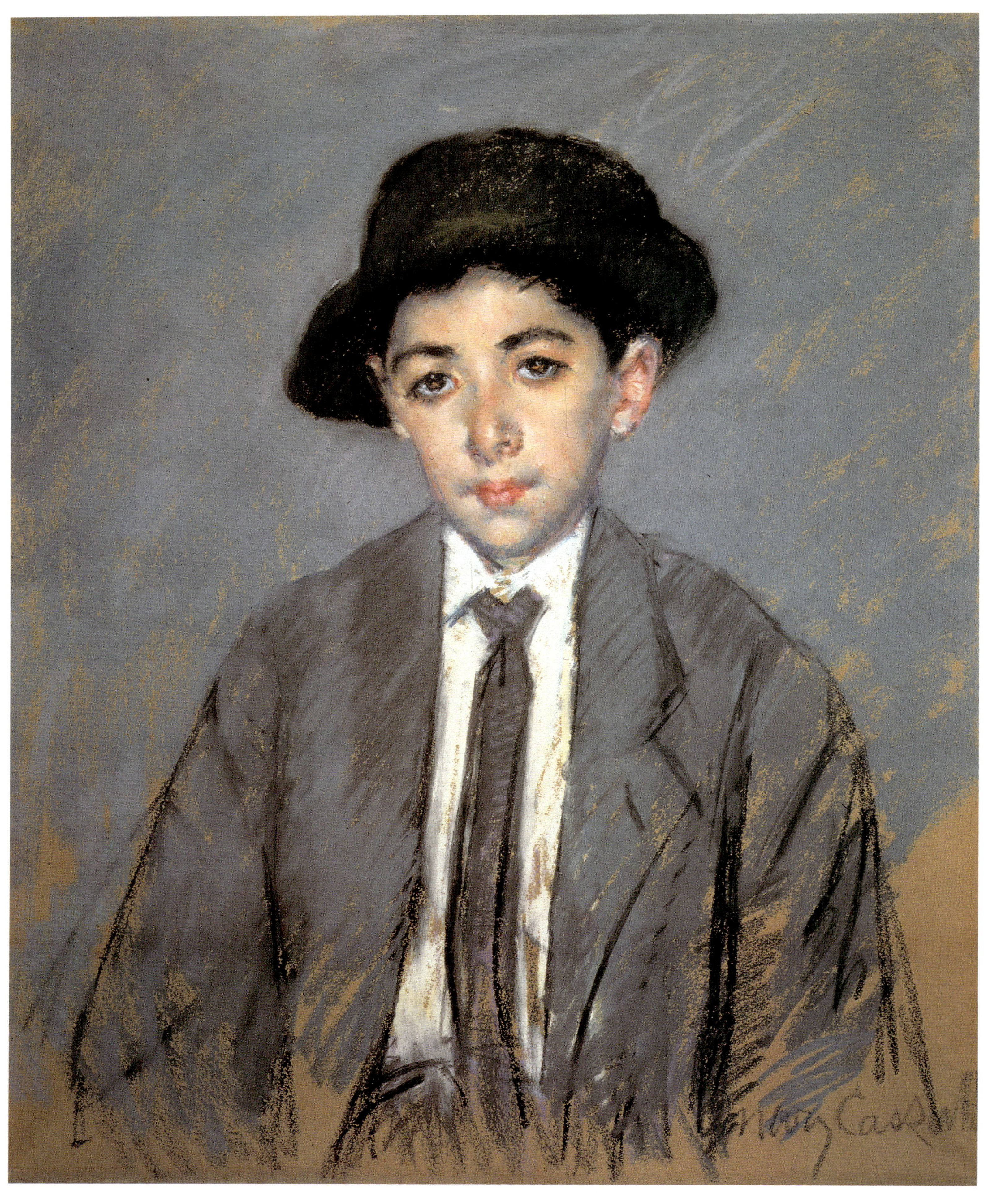

COLORPLATE 113. *Portrait of Charles D. Kelekian.* 1910. Pastel on paper. 26 × 20 ½ in. (66 × 52 cm). Private collection. Photograph courtesy of The Walters Art Gallery, Baltimore.

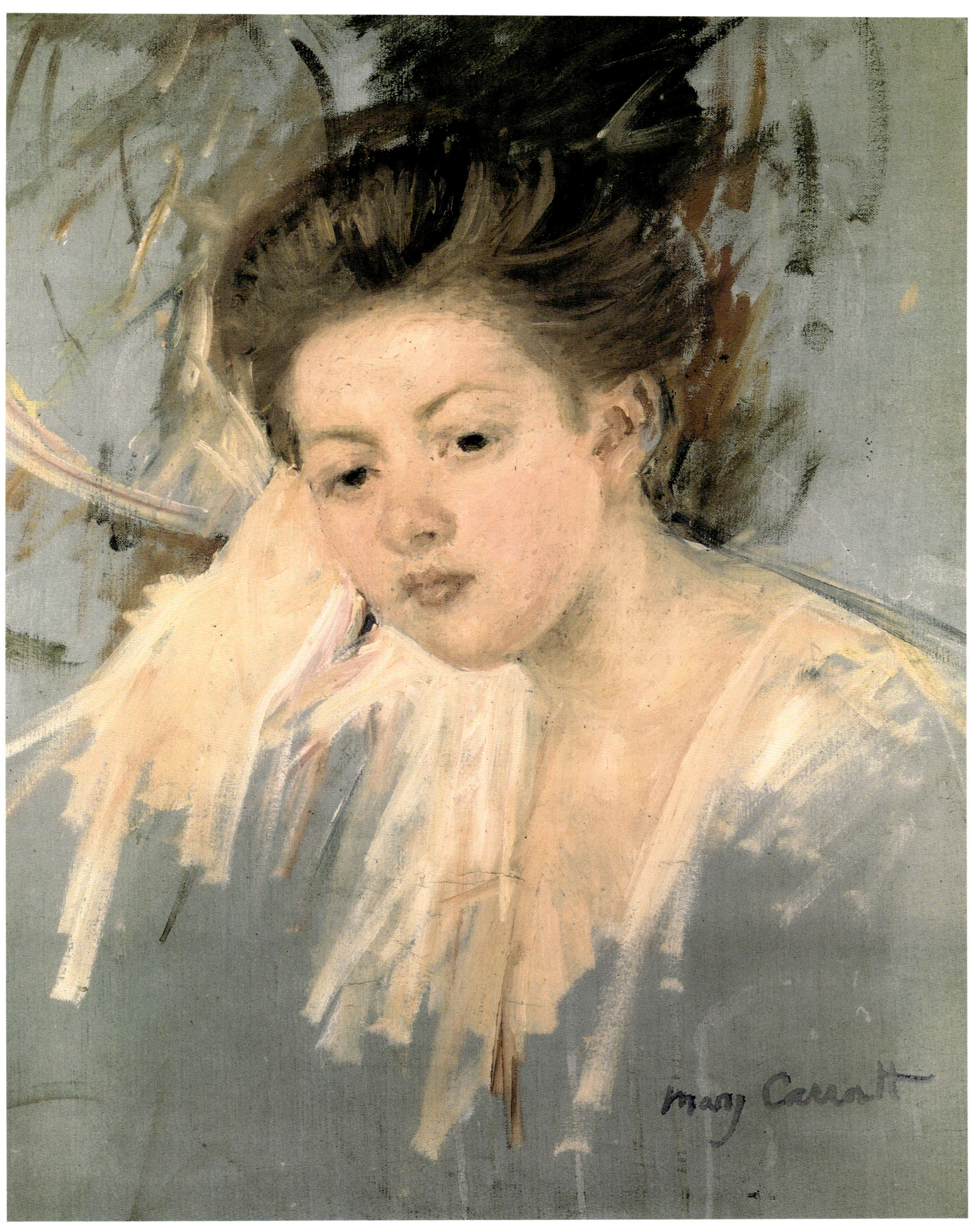

COLORPLATE 114. *Head of a Girl (Sketch for Denise at Her Dressing Table)*. c. 1909. Oil on canvas. 20 ¾ × 16 ¾ in. (53 × 42.5 cm). Private collection. Photograph: Giraudon/Art Resource, New York.

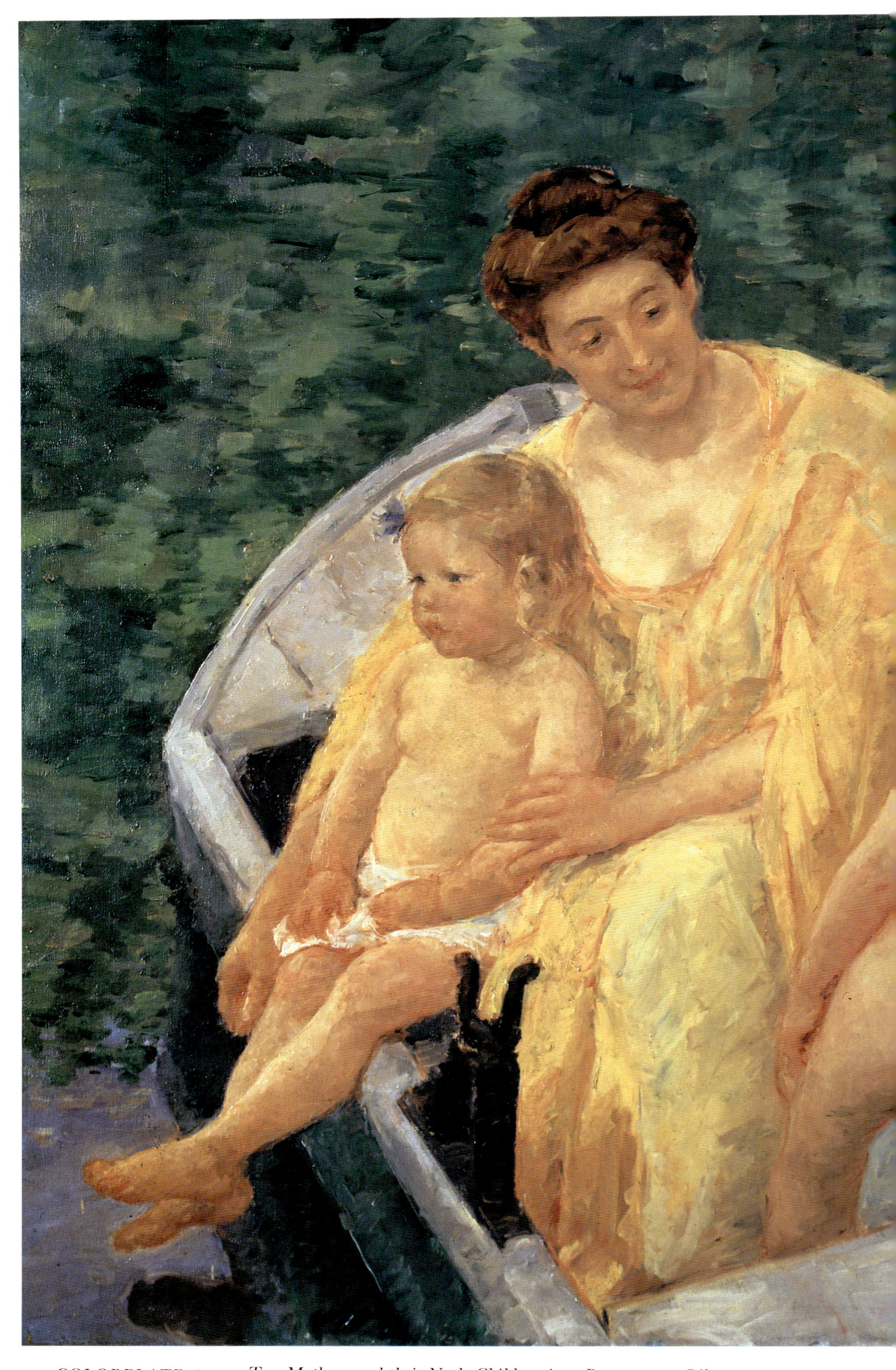

COLORPLATE 115. *Two Mothers and their Nude Children in a Boat.* 1910. Oil on canvas. 38 7/8 × 50 3/4 in. (98.7 × 129 cm). Musée du Petit Palais, Paris. Photograph: Giraudon/Art Resource, New York.

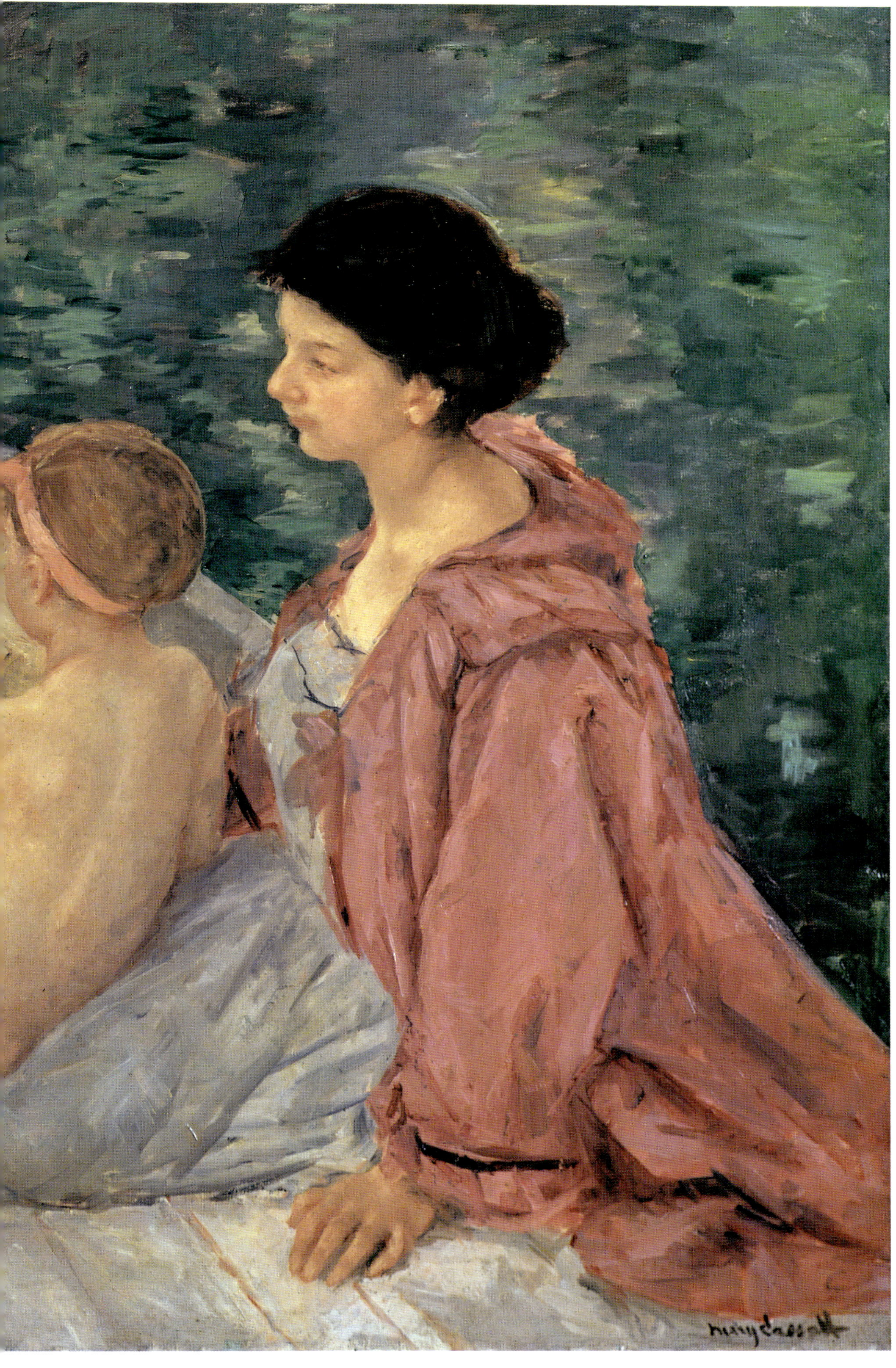

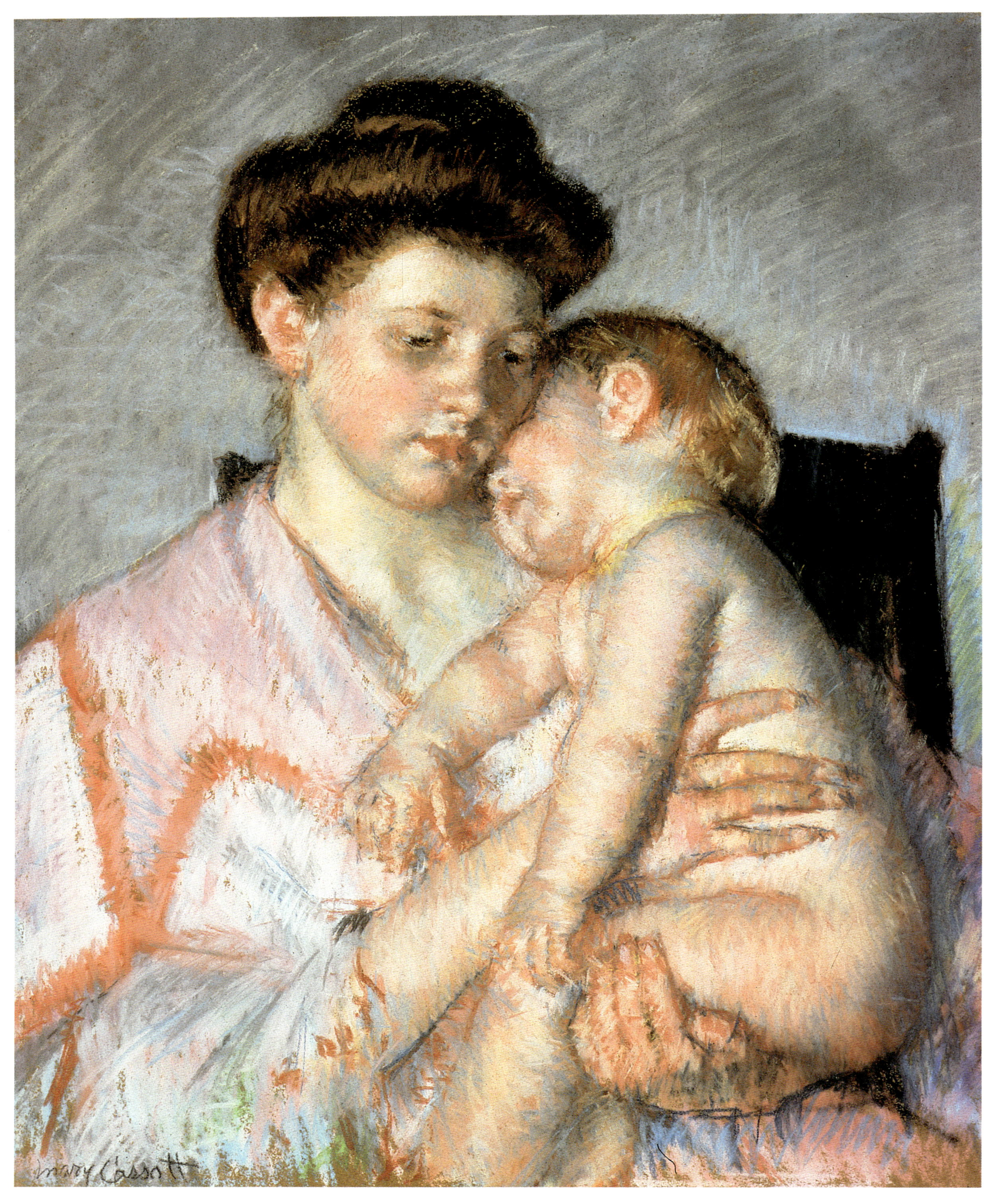

COLORPLATE 116. *Sleepy Baby*. c. 1910. Pastel on paper. 25 ½ × 20 ½ in. (64.7 × 52 cm). Dallas Museum of Art. The Munger Fund.

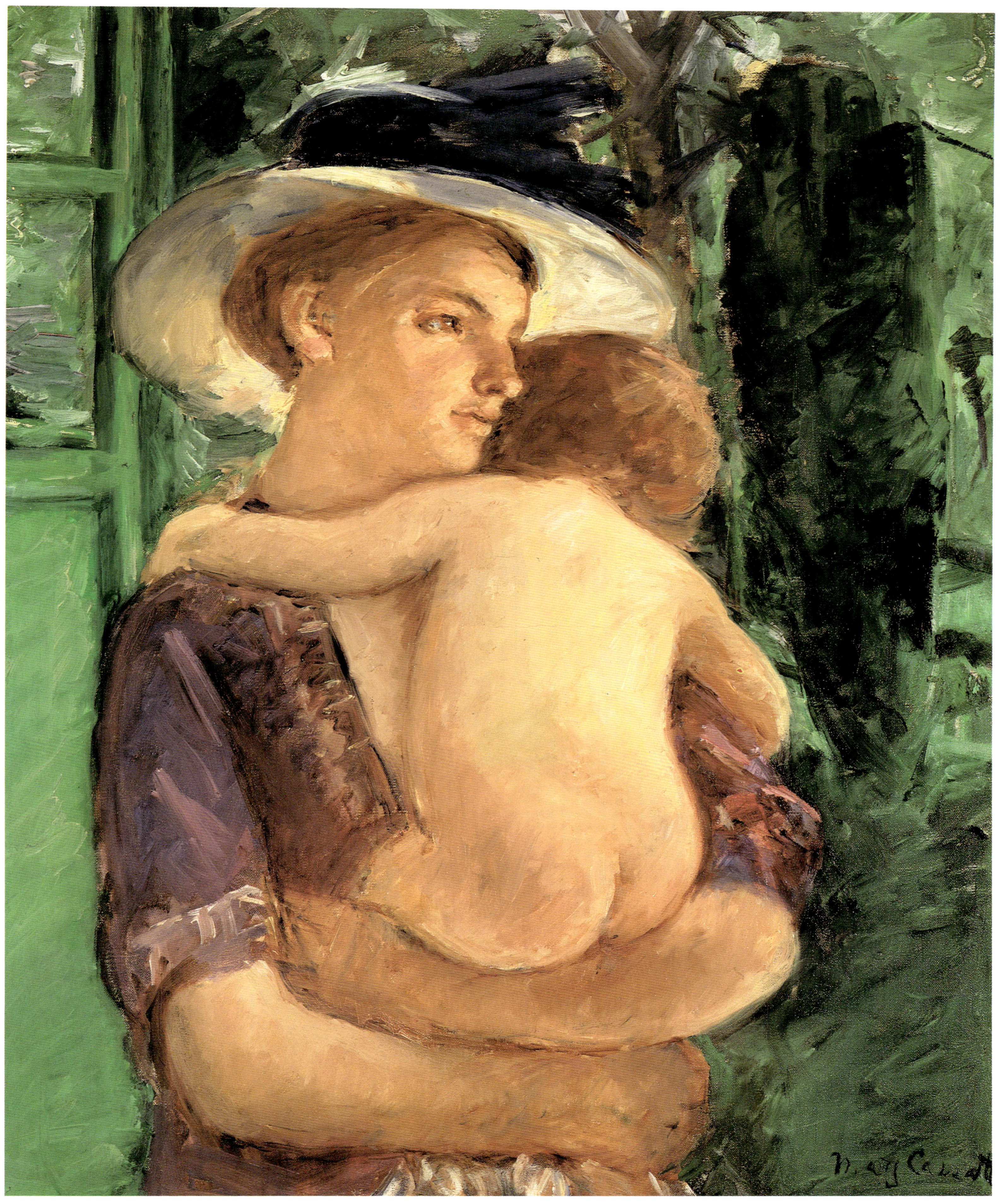

COLORPLATE 117. *Mother in Large Hat Holding Her Nude Baby Seen in Back View.* c. 1909. Oil on canvas. 31 3/8 × 25 in. (79.7 × 63.5 cm). Bill and Irma Runyon Art Collections, Texas A & M University Development Foundation. MSC Forsyth Center Galleries, College Station, Texas.

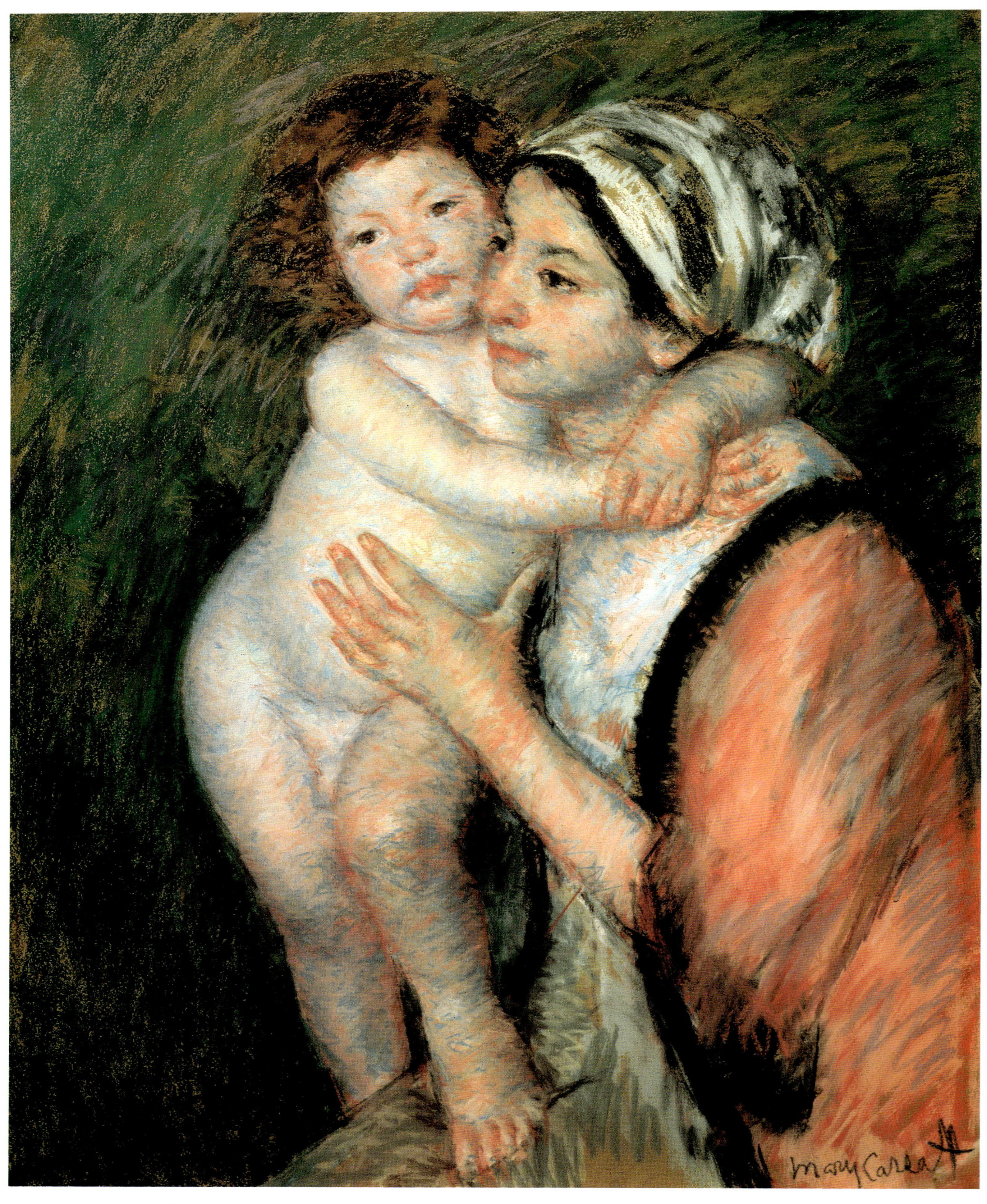

COLORPLATE 118. *Mother and Child.* 1914. Pastel on wove paper (now discolored) mounted on canvas, originally on a strainer. 32 × 25 5/8 in. (81.2 × 65 cm). The Metropolitan Museum of Art, New York, H.O. Havemeyer Collection. Bequest of Mrs. H.O. Havemeyer, 1929 (29.100.49). © 1988 The Metropolitan Museum of Art.

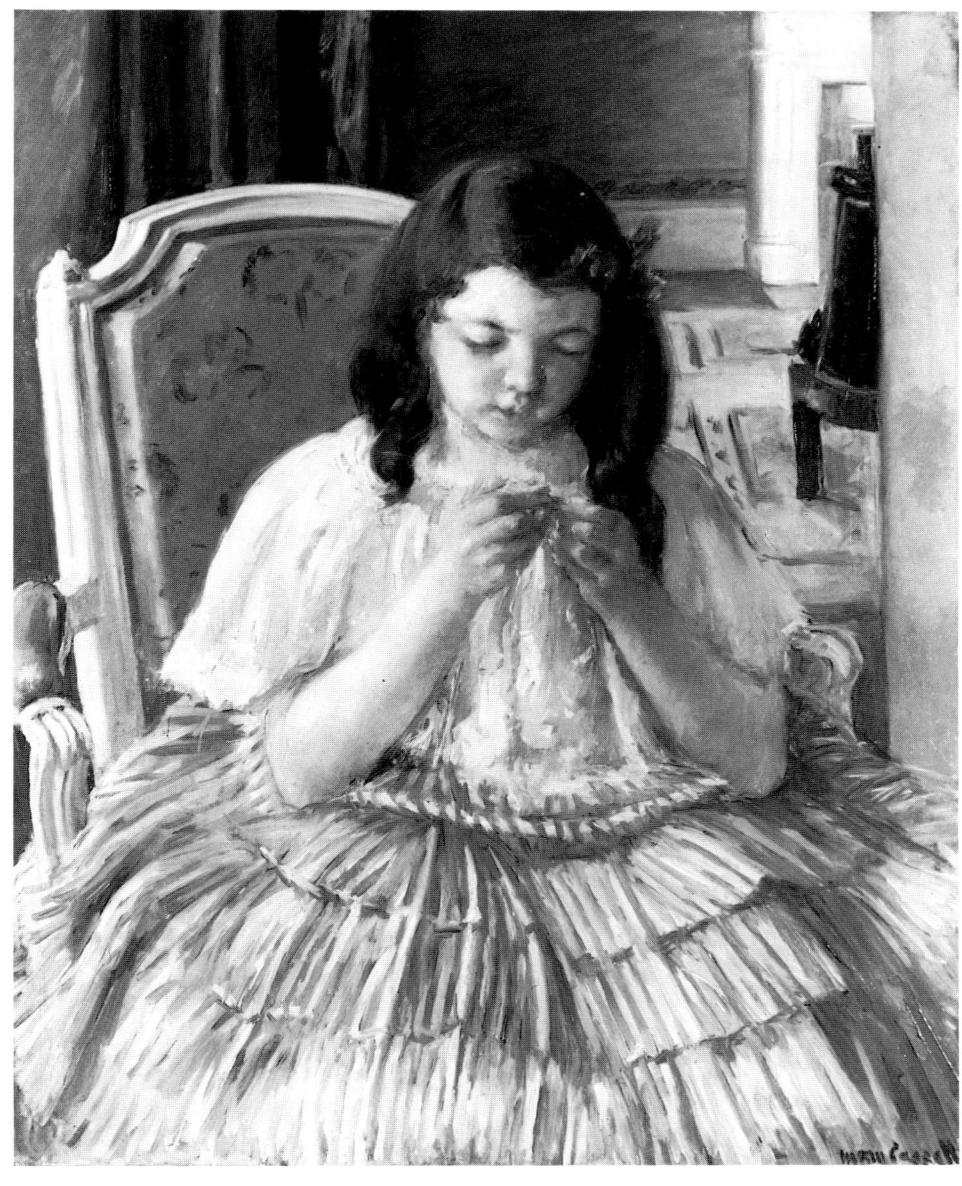

Françoise in Green, Sewing. c. 1908–1909. Oil on canvas. 32 × 25 ½ in. (81.3 × 64.8 cm). The Saint Louis Art Museum. Gift of Dr. Ernest G. Stillman.

capable artist's hands, were shrunken and folded on the quilt. When she began to talk they waved and flickered about her head; and the room became charged with the electric vitality of the old lady.

"Well," she fairly shouted, "have you ever seen such weather! My doctor says that in forty years there has not been such a storm." She was terribly put out that the weather had prevented her coming down to lunch. She would have ordered chicken but really hadn't expected me at the last moment. She hoped the Chateau Margot was really good. It was the last bottle of a case of wine presented to her by her brother J. G., just before his death some fifteen years back. It was all such bad luck. She had driven too far on Friday, and this terrible weather!

Miss Cassatt as usual did the talking. Her mind galloped along, shaking the frail human body, lying propped up so sadly thin and impotent. Every few minutes her memory would fail her, and the faithful Mathilde would lean over the bedhead, painfully intent on interpolating the missing links of the conversation. She could almost read her mistress' mind, and would make hurried suggestions to her. Miss Cassatt would pounce upon the right one and gallop along in her talk. Every now and then, for but a moment, she would gently subside, and Mathilde or I would inject a few remarks. What abysses and reinforcements of courage and life and enthusiasm still lay hidden inside the frail body, under the gentle exterior of an old lady's hospitality. Mathilde was to show me the little drawing of the family group done, I think, in Heidelberg, when she was quite a child. There she sat, with a book in her hand, prim, erect, intense; the corners of her eyes slightly raised, looking very straight and hard at one. She wished Mathilde to go and fetch the Egyptian jewelry of lapis lazuli and carnelian. Now there was a terrible snapping of fingers, and various words and suggestions were proffered. At last the jewelry was brought in and spread upon the bed.

"Mathilde," she suddenly shouted, "get Durand-Ruel's letter about my drypoints. I fancy that now I am vindicated. Did you ever hear of such an insult? You saw the prints too! Go and see Durand when you return to Paris. Such impudence!"

Miss Cassatt was becoming exhausted, and I told her that I should see her soon again. It was too bad the weather had prevented her coming down to lunch. She would motor down to Paris as soon as it got a little warmer. I think she hardly remembered me as I tiptoed out of the room. Down the long corridor, pausing to look at her drypoints and colored aquatints along the wall. Then through the darkened salon among the somewhat incoherent medley of Empire and Louis Philippe furniture. The drawing by Ingres over there hidden by the silk window curtain. Most of the Degas, the Courbets, and the Sisleys were in the Paris apartment. On a little table the set of dark blue English china so brilliantly painted in the *Lady at the Tea Table* in the Metropolitan. Then out through the cold glass-covered veranda where hung the Utamaros and one or two Hokusais. One last peep across the meadow, the chestnut trees, the little formal stream beyond. I drove away in the rain. I should never again talk with this extraordinary woman.

COLORPLATE 38

Her work had been the most important influence I had felt. Then too through her I had somehow lived more closely with her great contemporaries. She had known Berthe Morisot intimately; had seen much of Renoir during those last years at Grasse. Chiefly of course she talked of Degas, for whose work she had a passionate admiration. But it was as a great human being that she influenced me—perhaps the greatest human being I have ever known.

I first met her in 1912. She was then an old lady already becoming blind, and recovering from a nervous breakdown brought on in part by the death of her brother J.G., whom she adored. The qualities that made her very great to me were her integrity and her passion. She drew that almost impossible line between her social life and her art, and never sacrificed an iota to either. Socially she remained the prim Philadelphia spinster of her generation. When I used to bicycle over from Giverny to lunch with her, she would regale me with Washington Pie and Philadelphia White Mountain Cake and sherry. She loved to gossip about Philadelphians, and picked with relish on her family, certain of whom she adored. But she would never forgive them for not going to see her exhibitions in New York. She lived most of her life with her mother in her Paris apartment, or in the country at Beaufresne, and I fancy would have led much the same life had she never painted or left Philadelphia. Her moral code was as inflexible as were her ways of living. She was rather angered than shocked at the tardy discovery of certain irregular relations and an unexpected baby among a peasant family who lived at her gate.

It is extraordinary that a woman of such social rigidity could have preserved such white-hot passion for her art. It was only possible for a being mentally detached, of fanatical intensity, and an uncompromising fighter. Remember that she came to Paris a young girl, almost without preliminary tuition. She studied alone, and a few years later the early group of Impressionists were asking her to exhibit with them.

I recall with pleasure certain conversations—monologues. My ring at the door was answered by the barking and scampering of the ill-natured and overfed griffons who lived with Miss Cassatt. Their churlish yappings would finally subside to an asthmatic wheeze when the tea had been brought in; and they would settle like withered chrysanthemums upon the

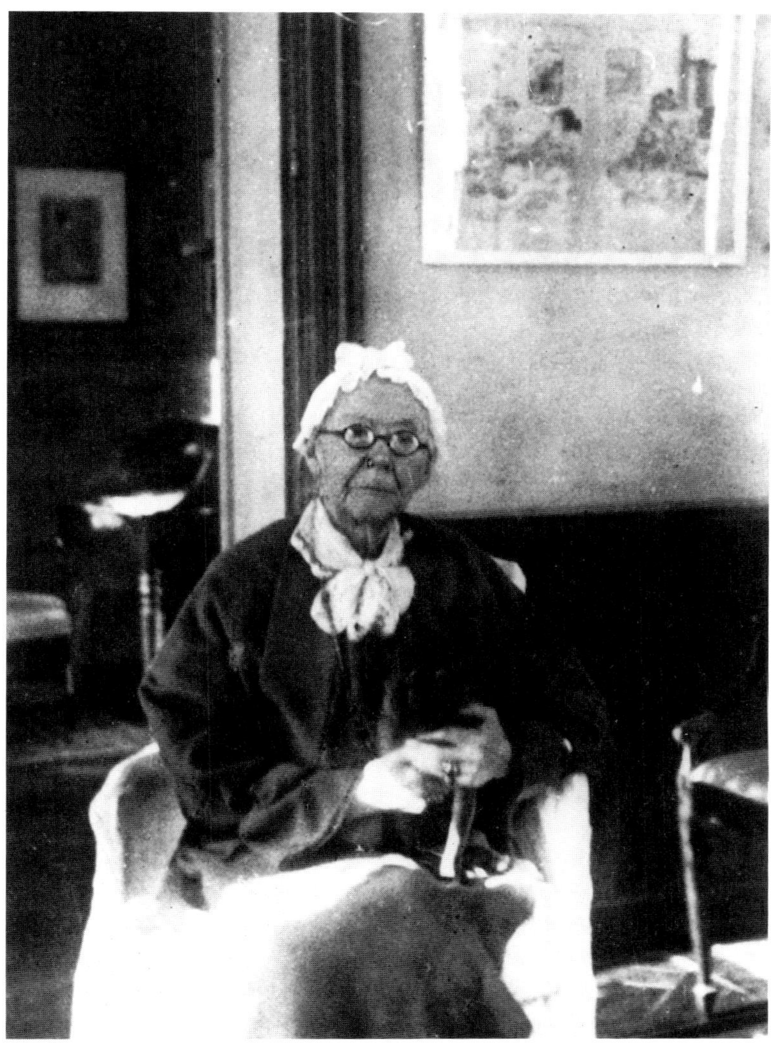

Photograph of Mary Cassatt at Beaufresne. 1925. Photograph courtesy of the Archives of American Art, Smithsonian Institution. The Frederick A. Sweet Papers. Location of original unknown.

rugs. I steeped myself in the old lady's reminiscent talk. It was my first year as an art student. G.B.: "And what do you think of John Sargent, Miss Cassatt?" Sargent, she said, had shown ability, and at one time Manet had spoken of him. But he preferred notoriety. "You know what Claude Monet said to me about Sargent? 'Miss Cassatt, *Sargent est un brave type mais quand il dejeune avec moi je ne parle pas la peinture.*' " I found that a judicious amount of opposition spurred her on. "But you will admit that he has painted some fine portraits?" "What!" she shouted, "have you seen that thing he did of my brother Alec? And did you know the price he charged? And did you notice the way he smudged in the background?" Her voice quivered. "I call it dishonesty. I told Alec he ought not to allow that thing in his house."

"Sargent est un brave type mais quand il dejeune avec moi je ne parle pas le peinture"; Sargent is a great fellow, but when he comes to lunch I don't talk about painting.

There were but few whom she tolerated among her contemporaries. G.B.: "And what do you think of Albert Besnard?" Miss Cassatt, snickering: "You know what Degas said about Besnard? '*Il a volé les plumes de nos ailes.*'" She quoted Degas frequently when I asked her own advice. G.B.: "What painters would you advise copying?"—for she believed in copying in the museums.—"Would Rembrandt or Rubens be good artists to copy?" Miss Cassatt: "No, Rembrandt is '*le dernier mot.*' " By this she meant that Rembrandt and Rubens were finished masters and that the purity of their line and design would be hidden under the brilliancy of their technique. Above all she valued line and design. "Do you know what Degas said?—'*Il faut se plier devant les primitifs.*' " She herself had copied Correggio in Parma as a young girl, and perhaps Moroni in Bergamo. She made me study his work one summer in museums. She had a veneration for Degas. What he felt was actually her law and standard. Pointing to a little grisaille on her wall she added, "—and no painter since Vermeer has mastered atmosphere the way he does." That was that. I have never seen a great and successful

"Il a vole les plumes de nos ailes"; He stole feathers from our wings.

"Il faut se plier devant les primitifs"; We must fall down on our knees in front of the primitives.

artist who so ungrudgingly acknowledged the debt to an earlier and lifelong influence. But it was not generosity with Miss Cassatt so much as her splendid detachment.

Many of Miss Cassatt's friends must have speculated, as I did, on the exact social relation between the two. She had been a young and brilliant disciple. They were both lonely idealists who lived in their art. And one personality fired and directed the other. How often, had I the courage, would I have asked the prim old lady point blank, "Was he ever your lover?" A couple of years ago Miss Cassatt was telling me about Degas' occasionally shabby or dishonest behavior. I have forgotten the occasion. I think she had sent an American buyer to his studio. Perhaps he was jealous. At any rate he said something about her painting which deeply embarrassed her. It was the particular indifferent intonation with which Miss Cassatt said: "After that for years I stopped seeing him," which revealed to me that relation about which I had been so romantically curious. Miss Cassatt's passion for Degas was a generous and detached enthusiasm for his work. About him socially she must have felt as any Philadelphia spinster might feel about the French bourgeois whom she frequently saw in business relations.

One day we peradventure spoke of Russians. Miss Cassatt: "If you have had dealings with them, as I have, you will never want to hear of them again. They have never produced art and never will." Without for the moment alluding to their literature I mentioned their music. "Music," said Miss Cassatt, "is a purely emotional art. The finest art is intellectual in its appeal." We never again spoke of Russians.

Miss Cassatt's mind was neither balanced nor analytic. It swept along enthusiastic and prejudiced. Like any artist's mind, good or bad, it saw things directly, did not arrive at truth through a process of ratiocination. Her mind was great because it inspired others to see great truths, through her passion and single-mindedness.

Like every artist, her ego was I suppose never satisfied; and she who had achieved such remarkable success must at times satisfy her pride by snatching too unnecessarily at sops of comfort. At one time she had wished to present to the Pennsylvania Academy of Fine Arts two portraits by Courbet. "I went to Durand-Ruel," she said, "and asked him the price, telling him I could not pay for them at the time. 'That's all right, Miss Cassatt,' he answered, 'I will take some of your work in exchange.' And do you know what the Academy had the audacity to write to me?" she shouted, "they thanked me and added that by the way they noticed that the Academy had no examples of my own work and would I send them something, hi! hi! hi! I told them I had been exhibiting for years at the Academy and they had never asked me my prices, although they had funds for buying contemporary American art."

Her family whom she adored caused her continual agonies. There is a particularly noble portrait of hers owned by the Metropolitan Museum. It was, as I remember, of a relative, Mrs. F. For many years it was kept by the family in the garret. "They liked the way the tea-cups were painted," tittered Miss Cassatt. But her day of revenge came. "They told me I would get the red ribbon if I allowed it to go to the Luxembourg. And do you know they had the impudence to offer the same honor to that woman Romaine Brooks! Well, they can't expect any of my things after that!"

"Lady at the Tea Table" (COLORPLATE 38). For the complete story see Cassatt's letter to Louisine Havemeyer on page 150.

Romaine Brooks (1874–1970), American painter known for androgynous figures and portraits.

Miss Cassatt was almost unaware of anything that happened in the world of art after 1900. Through occasional conversations with Durand-Ruel, Vollard and Jacacci she must have been dimly aware of certain names and tendencies that goaded her to fury. She never quite forgave Marie Laurencin for omitting noses on her portraits. "Why," she snapped, "I don't quite know what the world's coming to if they call that painting."

Marie Laurencin (1885–1956), French painter who worked with the Cubists and later focused on images of women—usually actresses and dancers—and sets for the ballet.

Vollard had presented her once with several little terracottas, perhaps by Clairette—when I first saw them across the room I thought they were Maillol's and asked her. "Well," she said, "Vollard told me the name. Yes, perhaps that was it. Do you know his work?" It seems almost inconceivable that she was unaware of Maillol's name.

Aristide Maillol (1861–1944), French Modernist sculptor.

Her political prejudices were as violent as were her artistic standards. Only they varied from year to year. Toward the end she became incensed with the French—for no reason that I can recall. They were becoming quite worthless and immoral. Earlier in 1915 she used to quote Schiller to me to show how the Germans had changed since the eighteenth century. The last year I saw her she became rather interested in contemporary American art. I rather think she felt that in so doing she was snubbing the French. Perhaps it was a sudden yearning for the country where she had been so little but where she knew she would always live. She had Mathilde accompany her to a little group of Americans that were exhibiting in Paris. I think I was never more flattered than when she told me that she had been led in front of one of my paintings and could make out that it was a still life. "But the others," she said, "I could not see very distinctly. It must have been a bad light."

I should hate to leave the impression that Miss Cassatt was a violently prejudiced, quarrelsome old spinster. She was all of this, and one was entirely unaware of it as one talked to her. She was a great and passionate idealist, the rare human being who could divert all her passion into her work and ideas. She did not have to "live" her art.

Art is a recreation of life, and enhances life by its power to make us live anew. Miss Cassatt, more than any man I ever knew, through the youthful intensity of her feeling, could make her hearer share her enthusiasm for ideas and her faith in ideas. If it is possible to love a purely detached enthusiasm, then I loved this prim old Philadelphia lady. How slim and upright she would sit in her white serge jacket and lace cap, her shawl sometimes spread over her knee, as she poured the tea in the apartment in the Rue Marignan—the wheezy, chocolate-eyed griffons subsiding in a coma of indigestion about her chair. And then as she caught on fire with some idea her eyes blazed and narrowed; her capable bony hands jerked hither and thither. The lace cap would slip to one side and the shawl slide from her knee. As the time to depart approached I would retreat step by step to the door. Once started she literally could not stop, and one was compelled to take one's leave by inches. She too would rise, snapping her fingers and talking ever louder, as she heard the visitor's voice recede toward the door. Usually she would follow me out on the landing, and perhaps scream over the banisters some bit of family gossip which she had saved from the last letter from Philadelphia. Such are the moments which I like to recall. And then there were the other moments when she must have sat alone, prim and straight and nearly blind, alone for months and years, nursing her passions and enthusiasms. It is not perhaps surprising that at the end of her great and finally successful career she said to the artist, Adolphe Borie, to whom she was devoted: "After all, woman's vocation in life is to bear children."

From *Journal des Debats*

Cassatt's Legacy

July 9, 1926

Miss Mary Cassatt, an American painter, chose French art. She just died, at eighty-two years of age, in her elective homeland. Nearly blind, she had not worked since the war, but, three years ago in Paris, one could have seen an exhibition of her works, and the discovery of a canvas, a pastel, or a print by this infinitely sensitive and graceful artist was always a source of joy. Was she not—along with Eva Gonzalez and Berthe Morisot—Impressionism's muse? She came to France very young, in order to pursue her artistic education, and soon formed friendships with Degas and Manet. The former's drawing undeniably influenced her burgeoning talent, but what was cruel precision in the painter of dancers became, in the American's work, scattered tenderness and charming intimacy. No colorist translated the emotions of young mothers, or the mischievousness of cherished children more variously than Mary Cassatt. The painter of the nursery, she captured with a free, bold, and always caressing hand the attitudes of the little ones, and the apprehensive, enveloping gestures of those who look as if they could be their elder sisters.

All is youth, freshness, and liveliness of line in the art of this spontaneous and refined artist. We know that she was generous and did much to spread a love for fine French painting in the United States. She is certain to live on, in the grateful memory of those in whom her art will always evoke the most touching poetry there is, that of childhood, maternal love, the hearth, the poetry of happiness.

From *Literary Digest*
"The Painter of Children"
July 10, 1926

Now that Mary Cassatt has become history—her death occurred June 15 at the age of eighty-three [*sic*]—there are many speculations as to how much she belongs to us. Pittsburgh was her birthplace, and Philadelphia gave her the rudiments of her art; but she had lived so long in Europe and become so identified with French art, that nothing now labeled "American" can seem to be applied to her. Her recent utterance that "no distinctive school of American art exists" seems to absolve her from any personal claim to alliance. Yet her fame, which has existed since the days of the great impressionists, Degas, Manet, Renoir, Berthe Morisot, is too much for us to surrender to any foreign ownership. The fact that, like Whistler and Sargent, she chose life-long exile from her native land, should not, says the Providence *News*, "preclude us from taking a great pride in her achievement." Heine and Byron lived away from their native land, but they were nevertheless the one German and the other English. "Mary Cassatt may not have been a great American according to the standards of Babbittry, but she brought this country a more precious fame than any Babbitt has ever brought or will bring." If there are those who will rise up to repel the words of the News, there is still this dictum of the New York *Telegram:*

> If she gave to France what ought to have been meant for America there is this to be said for her voluntary exile, that her shrinking nature had on the banks of the Seine a retreat where she could work and live such as she could not have found by the Hudson or the Delaware.
>
> After all the crop justified the foreign soil in her case as in that of Whistler.

Mary Cassatt will be remembered as the painter of children. "She has the eyes of a painter and in a measure the mind of a sister of charity," wrote Achille Segard, the great French critic. Also, she is "devoted to her art as if it were a religion." On this theme he makes a further observation:

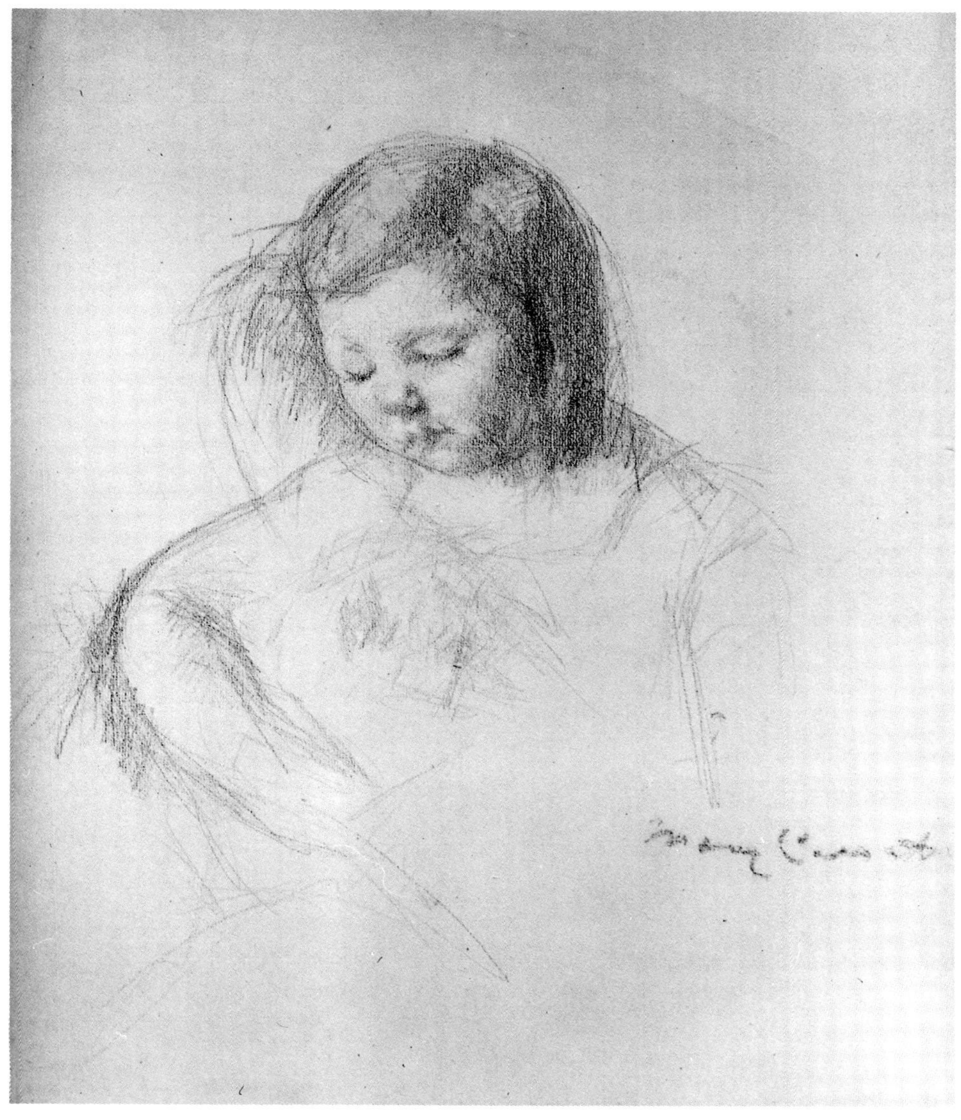

Portrait of Sara Looking Down. c. 1901. Pastel on paper. 22 × 18 in. (55.9 × 45.7 cm). Private collection. Photograph courtesy of Spanierman Gallery, New York.

> Her conception of life and art is profound and touching. One perceives that she has a strong feeling that the place of the child in human life is of limitless importance, hence he represents at one time both the present and the future, is the gage of immortality, the necessary medium for the continuation of the race and its perpetuation.

When, in 1874, Degas saw a canvas by her in the Salon and remarked: "That is genuine. There is one who does as I do," it was perhaps the beginning of that association in art that links her name with the impressionists. In *The Herald Tribune* is a forceful editorial that may be safely credited to the distinguished critic, Mr. Royal Cortissoz:

> Mary Cassatt was a remarkable woman, the comrade of those painters who under the banner of Impressionism achieved something like a revolution in modern art. The *mot* of Degas makes perhaps the best epitaph upon her whole career—"That is genuine." At the close of the famous exhibition of 1879 in which she and the others affirmed their independence there was a surplus in the treasury. With her share of it Miss Cassatt bought pictures by Degas and Manet. That, too, was like her. She lived utterly for art.
>
> She had the gift, the *flair,* but it took time before she found herself. Going abroad while she was still a young girl to be a painter, she strayed momentarily into the studio of Charles Chaplin, a

graceful Salonnier. Against his routine habit she promptly rebelled and sought instead the inspiration of the old masters. Rather oddly she found it first at Parma. This keen observer, this practitioner of an essentially French and modern directness, whose tenderness never lured her away from the exact statement of fact, actually began her apprenticeship by long saturation in the melting Correggiosity of Correggio. After Italy came Spain, but with a susceptibility to Rubens rather than to Velasquez in the stimulating pageant of the Prado, a susceptibility so ardent that it ultimately carried her to Antwerp and intense devotion to the works of the great Fleming. Yet these imitations were but preliminaries to the decisive development of her talent. That ensued in Paris.

The truth was her goal, and the newer French exemplars of it were her predestined counselors. She once told M. Segard, her biographer, what they meant to her. "I recognized my true masters," she said. "I admired Manet, Courbet and Degas. I hated conventional art. Now I began to live." The important point about this period in her life, too, is that she "began to live" as an individuality. Her associations never submerged her originality. There was an organic energy in her art. Even on what was in a sense her real debut, in 1879, Gauguin could shrewdly say of her: "Miss Cassatt has much charm, but she has more force." That force lifted her to high rank. It was as an equal that she foregathered with the Impressionist group. She and Degas were colleagues.

It is an amusing paradox in her history that her force, her penetrating vision, her technical clarity were wreaked largely upon the most fragile of themes. She excelled in pictures of children and their mothers. But her sentiment couldn't have drifted into sentimentality. She had too live a mind. She had too much taste. Apropos of her taste, it should be added that she was a most judicious connoisseur and had to do with the entrance of numerous fine pictures into divers American collections, private and public. Her judgment on a work of art was impeccable.

In the *Public Ledger,* Philadelphia, which gave her her first art training, thus remembers her:

> She made more than the beginning of her training here in America, and was a graduate of whom the Pennsylvania Academy has been justly proud. Her works are in the best American galleries as in the representative collections abroad, and her own country never failed in recognition of her merit, as when, twelve years ago, she received the gold medal of the Pennsylvania Academy. She painted with tender feeling and impressionistic breadth of technique the domestic intimacies, and instead of the formal imitation of classic tradition took motherhood and infancy for her favorite themes. Thus her work had a cogent human appeal that will cause it to be remembered when many an epic and heroic canvas is forgotten.

The Cassatts seem to give high authority to the efficacy of the melting-pot, tho they were here before that agency was supposed to begin functioning. Her brother, A.J. Cassatt, was president of the Pennsylvania Railroad and responsible for the great terminal station in New York. Says the New York *Telegram:*

> President Cassatt appears to have inherited the practical talents of his feminine Scots forebears, while Mary had the artistic endowment of the male French side of the family.

The Pittsburgh *Sun* regrets:

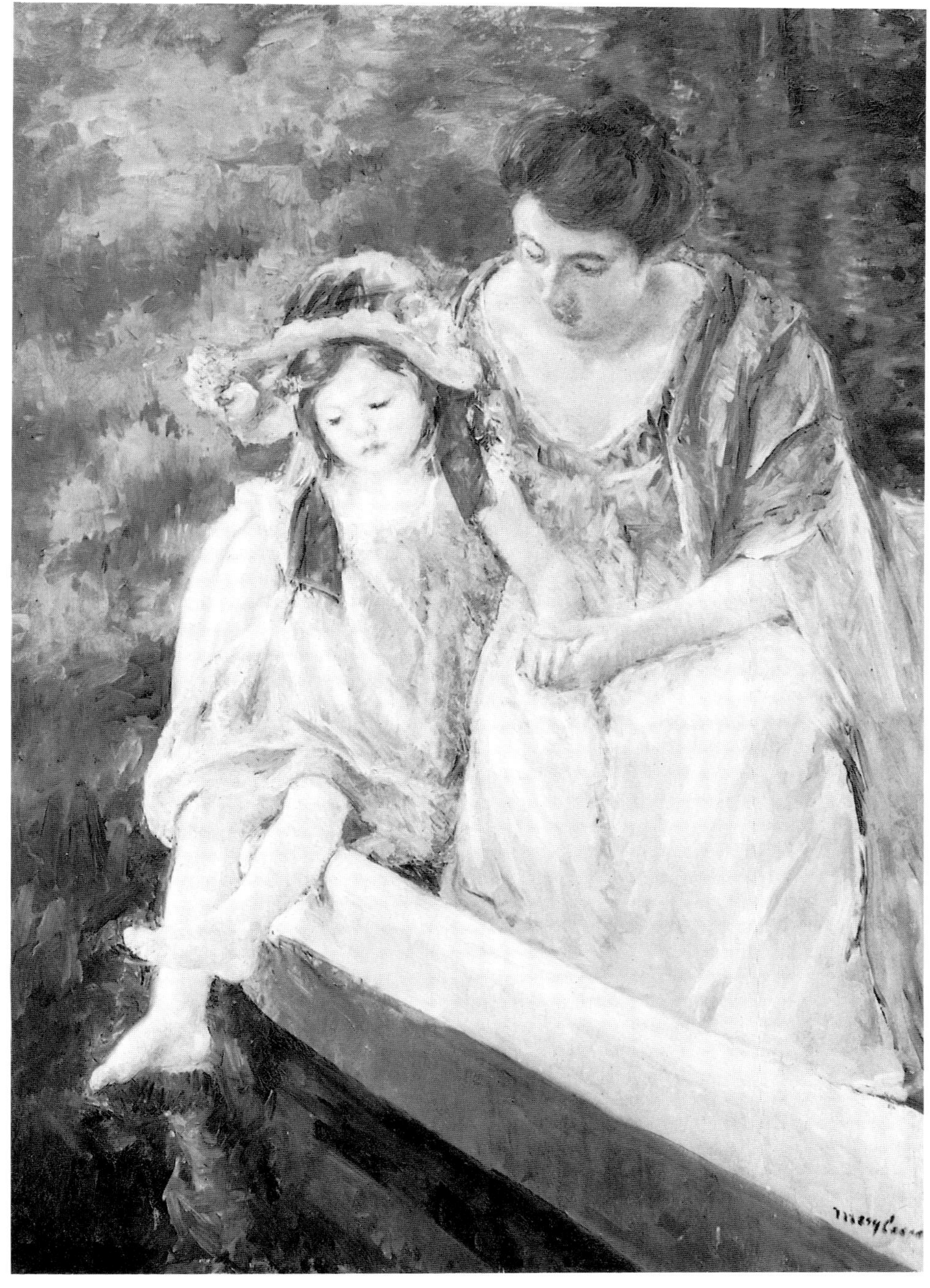

Mother and Child in a Boat. c. 1909. Oil on canvas. 45 ½ × 32 in. (115.6 × 81.3 cm). Addison Gallery of American Art, Phillips Academy, Andover, Massachusetts. Gift of an anonymous donor.

Pittsburgh can make no further claims than to have been the birthplace of this eminent woman. She received her training in art elsewhere. But Pittsburgh has changed since 1868. The international exhibition held annually attracts exhibitors from all countries of Europe; the permanent exhibit in the galleries of Carnegie Institute is the opportunity for an education in art for all. How Miss Cassatt, in her early days, would have welcomed such a collection!

There is one painting of Miss Cassatt's in the permanent collection in the gallery, *Young Women Picking Fruit,* the first picture purchased by the Patrons' Art Fund in 1922.

COLORPLATE 62

Just to show that people do not think alike, we add a letter written by the painter, Mr. Childe Hassam, to the New York *Herald Tribune.*

Miss Cassatt at the time of her death was one of the most distinguished living artists in the world, one of the two or three most eminent painter-etchers, and the most able and eminent woman who ever etched on copper or used the dry point; in fact, hers is the most notable woman's name in the history of the graphic arts. This seems not generally known by her countrymen, and by so few of the writers who have noted her death.

She was born in Pittsburgh, where a famous international exhibition is now held yearly, and it is perfectly safe to say that if an exhibition of her work had been held in New York while she was alive the director of the Carnegie Institute would not have rushed by the first train to New York to expend some $20,000 for one of her beautiful canvases (as he did for the Montmartre mediocrity with the Spanish name), any one of which is worth all, and more than all, of the recent exhibits by living European painters held here in this city (even with an introduction by Dr. Christian Brinton) or that are liable to be held here.

Like Whistler, Henry James and Sargent, she spent most all of her life in Europe, which she was used to and undoubtedly preferred. One lives where one likes, but she was an American, and it is worth calling attention to that fact in connection with the first few lines of this letter.

ROBERT HALLOWELL

Robert Hallowell (1886–1939), American painter and engraver, was the assistant director of the Works Project Administration (WPA) from 1935 to 1936.

From *The Survey*

Cassatt: A "Modern" American Woman

December 1926

A few years ago, standing before one of her own mother-and-child canvases, Mary Cassatt said to a young American woman painter, "You must choose. You can't be a painter and a mother too. Have you made your choice?"

"Yes," came the twentieth century reply, "I choose both!"

And she did. Whether wisely or not, or successfully or not, remains still to be seen.

What has been seen, and proved brilliantly, is that Mary Cassatt herself, by her devotion to her art; by her wise decision to do her work in what to her was the most congenial atmosphere (as it happened, France); and by her great native talent, came to be easily one of the half dozen most important figures in the history of modern American painting.

I say modern advisedly. For, though Mary Cassatt's work is wholly unmodern in the current use of that word, it is my belief that, when modern painting comes in for historical appraisal, the Impressionists, of which she was so to say a charter member, will be seen to be not only the founders of it all, but the most revolutionary group of painters the world has known for three centuries.

It should be remembered that when the Impressionists first showed their work at Durand-Ruel's in Paris the frames of their pictures were strewn with sous in denunciation of "this crazy pistol painting." Mary Cassatt had the vision to be among the crazy. She had the good sense to select one of them, Degas, as her master. And then—she had the gift to be herself.

American women who are sex-proud can afford to rejoice over the achievement of this rather prim, rather emphatic Philadelphia aristocrat,

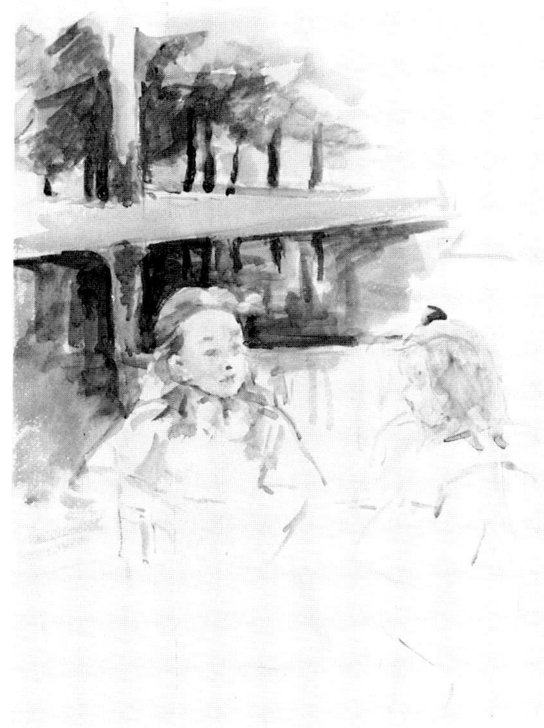

Augusta's Daughter and a Friend Seated Near a River Bank. c. 1910. Watercolor. 18 7/8 × 12 7/8 in. (47.9 × 32.7 cm). The Baltimore Museum of Art. The Cone Collection, formed by Dr. Claribel Cone and Miss Etta Cone of Baltimore, Maryland.

sister of a president of the Pennsylvania Railroad, who in spite of the French titles of her pictures and her French residence, belongs by the spirit of her work and its supreme craftsmanship to her native land.

From *Art et Decoration*

A Cassatt Retrospective

July 1931

Of the women artists who shared the dark hours, the disappointments, and the triumphs of the Impressonists, Mary Cassatt is one of those of whom the general public was least aware.

Though she lived in Paris, where she had made her home, for almost all her long life, most of her works went to her native America. It has been possible to mount only a few overall exhibitions.

Thus, we must be grateful to M. Reitlinger for the excellent retrospective that he offers us. Besides a few paintings and pastels, there were primarily sketches and studies that the artist had kept in her studio.

The Galérie A-M Reitlinger in Paris handled the exhibition and sale of the collection of Mary Cassatt's works inherited by Mathilde Valet.

Nothing is more indicative of a painter's talent than such drafts, these roughs, in which he reveals all of himself.

These drawings, hastily tossed down on sheets of every shape and color, disclose Mary Cassatt's continuous curiosity, her emotions, and her tenderness. As others express themselves with words, just so did she translate her thought into lines. Out of a summary drawing style that in a few lines indicates the essence of the subject emerges the interesting detail, emphasized with nervous hatchmarks—a face whose character struck her, aroused her sympathy, especially those artless attitudes of the children's bodies, the charming poses of mother love surrendering itself.

Quick strokes of watercolor and highlights in colored pencil reveal the colorist nearly as well as the canvases and those pastels, whose tones are so astonishingly fresh.

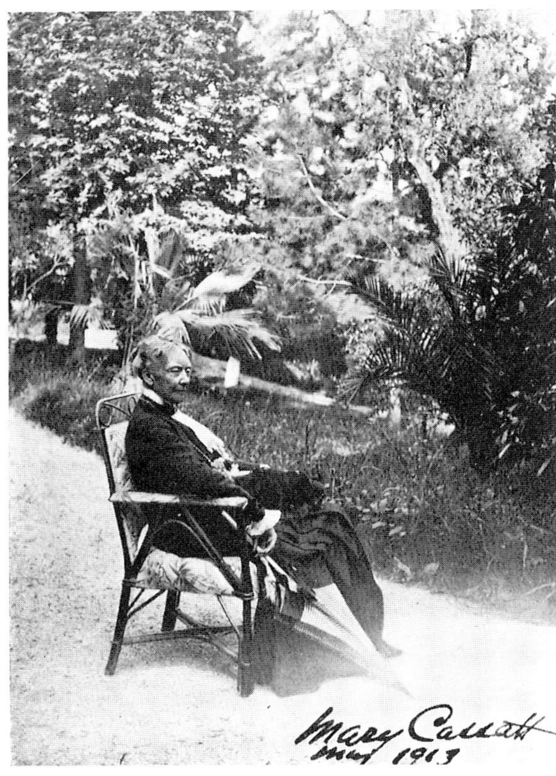

Photograph of Mary Cassatt seated, Grasse. 1913. Private collection.

But what stands out most in these undeniably candid pages, is the wholly synthesized, deliberately evocative, very pure classicism of an art that officialdom treated as a disturbance of the peace.

AMBROISE VOLLARD

From *Recollections of a Picture Dealer*

A Final Farewell

1936

Mary Cassatt owned a place at Mesnil-Beaufresne where she used to spend the summer. It was there that she died in 1926. The entire village followed the funeral procession. None but old Mathilde, her devoted maid, and a few intimates, knew the whole extent of her generosity, for Mary Cassatt accompanied her acts of beneficence by a dry, almost distant gesture, as though she felt shy of doing good.

In the cemetery, after the last prayers, the pastor, according to protestant custom, distributed to those present the roses and carnations strewn upon the coffin, that they might scatter them over the grave. Looking at this carpet of brilliant flowers, I fancied Mary Cassatt running to fetch a canvas and brushes.

SOURCE NOTES

Alexander J. Cassatt to his fiancée, Lois Buchanan; November 27, 1867
Philadelphia Museum of Art

Mary Cassatt and Eliza Haldeman to the Committee on Instruction; March 7, 1862
Pennsylvania Academy of the Fine Arts, Philadelphia

Eliza Haldeman to Samuel Haldeman; March 7, 1862
Pennsylvania Academy of the Fine Arts, Philadelphia

Mary Cassatt to Eliza Haldeman; March 18, 1864
Pennsylvania Academy of the Fine Arts, Philadelphia

Mary Cassatt to Eliza Haldeman; June 13, 1864
Haldeman Collection

Eliza Haldeman to Samuel Haldeman; December 4, 1866
Pennsylvania Academy of the Fine Arts, Philadelphia

Eliza Haldeman to Alice Haldeman; February 1867
Pennsylvania Academy of the Fine Arts, Philadelphia

Eliza Haldeman to Mary Haldeman; May 15, 1867
Pennsylvania Academy of the Fine Arts, Philadelphia

Eliza Haldeman to Samuel and Mary Haldeman; May 8, 1868
Pennsylvania Academy of the Fine Arts, Philadelphia

Mary Cassatt to Lois Cassatt; August 1, 1869
Philadelphia Museum of Art

Mary Cassatt to Emily Sartain; June 7, 1871
Pennsylvania Academy of the Fine Arts, Philadelphia

William Sartain to His Father, John Sartain; March 25, 1872
Historical Society of Pennsylvania

Emily Sartain to John Sartain; March 7, 1872
Moore College of Art, Philadelphia

Mary Cassatt to Emily Sartain; June 2, 1872
Pennsylvania Academy of the Fine Arts, Philadelphia

Mary Cassatt to Emily Sartain; January 1, 1873
Pennsylvania Academy of the Fine Arts, Philadelphia

Emily Sartain to John Sartain; May 8, 1873
Moore College of Art, Philadelphia

Emily Sartain to John Sartain; June 17, 1874
Moore College of Art, Philadelphia

Mary Cassatt to Ambroise Vollard; 1903
Archives of American Art, Smithsonian Institution

Mary Cassatt to J. Alden Weir; March 10, 1878
Mrs. Page Ely, Old Lyme, Connecticut

Mary Cassatt to Berthe Morisot; Fall 1879
Collection Denis Rouart, Paris

Robert Cassatt to Alexander Cassatt; May 21, 1879
Philadelphia Museum of Art

Katherine Cassatt to Alexander Cassatt; April 9, 1880
Philadelphia Museum of Art

Katherine Cassatt to her Granddaughter, Katharine Cassatt; April 15, 1881
Philadelphia Museum of Art

Mary Cassatt to Alexander Cassatt; June 22, 1883
Philadelphia Museum of Art

Katherine Cassatt to Alexander Cassatt; November 30, 1883
Philadelphia Museum of Art

Mary Cassatt to Louisine Havemeyer; February 4, 1915
The Metropolitan Museum of Art, New York

Mary Cassatt to Berthe Morisot; April 1890
Collection Denis Rouart, Paris

Mary Cassatt to Frank Weitenkampf; May 18, 1906
Brooklyn Museum Archives

Mary Cassatt to Bertha Palmer; October 11, 1892
Art Institute of Chicago

Mary Cassatt to Bertha Palmer; December 1, 1892
Art Institute of Chicago

Bertha Palmer to Mary Cassatt; December 15, 1892
Chicago Historical Society

Mary Cassatt to John H. Whittemore; December 22, 1893
J.H. Whittemore Co., Naugatuck, Connecticut

Mary Cassatt to Eugenie Heller; January 30, 1894
Thomas J. Watson Library, The Metropolitan Museum of Art, New York

Mary Cassatt to Paul Durand-Ruel; Summer 1894
Durand-Ruel Archives, Paris

Mary Cassatt to Rose Lamb; April 26, 1895
Museum of Fine Arts, Boston

Mary Cassatt to Eugenie Heller; c. February 1, 1896
Thomas J. Watson Library, The Metropolitan Museum of Art, New York

Mary Cassatt to Paul Durand-Ruel; January 22, 1898
Durand-Ruel Archives, Paris

Mary Cassatt to Theodate Pope; September 1903
Hill-Stead Museum, Farmington, Connecticut

Mary Cassatt to Harrison Morris; March 15, 1904
Pennsylvania Academy of the Fine Arts, Philadelphia

Mary Cassatt to John W. Beatty; September 5, 1905
Archives of American Art, Smithsonian Institution

Mary Cassatt to Joseph Pennell; November 17, 1905
Joseph Pennell Papers, Library of Congress

INDEX

Page numbers in *italics* denote illustrations.